Democratic Consolidation and Constitutional Endurance in Asia and Africa

Democratic Consolidation and Constitutional Endurance in Asia and Africa

Comparing Uneven Pathways

Edited by

TOM GERALD DALY
DINESHA SAMARARATNE

OXFORD
UNIVERSITY PRESS

OXFORD
UNIVERSITY PRESS

Great Clarendon Street, Oxford, OX2 6DP,
United Kingdom

Oxford University Press is a department of the University of Oxford. It furthers the University's objective of excellence in research, scholarship, and education by publishing worldwide. Oxford is a registered trade mark of Oxford University Press in the UK and in certain other countries

First Edition published in 2024

Published in the United States of America by Oxford University Press
198 Madison Avenue, New York, NY 10016, United States of America

British Library Cataloguing in Publication Data

Data available

Library of Congress Control Number: 2023948327

ISBN 978–0–19–289934–7

DOI: 10.1093/oso/9780192899347.001.0001

Printed and bound by
CPI Group (UK) Ltd, Croydon, CR0 4YY

For the activists, practitioners, and scholars who endure despite the odds . . .

Acknowledgements

This book project was originally conceptualised in 2019 in a series of conversations between us and Dr Asanga Welikala, Director of the Edinburgh Centre for Constitutional Law at the University of Edinburgh. The project's form, orientation, and design owe a very significant debt to Asanga's input and leadership, who drew from his diverse policy and academic background as well as his vibrant networks for this purpose. We thank him for this intellectual labour.

The institutional home for this book project has been the Laureate Program for Comparative Constitutional Law of the Melbourne Law School Australia. We thank Professor Adrienne Stone for her support over the course of this project. We also thank Gabrielle Dalsasso, the programme manager of the Laureate Program, for her support with the online workshops and all other logistics. We also thank our colleagues Darshan Datar and Toerien van Wyk for providing valuable research assistance at the book workshops in 2021.

A very special thank you to our research assistants James Choi and Max Stella for their excellent work on the draft chapters and the emergence of a unified manuscript. Thanks also to Amanda Halliday for support with editing.

Another special vote of thanks goes to Jamie Berezin, Lane Berger, Paulina dos Santos Major, and Brian Stone of Oxford University Press for abiding by this book project through the pandemic and the several other crises that the team endured while working on this project. Their support and guidance have been central to bringing this ship to harbour through some very choppy waters.

We also greatly appreciate the International Association of Constitutional Law (IACL) and the IACL–AIDC Blog for disseminating the insights presented in this edited volume. Being both former editors of the blog, it is gratifying to see it continue to expand its mission in serving as a truly global platform for constitutional experts across the world, including those parts of the world that are so often overlooked in global conversations.

We could not finish these acknowledgements without recognising that all works such as this are not collective enterprises only among editors and authors but also of a broader community. Effective scholarship can only ever be developed in conversation with others. We are fortunate to have a wonderful network of colleagues who have supported and encouraged us along the way. We thank, in particular, our colleagues at the Constitution Transformation Network (CTN) for their support. In many ways, this book reflects vital and ongoing intellectual and practical discussions about inclusive constitution-building and democracy-building that the CTN has pursued since its establishment in 2016, and we look forward to the further conversations this volume will hopefully foster.

Tom Gerald Daly and Dinesha Samararatne
1 December 2022

Contents

Detailed Contents

PART II. CASE STUDIES

List of Abbreviations

1MDB	1 Malaysia Development Berhad
ABSDF	All Burma Students' Democratic Front
ACC	Anti-Corruption Commission
ACHPR	African Charter on Human and Peoples' Rights
ADB	Asian Development Bank
AFPRC	Armed Forces Provisional Ruling Council
ALP	Arakan Liberation Party
ANDM	Amhara National Democratic Movement
ANFREL	Asian Network for Free Election
AP	Adalat Party
APRC	Alliance for Patriotic Reorientation and Construction
ARENA	Aliança Renovadora Nacional
ARSA	Arakan Rohingya Salvation Army
BN	Barisan Nasional
BSPP	Burma Socialist Programme Party
CDC	Constitution Drafting Commission
CDM	Civil Disobedience Movement
CEP	Council of Eminent Persons
CNF	Chin National Front
CRC	Constitutional Review Commission
CRPH	Committee Representing the Pyidaungsu Hluttaw
CSO	civil society organisation
DAP	Democratic Action Party
DDR	disarmament, demobilization, and reintegration
DKBA	Democratic Karen Benevolent Army
EAO	ethnic armed organisation
EC	Election Commission
ECLR	Eastern Corridor Rail Link
ECOWAS	Economic Community of West African States
EPRDF	Ethiopian People's Revolutionary Democratic Front
ERC	Electoral Reform Committee
FDC	Federal Democracy Charter
FDRE	Federal Democratic Republic of Ethiopia
FFP	Future Forward Party
FPTP	first past the post
GAD	General Administration Department
GBA	Gambia Bar Association
GDC	Gambia Democratic Congress
GDF	Gambia Democracy Fund

GDP	gross domestic product
GERD	Grand Ethiopian Renaissance Dam
GMC	Gambia Moral Congress
GPDP	Gambia Party for Democracy and Progress
GPU	Gambia Press Union
GST	goods and services tax
HDI	Human Development Index
HPR	House of Peoples' Representatives
HSR	high-speed rail
ICC	International Criminal Court
ICCPR	International Covenant on Civil and Political Rights
ICERD	International Convention on the Eradication of Racial Discrimination
IEC	Independent Electoral Commission
International IDEA	International Institute for Democracy and Electoral Assistance
IRC	International Reform Committee
ISEAS	Institute for Southeast Asian Studies
ITAK	Illankai Tamil Arasu Kachchi
JP	Jumhooree Party
JPCCA	Joint Parliamentary Committee for Constitutional Amendment
JSC	Judicial Service Commission
JVP	Janatha Vimukthi Peramuna
KNU	Karen National Union
KNU/NNLA PC	KNU/Karen National Liberation Army Peace Council
KVMRT	Klang Valley Mass Rapid Transit
LGA	local government area/local government authority
LTTE	Liberation Tigers of Tamil Eelam
MCA	Malaysian Chinese Association
MCO	movement control order
MDP	Maldivian Democratic Party
MIC	Malaysian Indian Congress
MNHRC	Myanmar National Human Rights Commission
MoU	memorandum of understanding
MRM	Maldives Reform Movement
MUDA	Malaysian United Democratic Alliance
NADD	National Alliance for Democracy and Development
NAWEC	National Water and Electricity Company
NCA	National Ceasefire Agreement
NCP	National Convention Party
NCPO	National Council for Peace and Order
NDR	Northern Development Region
NEBE	National Electoral Board of Ethiopia
NGO	non-governmental organisation
NHRC	National Human Rights Commission
NLA	National Legislative Assembly

NLD	National League for Democracy
NPP	National People's Party
NRC	National Reform Council/National Recovery Council
NRP	National Reconciliation Party
NRPC	National Reconciliation and Peace Centre
NSC	National Security Council
NUCC	National Unity Consultative Council
NUG	National Unity government
OECD	Organisation for Economic Co-operation and Development
OPDO	Oromo People's Democratic Organisation
PAC	Public Accounts Committee
PAS	Pan-Malaysian Islamic Party
PBK	Bumi Kenyalang (Sarawak) Party
PCS	Love Sabah Party
PDOIS	People's Democratic Organisation for Independence and Socialism
PDP—Laban	Partido Demokratiko Pilipino—Lakas ng Bayan
PDRC	People's Democratic Reform Council
PH	Pact of Hope
PIU	Police Intervention Unit
PKR	People's Justice Party
PNLO	Pa-O National Liberation Organisation
PPM	Progressive Party of Maldives
PPP	People's Progressive Party
PPRP	Palang Pracharath Party
PRC	Public Representations Committee on Constitutional Reform
PSB	Sarawak United Party
PT	Pheu Thai
RCSS	Restoration Council of Shan State
SAC	State Administration Council
SDR	Southern Development Region
SIPRI	Stockholm International Peace Research Institute
SLFP	Sri Lanka Freedom Party
SLORC	State Law and Order Restoration Council
SLPP	Sri Lanka Podujana Peramuna
SNLD	Shan Nationalities League for Democracy
SNNPR	Southern Nations, and the Nationalities and Peoples Region
SSR	security-sector reform
SST	sales and services tax
TNA	Tamil National Alliance
TPLF	Tigray People's Liberation Front
TRRC	Truth, Reconciliation and Reparations Commission
TRT	Thai Rak Thai
TULF	Tamil United Liberation Front
UDP	United Democratic Party
UEC	Union Election Commission

UMNO	United Malays National Organisation
UN	United Nations
UNDP	United Nations Development Programme
UNF	United National Front
UNOHCHR	United Nations Office of the High Commissioner for Human Rights
UNP	United National Party
UPC	Union peace conference
UPDJC	Union Peace Dialogue Joint Committee
UPFA	United People's Freedom Alliance
USDA	United Solidarity and Development Association
USDP	Union Solidarity and Development Party
WHO	World Health Organization

List of Contributors

Editors

Tom Gerald Daly is Convenor of the Constitution Transformation Network (CTN) at Melbourne Law School, Director of the Electoral Regulation Research Network (ERRN), and Director of the online knowledge platform Democratic Decay & Renewal (DEM-DEC, www.democratic-decay.org accessed 2 October 2023). He is also Associate Director of the Edinburgh Centre for Constitutional Law and serves on the Editorial Board of the *Journal of Public Law/Zeitschrift für öffentliches recht* (ZöR).

His comparative research, drawing on public law and political science, focuses on the decay and renewal of democracy from a global perspective, the contingent legitimacy of judicial review in different democratic contexts, constitutional design, and constitutional repair, with recent publications in the *International Journal of Constitutional Law*, *German Law Journal*, *Revista Suprema* (journal of the Supreme Court of Brazil), and *Law and Ethics on Human Rights*. As well as extensive experience in the university sector (principally at Melbourne, Edinburgh, and Copenhagen universities), Tom has worked in a variety of roles in government and international organisations, including designing a pan-continental African Judicial Network for the African Union and leading or working on constitutional, political, and judicial reform projects and reviews in states and territories including Ireland, Georgia, Kyrgyzstan, Lebanon, the Pacific, Palestine, Sri Lanka, Turkey, and Uzbekistan.

Dinesha Samararatne is a professor at the Department of Public & International Law of the University of Colombo, Sri Lanka. She is a senior fellow and co-convenor of the Constitution Transformation Network (CTN) at Melbourne Law School, Australia, editorial member of the *Indian Law Review* and Editor of the *University of Colombo Review*.

Her research interests include fourth-branch institutions, constitutional resilience, judicial review, women's rights and comparative constitutional law and comparative administrative law from a global south perspective.

Contributors

Adem Kassie Abebe (LLD) is Senior Programme Advisor at the Constitution Building Programme, International Institute for Democracy and Electoral Assistance (IDEA). He supports constitution, peace-building, and dialogue processes in transitions from conflict and authoritarianism to peace and democracy. Adem has edited books and published articles and chapters in prominent journals on comparative constitutional studies and practice. Adem serves as Vice-President of the African Network of Constitutional Law, in the Advisory Board of the *International Journal of Constitutional Law*, and as Extraordinary Lecturer at the University of Pretoria.

Jason Grant Allen is an Associate Professor of Law at Singapore Management University Yong Pung How School of Law. His book *Non-Statutory Executive Powers and Judicial Review* was recently published by Cambridge University Press and sets out a concept of official action and explores the nature of official power. Jason read law at the University of Tasmania, Universität Augsburg, and the University of Cambridge, the latter as a Poynton Scholar. This chapter draws on work undertaken while Jason was an Alexander von Humboldt Foundation post-doctoral fellow at the Humboldt-Universität zu Berlin Centre for British Studies.

Daniel Alphonsus has worked as an adviser at Sri Lanka's foreign and finance ministries. He read philosophy, politics, and economics at Balliol College, Oxford and public policy at the Harvard Kennedy School, where he was a Fulbright Scholar.

Mouli Banerjee is a PhD candidate at the Department of Politics and International Studies, University of Warwick. Her doctoral work focuses on how political parties in India interact with the legal ecosystem that regulates them and the interfaces between parties, the parliament, and judicial spaces in India.

Luwie Ganeshathasan (LLB (Colombo), LLM (Notre Dame)) is an Attorney at Law. Since January 2012, he has been involved in supporting public-interest litigation cases on issues of constitutional law, administrative law, and human rights law filed by the Centre for Policy Alternatives. He has authored several articles, policy briefs, and advocacy documents on issues related to constitutional reform and human rights. Between March 2015 and July 2018 he provided technical assistance on issues relating to electoral system reform to all political parties represented in the parliament of Sri Lanka and to civil society organisations including professional associations.

Joelle Grogan is a Research Fellow at UK in a Changing Europe, based at King's College London, and a Research Fellow at CEU Democracy Institute Budapest. Her primary focus is law and governance in times of crisis. Joelle was the convenor of the 2020 'COVID-19 and States of Emergency' and the 2021 'Power and the COVID-19 Pandemic' symposia, jointly hosted by the Verfassungblog, Democracy Reporting International, and the RECONNECT project. Joelle was advisor to the European Economic and Social Committee on COVID-19 and the rule of law and co-editor of the *Routledge Handbook on Law and the COVID-19 Pandemic*.

Satang Nabaneh is a Research Professor of Law and the Director of Programs at the University of Dayton Human Rights Center. As a scholar-practitioner, she teaches, advocates, and researches gender, sexualities, and race inequalities in the context of international human rights law, human rights in Africa, democratisation in Africa, and comparative African constitutional law. She is the Founder of Law Hub Gambia (https://www.lawhubgambia.com accessed 2 October 2023), an open-access legal information and knowledge institute in The Gambia. Recent publication includes the groundbreaking collection she co-edited, *The Gambia in Transition: Towards a New Constitutional Order* (Pretoria University Law Press, 2022).

Naw Janet is Programme Officer of the MyConstitution Programme at International IDEA. Her work focuses on supporting constitution-building and strengthening a well-informed constitutional and democratic culture in Myanmar. Prior to joining International IDEA, she worked at the Asia Foundation Myanmar, providing research assistance to the Myanmar Business Environment Index Project. Her research interests mainly concentrate on issues related to federalism, constitution-building in multi-ethnic societies, institutional design, oversight mechanisms, and minority rights.

Ohn Mar Zin is a graduate student in comparative politics at the American University in the United States. She was a Programme Officer at the International Institute for Democracy and Electoral Assistance's MyConstitution Programme. She supported constitution-building in Myanmar by working together with international and local experts in enhancing constitutional and federal knowledge of key political stakeholders, including representatives from Union and State/Region Parliament, the Constitutional Tribunal, the Supreme Court, political parties, civil society organisations, and ethnic armed organisations. Before joining International IDEA, she worked as a research associate for Myanmar Scholarship Alumni Association in assisting Pyidaungsu Hluttaw's research department.

Cheryl Saunders is a Laureate Professor Emeritus at Melbourne Law School and a convenor of the Constitution Transformation Network. She has specialist interests in comparative constitutional law on a global scale, including constitution-making and change, comparative method, and multi-level government. She was the founding Director of the Centre for Comparative Constitutional Studies, of which she remains an active member.

Wilson Tay Tze Vern is Senior Lecturer at Taylor's Law School, Taylor's University, Malaysia. He read law at University College London and subsequently obtained his LLM and PhD from the National University of Singapore (NUS). Wilson's current areas of teaching and research are constitutional law, administrative law, and health-care regulation. Previously, Wilson was Research Fellow at the Faculty of Law, NUS and Deputy Editor of the *Asian Journal of Comparative Law*. He has also previously served as Senior Assistant Registrar in the Judicial & Legal Service of Malaysia, based at the Commercial Division of the Kuala Lumpur High Court.

Khemthong Tonsakulrungruang is a Lecturer at the Faculty of Political Science, Chulalongkorn University. He works in the areas of constitutional law, the judiciary, and legal philosophy. He publishes articles and chapters on these topics, including in the *Routledge Handbook on Contemporary Thai Politics* (2020), *Thai Legal History* (2021), *Constitutional Courts in Asia* (2018), and in various journals, *Journal of Contemporary Thai Politics*, *Journal of International Constitutional Law*, and *Washington Journal of International Law*. He is also a regular contributor to blogs on constitutional law and Thai politics, namely, New Mandala, East Asian Forum, and I.CONnect.

Shanil Wijesinha is a Lecturer (Probationary) at the Faculty of Law, University of Colombo. His research interests include constitutional law, human rights law, and the judicial process.

He completed his undergraduate studies at the Faculty of Law, University of Colombo and holds a Master of Laws Degree from Harvard Law School. He has qualified as an attorney-at-law in Sri Lanka.

Julius Yam is an Assistant Professor at the University of Hong Kong and a Research Associate at the Programme for the Foundations of Law and Constitutional Government, University of Oxford. He holds an LLB from the University of Hong Kong and an LLM from the University of Chicago.

Mariyam Zulfa is currently a founder-member of Maldives Policy Advocacy Caucus (https://mpac.ac accessed 2 October 2023). A former Minister of Tourism in the cabinet of President Mohamed Nasheed, she is a graduate of the Melbourne University Law School and her research interests are in constitutional law and Maldives.

Kimana Zulueta-Fülscher (PhD) is Senior Advisor of the Constitution-Building Programme at International IDEA. She was previously Acting Head of the Programme and prior to that, Programme Manager of the MyConstitution Programme, located in Yangon (Myanmar). Her research and work focuses on comparative constitutional process and design, with a special emphasis on constitution-building processes in fragile and conflict-affected settings. Before International IDEA, Kimana was a senior researcher at the German Development Institute/Deutsches Institut für Entwicklungspolitik (DIE), where she worked and published in the area of political transformation in fragile contexts.

1

Decolonising Comparative Constitutional Law (and Democratisation Studies)?

Tom Gerald Daly and Dinesha Samararatne

1. Introduction: A Distorted Conversation

If the global conversation on building constitutional democracy were a wedding, we would always see the same democracies represented at the top table, with others scattered across the room at various degrees of proximity to the central guests. Some democracies would be seated close by, while many would be seated at the third-tier tables, far from the heat of the action, craning their necks to hear the speeches. Others would not feature on the invitation list, perceived as having no real connection to the gathering, viewed as misfits, or simply because the organisers did not think to invite them. If you asked those at the top table why they warrant their central position, they might respond reflexively, or even defensively: 'we have been a constitutional democracy for centuries', 'we are the cradle of modern democracy', 'we constructed a leading democracy after dictatorship', 'we are one of the biggest democracies in the world', or 'we are ranked as a top democracy by all international democracy assessments'. They might consider the very question to be an affront, even (or indeed, especially) if their democratic systems are experiencing serious challenges.

Perhaps one or two top-table guests might, with refreshing honesty, concede that their privileged position is owed not just to their democratic credentials but equally—or even primarily—to an admixture of geopolitical, historical, material, military, and epistemic power. Some, later in the evening, might even quietly admit that their imperial-colonial past means that they have at least two democratic stories: the construction of a viable constitutional democracy at home and the repression—often harsh, long-lasting, and only bitterly relinquished—of the democratic voice abroad: some rare acknowledgement of the 'chequered history through which democracies have emerged as well as functioned', as Nitasha Kaul puts it.[1] To say so out loud, however, might be to commit a grave error. The

[1] Nitasha Kaul, 'Democracy in the Non-West: Facts, Fictions and Frictions' in Centre for Bhutan Studies (ed), *Beyond the Ballot Box: Report from the Deepening and Sustaining Democracy in Asia Conference* (Centre for Bhutan Studies 2013) 116.

Tom Gerald Daly and Dinesha Samararatne, *Decolonising Comparative Constitutional Law (and Democratisation Studies)?* In: *Democratic Consolidation and Constitutional Endurance in Asia and Africa.* Edited by: Tom Gerald Daly and Dinesha Samararatne, Oxford University Press. © Oxford University Press 2024. DOI: 10.1093/oso/9780192899347.003.0001

conversation might stop abruptly, appalled faces turning to the taboo-breaking speaker before a loud voice intervenes to smooth over the proceedings with a genial story about how we are all in this together and headed for the same destination—'Getting to Denmark', in the rather problematic shorthand phrase employed by development professionals to denote development towards a state with well-functioning political and economic institutions: 'stable, democratic, peaceful, prosperous, inclusive, and [with] extremely low levels of political corruption'.[2]

That much of our global conversation on democracy-building is organised in this way does not mean that it is entirely futile, arid, meaningless, or hypocritical. However, it does mean that it is often exclusionary, closed, stale, and hindered by myriad forms of self-regard, self-delusion, and self-dealing, which arises perhaps more as a form of cultural mood music than any individual wrongdoing. On the current model, in both the academic and the political arenas, those at the top table decide what constitutional democracy 'is', what is valuable about it, how it should function, who counts as a democracy and who does not, whose deficiencies are scrutinised and whose are glossed over. Most importantly, they decide and narrate how viable and sustainable constitutional democracies are constructed, which often involves a re-telling of their own stories, nation-building myths, and democracy-building fables rather than listening attentively to others' experiences.

There is at least a laudable decades-long trend towards greater inclusion, but this has only marginally reconfigured the top table to include key states such as India, South Africa, and Colombia; the dynamic still generally involves the top table occasionally beckoning over other guests to pose specific questions—'How does Ethiopia organise its federal structure?' or 'Are there signs of judicial activism in Malaysia?'—questions designed to fill a gap in the top-table story of constitutional democracy; questions with pre-set parameters; questions that interrogate rather than opening a dialogue, leaving the summoned interlocutor standing instead of offering a seat; questions that leave many stories untold, or untold on their own terms. To be heard, interlocutors must employ the top table's idioms and connect with top-table preoccupations and anxieties, refracting their experiences in a form of triangulation and intellectual tribute that distorts, dislocates, and devalues articulation of their own democratic understandings, experiences, aspirations, and anxieties.

Of course, the metaphor of a wedding is itself problematic. Practically, it might suggest that the guests at each table are engaged in lively dialogue. However, certainly, if we think in geographic terms, conversations about democracy-building among neighbours, especially those of differing political-regime leanings, are often marked more by long silences and deep misunderstandings than shared understandings or stunted by an undue focus on what is happening, or has happened, at

[2] Francis Fukuyama, *The Origins of Political Order: From Prehuman Times to the French Revolution* (Profile Books 2011) 39.

the top table. In our wedding scenario, Asian and African guests would be placed at opposite ends of the venue, frustrating the potential for productive cross-regional conversations and maintaining the top table as the central point of focus and single common referent. (Indeed, 'Africa' and 'Asia' can themselves be problematic meta-geographical colonial constructions impeding alternative visions of the myriad transnational connections across these contiguous continents; a point we pursue in more detail below.)[3]

More fundamentally, our choice of wedding metaphor and imagery might be exclusionary, erecting obstacles to transnational understanding that might not be immediately obvious: weddings, after all, do not look the same everywhere. Who gets married and how varies significantly across cultures due to a range of factors, and the answer continues to change across time. Yet, across the world, we can at least say that all weddings will have key features that distinguish them from other occasions: individuals are being recognised publicly as a union (not necessarily limited to two individuals); the ceremony involves specific words and rites (whether civil or religious); there is some form of witness; and there is some form of communal celebration. If one of these elements is missing (e.g. communal celebration or formal dress), it will still count as a wedding. If some details are different (e.g. the bride's dress is colourful, or red, or white, or the groom carries a ceremonial sword), it will still count as a wedding. Yet, if other details are missing (e.g. there is no recognised office-holder to perform the ceremony or one person is purporting to marry themselves), it is patently *not* a wedding. We can argue, then, over the different details and models in between these two poles, but there is at least a cross-cultural baseline agreement about what a wedding is, what it is about, who is involved, and how it works. There is at least an agreement that simply claiming that an occasion is a wedding does not make it so if key elements are missing. So it is with constitutional democracy, but the problem remains: who gets to ask the questions about how to achieve sustainable constitutional democracy and what that destination truly means, and who gets to provide the answers?

2. This Book: Radically Re-orientating Our Centre

What factors drive constitutional change and sustain positive transformation? How are democratic values recognised, restored, and preserved through constitutional change? How can these questions be answered in a manner that is relevant

[3] As Gyan Prakash offers, '"Asia" emerged as a geographical category from the longue durée of colonialism': see Gyan Prakash (ed), *Design and Modernity in Asia: National Identity and Transnational Exchange 1945–1990* (Bloomsbury Publishing 2022) xiii. Similarly, it has been observed that the boundaries of 'Africa' have shifted depending on the governance priorities of colonial powers: see Martin W Lewis and Kären Wigen, *The Myth of Continents: A Critique of Metageography* (University of California Press 1997) chs 4 and 5.

to most of the world? These are the key questions that we raise in this edited volume, and we do so by configuring a very different 'top table' of states as our central focus. We draw from two geographical regions—Asia and Africa—and organise our analysis both jurisdictionally (with seven case studies that have experienced a democratising event in the past decade—Ethiopia, The Gambia, Malaysia, Myanmar, Sri Lanka, Thailand, and Maldives[4]) and thematically, building on the empirical surveys to offer analytical insights on seven themes arising from the case studies: the concept of 'office' and its relationship to political and constitutional development; the role of governing institutions in these processes of development; the roles played by political parties, which depart from established dominant 'Western' frameworks of thinking; the curious, diverse, and often marginal place of courts in our case studies; the often central importance of civil–military relations, which manifests in highly diverse ways; the salience and explanatory power of constitutional culture; and the impact of the COVID-19 pandemic.

Our aims are twofold: first is to make a contribution to the growing global comparative and inter-disciplinary literature on democratic consolidation, backsliding, and resilience through analysis of case studies that are otherwise understudied and which are rarely, if ever, compared to one another. Second, we aim to contribute to domestic constitutional debates in the case study countries by generating contextualised theoretical and comparative insights of relevance to the consolidation and development of constitutional democracy.

This collection has been developed at an inflection point for global democracy, where a perceived worldwide 'democratic recession'[5] has prompted seismic shifts in both comparative constitutional studies and democratisation studies. The recent rise of movements and trends of authoritarian populism, 'executive aggrandisement', 'autocratic legalism', institutional decay, party system degradation, hyper-partisanship, political corruption, political violence, identity politics, 'cultural backlash', and inter-ethnic tension in both longstanding stable constitutional democracies of the West and democracies of different vintages outside the West has generated a rapidly expanding body of literature on everything from the drivers of populism, neo-authoritarianism and neo-despotism to mechanisms for counteracting it, as comparative constitutional theorists, historians, political scientists, sociologists, and economists have addressed these issues from multiple angles.[6]

[4] Although 'The Maldives' and 'Maldives' are often used interchangeably, this collection tends to use 'Maldives'.

[5] Larry Diamond, 'Facing Up to the Democratic Recession' (2015) 26(1) Journal of Democracy 14.

[6] See e.g. Mark Graber, Sanford Levinson, and Mark Tushnet (eds), *Constitutional Democracy in Crisis?* (Oxford University Press 2019); Surendra Munshi (ed), *Democracy under Threat* (Oxford University Press 2017); Pippa Norris and Ronald Inglehart, *Cultural Backlash: Trump, Brexit and the Rise of Authoritarian Populism* (Cambridge University Press 2019); Steven Levitsky and Daniel Ziblatt, *How Democracies Die: What History Reveals about Our Future* (Penguin 2018); Jonah Goldberg, *Suicide of the West: How the Rebirth of Tribalism, Populism, Nationalism, and Identity Politics Is Destroying American Democracy* (Penguin Random House 2018); Aziz Z Huq and Tom Ginsburg, *How to Save a Constitutional Democracy* (University of Chicago Press 2018); Carolyn M Hendriks, Selen

At its heart, whether it adopts an institutionalist, theoretical, or sociological approach, this literature grapples with the major question of *how we can reconcile the relationship between constitutional democracy* (i.e. government based on the legitimacy of popular consent as well as the restraints of the rule of law) and the *forces that work against its social entrenchment* (including pure majoritarianism or exclusionary populism, ethnic nationalism, traditionalism, authoritarianism, or a mixture of some or all of these counter-ideologies).

One way to enter this unfolding global conversation would be to take it on its established terms, which have been largely hammered out on the anvil of Western realities. However, to take such an approach would reduce our case studies to mere additions and glosses to a global story whose frames are pre-set, somewhat rigid, and distortive. It might leave us looking in all the wrong places, seeking to understand the very different realities of our case studies through frames of populism while eliding forms of elite power (e.g. military power, business elites), an excessive focus on elected executives (e.g. overlooking monarchs), or proceeding from unhelpful assumptions (e.g. that political parties broadly operate in the same way everywhere). Our aim is to disrupt the dynamics of triangulation and intellectual tribute to 'top-table' epistemic centrality by centring our case studies as a different type of top table, as worthy of study on their own terms, in their own words, not because of perceived successes in democratic and constitutional development but because their stories provide rich insights into *both* successes and failures; the simultaneity of positive and negative trends; and questions of momentum, trajectory, and teleology. We might add that, together, the case studies have a population close to that of the United States—over 300 million individuals whose lives are directly affected by the quality of governance they experience, the extent to which their voices are heard in the halls of power, and the degree of protection they receive from the depredations of the state and dominant social, political, and economic forces. However, we offer this information merely to inform our reader not to fall into the trap of justificatory burdens for analysis that are not applied to analysis of top-table states.

Moving from the wedding metaphor employed above, an illuminating visual representation of our approach to radically reorientating our centre is the

A Ercan, and John Boswell, *Mending Democracy: Democratic Repair in Disconnected Times* (Oxford University Press 2020); Suzanne Mettler and Robert C Lieberman, *Four Threats: The Recurring Crises of American Democracy* (St Martin's Press 2020); Tímea Drinóczi and Agnieszka Bień-Kacała, *Illiberal Constitutionalism in Poland and Hungary: The Deterioration of Democracy, Misuse of Human Rights and Abuse of the Rule of Law* (Routledge 2021); Wojciech Sadurski, *Poland's Constitutional Breakdown: Freefall 2015–2018* (Oxford University Press 2019); Kim Lane Scheppele, 'Autocratic Legalism' (2018) 85 University of Chicago Law Review 545; Debasish Roy Chowdhury and John Keane, *To Kill A Democracy: India's Passage to Despotism* (Oxford University Press 2021); Tarunabh Khaitan, 'Killing a Constitution with a Thousand Cuts: Executive Aggrandizement and Party–State Fusion in India' (2020) 14(1) Law & Ethics of Human Rights 49; Emilio Meyer, *Constitutional Erosion in Brazil* (Hart Publishing 2021); Juliano Zaiden Benvindo, *The Rule of Law in Brazil: The Legal Construction of Inequality* (Hart Publishing 2022).

'authagraph' world map reproduced in Fig. 1.1 below. This is a re-engineering of the familiar Mercator–Miller projection map, which presents the world more accurately and allows for alternative presentations of familiar continental landmasses. In this version, Africa and Asia are placed centrally, with other continents in the periphery, and we have added pin symbols identifying the country case studies. This disrupts the totalising and 'slippery'[7] concepts of 'Global North' and 'Global South', pushing us to reflect instead on questions of core and periphery, of inclusion and exclusion, of epistemic dominance and epistemic injustice, which can cut across the North–South axis in both the global and regional arenas. Decolonising comparative constitutional law and democratisation studies, in this sense, challenges us to reimagine and reconceive the world we are analysing in spatial as well as intellectual terms. As an approach, it has strong affinities with Oklopcic's notion of 'comparing as (re-)imagining'.[8]

The Global North and Global South may be mutually constitutive, and epistemic and geopolitical power imbalances cannot simply be wished away, but we can, for now, for here, within the world of this project, utterly transform who counts as 'the centre' by transforming the (perceived) hinterland into heartland. What does it look like to conceptualise and theorise constitutional and democratic development afresh from the core we have fashioned for this collection? This challenge lies at the centre of our call to diversify and decolonise the field in terms of methodology, mindset, and practice, which is the main driving force for putting together this collection. The spatial–intellectual recalibration pursued here is one under-considered option to achieve an immediate, insurgent reordering in the context of a developing decolonising conversation focused on *permanently* decentring Europe and North America through a 'Southern turn' or 'facing South'.[9] This can trap us in an assumed positionality and relational bond, the Global North living rent-free in our heads even as we try to escape its influence, with the moment of achieving decentring always lying on a distant, unknowable, or recursive horizon.

While the principal contribution of the editorial introduction is often to draw out the main themes from the contributions, the seven thematic chapters as an organising strategy have cleared the ground for us to probe deeper into questions about knowledge-building, both at a theoretical level and a 'human' or practical

[7] Jean Comaroff and John L Comaroff, *Theory from the South OR How Euro-America Is Evolving toward Africa* (Paradigm 2012) 45.

[8] Zoran Oklopcic, 'Comparing as (Re-)Imagining: Southern Perspective and the World of Constitutions' in Philipp Dann, Michael Riegner, and Maxim Bönnemann (eds), *The Global South and Comparative Constitutional Law* (Oxford University Press 2020). It may be noted that this version of the authagraph map visually excludes the Pacific and New Zealand: in this sense, re-centering ourselves will always involve questions about exclusion and inclusion. What is important is that we navigate and acknowledge these choices expressly and thoughtfully.

[9] See e.g. Philipp Dann, Michael Riegner, and Maxim Bönnemann, 'The Southern Turn in Comparative Constitutional Law: An Introduction' and Florian Hoffmann, 'Facing *South*: On the Significance of An/Other Modernity in Comparative Constitutional Law' in Dann, Riegner, and Bönnemann, *The Global South* (n 8).

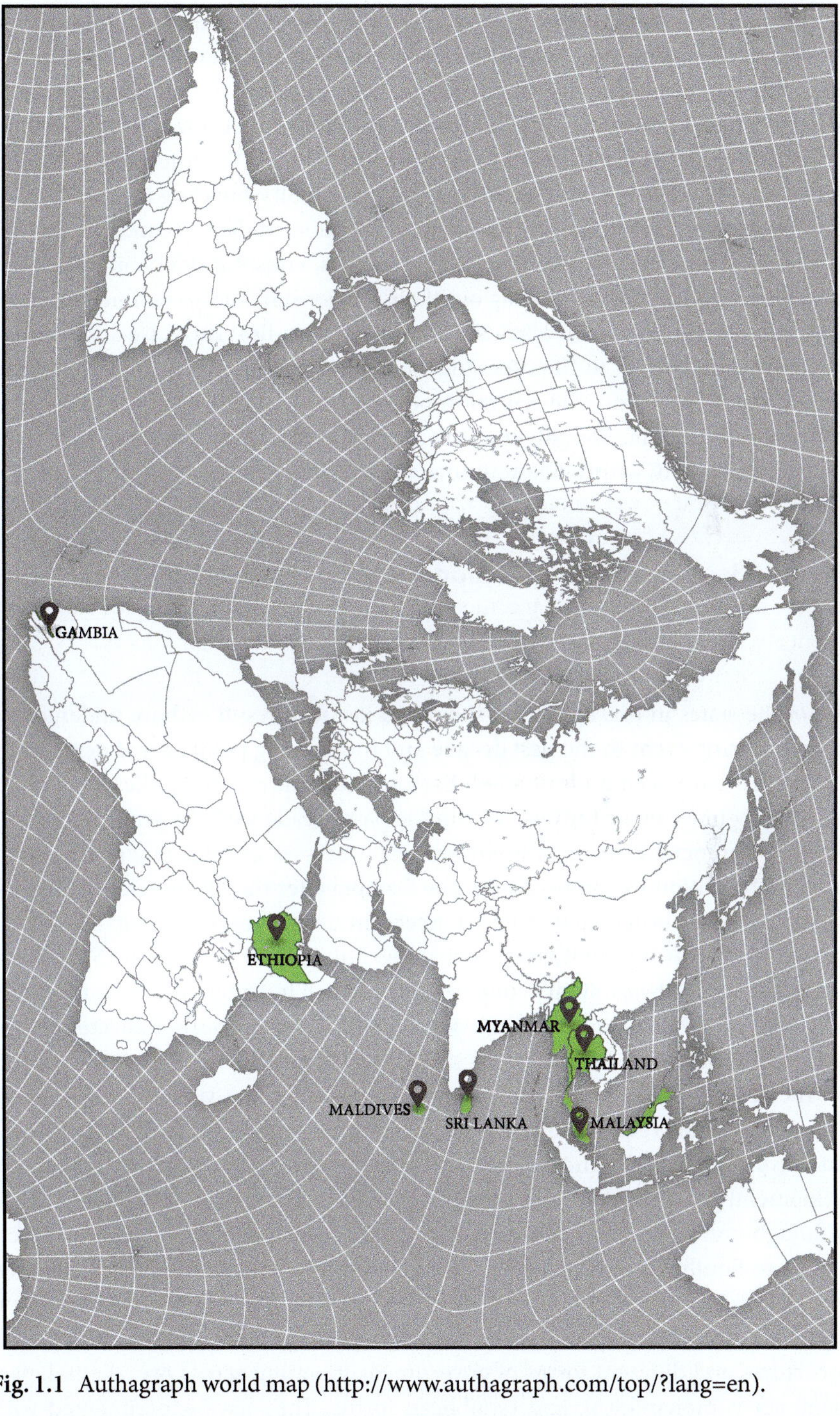

Fig. 1.1 Authagraph world map (http://www.authagraph.com/top/?lang=en).

level, generating insights into how practice and theory are co-constitutive in any comparative praxis. These reflections encompass three dimensions. First, we discuss our approach to comparative methodology and theory-building, seeking to articulate our frustrations with dominant methodologies in comparative constitutional law, our attempt to forge a different approach, and the importance of community, embeddedness, collaboration, and community-building in decolonising comparative constitutional law and democratisation studies. Second, we provide a brief overview of our two organising concepts, constitutional endurance and democratic consolidation, teasing out their relationship and sometimes antagonistic framing as well as their application to the case studies. Third, we discuss three key features common to the case studies, focusing on the cyclical nature of endurance and regression, the central importance of critical events and crises, and the multidimensional insights into institutions at the heart of change processes. Fourth, and finally, we provide a summary of each chapter.

3. Comparative Methodology and Theory-Building

3.1 The Case Studies

All of the states in this collection share two key features: they have undergone a democratising event in the past decade and the ensuing political and democratic transitions have been understudied. Each of the country case studies has experienced a regime change (or two) within the past decade with the promise of some form of democratic renewal. Some reform processes are still ongoing (e.g. the hopeful transition to democracy in The Gambia after the dictatorship of Yahyah Jammeh), while others have faltered, after some early successes (e.g. Sri Lanka's years of political instability and crisis after hopeful elections in 2015) or been starkly disrupted by a military coup (e.g. Myanmar). It is vital to better understand why some states have maintained a positive—albeit non-linear—trajectory while others have not.

The case studies and thematic analyses offer us comparative insight into understanding how the relationship between democracy-building, democratic reversal, and institutional endurance plays out in conditions of ongoing constitutional development, generally discussing events up to the cut-off point of 31 August 2021, although some have incorporated more recent developments. Spanning West Africa to Southeast Asia, as offered above, these are not countries that are often compared. In fact, the case studies differ on many counts. They include common law, civil, and mixed legal systems. They also include unitary, federal, and hybrid structures and different forms of government spanning across presidential, parliamentary, monarchical, and republican forms. They have experimented with different ideological regimes from socialism to capitalism and reflect diverse states of economic growth and development. Their historical evolution demonstrates both similarities in terms of uneven trajectories of democratic constitutional development and differences in constitutional institutions and cultures. Importantly, they represent differing experiences with Western colonialism prior to the decolonisation era, with two—Ethiopia and Thailand—lying outside this paradigm, while the remaining five states here gained independence between 1948 and 1965 during the collapse of the British Empire. Importantly, states (and different areas within states) experienced varying levels of direct colonial control. Some states also experienced Portuguese and/or Dutch colonisation (e.g. Maldives, Sri Lanka). Further comparison is offered in Tables 1.1–1.4 below (which use the term 'colony' to capture diverse arrangements) as well as sections 4 and 5 of this chapter.

3.2 A Different Model for Theoretical Development

As indicated above, this book seeks to theorise from understudied jurisdictions of the Global South, which is useful at two levels: (i) it adds to our understanding of the Global South and, more importantly, (ii) it has the potential to change the way

Table 1.1 Case studies: Central characteristics

Case study	Population*	Constitution**	State structure	Political system	Size***
Ethiopia	117.9 m	1994	Federal republic	Parliamentary	1.104 m km^2
Thailand	69.95 m	2017	Unitary monarchy	Parliamentary	513,120 km^2
Myanmar	54.81 m	[2008] 2021 coup	Unitary republic	Military junta	676,578 km^2
Malaysia	32.78 m	1957	Federal monarchy	Parliamentary	330,803 km^2
Sri Lanka	22.16 m	1978	Unitary republic	Presidential	65,610 km^2
The Gambia	2.487 m	1997	Unitary republic	Presidential	10,689 km^2
Maldives	543,620	2008	Unitary republic	Presidential	300 km^2

Source: This table was compiled by the editors, drawing on statistics from the World Bank (population) <https://data.worldbank.org/indicator/SP.POP.TOTL>, Constitute Project (constitution) <www.constituteproject.org>, and World Population Review (state size) <https://worldpopulationreview.com> all accessed 2 October 2023.

Table 1.2 Case studies: Constitutional endurance and replacement

Case study	Independence	Constitutions	Articles in current constitution	Amendments to current constitution (at November 2022)	Current constitution drafting/ review process
Ethiopia	N/a: never colonised (except: Italy 1936–1941)	4 (1994, 1987, 1955, 1931)	106	2	No
Thailand	N/a: never colonised	17 (2017, 2014 (int.), 2007, 2006 (int.), 1997, 1991, 1991, 1978, 1977, 1976, 1974, 1972, 1968, 1959, 1952 (rev.), 1949, 1947 (int.), 1946, 1932, 1932)	279	0	No
Myanmar	1948	3 ([2008]—coup 2021, 1974, 1948)	457 (and 5 schedules)	1	No formal process opposition Federal Democracy Charter
Malaysia	1957	1 (1957)	183 (and 13 schedules)	45	No
Sri Lanka	1948	4 (1978, 1972, 1948, 1947—Soulbury)	172 (and 9 schedules)	20	No
The Gambia	1965	3 (1997, 1970, 1965)	319 (and 4 schedules)	9	Drafting ongoing 2 draft constitutions (2019 and 2020)
Maldives	1965	7 (2008, 1997, 1968, 1953, 1942, 1932, 1931)	301 (and 3 schedules)	1	No

Source: This information is sourced by the editors from the case-study chapters in this collection and the Constitute Project <www.constituteproject.org> accessed 2 October 2023.

Table 1.3 Case studies: Political, systemic and democratic change

Case study	Systemic change	Coups
Ethiopia	Monarchy → republic Monarchy → one-party system Unitary → federal One-party system → multiparty system	1 1974 (3 attempts: 1960, 1989, 2019)
Thailand	Absolute monarchy → civilian government Civilian government → military government Military government → civilian government (Multiple cycles)	13 1932, 1933, 1939, 1947, 1951, 1957, 1958, 1971, 1976, 1977, 1991, 2006, 2014 (7 attempts)
Myanmar	Colony → independent state Civilian government → military government Military government → civilian government (Multiple cycles)	5 2021, 1988, 1962, 1853, 1837 (1 threatened 1958)
Malaysia	Colony → independent state Federation (with Malaya, Sabah, Sarawak, and Singapore, 1963) → federation (without Singapore, 1965)	0
Sri Lanka	Colony → independent state Parliamentary → presidential Presidential → semi-presidential	0 (1 attempt, 1962)
The Gambia	Colony → independent state Monarchy → republic Dictatorship → democratic transition	1 1994 (1 attempt, 2014)
Maldives	Absolute monarchy → constitutional monarchy Constitutional monarchy → presidential republic Presidential republic → constitutional monarchy Colony → independent state Constitutional monarchy → presidential republic (some features of semi-presidentialism) Presidential republic → democratic semi-presidential republic	0

Note: It may be noted that this table is not intended to be definitive; rather, it is intended to be illustrative of the relative and variable frequency of political change in the case studies. Coups are coded differently in a variety of data sets, and there is often contestation within a state as regards the numbers of coups. In Ethiopia, for instance, the 1974 event can be characterised as a revolution, while the 2019 event in Amhara region was characterised by the federal government as a coup attempt but characterised differently by others. See further, Alem Kebede, 'Ethiopia: The Role of the Military in the Political Order' in William R. Thompson (ed), *Oxford Research Encyclopedias: Politics* https://oxfordre.com/politics/display/10.1093/acrefore/9780190228637.001.0001/acrefore-9780190228637-e-1816?p=emailAMsnxSxWTXMxw&d=/10.1093/acrefore/9780190228637.001.0001/acrefore-9780190228637-e-1816 (published online, 19 November 2020) and 'Attempted Coup Leaves Ethiopia's Army Chief and 3 Senior Officials Dead' (*Reuters*, 23 June 2019).

Source: This table was compiled by the editors. The information is sourced from the case-study chapters in this collection, the Colpus data set (<www.johnjchin.com/colpus>) and the Cline Center data set 'Frequency of Coup Events from 1945 to 2022, by Country' <https://clinecenter.illinois.edu/project/research-themes/democracy-and-development/coup-detat-project/freq-table> both accessed 2 October 2023.

Table 1.4 Case studies: Democracy, rule-of-law, and development indices

Case study	Democracy (Freedom House)	Democracy (V-Dem Institute)	Rule of law (World Justice Project)	Human Development Index (UNDP)	Gross domestic product (bn) (International Monetary Fund 2020)
Ethiopia	23/100: not free	Electoral autocracy	0.39	0.498	96.61
Thailand	29/100: not free	Closed autocracy	0.50	0.800	500.29
Myanmar	9/100: not free	Closed autocracy	0.36	0.585	81.26
Malaysia	50/100: partly free	Electoral autocracy	0.57	0.803	337.28
Sri Lanka	55/100: partly free	Electoral democracy	0.50	0.782	80.68
The Gambia	47/100: partly free	Electoral autocracy (marked as possibly belonging in the 'electoral democracy' category)	0.49	0.500	1.83
Maldives	40/100: partly free	Electoral democracy	N/A	0.747	3.74

Source: This table was compiled by the editors from Freedom House, 'Countries and Territories' <https://freedomhouse.org/countries/freedom-world/scores> accessed 3 November 2022; V-Dem Institute, *Democracy Report 2022: Autocratization Changing Nature?* (2022) Table 1: 'Regimes of the World, 2010–2021'; World Justice Project Rule of Law Index<https://worldjusticeproject.org/rule-of-law-index> accessed 3 November 2022; and World Population Review, 'GDP Ranked by Country 2022' <https://worldpopulationreview.com/countries/by-gdp> accessed 3 November 2022.

we think about the field of comparative constitutional law (as well as democratisation studies).

Evidently, the existing cross-disciplinary literature has offered a range of explanatory theories in understanding, and normative theories in responding to, the global phenomenon of democratic backsliding, decay,[10] and crisis, with proffered solutions including recalibrating judicial review to address pathologies in the political system and process, enhancing 'fourth-branch' protections (e.g. through

[10] 'Democratic decay' is more commonly used to refer to democratic backsliding in an established liberal democracy but here is employed to also cover democratic reversal in younger, fragile, and hybrid democratic systems.

electoral and integrity bodies), re-tooling party selection of leaders, reforming economic models, and addressing the distortive effects of social media on democratic discourse and organisation. As such, it has provided new analytical insights and spurred reconsiderations of normative principles and institutional designs in the study of democratic backsliding and institutional resilience.[11]

Most importantly, recent analysis of challenges facing democracy has pushed a sea change in the comparisons made between 'the West and the rest'. Intensifying challenges to democratic governance in Western states mean that the perceived differences between 'well-functioning' democracies of the Global North and dysfunctional and less democratic states of the Global South (where analysis has tended to focus on poverty, conflict, and post-colonial implications) have become more open to question. These developments have been accompanied by comparative work that has become more genuinely comparative as between the West and the Rest in relation to the decay and endurance of constitutional democracy.[12] We see a shift from a stubborn standpoint of oppositional North/South mutual alterity (whether along presumed stable/fragile, rule of law/rule by law or legal innovation/adoption axes) to something more like what we might call a 'continuum of sameness'.[13] This shifts our gaze from labelling challenges as intrinsically 'Southern' to contemplation of the differing configurations and intensities of both factors promoting, and challenges for, maintaining sustainable constitutional democracy in our case study cluster.

However, genuine comparison needs to be pushed further and to incorporate a greater range of states than the 'canonical' Global South case studies that are prioritised in the literature, such as India and South Africa. We also need to revisit in more detail, and against a broader canvas, the major assumptions that underlie our understandings of societies' commitment to constitutional democracy, the view of constitutional democracy as the 'only game in town' for the political organisation of states, and the now discarded notion that constitutional democracy, once established, will only ever be a 'one-way street' to ever deeper consolidation.

[11] See e.g. Rosalind Dixon, *Democracy and Dysfunction: Towards a Responsive Theory of Judicial Review* (Oxford University Press 2023); Mark Tushnet, *The New Fourth Branch: Institutions for Protecting Constitutional Democracy* (Cambridge University Press 2021); Tarunabh Khaitan, 'Guarantor Institutions' (forthcoming; published online 22 September 2021) Asian Journal of Comparative Law https://www.cambridge.org/core/journals/asian-journal-of-comparative-law/article/guarantor-institutions/A2AF9B9E755BC1C270BC492F458FADAB; Tom Gerald Daly and Brian Christopher Jones, 'Parties versus Democracy: Addressing Today's Political-Party Threats to Democratic Rule' (2020) 18(2) International Journal of Constitutional Law 509; Ganesh Sitaraman, *The Great Democracy: How to Fix Our Politics, Unrig the Economy, and Unite America* (Basic Books 2019); and Shoshanna Zuboff, *The Age of Surveillance Capitalism: The Fight for a Human Future at the New Frontier of Power* (Profile Books 2019).

[12] See e.g. Graber, Levinson, and Tushnet (n 6); and Tom Gerald Daly, 'Democracy' in Jaakko Husa, Jan M Smits, and Catherine Valcke (eds), *Elgar Encyclopedia of Comparative Law* (Edward Elgar forthcoming).

[13] See Hoffmann (n 9) 55.

The latter, of course, could never be taken for granted in the countries to be studied in this collection, but we need a finer-grained account and comparison of the different reasons for this in these states. An older and unique example of such an approach is *The Role of the Judiciary in Plural Societies* edited by Neelan Tiruchelvam and Radhika Coomaraswamy. Published in 1987, this volume places the Philippines, India, Sri Lanka, the Mozambique, and Tanzania in comparison in assessing the role of courts in dealing with questions related to ethnic conflict, rights, and justice.[14]

Several decades later, this book accordingly seeks to theorise our understandings of democratic consolidation, backsliding, and constitutional endurance from a different standpoint to existing literature. All too often, theory elaborated on the basis of Western empirical realities (or of a select few Global South states, such as India and South Africa) is simply applied, albeit often in modified form, to understudied states that are treated as peripheral in the global constitutional conversation. As indicated above, we have sought to pursue a different model for constructing theory in this collection. Rather than setting out general theoretical frameworks and applying them to the case studies, we seek to derive general conclusions from particular case studies and to construct a better theoretical framework for comprehending what are complex realities.

This has been an iterative process, carefully managed through the editorial process and communicating effectively with both case study and thematic chapter authors, with the editors drawing out the insights from the case studies to the full. Shifting our approach in this way allows the experiences of these states to more fully inform our theoretical understandings of democratic consolidation and constitutional endurance—if not quite with a 'clean slate', at least less encumbered by existing understandings. One of the main strengths of this edited volume lies in exploring often-overlooked African and Asian states and placing them in conversation with each other. This approach allows us to maximise the insights to be gained from these case studies in a way designed to genuinely broaden and deepen the field.

This model also underlies our approach to structuring the book. In particular, we have opted for detailed thematic chapters, rather than a more general overview of key themes, for two reasons. First, many of the institutions, processes, and constitutional cultures in the types of states whose experiences we wish to foreground operate and interact in ways that strongly challenge our existing understandings

[14] Neelan Tiruchelvam and Radhika Coomaraswamy (eds), *The Role of the Judiciary in Plural Societies* (Frances Printer 1987). For a review of the book, see Arun K Thiruvengadam, 'Revisiting the Role of the Judiciary in Plural Societies (1987)—A Quarter Century Retrospective on Public Interest Litigation in India and the Global South' in S Khilnani and others (eds) *Comparative Constitutionalism in South Asia* (Oxford University Press 2013) 341.

of political order and constitutionalism (even in the Global South). We see it as important to develop a more systematic theoretical lexicon that can capture these differences, which impact on everything from constitutional pre-commitment, to 'organ-isation' of the political system as a network of offices, to reform momentum. Second, providing fuller attention to key dimensions and sources of democratic instability is essential to reading the case studies themselves against a broader context. We seek to move beyond what might seem like a wilderness of single instances to a nuanced understanding of shared constitutional features and pathologies in these carefully selected case studies in a way that avoids broad-brush rubrics such as 'constitutionalism of the Global South', which can often unhelpfully lump very disparate country experiences together simply on the basis that they do not belong to the Global North.

3.3 Context, Collaboration, and Community-Building

The collection brings together an international team of scholars and thought leaders with diverse cross-disciplinary knowledge encompassing law, history, and politics; policy experience; and in-country expertise, including both established thematic experts and emerging experts. In a literature still dominated by scholars from, based in, or educated in the Global North, in this volume, the intention has been to include a diverse range of voices and to facilitate their engagement with one another, with full gender balance across the contributors. The inclusion of new voices has helped to broaden representation in the literature and add nuance and diversity to the way in which the relationship between institutional resilience and democratic backsliding is understood.

The structure and development of this collection was designed to maximise its potential by inviting authors from the case-study jurisdictions to write the case-study chapters, sequencing the thematic chapters to be written after the case-study chapters and conducting workshops for the drafts. We designed the process to develop single-jurisdiction case studies over a period of time and in conversation with each other. At the same time, the case studies fed into the development of the thematic analysis. First, we invited scholars or practitioners who were intimately familiar with constitutional developments of the jurisdiction to draft their analysis. At the same time, authors invited to make a thematic contribution developed their own first drafts. We then met virtually across six webinar workshops in June 2021 to discuss these drafts. The aim of the workshops was to provide a platform for comparison, discussion, and reflection on the different experiences, perspectives, and challenges addressed in the chapters. The thematic authors had the opportunity to listen and learn from the experts on each jurisdiction at these workshops. The second stage involved the substantive revision of all chapters based on this exchange of ideas.

To some extent, this approach resonates with the notion of 'slow comparison' proposed by Dann and others.[15] Comparison, in our efforts, was individual but benefited from insights shared from other similarly situated jurisdictions. They further benefited from thematic inquiries. To this extent, the comparative work and methodology in this volume is essentially collaborative. Throughout the development of the collection, we have remained acutely aware that each constitutional system is its own creature, embedded within its own unique matrix of cultural, legal, and political traditions and understandings, which requires not an artificial scholarly positionality of undefined 'elevation' but one of 'embeddedness'. However, while each of the case studies is a single-jurisdiction study, fully understanding any system in context requires creative collaboration between both the 'insiders' and 'outsiders' in an ethos of open, reflective, and iterative dialogue based on the shedding of assumptions, attentiveness, and a form of intellectual kinship. It has required all of us to openly acknowledge the limitations of our understanding but has also required us to question why we think about specific challenges, concepts, and frameworks, or institutions in the way that we do. We can never fully bridge the insider–outsider gap, but focusing closely on what that gap looks like can help us to better address this deep challenge of comparison in constitutional law, which so often limits its prospects. It is also our hope that this is not just a community for now but part of a community-building exercise that can enrich all of our work and collectively provide intellectual and mutual supports that strengthen over time. While we can continue to issue claims to the centre for recognition, for inclusion, and for equity, we can work to incrementally construct our alternative sites and networks of intellectual exchange.

The presence of contributors from the Global North not only reflects this need for insider–outsider collaboration but also reflects the relevance of the empirical and thematic analysis far beyond the seven case studies. In this connection, it may be noted that these authors, too, come from systems that are, in many ways, 'peripheral' in the global conversation on constitutional democracy (e.g. Australia, Ireland, New Zealand), which has helped in fostering understandings of how knowledge and theory are constructed 'in the shadow of global constructions',[16] although how each of us experiences this differs greatly from state to state depending on recognition at the Global North 'top table', cultural linkages, and geographic proximity to the most active sites of intellectual engagement as well as access to material resources. Finally, this form of aggregative comparison also requires

[15] See e.g. Dann, Riegner, and Bönnemann, 'The Southern Turn' (n 9) 35.

[16] Carlos Arturo Villagrán Sandoval, 'Interrogating "Constitutionalism of the South" and New Pathways for Research: The Case for a Central America in the Global Debate' (*Völkerrechtsblog*, 8 August 2017) https://voelkerrechtsblog.org/interrogating-constitutionalism-of-the-south-and-new-pathways-for-research-the-case-for-a-central-america-in-the-global-debate/.

collaboration with the reader, inviting them to examine their own preconceptions and understandings and inviting them to read actively by engaging in their own process of comparison from their knowledge base.

4. Our Organising Concepts: Democratic Consolidation and Constitutional Endurance

Before closing our introduction with a summary of the chapters, it is worthwhile to set out and interrogate the overarching conceptual framework for this collection. As the book's title suggests, and reflecting the collection's cross-disciplinary nature, our two main organising concepts are constitutional endurance and democratic consolidation, which connect two major fields: comparative constitutional studies[17] and the field of 'consolidology' in political science. As discussed below, these two concepts capture different dimensions of shifts towards, and away from, constitutional democracy in this collection and are complementary while also generating productive conceptual and analytical tensions. Endurance highlights the idea of continuity, stability, and resilience, while consolidation expresses the idea of movement, change, adaptability, trajectory, and teleology. Evidently, endurance does not mean the absence of change; change and reform may be central to resilience. Conversely, consolidation does not merely relate to the implementation of a specific single constitution: indeed, processes of democratisation may transcend specific constitutional texts.

We might first clear the conceptual ground with two observations. For the purposes of this collection, we eschew any assumption of Western-style liberal democracy as the destination point. However, this does not mean the absence of any foundational normative commitment or a lapse into relativism. We understand democracy broadly, as a political system comprising, at minimum, full, free, and fair elections; protection of core liberal and democratic rights; and meaningful constraints on government. In this manner, we seek to avoid foreclosing the possibility of post-liberal, non-liberal, or perhaps 'alt-liberal' visions of democracy. This does not, however, entail any acceptance of the concept or narrative of 'illiberal democracy' in the Hungarian or Singaporean senses, whose excessive centralisation of power and denial of political pluralism runs contrary to our basic predicates for a 'true' democracy.[18] Moreover, we should keep in mind Linz and

[17] We are mindful here that some authors, such as Oklopcic, take issue with the nomenclature of 'comparative constitutional studies', preferring the term 'comparative constitutional inquiry'. We employ 'studies' here as the cross-disciplinary term with the most recognition. See Oklopcic (n 8) 81–91.

[18] See e.g. Renáta Uitz, 'Can You Tell When an Illiberal Democracy Is in the Making? An Appeal to Comparative Constitutional Scholarship from Hungary' (2015) 13(1) International Journal of Constitutional Law 279; and Jan-Werner Müller, *What Is Populism?* (University of Pennsylvania Press 2016) chs 1 and 2. This is, of course, a conceptual minefield: Tucker, for instance, sees a stark contrast

Stepan's distinction between 'liberalisation', which may involve limited measures (e.g. easing censorship), and 'democratisation', which relates to more fundamental political regime transformation, as well as their observation that while 'transitions may begin that are never completed', this does not mean return to the *status quo ante*.[19] We also must remain alive to the fact that some claims for 'decolonisation' in the political sphere, or for the construction of an autochthonous democracy, can merely provide rhetorical cover for unconstrained—or at least, highly exclusionary—executive or majoritarian power, although this is certainly not universal.

In addition, taken together, and relying on data sets from both Freedom House and the Varieties of Democracy Institute (V-Dem), we can view our case studies at the time of writing as falling into two broad camps: three 'harder' authoritarian regimes (Ethiopia, Myanmar, and Thailand, which are categorised as 'not free', 'closed autocracy', or 'electoral autocracy') and four 'hybrid' regimes featuring a blend of democratic and authoritarian characteristics (The Gambia, Malaysia, Maldives, and Sri Lanka, which are categorised as 'partly free' and either 'electoral autocracy' or 'electoral democracy', with the latter having much higher Freedom House scores). Of course, such indices are seriously limited and can only ever tell us pieces of a complex truth.[20] Here, triangulation and comparison of indices, and their testing against qualitative analysis, helps to avoid the possible trap of over-reliance on naked data sets. Moreover, these cannot be viewed as entirely hard or traditional categories: the four 'hybrid regimes' lie along different points of the 'ever-widening grey zone'[21] between the poles of recognisable liberal democracy and authoritarianism, and some scholars prefer the nomenclature of a 'new despotism' to capture a strange new species of state-regulated extractive capitalism that seeks to leap-frog to economic modernity by placing emphasis on privatisation of life rather than encouraging the growth of the public square.[22] Even in authoritarian states, governance practices have changed, with 'modern authoritarianism' making concessions to the international arena (e.g. economic openness, limited political competition) to maintain power and a semblance of legitimacy.[23] Neither are they

between Hungary as a 'populist neo-illiberal democracy' and Singapore's 'liberal authoritarianism'. See Aviezer Tucker, *Democracy against Liberalism: Its Rise and Fall* (Polity Press 2020).

[19] Juan Linz and Alfred Stepan, 'Democracy and Its Arenas' in Juan Linz and Alfred Stepan (eds), *Problems of Democratic Transition and Consolidation. Southern Europe, South America, and Post-Communist Europe* (John Hopkins University Press 1996) 3–4.

[20] Kim Lane Scheppele, 'The Rule of Law and the Frankenstate: Why Governance Checklists Do Not Work' (2013) 26(4) Governance 559.

[21] András Bozóki, 'Illiberal Democracy Belongs to the Hybrid Regimes: Reflections on Jeffrey C. Isaac's Illiberal Democracy' (Public Seminar, 2 August 2017).

[22] See John Keane, *The New Despotism* (Harvard University Press 2020).

[23] See Andrew Puddington, *Breaking Down Democracy: Goals, Strategies, and Methods of Modern Authoritarians* (Freedom House June 2017).

static. Assessment frameworks are descriptive but not predictive: they can paint a picture of the present but not of what is to come, reminding us that many of the democratising events in our case studies were something of a surprise.

This brings us to the first conceptual framework, democratic consolidation, which is essentially contested but nevertheless useful. Democratisation theory, developed by political scientists alongside the global expansion of democracy (the 'third wave of democratisation', which swept across Southern Europe, Latin America, Asia, and Africa from the 1970s into the late 1990s), separates the overall democratisation process into two phases: 'transition to democracy', defined as the movement towards full, free, and fair elections in post-authoritarian states, whether through revolution, a political pact, or the gradual ceding of power by an authoritarian regime; and 'consolidation of democracy', which might be defined as the development of a minimal level of democratic governance in the period following the first democratic elections.[24]

Three starting observations can be made here. First is that theorists diverge sharply on when a constitutional democracy might be considered to be 'consolidated', which ultimately depends on the underlying definition of democracy itself. For those adhering to a more minimal procedural conception centred on the electoral process, consolidation can be considered achieved when, for instance, a state has experienced two peaceful transitions of power through full, free, and fair elections, and there are no significant threats to democratic rule.[25] This, however, has been criticised as bringing a range of West-centric assumptions into play, exemplified by Huntington's 'two-party turnover' test for consolidation (requiring two alternations of parties in government), criticised by Schmitter as revealing an 'Anglo-Saxon bias' in its excessive adherence to the model of strong, two-party systems in Anglo-Saxon countries such as the United States and the United Kingdom, and for over-inclusion of states within the democratic fold.[26] Second, alternative frameworks place additional emphasis on the rule of law and the protection of civil liberties and fundamental rights.[27] However, in the 1990s, this gave rise to forbiddingly complex frameworks for assessing whether consolidation had, in fact,

[24] See e.g. Philippe Schmitter and Javier Santiso, 'Three Temporal Dimensions to the Consolidation of Democracy' (1998) 19(1) International Political Science Review 69, 72, 77. An alternative conceptual framework from the 1990s, aimed at examining 'quality of democracy', places much less emphasis on the temporal aspects of democratisation and has never quite supplanted the other two.

[25] Samuel Huntington, *The Third Wave: Democratization in the Late Twentieth Century* (Oxford University Press 1991) 266.

[26] Philippe Schmitter, 'The Consolidation of Political Democracies: Processes, Rhythms, Sequences and Types' in Geoffrey Pridham (ed), *Transitions to Democracy: Comparative Perspectives from Southern Europe, Latin America and Eastern Europe* (Dartmouth 1995) 550.

[27] Philippe Schmitter, for instance, made use of a bipartite classification of procedural and structural *minima* encompassing 'civic rights of contestation and association, secret ballots, universal suffrage and "the rule of law"' and 'regular elections, multiple political parties, associational recognition and access, and an accountable executive'. See Schmitter, 'The Consolidation of Political Democracies' (n 26).

been achieved.[28] Recent patterns of regression across third-wave democracies have raised further questions about whether third-wave analysts underestimated the timescales needed to entrench self-sustaining constitutional democracy, including not only implementing a new constitution but also fostering a very different constitutional culture.

Third, and perhaps most importantly, these frameworks related to 'third-wave' democratisation processes that were, compared to our seven case studies, far more linear, usually involving a rather clear shift from authoritarian rule to democratic rule, including a change of government, a new constitution in an overtly democratic cast, and new institutions, for example a new constitutional court or a shift to a multiparty system in states such as Spain, Hungary, Brazil, or South Korea. In this sense, democratic consolidation and the entrenchment and implementation of a new constitution could be viewed as coextensive. Among our case studies, Maldives or The Gambia come closest to this paradigm, the former facing the challenge of faithful implementation of the text and spirit of its first democratic Constitution adopted in 2008, the latter facing the challenge of installing a new constitution capable of giving voice to the democratic transition following the ousting of dictator Yahya Jammeh in 2016. Across the other case studies, the dominant picture is one of 'ambiguous transitions'[29] evincing greater fluidity, complexity, and non-linearity—the 'uneven pathways' of this collection's title—as well as heightened antagonism between the constitutional framework and democratic development, raising the difference between 'big bang' constitutional change and incremental change and the constraints of attempting democratisation within the framework of an ambivalently democratic constitution, discussed further below.[30]

Two additional points should help to clarify our employment of this framework. First, it is important to recognise that the international context for these

[28] Alfred Stepan and Juan Linz constructed perhaps the most complex formula for democratic consolidation, as involving three separate but interrelated elements: (i) *behavioural* consolidation (the absence of any significant anti-democratic movements in a polity); (ii) *attitudinal* consolidation (requiring public support for democracy as the most legitimate form of government); and (iii) *constitutional* consolidation (entailing the submission by all political and other actors in the regime to a specific framework of laws, institutions, and procedures; 'the rule of law'). 'Democratic consolidation' was further subdivided into five 'arenas', each with its own guiding principles, provided in parentheses here: *civil society* (freedom of association and expression); *political society* (free, fair, and regular elections); *rule of law* (unconditional adherence to the Constitution); *state apparatus* (usable and effective bureaucracy); and *economic society* (institutionalised market economy). Linz and Stepan suggested that progress in these 'arenas' could be assessed against any or all of the three overarching subtypes of consolidation to provide a better picture of the overall consolidation process. See Linz and Stepan, 'Democracy and Its Arenas' (n 18).

[29] See e.g. Kinkino Kia Legide, 'Exploring the Limits and Challenges of Compliance with Transitional Justice in the Context of Ambiguous Transitions: The Case of post-2018 Ethiopia' (2022) 13(1) Journal of Law and Conflict Resolution, 1–26.

[30] See e.g. Cheryl Saunders, 'Session IV Conclusions' from the Second Melbourne Forum on Constitution Building in Asia and the Pacific, "From Big Bang to Incrementalism: Choices and Challenges in Constitution Building"' (Manila, 3–4 October 2017) <https://law.unimelb.edu.au/__data/assets/pdf_file/0004/2607394/Report-conclusions-Saunders.pdf> accessed 3 November 2022

developments has itself changed since the third wave of democratisation was at its peak in the 1990s. Whereas post-1974 (and certainly post-1989) theorists tended to assume a single destination (some form of 'getting to Denmark', albeit often a more neoliberal and 'low-intensity' democracy than the real Denmark itself), we now live in not merely a multipolar world but a multi-model world, where Danish democratic imaginaries compete with 'getting to China' or 'getting to Singapore', while many other empirical referents (including neocolonial powers like the United States and old colonial powers like the United Kingdom and France) are facing serious democratic challenges. That said, on the positive side, compared to the transitions of the third wave, we now do not lack for other 'Denmarks': why do we not speak of getting to Botswana, South Korea, Uruguay, Seychelles, or Tuvalu, all of which have highly regarded non-Western democratic systems? Second, our case studies suggest that we should focus not only on empirical referents for a 'final destination' but also on intervening destinations: depending on a state's starting point, the aim might be first to get to Malaysia, Mongolia, South Africa, or Uruguay. Evidently, the very notion of a destination must be handled carefully: our destinations are not static as both democratic practice and democratic understandings are continually changing.

The second conceptual framework, constitutional endurance, owes its origins to the work of Elkins, Ginsburg, and Melton, offering empirical assessment of the endurance of national constitutions and identifying a positive correlation between constitutional longevity and democratic quality, political stability, rights protection, and economic performance.[31] This has had a significant impact in comparative constitutional law, prompting reflection on the 'quest for stability'[32] and the optimal balance between constitutional rigidity (setting down effective rules of the game superior to 'ordinary' politics) and flexibility (allowing for continual updating of, and avoiding ossification, of the constitutional order).

While the literature appears somewhat undecided on whether greater ethnic diversity may negatively affect constitutional endurance due to the heightened difficulties in agreeing the rules of the game,[33] it is clear that ethnic divisions have affected the trajectory of democratisation in our case studies, reflected here most starkly in Ethiopia's ethnically based federal structure and Myanmar's estimated 135 ethnic groups (across 8 major groups) but also in Malaysia's ethnocentric

[31] See Zachary Elkins, Tom Ginsburg, and James Melton, *The Endurance of National Constitutions* (Cambridge University Press 2009). See also Dag Anckar, 'Democracy and Constitutional Endurance' (2014) 10(1) Taiwan Journal of Democracy 23.

[32] See Giacomo Delledonne, 'Crisis, Emergencies and Constitutional Change' in Xenophon Contiades and Alkmene Fotiadou, *Routledge Handbook of Comparative Constitutional Change* (Routledge 2021).

[33] See Andreas P Kyriacou and Francisco José López Velásquez, 'An Examination of the Long-Term Determinants of Constitutional Endurance: Geography, Diversity, and Historical Legacies' (2015) 171(3) Journal of Institutional and Theoretical Economics 432, 436. Cf Elkins, Ginsburg, and Melton (n 31) 138.

politics and the struggles between the Sinhalese majority and Tamil minority in Sri Lanka, among others.[34] Moreover, approaching this expanding literature with a decolonial lens, one finds that it can all too easily slip into familiar (neo)colonial frames and analytical registers. Consider, for instance, a 2015 study building on the constitutional endurance framework to offer that countries with a greater percentage of land in the tropics (used as a proxy for extractive industries and the institutionalisation of inequalities) are at a higher risk of constitutional failure or that the 'genetic distance' of a country from the United States may be a factor in constitutional endurance: 'the bigger the differences, the more difficult it becomes to understand and adapt complex technological and institutional innovations coming from the U.S.'.[35] The same study offers, in addition, that 'a longer colonial experience reduces the risk of constitutional failure'[36] and positively compares the benefits of British colonisation with French colonisation, for instance, as regards the durability of the constitutional order.

None of this is couched in any language acknowledging what might be deeply problematic cultural assumptions underlying the framing and interpretation of the statistical data or the deficiencies in comparison: it is one thing to note the greater durability of institutions in former British colonies compared to their French counterparts, for instance (which is relevant to five of our case studies), but this utterly marginalises the unanswerable but necessary question of how a community or polity may have developed without the predations of colonisation. For anyone reading such studies in a 'peripheral' post-colonial state in the Global South (or, indeed, the Global North), there are very uncomfortable echoes of the purportedly objective pseudo-scientific treatment of governance, politics, and race of the nineteenth and twentieth centuries, even if such work is produced in good faith.

That said, the concept of constitutional endurance provides useful intellectual resources for analysing and understanding the broader context of the democratising episodes in our seven case studies. First, it trains our mind on constitutional longevity. Taking Africa and Asia as starting categories, and removing Latin America as a hotspot of constitutional replacement, recent research suggests that the average duration of a constitution in sub-Saharan Africa is 17.14 years, whereas it is 61.4 years in the rest of the world (including Asia).[37] However, our suite of states includes notable diversity in basic constitutional endurance: as Table 1.4 shows, we see a spectrum from Malaysia, which has had the same constitution

[34] Here, we are cognisant of studies on the very creation of 'ethnicity' as a concept during the Empire which should inform constitutional discourse. See e.g. Mahmood Mamdani, *Define and Rule: Native as Political Identity* (Harvard University Press 2012).

[35] Kyriacou and López Velásquez (n 33) 434, 436.

[36] Ibid, 444.

[37] Niall Ferguson and Daniel Lansberg-Rodríguez, *The Constitution of Disposability/Constituciones desechables* (Fundación para el progreso 2017) 65.

since independence in 1957 (65 years), to Thailand, where no less than 17 constitutions have been promulgated since 1932, most recently in 2017. In fact, only four countries worldwide have had more constitutions, all located in Latin America and the Caribbean.[38] The other case studies have had much fewer constitutions, ranging between three (Myanmar) and seven (Maldives). The constitutions in force date from the 1950s, 1970s, 1990s, and 2000s. Providing an average figure for constitutional durability across the seven states would therefore be misleading.

In Thailand, which has been a central case study for the endurance literature, the replacement rate correlates, to a significant extent, with the frequency of coups, and we see some negative correlations, as one might expect, with democratic performance: as Table 1.4 indicates, the country has a low Freedom House score of 29/100, and is categorised as a 'closed autocracy' by the V-Dem (Varieties of Democracy) Institute. In this connection, the constitutional endurance framework makes a useful distinction between 'churn' (frequent constitutional replacement alongside institutional continuity) and 'cycling' (irresolvable competition between two groups, which produces constitutional replacement dynamics when power alternates).[39] Myanmar has, at first blush, a much better basic record on constitutional survival, with three constitutions since 1948; yet, it is also categorised as a 'closed autocracy' by V-Dem but with a much lower Freedom House score of 9/100. However, this simply underscores the air of unreality generated where a constitution is not formally suspended, abrogated, or replaced following a military coup: in Myanmar, we see claims from the military junta that the 2008 Constitution remains in force, despite the impossibility of its application since the coup took place in February 2021, and against the insistence by the opposition (partly in exile) that the Constitution is no longer in force. Constitutional endurance, in such a scenario, is a chimera, especially where the repudiation and rupture of democratic governance enshrined in the Constitution is so much swifter and overt than other forms of decay, backsliding, or reversal[40] and where the opposition has adopted an interim framework, the Federal Democracy Charter, the latter underscoring the resilience of the democratic movement in the face of the strongest headwinds.[41] Further complicating the picture, when we look at the United Nations Development Programme's Human Development Index in Table 1.4, Thailand is one of the top two performers (alongside Malaysia, with its 1957 Constitution) and

[38] Ecuador (20), Haiti (24), Venezuela (26), and Dominican Republic (33). See Ferguson and Lansberg-Rodríguez (n 37) 61–64.

[39] Elkins, Ginsburg, and Melton (n 31) 23–24.

[40] On the conceptual and practical distinctions between democratic decay and democratic breakdown, see e.g. Tom Gerald Daly, 'Breaking Down the Meaning of Constitutional Breakdown' in Ulad Belavusau and Aleksandra Gliszczyńska-Grabias (eds), *Constitutionalism under Stress: Essays in Honour of Wojciech Sadurski* (Oxford University Press 2020).

[41] See in this collection Ohn Mar Zin, Naw Janet, and Kimana Zulueta-Fülscher, Chapter 13 'Myanmar's Transition to Peace and Democracy: The Journey Reversed' [PAGE NUMBER, p.2, p.18, p.23 manuscript].

has the highest gross domestic product (GDP) of all seven case studies. Its rule-of-law score from the World Justice Project (WJP) also compares well to the other case studies with more durable constitutions, which are all 'middle performers' in the WJP Index's 140-country data set—although all are on a downward trend in that index.

The constitutional endurance framework is clearly useful, then, but it must be carefully approached. Our case studies warn us not to fetishise constitutional endurance as an end in itself: if a state has a constitution that is more authoritarian in character, its replacement by a more democratic text is surely welcome. Here, there is wide variation in constitutional rigidity. Myanmar's 2008 Constitution, before the 2021 coup, is indicative of the problems raised by a hybrid text enshrining a 'disciplined' democratic regime contemplated by the armed forces according a veto to the armed forces regarding amendment.[42] At the other end of the spectrum, as Zulfa notes, the 2008 Maldivian Constitution dispensed with special amendment requirements in previous constitutions, requiring merely a majority vote in parliament, which is viewed as problematically stacking the odds towards hyper-presidentialism in a text that has already enshrined expansive executive presidential powers.[43] The longer-lived Malaysian and Sri Lankan constitutions have been amended 45 and 20 times, respectively, with flexibility producing many deleterious effects on the protection of fundamental liberties and checks and balances.[44]

Yet, this is not simply about constitutional updating: our case studies also indicate what might be viewed as 'intra-constitutional cycling'. In Sri Lanka, for instance, we see a tug-of-war of amendments as two political blocs with competing visions of the constitutional and political order gain the upper hand: between an empowered executive presidency and a more balanced 'semi-presidential' power relationship between president and parliament. Whether constitutional length is an impediment to the text operating as an effective co-ordination mechanism is an additional question: four of the seven case studies have constitutions of near, or over, 300 articles, placing them at the highest end of the global scale. The Constitution of Myanmar is the longest, at 457 articles in total.

[42] See the discussion of the 'Seven Step Roadmap to Disciplined Democracy', ibid, [PAGE NUMBER, p.5 manuscript].

[43] See in this collection Mariyam Zulfa, Chapter 11 'Maldives Constitution 2008: Winds of Change at the Fifteenth-Year Crossroads' [PAGE NUMBER, p. 9 manuscript].

[44] In Malaysia, for instance, the sheer scale of change is further revealed when one considers that the 45 amendment Acts have made over 600 textual alterations to the Federal Constitution since 1957. See e.g. Andrew Harding, *The Constitution of Malaysia—A Contextual Analysis* (Hart Publishing 2012) 103: updated to November 2022 in this collection by Wilson Tay Tze Vern, Chapter 15 'Making Progress on a Rocky Path: Democratic Consolidation and Endurance in Malaysia, 2018–2021'.

5. Three Key Features

While summaries of the chapters are provided at the end of the introduction, it may be helpful, here, to draw out three further key features of the constitutional landscapes covered in this collection.

5.1 Constitutional Change: Endurance and Decay as Cyclical

The jurisdictional analysis in this collection reveals that endurance and decay tend to have a recurrent pattern. Observing this pattern compels us to revisit the manner in which we approach constitutional developments. As illustrated in the case studies, it is difficult to predict when and how political opportunities for constitutional change come about. It is even harder to predict when political opportunities for democratisation come about.

However, when they occur, the case studies suggest that those moments were interpreted as moments for transition to democratisation and constitutional endurance. In most of our case studies, within a short period of time, there was a return to more authoritarian government. If this is, in fact, the experience in constitutional change, how should that inform the way we think about constitutional endurance and democratic decay? The case studies reveal the way in which the same constitutional actors and institutions can radically alter their constitutional commitments to contribute to democratic decay, as we see in Ethiopian Prime Minister Abiy Ahmed's shift from substantive commitment to democracy, to mere rhetorical use of democratic language, the military's shifting positions in Thailand and Myanmar, or the heightening repression of the Malaysian government during the COVID-19 crisis. What factors contribute to such behaviour? In what ways can constitutional practice respond to such developments? The thematic analysis offered in this volume suggests that political parties play a crucial role here. Civil–military relations is another dimension which can be both a driver of such cyclical experiences and the means by which constitutional endurance can be undermined.

From a practice perspective, anticipating a cyclical progression between constitutional endurance and democratic decay can be very useful. It can help constitutional actors who are often in the minority to strategise differently about their principled interventions and about sequencing of reforms. It will also help to manage expectations and limited resources in more sustainable ways. Importantly, many of the case studies underline that a democratising episode, even if stymied or reversed, leaves traces in the body politic. For that reason, rather than speaking of linear 'pendulum swings' or static cycling, we could use the metaphor of a spiral or corkscrew.

5.2 Critical Events and Crises

In the jurisdictions examined in this edited volume, several critical events occurred during the writing process itself, and authors, mostly based in-country, had the unenviable task of updating their analysis to account for such developments.

All seven case studies were inevitably affected by the COVID-19 pandemic, which has evidently had a significant impact worldwide on democratic practice and developments. The case study cluster presents a range of diverse experiences, including how the pandemic affected democratisation, albeit in different ways and to different extents. In some, the effect appears minimal, or at least manageable, to date. In others (e.g. Sri Lanka, Ethiopia, or Malaysia) the impact has been dramatic and goes directly to the concerns of this volume. The pandemic occurred at the mid-point stage in developing this edited volume, giving rise to several conceptual and practical challenges which we reflect on further below. At a minimum, it required that we review and expand the substantive focus of the volume, including the addition of a thematic chapter. Suffice to say that, while it was disruptive, it provided us with a useful foil to examine the relevance of crises to constitutional endurance, democratic consolidation, and democratic decay. It is notable that preliminary assessment of the pandemic's impact worldwide suggests that this impact has been asymmetric: while many established democracies have shown resilience, declines are viewed as concentrated in hybrid and authoritarian states due to abuse of emergency powers and a hike in political repression.[45]

In addition to the COVID-19 pandemic, several jurisdictions experienced additional political and economic crises, including the outbreak of conflict in Ethiopia, a military coup in Myanmar, and severe economic crisis in Sri Lanka. Dealing with the impact of these developments for scholarship, for professional commitments, and to all concerned at a personal level gave us the opportunity to learn more deeply about the demands of meaningful comparative work. Contributing to the global knowledge pool on constitutional endurance and decay while dealing with the multidimensional critical events, and sometimes a crisis, was difficult, to say the least. The authors had deep and rich insights and interpretations on the constitutional developments that they were examining. However, many of us lacked the intellectual, cultural, and economic resources that are necessary for translating that to scholarship. In seeking to bridge this gap in producing this volume, we have been reminded of the need to think of solidarity at multiple levels: personal, institutional, intellectual, and beyond. It should encourage us to review practices of knowledge development to ask what must change if knowledge production is to be more inclusive and representative.

[45] See e.g. International IDEA, *Global State of Democracy Report 2021: Building Resilience in a Pandemic Era* (International IDEA December 2021).

While many of these crises, of course, have laid bare the deficiencies in governance that trouble us in this collection, they have also reminded us of the reserves of strength, resilience, determination, and innovation that can be found in the face of such adversity, both in the scholarly communities and the wider societies in which they are embedded. Interestingly, considering the key finding of Elkins, Ginsburg, and Melton that crisis does not necessarily impact upon constitutional endurance, to date, these crises have not (yet) led to constitutional change—although that is debatable in the context of Myanmar, as discussed above. Finally, events in both our case studies and Global North democracies alike require us to reflect on how we tend to think of crises as acute phenomena, overlooking the importance of latent crisis or chronic crises (e.g. concerning the legitimacy of the political system or ruling elites), which may not present an existential threat to the constitutional order but continually reveal its structural deficiencies.[46] This is not only an important contextual feature but also one that Global North democracies need to better comprehend.

5.3 New Old Actors

This volume also offers new perspectives on constitutional actors. The monarch in Thailand and the military in Myanmar, Sri Lanka, and Thailand, for instance, make a significant impact on constitutional governance. Civil–military relations, in particular, is an area that is marginal to scholarly inquiries about constitutional endurance and decay, except as actors that place constitutional governance at risk. The collection also challenges us to see familiar actors with fresh eyes, including Mouli's observation that the existing literature tends to assume that there is a broad global understanding of 'what a party is', overlooking the salience of the 'past lives' of parties as grassroots or social organisations in post-colonial and Southern states. More fundamentally, the first thematic chapter trains our minds on the importance of 'office' in processes of constitutional change and continuity, which helpfully disaggregates and reframes how we tend to focus on institutions and institutional frameworks. Finally, the post-colonial case studies remind us that, while democratic institutions can be framed in some way as a colonial inheritance, a significant part of that inheritance is clearly a legacy of 'authoritarian shadows' bequeathing an array of laws and tools to stifle democratic organisation and expression to contemporary governments.[47] We see similar dynamics in any state seeking to transition from authoritarian or undemocratic rule more generally, as indicated by

[46] See Benjamin M Studebaker, 'Legitimacy Crises in Embedded Democracies' (2023) 22 Contemporary Political Theory 230.

[47] See e.g. Dag Anckar, 'Democracy as a Westminster Heritage' (2011) 7(1) Taiwan Journal of Democracy 56; Ravi Ahuja, 'Authoritarian Shadows: Indian Independence and the Problem of Democratisation' (2018) 46(5–6) Social Scientist 3.

references to a 'tradition of authoritarianism' in Ethiopia and Maldives, for instance, encompassing a spectrum from monarchical to one-party to dominant-party rule.

6. Summary of the Book

As the discussion above suggests, this book is designed to be of interest to a diverse international audience of scholars; teachers; and students of law, history, politics, and development. There are a variety of 'entry points' to the book for scholars and practitioners, whether one is interested in law and development, the dynamics of democratisation, democratic backsliding, constitutional design, the interface between law and politics, post-colonial studies and decolonisation, federalism, or conflict and peace-making. The text has been written with the aim of achieving maximum clarity and is structured in a way to aid the reader, with a logical flow from the introductory framing chapter, to the seven thematic chapters, and finally the seven country-specific case studies. The editors have encouraged cross-references between chapters to ensure that the collection works as a coherent and meaningful meeting of minds across all authors.

6.1 Thematic Chapters

In Chapter 2, the first thematic chapter, Jason Grant Allen draws on the seven case studies to elaborate a key theme in, and conceptual framework for understanding, any process of constitutional development: public office. He defines offices as institutionalised jural positions whose content (i.e. rights, powers, duties) determines the official's position vis-à-vis other officials and subjects of various status. Constitutional orders, by turn, are networks of offices. Office, for Allen, has been relatively neglected in modern Western public law theory but is fundamental to understanding any politico-legal order (Western or non-Western, modern or pre-modern). His framework of analysis opens up several perspectives on 'constitutional development'. First, it provides a model for tracking changes over time as (i) changes to the content of offices within a stable catalogue of offices and (ii) changes to the overall catalogue of offices. Second, it provides a framework to conceptualise the interaction between competing constitutional orders, such as the official state constitutional order and parallel religious or ethnic social orders that bolster or compete with it. Third, it provides a framework within which to articulate a minimum normative concept of 'constitutionalism' that could avoid some of the usual objections lodged against ideas of democracy and the rule of law in the post-colonial context.

Chapter 3, by Kimana Zulueta-Fülscher, explores the role of governing institutions as either catalysts, allies, or potential obstacles to reform by analysing the structure and character of these institutions in the seven case studies. Central to this chapter is the very complex relationship between (and within) the executive and the legislature in parliamentary monarchies or republics and presidential, semi-presidential, and assembly-independent systems. Looking at these systems, the chapter also focuses on the relationship between the political, the electoral, and the political party system in an attempt to assess whether and how this interaction may have contributed or not to stable and resilient governments with enough power to push through reforms. It stands out that all seven countries have endured significant setbacks to reform processes mostly aimed at consolidating democracy by way of increasing the accountability of state institutions and rebalancing executive–legislative relations. Some of the factors contributing to these (temporary) failures include the highly fragmented and weak nature of many opposition coalitions; the personalised nature of political parties and high levels of party corruption, which result in weak parliaments that fail to serve in their oversight capacity; the general fluidity of the political party system; and short-termism of many political leaders and their electorate. Underlying the latter are two different world views—liberal-republican and communitarian and/or ethno-nationalist—that help build narratives and expectations as to the way politics is practiced and the role and aim of governing institutions in processes of democratic consolidation.

Chapter 4, by Mouli Banerjee, provides a 'state-of-the-field', critical overview of the role of political parties in democratic transitions, especially in nation states of the Global South. With specific references to the seven case studies, the chapter maps the patterns that emerge in the interactions between party politics and fluxes in regimes within nation states. It conceptualises the role of political parties in democratic strengthening or backslides along two broad thematic parameters: first, in relation to the historical, legal, and institutional contexts within with parties exist; and second, in relation to the dynamic roles parties play as agents. The chapter focuses on parties as individual units instead of party systems and touches upon questions of party constitutionalisation; party bans; party finance; party institutionalisation; and the linkages between political parties and business elites, autocratic or military regimes, populist leaders, and dynastic politics. It also sheds light on the previous lives of parties as grassroots or social organisations and locates post-colonial parties in their historical context. By doing so, the chapter understands parties as heterogenous, constantly shifting, dynamic entities and provides the thematic rubrics against which the place of parties in democratisation processes in the selected case studies in this volume, as well as in other states in transition globally, can be better understood.

Chapter 5, by Julius Yam, draws on the case studies to challenge two common ways of understanding constitutional courts in transitional regimes—the

'Descriptive View' and the 'Normative View'. The Descriptive View describes constitutional courts as active participants in transitional politics, while the Normative View suggests that successful transition requires constitutional courts taking up a democracy-building role. The chapter argues that both have failed to properly account for the exceptionality of regime change. The exceptional nature of transitions suggests that there is tremendous diversity among the paths of transitional regimes, patterns of constitutional politics, and courts' involvement during transitional periods. The fact that courts are operating in transitional regimes tells us very little about their actual judicial roles. The exceptional nature of transitional regimes also has normative implications. The chapter contends that the exceptionality of regime change can potentially work against judicial intervention. Exceptionality, in and of itself, is not a justification for a stronger judicial role. It is argued that there are situations where it is, in fact, desirable for courts to stay out of transitional politics.

Chapter 6, by Shanil Wijesinha and Daniel Alphonsus, examines two primary issues: (i) the connection between constitutions and civil–military relations and (ii) how security-sector reform intersects with democratic consolidation and constitutional endurance, especially at moments of democratic transition. Drawing from literature on militarisation, they examine how constitutional features regulate and influence civil–military relations, that is, the balance of power between civilian authorities and the security sector. This includes analysis of the executive powers of the head of state, the role and powers of the commander-in-chief, the role of the military, and the 'military imprint'. It also reflects on the limitations of constitutions and constitutional reform as tools to balance civil–military relations and how contextual factors and the balance of power foreground any such effort. Finally, they consider strategies for recalibrating unbalanced civil–military relations.

Chapter 7, by Cheryl Saunders, examines the relevance of culture for the establishment and resilience of constitutional democracy. Her analysis seeks both to understand the impact of culture on constitutional endurance and to identify responses that may be useful to maximise resilience. Drawing on the range of experiences with democratisation across the seven country case studies, the analysis begins by exploring the properties of culture that have a bearing on constitutional democracy and identifying the variety of communities with whom aspects of culture might be associated. A necessarily stylised distinction is drawn between three phases in making and maintaining democratic constitutions: the period during which the foundations are laid, implementation of a new or changed constitution, and consolidation over time. The findings of the chapter endorse the relevance of culture. They also point to some critical questions that remain unresolved about how constitutional culture can be adapted within a confined time frame to support extensive constitutional change.

The final thematic chapter, by Joelle Grogan, reflects on whether the COVID-19 crisis has served as a catalyst for deeper commitment to constitutional consolidation, and proof of the resilience of democratic institutions in the case studies, or as a means of furthering democratic decay and deconsolidation. It traces the central themes, questions, and issues raised by the case studies as regards the measures adopted in response to the COVID-19 pandemic. It connects this with an examination of whether the predicted dangers of the abuse of emergency powers took place and whether countries were successful in limiting the potential for abuse as well as preventing or sanctioning it. It also considers the degree to which constitutional limits on the use of emergency powers during a pandemic, as well as provisions for parliamentary oversight and judicial scrutiny, have provided an effective safeguard against the abuse or misuse of power during the pandemic among the case studies.

6.2 Case Studies

In Chapter 9 Satang Nabaneh presents the first case study, focusing on The Gambia. She examines how, after 22 years of uninterrupted authoritarian government headed by Yahya Jammeh, in 2017, The Gambia formally began the transition to democracy after the 'unprecedented' 2016 presidential elections. Observing that incumbents in semi-competitive authoritarian regimes often retain power despite having to regularly compete in multiparty elections, she highlights that what happened in The Gambia is the first time in post-colonial Africa's political history that a 'military-turned-civilian' dictator lost an election. For Nabaneh, this transition sparks a key question: what are the prospects for democratic consolidation and constitutional endurance in the Gambian case? While conventional assumptions categorised The Gambia as a 'least likely' case, she argues that there is a fair chance for democratic consolidation, given The Gambia's context of the withering of an authoritarian regime and its replacement by a democratic government. This chapter gives an overview of the constitutional change processes, the role of governing and judicial institutions, and the influence of entrenched political culture on democratic constitutional performance after more than two decades of autocratic rule.

Chapter 10, by Adem Kassie Abebe, describes and interrogates the (hopes for) transition to democracy in Ethiopia that was set off by the protest-induced reshuffle within the ruling party in April 2018 (mainly up to October 2020). In addition to describing the main issues, actors, and reforms in the transition, the chapter outlines some insights relevant to policy and scholarly understanding of political transitions and constitutional design. The chapter observes that the transition not only failed to deliver democracy but has also degenerated into civil war, necessitating a more confounding double transition from conflict to peace and to democracy. The chapter highlights the importance of constitutional arrangements, even in authoritarian settings; the need to build a coalition of democracy to backstop a transition and ameliorate inherent vulnerabilities to conflict; and the criticality of reforms outside the legal and constitutional framework. The chapter concludes with observations on the magnetic pool of a socio-political tradition of authoritarianism in stalling, and even reversing and worsening, democratic and constitutional transitions.

Chapter 11, by Mariyam Zulfa, examines the introduction of multiparty democracy and multi-candidate elections in Maldives for the first time in its constitutional history in 2008. Since then, party politics has gained ground with ten parties active on the ground today. Experience since the new Constitution's inception has shown that no one political party has attained the constitutionally required 50 per cent + 1 votes in the first round. Zulfa offers that the resultant coalition-making is anomalous to the presidential system upon which the Constitution is predicated and requires review. She argues that the embeddedness of a constitutional culture resulting from centuries of monarchical—and later authoritarian—rule, as well as the relative youth of political parties, manifested in their lacking liberal ideological bearings and continued factionalisation and disagreements amongst party elites, which are all signposts for review as the democratisation process embraces more citizen participation. The Maldivian case study illustrates that constitution-making processes are sites for power play by political elites. While political parties create a space for greater public participation, something more is required for the true benefits of individual rights guaranteed by the Constitution to flow to the people and to entrench institutional resilience.

Chapter 12, by Luwie Ganeshathasan, analyses the failures of Sri Lanka's 2015-2018 constitutional reform process. The chapter starts with a brief explanation of the country before addressing Sri Lanka's constitutional evolution since its independence. This includes discussion of fraught ethnic relations, majoritarian politics, and secessionist claims. The central focus of the chapter is the political change that occurred in January 2015 with the election of President Maithripala Sirisena. Special attention is paid to the Nineteenth amendment to the Constitution of 1978 enacted during this period and the larger constitutional reform process, including a discussion on the manner in which the political opposition to these reforms manifested itself both within and outside the government. This chapter also provides a brief comment on Sri Lanka's response to COVID-19 and the pandemic's impact on constitutional governance. In the final section, Ganeshathasan reflects on the reasons for the failure of the 2015–2018 reform effort, discussing the failures both in terms of process and substance that allowed the momentum and public support for curtailing the powers of the executive president to be squandered and which provided ammunition for a counter-narrative as to why a stronger executive president was, in fact, needed.

Chapter 13, by Ohn Mar Zin, Naw Janet, and Kimana Zulueta-Fülscher, explores Myanmar's political journey from colonial times to the 2021 military coup d'état, which reversed ten years of a difficult, yet hopeful, transition to peace and democracy. After decades of military rule, Myanmar's shift to a civilian government in 2010, under a military-sponsored constitution, constituted a significant turnaround, which paved the way for the start of a transition to peace, democracy, and economic development. However, the 2008 Constitution guaranteed key institutional powers to the armed forces, which ensured that it controlled key ministries in the executive, and afforded the possibility to veto constitutional amendment proposals in the Union Parliament. The armed forces, and its Commander in Chief, thus remained key actors—and potential veto players—in Myanmar's myriad transitions. This chapter looks closely at the democratic transition, first under the military-sponsored Union Solidarity and Development Party (USDP) and, since 2015, under the government of Aung San Suu Kyi's National League for Democracy (NLD). It also describes the way in which the very fragile and politically charged dynamics between the NLD, the armed forces, and a myriad ethnic groups and their representatives challenged progress in the peace negotiations and, as a result, on constitutional reform and the planned transition towards federalism and institutional reform. The coup d'état on 1 February 2021, after the NLD again won the November 2020 elections by a landslide, constituted a setback, though it allowed the emergence of a stronger resistance movement against the armed forces.

Chapter 14, by Khemthong Tonsakulrungruang, argues that Thailand has suffered from a phenomenon known as 'abusive constitutionalism', where not only does a constitution not produce vibrant democracy, but also we see constitutional change employed by an authoritarian leader to entrench his rule and undermine democracy. This chapter traces Thailand's rapid decay from 2014 to 2020, where a military junta ordered the drafting of the 2017 Constitution and conditioned its electoral victory. However, this chapter argues that the junta could not act alone. A network of anti-democratic elites (namely royalists, the military, the judiciary, and business conglomerates) is responsible. They are bound by the political, economic, and most importantly ideological ties of 'Thai-style democracy', which places nationalism, royalism, and moralism over democratic values, such as rights and liberties, a free and fair election, and the supremacy of the Constitution. Tonsakulrungruang explores how the anti-democratic network develops such a concept and discusses the impact of abusive constitutionalism.

In the final case study, Wilson Tay Tze Vern examines the significance of Malaysia's 'regime change' in the general election of 2018 and its tumultuous aftermath. He contextualises the 'regime-change event' within the ethnocentric landscape of Malaysian politics, setting out the prelude to the landmark events of 2018. He also explains why the driving forces behind the watershed moment of 2018 were able to make only limited reforms at best and ultimately lost their grasp on power altogether. Nonetheless, his analysis sounds a note of hope, arguing that, despite the appearance of the 'old guard' having returned to power, the Malaysian political landscape has been altered in profound and long-lasting ways which bring Malaysia closer towards genuine multiparty democracy. Constitutional mechanisms for a transition of power at federal level have been successfully tested and developed, marking further steps in the country's path towards a mature democracy. Most importantly, the political crises that have rocked Malaysia in recent years have served to underscore the resilience of constitutional democracy and institutions in the country. While the practices and principles of constitutional democracy have been severely tested by the political turmoil of 2018–2021 and the concurrent onset of the COVID-19 pandemic in Malaysia, and have held firm, he sees grounds for cautious optimism as we look to the future.

7. Concluding Reflections: Seeing Non-linear Constitutional Change through New Eyes

Anyone who has come to this book will probably share at least some of our fundamental normative commitments concerning the importance of constitutional democracy (broadly construed) as a form of political order and the importance of better understanding its myriad manifestations across our shared world. They might also share some of our frustrations with the state of the existing global conversation on democracy-building and democratic decay and might, therefore, be sympathetic to our intellectual and methodological responses to these frustrations. We are at a moment where not only is momentum building around critiques of how we approach comparative constitutional law and the study of democratisation, but also real-world events are challenging us to confront—and in some cases shred, or at least unbind ourselves from—established theoretical and conceptual assumptions and binaries. We might summarise our aim in this book as exploring the relationship between democracy-building, constitutional endurance, and democratic decay in five central ways: (i) accounting for the onset of democratising events; (ii) accounting for constitutional endurance (also known as institutional resilience); (iii) accounting for the reversal of democratisation (understood here as democratic decay, backsliding, or deconsolidation) or even the breakdown of democracy entirely; (iv) based on (i), (ii), and (iii), reviewing the heuristic model of liberal constitutional democracy that has served constitution-making across the world in the past several decades; and (v) questioning assumptions and practices associated with the dominant model that might have contributed to its current precarity; and based on all of the above, offering normative prescriptions and institutional reform options for guarding against backsliding and strengthening resilience.

However, our aim here is not to be definitive or to push an inflexible methodological model or world view. Rather than presenting ourselves as holding all the answers, we want to be understood as trying to ask unasked questions; to shine a light on understudied contexts; to provide a platform to new voices; and to prompt reflection, responses, and engagement from the overlapping scholarly and practitioner communities across the Global South and Global North. We urge our readers to seek us out, to challenge us, and to join us in this project. In this connection, one collection cannot address all of the possible questions that arise concerning democratic consolidation and constitutional endurance in the Global South: key questions for future work include issues such as prevalent corruption, the salience of multi-level governance, the roles played by international actors in democratising events (especially 'non-paradigmatic' events), and the salience of constitutional replacement in neighbouring countries, where the literature suggests a 'contagion' effect that might be missed in analysis that focuses solely on the domestic arena.[48]

While this collection does not paint a generally rosy picture, it reminds us that broad global narratives such as 'democratic recession' can hide a range of positive developments that buck the perceived dominant downward trend and which may still, over time, bear fruit. Most importantly, we hope that readers come away from this book with a renewed resolve to avoid any temptation to simply label any country contexts as 'too complicated' and to view the states here not as mere 'reservoirs of raw fact'[49] but as repositories of insight. While we can never capture the full reality, we can always get a better picture of what trends are dominant, what is the direction of travel, and what lessons we can learn from even unsuccessful democratising events.

One final point to be made concerns accessibility: it is not sufficient to simply produce knowledge in the English language. Our hope is that this work will also be translated into other languages, especially the languages of the case studies, to reach and be in dialogue with audiences that must remain central in our mental frames, namely, those located in our radically reorientated centre.

[48] Kyriacou and López Velásquez (n 33) 432, 435.
[49] Comaroff and Comaroff (n 7), cited in Hoffmann (n 9) 55.

PART I
THEMATIC CHAPTERS

This Part comprises seven thematic chapters offering analytical insights on seven themes arising from the case studies: the concept of 'office' and its relationship to political and constitutional development; the role of governing institutions in these processes of development; the roles played by political parties, which depart from established dominant 'Western' frameworks of thinking; the curious, diverse, and often marginal place of courts in the case studies; the often central importance of civil–military relations, which manifests in highly diverse ways; the salience and explanatory power of constitutional culture; and the impact of the COVID-19 pandemic.

2
Public Offices in Processes of Constitutional Development

Jason Grant Allen

1. Introduction

The foundation of this volume is a collection of case studies dealing with jurisdictions undergoing some process of constitutional change. These include both smaller states (such as Maldives) and larger ones (such as Ethiopia) which lie outside the typical comparative constitutional law circuit. One professed aim of the volume is to take a fresh look at the dynamics of how constitutions are created, altered, and degraded, not ignoring the conventional scholarship but attempting to transcend its conventions by looking at a somewhat novel data set. The deeper aim is to develop new theoretical resources for studying processes of constitutional development—which resources could be applied, subsequently, to the usual subjects of study and, indeed, to established democracies themselves.

In this spirit, this thematic chapter approaches *processes of constitutional development* through the lens of a concept that is also somewhat eccentric to mainstream constitutional law scholarship: the concept of *office*. My central claim is that any study of constitutional change can be (best) understood as a study of changes within the network of offices that structures and animates what we think of as the 'constitution' of an organised political community. If I am right, then stories of constitutional change are stories of changes to *offices themselves* (e.g. the powers that inure in them, procedures of appointment and demission) and, to the extent it differs, of changes to *relations between offices* (e.g. cross-institutional accountability *versus* immunity, hereditary *versus* meritocratic selection). It would provide a mode of comparison between very different constitutional situations both in contemporary societies and across time. Understanding what an office is, and how offices connect individuals to institutionalised social roles, is therefore fundamental to understanding processes of constitutional development. This is so regardless of the direction of change and how we evaluate it—that is, regardless of whether the direction of travel is towards 'democratic consolidation', 'constitutional endurance', or 'authoritarian backsliding'. All of these processes can most accurately be modelled as changes to the network of offices that structures the political life of the relevant political community. If this is correct, then office is a central category

Jason Grant Allen, *Public Offices in Processes of Constitutional Development* In: *Democratic Consolidation and Constitutional Endurance in Asia and Africa.* Edited by: Tom Gerald Daly and Dinesha Samararatne, Oxford University Press. © Oxford University Press 2024. DOI: 10.1093/oso/9780192899347.003.0002

for understanding the core concerns of the case studies and the themes running through this volume as a whole.

2. The Search for an Organising Concept

A number of intersecting themes emerge from the case studies. The challenge is to find a concept with which to organise them into a set of commensurable experiences rather than so many instances—accepting some inevitable loss of resolution.

One common theme is the role of ethnic and religious politics in constitutional development, which features strongly in the case studies on Ethiopia, Malaysia, Myanmar, Sri Lanka, and The Gambia. A frequent story is that of political leaders subverting a constitution by using the powers granted to them by that constitution to favour one or the other ethnic group. Ethno-politics is closely related to the idea of 'nation-building' in the sense of constructing a new imagined community as the primary target of political loyalty.[1] In many of the case-study countries, there is no homogeneous community of ancestry, language, or religion coterminous with the geographical boundaries of the post-colonial state. For example, Ethiopian constitutional history since 1974 has been characterised by a form of federalism between ethnic blocs in the country's various regions. The civil war (current at the time of writing) between the central government and the Tigray region is the latest iteration. Current Malaysian politics, and the promise of a new government formed by a coalition of traditional opposition parties, also illustrates the difficulty of ethnically based political mobilisation.

A second, closely related, theme is the dynamic of federal arrangements between a centre and one or more peripheries. Alongside Ethiopia, Myanmar provides a study in the difficulties of negotiating an ethno-federal constitutional form. Myanmar's post-colonial Constitution of 1948 created a federation including numerous autonomous regions; instabilities in this constitutional framework led to a coup and long-standing military rule. Ethnic and federal tensions have characterised Myanmar's punctuated experience with democracy, too.

Another important theme characterising multiple case studies' constitutional pathway is the interaction between some '*ancien régime*' of institutions (often comprising pre-colonial and colonial-era institutions alike) and some new constitutional order (often the result of an independence/decolonisation process and often in multiple iterations reflecting pivotal constitutional watersheds such as a *coup d'état* or a new constitutional document). For example, even under Myanmar's 2008 Constitution, the military has held over constitutional prerogatives, such as the power to appoint 25 per cent of parliamentary representatives in the federal

[1] See Benedict Anderson, *Imagined Communities: Reflections on the Origin and Spread of Nationalism* (Verso 1983).

regions. In Maldives, we see an ancient Sultanate being replaced, in fits and starts over the twentieth century, with various forms of presential and parliamentary rule on loosely British models—before the passage of a landmark democratic constitution in 2008. In other cases, such as Malaysia, we see ancient monarchies surviving colonialism, independence, and democratisation to the present, where they interact with the current affairs of Malaysian constitutional politics: ethnic tension, party politics, corruption scandals, and a state of emergency induced by the COVID-19 pandemic.

The focus on arrangements of institutions begins to hint towards the focus of the chapter—'processes of constitutional development'—because it is institutions (presidents, political parties, militaries but also potentially non-state institutions such as religious orders or militias) and the relations between them are so often the locus of such developments (for good or ill). Another pervasive theme, in this regard, is the diversion of state resources by officials to favour sectional constituencies at both the central and regional level. For example, in The Gambia, Yahya Jammeh systematically diverted state resources to his ethnic power base while pursuing discriminatory and exclusionary policies against others. So, too, is systemic corruption, turning the state into a *cosa nostra* rather than a *res publica*, as in the recent 1 Malaysia Development Berhad (1MDB) scandal in Malaysia.[2] Closely related to this, again, is the 'weaponisation' of state bureaucracies and resources—even the law itself, in the permutation of 'rule of law' into 'rule by law'—to serve interests other than the general interest. These form the backdrop for, and inform, debates about the form of state that should be developed.

Other thematic chapters deal with many of these themes in detail. In this chapter, I wish instead to search for an organising concept to study these themes in a systematic fashion. Such a concept should allow us to understand the mechanics of what is actually going on—on a conceptual level—when a president extends his or her tenure unilaterally or a constitutional amendment gives judges stronger protections from political dismissal, for example. It should allow, and indeed enable, better comparative study of processes of constitutional development across geography, time, and different social conditions—looking past the plumage and providing a view of the bones and sinews of a 'constitution'.

That skeletal structure of any constitution can be understood as a *network of offices*. My claim is not that office is the *only* conceptual framework for understanding processes of constitutional development, nor do I need to insist that it is necessarily the best. But I do think it provides a crucial perspective on understanding what is going on. An 'office' is an institutionalised social role with implicit jural positions

[2] 'Our thing' in the parlance of Southern Italian organised crime syndicates *versus* 'public thing' in the parlance of Western political theory since the ancient Roman republic. For a brief account of the 1MDB scandal, see in this collection Wilson Tay Tze Vern, Chapter 15 'Making Progress on a Rocky Path: Democratic Consolidation and Constitutional Endurance in Malaysia, 2018–2021' [PAGE NUMBER, p. 6 manuscript].

vis-à-vis other actors, including both individual subjects and other officials. Constitutional developments can be understood as (i) changes to the composition of that network of offices, typified in post-independence or post-revolutionary reforms or (ii) incremental evolution of the content of extant offices, that is, the powers they wield and the duties they owe *vis-à-vis* the public and other offices. For example, the classic question of parliamentary *versus* presidential *versus* military rule boils down to a question of *which officials* exercise *what powers*—or in the distribution of competence between offices in different levels of (centralised and decentralised/regional) government. This is a meaningful and informative analysis of any process of constitutional development in any society. On this view, for example, the competition of personal, sectional (e.g. ethno-religious), and broader social interests can be told as a story of individuals aligned with one set of interests capturing offices that are meant to serve the common good of the whole society and using their powers *virtute officii* to promote their own personal interests (simple corruption) or the interests of their class, ethnic, or religious group.

3. Mapping Changes of Political, Legal, and Constitutional State

In order to describe processes of constitutional development, it is helpful to unpack what, exactly, that term means. To avoid assuming liberal democracy as the ultimate goal of constitutional development, let us first consider *constitutional change* irrespective of the direction of travel in the first instance. To that end, let us indulge in a closer examination of the terminology.

How does *constitutional* change differ from *political* change and *legal* change? When a new party comes to power (by whatever means), new people come to occupy offices within the various branches of government and use that position to change the political agenda pursued by the state. This may spell a policy sea change but is not 'constitutional' without something more. Likewise, the law of the land can be changed in ways that affect the lives and interests of citizens fundamentally (again, effected by persons occupying offices in the legislative, executive, and judicial branches of government using their powers to make new law of different forms). But, without more, even important legal changes are not necessarily 'constitutional' in nature.

While there is no accepted technical meaning, by constitutional change we generally mean some *structural* change to the institutions which organise the relevant body politic in a way that is intended to be enduring in nature. The metaphor implicit in 'organisation' is of specialised roles that forge individuals into a corporate entity capable of joint action. Constitutional change is a change to the way that political body is made up and animated, rather than just what it does or how it does so. For example, the Second Republican Constitution shifted the balance of power in the Sri Lankan Constitution from a parliamentary system (on the British Westminster model) to an executive presidency with substantial powers over parliament, as well as introducing justiciable fundamental rights and a different system for electing parliamentary representatives. These are all changes to the way the organised political community of Sri Lanka is constituted and acts as one 'body' through 'organs'.

As I have argued elsewhere, 'constitution' connotes some fusion of legal and political institutions and processes distinct from ordinary 'politics'. A constitution can be understood as a complex network of shared institutions, social practices, and symbols that organises the common life of a political community, with a degree of stability over time. This fusion of politics and 'organic' law is intended to keep politics within a certain set of parameters. A constitution is something that a state *is* rather than just something it *has*; our focus should be on the way that communities order their associational life rather than on documents—as important as declarations of independence, bills of rights, and (written) constitutions are.[3] A study of constitutional development is the study of the totality of institutions (in the broadest sense) that structure the life of a political community.

How, then, do we describe *processes* of constitutional change? The English word comes to us via Old French (from *procés* or 'journey'), implying transitive movement from one point to another. That movement, however, is through time, not space, and the transition is from one *form of organisation* to another. A focus on process thus asks about changes from one 'state of a constitution' (in the sense of a set of facts obtaining at a particular point in time) to another.

Through this admittedly trite exercise in linguistic analysis, we are brought to a simple question that points clearly to the kind of concept we need. When talking about changes in the constitution of a state over time, *what is actually being changed*? The short answer is: offices, broadly defined, are being changed, within the relevant institutional apparatus of the political community in question. What exactly an office is, and how it changes, is the subject matter of this chapter.

3.1 Constitutionalism and the Westphalian State

Although the Westphalian nation-state model has driven most post-colonial processes of constitutional development, the statist paradigm is empirically weakest in the context of post-colonial states.[4] While states are (and will likely remain) a very important category of geopolitical organisation, the state cannot demand the

[3] Jason Grant Allen, 'What Is Transitional Constitutionalism and How Do We Study It?' (2014) 3(4) Cambridge Journal of International and Comparative Law 1098, 1099.

[4] See generally Brian Z Tamanaha, *Legal Pluralism Explained: History, Theory, Consequences* (Oxford University Press 2021), particularly ch 2.

conceptual primacy it once did.[5] Ideally, we should be able to develop a concept of office that is fit for application to such states *and* to other organised political communities such as tribes, churches, or corporations that exist below, above, across, and between states. The case studies themselves show, in their complex federal arrangements, just how important non-state associations are in constitutional theory. In many cases, the national state is a (more or less crude) imposition from outside. However, it would also seem like one that is here to stay as very few political groupings disclaim the state form. The explanatory value of a state-agnostic concept of office, then, would seem precisely to allow analysis of state and non-state formations according to a common conceptual framework that sidesteps (without denigrating or taking a substantive position in) the statist/pluralist debate.

This notwithstanding, the state does provide a convenient frame of reference for heuristic purposes at least. Modern theory sees the state as an emergent product of *territory*, *government*, and *people*, for example in Georg Jellinek's 'three element theory'.[6] Although things like secession events are important forms of constitutional development (e.g. in the 1976 *Vaddukoddai* Resolution for an independent Tamil state in Sri Lanka), we are not concerned just with extreme events like territorial expansion or (voluntary or forced) changes to the composition of a population. Thus, leaving the equally important ideas of territory and people to one side, 'processes of constitutional development' would seem to implicate changes to the 'government' element, and that requires a working theory of what a 'government' actually is.

The answer is suggested by the case studies themselves, all of which deal in detail with the dynamics within and between particular offices within the different branches of government, including the executive, legislature, judiciary, and military. The offices discussed (such as president and prime minister, to use one example that arises frequently) are absolutely central to the dynamics of constitutional development at play. These roles seem to be the chairs at stake when politics, for example, is described as a 'game of musical chairs'. The case studies could, in fact, be read as historical analyses of officials interacting (i) with outside entities, such as other states and international organisations; (ii) with other officials within the state; and (iii) with citizens and subjects within their own state.

Of course, there is hybridity—for example, in the question of federal politics and de facto or de jure autonomous federal units, which are common in case studies such as Ethiopia and Myanmar. These external, horizontal, and vertical dynamics of official action determine, to a large extent, the stability and endurance (or

[5] See e.g. Joseph Raz, 'Why the State?' in Nicole Roughan and Andrew Halpin (eds), *In Pursuit of Pluralist Jurisprudence* (Cambridge University Press 2017) ch 7.

[6] See generally Georg Jellinek, *Allgemeine Staatslehre* (Häring Verlag 1900); Jens Kersten, 'The Normative Power of the Factual: Georg Jellinek's Phenomenological Theory of Reflective Legal Positivism' in Torben Spaak and Patricia Mindus (eds), *The Cambridge Companion to Legal Positivism* (Cambridge University Press 2021) 248–71.

otherwise) of the constitution under study. My claim is simply that taking an office-based approach to processes of constitutional change can, in fact, take us a long way in understanding the processes at play and comparing experiences in different times and places. This suggests a categorical, but normatively modest, claim: a 'constitutional' system is one characterised by some degree of *permanence in the offices* associated with it, whatever specific form the geopolitical association takes.

3.2 Office, Status, and Role (in Western Modernity and Beyond)

Taking an office-based approach to processes of constitutional change requires a well-developed concept of office itself. Unfortunately, such a concept is oddly lacking. The purpose of this section is to sketch the contours of a concept appropriate to studying processes of constitutional development in diverse societies.

I take *an office* to be an institutionalised social role that implies a certain jural status in the sense that it comes with (or *itself is*) a bundle of interwoven powers and duties.[7] Offices, as opposed to private statuses, are bestowed on an individual by society, often with rituals full of symbolism, and are always for purposes that transcend that individual's private interests. The concept of office is not limited to the political—offices are also found in private law associations (such as corporations) and in religious ones (such as churches). Offices, however, are central to the very idea of political life and are typified by offices such as 'king', 'prime minister', or 'president'.

One nineteenth-century American treatise on the law of offices helpfully defined an office as 'the right, authority and duty, created and conferred by law, by which for a given period … an individual is invested with some portion of the sovereign functions of government, to be exercised by him for the benefit of the public'.[8] The relevant period might be fixed by law or at the pleasure of the creating power, although any role which is too precarious may be something less office-like and more employment-like.[9] What is really determinative in distinguishing an 'official' from a mere state employee, however, is the delegation of a (limited) bundle of the sovereign authority: 'that some portion of the sovereignty of the country, either legislative, executive or judicial, attaches, for the time being, to be exercised for the public benefit'.[10]

[7] Moral incidents also attach to offices, but I am more concerned with the legal ones. Their interrelation will depend on one's view of law. Cf Nicole Roughan, 'The Official Point of View and the Official Claim to Authority' (2018) 38(2) Oxford Journal of Legal Studies 191.

[8] Floyd R Mechem, *A Treatise on the Law of Public Offices and Officers* (Callaghan & Co 1890) I:1, 4, I:4, 5.

[9] See Janet McLean, 'Between Sovereign and Subject: The Constitutional Position of the Official' (2020) 70(2) University of Toronto Law Journal 167.

[10] Mechem (n 8) 5.

The conceptual resources nearest to hand in constructing a concept of office are not found in Western modernity so much as Western early modernity and the European Middle Ages, stretching back to the classical civilisations of the Mediterranean. As I have explained elsewhere, the concept of office in Anglophone public law, at least, declined precipitously during the administrative reforms of the eighteenth and nineteenth centuries as the traditional system of offices was swept away to make room for a modern, managerialist bureaucracy.[11] However, if we approach office at the right level of abstraction, there are certain structural features that—albeit described in a modern Western idiom—are capable of broader application and reflect, to a greater or lesser degree, non-Western modes of political organisation too. In the present context, as we are searching for concepts and categories of general application across very different (and non-Western) societies, it is convenient to explore the concept of office in a broader context.

In the Western tradition, Melissa Lane has recently set out in fascinating detail the role of office in Greek (particularly Athenian) constitutional thought.[12] In *Politics*, Aristotle describes a constitution (*politeia*) as an 'order' (*taxis*) of offices:

> A constitution arises when the hierarchical power of command is transmuted into the lineaments of offices defined by their ordering and limiting features: their legal capacities, their terms, their mode of selection, and the controls exercised over them. Indeed there is an important linguistic and conceptual interplay in Attic Greek between the noun for office (*he arche*) and the verb for "to rule" (*archein*) which can also become, especially in participal constructions, a way to refer to 'officeholders'.[13]

The Roman statesman Cicero's treatise on government—entitled *De Officii*—admonished those involved in government to place the common weal above their personal interests and the interests of 'some one party' within it; the administration of government, he says, 'like the office of a trustee, must be conducted for the benefit of those entrusted to one's care, and not of those to whom it is entrusted'.[14] Indirectly, this classical tradition informs modern conceptions of public office,

[11] See Jason Grant Allen, *Non-Statutory Executive Powers and Judicial Review* (Cambridge University Press 2022) ch 6; see also Norman Chester, *The English Administrative System 1780–1870* (Clarendon Press 1981).

[12] See Melissa Lane, 'The Idea of Accountable Office in Ancient Greece and Beyond' (2020) 95(1) Philosophy 19.

[13] Ibid, 23; citing *inter alia* Alex McAuley, 'Officials and Office-Holding' in Hans Beck (ed), *A Companion to Ancient Greek Government* (Blackwell 2013) 176. On the state's nature as a network of offices, see also Michael J Braddick, *State Formation in Early Modern England c. 1550–1700* (Cambridge University Press 2000) 11, 45.

[14] Cicero, *De Officiis* (Walter Miller tr, William Heinemann Ltd 1913) I:25, 87. The terms used in the original Latin are, of course, not 'guardianship' and 'trust' but rather '*tutela*' and '*commissi*'—the point, however, is carried by these Roman law cognates adequately.

with additions from ecclesiastical law and Roman private law, from which ideas of trust, in particular, were borrowed.[15]

The historical transition by which offices came to be seen as institutional structures occupied by persons from time to time, rather than *personal* statuses, explains much about the emergence of the 'state' and, indeed, of 'constitutional law' in the Western tradition. Jean Bodin, who coined the term 'sovereignty', is known for his advocacy of absolute royal power, but he actually presented something like Jellinek's three-element doctrine *avant la lettre*: it is 'neither the wals, neither the persons, that maketh the citie, but the union of the people under the same soveraigntie of government'.[16] Bodin's theory of state was office-centric, and, as Daniel Lee and others have argued, once office is (re)incorporated into our understanding of his account, Bodin's theory is less absolutist than it first appears.[17] In particular, Bodin stresses whether a public functionary is to be seen as an 'officer' or a 'commissioner'. The main criterion for determining this is the functionary's security of tenure in his role—does he have a proprietary interest in it or does he hold it only on the monarch's pleasure? Bodin associated the former with 'lawful' and the latter with 'arbitrary' rule.[18]

Looking to the seminal work of the Anglophone social contract tradition, Thomas Hobbes's *Leviathan* describes a system of government established 'by art', namely, through the erection of an 'abstract seat of power' separate from the individual human beings that occupy it. The sovereign 'is no person, nor has capacity to do anything' except through (human) representatives.[19] As Martin Loughlin has

[15] See in particular Daniel Lee, '"Office Is a Thing Borrowed": Jean Bodin on Offices and Seigneurial Government' (2013) 41(3) Political Theory 409; Daniel Lee, 'Private Law Models for Public Law Concepts: The Roman Law Theory of Dominium in the Monarchomach Doctrine of Popular Sovereignty' (2008) 70 Review of Politics 370; see (Claude Nicolet, *The World of the Citizen in Republican Rome* (PS Fallas tr, University of California Press 1980) 21; Joseph Canning, *A History of Medieval Political Thought 300–1450* (Taylor & Francis 2006) 9.

[16] Jean Bodin, *The Six Bookes of a Commonweale* (Richard Knowles tr, Kenneth McRae ed, Cambridge University Press 1962 [1606]) I:2, 10.

[17] See in particular Daniel Lee, *Popular Sovereignty in Early Modern Constitutional Thought* (Oxford University Press 2016); Lee, 'Office Is a Thing Borrowed' (n 15); Benjamin Straumann, *Crisis and Constitutionalism: Roman Political Thought from the Fall of the Republic to the Age of Revolution* (Oxford University Press 2016); McLean, 'Between Sovereign and Subject' (n 9).

[18] As Daniel Lee explains, Bodin saw 'seigneurial' government as government by the sovereign's arbitrary will; the 'subjects' of such a regime were, effectively, slaves. Of course, power could be delegated by the sovereign to be exercised by others, but this delegation was precarious and could be revoked at any time. Bodin contrasted this to the 'lawful' mode of rule in which power is (*via* a somewhat complicated and paradoxical line of reasoning) laid 'in trust' upon officers to exercise on behalf of the (thereby de-politicised) sovereign, who could not revoke the trust without some cause. A well-ordered state, he argued, stood by virtue of officers and was distinct from a state where functionaries ruled by commission. There is an ambiguity here. In Bodin's scheme, as in English law, office is seen as a form of property and the tenure of this property ensures lawful rule. But (private) property is also a force conducive to personalism. Bodin borrowed on Roman private law concepts here, like others, to forge early modern European public law. See Lee, 'Private Law Models' (n 15); Daniel Lee, 'Sources of Sovereignty: Roman *Imperium* and *Dominium* in Civilian Theories of Sovereignty' (2012) 1 Politica Antica 79; Lee, 'Office Is a Thing Borrowed' (n 15) 420.

[19] Thomas Hobbes, *Leviathan* (Richard Tuck ed, Cambridge University Press 1996) 3, 184.

observed, this illustrates the critical importance of office to the very idea of 'public law': office distinguishes the powers and duties which attach to a post from the personal attributes of the post-holder, which creates a 'public realm'.[20] Again, Hobbes is known for his royal absolutism, but once the structural role of officials is appreciated, there are good reasons to view his absolutism as more attenuated.[21]

In sum, as Conal Condren writes, office was a crucial category of thought in European early modernity, in which so many of the classic ideas of modern state theory were forged. Medieval and early modern Europeans shared the ubiquitous presupposition that proper official action was action by the office as a *persona* separate from the official; conversely, improper conduct was conceptualised as abuse of office. At its most extreme, abuse of an office 'sloughed off' the *persona*, erasing the moral identity and social standing generated by association with it.[22] This idea is incipient with AV Dicey's seminal nineteenth-century concept of the rule of law—and his antagonism towards a distinct body of 'administrative law'. But, for example, compared to the ancient Athenians, who also dealt with the personal *versus* collegiate liability of officials for wrong-doing,[23] Dicey is illustrative of the anaemic office concept characteristic of English public law in modernity.[24] Janet McLean explains:

> When Dicey uses the word 'official' throughout [...] his constitutional treatise, it is denuded of all the special public law controls that defined and constrained an official *qua* official in the eighteenth and early nineteenth centuries. Indeed, the central thrust of Dicey's invocation of the rule of law is that there should be no special category of law for officials. Officials should be treated more like citizens than sovereigns, and they are not considered to have any mediating role.[25]

Officials, of course, occupy a position *between* sovereign and subject inasmuch as they exercise delegated powers of sovereignty—in fact, 'sovereignty' itself is a *product* of the appointment of officials. Officials themselves are both organs of that power and subjects of it themselves in their private capacity.

Looking beyond the Western tradition, we have already encountered ancient monarchies in Southeast Asia; it is trite but necessary to point to ancient traditions

[20] Martin Loughlin, *The Idea of Public Law* (Oxford University Press 2003) 157.

[21] See Evan Fox-Decent, *Sovereignty's Promise: The State as Fiduciary* (Oxford University Press 2011); David Dyzenhaus, 'Hobbes' Constitutional Theory' in Ian Shapiro (ed), *Leviathan: Or The Matter, Forme, & Power of a Common-Wealth Ecclesiasticall and Civill* (Yale University Press 2010) 453–80.

[22] Conal Condren, *Argument and Authority in Early Modern England* (Cambridge University Press 2006) 6.

[23] See Lane (n 12) 26.

[24] For an excellent overview of Dicey's tendency to 'disaggregate' the government, and (in my view) thereby undermine the very office concept on which his theory of public law depends, see Janet McLean, 'The Crown in Contract Law and Administrative Law' (2004) 24(1) Oxford Journal of Legal Studies 129.

[25] McLean, 'Between Sovereign and Subject' (n 9) 180.

of complex administration in South Asia and East Asia as well.[26] Colonial history is replete with examples of local kings, chiefs, and other constituted leaders being incorporated into the formal structure of (for example) the British Empire and into the administrative apparatus of the colonial state. Indeed, it was only after direct rule in India that Queen Victoria styled herself an 'Empress', that is, a Queen of Queens.[27] An interesting, but underexplored, feature of some colonial histories was the assumed categorical (if not substantive) parity between the contracting parties—consider the Treaty of Waitangi between the Māori *rangatira* and representatives of the Crown[28] or the numerous cession treaties that use the title 'King' for West African political leaders.[29] Richard Bradley, who was sent in the 1780s to procure an island in the Gambia River for the British government, wrote back with unhappy news of limited chiefly power:

> [I]n concluding this business I experienced difficulties which I had no idea of when I engaged with Your Lordship to undertake it. The Principal Men of the Country disputed the right of the Chief to dispose of the Island, and to obtain their Consent the expence of the Purchase was increased.[30]

One inroad into a non-Western, pre-modern, but surviving tradition of office is the work of Cambridge anthropologist Meyer Fortes, who studied political leadership in West African societies in the mid-twentieth century. His work in West Africa inspired a general theory of office, personality, and corporation that Fortes astutely compared back to British constitutional arrangements. There is an obvious caveat in using the work of a mid-twentieth-century British anthropologist in this

[26] See e.g. Ch'ien Mu, *Traditional Government in Imperial China: A Critical Analysis* (Chün-tu Hsüeh and George O Totten trs, Chinese University Press 1982). On the sale of venal offices, which bears obvious parallels to the European experience, see RM Marsh, 'The Venality of Provincial Office in China and in Comparative Perspective' (1962) 4(4) Comparative Studies in Society and History 454. On India, see Harnam Singh, 'The Indian States: A Study of Their Constitutional Position' (1949) 64(1) Political Science Quarterly 95; HN Sinha, 'Constitutional Position of the Orissa States' (1940) 2(1) Indian Journal of Political Science 63; CL Tupper, 'Indian Constitutional Law' (1903) 5(1) Journal of the Society of Comparative Legislation 90.

[27] See e.g. Harshan Kumarasingham, 'A New Monarchy for the Commonwealth? Monarchy and the Consequences of Republican India' in Robert Aldrich and Cindy McCreery (eds), *Crowns and Colonies: European Monarchies and Overseas Empires* (Manchester University Press 2016).

[28] Article 1 of the Treaty of Waitangi (1840) reads:

> The Chiefs of the Confederation of the United Tribes of New Zealand and the separate and independent Chiefs who have not become members of the Confederation cede to Her Majesty the Queen of England absolutely and without reservation all the rights and powers of Sovereignty which the said Confederation of Individual Chiefs respectively exercise or possess, or may be supposed to exercise or to possess over their respective Territories as the sole sovereigns thereof.

[29] See e.g. *Cession of the Island of Buma* by the 'King of Biafra' in Edward Hertslet, *British Colonies, Protectorates, and Possessions in Africa Vol I* (3rd edn, Routledge 1967) 36.

[30] As reproduced in Stuart Banner, 'Terra Nullius? Anthropology and Property Law in Early Australia' (2005) 23(1) Law and History Review 95, 98.

manner: this body of scholarship was often regarded by administrators, and acknowledged by scholars themselves, as a tool of colonial administration.[31] That said, it provides an organised body of learning on non-Western societies couched in terms that are readily integrated with the lexicon of constitutional and political theory as used by Western and non-Western scholars today. It has helped me to formulate my own conception of kingship in the British tradition considerably, and for that reason, I have returned to it often.[32]

A seminal study deals with Ashanti kingship and chiefship.[33] Classical anthropology had stressed relations and disjunctions between physical or biological phenomena and socially constituted phenomena (e.g. biological *versus* social parenthood, as in cases of adoption), but, according to Fortes, such an approach left some important questions unanswered. His key to exploring these questions was to ask why *ritual* is so important in marking changes of social status.[34]

Rather than starting with the Roman origins of the English term 'office', Fortes starts with the pervasive duality found, in various societies, between the internal or private self and the outward, public self that both situates the individual in society and (in so doing) structures the associational life of the society itself. Office, he argues, is 'not an artifice of modern sociological theory' but is 'so essential to the management and comprehension of the social relations of persons and groups that it is present in all social systems' in some form.[35] In an address to the Royal Anthropological Institute 'On Installation Ceremonies',[36] Fortes observes that office should be regarded as a 'special variant of the general phenomenon of status in social structure'; the central question (contrary to contemporary prevailing opinion) was 'whether office invariably carries power and authority'.[37] An office

[31] See Meyer Fortes and EE Evans-Pritchard, 'Introduction' in Meyer Fortes and EE Evans-Pritchard, *African Political Systems* (Oxford University Press 1940) 1; Richard Brown, 'Passages in the Life of a White Anthropologist: Max Gluckman in Northern Rhodesia' (1979) 20(4) Journal of African History 525; see generally Lyn Schumaker, *Africanising Anthropology: Fieldwork, Networks, and the Making of Cultural Knowledge in Central Africa* (Duke University Press 2001) on the 'Manchester School', whose founder drew on Fortes's work. Personally, I think it is problematic to call Jewish anthropologists like Fortes and Gluckman 'white' during the time of a genocidal regime that held they were *not*. This pulls us into the strange world of Jews' placement in (i) Apartheid, (ii) Nazi racialogy, and (iii) colonial British society. For what it is worth, Fortes himself attributed his interest in the study of race and class, through which he came to anthropology, as a result of his experience of South African racial politics and being the son of Jewish immigrants: see Susan Drucker-Brown, 'Notes towards a Biography of Meyer Fortes' (1989) 16(2) American Ethnologist 375, 382; Moses Anafu, 'Meyer Fortes: A Personal Memoir' (1983) 8(2) Cambridge Journal of Anthropology 9, 13.

[32] See Jason Grant Allen, 'The Office of the Crown' (2018) 77(2) Cambridge Law Journal 298, 304.

[33] Ashanti society knows both chiefs and kings, and these two offices bear structural parallels. They exist in a hierarchical structure, but it is unclear to me where the line between chiefship and kingship ought to be drawn; the *Asantehene* Osei Tutu II would certainly be referred to as a 'king' in English, but other 'chiefs-of-chiefs' may not.

[34] Meyer Fortes, 'Ritual and Office in Tribal Society' in Max Gluckman (ed), *Essays on the Ritual of Social Relation* (Manchester University Press 1962) 55.

[35] Ibid, 58.

[36] Meyer Fortes, 'Of Installation Ceremonies' [1967] Proceedings of the Royal Anthropological Institute of Great Britain and Ireland 5.

[37] Ibid, 6. Citations omitted.

is a 'perpetual institutional entity' that is 'owned by society' and separate from its temporary holder:

> [H]owever metaphysical this may sound, it comes nearer to the reality than do the traditional anthropological interpretations. Evans-Pritchard's re-analysis of divine kingship of the Shilluk offers a striking illustration. He shows how the office is set apart from its incumbents, and how this is objectified in the effigy of Nyakang, and is dramatized in the mock battle of accession rites. His epigrammatic summing up 'The kingship captures the King' makes the point clear.[38]

As I have glossed it elsewhere, taking the above points together, Fortes's anthropology of office posits the following structural properties. First, office and officeholder are distinct from one another; that is, there is a segregation between the 'perpetual and self-identical office' and the 'transient and mortal holder'. The officeholder is not the office *qua* political corporation but is invested through a fiction with qualities *as if* he or she were the office. Second, offices are perpetual and entail succession, as suggested by the aphorism 'The King is dead, long live the King' (or, as Fortes rephrased it, 'The King is dead, the Kingship lives forever'). A corporation unifies several individuals into a juristic entity. An office unifies individuals across time, making succession delicate and the conceptual independence of the office much more important; the death or demission of the officeholder potentially disrupts the ideal perpetuity of the office itself.[39] Third, offices have outward and visible trappings and material insignia which objectify their function and the jural implications of office-holding, that is, the incumbent's powers and duties. Fourth, officeholders must conform to certain modes of behaviour connected with the office: the powers of an office are always, inherently, connected to and conditioned by duties. Fifth, offices have a moral and jural sanction from society, either directly (e.g. through popular acclamation) or indirectly (e.g. through other representative officeholders). Finally, the insignia of office are socially conferred, generally by means of ritual.[40]

The comparative investigation of ritual installation sheds further light on the structural features of office. Fortes proffers an ethnography of the subject using the Provost of King's College, Cambridge by way of example, comparing it to the

[38] Ibid, 6–7. Citations omitted.

[39] The late medieval French practice of maintaining an effigy of the dead king until the day of his funeral, which continued until the installation of Louis XIII, is instructive here; the effigy would be carried around and even presented with food, but, according to Mayer, 'the effigy was not believed to hold the soul of the late king, it was only an "as if" aspect of the late king's continuance: and this referred less to his actual person than to his status, the dignity of kingship which continued until his internment': Adrian C Mayer, 'The King's Two Thrones' (1985) 20(2) Man 205, 212. This change reflects changes to the process of installation, which I cannot go into here.

[40] This list is adapted from Burkhard Schnepel, 'Corporations, Personhood, and Ritual in Tribal Society: Three Interconnected Topics in the Anthropology of Meyer Fortes' (1990) 21(1) Journal of the Anthropological Society of Oxford 1, 8.

installation ceremonies of the Archbishop of Canterbury, the Bishop of Ely, and the Queen.[41] Looking past the 'splendidly dramatized symbolism' in these ceremonies, he sets out the features they share with such ceremonies in other parts of the world, which number seven. First, the candidate must be recognised as legitimately entitled to accede to the office. Second, the tenant cannot take possession of the office by his own unilateral action—office is conferred by functionaries who often do not hold the office themselves. Third, office is conferred by representatives of the community, in its name, and often in the name of some superior politico-jural or religious authority recognised in the charter of the office. Fourth, a number of distinct steps mark the installation to the office, for example a step of *accession* (in which the office—but not yet its powers and duties—is put into the holder's hands), followed by a rite of *investiture* (in which the office is formally entrusted to the holder), followed by the *installation* proper (which finally transfers the lawfully vested capacities and appurtenances of the office). Fifth, while many rites are carried out in private, there is a public element as the community must participate, whether through its representatives and/or as a congregation. Sixth, a recurrent theme is the concern to demonstrate that the office has a reality and continuity, 'one might almost say immortality', as an institutional complex that is separate from, and prior to, its succession of holders—often through enduring material relics and regalia. Finally, the actual installation ceremony finally places the incumbent in office such that the office-holder can exercise their powers and is subject to its duties: the individual merges with their office, putting their former lay self aside for the duration of their incumbency.[42]

A general concept of office, then, is of an institutionalised social role to which an individual accedes and in which they wield powers and are subject to duties that are separate to their private ones—to the extent that they act, as it were, in a separate capacity. The incidents of any office could be mapped more or less formally (e.g. using a scheme such as WN Hohfeld's scheme of jural relations or any other comparable scheme[43]) to comprise a map of the constitution as a graphic 'network of offices', and changes to that network could be mapped dynamically over time. As Neil MacCormick writes,

> The law of a modern state is indeed an institutional order of great and bewildering complexity . . . Yet behind the complexity, it is possible to discern simplicity. A state has, as such, a constitution. This is a complex of explicit rules, implicit rules, and conventions, that essentially establish three types of institutional agencies, namely, of course, judiciary, legislature, and executive.[44]

[41] Fortes, 'Of Installation Ceremonies' (n 36) 5, 8.

[42] I have paraphrased this list from ibid, 8–9. Citations omitted.

[43] See Allen, *Non-Statutory Executive Powers and Judicial Review* (n 11) ch 7; Wesley N Hohfeld, 'Fundamental Conceptions as Applied in Judicial Reasoning' (1917) 27 Yale Law Journal 711.

[44] Neil MacCormick, 'Norms, Institutions, and Institutional Facts' (1998) 17 Law and Philosophy 301, 326.

These rules, and the offices they instantiate, change over time—often through implicit and conventional as much as explicit means. This provides a useful logical framework for studying processes of constitutional development over time and might render such processes in different societies more readily comparable.

4. Putting the Office Concept into Action

Broadly speaking, there are two obvious modes of constitutional change. The first mode is the decommissioning of old offices and the creation of new ones. This is perhaps the textbook case of regime change whereby the table is swept more or less clean of the *ancien régime* complete with not only a turnover of the personnel formerly engaged in ruling but also the offices and institutions in which they do so. Historically, the paradigm example is the French Revolution in which the complex offices and statuses of the feudal system were swept aside in the 'Reign of Terror'.[45]

This mode of constitutional change has been the experience in Ethiopia, which experienced a change from hereditary monarchy in 1974, through a protracted civil war, to an unstable communist military regime, to today's fragile ethno-federalist Constitution. It has also been the experience in The Gambia, where independence occurred first as a form of home rule under the British monarchy in 1965, evolving to a republican constitution in 1970, and experiencing drastic rupture only following a military coup in 1994. It has also been the experience in Myanmar, which moved directly to a republican form upon independence and experienced decades of communist military rule. Despite their important differences, these case studies show the difficulty of establishing brand new constitutions *qua* networks of offices. It seems that when things are in flux, older political loyalties play an outsized role in determining the success or otherwise of the new order. In many cases, those older loyalties are ethnic and religious. In such situations, ethnic competition has been a competition for control of the state apparatus—and its military apparatus, especially.

The post-colonial experience of Malaysia, Sri Lanka, and Maldives has been more nuanced, however, and Thailand did not experience direct colonisation. In all of these case studies, we see a second mode of change. In this mode, processes of constitutional change are driven by changes to the *content* of extant offices and relations between them. Of course, where only the name remains, it is hard to see any difference between modification of an old office, on the one hand, and the destruction of the old and creation of a new one, on the other. But there is a degree of continuity in, for example, pre-colonial monarchies that have survived through to the present day that is essential to understanding their constitutional pathway.

[45] See e.g. Alexis de Tocqueville, *The* Ancien Régime *and the French Revolution* (Gerald Bevan tr, Penguin 2008).

Modern Malaysia, for example, is an elective monarchy in which a collegiate body of (mostly) sultans elect a 'Paramount Ruler' or *Yang di-Pertuan Agong* for a term of years. This ancient system has been effectively incorporated into a broadly Westminster-style parliamentary system,[46] complete with the all-important conventions such as royal action on advice of elected ministers responsible to the legislature. What exactly it means to be *Yang di-Pertuan Agong* has changed over the past two centuries despite much continuity in regalia, appointment, title, and honorifics. Studying processes of Malaysian constitutional development involves, at the very least, some descriptive account of how the office of *Yang di-Pertuan Agong* has changed over time—what powers it holds, what duties it implies, what mechanisms exist to enforce those duties, and what kind of social consensus supports the office. This is essential for explaining not only how the office could survive British imperialism but also contemporary politics, for example in the powers of the *Yang di-Pertuan Agong* in relation to the prime minister around things like declarations of emergencies, as illustrated by the events of 2020 set out in the case-study chapter on Malaysia in Chapter 15 of this collection.

4.1 Modelling Competition between the State and Its Rivals

In many of the case study countries, we can observe competition between a post-colonial constitution made for something built on the model of a modern nation state with older and deeper ethnic loyalties. In others, we can observe the role of sub-state associations like political parties assuming primacy as a locus of official loyalty rather than the state they are meant to serve. In both cases, what usually results is the diversion of resources that should be allocated within the whole political community to a section of it only. As we saw from Cicero, above, this problem is likely as old as politics.

The office concept is useful in both of these scenarios because it allows us to understand what is going on, both at a societal and an individual level. At a societal level, it would seem that there are not one but two or more 'constitutions' in operation. This articulates quite naturally with a legal pluralist approach to legal order. On an individual level, it also helps us to understand what is actually happening. In a tribal society, for example, where officials use their offices to channel social goods towards their in-group, the officials are not 'just' being dishonest and corrupt; their wrongdoing is the subversion of a state office to the *normative imperatives of a competing political association*. Although this is speculative, it may even be possible to

[46] See generally Harshan Kumarasingham, 'Eastminster—Decolonisation and State-Building in British Asia' in Harshan Kumarasingham (ed), *Constitution-Making in Asia—Decolonisation and State-Building in the Aftermath of the British Empire* (Routledge 2016) ch 1.

map the constitution of a sub-state association and track its patterned interactions with the constitution of the state on this basis.[47]

The same can be observed in societies where religious institutions, which generally display ideal-typical offices, are implicated into the political system. It is sometimes easy to forget from a modern perspective, which takes the state as a given, but the Westphalian state form itself is, of course, a product of the dynamic between organised religion and territorial politics in early modern Europe. Here, for example, we could compare the experience in Sri Lanka and Thailand and examine both through the lens of office. In the former, Buddhist monks are allowed to be politically active and even to hold political offices. Their role in nationalist Sinhala politics is well documented.[48] In Thailand, the Buddhist *sangha* (monastic community) has interacted with state politics in complex ways.[49] Despite successive bans from participation in politics, monks are involved in politics and in the broader project of building a robust national loyalty in a society ridden with political tension. The *sangha* itself is an important constitutional institution.

Religious associations, like ethnic ones, seem to command a high degree of political loyalty in individuals, and the actions of their leaders can be of critical importance to the form—and ultimate success—of constitutional developments. In many cases, the offices of a religious institution may actually just be offices within the relevant constitution. As I have argued previously, most people live closer to pre-, post-, sub-state political associations such as tribes and religious traditions than they do to 'their' nation state, and in the decades since the Second World War supra-state institutions have assumed increased importance:

> In phases of constitutional transition, these institutions come to fill any void left by the state—from United Nations peacekeeping missions or religious customary law filling the void in a 'failed state', non-state law breaks through weak or unpopular state institutions.[50]

In all cases, this can be understood as the resurgence of an alternative 'network or offices' or the defection of state officials to a pre-state normative order in preference to the state they are ostensibly appointed to serve.

[47] It could perhaps also be linked to Martin Loughlin's account of a 'formal' and 'material' constitution—possibly a factor in the stability of a constitutional order being the internal coherence of those two. See e.g. Martin Loughlin, 'Political Jurisprudence' (2016) 16 Jus Politicum 15.

[48] See Suren Raghavan, *Buddhist Monks and the Politics of Lanka's Civil War: Ethnoreligious Nationalism of the Sinhala Saṅgha and Peacemaking in Sri Lanka, 1995–2010* (Equinox Press 2018).

[49] See Katewadee Kulabkaew, *The Politics of Thai Buddhism under the NCPO Junta* (Institute of Southeast Asian Studies–Yusof Ishak Institute 2019).

[50] Allen, 'What Is Transitional Constitutionalism and How Do We Study It?' (n 3) 1104.

4.2 Towards a Minimum Normative Concept of 'Constitutionalism'

As elaborated above, the living core of the concept of office is the distinction between the office and the person occupying it. The case studies in this volume, and the broader literature, show that a major issue in constitutional development is the blurring of this line between office and incumbent. For example, the rules governing accession to, and termination from, an office might be amended in order to ensure a populist ruler's tenure. Admitted prerogatives such as declaring a state of emergency—vital in times of real need—might be used in an opportunistic way in order to postpone elections or hand over power. In my view, a clear view of what an office is, how it is created by society and conferred on an individual, could be extremely helpful in teasing out the mechanisms by which official rule is degraded into personal rule and to articulate clear and peremptory norms governing the use of high officials' powers.

In a sense, all states have a 'constitution', even brutal dictatorial ones. I began this chapter with the express intention of avoiding any normative conceptions of constitutional development that might imply liberal parliamentary democracy as the preferred, or only acceptable, form of constitutional state. This commitment is genuine, despite my personal commitments to that form of political organisation. However, it seems arguable that the concept of office as impersonal public service in a special capacity could entail some minimum normative conception of 'constitutionalism' in the sense that not all relationships of domination and subordination could really be described as 'official' or even 'political' at all. In their seminal study of African political systems (and, whether aware of it or not, echoing Bodin), Fortes and Evans-Pritchard argue:

> [A] king's power and authority are composite. Their various components are lodged in different offices. Without the co-operation of those who hold these offices it is extremely difficult, if not impossible, for the king to obtain his revenue, assert his judicial and legislative supremacy, or retain his secular and ritual prestige... Every one who holds political office has responsibilities for the public weal corresponding to his rights and privileges. The distribution of political authority provides a machinery by which the various agents of government can be held to their responsibilities.[51]

If something like offices are found in every society and in every constitutional order, there might be an office-based argument for some minimum conception of

[51] Fortes and Evans-Pritchard, 'Introduction' (n 31) 12.

power limited by separation and apportionment throughout an apparatus of administration, too.

More exciting still is the normative implication of office itself as a status that is socially (i.e. multilaterally) constructed and endowed on a person. A perennial theme in the study of constitutional developments in the Global South is the perception, right or wrong, that (liberal) democracy is a Western idea that has been imposed, often through processes of colonisation and decolonisation, on other political cultures and traditions. Adopting an office-based approach might, perhaps, reframe some of the usual debates in this context. First, it offers one doorway through which non-Western traditions of political leadership might enter contemporary constitutional discourse. If pursued, this approach could potentially provide a more neutral conception of the 'democratic constitutional state' for analysis of constitutional developments in post-colonial states. More ambitiously, provided we can arrive at a concept of 'office' that is not inherently Western or modern, office could provide a stub from which to develop a conception of 'constitutionalism' including the rule of law and democracy that draws on epistemological reference systems endemic to the Global South, as well as the canonical Western ones.

While I am not the scholar to do it,[52] truly expanding the concept of office beyond Western modernity could, perhaps, provide a common framework within which to study very different societies (with all the usual caveats that apply against folk ethnography and historical anachronism). In my view, there is a good case to be made that the inherently limited nature of 'official power' is a universal theme in all traditions of constituted political authority. Office is the bridle by which communities harness the action of (hopefully extraordinary) individuals and, simultaneously, keep that power in check. The terms on which offices are bestowed, withdrawn, and made accountable determine the substantive characteristics of the constitutional order that results—elite or popular, autocratic or deliberative, conscientious or dismissive of the law.

The role of the public official, at base, is to act (whether in a representative, expressive, coercive, or other manner) as an 'organ' on behalf of an 'organised' political community. The idea is that a group of subjects are elevated to a status of 'active citizenship' in which they can act for, and on, the community as a whole. The attribution of such a status, according to Jellinek, necessarily *limits* official power:

> A power to rule becomes legal by being limited. Law is legally limited power. The potential power of the ruling commonwealth is greater than its actual power. Through auto-limitation it gains the character of legal power. Such auto-limitation

[52] Because 'office', as I have presented it, is a concept informed most directly by European legal history and analytical philosophy in the Western tradition, there is a danger that this kind of approach not only puts experiences from the Global South (i.e. the case studies) into a preconceived theoretical box (i.e. office) but also smuggles Western values (e.g. democracy and the rule of law) surreptitiously into the concept of 'constitutional development'.

> is not arbitrary, i.e., whether the state actually wants to cultivate this is not something that lies at the state's pleasure. The limitation is, in type and extent, disclosed through the entire antecedent process of history. *Staatsgewalt* is thus not power [*Gewalt*] per se, but power exercised within internal legal limits, and hence legal power.[53]

A focus on office, and the idea that official power is inherently subject to legal limits, shifts our focus towards the normativity immanent within socio-political organisation itself rather than the imposition of exogenous imperatives upon assumed social structures. My claim is that the 'organ-isation' of a political community generates its own inherent but limited normativity. This minimal normativity provides the basic conceptual structure and content of the concept of 'constitutionalism' and permits us to present a slightly thicker concept of 'constitutional development'.

Bernard Williams's classical argument for the priority of the 'political' over the 'moral' might offer one such possibility.[54] According to Williams, both deontological and utilitarian approaches to political philosophy treat the moral as something *prior to*, and therefore existing *independently of*, the political. Whether they present politics as the instrument of the moral or present the moral as a set of constraints on what politics can rightfully do, 'political theory is something like applied morality'.[55] In contrast to this approach, Williams advocated a theory of political realism in which the demands and constraints of legitimacy arise from the nature of politics *itself*. This starts with the 'first political question': the Hobbesian question of how to secure 'order, protection, safety, trust, and the conditions of cooperation'.[56] Debate naturally centres on whether that necessary condition of legitimacy (i.e. an ordered state) is sufficient in itself, but the more important point is that this minimum necessary condition already starts to imply some minimal propositions of political morality. First and foremost, the purported cure cannot be worse than the affliction—even Thomas Hobbes did not think that a reign of terror could save people from the terror of his state of nature.

As such, Williams argued that the *mere idea* of meeting the basic legitimation demand implies a sense in which the state must offer a justification of its power to *each subject*.[57] He used the example of a community of dissentients living within the borders of an organised geopolitical community. They are subject to its official power structures but are radically disadvantaged relative to their fellow subjects. (This was, indeed, the condition for many of the religious dissenters of early

[53] Georg Jellinek, *Allgemeine Staatslehre* (3rd edn, Springer 1932) 386, as translated in Martin Loughlin, *Foundations of Public Law* (Oxford University Press 2012) 217. Emphasis added.

[54] See Bernard Williams, *In the Beginning Was the Deed* (Geoffrey Hawthorn ed, Princeton University Press 2007) ch 1; Tully Rector, 'The Structure of Global Injustice: A Realist Account' (DPhil thesis, Freie Universität Berlin 2019).

[55] Williams (n 54) 2.

[56] Ibid, 3.

[57] Ibid, 4.

modern Europe who generated so much of our political philosophy and is echoed in the overarching theme of ethnic and other minorities in the case studies.) There is nothing that can be said *to this group* to explain why they should voluntarily submit to those power structures rather than revolting. Using the example of the Helots in ancient Sparta, Williams argued that such a situation is rather one of continuing warfare rather than any kind of 'political' condition:

> The situation of one lot of people terrorising another lot of people is not *per se* a political situation: it is, rather, the situation in which the existence of the political is in the first place supposed to alleviate (replace). If the power of one lot of people over another is to represent a solution to the first political question, and not itself be part of the problem, *something* has to be said to explain (to the less empowered, to concerned bystanders, to children being educated in this structure, etc.) what the difference is between the solution and the problem, and that cannot simply be an account of successful domination. It has to be something in the mode of justifying explanation or legitimation.[58]

If this is a 'moral' principle, argues Williams, it is not a morality that is *prior to* politics but one which is *inherent in* the idea of politics itself. While it looks a lot like an account based on the rights of the person on a Kantian view, for example, it is more modest and rests on a foundation that purports to a kind of factuality that the Kantian account cannot. As Tully Rector has argued, the demands of the rule of law that are generated from the nature of politics—from the ontology of political organisation itself—*just are* the necessary prerequisites for associational life to exist at all. To violate them is not to 'act wrongly'; it is to undermine the nature of a political association and denature it into a structure of domination between groups.[59]

This speaks, in particular, to the persistent theme not only of personalism (in which a constitutional state degrades into a crony network of insiders dominating a society of outsiders) but also of ethnic and religious federalism (where a constitutional state degrades, as in the Helot example, into a relationship of domination between one group that has weaponised the apparatus of state and its competitors).

5. Conclusion

In this chapter, I have urged the importance of the category of office to understand processes of constitutional change and attempted, by way of reference to historical sources and also to the contemporary case studies, to sketch out (i) what an

[58] Ibid, 5.
[59] Rector (n 54) 6.

adequate concept of office might look like and (ii) what it might reveal about constitutional development if adopted as a frame of enquiry.

This account of office provides a quasi-formal system for analysis of processes of constitutional development, which is useful in at least three respects. First, it could be used to *compare* offices in different systems or in the same system over time. For example, what is the jural position of a US judge compared to a South African judge? How are they both selected, appointed, demitted, remunerated, and held to account for misconduct? Or, for example, what is the jural position of the Maldives President under the Constitution (of 1932 or 2008) compared to the traditional jural position of the Sultan?

Second, it could also be used to describe the *dynamics* of the process of constitutional development over time. I have suggested that the two ideal processes of 'constitutional development' are (i) abolishing and replacing offices and (ii) changing the jural incidents that attach to the offices within a continuing, complex structure. Either of these approaches, for example, could be taken to establish a representative democracy in a traditionally autocratic monarchy or convert a representative democracy into an autocratic one-party state. I would not venture any categorical claims about the relative merits of either approach, but there would seem to be intuitive appeal to maintaining a set of status functions that is familiar and enjoys popular loyalty even while changing the powers and duties attached to relevant posts. To me, this would seem to provide a particularly attractive framework for examining the interplay of parallel or competing political communities—for example, in contested federal systems or in systems where the status functions of a religious legal system compete with those of a top-down imposed secular state modelled along Western lines.

Third, the concept of office I have suggested provides a way to argue for a minimum internal morality, as it were, of a 'constitutional' system understood as a system in which political power is legally bundled and bestowed on individuals in an enduring structure. I claimed (categorically) that official power is limited power; although the examples I have provided cannot, by a long shot, make this claim out, I think they put the onus on advocates of unlimited political authority to rebut the argument. If I am right, the very idea of 'official power' is a protean, but powerful and intuitive, idea of popular sovereignty that speaks against both dominative ethnic politics and for something like 'democracy' (very) broadly defined. The minimal normativity inherent in office, I think, reflects the constitutional aspirations of all reasonable people and of the contributors to this volume in particular. Perhaps, in time, it might become a fixture of scholarly analysis—and constitutional rhetoric—in processes of constitutional transition.

3

The Role of Governing Institutions in Attempted Reform Processes

Kimana Zulueta-Fülscher

1. Introduction

Governing institutions or institutions of (representative) governments are traditionally understood as those bodies in charge of creating, amending, and implementing laws and regulations in a given polity, commonly including an executive, a legislature, and a judiciary as three separate powers. Governing institutions can be key in reform processes, as catalysts and allies but also potentially as obstacles to reform. These roles may be either consistent across institutions or paradoxical in those cases where different institutions (or key individuals within those institutions) may not agree to the nature or direction of particular reforms and may block other institutions or individuals from pursuing them.

One way to start to examine the nature and structure of governing institutions is to assess the government system as provided for by the Constitution. In this edited volume, the seven case studies represent examples of a wide variety of systems of government, including parliamentary monarchies (Malaysia, Thailand), a parliamentary republic (Ethiopia), presidential systems (The Gambia, Maldives), one semi-presidential system (Sri Lanka), and one assembly-independent system (Myanmar, which became a military junta in 2021). Central to this chapter will be the relationship between the executive and the legislature in each of these systems.

An important part of the literature on executive–legislative relations distinguishes between these different types of government systems, with parliamentary systems at one end of the spectrum, characterised by the 'mutual dependence' of the executive and the legislature, with the prime minister indirectly elected by the directly elected parliament, and presidential systems at the other end of the spectrum, characterised by the fact that the president and the legislature are separately and directly elected, marking their 'mutual independence'.[1] What follows

[1] Alfred Stepan and Cindy Skach, 'Constitutional Frameworks and Democratic Consolidation: Parliamentarianism versus Presidentialism' (1993) 46(1) World Politics 1.

Kimana Zulueta-Fülscher, *The Role of Governing Institutions in Attempted Reform Processes* In: *Democratic Consolidation and Constitutional Endurance in Asia and Africa*. Edited by: Tom Gerald Daly and Dinesha Samararatne, Oxford University Press. © Oxford University Press 2024. DOI: 10.1093/oso/9780192899347.003.0003

from this distinction, as a broad generalisation, is that parliamentary systems are thought to be, for the most part, collaborative systems, in which the government seeks the consent of a majority of representatives in parliament to stay in power and to legislate. Presidential systems can be more conflictual, especially in those cases where the majority in the legislature is not the president's party or coalition. While the president does not depend on the legislature to reach or stay in power, legislating may become more difficult if a majority in parliament does not see eye to eye with the president, at least on particular policies that need new or amended legislation.[2]

This distinction between parliamentary and presidential systems falls short of reflecting not only the varied systems of government this edited volume deals with but also particularly the complex relationships between (and also within) the executive and the legislature in the respective countries. Not only is it the case that, for some of these countries (particularly Myanmar, Sri Lanka, and Thailand), divisions within the executive further complicate the already complex relationship between the executive and the legislature, but also the make-up of parliament itself, as cohesive or fragmented, efficient or representative,[3] also indicates whether the executive can systematically rely on legislative support or whether both powers will need to negotiate and compromise to advance their respective agendas.

This chapter explores the relationship between the executive and the legislature across the aforementioned seven case studies. In looking at executive–legislative relations, issues related to government formation and dismissal and the legislative and constitutional amendment processes are, of course, key. Looking specifically at parliamentary, presidential, and hybrid systems, the chapter also focuses on the relationship between the electoral system and the resulting party framework in order to assess whether, and how, this interaction contributes or not to stable and resilient governments with enough power to push through reforms if they so choose. The sometimes complex relationship between the armed forces and the executive is also briefly probed. Next, the chapter explores ways in which governing institutions constitute catalysts, allies, or obstacles to reform in all seven countries. To conclude, key factors that may have contributed to the gridlock or outright failure of these reform processes are identified.

[2] See Matthew S Shugart and John M Carey, *Presidents and Assemblies: Constitutional Design and Electoral Dynamics* (Cambridge University Press 1992); Giovanni Sartori, *Comparative Constitutional Engineering: An Inquiry into Structure, Incentives and* Outcomes (New York University Press 1994); Jose Antonio Cheibub and Fernando Limongi, 'From Conflict to Coordination: Perspectives on the Study of Executive–Legislative Relations' (2010) 1(1) Revista Ibero-Americana de Estudos Legislativos 38.

[3] Shugart and Carey (n 2).

2. Executive–Legislative Relations

2.1 Parliamentary Systems

Parliamentary systems do not per se allow for a separation of power between the legislature and the executive as governments in these systems need to be appointed, supported, and sometimes dismissed by a parliamentary vote.[4] Governments in parliamentary systems usually depend on a given parliamentary majority, with this parliamentary majority being constituted by a single party, or different parties (some of which may chose to remain outside of government), or of a coalition of parties established either before or after elections have been held. This parliamentary majority will ideally allow them to make policy decisions and, in turn, legislate. Sometimes, no party or coalition can wield a parliamentary majority, and hence, minority governments are formed.

Out of the three countries reviewed in this volume that have a parliamentary system of government, two have had long-running and fairly cohesive ruling coalitions formed out of ethnically based political parties, that is, Malaysia and Ethiopia. Single-member constituencies with a majoritarian 'first-past-the-post' electoral system have allowed these coalitions to win sufficient majorities in parliament to unilaterally legislate or even amend their respective constitutions. Arguably, this winner-takes-all electoral system threatens opposition parties or coalitions with becoming irrelevant over time or being weakened to the point of not constituting a real government alternative.[5] But at the same time, the fact that government coalitions are mostly multi-ethnic means that intra-coalition negotiations will be necessary in order to legislate and adopt constitutional amendments.

Beyond this, both Malaysia and Ethiopia are federal systems with bicameral parliaments. Noteworthy is the fact that Ethiopia's upper house—the House of Federation—is not involved in the regular legislative process and does not represent its constituent units but is composed of representatives of ethnic groups and functions as an arbiter of constitutional and intergovernmental disputes related to the right to self-determination of ethnic groups. At the same time, Ethiopia's upper house is mostly occupied by representatives of the ruling coalition. The Malaysian senate—Dewan Negara—is partly indirectly elected by the state legislative assemblies (26 senators) and partly appointed by the king (40 senators), and four senators are appointed to represent particular federal territories. It is also constitutionally restricted to constitute a 'chamber of review and reflection' in that it allegedly only exists to 'improve the quality of legislation' and provide a discussion

[4] Sartori (n 2) 101.
[5] Ibid, 33–34.

forum around the details of the proposed legislation.[6] Hence, the upper house has delaying powers at most.[7] If the senate does not approve or propose amendments to a legislative bill within a year of submission, the lower house can still send the original bill to the king for enactment.

In Thailand, the biggest reform push to its parliamentary monarchy took place in 1997, with the adoption of a new progressive constitution meant to strengthen the prime minister's leadership. The Constitution changed the electoral system to the lower house—to a mixed member system where 100 members were elected through party lists and 400 members through a plurality 'first-past-the-post' electoral system—that favoured large political parties, and was aimed at strengthening the party system and parliament's effectiveness.[8] Government stability was also to increase by way of making it more difficult for parliament to initiate and execute a vote of no confidence in the prime minister.[9] In addition to this, the Constitution also provided for stronger checks and balances to eradicate corruption.

The mixed-member system was slightly changed with the 2007 Constitution, with 400 members of parliament elected through single-member constituencies and 80 members through a proportional representation electoral system. And again, the 2017 Constitution changed the ratio to 350 members elected through 'first-past-the-post' and 150 members using proportional representation. Crucially, the Senate was a fully elected institution (with a total of 200 senators) in 1997, meant to play a key role in appointing oversight institutions and to guarantee a certain degree of insulation from the corrupting influence of political parties—senators were not allowed to be members of political parties. In 2007, this changed, and members of the Senate were partly elected (76 senators) and partly appointed (74 senators), and in 2017, they became fully appointed by the armed forces (250 senators). The Senate, in turn, has significant legislative, oversight, and appointment powers. Critically, the king appoints members to the Constitutional Court, the Election Commission, the Anti-Corruption Commission, and the Auditor General on the advice of the senate.[10] Beyond this, the king's role is particularly significant in that he commands the armed forces and has the power to intervene

[6] Elliot Bulmer, 'Bicameralism: International IDEA Constitution-Building Primer 2' (*International Institute for Democracy and Electoral Assistance* (*International IDEA*), 2 August 2014) <www.idea.int/publications/catalogue/bicameralism> accessed 28 September 2021.

[7] Constitution of the Federal Democratic Republic of Ethiopia (1995) art 68.

[8] Beyond this, and in order to prevent last-minute party-switching, MPs were required to be registered members of political parties at least 90 days before the election date.

[9] A two-fifths vote of the House was required for a vote-of-no-confidence debate to be initiated against a prime minister. The motion must also contain the name of an alternative premier to replace the incumbent. A successful vote of no confidence required a majority of at least half of the House. A similar process could initiate a no-confidence motion against an individual minister; this required only one-fifth of the signatures of the House members. These measures were aimed at increasing the stability of governments.

[10] Adem Kassie Adebe, 'Senate Reforms in Constitution-Making Processes in 2016' in *International IDEA: Annual Review of Constitution-Building Processes 2016* (International IDEA 2017) 51.

in politics when politicians succumb to 'corruption and selfishness', as Khemthong Tonsakulrungruang writes (more on this in section 2.2).[11]

2.2 Presidential Systems

Presidential systems are defined by the separation of the executive from the legislature. The president is directly elected, and both the term of the president and the assembly are fixed and not dependent on each other's confidence. Beyond this, the president has some legislative authority, alongside the assembly. And hence, while the emergence and survival of both branches are independent of each other (neither can parliament usually call for a vote of no confidence on the president nor can the president dissolve the assembly), their responsibilities may overlap regarding the power to legislate.[12] Presidents may have the power to initiate and sometimes promulgate legislation, partially or fully veto legislation (which sometimes the assembly can override by a qualified majority voting), and sometimes also call for (binding or advisory) referendums on particular legislation.

The two presidential systems in this edited volume, The Gambia and Maldives, are both unicameral and have been governed, for decades (if not centuries), by authoritarian regimes. In The Gambia, (former) army lieutenant Jammeh came to power through a coup d'ėtat in July 1994, suspending the existing 1970 Constitution, and drafting a new constitution, which came into force in 1997. This constitution transformed the system of government from a hybrid to a full presidential system, and Jammeh managed to stay in power until he was voted out in December 2016. The National Assembly is elected through single-member constituencies and a 'first-past-the-post' electoral system, and the president is elected by a plurality vote. Unlike other presidential systems, though, the president of The Gambia can be removed from office not only through impeachment but also through a two-thirds vote of no confidence in parliament, to be followed 30 days later by a referendum on the motion to either endorse or reject the decision of the National Assembly.[13] This would theoretically weaken the powers of the presidency as the presidency would also be accountable to parliament throughout the president's term in office. But the reality is that the governing party has benefited from having a significant majority in parliament, at least until 2016, and hence, a vote of no confidence has never been called. Regarding general legislation, members of the National Assembly and

[11] See in this collection Khemthong Tonsakulrungruang, Chapter 14 'Coup and Decay: How Thai-Style Democracy Abuses Constitutionalism'.

[12] Shugart and Carey (n 2) 18–19.

[13] Impeachment needs to be supported by at least half of the members of the Assembly, in which case the speaker would request the Chief Justice to create a tribunal to look into the allegations. If the tribunal finds that the accusations are substantiated, then the Assembly needs to vote the motion by at least two-thirds of its membership. See Constitution of the Republic of Gambia (1996), arts 63(3) and 63(4).

members of the cabinet may introduce a bill or a motion to be debated and voted upon by the Assembly and then promulgated by the president. But the president may decide to request the National Assembly to reconsider this bill/motion, which the Assembly can only override through a qualified majority vote of two-thirds.[14] Regarding constitutional amendment, the National Assembly needs to approve the amendment bill by a three-quarters majority in both the second and third reading of the bill[15] and then submit it to the president for his or her assent. If the president fails to assent within 30 days, a referendum shall be held, and if at least 50 per cent of those eligible to vote take part in the referendum and support the bill by not less than 75 per cent, then the president has to assent within seven days.

Maldives' short and convoluted constitutional history started with the framing of its absolute monarchy in 1932. It continued with a short-lived republican constitution in 1953 (abolished in 1954), and a renewed attempt at republicanism in 1968. President Maumoon Abdul Gayoom (1978–2008) enacted a new constitution in 1998, which provided for a system that again concentrated powers in the executive and where the president was to be selected by parliament and then supported or rejected in a popular referendum. The president had the power to appoint 8 out of 50 members of parliament as well as the judges of the High Court and other courts, the auditor-general, and the commissioner of elections. No other independent institutions were provided for. Political parties were only allowed starting in 2005. The sixth, and first democratic, Constitution, adopted in 2008, enacted a full presidential system, where the president is to be directly elected using a two-round electoral system. This means that if a candidate does not win more than 50 per cent of all votes in the first round of elections, a second-round election needs to be called for the two candidates with the highest number of votes to run against each other. Beyond this, the 2008 Constitution revoked the rights of the president to appoint members of parliament, and parliament had to approve (and could also dismiss members of parliament via a vote of no confidence) the cabinet appointed by the president,[16] unlike in The Gambia. The president can only be removed from office via impeachment, as in other presidential systems, whereby at least one-third of all representatives in parliament needs to present an impeachment motion, and at least a two-thirds majority of the total membership in parliament is needed to impeach the president.[17] Grounds for impeachment are wide open in that any violation of Islam or the law, serious misconduct, and inability to perform the office's responsibilities can be grounds for impeachment. The large majority needed to approve an impeachment makes the latter an unlikely occurrence. Legislative authority, on the other hand, rests with parliament, including the amendment of the

[14] Ibid, art 100.
[15] Ibid, art 226.
[16] Constitution of Maldives (2008) art 129c, 101.
[17] Ibid, art 100.

Constitution. Amending the Constitution, however, needs the support of more than three-quarters of members of parliament, and (depending on the exact provision to be amended) also needs a referendum, after which the president has to give his or her written consent. And while the president can refrain from assenting to a constitutional amendment, parliament can then call a referendum, and if the referendum ratifies the given amendment, the president needs to consent. For any other bill, the president can request reconsideration or amendment of the given bill, which can be overridden by the vote of a majority of the total membership in parliament. If the president does not assent to the bill or returns it to parliament for reconsideration, the bill is deemed to have been assented to and shall be published as is in the *Government Gazette* within 15 days of receipt by the president's office.[18]

2.3 Structure of Government in Comparison: Hybrid Systems

Sri Lanka is one of a few countries in Asia with a semi-presidential system of government with a double-headed executive comprising a directly elected president and a directly elected parliament that selects a prime minister to lead the government. It was the Second Republican Constitution that instituted this system of government in 1978, away from the post-independence, Westminster-style parliamentary system it had entertained since 1946—similar, in many ways, to the Malaysian system of government, which had been transformed into a parliamentary republic in 1972. Under this system, the president is elected using the alternative vote system, whereby voters state up to three preferences of candidates for the presidency. This system is supposed to make the presidential election more inclusive as presidential candidates would need to appeal to voters in all, and not just selected, constituencies.

The 1978 constitutional dispensation gave broad powers to the executive, with the president constituting both the head of state, government, and the armed forces. At the same time, the powers of the president, and broadly executive–legislative relations, have been contested ever since the Constitution entered into force. The 2001 Seventeenth Amendment to the Constitution managed to limit the powers of the president, mainly regarding appointments to key institutions and positions in government, but the latter was undermined and ignored. The 2010 Eighteenth Amendment to the Constitution repealed the Seventeenth Amendment and, again, strengthened the powers of the president, who was directly elected for a six-year term without term limits. Between 2010 and 2015, the president could appoint the prime minister, the cabinet, and judges of the Supreme Court, amongst others, constituting a president–parliamentary system.[19] The president could also

[18] Ibid, art 91.
[19] Shugart and Carey (n 2) 24.

remove the prime minister and prorogue or dissolve parliament, which weakened parliament vis-à-vis the presidency. The president could only be removed through impeachment, which requires a referral to the Supreme Court by a two-thirds vote in parliament, and upon the Supreme Court's findings another vote of two-thirds for the president's removal. Reaching a two-thirds majority in parliament is not easy due to an electoral system in parliament based on proportional representation and a political party structure made up of more or less large and fragile coalitions. The 2015 Nineteenth Amendment, as we will see in section 2.4, again repealed the Eighteenth Amendment and significantly curtailed presidential powers, albeit only for a short period of time.

Myanmar is a sui generis case in that, until very recently, it was the only country in the world that had an assembly-independent system of government wherein both houses of parliament selected a president amongst three proposed vice-presidents, but the president was not removable by the assembly through a vote of no confidence but only via impeachment.[20] The military-drafted 2008 Constitution included broad grounds for impeachment as well as grounds for the president's office to fall 'vacant', which include his or her resignation, death, permanent disability or 'any other cause'.[21] The single-member constituency, 'first-past-the-post' electoral system was meant to give a large majority to big national vis-à-vis smaller and/or ethnic-based parties. Beyond this, and before the military coup of 1 February 2021, the commander-in-chief of the armed forces nominated military personnel to at least 25 per cent of the seats in both houses, and three key ministers to the government, that is, interior, defence, and border affairs. This gave the commander-in-chief power over the entire security apparatus and effectively prevented elected representatives in parliament from amending a constitution the armed forces had drafted to protect their own economic and political interests. Constitutional amendments would need more than 75 per cent approval in both houses of parliament. After the coup, the commander-in-chief had the acting president call a state of emergency, with the automatic transfer of all legislative, executive, and judicial powers to the commander-in-chief.[22]

2.4 Role of the Armed Forces in Supporting or Hampering Policymaking

The relationship between the executive and the armed forces, at least in some of the countries assessed in this volume, requires focused attention. In both Myanmar and Thailand, the armed forces have had key decision-making roles within

[20] Ibid, 26.
[21] Constitution of the Union of Myanmar (2008) s 73(a).
[22] Ibid, s 419(a).

governing institutions. In Myanmar, after the 1962 coup, the Myanmar armed forces—or Tatmadaw—took over power, which they only partially and slowly released, according to the 2003 'Seven Step Roadmap to Democracy', after the 2010 elections. The Tatmadaw entered into a power-sharing arrangement with civilian authorities whereby the former could administer and adjudicate its own affairs without being accountable in any way to civilian power (section 20(b)) and could veto constitutional amendments. On 1 February 2021, the commander-in-chief, though, acted on the realisation that the 2008 Constitution did not automatically provide for the Tatmadaw to override elections. The Tatmadaw took over power once again, declared an unconstitutional state of emergency, ordering the arrest of high-level state officials, including the President of Myanmar and State Counsellor Daw Aung San Suu Kyi, and the murder of more than 1,000 peaceful protesters. Civil war has since ensued throughout the country.

In Thailand, the king is the head of the armed forces, and the armed forces have played a crucial role in politics, guided as they were by an 'ultra-conservative nationalist ideology', acting as guardians of 'Thai-style democracy' against the instability and corruption increasingly linked to liberal democratic politics. As a result, since the 1932 transition to democracy, Thailand has suffered a total of 13 coups d'état, two since the 1997 Constitution entered into force, and has been the perpetrator of major massacres and other crimes with absolute impunity. The two latest constitutions of Thailand—2007 and 2017—were, similar to the 2008 Myanmar Constitution, drafted at the behest of the armed forces to protect both their political power and economic interests. In both countries, the armed forces are heavily invested in not only legal but also illegal, and highly profitable, economic activities.

At the other end of the spectrum, in Malaysia, the king is also the supreme commander of the armed forces, as is the case in Thailand. However, the Malaysian armed forces have neither sought nor exercised any role in government. Beyond this, the monarchy is widely perceived as having played a crucial stabilising role in times of political crises.[23] The role of the armed forces has been more variable in the other four countries.

In Ethiopia, the blend of the state and the party at its helm means that the party or faction in control of state institutions also controls the armed forces. The Tigray People's Liberation Front (TPLF) had been the dominant force since the end of the civil war in 1991, but once Prime Minister Abiy Ahmed came to power in 2018, he initiated a security sector reform also aimed at professionalising the army and diversifying its leadership. The most immediate effect was the diminishing presence and power of TPLF leaders in the security apparatus, which, in turn, heightened the TPLF's distrust towards the federal government and arguably accelerated

[23] See in this collection Wilson Tay Tze Vern, Chapter 15 'Making Progress on a Rocky Path: Democratic Consolidation and Constitutional Endurance in Malaysia, 2018–2021'.

the ongoing conflict between the TPLF and the federal army. In Sri Lanka, the militarisation of politics has also persisted since the end of the 25-year civil war in 2009, aggravated since the August 2020 parliamentary elections, which gave President Gotabaya Rajapaksa's party a vast majority in parliament.[24] In the name of professionalising politics, as well as more circumstantially dealing with the COVID-19 pandemic and other crises, President Rajapaksa has used his parliamentary majority to appoint (retired) military figures to high-level administrative positions.[25] Both Maldives and The Gambia entertain small armed forces, which are nominally under the control of civilian authorities, with the president acting, in both cases, as commander-in-chief. At the same time, in neither country have the armed forces always been apolitical, in both cases supporting or undermining elected officials if the latter appeared to contest their acquired benefits. The main concern here appears to be less one of constitutionally establishing civilian control over the armed forces and more about maintaining it, partly, at least, by way of creating and maintaining an apolitical military.

3. The Role of Governing Institutions in Reform Processes

Governing institutions can be catalysts, supporters, or obstacles to reform, and their role may be consistent where those institutions follow one and the same agenda towards or against reform or, paradoxically, in those cases where different institutions (or key individuals within those institutions) do not agree to the nature or direction of particular reforms. I will address each case study separately in this section to then identify key factors that may have contributed to the rise and fall of these reform movements and processes in section 4.

Following the same order as above, Malaysia is first on the list. A first-past-the-post electoral system favouring coalitions of ethnic-based political parties with territorially concentrated constituencies had resulted in the same coalition ruling from 1957 to 2018, mostly with large, two-thirds, majorities in parliament. The last prime minister, who governed from 2009 to 2018, had been marred at the end of his term by maladministration and a big corruption scandal, turning public opinion against him and against the de facto one-party system. This motivated a number of ideologically diverse opposition parties to unite in coalition against the incumbent prime minister and campaign for reform, including fiscal reforms but also weakening the prime minister's power; increasing parliamentary autonomy;

[24] Sudha Ramachandran, 'Sri Lanka: Where Generals Fight the Coronavirus, Food and Fiel Shortages' (*The Diplomat*, 3 September 2021) <https://thediplomat.com/2021/09/sri-lanka-where-generals-fight-the-coronavirus-food-and-fuel-shortages> accessed 3 October 2021.

[25] Salman Rafi Sheick, 'Rajapaksas Marching Sri Lanka towards Military Rule' *Asia Times* (21 January 2021) <http://asiatimes.com/2021/01/rajapaksas-marching-sri-lanka-towards-military-rule> accessed 3 October 2021.

and strengthening checks and balances by, for instance, decreasing the influence of the executive on the selection of judges, increasing the power of judicial review regarding government actions and new legislation, or increasing the independence of the Elections Commission.[26] This coalition of parties (Pakatan Harapan, PH or Pact of Hope), made up of multiracial social-democratic, secular and reformist, moderate Islamists, and ethnic Malay-and-indigenous parties, won the elections against any prognosis, and formed a government. But the coalition did not hold long, as internal bickering between two of the main coalition leaders led the prime minister to resign, in principle in order to instil fear in the coalition partners of a return to the old and therefore revive their support for him. While PH regrouped and claimed a renewed majority, so did the opposition. A motion to hold a confidence vote on the (then interim) prime minister never took place, but the king decided to hand the prime ministership to the opposition (and former government) leader, who then unseated PH on 1 March 2020.[27] Many of the coalitions' electoral promises therefore remained unfulfilled. By January 2021, the new government had consolidated power through the proclamation of a constitutional state of emergency, allegedly in response to the COVID-19 pandemic, suspending parliament, postponing all scheduled elections, and giving the federal government the power to rule by decree. According to Wilson Tay Tze Vern, after only a two-year period of hope, the country was back to square one.[28]

Also in Ethiopia, the war against the Dergue communist regime ended in 1991, with the triumph of ethnonationalist forces and the establishment of the Peoples' Revolutionary Democratic Front (EPRDF), a coalition of four ethnic-based parties that represented the country's four main ethnic regions (Oromo; Amhara; Tigray; and the Southern Nation, Nationalities and Peoples Region) alongside affiliated parties from the other five regions. The EPRDF was controlled by the smallest but military strongest ethnic group—the Tigray—through the TPLF, which, under the 1995 Constitution, governed with a heavy hand for more than 20 years. In 2015, popular protests in two of the biggest regions allowed, according to Adem Abebe, for reformist elements within the governing coalition to push for change. The TPLF eventually reacted by selecting a new prime minister in April 2018—the first Oromo prime minister in Ethiopia's recent history—Abyi Ahmed Ali. While structural reforms to governing institutions were not an immediate objective of his administration, Abiy did lead the transformation of the EPRDF into a membership-based party, away from its previous consociational structure, which fundamentally changed both intra-party and intra-government dynamics between the different

[26] Cassey Lee, 'Making Sense of Malaysia's Institutional Reforms' (2018) 78 ISEAS Perspective <www.iseas.edu.sg/wp-content/uploads/pdfs/ISEAS_Perspective_2018_79@50.pdf> accessed 28 September2021.

[27] Asanga Welikala, 'The Dismissal of Prime Ministers in the Asian Commonwealth: Comparting Democratic Deconsolidation in Malaysia and Sri Lanka' (2020) 91(4) Political Quarterly 792.

[28] See in this collection Tay Tze Vern (n 23).

coalition parties. This transformation not only led the TPLF to leave the coalition but also led to heightened intra-Oromo contestation as some Oromo had grown weary of Abyi's pan-Ethiopian rhetoric and his perceived closeness to the Amhara. Most importantly, though, Abyi had managed to estrange the powerful but numerically small TPLF. Both the TPLF and the Oromo opposition had high hopes that elections initially scheduled for May (and then August) 2020 would provide them with an opportunity to challenge Abyi's (new) Prosperity Party. A state of emergency declared in April 2020, in response to the COVID-19 pandemic, served to extend the parliamentary term, with elections delayed for a maximum of one year. The TPLF did not accept the delay, which had been rubber-stamped by the upper house, and unilaterally organised regional elections in September 2020. The civil war started in October 2020, with members of neither party recognising each other, and has only confirmed Abyi's perception that a heavy hand is needed now more than ever. Reforms were delayed until after the elections, which were held in July and September 2021, with Abyi's new Prosperity Party winning by a landslide and some opposition parties boycotting.

Thailand engineered its own constitutional and institutional reform in 1997 and has arguably experienced a process of democratic reversal ever since. The 1997 Constitution, which was hailed as the first democratic constitution in Thailand's recent history, was, for the most part, dismantled after the 2006 coup d'état and the drafting of the 2007 Constitution. Highly popular Prime Minister Thaksin Shinawatra (2001–2006) had been able to hollow out all oversight institutions, including the elected senate, the judiciary, and even civil society and the media, thereby evading the law, enriching himself, and silencing all opposition. In brief, the 1997 Constitution, while good on paper, had been unable to build a sense of the common good and the need to hold the executive accountable. The 2007 Constitution attempted to prevent another concentration of powers in the executive by both reinforcing the judiciary and independent oversight agencies and weakening governance by way of weakening political party representation in (and therefore fragmenting) the lower house, establishing a semi-appointed senate and increasing the powers of the king to intervene in politics.[29] These constitutional changes were not enough to prevent another Shinawatra family member—Yingluck Shinawatra—becoming prime minister (2011–2013). Her continuous abuse of the government coalition's majority in parliament motivated traditional elites to stage street protests against her and her government, which ultimately led to General Prayuth Chan-ocha staging another coup, again with the Crown's endorsement. The 2007 Constitution was suspended, and a long and drawn-out constitutional drafting process concluded with a new constitution

[29] Björn Dressel, 'Thailand's Elusive Quest for a Workable Constitution, 1997–2007' (2009) 31(2) Contemporary Southeast Asia 305–07; see also Allen Hickey, 'The 2007 Thai Constitution: A Return to Politics Past' (2007) 19(1) Crossroads: An Interdisciplinary Journal of Southeast Asian Studies 128.

entering into force in 2017. This Constitution further weakened the executive by again favouring small-to-mid-sized parties in the 500-member lower house and with a fully appointed senate. The first prime minister after the Constitution entered into force—General Prayuth—was selected by a joint sitting of both houses. The 2017 Constitution also expanded the role of the judiciary and fourth-branch institutions, with the counter-corruption agency able to remove politicians from their posts 'if they acted immorally'. And it also gave these institutions a key role throughout the legislative process in that the introduction of new bills depended on their advice or recommendation, and these bills needed their approval even after the Assembly had consented.[30]

In The Gambia, in ways similar to Malaysia, the opposition to long-term authoritarian president, Yahya Jammeh, managed to defeat him in presidential elections held on 1 December 2016. Adama Barrow became the new president, supported by a coalition of seven political parties, civil society groups, and one independent candidate. Jammeh did not immediately accept the results, filing a petition first to contest the validity of the election results and then declaring a constitutional state of emergency that his party (the Alliance for Patriotic Reorientation and Construction (APRC), which still dominated the Assembly) approved, thereby extending both his and parliament's term by 90 days. The international community had to intervene for Jammeh to leave for Equatorial Guinea. The opposition United Democratic Party (UDP) won a majority of seats in parliament in elections held in April 2017, and a process started to draft a new constitutional dispensation in The Gambia, which was tabled before the National Assembly on 14 September 2020. Before the National Assembly's vote on the bill, there was contestation within the UDP as to the length of Barrow's presidency. He announced, at the start of his presidency, that he would only stay for three years and then call for elections but soon announced he would stay for his full term. The contention led to estrangement between the leader of the UPD, Ousainou Darboe, and the President, who dismissed Darboe as vice-president in March 2019. The constitutional bill included critical checks on presidential powers, as well as term limits, but did not reach the required majority in the National Assembly. Amongst others, eight parliamentarians[31] expelled from the UDP for openly siding with President Barrow, in addition to those parliamentarians representing the APRC, voted against. Efforts to mediate between President Barrow and opposition leader Darboe for an amendment of the constitutional bill that would ensure its adoption in the National Assembly ended in fiasco.

[30] Constitution of the Kingdom of Thailand (2017), ss 126 and 127.

[31] Laura Angela Bagnetto, 'Widespread Disappointment in Gambia after New Constitution Voted Down' (*Radio France Internationale*, 25 September 2020) <www.rfi.fr/en/africa/20200925-widespread-disappointment-in-gambia-after-new-constitution-voted-down> accessed 28 September 2021.

Maldives held its first democratic elections in October 2008. For the first time, different political parties were allowed to compete for the presidency, and Mohammed Nasheed from the Maldivian Democratic Party (MDP) won the elections in the second round. He was ousted from power in 2012, before his term was over, by opposition forces supported by parts of the Maldivian armed forces. In 2013, Nasheed again won two consecutive elections with 46 per cent of the vote but was outrun by an alliance of parties that supported presidential candidate Yameen Abdul Gayoom, brother of former President Maumoon Abdul Gayoom and second in the race for the presidency. The coalition that supported Yameen fell apart before long as the two brothers became political adversaries. Still, Yameen became an increasingly authoritarian leader, banning opposition leaders from running for office or persecuting them[32] as well as journalists and other civil society representatives, undermining the system of justice, and finally himself being involved in money laundering and eventually accused and prosecuted for corruption by the Supreme Court.[33] In February 2018, Yameen called a constitutional state of emergency in response to the Supreme Court ordering the retrial of several political leaders and the reinstatement of 12 suspended opposition members of parliament.[34] Yameen's brother Maumoon established a strategic coalition before the September 2018 elections with the MDP and other parties that resulted in MDP's presidential candidate Solih winning the presidency in the first round. In the April 2019 parliamentary elections, former President Nasheed won a seat as an MDP member of parliament as part of a larger MDP majority and became speaker of parliament. Solih's reformist agenda, which could have been supported by the MDP majority in parliament, was, to a certain extent, neutralised by all other parties in the government coalition. This became very clear after Nasheed became the target of a terror attack in May 2021, when combating Islamic extremism rose again to the top of the agenda and caused a rift between President Solih and former President Nasheed as both men disagreed on the best approach to respond to the threat.

Executive–legislative relations were at the centre of another short-lived reform process, in Sri Lanka. Catalyst to this reform process was the election of Maithripala Sirisena as president of the republic in January 2015. Sirisena, a senior minister in the outgoing government, announced, in November 2014, that he would run as the opposition's candidate in the next presidential election. Once he became president, Sirisena also became the Secretary General of his political party—the Sri Lanka Freedom Party (SLFP)—a post the outgoing president, Mahinda Rajapaksa, had

[32] Patricia Gossman, 'No Need for Sorcery to Stifle Democracy in the Maldives' (*Human Rights Watch Blog*, 24 August 2018) <www.hrw.org/news/2018/08/24/no-need-sorcery-stifle-democracy-maldives> accessed 28 September 2021.

[33] Shahudha Mohamed, 'High Court Sustains Ex-Pres Yameen's 5-Year Sentence' (*The Edition*, 21 January 2021) <www.edition.mv/ex_vp_ahmed_adeeb/21653> accessed 28 September 2021.

[34] UN Human Rights Office of the High Commissioner, 'Maldives State of Emergency: 'All-Out Assault on Democracy' (*Zeid*, 7 February 2018) <www.ohchr.org/EN/NewsEvents/Pages/DisplayNews.aspx?NewsID=22640&LangID=E> accessed 30 September 2021.

held during his tenure. The SLFP led the United People's Freedom Alliance (UPFA). During the campaign, Sirisena accused Rajapaksa of nepotism and corruption and vowed to reduce the president's excessive powers with a return to a more balanced relationship between the president and the prime minister or a change from a president–parliamentary to a premier–presidential system.[35] Sirisena immediately appointed opposition leader, Ranil Wickremensinghe, as prime minister. In April 2015, the outgoing parliament passed a constitutional amendment significantly curtailing the powers of the presidency. But parliamentary elections in August 2015 did not result in a significant majority for the opposition's coalition, led by Wickremensinghe.[36] The UPFA and the opposition decided to establish a National Unity Government, led by Wickremensinghe. But Rajapaksa, who had been elected to parliament as a member of the SLFP (leader of the UPFA), opposed the government of national unity and defected by creating a new party, the Sri Lanka Podujana Peramuna (SLPP), taking with him a number of representatives loyal to him. According to Luwie Ganeshathasan, this made constitutional reform an uphill battle as parliament further fragmented, and those political parties initially in favour of structural reform significantly diminished in size. The coalition in government also started to disagree on the content (and the process itself) of a new constitutional dispensation, thereby protracting the process until, in February 2018, local authority elections resulted in the SLPP consolidating its power vis-à-vis both the SLPF-led UPFA and the opposition United National Party coalitions. After the elections, Wickremensinghe survived a vote of no confidence in parliament, initiated by the SLPP, but was then unconstitutionally removed from power in October 2018 by President Sirisena, to return to power following a Supreme Court resolution on the unconstitutionality of his removal. The government coalition, though, was in shambles, and Gotabaya Rajapaksa, Mahinda Rajapaksa's brother, easily won the November 2019 presidential elections and called for parliamentary elections, which were finally held in August 2020, with the SLPP winning by a landslide and Mahinda Rajapaksa becoming the new prime minister—a lost opportunity.

Myanmar is arguably one of the most tragic examples. When the authors of the Myanmar case study started to draft their chapter, they conceived their narrative as recounting a difficult and highly constrained reform process that had arguably started with the first elected administration in 2010 and started to consolidate with the first government of Aung San Suu Kyi's National League for Democracy (NLD) in 2015. Reforms, while still ongoing, had already managed a significant opening of Myanmar society to the outside world and a steep development curve, which was pushing the boundaries of both transitions to peace and democracy. But a constitution drafted by Myanmar's armed forces precisely to allow the latter to maintain

[35] Shugart and Carey (n 2) 23–24.

[36] Wickremensinghe led the United National Party (UNP) and led United National Front (UNF).

control over both their interests and the direction of reform had also allowed its main foe, the NLD, to control a significant majority of seats in both houses of parliament, and therefore the presidency, a significant part of the executive, the judiciary, and all other regulatory and oversight institutions. With another decisive win in the November 2020 elections on the part of the NLD, the commander-in-chief, who arguably had pretensions of becoming the next president of Myanmar, was unable to have these institutions, particularly the Union Election Commission, 'dance to his tune' and hence decided to stage a coup on 1 February 2021, declare an unconstitutional state of emergency, and essentially bring Myanmar back to square one.

4. Factors Contributing to Failure (or a General Theory on the Causes for Failure)

And hence we have seven countries, all of which have recently endured setbacks to reform processes aimed mostly at consolidating democracy by way of increasing the accountability of state institutions and oftentimes by way of rebalancing executive–legislative relations. In this section, we will explore some of the factors that may have contributed to these setbacks, particularly from the perspective of governing institutions.

As a caveat, the reader may want to bear in mind that inter-country variation makes comparisons between the seven case studies difficult, to say the least. Perhaps the only element that all countries have in common is the fact that recent attempts to reform governance systems have all had serious setbacks. Hence, one of the first and rather obvious conclusions relates to the fact that reform processes are hard. Extant political, economic, and social dynamics and interests take a long time to change, and any one critical juncture aimed at reforming the system needs to be followed by years—sometimes decades—of robust and unwavering political support and commitment not only from the elites but also from the general citizenry. Changes to the system need to be perceived to protect interests and provide necessary goods and services before long as expectations regarding the impact of governance reforms on general livelihoods are often high and sometimes unrealistic. As a consequence, perceived underperformance can be used by opportunistic elites, such as we have seen in Sri Lanka, to leverage their power to turn the citizenry against reforms. Short-termism often prevails in these instances.

In many of the cases reviewed in this volume, opposition coalitions are highly fragmented, with constituent parties' main objective constituting the deposal of the 'old regime'.[37] While the narrative of these reform-orientated opposition coalitions

[37] See also Welikala (n 26) 792.

is often one that targets system failures in general and the decay of governing institutions more specifically, details regarding how to tackle failure and decay are often missing. As parties concentrate on their candidate(s) winning the elections, not enough weight is given to specifying the strategy to reform the governance system, to make it more accountable, more transparent, and less corrupt. Once in government, ideological (and other types of perhaps even more personal) differences between coalition parties (and their leaders) come to the fore, delaying or attenuating key reforms and thereby offering an opportunity to anti-reformists to reach power or to the former government party or coalition to regroup and return to power. Such has been the case in Malaysia, Maldives, and Sri Lanka.

Political parties themselves are, for the most part, weak and personalised, with no discernible agenda or programme and no internal democratic procedures. This, in addition to high levels of intra-party corruption, often leads to particular members of parliament floor-crossing or party-splintering, which, in turn, leads to a permanent fluidity in the political party system, as is currently the case in Malaysia, Maldives, and Thailand. Beyond this, the personalisation and lack of internal democracy of political parties often means that leaders are given vast amounts of intra-party power that often translates into authoritarian tendencies, at least once they are at the helm of governing institutions, such as in Ethiopia, The Gambia, Myanmar, or Thailand. The COVID-19 pandemic has offered an added opportunity for these leaders to amass power, sometimes resulting in backlash against their reforms, however timid, in the form of a coup d'état in Myanmar or an open civil war in Ethiopia. In other instances, leaders that were supposed to drive the reform process often realise, once in power, that those reforms would personally impact them and their entourage, perhaps impairing their chances to win the next elections, hence reverting back to defending a more beneficial status quo, as happened in The Gambia, Malaysia, and Sri Lanka.

The weakness and personalisation of political parties often contributes to the fragmented nature of party coalitions and vice versa. But beyond this, weak and personalised political parties also generate weak parliaments that, for the most part, fail to serve in their oversight capacity. The reason for this is that these types of parties often 'lack the sort of internal coherence, cohesion and discipline that would allow them to act purposefully and consistently within parliament',[38] for instance engaging the government in hearings or interpellations.[39] The resulting volatility of party coalitions often also results in members of parliament engaging in short-term political calculations meant to prevent them from losing power rather than strengthening the transparency and accountability of the executive. In some cases, the party or coalition in government commands a significant majority

[38] Carlos Santiso, 'Legislatures and Budget Oversight in Latin America' (2004) 4(2) OECD Journal on Budgeting 69.

[39] Ibid, 47.

in parliament, such as in Myanmar. In these cases, incentives on the part of the governing party in the legislature to oversee the executive are anyway limited.[40] Party personalisation further stifles members of parliament from questioning the actions taken by the government's leadership, also for fear of retaliation, such as in Thailand and arguably also Ethiopia, and hence legislative oversight is further weakened, which, in turn, strengthens the hand of the executive. Moreover, the judiciary and also fourth-branch institutions, with some exceptions in the case studies reviewed in this volume (such as Sri Lanka), are often weak and lack independence and therefore do not necessarily constitute an alternative to overseeing the government's actions.

Underlying these potential factors one can also find, in very rough terms, two different world views, one where individual equality and freedom is at the centre—a pan-ethnic, perhaps anti-nationalist, and more or less social but critically liberal (sometimes republican) perspective—and perhaps a stronger one, where group rights and identity are at the centre—a mostly communitarian ethno-nationalist perspective. Different parties and actors represent these different world views to different degrees, often cutting across governing coalitions and their constituencies, as has been the case in Sri Lanka but also in Malaysia and in Ethiopia. In and of themselves, these different world views say little about the way in which politics is practiced, the 'political culture' of a country's agents. But what they may do is offer different narratives to explain the medium- or long-term goal of politics, narratives that build expectations as to the way in which politics is practiced; the nature of political parties and the electoral process; the way in which actors and institutions collaborate or compete to ensure the system is able to respond to the body politics' needs and demands; and, in this sense, the role and the aim of governing institutions in processes of democratic consolidation. Perspectives that have emerged out of these different world views have often clashed, sometimes resulting in ephemeral reform coalitions.

5. Conclusion

As mentioned at the start of the chapter, governing institutions have played different roles in countries' reform processes, acting as catalysts, allies, or obstacles to reform. Executive–legislative relations specifically have been the main object of reform processes in countries like Sri Lanka, where one of the key elements in the discussion was about attenuating the power of the executive president vis-à-vis the prime minister and increasing the government's responsiveness and accountability vis-à-vis parliament; or in The Gambia, where the central tenet included

[40] See for instance Richard E. Messick, 'Strengthening Legislatures: Implications from Industrial Countries' (Public Sector Notes, No 63, Open Knowledge Repository—The World Bank, March 2002).

the readjustment of the powers of the presidency vis-à-vis parliament to prevent a return to its authoritarian past; or even in Thailand, where initial reforms to strengthen parliament were reversed to give non-elected agents (i.e. the Crown and the armed forces) the main prerogative over key policy decisions. But in these and most other settings, executive–legislative relations were also one of the key elements hampering reform.

To be sure, reform processes are seldom straightforward and swift. But particularly when thinking about the role of governing institutions as both subjects and objects of reform, we need to carefully examine the nature of the political leadership and the political party system, the way politics is practiced, the volatility of governing coalitions, the potential fragmentation of parliamentary institutions, the power asymmetries between the executive and the legislature, and the latter's impact on the effectiveness (or lack thereof) of governing institutions, especially when difficult reforms are on the agenda. Time is rarely on the side of the reformers.

4

Here, There, and Everywhere

Locating the Political Party in Democratic Transitions and Backslides

Mouli Banerjee

1. Introduction

The political party as an object of study occupies an interesting position across different fields of scholarship. Intuitively, it is difficult to imagine a modern representative democracy, following Schattschneider's famous but controversial observation, without political parties.[1] At the same time, much of mainstream democratic theory still considers parties 'one-dimensionally, as monolithic entities or mysterious black boxes'.[2] Across disciplines, there is also a variance in the approaches to understanding the role of political parties in democracies—legal scholars have focused on the regulation of parties and party systems, and scholars of political science, political anthropology, and sociology have focused on how parties operate in practice, how they organise internally and externally, and how that affects democratic orders.[3] In the mainstream and established literature on parties, however, a normative understanding of the party as a necessary vessel for representation, accountability, and policymaking in a democracy persists.[4] This, fused with the growing academic interest recently in decoding the global patterns of democratic backslides, has allowed us to zero in on the role of political parties within nation states as a crucial variable in democratic decline.[5]

However, if, as Tom Daly and Brian Christopher Jones have very catchily proposed, 'the growing threat to liberal democracy worldwide is, in many ways, a political party threat',[6] decoding the threat (or conversely the role of the party in

[1] EE Schattschneider, *Party Government* (Farrar & Rinehart Inc 1942).

[2] Ingrid van Biezen and Michael Saward, 'Democratic Theorists and Party Scholars: Why They Don't Talk to Each Other, and Why They Should' (2008) 6 Perspectives on Politics 21, 25.

[3] Stephanie L Mudge and Anthony S Chen, 'Political Parties and the Sociological Imagination: Past, Present, and Future Directions' (2014) 40 Annual Review of Sociology 305.

[4] Vicky Randall, 'Political Parties and Democratic Developmental States' (2007) 25 Development Policy Review 633.

[5] Tom Gerald Daly and Brian Christopher Jones, 'Parties versus Democracy: Addressing Today's Political Party Threats to Democratic Rule' (2020) 18 International Journal of Constitutional Law 509; David Runciman, *How Democracy Ends* (Profile Books Ltd 2018).

[6] Daly and Jones (n 5).

Mouli Banerjee, *Here, There, and Everywhere* In: *Democratic Consolidation and Constitutional Endurance in Asia and Africa*. Edited by: Tom Gerald Daly and Dinesha Samararatne, Oxford University Press.
DOI: 10.1093/oso/9780192899347.003.0004

keeping this threat at bay) requires understanding the party's *different* meanings—as a subject, an agent, and as an organisational entity institutionalised within a democracy's frameworks. Most of the scholarship locates *global* patterns across parties and individual politicians, linking them—from the United States, Hungary, Poland, and Germany, to India, Brazil, and the Philippines, for example. The literature in doing this works intuitively and assumes that there is a broad global understanding of 'what a party is' and that this is a broadly stable definition. Pippa Norris and Ronald Inglehart, in their recent attempt to classify and create a global typology of populist parties, also acknowledge this problem of potential 'concept-stretching and boundary issues'[7] arising from lumping 'political parties' in their democratic or non-democratic tendencies into the same categories. This volume, consciously selecting not only Global South case studies of states in transition but also particularly Global South states that have had comparatively little mainstream work done on them, provides an opportunity, instead of engaging with established frameworks within which parties are studied, to work counterintuitively and reimagine these frameworks.

2. Parties versus Systems: On the Design of This Chapter

In a thematic chapter meant to provide a broad overview of the role of political parties in constitutional endurance and democratic weakening drawing interlinkages and patterns between the seven case studies in this volume, the possibilities of enquiry are both endless and, of course, limited by practical constraints. The factors and patterns located here are therefore not exhaustive. This chapter attempts to avoid slotting the case studies into categories of party behaviour pre-established in the existing literature or forcing a comparative analysis between the case studies. Instead, it is designed, rather loosely, in terms of interesting patterns that appear in these cases and how these patterns complicate the mainstream scholarship. Therefore, I have chosen to keep political parties as individual organisations the primary unit of analysis instead of delving deep into the kind of *systems* the parties are located in—electoral systems, party systems, political (parliamentary, presidential, or semi-presidential, for example)—and the interactions of parties with these systems. Later sections of this chapter contextualise some parties in their systems, and the volume as a whole, through the other thematic chapters, allowing for a holistic reading of these interacting systems.

Keeping this in mind, I have broadly located the patterns of the roles parties play in political transitions or constitutional and democratic endurance emerging from the case studies in this volume in two categories: questions of context and

[7] Pippa Norris and Ronald Inglehart, 'Classifying Parties' in Pippa Norris and Ronald Inglehart (eds), *Cultural Backlash: Trump, Brexit, and Authoritarian Populism* (Cambridge University Press 2019) 215.

questions of agency. The former takes the history and structures of power and the institutional set-ups which shape these parties and determine their roles into account, and the latter comprises locating the actions of parties, not just as organisational units but as a collective of agents strategising for democratic strengthening or weakening within a system. The boundaries between the two categories are, of course, porous, but this arbitrary conceptual categorisation facilitates a constitutive reimagination of political parties and allows us to prompt new lines of thought. For example, how is our intuitive understanding of parties complicated by considering the lives of parties as social organisations before and after constitution-building? Where does post-coloniality figure or not figure in all this, especially when we transport a largely European/Global North understanding and scholarship on party law nexus to the study of systems in the Global South?

3. The Party Regulated, the Party Regulating: Finances, Bans, Suppression

What kind of a threat to democracy (or a positive agent strengthening a democracy) a political party is depends, to an extent, on the existent party laws or constitutional frameworks that govern and control what kinds of parties enter which political arena in a state. Party scholarship, both in legal studies and in political science, in an attempt to locate the party as an entity in its regulatory ecosystem within any nation state, focuses on the ties of the party to the state, through party laws, regulations, and state constitutions.[8] Besides codification into national constitutions, party regulation comprises the bodies of law that regulate the functioning of political parties—on party registration, political finance, elections, campaigns, and party constitutions (when justiciable), as well as legislative statutes, administrative rulings, and court decisions.[9] In this section, I touch briefly, in relation to the case studies, on two kinds of institutional set-ups: those that allow a party *to exist* (i.e. how parties get registered, how they recruit members and field candidates for elections, how they communicate with the people they represent, and so on and when they are prevented from doing these things) and those that allow the party *to function* (i.e. how parties finance themselves, what kind of entities they are in terms of internal organisation and audits, and what their relationship and accountability to the state is).

Older liberal constitutions considered political parties only 'intermediary organisations' in a democracy[10] and did not codify them into constitutional frameworks.

[8] Lauri Karvonen, 'Legislation On Political Parties' (2007) 13 Party Politics 437; Ingrid van Biezen, 'Constitutionalizing Party Democracy: The Constitutive Codification of Political Parties in Post-War Europe' (2012) 42 British Journal of Political Science 187.

[9] Dan Avnon, 'Parties Laws in Democratic Systems of Government' (1995) 1 Journal of Legislative Studies 283; Van Biezen, 'Constitutionalizing Party Democracy' (n 8).

[10] Van Biezen, 'Constitutionalizing Party Democracy' (n 8).

It is important to locate this phenomenon within the rubrics of the traditional liberal democracy, which saw no connection between the parliamentary order (established by the constitution) and political parties as entities.[11] Newer constitutions in Europe (and in Latin America, too, starting with Costa Rica in 1949) post the Second World War saw waves of rapid party constitutionalisation, and similar amendments soon followed in older European constitutions.[12] Comparative analyses of party constitutionalisation in post-war European states show that regularisation of parties through stronger legislation/constitutionalisation led to more efficient democracies.[13] Post-conflict or conflict-prone states also opt for heavier party regulation in their efforts at democratic rebuilding.[14] States with non-democratic pasts regulate parties more, and if the regulation of parties happens in an already democratic state, it consolidates its democratic nature.[15]

3.1 Party Suppression through Party Laws

This liberal-democratic approach to constitutionalism carries a normative assumption that such constitutionalisation, whereby 'an increasing range of public life is ... subjected to the discipline' of the state,[16] adds to the accountability, and therefore efficiency, of institutions in a democracy.[17] This assumption does not hold up, not only for authoritarian regimes but also, often, for democracies in transition and fragile democracies. Whereas in more substantive, stable democracies, party suppressions and regulation help curb anti-democratic party practices,[18] in non-democratic states, they are used by ruling parties to limit opposition.[19] Authoritarian regimes consistently ensure the lack of viable parties by repressing or co-opting possible oppositions, enacting constitutional measures or party laws that make it harder for new parties to register or compete in elections. In Egypt

[11] Pepijn Corduwener, 'Democracy and the Entanglement of Political Parties and the State: Party–State Relations in 20th-Century France, Italy, and Germany' (2020) 53 Comparative Political Studies 40.

[12] Ingrid van Biezen, 'State Intervention in Party Politics: The Public Funding and Regulation of Political Parties' (2008) 16 European Review 337; van Biezen, 'Constitutionalizing Party Democracy' (n 8).

[13] Van Biezen, 'Constitutionalizing Party Democracy' (n 8).

[14] Van Biezen, 'State Intervention in Party Politics' (n 12).

[15] Avnon (n 9); Gur Bligh, 'Defending Democracy: A New Understanding of the Party-Banning Phenomenon' (2013) 46 Vanderbilt Journal of Transnational Law 1321.

[16] Martin Loughlin, 'What Is Constitutionalisation?' in Petra Dobner and Martin Loughlin (eds), *The Twilight of Constitutionalism?* (Oxford University Press 2010) 61.

[17] Ingrid van Biezen and Fernando Casal Bértoa, 'Party Regulation in Post-Authoritarian Contexts: Southern Europe in Comparative Perspective' (2014) 19 South European Society and Politics 71; Ingrid van Biezen and HMTD ten Napel (eds), *Regulating Political Parties: European Democracies in Comparative Perspective* (Leiden University Press 2014).

[18] Bligh (n 15); Giovanni Capoccia, 'Militant Democracy: The Institutional Bases of Democratic Self-Preservation' (2013) 9 Annual Review of Law and Social Science 207.

[19] Karvonen (n 8).

under Abdel Fattah el-Sisi, parties that tried to destabilise the regime were consistently banned, allowing him to run for president unopposed repeatedly.[20]

This is a pattern visible across the country-specific case studies in this collection as well. Nearly all of them have constitutions that, in some form or another, constitutionalise political parties. Myanmar's Constitution has a separate chapter (X) on political parties, their formation, and 'the right of Non-Existence of Political Parties' (chapter X part 2 article 407).[21] The Gambia's Constitution also has a separate section (part III section 84) laying down the rules and restrictions for party registration, party finance, and clauses for party deregistration.[22]

Thailand has had a history of party bans, from largescale bans by successive military governments since 1932, and then for not meeting electoral criteria until 2006.[23] Party laws were enacted in Thailand as early as 1955, and the 1997 Constitution also explicitly contained measures for dissolving parties.[24] The most unprecedented and notable slew of party bans in Thailand, using the mechanisms provided for in the 1997 Constitution, happened, however, between 2006 and 2008 with the dissolution of Thaksin Shinawatra's Thai Rak Thai (TRT) party, Pandin Thai, Pattana Chart Thai Prachatipatai Kaona, and then Palang Prachachon (which was accused of being a Thaksin-aligned cover for TRT) in 2007 and Chart Thai and Matchimatipatai in 2008.[25] Following the 2014 military coup, all parties were suspended; it is interesting to note that the 2017 Constitution spells out the regulations and restrictions on forming a party[26] but contain nothing explicitly on party bans.

Since the end of the military rule, Ethiopia has had the Ethiopian People's Revolutionary Democratic Front (EPRDF), a one-party dominant coalition, in power until 2019. Ethiopia's institutional design has had a detailed system of party regulation, from constitutional provisions to proclamations, which set the criteria for parties to be recognised and financed.[27] This regulatory ecosystem, however, has been actively in favour of the EPRDF coalition and operationalised to suppress the opposition parties.[28] As Adem K Abebe's case study chapter in this volume also

[20] Natasha Ezrow, 'How Can the Liberal Democratic Cause Be Advanced in the Middle East?' in Ivor Crewe and David Sanders (eds), *Authoritarian Populism and Liberal Democracy* (Springer International Publishing 2020).

[21] 'Myanmar's Constitution of 2008 with Amendments through 2015' (*Constitute*) <www.constituteproject.org/constitution/Myanmar_2015.pdf?lang=en> accessed 3 October 2021.

[22] 'Gambia (The)'s Draft Constitution of 2020 Draft of 29 Mar 2020' (*Constitute*, 29 March 2020) <www.constituteproject.org/constitution/Gambia_2020D.pdf?lang=en> accessed 3 October 2021.

[23] Aim Sinpeng, 'Party Banning and the Impact on Party System Institutionalization in Thailand' (2014) 36 Contemporary Southeast Asia: A Journal of International and Strategic Affairs 442.

[24] Ibid.

[25] Ibid; Aurel Croissant and Paul Chambers, 'Unravelling Intra-Party Democracy in Thailand' (2010) 18 Asian Journal of Political Science 195.

[26] 'Thailand's Constitution of 2017' (*Constitute*) <www.constituteproject.org/constitution/Thailand_2017.pdf?lang=en> accessed 3 October 2021.

[27] Kassahun Berhanu, 'Party Politics and Political Culture in Ethiopia' in Mohamed Abdel Rahim Mohamed Salih (ed), *African Political Parties: Evolution, Institutionalism and Governance* (Pluto Press 2003).

[28] Ibid.

confirms, after the 2005 elections this institutional set-up allowed for crackdowns on the opposition and the manufacturing of state support.

3.2 Business Elites, Transnational Networks, and Party Financing

Existing scholarship on party financing indicates the push for understanding parties as 'public' entities in order for their funding practices to be transparent and accountable.[29] The problem, however, remains that much of this is disproportionately Global North focused.[30] A few recent works take note of this lacuna.[31] It is, of course, difficult to find much transparency and information on the aspects of political funding in the case of authoritarian regimes or fragile democracies, but the case studies in this collection indicate that political financing in weaker democracies, in both electoral and non-electoral contexts, concerns power networks beyond the parties as organisations and involves political and business elites, with often transnational implications to these networks. It is worth, perhaps, mentioning here certain interesting observations that emerge on party funding in relation to our case studies.

Ethiopia, as previously mentioned, has a very strong set of party laws, but until 2019, it had no law specifically aimed at regulating issues of political financing. These were all dealt with through the revised Political Parties Registration Proclamation No 573/2008.[32] After his election, Abiy Ahmed initiated reforms in party laws, which resulted in the passing of the Ethiopian Electoral, Political Parties Registration, and Election's Code of Conduct Proclamation No 1162/2019, which brought all the party laws together under one proclamation. Among other things, the new law prohibits foreign donations and contributions to party financing, and while recognising that private donations are a legitimate source of income for parties, the law now requires the donors to declare their identification and citizenship.[33] This has come to be a big blow to the opposition parties, who

[29] Van Biezen, 'State Intervention in Party Politics' (n 12).

[30] Richard Gunther and Larry Diamond, 'Species of Political Parties: A New Typology' (2003) 9 Party Politics 167.

[31] Erik Mobrand, 'Constitutionalization of Political Parties in East and Southeast Asian Democracies' (NUS Centre for Asian Legal Studies (CAS) Working Paper, 2018) <https://law.nus.edu.sg/wp-content/uploads/2020/04/CALS-WPS-1805.pdf> accessed 20 November 2023; Aradhya Sethia, 'Where's the Party?: Towards a Constitutional Biography of Political Parties' (2019) 3 Indian Law Review 1; Aradhya Sethia, 'Where's the Money?: Paths and Pathologies of the Law of Party Funding' (2019) 1 NLUD Journal of Legal Studies.

[32] Zelalem Degifie, 'Party-Political Financing, Democracy, and Constitutionalism in Ethiopia' in Zelalem Degifie (ed), *Democracy, Elections, and Constitutionalism in Africa* (Oxford University Press 2021) 302 <https://oxford.universitypressscholarship.com/view/10.1093/oso/9780192894779.001.0001/oso-9780192894779-chapter-12> accessed 28 September 2021.

[33] Ibid, 304.

have relied substantially on donations from the Ethiopian diaspora,[34] while the in-country private donations have largely been for the parties in power, that is, the EPRDF.[35] It has been noted, in view of the party suppression post the 2005 elections, that businesses already considered backing the opposition risky, and now, with the new law, while there seems to be a big push for higher transparency, the need for donor identification has made it even less lucrative for businesses to finance the opposition.[36]

In contrast to this, Malaysia does not have any clear laws to govern party financing yet; all political parties register with, and submit yearly audits of, their finances to the Registrar of Societies.[37] However, these reports are not accessible to the public,[38] and political financing in Malaysia therefore has a transparency problem. The Registrar of Societies regulates parties just the same as any other social organisation and allows political parties in Malaysia to run and profit from corporate enterprises or 'political business'.[39] The United Malays National Organisation's (UMNO) membership and focus, over the 1980s, moved from mass support to the support of business elites, with one of UMNO's important coalition partners, the Malaysian Chinese Association, being led and funded by business elites.[40] Conversations and public demands around political funding and the need to curb corruption have been consistent through the decades—from the Asian Financial Crisis in the 1990s, and the *reformasi* movement, to the Coalition for Clean and Fair Elections, formed with opposition parties coming together in 2006.[41] But a renewed surge in this demand was witnessed, specifically focused on party funding, in the aftermath of the 1Malaysia Development Berhad scandal (1MDB) scandal in 2016 involving the then prime minister, Najib Razak.[42] Following this, the UMNO set up a Consultative Committee, which came up with recommendations for financing regulations. Interestingly, it has been noted that the opposition parties, which also receive funding from private donors, not only did not support the committee's recommendations but also had been against reforms in party financing since before the 1MDB scandal.[43] In 2018, the Pakatan Harapan alliance came into power with political financing reform and the introduction of a Political Financing Control Act as one of its agendas.[44] However, Malaysia seems

34 Ibid, 304.
35 Ibid, 311.
36 Ibid, 311.
37 Edmund Terence Gomez, 'Monetizing Politics: Financing Parties and Elections in Malaysia' (2012) 46 Modern Asian Studies 1370; Sebastian Dettman and Edmund Terence Gomez, 'Political Financing Reform: Politics, Policies and Patronage in Malaysia' (2020) 50 Journal of Contemporary Asia 36.
38 Dettman and Gomez (n 37).
39 Gomez (n 37).
40 Ibid.
41 Dettman and Gomez (n 37) 41.
42 Ibid.
43 Ibid, 47.
44 Ibid, 51.

to still be waiting on this reform. This links also to the power networks and loyalties that travel from one party to another—some of the most powerful leaders in the Pact of Hope (PH) were once United Malays National Organisation (UMNO) party members.[45]

Political parties thus often become carrier organisations for existing elites and their political ambitions, and this is reflective of the larger political systems in place within these states. This brings up other possible lines of enquiry with regard to understanding political parties within their specific democratic or undemocratic contexts. For example, it then becomes important to factor in how different political societies respond to questions of party loyalty, party allegiances, and the extent of normative relationship a state or society has with questions of party defections and party splits. Additionally, it also allows us to re-evaluate the relationship of political parties with voting patterns—do the voters vote for political parties; are votes in a state and, in particular, elections along ideological lines that parties stand for; or do voters elect leaders that can signal democratic change, irrespective of which parties they affiliate with in a given moment?

These questions of context, as they become apparent in these examples from the case studies, reflect how the institutional frameworks around what political parties are within a specific nation-state determine how parties stay in power and how parties in power operationalise these set-ups—sometimes in opposition to each other and sometimes in collusion when it serves the political purpose. It also allows us to think in terms of how transnational politics and money networks contribute to both the strengthening, and sometimes weakening, of democracies.

4. Populism, Leaders, and Military Regimes: The Party as a Front

The question of populism has received a lot of academic attention in recent years, with a substantial range of scholarship focused on the rise of populism, illiberal parties, and their threat to liberal democracies. Traditionally understood to be a concern for non-democratic systems and not stable liberal democracies,[46] recent scholarship has shown how 'cartel party' formations[47] have given way to the diminished trust of the people in mainstream parties and their party politics, which are often understood as elitist and distanced from the people,[48] coinciding with the

[45] Ibid, 49.

[46] Ivor Crewe and David Sanders, 'Introduction' in Crewe and Sanders, *Authoritarian Populism and Liberal Democracy* (n 20).

[47] Richard S Katz and Peter Mair, 'The Cartel Party Thesis: A Restatement' (2009) 7 Perspectives on Politics 753.

[48] Ruth Wodak, Majid KhosraviNik, and Brigitte Mral (eds), *Right-Wing Populism in Europe: Politics and Discourse* (Bloomsbury 2013).

rise of populist parties in countries across Europe. However, the literature often generalises populist parties under one umbrella where, really, populism can be mapped across a spectrum.[49] The case studies in this volume allow for the analysis of certain kinds of populist party formations which manage to capture public support, ranging from parties that are created as fronts for the ambitions of individual political leaders to those that create semblances of legitimacy for military regimes.

At this juncture in the chapter, it is worth looking at shell parties as a specific type of political party, especially within Global South states. This subsection conceptually connects the 'shell party', or the formation of a party as a front, with the later sections on coalition-building and the importance of taking any particular party's origins and organisational history into consideration while analysing its role in a moment of political transition. Traditionally a feature more often of presidential systems, shell parties could be understood as smaller parties, with comparatively less public appeal or mass outreach, which work to prop up individual populist leaders for elections. Populist and authoritarian presidential candidates have repeatedly used this ploy, for example Fernando Collor de Mello, in Brasil in 1989,[50] and Peru's Alberto Fujimori in 1992 (whose success resulted in similar patterns being repeated by subsequent political elites, shaping Peru's party system).[51] The Philippines' Rodrigo Duterte also campaigned successfully riding on the nomination of Partido Demokratiko Pilipino—Lakas ng Bayan (PDP—Laban), which, at the time, had only a single legislative seat and is now the ruling party in the Philippines.[52] The shell or front parties that appear in the case studies in this volume vary in types; for some, like in Sri Lanka, their popularity is also related to the strength of dynastic politics as, in many Global South states, in some cases, they act as a legitimation of the authority of the military, and some reflect the personal ambition of individual politicians.

In the Sri Lankan case, it is worth looking at the popular rise of the Sri Lanka Podujana Peramuna (SLPP), which was launched in 2016, after Mahinda Rajapaksa's defeat in the 2015 elections, as a front party for Rajapaksa. The SLPP brought together a coalition of several minority parties and the members of the (dissolved in 2019) United People's Freedom Alliance.[53] The SLPP's dramatic rise owed much to weak inter-party relations of the ruling coalition,[54] and the majority

[49] Norris and Inglehart, 'Classifying Parties' (n 7).

[50] Kurt Weyland, 'The Rise of Latin America's Two Lefts: Insights from Rentier State Theory' (2009) 41 Comparative Politics 145.

[51] Steven Levitsky and Maxwell A Cameron, 'Democracy without Parties? Political Parties and Regime Change in Fujimori's Peru' (2003) 45 Latin American Politics and Society 1.

[52] Thomas Power and Eve Warburton (eds), *Democracy in Indonesia: From Stagnation to Regression?* (ISEAS Publishing 2020).

[53] A Rameez, 'Rise of Sri Lanka Podujana Peramuna (SLPP): Causes, Consequences and Challenges' (2020) 13(1) KALAM International Research Journal 1 <http://ir.lib.seu.ac.lk/handle/123456789/5228> accessed 3 October 2022.

[54] Ibid.

it held in the Sri Lankan parliament allowed it to reverse the 19th Constitutional Amendment and pass the controversial 20th Constitutional amendment.[55]

As opposed to anti-establishment parties in liberal democracies or systems co-opting populist parties in illiberal democracies, in regimes with military or authoritarian tendencies, parties in power often only act as the mouthpiece of the executive or the military, as in the case of the Aliança Renovadora Nacional (ARENA) in Brazil during the military rule,[56] the Union Solidarity and Development Party (USDP) in Myanmar, and the Palang Pracharath Party (PPRP) in Thailand. In the case of two countries in this collection's case studies, both with parliamentary systems in place, Myanmar's USDP and Thailand's Democrat Party (which stood out by not getting dissolved in the slew of party bans between 2006 and 2008) are arguably proxy parties for their country's military. However, as the examples in the latter sections of this chapter will hope to elucidate, this parliamentary set-up ensures a certain level of vertical party institutionalisation and necessitates forms of inter-party power relations that make them different from shell parties described above.

One slightly different pattern that emerges through the case studies in this volume is that of an individual political leader's ambitions leading to the formation of a new party, as in the case of Ethiopia and Abiy Ahmed's Prosperity Party and Adama Barrow's National People's Party (NPP) in The Gambia.[57] Section 5 delves a little further into the role and efficacy of Ahmed's Prosperity Party, and I touch upon the NPP again in the section on coalitions, but it is worth mentioning these two examples here separately for it projects a distinctly different role of the political party in states experiencing political transitions (the role of a brand new political party as a 'solution' or a fresh start into a democratic imagination), irrespective of the success or failure of this vision.

This also takes us back to the beginning of this chapter and the intuitive acceptance of parties as necessary vehicles of ideologies and change within political systems. Even when they serve, in practice, as proxies for undemocratic regimes and institutions or when they work as platforms for individual political leaders and their ambitions, registered parties offer a kind of institutional legitimacy, a brand of the *collective* that unaffiliated political players cannot tap into as easily. Political parties are thus simultaneously actors themselves as heterogenous organisational units as well as the umbrellas under which political leaders and groupings enact many performative 'claims of representation'.[58] Conceptualising them as such lets us reimagine them in their dynamic and shifting meanings.

[55] Neil DeVotta, 'Sri Lanka: The Return to Ethnocracy' (2021) 32 Journal of Democracy 96.

[56] Ezrow (n 20).

[57] 'Adama Barrow, Full Text Of President Barrow's Speech At NPP Launch Ceremony—The Fatu Network' (*Fatu Network*, 30 January 2021) <https://fatunetwork.net/full-text-of-president-barrows-speech-at-npp-launch-ceremony> accessed 3 October 2021.

[58] Michael Saward, *The Representative Claim* (Oxford University Press 2010) <https://oxford.universitypressscholarship.com/view/10.1093/acprof:oso/9780199579389.001.0001/acprof-9780199579389> accessed 3 October 2022.

5. The Other Lives of Parties: Contextualising Parties as Organisational Entities

The selection of case studies here also allows us to consider an aspect that is yet to be fully explored within party scholarship—how the original organisational identity and context of the collectives that eventually become registered as 'political parties' affects what roles these parties play in these nation states.

The role of political parties in drafting constitutions has been established in much of the literature, which attributes a positive role in general to participatory constitution-making.[59] However, as empirical evidence indicates, as in the case of both Ethiopia and Thailand, participatory processes of constitution-making did not necessarily contribute to stronger democratic institutions.[60] Ethiopia's 1994 Constitution is unique and much studied for its ethnic decentralisation model. The domination of a single party, the Tigray People's Liberation Front (TPLF), in the drafting process, skewed the participatory constitution-making process.[61] As Yash Ghai has famously observed, when the goal of decentralisation, as in Ethiopia, is national integrity and some amount of autonomous rule for multiple ethnicities, the focus on constitutionalism becomes secondary.[62] However, another important aspect of this process is the historical context of the TPLF before it became a party. This has arguably affected not only the 1994 Constitution and subsequent Ethiopian one-party/coalition dominant politics but also the current democratic backslide unfolding in Ethiopia, with the dismantling of the ethnic party coalition and the formation of Abiy Ahmed's Prosperity Party. The deep roots of the TPLF as a social and grassroots movement against the military regime, from 1976 to 1991[63] (i.e. its past life before it was a viable 'political party') is crucial to understanding how the party's networks operate and how it shapes Ethiopian politics.

In Myanmar, too, the USDP's existence as a front for the military regime must be contextualised by keeping in mind the history of the United Solidarity and Development Association (USDA), which operated as the military's political network in Myanmar, as a social organisation, while consistently referring to itself as 'the party' and mobilising the masses against the National League for Democracy (NLD), much before it finally registered as the USDP in 2010 to contest elections.[64]

59 Tom Ginsburg, *Comparative Constitutional Design* (Cambridge University Press 2012) <http://ebookcentral.proquest.com/lib/warw/detail.action?docID=862413> accessed 3 October 2022; Tom Ginsburg, Zachary Elkins, and Justin Blount, 'Does the Process of Constitution-Making Matter?' (2009) 5 Annual Review of Law and Social Science 201.

60 Ginsburg, Elkins and Blount (n 59).

61 Jamal Benomar, 'Constitution-Making after Conflict: Lessons for Iraq' (2004) 15 Journal of Democracy 81.

62 Yash Ghai, 'Ethnicity, Decentralization, and Constitutionalism: A Comparative Perspective' in Charles M Fombad and Nico Steytler (eds), *Decentralization and Constitutionalism in Africa* (Oxford University Press 2019).

63 John Young, 'Ethnicity and Power in Ethiopia' (1996) 23 Review of African Political Economy 531.

64 Ye Htut, *Myanmar's Political Transition and Lost Opportunities, 2010–2016* (ISEAS 2019).

This aspect of the past lives and the afterlives of political parties and party systems, before and after constitutions and regimes, is particularly notable in the case of the Global South and often post-colonial nation states. The impact of this is understudied in mainstream party scholarship, which, in general, not only relies on a Western liberal democracy as the primary framework of reference but also draws parallels between political systems in European or North American democracies, with political systems arising out very different Global South contexts. A decontextualised reading of the role of parties in democratic decay often ignores this history and how it shapes the role of political parties within a liberal or illiberal democracy.

6. Coalitions, Dynasties, and Power Networks: Party and Party System Institutionalisation

The trouble with a thematic chapter on political parties and democratic institutions is that it cannot be complete without considering the aspects of party politics that have been most researched in political sciences, and at the same time, a subsection could never fully do justice to it. In the vast literature, however, there are some confluences: much of the literature focuses on the voter response to intra-party issues.[65] While the direct co-relation between more democracy and higher party institutionalisation (i.e. clearer intra-party organisation) is uneasy,[66] one could still surmise that parties with democratic intent are better positioned to succeed when equipped with stronger inter-party and intra-party organisation. A lot of the discussion until now in this chapter has already touched upon these aspects. Keeping these factors in mind, I limit myself here to some inferences from a few of the case studies in this book, interlaced with examples from some additional nation states.

6.1 The Impact of Party Systems and Institutionalisation

Continuing from the argument in section 5 regarding the other lives of parties, contextualisation is key. Thailand's weakly institutionalised party system, for example, can be attributed to the lack of grassroots movements or a bottoms-up party formation, which scholars have chalked up to the fact that Thailand was never colonised, and therefore, that it did not have a mass-based freedom or social

[65] Ron Lehrer, 'Intra-Party Democracy and Party Responsiveness' (2012) 35 West European Politics 1295.

[66] Vicky Randall and Lars Svaasand, 'Party Institutionalization in New Democracies' (2002) 8 Party Politics 5; Gideon Rahat, Reuven Y Hazan, and Richard S Katz, 'Democracy and Political Parties: On the Uneasy Relationships between Participation, Competition and Representation' (2008) 14 Party Politics 663.

movement culminating in its initial party groupings.[67] Consequently, its first party, the People's Party formed in 1932, and subsequent party formations, have been elite-led and concentrated at the top, resulting in a weak party system.[68] Between 1997 and the 2006 coup, despite attempts to develop their organisational bases, the major parties in Thailand remained elite-based and centralised without achieving high levels of party institutionalisation[69] or mass integration.

The inter- and intra- party issues in another military-controlled regime, Myanmar, are also worthy of attention. In Myanmar's 2008 Constitution, drafted by the military regime and ostensibly with public support, it is interesting to note, the Preamble makes explicit reference to the history of changes in the nation's party systems:

> In order to gain independence speedily, the Constitution was hastily drafted, and it was adopted by the Constituent Assembly on 24th September 1947. After attaining independence, Parliamentary Democracy System was practised in the State in accord with the Constitution of the Union of Myanmar. However, as democratic system could not be effectively materialized, the new Constitution of the Socialist Republic of the Union of Myanmar was drafted based on the single party system, and after holding a National Referendum, a socialist democratic State was set up in 1974. The Constitution came to an end because of the general situation that occurred in 1988. Later, due to public aspirations, the State Peace and Development Council made efforts to adopt a multi-party democratic system and market economy in accord with the National situation.[70]

The Basic Principles also include, under Article 6(d), the 'flourishing of a genuine, disciplined multi-party democratic system'.[71] While it is ostensibly, on paper, an acknowledgement of multiparty-ness being an indicator of democratisation, in effect, it works as a legitimisation strategy for the Myanmar military regime.[72] But the party problems in Myanmar are twofold; on the one hand, there is the military and military-backed USDP, but on the other hand, there are also issues of ethnic and geopolitical suppression by the National League for Democracy (NLD). Before coming to power in 2015, the NLD had criticised the military line of argument on ethnic strife, which saw the only way forwards in peace negotiations

[67] Erik Martinez Kuhonta, 'Social Cleavages, Political Parties, and the Building of Performance Legitimacy in Southeast Asia' in Nancy Bermeo and Deborah J Yashar (eds), *Parties, Movements, and Democracy in the Developing World* (Cambridge University Press 2016) <www.cambridge.org/core/product/identifier/9781316661581%23CN-bp-3/type/book_part> accessed 3 October 2022.

[68] Ibid.

[69] Croissant and Chambers (n 25).

[70] 'Myanmar's Constitution of 2008 with Amendments through 2015' (n 21).

[71] Ibid.

[72] Aurel Croissant and Jil Kamerling, 'Why Do Military Regimes Institutionalize? Constitution-Making and Elections as Political Survival Strategy in Myanmar' (2013) 21 Asian Journal of Political Science 105.

being to sign the National Ceasefire Agreement (NCA).[73] However, after coming to power, the NLD could not maintain the same position and chose to toe the military line, backing the NCA, which has not been a success.[74] Another crisis whose mismanagement has put Myanmar under the global spotlight is the dispossession of the religious and ethnic minority group of the Rohingya Muslims. This is interesting to mention, especially in relation to the role of parties in democracies, because, ostensibly, the NLD's stand coincided with popular mass vitriol against the Rohingyas[75] and did not depreciate their popular democratic legitimacy within the country. However, it did put Aung San Suu Kyi's party's and her own commitment to liberal democracy under deep suspicion internationally.[76]

The ebb and flow in the optimism relayed in the scholarship on Malaysia's party system and its relationship to democracy is, again, interesting. In 2008, a formal coalition that saw opposition parties the PKR (People's Justice Party), PAS (Islamic Party of Malaysia), and the Democratic Action Party (DAP), with very different electoral bases and ideological standpoints, collaborate under the Pakatan Rakyat banner to win significant victories in elections brought hope that the dominant Barisan Nasional (National Front, BN) could be overthrown.[77] The opposition's coalition strategically fielded candidates to play to the ethnic composition of different constituencies, whereby PAS competed from Malay majority areas, DAP from the ethnically Chinese areas, and the PKR from the mixed areas, creating the possibility of potential cross-ethnic cooperation in Malaysian party politics.[78] By 2009, however, with the Perak Constitutional Crisis and the defection of three state legislators from the Pakatan Rakyat coalition, the BN had managed to destabilise this optimism.[79] Almost a decade later, as Wilson Tay Tze Vern describes in his case study in Chapter 15 in this volume, the coming of a new political party, Bersatu, in time for the general elections of 2018, brought back the possibility of ethnic and religious cooperation under the coalition, Pakatan Harapan. The regime change, however, as described by Tze Vern, has been far from stable.

[73] Maung Aung Myoe, 'Partnership in Politics: The Tatmadaw and the NLD in Myanmar since 2016' in Chit Win and others (eds), *Myanmar Transformed?: People, Places and Politics* (Institute of Southeast Asian Studies (ISEAS)—Yusof Ishak Institute 2018) <www.cambridge.org/core/books/myanmar-transformed/partnership-in-politics-the-tatmadaw-and-the-nld-in-myanmar-since-2016/29B0F34519018F869DB4095654909E3D> accessed 5 June 2021.

[74] Matthew Walton, 'Reflections on Myanmar Under the NLD so Far' in Chit Win and others (n 73) <www.cambridge.org/core/books/myanmar-transformed/reflections-on-myanmar-under-the-nld-so-far/629E5A9BFA08C5CF4D862B13542BCDFE> accessed 3 October 2022.

[75] Ibid.

[76] Myoe (n 73).

[77] Maznah Mohamad, 'Malaysia—Democracy and the End of Ethnic Politics?' (2008) 62 Australian Journal of International Affairs 441.

[78] Ibid.

[79] Chin-Huat Wong, James Chin, and Norani Othman, 'Malaysia—Towards a Topology of an Electoral One-Party State' (2010) 17 Democratization 920.

6.2 Dynasties and Loyalties: Parties as Vehicles for Unreliable Power Negotiations

Similar to the Malaysian vision of coalition-building for democracy, the 2015 Sri Lankan elections also indicated rising optimism in the Wickremesinghe–Sirisena coalition-building, but this coalition also saw differences within the administration, resulting in faltering governance, and contributed to the eventual 2018 constitutional crises.[80] Dynastic politics not only returned to power in Sri Lanka, with the Rajapaksa family and their new party, the SLPP, in government and occupying presidential and prime ministerial as well as key cabinet positions, but also scholars have noted that the recent constitutional changes passed by the Rajapaksa government allowed for an even longer dynastic regime in the future.[81]

Conversely, in the case of Maldives, as Mariyam Zulfa's Chapter 11 in this collection also traces, a strategic coalition of the opposition parties behind Solih followed the fall-out within another political dynasty—the Gayoom brothers. Maldives' party system is an example of fickle power coalitions typical of weak democracies, where party allegiances are unreliable and unstable. The democratic hope after Nasheed had ousted the Gayoom regime in the 2008 elections receded with Yameen Abdul Gayoom's coup, and in 2013, the party loyalties had reversed: all of Nasheed's supporting parties had pledged their loyalties to Gayoom and his Progressive Party of Maldives (PPM).[82] Gayoom's children also received key positions in that government,[83] solidifying the dynastic roots within political institutions. But with the disagreements within their dynastic politics, in the 2018 elections, the opposition managed to unite behind Solih, ushering in a positive regime change to democracy.[84]

The transition of The Gambia into democracy was also one of optimism, bolstering the argument on the collaborative potential of political parties. The opposition in The Gambia, after decades of failed attempts to cooperate to overthrow Jammeh, was finally successful in 2016. In 2001, many of the major parties banned at the beginning of Jammeh's coup were 'un-banned', but the opposition parties could not agree on one presidential candidate to back.[85] In 2005, again, the opposition faced the same problem, even though they had managed a formal coalition: the National Alliance for Democracy and Development (NADD).[86] With

[80] Amanda Cats-Baril, 'Coalition for Constitutional Change: Sri Lanka's Constitutional Crisis and Maldives' 2018 Elections' in Adem Abebe and others (eds), *Annual Review of Constitution-Building: 2018* (International Institute for Democracy and Electoral Assistance (International IDEA 2020) 22–35.

[81] DeVotta (n 55).

[82] Fathima Musthaq, 'Shifting Tides in South Asia: Tumult in the Maldives' (2014) 25 Journal of Democracy 164, 166.

[83] Ibid.

[84] Abebe and others (n 80).

[85] David Perfect, 'The Gambia under Yahya Jammeh: An Assessment' (2010) 99 Round Table 53.

[86] Ibid.

every election, Jammeh had been winning by an increasing margin, although at the cost of in-fighting within his own party, Alliance for Patriotic Reorientation and Construction (APRC).[87] The Gambian opposition's success in the 2016 elections was owed, to a great extent, to strategically pushing the independent, non-party affiliated candidate instead of trying to negotiate for a candidate from one of the opposition parties.[88] It is also in light of this that the negotiation and collaboration unfolding at the moment, between Barrow's NPP (which, as noted before in this chapter was launched with a declaration for a new kind of democratic party politics) and Jammeh's APRC[89] brings further doubts for The Gambia's democratic future.

7. Conclusion: Locating the Party as an Organisation

Nation states experiencing rapid changes in their democratic status, like the Global South case studies in this volume, might present a harder task when looking to thematically chart the role of political parties within regimes. More stable regimes, in comparison, provide a more long-term view of parties and party systems. However, looking at parties as agents in systems in flux allows us a unique opportunity to locate parties in their specific contexts and therefore destabilise the liberal democratic conceptualisations about political parties. This fits in with my attempt, in this chapter, to focus on parties as individual units instead of party *systems*.

As this chapter has tried to elucidate with examples, political parties really are essentially carriers of political motivations, and their role in the sustenance or the deterioration of a democracy is largely circumstantial. This is evident in the case studies in this collection, but it also holds globally. Centrist, mainstream political parties can turn populist, like Macron's En Marche!,[90] and in set-ups where democratic regimes were previously thought untenable, like countries in the Arab world, parties like those in Tunisia proved a democratic exception.[91] Another important facet of party politics and its rapid reorientation globally today, which is important to mention even if a detailed analysis is beyond the scope of this chapter, is the role and use of social media by political parties, whether located at the moderate centre,

[87] David Perfect, 'The Gambian 2016 Presidential Election and Its Aftermath' (2017) 106 Round Table 323.

[88] Ibid.

[89] Achraf Tijani, 'Gambia: Will Jammeh Help Adama Barrow Secure a Second Term?' (*The Africa Report*, 2021) <www.theafricareport.com/127918/gambia-will-jammeh-help-adama-barrow-secure-a-second-term> accessed 3 October 2021.

[90] Charles Barthold and Martin Fougère, 'How You Can Tell Emmanuel Macron Is Actually a Populist—And Why It Matters' (*The Conversation*, 5 March 2020) <https://theconversation.com/how-you-can-tell-emmanuel-macron-is-actually-a-populist-and-why-it-matters-130496> accessed 5 June 2021.

[91] Ezrow (n 20).

at ideological fringes, at positions of authoritarian power, or rallying against it, and how this is fundamentally changing traditional politics.[92]

I have attempted, in keeping with the spirit of this collection, to sidestep much of the Global North-focused party analysis. While generalised inferences or establishing causal links between party behaviour and democracies can lead to contradictory formulations, it is perhaps possible to formulate two general takeaways from this chapter—first, that what 'a party' is depends heavily on the institutional context and the legal and constitutional frameworks within the particular nation state; second, in systems where institutions are in a constant flux, parties too are constantly shifting, dynamic entities. Gabriel Negretto encapsulates this perfectly:

> regardless of the analytical perspective we adopt, the claim that institutions matter hinges on the assumption that institutions are stable. But while the assumption of institutional stability is plausible in some contexts, in others it is not. And when institutions themselves are in flux, analysis of the underlying game that leads to institutional change provides a better and deeper understanding of the institutional setting than simply taking rules as a given from which outcomes are derived.[93]

This is especially fitting for the fragile or fluctuating democracies that this collection chooses to bring together. I have tried to not force a relationship between the case studies, and yet, hopefully, some broader patterns have emerged in this chapter. Parties that endure, like the USDP in Myanmar, or parties which, when dissolved, plummet the state into conflict, like the EPRDF in Ethiopia, derive their deep roots from their pre-party organisational strengths. It is also useful to differentiate between the change spurred by a party leader and that by parties as organisations. One could argue, perhaps, that while democratic retrogression spurred by individuals is more visible, institutional capture by parties is often more insidious. It involves a more silent process of system change and collaboration with other networks of capital and power, like business elites or the military, for example. Thus, where the party is located on these constantly shifting maps of political change is always a combination of its institutional context and the limits of its agency, and it is in charting these dynamic positions that we can encapsulate their roles in democratic backsliding, democratic strengthening, or constitutional endurance.

[92] CBC Radio, 'Are Digital Technologies Making Politics Impossible?' (25 November 2016) <www.cbc.ca/radio/spark/336-bad-driving-social-media-influence-and-more-1.3863844/are-digital-technologies-making-politics-impossible-1.3863855> accessed 3 June 2021; John Postill, 'Populism and Social Media: A Global Perspective' (2018) 40 Media, Culture & Society 754.

[93] Gabriel L Negretto, *Making Constitutions: Presidents, Parties, and Institutional Choice in Latin America* (Cambridge University Press 2013) 242 .

5
Constitutional Courts and the Exceptionality of Regime Change

Julius Yam

1. Introduction

There are two complementary views when it comes to discussions about the relationship between constitutional courts and transitional regimes: (i) constitutional courts tend to be active participants in transitional politics (the 'Descriptive View') and (ii) successful transition requires constitutional courts taking up a democracy-building role (the 'Normative View'). The Descriptive View is a descriptive claim and an attempt to use the political regime in which a court is situated (which, in this case, is a transitional regime) to characterise judicial involvement in constitutional politics. There is a tendency by comparative scholars to categorise courts based on regime type: for instance, they would associate courts in democracies as strong and those in authoritarian regimes as subservient.[1] The Descriptive View extends the regime-type approach to understanding constitutional courts in transitional regimes, treating them as central actors in transitions and possessing the necessary capabilities to guide the transition. Some of the more widely discussed experiences, such as the constitutional courts in post-apartheid South Africa, post-war Germany, post-Franco Spain, and Colombia during the late 1990s, seem to support this view.[2]

The Normative View is a normative claim, arguing that judges should guide, or even lead, the democratisation project. Many scholars and policymakers assume that democratisation and constitutionalism go hand in hand. In particular, it has been argued that courts should step up and actively safeguard a vulnerable

[1] See Tamir Moustafa, 'Law and Courts in Authoritarian Regimes' (2014) 10 Annual Review of Law and Social Science 281; Gretchen Helmke and Frances Rosenbluth, 'Regimes and the Rule of Law: Judicial Independence in Comparative Perspective' (2009) 12 Annual Review of Political Science 345.

[2] See Heinz Klug, 'South Africa's Constitutional Court: Enabling Democracy and Promoting Law in Transition from Apartheid' (2008) 3 Journal of Comparative Law 174; Francesco Biagi, *Three Generations of European Constitutional Courts in Transition to Democracy* (Cambridge University Press 2020); Julio Faundez, 'Democratization through Law: Perspectives from Latin America' (2005) 12 Democratisation 749; Bojan Bugaric, 'Courts as Policy-Makers: Lessons from Transition' (2001) 42 Harvard International Law Journal 247; Michaela Hailbronner, 'Transformative Constitutionalism: Not Only in the Global South' (2017) 65 American Journal of Comparative Law 527.

Julius Yam, *Constitutional Courts and the Exceptionality of Regime Change* In: *Democratic Consolidation and Constitutional Endurance in Asia and Africa*. Edited by: Tom Gerald Daly and Dinesha Samararatne, Oxford University Press.
 DOI: 10.1093/oso/9780192899347.003.0005

constitutional order that is seeking transformation.[3] The exceptionality of the transitional process has often been used to justify courts taking a more expansive role.[4]

Based on the experiences of this volume, this chapter challenges both views and argues that they have failed to properly account for the exceptionality of regime change. The exceptional nature of transitions suggests that there is tremendous diversity among the paths of transitional regimes, patterns of constitutional politics, and courts' involvement during these periods. The fact that courts are operating in transitional regimes tells us very little about their actual judicial roles. The exceptional nature of transitional regimes also has normative implications. The chapter contends that the exceptionality of regime change can potentially work against judicial intervention. Exceptionality, in and of itself, is not a justification for a stronger judicial role. There are conditions where it is, in fact, desirable for courts to stay out of transitional politics.

Before outlining the road map of the chapter, two definitional issues need to be addressed. The term 'constitutional court' here is used broadly to refer to courts with jurisdiction to address constitutional questions. It accordingly covers different models of constitutional courts, such as the centralised, Kelsenian model (where a separate court exercises exclusive constitutional jurisdiction), the diffused model (where any court within the system has constitutional jurisdiction), and the French model (where the court, more commonly known as the constitutional council, exercises an advisory function and makes recommendations on constitutional questions). Transitional regime is defined as a state undergoing regime change.[5] A transitional regime is an interim arrangement and commences at the initiation of transition, which can be a single event, such as an election, or a process, such as constitutional reform. A central feature of transitional regimes is a high degree of uncertainty about the rules of the game and how constitutional developments will unfold.[6] This uncertainty is assessed from the perspective of current actors involved in the transitional process. Democratisation is only one of many possible outcomes, and a transitional regime can end up at the same, or an even worse, position than where it started. Hence, a transitional regime is not synonymous with a new democracy.

The rest of this chapter is divided into four sections. Section 2 begins by outlining how comparative constitutional scholars are accustomed to using the

[3] See Samuel Issacharoff, 'Constitutional Courts and Democratic Hedging' (2011) 99 Georgetown Law Journal 961; László Sólyom, 'The Role of Constitutional Courts in the Transition to Democracy: With Special Reference to Hungary' (2003) 18 International Sociology 133.

[4] See Nicholas W Barber and Adrian Vermeule, 'The Exceptional Role of Courts in the Constitutional Order' (2016) 92 Notre Dame Law Review 817; Ruti Teitel, 'Transitional Jurisprudence: The Role of Law in Political Transformation' (1997) 106 Yale Law Journal 2009.

[5] See Nancy Bermeo, 'Rethinking Regime Change' (1990) 22 Comparative Politics 359.

[6] This is arguably the most common way to define a transitional regime, but using uncertainty as a definition can create fuzzy boundaries. See Andreas Schedler, 'Taking Uncertainty Seriously: The Blurred Boundaries of Democratic Transition and Consolidation' (2001) 8 Democratization 1. Nevertheless, this way of defining a transitional regime is sufficient for the purposes of this chapter.

regime-type approach. Understanding the regime-type approach helps to unpack the intuition behind extending it to constitutional courts in transitional regimes. Section 3 then argues why the Descriptive View is misguided and how the exceptional circumstances around transitional contexts make it highly challenging to apply the regime-type approach in understanding the relationship between constitutional courts and transitional regimes. Section 4 returns to a more fundamental normative question about what role constitutional courts should play in periods of regime change. In contrast with the Normative View, it will be argued that judicial intervention would only be desirable if a court possesses at least two qualities: social legitimacy and judicial independence. Nevertheless, these qualities are often missing because of transitional politics. This creates some doubts as to whether judicial intervention in transitional politics should always be welcomed. Section 5 offers concluding remarks.

2. The Regime-Type Approach and Its Allure

To figure out where the Descriptive View comes from and its flaws, we need to first understand what the regime-type approach is. The regime-type approach is one of the most common ways for comparative constitutional scholars today to compare courts across different geographical locations and time periods.

As the field of comparative constitutional law grew, the gap between law and politics has become increasingly blurred. In fact, these disciplinary boundaries, it has been argued, only impede the development of the field, and some suggest renaming the field as comparative constitutional studies instead.[7] Semantics aside, it seems to be widely accepted today that constitutional law and judicial studies are subjects that are heavily conditioned by politics.

A logical extension of this assumption would be to categorise courts based on the political regime in which a court exists. If it is believed that constitutional law is impacted by constitutional politics, then there are good reasons to suspect that constitutional law and judicial politics are shaped, at least partly, by regime-type politics. Stephen Gardbaum, for example, writes, 'the political space available for more independent, robust, and consequential constitutional courts is in significant part a function of the general political regime in which it operates'.[8]

This intuition based on regime type is very attractive because it means that comparative studies on courts can be conducted based on macro-political features. More importantly, these features—such as the design of the political system,

[7] Ran Hirschl, *Comparative Matters: The Renaissance of Comparative Constitutional Law* (Oxford University Press 2014).

[8] Stephen Gardbaum, 'What Makes for More or Less Powerful Constitutional Courts' (2018) 29 Duke Journal of Comparative & International Law 1, 24.

number of veto players, and electoral competitiveness—are not hard to empirically identify. The convenience of this hypothesis has facilitated cross-jurisdictional and cross-disciplinary discussions, leading to the development of many interesting comparative constitutional and judicial theories.

The remainder of this part overviews how the regime-type approach has been applied. The survey here is by no means comprehensive, but it seeks to highlight a common thread that exists within a body of literature in comparative constitutional law, that is, the use of regime type to explain different aspects of the relationship between courts and constitutional politics.[9]

Independent courts have been traditionally linked with democracies. This perception perhaps stems from international rule-of-law programmes led by the United States during the 1990s and has since shaped the strategies pursued by transnational and international policy organisations.[10] Scholars used to be occupied by the dichotomy of independent courts in democracies versus subservient courts in authoritarian regimes.[11] As the field progressed, the regime-type approach was used in an increasingly fine-grained way and the traditional dichotomy has proven to be too broad-brush. Courts in democracies were not always alike. Mark Ramseyer's comparison of the US and Japanese courts, for instance, showed two very different courts, despite both operating in what can only be called democracies.[12] He finds that the US courts were a lot more independent than their Japanese counterparts, and the explanation he proposes is based on the level of competitiveness of a democratic system. A more electorally competitive democracy is likely to produce a more independent judiciary. The reason for this, he posits, is that political powers are more diffused in dynamic political environments, making it less likely for any single political entity to exert pressure and influence on courts. Extending Ramseyer's theory, Tom Ginsburg argues that independent courts are more likely to emerge in new democracies with a more competitive political system than those ruled by a dominant political coalition.[13] Po Jen Yap has made a similar argument in the context of Asian democracies, observing that courts in competitive democracies are likely to take a central role in democratic consolidation, whereas those in fragile democracies and democracies with a single party tend to be politicised and weak.[14]

[9] For a more extensive overview of the literature, see Helmke and Rosenbluth (n 1). For a critique of the regime-type approach, see Mark A Graber, 'Constitutional Politics in the Active Voice' in Diana Kapiszewski, Gordon Silverstein, and Robert A Kagan (eds), *Consequential Courts: Judicial Roles in Global Perspective* (Cambridge University Press 2013).

[10] David Trubek, 'The "Rule of Law" in Development Assistance: Past, Present, and Future' in David Trubek and Alvaro Santos (eds), *The New Law and Economic Development: A Critical Appraisal* (Cambridge University Press 2006).

[11] See Moustafa (n 1) 294.

[12] Mark Ramseyer, 'The Puzzling (In)Dependence of Courts: A Comparative Approach' (1994) 23 Journal of Legal Studies 721.

[13] Tom Ginsburg, *Judicial Review in New Democracies: Constitutional Courts in Asian Cases* (Cambridge University Press 2003).

[14] Po Jen Yap, *Courts and Democracies in Asia* (Cambridge University Press 2017).

The regime-type approach is by no means limited to democracies. Similar studies on courts in authoritarian regimes are emerging. These courts seem different to those in democracies, but most of them are more than 'window dressing for dictators'.[15] The regime-type approach has been used to reveal behavioural variations among courts in different kinds of authoritarian regimes. Brad Epperly's large-N study finds that courts in authoritarian regimes exhibit varying levels of judicial independence.[16] More specifically, it seems that courts in hybrid regimes—which are regimes that are neither fully democratic nor fully authoritarian—are more likely to be more autonomous than those in pure authoritarian regimes. His findings confirm that the electoral logic of judicial independence suggested by Ramseyer can be activated under nominally competitive environments. Providing an alternative explanation, Eric Ip argues that there is a higher chance for strong and independent courts to emerge in hybrid regimes than pure authoritarian regimes because of the high political transaction cost environment of hybrid regimes.[17] Hybrid regimes are characterised by their ideological divides and relatively decentralised political structures. This makes it harder for hybrid-regime incumbents to govern at will and, as a result, creates more space for judicial manoeuvring. Looking at a more specific regime type (unstable authoritarian regimes with a high incumbent turnover rate), Gretchen Helmke uses the case study of Argentina to show that judges have a propensity to rule against the government when the incumbent begins to lose power.[18] In unstable authoritarian regimes where coalitions often shift, she argues that judges are incentivised to align with the incoming elites so as to preserve the judges' own interests. Her theory, which she calls the strategic defection theory, helps explain fluctuating moments of judicial assertion in this particular kind of authoritarian regime. Some have also suggested that authoritarian regimes with developing or developed economies would tend to have more independent courts because semi-independent courts are needed to boost investors' confidence.[19]

3. Courts in Transitional Regimes?

The attraction of the regime-type approach should be obvious by now. With its political-institutional focus, the approach offers relatively clean explanations to account for judicial-political dynamics across a wide range of jurisdictions that may not, at first sight, seem to be comparable. It has unleashed convenient frameworks

[15] Moustafa (n 1) 281.

[16] Brad Epperly, *The Political Foundations of Judicial Independence in Dictatorship and Democracy* (Oxford University Press 2019).

[17] Eric Ip, *Hybrid Constitutionalism: The Politics of Constitutional Review in the Chinese Special Administrative Regions* (Cambridge University Press 2019).

[18] Gretchen Helmke, *Courts under Constraints: Judges, Generals, and Presidents in Argentina* (Cambridge University Press 2012).

[19] Moustafa (n 1) 285.

that unveil common ways in which macro-politics might impact courts and, as a result, significantly advanced the field of comparative constitutional studies.

It would, then, only seem natural to extend the regime-type approach to another category of political regime—transitional regimes. And, indeed, constitutional courts in transitional regimes are commonly associated with certain attributes. Courts can be thought of as intensely involved in the transitional process, capable of dictating the pace and direction of the transition, and it can be thought that judicial contributions would positively impact interim developments.[20] There are at least two factors that have contributed to this association between courts and transitional regimes.

First, it might be that paradigmatic cases (such as the post-apartheid South African Constitutional Court and the post-war German Constitutional Court) have had a huge influence on people's perception about constitutional courts. The vast number of discussions generated by these examples enlarged the perceived role of a constitutional court. These discussions created not only a belief that transition and consolidation needed strong constitutional courts but also a sense that there were many other constitutional courts that were like these paradigmatic cases. Anecdotal evidence has further cemented this view as a number of constitutional courts highly featured in the literature—such as those in Italy, Spain, Czech Republic, Indonesia, Korea and Colombia[21]—have played a similarly important part in these countries' transitional projects.[22]

Second, the decades following the Second World War saw the establishment of constitutional courts becoming part of the model of democratisation.[23] Constitutional courts symbolised a clean break from their states' authoritarian past. Many post-war and post-Communist countries followed, in particular, post-war Germany in adopting the Kelsenian institutional design in setting up a separate, dedicated court with centralised power of constitutional review. These courts were armed with strong forms of judicial review powers and enjoyed explicit constitutional authority to implement the Constitution. This model for democratisation was so popular that constitutional courts have become a feature in most new

[20] These points are more often treated as an assumption or found in passing remarks in the literature. See e.g. Bugaric (n 2); Hailbronner, 'Transformative Constitutionalism' (n 2); Issacharoff (n 3); Teitel (n 4) 2032–34; Kim Lane Scheppele, 'Democracy by Judiciary. Or, Why Courts Can Be More Democratic than Parliaments' in Adam Czarnota, Martin Krygier, and Wojciech Sadurski (eds), *Rethinking the Rule of Law after Communism* (Central European University Press 2005).

[21] See Biagi (n 2); Marcus Mietzner, 'Political Conflict Resolution and Democratic Consolidation in Indonesia: The Role of the Constitutional Court' (2010) 10 Journal of East Asian Studies 397; Ginsburg (n 13); Faundez (n 2).

[22] It is also worth noting that these courts provided institutional models for one another. The South Korean constitutional court, for example, was used as a 'template' by Indonesia, whereas the German constitutional court was 'directly emulated' in Spain and South Korea. See Tom Gerald Daly, *The Alchemists: Questioning Our Faith in Courts as Democracy-Builders* (Cambridge University Press 2017) 82.

[23] See ibid, ch 2.

constitutions in the past several decades.[24] This is perhaps another reason why there is a tendency among scholars and policymakers to have positive associations when it comes to courts and transitional regimes.

An attentive reader of this volume will have already noticed the problem of this view. There is tremendous diversity in the involvement of courts in transitional politics.[25] A cursory look at the examples in this volume suggests that there is a variety of roles played by courts in different transitional moments. We have constitutional courts that are relatively inactive (such as Myanmar),[26] but judicial inactivity surprisingly had a major impact on transitional politics in The Gambia.[27] Among those heavily involved in transitional politics, there were some that consistently preserved the interests of the status quo (such as Thailand)[28] and others that strove to facilitate regime change by dislodging the incumbent (such as Maldives).[29] Aside from ideological heterogeneity, their impact on regime change ranged from bringing a constitutional crisis to an end (or, at least, in Sri Lanka, temporarily halting it)[30] to further deepening pre-existing political divides (such as Maldives).[31] More interestingly, their historical roles did not determine the roles they played in regime-change moments. The fact that they were largely irrelevant actors in normal times does not mean that they would be necessarily irrelevant in regime-change moments (such as Ethiopia).[32] Not to mention that these constitutional courts were structured quite differently in their respective transitional periods. Unlike the South African and German experiences, many courts, here, did not experience judicial reform at transitional moments that would enhance their constitutional position. In fact, some of the courts were simply too weak to participate in constitutional politics during transition. For example, constitutional review was historically restricted in Malaysia, and the wings of the Federal Court remained clipped during the transition.[33]

[24] Tom Ginsburg and Mila Versteeg, 'Why Do Countries Adopt Constitutional Review?' (2014) 30 Journal of Law, Economics, & Organization 587.

[25] Courts are not monolithic entities, and there may even be behavioural variations within the judiciary and among judges on the bench because of judicial politics during transitional periods, though this is beyond the scope of this chapter.

[26] See in this collection Ohn Mar Zin, Naw Janet, and Kimana Zulueta-Fülscher, Chapter 13 'Myanmar's Transition to Peace and Democracy: The Journey Reversed'.

[27] See in this collection Satang Nabaneh, Chapter 9 'Prospects for Democratic Consolidation in The Gambia: A Cup Half Full, Half Empty, or More?'.

[28] See in this collection Khemthong Tonsakulrungruang, Chapter 14 'Coup and Decay: How Thai-Style Democracy Abuses Constitutionalism'.

[29] See in this collection Mariyam Zulfa, Chapter 11 'Maldives Constitution 2008: Winds of Change at the Fifteenth-Year Crossroads'.

[30] See in this collection Luwie Ganeshathasan, Chapter 12 'Sri Lanka's Chronic Inability to Sustain Democratic Reform'.

[31] See in this collection Zulfa (n 29).

[32] See in this collection Adem Kassie Abebe, Chapter 10 'Ethiopia's Transition: Will the Country Stem Descent to Its Tradition of Authoritarianism?'

[33] See in this collection Wilson Tay Tze Vern, Chapter 15 'Making Progress on A Rocky Path: Democratic Consolidation and Constitutional Endurance in Malaysia, 2018–2021'.

In short, significant variations exist among constitutional courts in transitional regimes regarding their institutional structure, capabilities, level of constitutional involvement, social impact, and ideological inclination. Some courts, of course, participate in transitional politics and make significant contributions to democratisation, but this is hardly reflective of the full picture.

The fact that the Descriptive View is only partial is because the two factors outlined above that had contributed to the paradigm are skewed. The influence of the classic cases is not only huge but also disproportionate. Freeing ourselves from existing experiences, we find that this impression suffers from a sampling bias, as this volume shows., maybe because we have not looked hard enough, maybe because examples that do not conform with the dominant narrative were not given sufficient attention, or maybe because we have been only interested in cases that meet the predefined standards of success. Whatever the reasons might be, there are many cases out there that do not fit with the paradigm but should be counted towards the bigger picture.

Furthermore, the classic cases used to support the Descriptive View seemed to follow a similar transitional pattern, involving a new constitution as a 'binding blueprint',[34] a newly structured constitutional court that enjoys explicit constitutional authority to implement the Constitution, a polity largely committed to the democratisation project, and a steady and gradual progression towards that goal. The elements mentioned are far from guaranteed though. Unlike the South African Constitutional Court, most courts do not have the explicit constitutional mandate to play a transformative role. In fact, while it is relatively rare not to have a new constitution during a transitional context,[35] many regime-change moments do not involve the establishment of a new constitutional court.[36] It is also common to see the authoritarian past and hegemonic interests corrupting the transitional process, creating barriers to courts asserting themselves. Transitions are also frequently zigzagging and not as linear as one might assume. If there is one lesson that can be drawn from the case-study chapters of this volume, it is that the pathways for constitutional democratic developments are rarely even. The states studied here have all experienced some kind of democratising moment that would supposedly bring them closer to the democratic end. But, as we have seen, their trajectories turned out to be quite different. The Gambia is an encouraging example, where modest progression can be observed, but the others seem to be taking a detour or heading the other way. Contrary to what many had hoped, a lot of the democratising moments ended up becoming steps towards authoritarian entrenchment. Even among those undergoing democratic backsliding, the pace of retrogression has also varied.

[34] Hailbronner, 'Transformative Constitutionalism' (n 2) 545.
[35] Argentina's democratic transition in 1983 is an example of this exception.
[36] Daly, *The Alchemists* (n 22) 88–89.

An even more basic point is that, even if the formation or strengthening of a constitutional court coincided with the period of transition, its mere establishment or empowerment does not promise a fixed judicial role. The waves of constitutional courts during the post-war decades and after the collapse of communism brought a sense of optimism about the potential of court-centric democratisation. The setting up of a new constitutional court may be a natural response to authoritarianism considering the history of many states striving to democratise, but it does not automatically lead to a constitutional court that will be actively involved in transitional politics or willing or capable of making democratic contributions.

My critique here suggests that it would be challenging to extend the regime-type approach to transitional regimes. It is perhaps possible to apply the approach in ways that are more sensitive to the *different kinds* of transitional regimes. Indeed, similar features in relation to judicial politics during transition can be observed. For instance, the issues that courts are asked to deal with are likely to be mega-political in nature, where the political stakes are so high that a constitutional decision can have significant impact on the very fabric of the polity. Whether judges admit it or not, law often becomes intrinsically tied up with politics in these moments. Furthermore, the political environment is highly unstable, and political coalitions are likely to be shifting during those times. This creates a more complex socio-political backdrop for the courts and makes it harder for judges to accurately forecast potential responses from different political actors. These judicial-political features of transitional contexts are illuminating to the extent that they point to the kinds of challenges potentially faced by constitutional courts during these periods. However, this still leaves open an array of possibilities regarding how courts would actually respond to these challenges. The fact that transitional moments are typically uncharted territories for judges further opens the space for judicial creativity. As a result, there is a limit as to how helpful the regime-type approach can be in understanding courts in transitional regimes. Judicial experiences during transition tend to be quite distinct because of the idiosyncrasies of regime change. Historical or contextual approaches might, instead, offer greater intellectual yield if the goal is to have a deeper understanding of constitutional-judicial politics in transitional contexts.

4. The Exceptional Normative Role?

At the moment, based on the experiences we have looked at, it seems rather unlikely that we can learn much about constitutional courts in transitional regimes through the regime-type approach because of the exceptional nature of a transitional regime. The commonalities among transitional regimes seem to be their high degree of uncertainty and instability, as well as their moments of 'intense flux'.[37] We have

[37] Ibid, 152.

seen how regime change can have different causes, and be of different paces, and that the direction of regime change is hard to foresee. The political-institutional patterns of transitional regimes are, by definition, inconsistent and unpredictable. Accordingly, transitional regimes seldom impact courts in consistent and predictable ways, and the impact of courts on regime change can be equally inconsistent and unpredictable. Such diversity in judicial involvement should, then, not come as a surprise.

The exceptional nature of transitional regimes not only forces us to acknowledge the many different judicial roles undertaken by courts but also prompts reflection about how constitutional courts *should* position themselves during regime-change periods. The Normative View describes an expectation, widely shared in the field, that courts need to take up the role of a democracy-builder because successful transition depends on it. On this view, courts need to assert themselves forcefully to make sure that the transition unfolds within the bounds of the Constitution. Marcus Mietzner, for instance, observes '[t]hat constitutional courts can play a positive role in the stabilization of transitional democracies is not a new theoretical insight'.[38] Or, as Alec Stone Sweet writes, 'it appears that the more successful any transition has been, the more likely one is to find an effective constitutional or supreme court at the heart of it'.[39] Miguel Schor argues that '[a]ctivist courts ... can play a key role in ushering in needed democratic transformations in transitional democracies',[40] and Francesco Biagi's recent study of European constitutional courts finds that, in the context of democratic transition and consolidation, 'the role played by the constitutional courts is of the utmost importance'.[41] László Sólyom makes a similar point, that constitutional courts are 'inseparable from democratic changes'.[42]

One of the motivations of the Normative View is the exceptional circumstances of transition. The judiciary is thought of as the main guarantor of the Constitution. Regime-change moments put pressure on the constitutional order. There is great uncertainty in these times about the future of the state. Passions run high, and interim reform negotiations can easily morph into violent conflicts that might put the Constitution at existential risk. The significance and the consequentiality of transition have accordingly been used a reason to justify judicial intervention. Putting this sort of argument in more exact terms, Nick Barber and Adrian Vermeule have suggested that, in rare moments when the Constitution is thrown into dispute, courts have 'no option but to take it upon themselves to rule upon ... the validity

[38] Mietzner (n 21) 398.

[39] Alec Stone Sweet, 'Constitutional Courts' in Michael Rosenfeld and András Sajó (eds), *The Oxford Handbook of Comparative Constitutional Law* (Oxford University Press 2012) 827.

[40] Miguel Schor, 'An Essay on the Emergence of Constitutional Courts: The Cases of Mexico and Columbia' (2009) 16 Indiana Journal of Global Legal Studies 173, 176.

[41] Biagi (n 2) 15.

[42] Sólyom (n 3) 135.

of the very constitutional order'.[43] Ruti Teitel also contends that during transitional times, a constitutional court needs to take on a transformative role and that the usual counter-majoritarian objections are justifiably suspended.[44] The idea is that even at the risk of overstepping their constitutional boundary and violating separation of powers principles, an expansive judicial role is necessary in order to safeguard a constitutional democratic project that is struggling to maintain its course.[45]

The Normative View is making two assumptions here. The first is that without judicial intervention, transition will likely derail. Or alternatively, judicial contributions towards regime change are likely positive. The second assumption is that constitutional courts have the power and capacity to make positive changes. The problem with the Normative View is that, both in theory and practice, judicial intervention can sometimes lead to bad outcomes *and* that constitutional courts may sometimes lack the ability to make positive changes to begin with.[46] Advocates of the Normative View argue that political actors in transitional regimes tend to lack the experience, legitimacy, and competence to lead the process because a mature political system is lacking and constitutional norms are not entrenched yet.[47] It is unclear, however, why the same concerns should not apply to judges as well. The same factors that are influencing political actors during regime-change moments (such as a lack of public trust and a highly polarised political environment) can impair judges' ability to guide the transitional process effectively as well. Furthermore, for states coming out of authoritarianism, years or decades of authoritarian rule would have likely entrenched a particular kind of judicial culture in transitional regimes, and identifying judges who are able to maintain their independence and are not politically compromised during regime-change moments can be a challenge.[48] Some of the negative impacts of transitional politics on constitutional courts will be discussed shortly. Regardless, examples of counterproductive constitutional courts during transition are not hard to find,[49] and some of them have been briefly

[43] Barber and Vermeule (n 4) 818.

[44] Teitel (n 4) 2032–34.

[45] Similar in spirit, Owen Fiss argues that standards of judicial independence should be set aside in transitional context and that court-packing and other political interferences are justified when they function to ensure that the judiciary is playing a role that is conducive to democratisation. The distinction between justifiable and unjustifiable political interferences during transition will not be addressed here, but Fiss's argument is another illustration of how the exceptionality of transitional contexts animates different lines of argument that may seem, at first sight, to be contrary to accepted principles of democracy and constitutionalism: Owen Fiss, 'The Right Degree of Independence' in Irwin P Stotzky (ed), *Transition to Democracy in Latin America: The Role of the Judiciary* (Westview Press 1993).

[46] One might rightly argue that the accounts cited in the preceding two paragraphs are more nuanced upon elaboration. My point is simply to use those quotes to illustrate a general attitude within academia and the policy sector towards courts in transitional regimes, which has, in practice, created an expectation of courts that is sometimes impossible to live up to for reasons discussed in this chapter.

[47] Teitel (n 4) 2033.

[48] See e.g. Melissa Crouch, 'The Challenges for Court Reform after Authoritarian Rule: The Role of Specialized Courts in Indonesia' (2021) 7 Constitutional Review 1.

[49] Another example can be found in Mongolia, where, after its 1996 parliamentary elections, Mongolia's constitutional court decided to ban sitting members of parliament to take ministerial

outlined above already. The exceptionality of transitional times will work against judicial intervention when there are good reasons to believe that a constitutional court will exacerbate the problems arising out of transition, causing irreversible damage to the democratisation process and constitutional order.

The Normative View seems to be applicable *only* when a constitutional court possesses at least two important qualities: judicial independence and social legitimacy. By judicial independence, I am referring to both de jure and de facto judicial independence; that is, sufficient constitutional protection must exist to create space for judicial manoeuvring and that judges must not be subjected to undue pressure from the political actors. Social legitimacy refers to the idea that a constitutional court and its decisions must be perceived as legitimate.[50] It is a concept closely tied with judicial power as social legitimacy affects a court's efficacy and effectiveness. Unfortunately, constitutional courts in many transitional contexts, it will be argued, lack either or both qualities because of the exceptional circumstances of transition.[51]

Judicial independence has been described as a tenet of a constitutional democracy. Judicial intervention during transition becomes pointless if the courts are called on to simply legitimate the actions of whoever's political pocket the courts are in. The idea of the Normative View is that judicial intervention seeks to ensure that political actors across the political spectrum are abiding by the constitutional rules and principles while they are competing for power during the regime-change process. It defeats the purpose if judges are simply acting as an instrument of whichever political faction they are aligned with. Of course, judicial decisions on transitional politics would inevitably benefit certain social groups more than others. The guiding principle, though, is that the constitutional judges' duty should always lie in the Constitution as opposed to some political group.

There are good reasons to suspect that judicial independence is likely weak during transitions. It comes as no surprise that judicial independence is not well protected in the constitutions of authoritarian regimes,[52] and transitional regimes

posts. See Tom Ginsburg and Gombosuren Ganzorig, 'When Courts and Politics Collide: Mongolia's Constitutional Crisis' (2001) 14 Columbia Journal of Asian Law 309. See also Bugaric (n 2).

[50] Richard H Fallon Jr, *Law and Legitimacy in the Supreme Court* (Harvard University Press 2018) 6. The concept of social legitimacy is also sometimes referred to as public support or diffuse support. See also Gregory A Caldeira and James L Gibson, 'The Etiology of Public Support for the Supreme Court' (1992) American Journal of Political Science 635.

[51] Relatedly, courts suffering from resource constraints, as Siri Gloppen argues, may also be particularly vulnerable to political control and find it hard to play a significant role in countries seeking democratic transformation. The problem of inadequately resourced courts is a common problem in transitional countries with poorly developed economies. See Siri Gloppen, 'The Accountability Function of the Courts in Tanzania and Zambia' in Roberto Gargarella, Siri Gloppen, and Elin Skaar (eds), *Democratization and the Judiciary: The Accountability Function of Courts in New Democracies* (Routledge 2004).

[52] James Melton and Tom Ginsburg, 'Does De Jure Judicial Independence Really Matter? A Reevaluation of Explanations for Judicial Independence' (2014) 2 Journal of Law and Courts 187

that carry on using their old constitutions are simply perpetuating a framework that offers little protection to judicial institutions. Even if the new Constitution decides to add in judicial independence clauses or that these protections already formally exist, judicial independence on paper by no means guarantees de facto judicial independence.[53] Conflicting actors during transition are strongly incentivised to capture constitutional courts, with the full knowledge that these judges are key veto players that can potentially change the game. Hence, all eyes will be on the constitutional court, should it decide to participate in, or be drawn into, constitutional politics. The weakest branch, however, does not have the tools to resist the kind of immense pressure coming from complex transitional questions. The pen is no match for the sword, and the Constitutional Tribunal in Myanmar was essentially irrelevant during the 2021 coup because pre-existing members were being replaced by the military not long after the military took over the government. There are, of course, many other ways for those in power to assert their influence over courts aside from controlling judicial appointment, and I shall not rehearse them here.[54] My point is simply that, because the stakes are extremely high during transition and a constitutional court is generally believed to be a consequential actor, it will easily become a vulnerable target. It is accordingly doubtful as to how much de facto independence a constitutional court usually enjoys during transitional times.

Social legitimacy is an important currency in regime-change moments as well. Transition creates uncertain moments that are in need of resolution and clarity. A court is called in with the hope of authoritatively putting a controversy to bed. Its ability to do so is precisely a function of the social legitimacy it enjoys. Lacking social legitimacy, a court's decision may be *seen* as biased, and political actors may choose to ignore the court's rulings. The involvement of a court that is thought of as illegitimate by the people would then not only perpetuate the underlying political conflict but also intensify doubts over the validity of the constitutional order, putting the entire system at greater risk.

As important as social legitimacy is, the tricky thing about it is that it cannot be earned overnight. What this means is that the history of an institution would influence its current form. Pre-transition conditions, especially when the state is coming out of authoritarianism, are unlikely to provide opportunities for constitutional courts to build social legitimacy. Despite the judges' best intentions, a constitutional court that is tainted by the authoritarian past will likely lack the public trust and confidence to make effective and positive changes to the transition. For example, the reasoning of the recommendation offered by the Council of Constitutional Inquiry in Ethiopia in relation to the question of parliamentary term limit during the COVID-19 pandemic was thought by experts to be legally

[53] Ibid.
[54] See Gerald N Rosenberg, 'Judicial Independence and the Reality of Political Power' (1992) 54 Review of Politics 369, 376–77.

plausible, but the fact that it has always been a politically appointed body that is perceived as biased meant that its recommendation to extend the term limit had minimal legitimating effect on the constitutional question.[55] The polarised atmosphere that usually comes with transitional politics makes it even harder for a constitutional court to convince people on mega-political issues.

A solution to replenish social legitimacy is to perhaps 'purify'[56] the constitutional court by appointing reformist judges, requiring all pre-existing judges to go through a review process,[57] or more fundamentally redesigning the entire institution to symbolise a clean break from the past. This is plausible in theory, though much would depend on how the judicial (re)configuration is implemented. In addition, as noted previously, the establishment or reform of the constitutional court does not always coincide with transition. Old court structures are likely to persist during transitions, as we see in the case studies of this volume. This purification process that confers a moral mandate to the constitutional court during transition is not as common as one might expect.

Another solution would be for those in power to invest efforts in developing the social legitimacy of a constitutional court. The bench in The Gambia, for example, used to be filled by foreign judges that were hand-picked by its former leader, Yahya Jammeh. In an effort to replenish the judiciary's social legitimacy during the transition, the new government made active efforts to 'Gambianise' the judiciary by appointing more local judges. This is an encouraging attempt to develop the judiciary in the long run and may complement the judges' own strategies in building political support. As I pointed out, however, the cultivation of social legitimacy takes time, and the effects of these strategies may *not* be as *immediate* as some might hope, especially if a constitutional court wants to assert itself with regard to transitional issues. Or at times, these strategies may simply be *ineffective* because, as Melissa Crouch writes, 'the legacies of judicial culture are not easily overcome by institutional reform'.[58] Institution-building requires long-term efforts to improve the internal culture of the judiciary and rebuild public trust, amongst other things. In any event, far-sighted strategy of this sort cannot be observed in many of the case studies in this volume.

Perhaps a reason as to why a constitutional court does not always get to reset and replenish its social capital is because the two solutions mentioned depend on the

[55] Credits to Adem Abebe for mentioning this point. See in this collection Abebe (n 32) [PAGE NUMBER, p.14 manuscript].

[56] Wojciech Sadurski, *Rights before Courts: A Study of Constitutional Courts in Postcommunist States of Central and Eastern Europe* (Springer 2008) 43.

[57] For example, to address systemic corruption, the 2010 Kenyan Constitution established a vetting process which all sitting judges must go through: Tom Gerald Daly, 'The Judiciary and Constitutional Transitions' (IDEA Workshop Report, 14–15 November 2014).

[58] The example Crouch gives is judicial reform in Indonesia after authoritarian rule, where the increased appointment of non-career judges has limited effects in changing corrupt practices within the judiciary and the judiciary's social legitimacy: Crouch (n 48) 19.

will of political actors. Rebuilding the image of the constitutional court may not be on the top of the political actors' agenda as there may be more pressing topics to attend to such as the propriety of a national election, the formation of a new government, designing a new socio-economic structure, or holding perpetrators accountable, to name just a few. It may not be until a wholesale constitutional reform process takes place that the restructuring and strengthening of the judiciary is considered. In this instance, a constitutional court, especially in the earlier years of transition, can only play with the cards it is dealt with and try to earn the trust of the public over time. Not to mention that incumbents may not have the incentives to rebuild a constitutional court as a politicised court may be a way for agents of the past to cling to power and maintain their influence.

My argument is not that the role of constitutional courts during transitional times should always be limited; it is that the debate about whether constitutional courts should adopt a transformative or a confined role during transition can only lead us so far because the circumstances faced by constitutional courts during transitional times can vary a lot and conclusions cannot be easily drawn on that level of generality. The normative role of a constitutional court would depend on the conditions it faces. For example, it would make sense for a constitutional court to actively guide the transition process if it is an independent and socially legitimate institution that possesses the necessary competence to adjudicate on complex constitutional issues arising out of transitional politics because such a constitutional court has the qualities to make principled decisions that might potentially enable the democratisation process. The German Constitutional Court is perhaps the closest example in this respect. The Nazi past provided the impetus for a newly established constitutional court to take on an activist role, at least in the early years of the transition.[59] Its power to assert itself authoritatively in the beginning came, in part, from the new Constitution and the symbolic values attached to its establishment.[60]

As already suggested, however, the real problem is that conditions are rarely favourable for constitutional courts during transition periods. Even the South African Constitutional Court, arguably one of the most esteemed constitutional courts in the transitional constitutionalism literature, was found to be weak in terms of social legitimacy during the first decade of transition, as surveys show.[61] If a constitutional court is socially illegitimate but independent, it should perhaps focus its energy on institution-building first. Its ability to influence mega-politics

[59] See Michaela Hailbronner, 'Rethinking the Rise of the German Constitutional Court: From Anti-Nazism to Value Formalism' (2014) 12 International Journal of Constitutional Law 626.

[60] Ibid. However, Hailbronner argues that the Nazi thesis at most provides a partial explanation for the first few years of transition. She attributes the rise of the German constitutional court mainly to the judges' success in reconciling transformative constitutionalism with Germany's formalist and hierarchical legal culture.

[61] James L Gibson and Gregory A Caldeira, 'Defenders of Democracy? Legitimacy, Popular Acceptance, and the South African Constitutional Court' (2003) 65 Journal of Politics 1.

is handicapped because of the lack of public support. Such a court may wish to restrict the judicial role to less contentious issues when its position is weak and begin experimenting on cases with social significance when it gradually earns the confidence of the people through demonstrating its professionalism and impartiality in cases of lower political stakes.[62] This is similar to what the South African Constitutional Court has done. According to Theunis Roux, the emergence of the South African Constitutional Court was largely attributable to its strategies in maintaining its institutional strength in the face of the dominant political party at the time, the African National Congress.[63] The court steered cleared of direct confrontation with the party and built its constitutional superiority by exploiting the power dynamics between the public and internal party politics. In other words, the court had to be extra clever in navigating the spaces if it wanted to assert its authority sustainably.

The conditions required to implement the approach suggested do not always exist in transitional contexts, however. As mentioned, moments of intense flux define transitional regimes, and courts may not be presented with the necessary range of options to build their legitimacy incrementally. To put it differently, most cases presented to constitutional courts during transitional periods may be considered politically salient, and courts may enjoy little room for manoeuvring because of the nature of the circumstances. Without the necessary time and space, courts will not be able control their agenda. In these instances, courts are forced to confront regime-defining cases, despite their lack of social legitimacy. But even in these instances, judges should try their best to pick their battles very carefully and, when crafting their judgments, be mindful of the social constraints they are under and the socio-political implications of their decisions.

Most of the constitutional courts explored in this volume are, unfortunately, neither socially legitimate nor independent. When a constitutional court is not independent, regardless of whether it is perceived as legitimate or not, it is best for judges to be detached from transitional politics. Despite being armed with the power to destabilise authoritarian networks, for instance, time and again, the constitutional court in Thailand has done the opposite of what democracy advocates had hoped and stepped in to block any attempts that might threaten the monarchy's interests.[64] There is no reason why we should welcome an activist court when it is essentially a remnant of the authoritarian past seeking to preserve pre-existing hegemonic interests. If anything, committed judges within the judiciary, if there are any, should instead focus on ways to reform the court and convert loyal

[62] For the virtues of judicial incrementalism, see Jeff King, *Judging Social Rights* (Cambridge University Press 2012) ch 10.

[63] Theunis Roux, *The Politics of Principle: The First South African Constitutional Court, 1995–2005* (Cambridge University Press 2013).

[64] See in this collection Tonsakulrungruang (n 28).

judges by mobilising political allies within the government and in the public.[65] The idea that political actors during transitional periods may lack experience, capacity, and/or legitimacy to lead the transition is irrelevant if there is no a priori reason to believe that bringing in a constitutional court would help mitigate or solve constitutional problems arising from inadequate political actors.

5. Conclusion

The new and fascinating case studies of contexts underexplored in comparative constitutional studies are enrichening our understanding of the behavioural diversity of constitutional courts in transitional regimes and challenging pre-existing assumptions about them. While the regime-type approach has helped advance the field of comparative judicial studies in many ways, this chapter has questioned current approaches to using the regime-type approach to studying courts in transitional regimes. The Descriptive View and the Normative View, as presented in this chapter, are likely based on flawed assumptions since transitional paths tend to be quite exceptional. That is, of course, not to deny the possibility of extending the regime-type approach to transitional regimes. Whether this is feasible will, to a large extent, depend on the research question one is seeking to answer. For instance, one may argue that the regime-type approach helps highlight the challenges commonly faced by courts in transitional regimes—such as a lack of infrastructure, being constantly asked to decide on politically salient cases, limited space for strategic manoeuvring, and an institutional culture that is an extension of the polity's authoritarian past. Useful lessons can be drawn from different courts' experiences in addressing these common challenges. Furthermore, a distinction to be made that might help us study courts in transitional regimes is to disaggregate the different kinds of transitional regimes. Transitions, for example, can be gradual or abrupt, and the rhythm of transition may also raise different questions for courts. It remains to be seen the extent to which we can learn from using the regime-type approach to transitional contexts.

Acknowledging the exceptionality of regime change affects how we should understand the normative role of constitutional courts. Such exceptionality can cut both ways. On the one hand, it necessitates a neutral arbiter to save the constitutional order, which then provides a prima facie moral justification for judicial intervention. This seems to be the traditional view. On the other hand, the exceptionality of transition may generate challenges of significant implications to the polity and the court. The same factors that are undermining political actors' ability to lead the transitional process may be impacting judges, though perhaps

[65] See Ezequiel González-Ocantos, *Shifting Legal Visions: Judicial Change and Human Rights Trials in Latin America* (Cambridge University Press 2016).

in different ways. If a constitutional court fails to handle these challenges properly, the transition might take a turn for the worse because of judicial intervention. Furthermore, the complexity and consequentiality of transitional politics can undermine a constitutional court's ability to make positive contributions, as I have argued. In short, the conditions may not always exist for constitutional courts to play a transformative role. The appropriate normative role of a constitutional court would very much depend on whether it is an independent and socially legitimate institution. When there are strong reasons to suspect that judicial intervention will lead to bad outcomes, there is a case to be made for courts to take a back seat and afford room to other constitutional actors, to learn to find a solution together, and to work towards the goal of popular self-governance in a sustainable and peaceful manner.

6
Civil–Military Relations

Shanil Wijesinha and Daniel Alphonsus

1. Introduction

Security-sector reform is not a sufficient condition for a successful transition from authoritarianism to constitutional democracy. But it is often a necessary condition.[1] Therefore, the relationship between civilian authorities and the security sector—or civil–military relations—is a vital element of democratic consolidation. It is also germane to constitutional endurance. Issues relating to democratic backsliding and the persistence of democratic gains often intersect with the interests of security-sector agencies and questions about security sector reform, as demonstrated by the case study countries.

This chapter seeks to analyse civil–military relations primarily through the lens of constitutional law as exercised and embedded within the case-study countries. It hopes to examine constitutional features which regulate and influence civil–military relations, both in theory and practice. Given the multiple elements that together constitute the civil–military complex and shape the balance of power between the civil and military domains, it also reflects on the limitations of constitutions and constitutional reform as tools to regulate and influence civil–military relations.

The principal concern of this chapter is framing civil–military relations as a question about how civilian authorities regulate and influence actors who have a monopoly over violence, that is, how the security sector's power can be balanced relative to civilian authority. Note that, here, the security sector is thought of as broadly including all security agencies, such as the armed forces, police, intelligence agencies, and militias. Our analysis assumes the desirability of civilian control over the security sector. Consequently, 'imbalanced' civil–military relations refer to situations in which such civilian control and influence has diminished or where security-sector control and influence has increased, both formally and informally, effectively and potentially. Our analysis also concedes that this balancing

[1] Sumit Bisarya and Sujit Choudhry, 'Security Sector Reform in Constitutional Transitions' (International IDEA Policy Paper No 23, International Institute for Democracy and Electoral Assistance (International IDEA) and the Centre for Constitutional Transitions, 5 October 2020) 8.

Shanil Wijesinha and Daniel Alphonsus, *Civil–Military Relations* In: *Democratic Consolidation and Constitutional Endurance in Asia and Africa*. Edited by: Tom Gerald Daly and Dinesha Samararatne, Oxford University Press.
 DOI: 10.1093/oso/9780192899347.003.0006

must be achieved without compromising the legitimate role of security agencies, including within the democratic transition.

This chapter is organised into five sections. First, we situate this chapter within the literature on civil–military relations and militarisation. Second, we briefly explore the relevant domestic context within each case-study country. This foregrounds the discussion to follow, where, third, we map these features onto the Constitution and constitutional framework of each country. Here, our approach is empirical. The primary aims of this section are to identify and categorise constitutional features which regulate and influence civil–military relations.

Fourth, we interrogate the experience of the case-study countries in the light of the normative question of how constitutions should regulate and influence civil–military relations. Here, our approach is empirical and critical. It presents the ideal institutional structure and design for regulating civil–military relations and then seeks to evaluate the potential for, and limitations of, such institutional architecture by mapping it onto the experiences of the case-study countries.

Fifth, and finally, we turn to the strategic question of how to recalibrate imbalanced civil–military relations, particularly at moments of democratic transition. It seeks to understand the contextual features which sustain a balance of power weighted towards the security sector and explores strategies that may be deployed to achieve equilibrium. Here, our approach is prescriptive.

1.1 Civil–Military Relations and Militarisation

1.1.1 Civil–military relations

Our usage of the term 'civil–military relations' situates itself within the larger corpus of literature on the subject. These is no standard classification of civil–military relationships.[2] Military regimes have been disaggregated by *role* (e.g. as 'moderators, guardians or rulers' or 'arbitrator and ruler praetorian regimes') and by *types*, such as military juntas (or stratocracy), presidential types, and regimes which are founded by a military coup but display features such as a civilian cabinet, a party system, and a legislature.[3] The lack of a 'rigid dichotomy' between civil and

[2] Morris Janowitz, *The Military in the Political Development of New Nations: An Essay in Comparative Analysis* (University of Chicago Press 1964) cited in Ronald May and Viberto Selochan (eds), *The Military and Democracy in Asia and the Pacific* (ANU Press 2004) 5).

[3] Eric Nordlinger, 'Soldiers in Mufti: The Impact of Military Rule upon Economic and Social Change in the Non-Western States' (1970) 64(4) American Political Science Review 431–48; Amos Perlmutter, *Political Roles and Military Rulers* (Frank Cass & Co 1981); Samuel E Finer, 'Military Regimes' in Vernon Bogdanor (ed), *The Blackwell Encyclopaedia of Political Science* (Blackwell, 1991) 366–67 cited in May and Selochan (n 2) 5–6. For a detailed discussion, see May and Selochan (n 2) 5–9.

military regimes has been observed, with civil–military relations being described as a continuum between 'civilocracy' and 'militocracy'.[4]

All these definitions, typologies, and observations are analytically useful in general. More specifically, they are relevant to our analysis as they help us to think of civil–military relations in three ways: (i) the relationship between military and political power, especially political agents and institutions; (ii) the perception, including the military's own perception, of the military's role in the polity and in larger society; and (iii) the structural and institutional organisation of military power, including political power. Moreover, the framing of civil–military relations as a continuum affirms our decision to analyse civil–military relations primarily through the lens of the balance of power between civilian actors and the security sector.

1.1.2 Militarisation

This chapter also seeks to situate itself within the corpus of literature relating to militarisation. Enloe defines 'militarisation' as

> the step-by-step process by which something becomes controlled by, dependent on, or derives its value from the military as an institution or militaristic criteria.[5]

Militarisation has also been recognised as a process wherein societal norms and institutions are dominated by the military establishment.[6] Such an understanding of militarisation coheres within the literature on civil–military relations, which recognises the role of the military as evolving and dynamic and exerting both formal and informal power and influence over the state apparatus and political system, even when soldiers are 'sound asleep in their barracks'.[7] This raises several pertinent questions for this chapter.

First, evaluating imbalanced civil–military relations prompts us to analyse situations in which institutions are controlled by the security sector. But that is insufficient. The process of evaluations also leads us to consider the mainstreaming and legitimising of militaristic values and ideology as normative or persuasive criteria within society and the state. What is relevant for this chapter is how such mainstreaming and legitimising of militaristic values and ideologies interface with the Constitution, including situations when militaries design and enact

[4] Anton Bebler, 'Typologies Based on Civilian-Dominated Versus Military-Dominated Political Systems' in Anton Bebler and Jim Seroka (eds), *Contemporary Political Systems: Classifications and Typologies* (Lynne Rienner 1990) 261–74 cited in May and Selochan (n 2) 6.

[5] Cynthia Enloe, *Manoeuvres: The International Politics of Militarizing Women's Lives* (University of California Press 2000) 291.

[6] See Chulacheeb Chinawanno, 'Militarisation in Thai Society' in Peter Wallensteen and others (eds), *Global Militarisation* (Westview Press 1985).

[7] Samuel Huntington, *Political Order in Changing Societies* (Yale University Press 1968) 221 cited in May and Selochan (n 2) 6; Bebler (n 4) 261–63.

constitutions, when analysing the 'military imprint' on the substance of constitutions,[8] and in relation to the interpretation of constitutions and democratic values.

Second, it urges us to scrutinise all domains and arenas of decision-making, not just those which are traditionally regarded as relating to the military. For example, Enloe argues that even a pair of sneakers is militarised when the employers call on local militarised security forces to suppress trade union activity or ally with governments who use national security as a justification to deny trade union activity.[9] In this way, decision-makers who animate the militarising process are not only colonels and soldiers but also non-military persons.[10] This compels us to recognise that a constitutional lens may not adequately bring into focus all arenas of militarisation. However, these arenas remain relevant to our inquiry from the point of view of democratic consolidation and constitutional endurance. For example, we are reminded that at moments of democratic consolidation and transition, any reform effort—in particular, security-sector reform—cannot be limited to textual constitutional reform. These must be accompanied by efforts to unlearn and disentangle military ideology from democratic institutions and consciousness and to (re)learn and (re)legitimise democratic and constitutional values.

2. Case Studies

2.1 Historical Features

All countries except for Thailand—and perhaps Ethiopia, which was under occupation by Italy for a short period of time—were colonised by European powers. As a result, the militaries of these countries generally trace a direct lineage to the colonial armies tasked with subjugating the civilian population.

The military has played a significant role in the historical and political trajectory of all countries. In several countries (Ethiopia, The Gambia, Maldives, Myanmar, and Thailand), armed forces and armed groups have resorted to military coups, overthrowing democratically elected governments or other military regimes. In Malaysia and Sri Lanka, the military played a significant role in responding to violence by communist insurgencies and the Liberation Tigers of Tamil Eelam (LTTE). Foreign militaries have also played significant—and diverse—roles. For example, in The Gambia, the Economic Community of West African States

[8] See in this collection Ohn Mar Zin, Naw Janet, and Kimana Zulueta-Fülscher, Chapter 13 'Myanmar's Transition to Peace and Democracy: The Journey Reversed'.
[9] Enloe (n 5) 291.
[10] Ibid, 292.

(ECOWAS) intervened, including through military means, in the aftermath of the constitutional crisis following the presidential election in 2016.[11]

2.2 Exercise of State Power by Present and Former Military Officials

In all countries (although to obviously different degrees), military officials have exercised executive and legislative power by (i) the process of political appointments, (ii) successfully participating in elections, and (iii) through constitutional provisions enabling such exercise of power. In many case-study countries, armed groups which took over state power in a coup thereafter contested (and won) elections. In Myanmar, after military coups, the Tatmadaw (i.e. the armed forces) have governed Myanmar through political parties and institutions and have contested in elections through political parties which are a thinly veiled extension of the military, such as the Union Solidarity and Development Party (USDP). Extraordinarily, elected civilian governments and the Tatmadaw share legislative and executive power at the Union and state/region levels. In Thailand, the military contest in popular elections through the Palang Pracharath party (PPRP) and, after military coups, have governed through entities including the National Council for Peace and Order (NCPO).

Former military officials have successfully contested in both presidential and parliamentary elections (Ethiopia, Maldives, and Sri Lanka) and exercise various forms of executive power through political appointments.

Former and present military officials are often appointed to institutions which have security-orientated functions and mandates. For example, in Malaysia, the Chief of Defence Forces and the Inspector General of Police are permanent members of the National Security Council.[12] In the case-study countries, former and present military officials are also appointed to institutions which have no demonstrable security function or mandate. In Sri Lanka, both former and present military officials have been appointed to 'task forces' on subjects ranging from poverty alleviation, to archaeological heritage, to societal discipline.[13]

[11] See in this collection Satang Nabaneh, Chapter 9 'Prospects for Democratic Consolidation in The Gambia: A Cup Half Full, Half Empty, or More?'

[12] Malaysia, National Security Council Act 2016 (Act 776) ss 2–6.

[13] Task Force for Poverty Eradication and Livelihood Development, Gazette Extraordinary No 2159/64 (25 January 2020) <http://documents.gov.lk/files/egz/2020/1/2159-64_E.pdf>; Task Force for Economic Revival and Poverty Alleviation, Sri Lanka, Gazette Extraordinary No 2172/9 (22 April 2020) <http://documents.gov.lk/files/egz/2020/4/2172-09_E.pdf>; Presidential Task Force for Archaeological Heritage Management in the Eastern Province, Gazette Extraordinary No 2178/17 (2 June 2020) <http://documents.gov.lk/files/egz/2020/6/2178-17_E.pdf>; Presidential Task Force to Build a Secure Country, Disciplined, Virtuous and Lawful Society, Sri Lanka, Gazette Extraordinary No 2178/18 (2 June 2020) <http://documents.gov.lk/files/egz/2020/6/2178-18_E.pdf> all links accessed 10 October 2021.

Former and present military officials may also be appointed to institutions mandated to initiate reform, including constitutional reform. In Myanmar, such officials were appointed to institutions including the National Reform Council and the National Legislative Assembly.

Former and present military officials have also been appointed to key posts in the public service and in public administration. For example, in Sri Lanka, retired military officials have been absorbed into the public service as heads of departments and authorities coming within the purview of ministries.[14] As of January 2021, at least 28 former or present military and intelligence officials had been appointed to key administrative posts.[15]

2.3 Deployment of the Military for Functions Unrelated to National Security

In all countries, the military has been 'summoned from the barracks' and deployed to perform various tasks and functions unrelated to national security. Such deployment has been ordered by regimes which came into power after democratic transition as well as military regimes. In The Gambia, Yahya Jammeh deployed armed forces to arrest protesters, including members of opposition political parties, in response to an attempted coup in 2014.[16] In Maldives, former President Mohamed Nasheed—the first democratically elected president—deployed the military to arrest and detain the Chief Judge of the Criminal Court, Judge Abdulla Mohamed. The deployment of the military is often, but not always, accompanied by a declaration of a state of emergency.

The most recent iteration of summoning the military from the barracks for functions unrelated to security has been in the response of most countries to the COVID-19 pandemic. In Sri Lanka, the entire national effort to combat COVID-19 was headed by present or former military officials.[17] The military also played a central role in activities such as contact-tracing, running quarantine centres, and distributing relief.[18]

[14] See Sri Lanka, Gazette Extraordinary No 2168/8 (26 March 2020) <http://documents.gov.lk/files/egz/2020/3/2168-08_E.pdf> accessed 10 October 2021.

[15] Human Rights Council, 'Report of the Office of the High Commissioner for Human Rights' (UN Doc A/HRC/46/20, 27 January 2021) para 22.

[16] See in this collection Nabaneh (n 11).

[17] The Diplomat, 'Sri Lanka: Where Generals Fight the Coronavirus, Food and Fuel Shortages' (*The Diplomat*, 3 September 2021) <www.thediplomat.com/2021/09/sri-lanka-where-generals-fight-the-coronavirus-food-and-fuel-shortages> accessed 11 October 2021; Sri Lanka, Gazette Extraordinary No 2168/8 (n 14).

[18] The Hindu, 'Sri Lankan Military Is Helping the Country Fight the Pandemic' (*The Hindu*, 15 April 2020) <www.thehindu.com/news/international/covid-19-sri-lankan-military-is-helping-the-country-fight-the-pandemic/article31350778.ece> accessed 11 October 2021.

3. Constitutions and Civil–Military Relations

3.1 Constitutional Features which Regulate and Influence Civil–Military Relations

The case studies reveal some discernible features of constitutions which regulate and influence civil–military relations, both directly and indirectly. Civil–military relations are also regulated and influenced by constitutional practice, for example, in the manner that provisions are interpreted or applied over a period that often precedes and endures beyond moments of democratic transition.

This section seeks to identify the constitutional framework which animated the examples cited in the summary of the case studies. The examples provided are not intended to be an exhaustive survey, nor do they suggest that these constitutional provisions are causally bound to the outcomes we discuss. However, they illustrate the constitutional spaces within which civil–military relations are shaped, provide a lens through which civil–military relations in other countries can be evaluated and understood, and lend themselves to categorisation.

3.1.1 Executive powers of the head of state

In the case-study countries (during periods of non-military rule), we observe both presidential (The Gambia, Maldives, Myanmar, Sri Lanka) and parliamentary (Ethiopia, Malaysia, and Thailand) systems of government. Malaysia and Thailand are also constitutional monarchies. The executive powers exercised by nominal and effective heads of state regulate and influence the balance of civil–military relations in several ways.

3.1.1.1 Powers of appointment and assigning subjects and functions to ministries

Heads of state appoint ministers and secretaries to ministries, high posts, and officials within the public service. Powers of appointing cabinet and non-cabinet ministers are often complemented by the power to assign subjects and functions and create departments within such ministries.

In Myanmar, the constitutional provisions are exceptional in that the Tatmadaw is constitutionally empowered to appoint defence services personnel as the ministers and deputy ministers of defence, home affairs, and border affairs.[19] Such personnel are not required to retire or resign from the defence services during their tenure as minister.[20] Even during times of civilian rule, this creates a double executive system, which poses substantial challenges to balancing civil–military relations. Departments coming under the direct control of the military have allowed for authority over matters that are not military concerns. For example, the

[19] Constitution of Myanmar, arts 232 and 234.
[20] Ibid, art 232(j).

2012 Ward or Village Tract Administration Law,[21] which is administered by the Ministry of Home Affairs,[22] provides for the management and supervision of administrators at ward and village tract levels. Some functions and duties of administrators relate to security, but these also include matters such as the registration of births and deaths, local development activities, permission to hold public events, and even the regulation of livestock ownership.[23]

In Sri Lanka, the president appoints cabinet, non-cabinet and deputy ministers (in consultation with the prime minister, where deemed necessary); appoints secretaries to all ministries; determines the number of cabinet ministers, ministries, and the assignment of subjects and functions to such Ministries; and can change the assignment of subjects, functions, and composition of cabinet and non-cabinet ministers.[24] The president can assign subjects and functions to him- or herself and remains in charge of any subject or function not assigned to a minister.[25] The president also appoints, after seeking the observations of the Parliamentary Council, the members of independent commissions,[26] high posts and institutions associated with the judiciary,[27] and other high posts.[28] The president is the head of the cabinet of ministers,[29] which, among other things, exercises powers of appointment, promotion, transfer, disciplinary control, and dismissal over public officers and all heads of departments.[30] Finally, the president appoints the governor for each province.[31] Many of these powers have been utilised to appoint former or present military officials to such positions. The procedure by which officials to high posts and independent commissions are appointed lacks adequate checks and balances

[21] This was enacted under art 289 of the Constitution of Myanmar, which provides that 'Administration of ward or village-tract shall be assigned in accord with the law to a person whose integrity is respected by the community.'

[22] Thinzar Shunlei Yi, 'Myanmar: Under the Name of Democracy, the Military Rules' (*Civicus*) <www.civicus.org/index.php/re-imagining-democracy/stories-from-the-frontlines/3422-myanmar-under-the-name-of-democracy-the-military-rules> accessed 15 October 2021. Under civilian rule in 2018, the General Administration Department (GAD) came within the purview of the civilian-controlled Ministry of Union Government, but further reform was required due to the imprint from 'decades of military control and the fact that both the ministry and the GAD still include[d] large numbers of retired military officers or staff with military connections'. See in this collection Ohn, Janet, and Zulueta-Fülscher (n 8).

[23] Yi (n 22).

[24] Constitution of Sri Lanka, arts 44–46 and 52. See also art 47(1) for limitations imposed on the number of cabinet, non-cabinet, and deputy ministries.

[25] Ibid, art 44(1) and (2).

[26] Elections Commission, Public Service Commission, National Police Commission, Human Rights Commission of Sri Lanka, Commission to Investigate Allegations of Bribery and Corruption, Finance Commission, Delimitation Commission.

[27] Chief Justice, Judges of the Supreme Court, President and Judges of the Court of Appeal, Members of the Judicial Service Commission other than the Chairman.

[28] The Attorney General, Auditor General, Parliamentary Commissioner for Administration, Secretary General of Parliament, Inspector General of Police; Constitution of Sri Lanka, art 41A, including Sch I and II thereto.

[29] Constitution of Sri Lanka, art 43(2).

[30] Ibid, art 55(1) and (2).

[31] Ibid, art 154B.

to protect against state capture. The power to determine subjects and functions of ministries has also been exercised in ways which skew civil–military relations.[32] The president also appoints the heads of the army, navy, and air force.[33]

In Thailand, the king (who is the head of state)[34] appoints and removes judges and justices, and before taking office, they swear an oath of loyalty to the king and agree to faithfully perform their duties in the name of the king.[35] The king selects and appoints the president and councillors of the Privy Council, who have the duty, among other things, to 'render advice to the King on all matters pertaining to His functions'.[36] The king has exercised this power to maintain a good relationship with the army and the judiciary by appointing retired supreme court and constitutional court judges and army generals to the Privy Council.[37]

Institutional capture—whether through powers of appointment or otherwise—sustains an ecosystem within which militarisation thrives. In Thailand, democratic consolidation has consistently been attacked by three actors: the mob, the court, and the armed forces.[38] The security sector turns a blind eye to pro-royalist protesters while violently cracking down on those who are engaged in electoral politics.[39] The resulting chaos is attributed to inherent weaknesses of constitutional democracy, thus justifying a return to military rule to restore order and stability.[40] The judiciary has partnered in transitions to military rule by legitimising violent protests and consistently confirming the legality of coups.[41] The Elections Commission has enabled democratic backsliding—for example by turning a blind eye to the large donations made by corporations and government agencies to the PPRP.[42] The Constitutional Court has also partnered in democratic backsliding, for example by declaring elections to be void[43] and dissolving the Future Forward Party.[44] There are countless other examples of how democratic backsliding and consolidation of military rule in Thailand has been achieved through a range of institutions and officials engaged in a multi-pronged assault.[45]

[32] See e.g. the subjects and functions allocated to the Ministry of Defence in Sri Lanka, Gazette Extraordinary No 2153/12 (10 December 2019) <http://documents.gov.lk/files/egz/2019/12/2153-12_E.pdf> accessed 10 October 2021.
[33] Constitution of Sri Lanka, art 61E.
[34] Constitution of Thailand, s 2.
[35] Ibid, ss 190 and 191.
[36] Ibid, s 10.
[37] See in this collection Khemthong Tonsakulrungruang, Chapter 14 'Coup and Decay: How Thai-Style Democracy Abuses Constitutionalism'.
[38] Ibid.
[39] Ibid.
[40] Ibid.
[41] Ibid.
[42] Ibid.
[43] BBC News, 'Thai Court Rules General Election Invalid' (21 March 2014) <www.bbc.com/news/world-asia-26677772> accessed 2 November 2021.
[44] See in this collection Tonsakulrungruang (n 37).
[45] Ibid.

It is entirely appropriate for the head of the executive to exercise executive power. However, the case-study countries demonstrate that where such powers are exercised without adequate checks and balances, and where the institutions designed to impose checks and balances have been subject to state (and military) capture, such power can be used instrumentally to skew civil–military relations. This can occur in different ways, including through appointing former or present military officials (or loyalists willing to advance such militarisation) to positions in the government and public service; bringing subjects, functions, and departments under the control of such officials; institutional capture; and by sustaining an eco-system within which militarisation thrives.

3.1.1.2 Presidential pardons

In all case-study countries, the head of state is granted the power of pardon subject to conditions and procedures.[46] Such powers have been used widely and in various contexts. They can be exercised as a means of democratic consolidation, for example, by reversing the outcomes of politically motivated trials in ways which have implications for civil–military relations. In Myanmar, one of the topmost priorities of the State Counsellor Aung San Suu Kyi's government after nearly 50 years of military rule was to release political prisoners and student activists.[47] On the other hand, powers of pardon can also be exercised to reverse democratic gains and accountability and fortify militarisation. For example, in Sri Lanka, President Gotabhaya Rajapaksa pardoned former Army Staff Sergeant Sunil Ratnayake, who was found guilty of the murder of eight civilians in the 'Mirusuvil massacre'.[48]

Even though often the distinction between these different uses of powers of pardon is self-evident, there are also examples which are more ambiguous. Pardons have been granted by military rulers in ways that ostensibly appear to further justice. In Myanmar, Senior General Min Aung Hlaing pardoned more than 23,000 prisoners, including a few political prisoners.[49] Moreover, heads of state *after* democratic transition have pardoned members of security forces in ways that appear to weaken accountability—for example in Myanmar, where former President Win Myint granted amnesty to more than 8,500 prisoners, including nearly 2,000

[46] Constitution of Ethiopia, art 71; Constitution of The Gambia, article 82; Constitution of Malaysia, art 342; Constitution of Maldives, art 115(s); Constitution of Myanmar, art 204(a); Constitution of Sri Lanka, art 34; Constitution of Thailand, s 179.

[47] ABC News, 'Myanmar's Aung San Suu Kyi Vows to Press for Political Prisoner Release (8 April 2016) <www.abc.net.au/news/2016-04-08/myanmars-suu-kyi-vows-to-press-for-political-prisoner-release/7309462> accessed 16 October 2021; ABC News, 'Myanmar's President Htin Kyaw Pardons More Political Prisoners, Journalists' (17 April 2016) <www.abc.net.au/news/2016-04-17/myanmar-president-pardons-more-political-prisoners-journalists/7333222> accessed 16 October 2021.

[48] News First, 'Presidential Pardon to Fmr. Army Staff Sergeant Sunil Ratnayake' (*News First*, 26 March 2020) <www.newsfirst.lk/2020/03/26/presidential-pardon-to-fmr-army-staff-sergeant-sunil-ratnayake> accessed 16 October 2021.

[49] The Associated Press, 'Myanmar Junta Pardons Prisoners, to Attend Regional Summit' (19 April 2021) <https://www.asahi.com/ajw/articles/14333353> accessed 16 October 2021.

members of security forces.[50] The manner in which powers of pardon are exercised as a political tool by all regimes fortifies their legitimacy of use in all contexts.

It is also pertinent to note that powers of pardon are often used in conjunction with days of national and religious importance (Myanmar, Sri Lanka, Thailand). Thus, granting pardons becomes a routine (and expected) constitutional practice. This also intersects with religious legitimacy, which military rulers may rely on to consolidate their influence.[51]

3.1.1.3 Declaration of states of emergency and powers to deploy the military

In all case-study countries, the Constitution provides for the procedure to be followed when declaring states of emergency and safeguards such as parliamentary oversight. The power to declare states of emergency has a substantial influence on civil–military relations as it enables the armed forces to be called out of the barracks and perform tasks within civilian spaces.

With the exception of Ethiopia, where the power to declare an emergency is vested in the Council of Ministers of the Federal Government and sometimes in the House of Peoples' Representatives,[52] all other constitutions vest the power to declare an emergency in the head of state. Such declarations have been used for various purposes and exigencies, including civil war (Ethiopia[53]), efforts to retain power after losing elections (The Gambia[54]), controlling COVID-19 (Malaysia[55]), consolidating political power (Maldives[56]), carrying out a military coup (Myanmar[57]), regulating food distribution (Sri Lanka[58]), and responding to anti-government protests (Thailand[59]).

[50] *Garda*, 'Myanmar: President Pardons 8500 Prisoners in Thingyan Amnesty' (*Garda*, 17 April 2018) <www.garda.com/crisis24/news-alerts/110301/myanmar-president-pardons-8500-prisoners-in-thingyan-amnesty> accessed 16 October 2021.

[51] For a further discussion about the 'religious legitimacy' of military and authoritarian regimes, see section 5.2.6 below.

[52] Constitution of Ethiopia, art 93.

[53] Abiy Ahmed, 'Ethiopia Declares State of Emergency in Opposition-Ruled Tigray' (*Al Jazeera*, 4 November 2020) <www.aljazeera.com/news/2020/11/4/ethiopia-declares-state-of-emergency-in-opposition-tigray-region> accessed 16 October 2021.

[54] BBC News, 'The Gambia's President Declares State of Emergency' (17 January 2017) <www.bbc.com/news/world-africa-38652939> accessed 16 October 2021.

[55] BBC News, 'Malaysia Declares Covid State of Emergency Amid Political Challenges' (12 January 2021) <www.bbc.com/news/55625448> accessed 16 October 2021.

[56] United Nations Office of the High Commissioner for Human Rights (UN OHCHR), 'Maldives State of Emergency 'All-Out Assault on Democracy'—Zeid' (7 February 2018) <www.ohchr.org/en/NewsEvents/Pages/DisplayNews.aspx?NewsID=22640&LangID=E> accessed 16 October 2021.

[57] Reuters, 'Statement from Myanmar Military on State of Emergency' (*Reuters*, 1 February 2021) <www.reuters.com/article/us-myanmar-politics-military-text-idUSKBN2A11A2> accessed 16 October 2021.

[58] Economy Next, 'Sri Lanka Food Emergency Regulations: Opposition Alleges Creeping Authoritarianism' (*Economy Next*, 1 September 2021) <www.economynext.com/sri-lanka-food-emergency-regulations-opposition-alleges-creeping-authoritarianism-85673/#modal-one> accessed 16 October 2021.

[59] International Commission of Jurists, 'Thailand: Lifting of Serious Emergency Situation in Bangkok Is Welcome, But Emergency Laws Remain Deeply Problematic—ICJ Briefing Paper' (27 October 2020)

All constitutions (except The Gambia[60]) provide for grounds and purposes for which states of emergency can be proclaimed. Reflecting on the constitutional provisions of the case-study countries, two observations can be made. First, an 'emergency' is often defined as an all-encompassing typology including disparate issues such as national security, law and order, natural disasters, and health emergencies. For example, a state of emergency can be declared in Ethiopia in the event of 'an external invasion, a breakdown of law and order which endangers the constitutional order and which cannot be controlled by the regular law enforcement agencies and personnel, a natural disaster, or an epidemic'.[61] Second, typologies of states of emergency are often nebulous and indefinite. Such ambiguity grants extensive powers to the head of state to declare an emergency in circumstances not explicitly provided for. For example, in Malaysia, an emergency can be proclaimed where a grave emergency threatens the security, or the economic life, or public order in the Federation.[62] Issues caused by all-encompassing and nebulous typologies of emergency and the desirability of a narrower, well-defined approach in which different procedures and approvals are constitutionally prescribed for different types of emergencies is an area of research that warrants more attention—especially in the light of the declaration of states of emergency and the militarised response to the COVID-19 pandemic. For example, in Maldives, a state of 'public health emergency' can be declared under the Public Health Protection Act, which vests critical powers (including declaration of the state of emergency) in the minister for health and the director general of public health.[63]

Constitutions often explicitly refer to derogation from fundamental rights during states of emergency. Suspension and limitation of fundamental rights through decrees and regulations enacted by the executive, especially in the context where armed forces are granted police powers and measures, could have a profound impact on civil–military relations. In addition to the usual safeguard of parliamentary oversight, many constitutions also have specific provisions regulating derogation from fundamental rights. During times of emergency in Maldives, the president is precluded from restricting an extensive list of rights, including the right to life, freedom of expression, freedom of the media, and fair trial rights;

<www.icj.org/thailand-lifting-of-serious-emergency-situation-in-bangkok-is-welcome-but-emergency-laws-remain-deeply-problematic-icj-briefing-paper> accessed 16 October 2021.

[60] Constitution of The Gambia, art 34(1).
[61] Constitution of Ethiopia, art 93(1).
[62] Constitution of Malaysia, art 150(1) and (2).
[63] Public Health Protection Act No 7/2012; Zunana Zalif, 'Maldives Extends State of Public Health Emergency for 18th Time' (*Raajje*, 1 September 2021) <https://raajje.mv/105833> accessed 25 October 2021. It is fitting to mention, however, that the Maldivian president can declare a state of emergency in certain events, including 'dangerous epidemic disease', but this was not resorted to. See Constitution of Maldives, art 253.

and all measures should also be consistent with the obligations of Maldives under international law.[64]

Some case-study countries have constitutional provisions and laws which enable the deployment of the military without a declaration of emergency. This sustains militarisation by blurring the distinction between the mandates of the police and the armed forces. It also mainstreams military responses to issues unrelated to national security and creates de facto states of emergency without applicable constitutional safeguards. In The Gambia, the president can give directions to a commander to deploy the forces under their control for the purpose of maintaining and securing public safety and public order.[65] In Malaysia, the National Security Council Act 2016 ('NSC Act') gives the prime minister the power to declare an area to be a 'national security area' in defined circumstances and based on the advice of the NSC.[66] The NSC can deploy security forces or relevant government entities within such areas to exercise extensive powers.[67] For example, security forces can arrest any person found—or suspected of—committing an offense under the laws that apply in the security area.[68] The NSC Act also enables magistrates or coroners to dispense with the holding of an inquest in relation to the death of a member of the security forces or anyone killed by operations of the armed forces in the security area.[69] In Sri Lanka, the president is empowered to call out the armed forces in circumstances 'endangering the public security' in any area where the president is of the opinion that the police are inadequate to deal with such situation.[70] In practice, the president calls out the armed forces to maintain public order without referring to the circumstances which endanger public security and the inadequacy of the police to deal with the situation.[71]

Constitutional and other legal provisions in Myanmar and Thailand contain extraordinary grants of power to the armed forces to declare martial law and exercise state powers during times of emergency, which have been evoked and relied upon to justify military takeovers. In Myanmar, for example, where a state of emergency could cause 'disintegration of the Union, disintegration of national solidarity and loss of sovereign power or attempts therefore by wrongful forcible means such as insurgency or violence', the commander-in-chief of the defence services has the right to 'take over and exercise State sovereign power' in accordance with the provisions of the Constitution.[72] This provision was invoked by the military junta after

[64] Constitution of Maldives, arts 254 and 255.
[65] Constitution of The Gambia, art 188.
[66] National Security Council Act 2016 (n 12) s 18(1).
[67] Ibid, s 19.
[68] Ibid, s 25.
[69] Ibid, s 35.
[70] Public Security Ordinance, No 25 of 1947 (as amended), s 12.
[71] See e.g. Sri Lanka, Gazette Extraordinary No 2245/34 (17 September 2021) <www.documents.gov.lk/files/egz/2021/9/2245-34_E.pdf> accessed 16 October 2021.
[72] Constitution of Myanmar, art 40(c).

overthrowing the government in February 2021.[73] Further, in Thailand, the military authority is empowered to declare martial law in localities where it is necessary to do so as a matter of urgency and in order to maintain law and order.[74] In 2014, the military relied on such powers when it declared martial law during the caretaker government of former Prime Minister Thaksin Shinawatra.[75]

3.1.1.4 (Extra-)Constitutional practice and residual powers

Heads of state may engage in acts which appear to be justified through constitutional practice but may have a tenuous (if any) legal basis in the Constitution. For example, in Sri Lanka, the president has appointed 'task forces' on diverse issues.[76] Gazette notifications establishing such task forces refer to 'Article 33 of the Constitution'.[77] This does not explicitly include the power to establish task forces.[78]

Task forces have been an arena of militarisation in two ways; first through the appointment of current and former military officials as members of such task forces[79] and, second, by creating a parallel administration to institutions and officials who are legally empowered to perform tasks in terms of the Constitution and written law, thus undermining these institutions and officials.[80]

It is fitting to note that the practice of appointing task forces has continued under successive regimes,[81] including the regime after the moment of democratic transition. The claimed constitutional basis for all such task forces is either identical to

[73] Al Jazeera, 'Full Text of Myanmar Army Statement on State of Emergency' (*Al Jazeera*, 1 February 2021) <www.aljazeera.com/news/2021/2/1/full-text-of-myanmar-army-statement-on-state-of-emergency> accessed 17 October 2021. The prior condition of the declaration of a state of emergency by the President seems to have been disregarded—see Constitution of Myanmar, arts 417 and 418.

[74] Constitution of Thailand, s 176; Martial Law Order 1914 <www.icj.org/wp-content/uploads/2012/12/Thailand-Martial-Law-1914-eng.pdf> accessed 2 November 2021.

[75] Reuters, 'Thailand's Army Declares Martial Law, Says Not a Coup' (*Reuters*, 20 May 2014) <www.reuters.com/article/uk-thailand-protests-martial-idUKKBN0DZ1YU20140520> accessed 2 November 2021.

[76] See e.g. the task forces listed in n 13.

[77] See Gazette notifications referred to in nn 13 and 14.

[78] See Centre for Policy Alternatives, 'The Appointment of the Two Presidential Task Forces: Discussion Paper' (June 2020) 4–6 <www.cpalanka.org/wp-content/uploads/2020/06/Commentary-Two-Task-Forces-CPA-Final.pdf> accessed 10 October 2021.

[79] Ibid, 7; Sri Lanka, Gazette Extraordinary No 2074/11 (5 June 2018) <www.documents.gov.lk/files/egz/2018/6/2074-11_E.pdf> accessed 16 October 2021.

[80] Centre for Policy Alternatives, 'Discussion Paper' (n 78) 7–12. For an excellent discussion of the phenomenon of a parallel military administration establishing a 'shadow state', see Ambika Satkunanathan, 'The Executive and the Shadow State in Sri Lanka' in Asanga Welikala (ed), *Reforming Sri Lankan Presidentialism: Provenance, Problems and Prospects* (Centre for Policy Alternatives 2015).

[81] Sisira Jayasuriya and others, 'Post-Tsunami Recovery: Issues and Challenges in Sri Lanka' (ADB Institute Research Paper Series No. 71, 2006) <www.adb.org/sites/default/files/publication/157220/adbi-rp71.pdf> accessed 16 October 2021; Relief Web, 'Sri Lanka: President Appoints New Task Force to Rebuild North' (14 May 2009) <www.reliefweb.int/report/sri-lanka/sri-lanka-president-appoints-new-task-force-rebuild-north> accessed 16 October 2021; Sri Lanka, Gazette Extraordinary No 2074/11 (n 79).

the present regime[82] or equally ambiguous.[83] This raises pertinent questions about how (extra)constitutional practices can persist across regimes in ways that may seem innocuous but which construct pathways to militarisation.

3.1.2 The role and powers of the commander-in-chief

Two general observations about constitutional provisions relating to the commander-in-chief are as follows. First, constitutional provisions, more often than not, specify who holds the title of commander-in-chief without expounding on what authority this title entails. This permits the head of state to exercise powers in relation to the security sector which do not have a clear basis other than their designation as commander-in-chief. Sometimes, the Constitution may grant powers to the president which relate to their authority as commander-in-chief without explicitly mentioning it. Powers to deploy the military within the state in times of emergency and otherwise, and to appoint the heads of the armed forces, are examples of this.

Second, it is often the case that all that is revealed in constitutional provisions concerning the commander-in-chief is that the highest military authority and the highest civilian office are granted to the same person, fusing military and civilian supremacy.[84] Analysis unpacking what this 'fused dominion' entails appears to be scarce and underdeveloped in constitutional law, particular in the case-study countries.[85] This is notable as the meaning and consequences of granting fused dominion vary drastically between countries and forms of government. In one understanding of fused dominion, described as the *consolidationist model*, the power of civilian (or military) office can be enhanced by fusing it with the powers of the other—for example where military capability is construed as a legitimacy condition for governance or when civil authority is absorbed into military command. Alternatively, the vesting of military supremacy in a civilian leader whose own powers are subject to checks and balances can be a means by which the military's powers are checked without functionally fusing with the military—described as the *separationist model*.[86] Through the separationist model, civilian control of the military is ensured through a civilian commander-in-chief, while other civilian institutions check the powers of the commander-in-chief.[87] The

[82] See Centre for Policy Alternatives, 'Structures to Deal with COVID-19 in Sri Lanka: A Brief Comment on the Presidential Task Force' (April 2020) 4 (n 7) <www.cpalanka.org/wp-content/uploads/2020/04/FINAL-Presidential-Task-Force-on-COVID19-April-2020-copy.pdf> accessed 16 October 2021.

[83] The three task forces appointed in the aftermath of the tsunami were seemingly being brought under the Presidential Secretariat. See World Health Organization (WHO), 'Sri Lanka Tsunami Situation Report' (14 February 2005) <www.reliefweb.int/report/sri-lanka/sri-lanka-tsunami-situation-report-14-feb-2005> accessed 16 October 2021.

[84] David Luban, 'On the Commander-in-Chief Power' (2008) 81 Southern California. Law Review 477, 483.

[85] For an example of excellent analysis on this fused dominion with reference to the United States of America, see ibid, 482–88.

[86] Ibid, 483–89.

[87] Ibid, 491.

danger of the consolidationist model, amongst other things, is that we may mistake the commander-in-chief of the armed forces for the 'commander-in-chief of the country, its industries and inhabitants'.[88] This analysis is useful to foreground the discussion of the case-study countries to follow as it illustrates how different understandings of the role of the commander-in-chief can have a decisive bearing on civil–military relations.

Each case-study country recognises fused dominion. In The Gambia, the president is 'the Head of State and of the Government and Commander-in-Chief of the Armed Forces'.[89] In Ethiopia, the prime minister is the chief executive, the chairman of the council of ministers, and the commander-in-chief of the national armed forces.[90] In Maldives, the president is the head of state and the government and the commander-in-chief of the armed forces.[91] In Malaysia, the Yang di-Pertuan Agong is the Supreme Commander of the armed forces[92] and is also the supreme head of Malaysia.[93] In Sri Lanka, the president is the head of state, the executive, and the government and is the commander-in-chief of the armed forces.[94] In Thailand, the king is the head of the state and is the 'Head of the Thai Armed Forces'.[95] Unlike in other countries under consideration, in Myanmar, the president appoints a person proposed and approved by the National Defence and Security Council as the commander-in-chief of the defence services,[96] and command of the armed forces is vested in the defence services.[97] The commander-in-chief also nominates (and the president appoints) the ministers of defence, home affairs, and border affairs from among military officials.[98] Here, fused dominion takes on a distinct character as the commander-in-chief of the armed forces is a military official who also exercises powers often exercised by civilian heads of state. In each country, whether fused dominion is consolidationist or separationist would depend, to a large extent, on institutional design. But, as we will see, it would also be subject to more subjective factors such as the profile, personality, and ambition of the commander-in-chief.

Unlike other case-study countries,[99] the Constitution of The Gambia expounds on the powers of the president *qua* commander-in-chief, for example, by subjecting

[88] *Youngstown Sheet & Tube Co v Sawyer* 343 US 579, 643–44 (1952) (Jackson J, concurring) cited in Luban (n 84) 487.

[89] Constitution of The Gambia, art 61.

[90] Constitution of Ethiopia, art 74(1).

[91] Constitution of Maldives, art 106(b).

[92] Constitution of Malaysia, article 41.

[93] Ibid, art 32(1).

[94] Constitution of Sri Lanka, art 30(1).

[95] Constitution of Thailand, ss 2 and 8.

[96] Constitution of Myanmar, art 342.

[97] Ibid, art 338.

[98] Ibid, art 232(b)(ii) and (c).

[99] The only exception is Maldives, where the president *qua* commander-in-chief is authorised to order the deployment of the armed forces in defence of the Republic or as part of an international undertaking, which is subject to the approval of the People's Majlis—Constitution of Maldives, art 243(b). However, no other explicit powers are granted.

the operational and administrative control over the armed forces to the authority and directions of the president,[100] recognising the 'general power and authority' of the president *qua* commander-in-chief,[101] and granting powers to deploy the armed forces within The Gambia to maintain and secure public safety and order.[102] The only limitation on the power of the president *qua* commander-in-chief is that, whenever practicable, they must consult the National Security Council when exercising their powers.[103] This demonstrates a consolidationist model of fused dominion as it enhances the powers of the civilian head of state by merging it with military power. The Gambian experience demonstrates the manner in which this could skew civil–military relations. For example, after his electoral defeat to President Barrow, former President Jammeh sent the armed forces to take over the elections commission.[104] Ultimately, diplomatic and military intervention by ECOWAS was necessary to ensure a transfer of power to President Barrow.

In all other case-study countries, the powers of the commander-in-chief are not expounded in the Constitution with as much detail. Notwithstanding this fact, the case studies demonstrate how heads of state exercise powers over the security sector, including a degree of operational control and ability to deploy the armed forces to perform policing functions, often in politically charged situations. In Ethiopia, after Abiy Ahmed was appointed as prime minister in 2018, he sacked members of the TPLF, which was a coalition partner, from key security posts; arrested generals on charges of corruption; and introduced reform within the military to counter Tigrayan dominance of the armed forces.[105] There are concerns that security-sector reform was politicised by Abiy Ahmed—for example arresting former high-ranking officers on live television by heavily armed security personnel and targeting officials from Tigray who long controlled the military and intelligence services.[106] In Maldives, former President Nasheed ordered the armed forces to arrest and detain the Chief Judge of the Criminal Court—which unleashed a series of events which ended in his forceful removal from power by the military and the police.[107]

[100] Constitution of The Gambia, art 188(1).

[101] Ibid, art 188(2).

[102] Ibid.

[103] Ibid, art 188(3).

[104] Ruth Maclean, 'Gambian Military Takes Over Offices of Electoral Commission' *The Guardian* (London, 13 December 2016) <www.theguardian.com/world/2016/dec/13/gambian-military-takes-over-offices-of-electoral-commissionyahya-jammeh> accessed 16 October 2021.

[105] Jason Burke, 'Rise and fall of Ethiopia's TPLF—From Rebels to Rules and Back' *The Guardian* (London, 25 November 2020) <www.theguardian.com/world/2020/nov/25/rise-and-fall-of-ethiopias-tplf-tigray-peoples-liberation-front> accessed 16 October 2021.

[106] See in this collection Adem K Abebe, Chapter 10 'Ethiopia's Transition: Will the Country Stem Descent to Its Tradition of Authoritarianism?'; Emmanuel Igunza, 'Ethiopia's PM Abiy Ahmed Takes on the Military' (*BBC News*, 15 November 2018) <www.bbc.com/news/world-africa-46221240> accessed 16 October 2021.

[107] Azra Naseem, 'Gone at Gunpoint' (*Himal Southasian*, 11 February 2012) <www.himalmag.com/gone-gunpoint> accessed 17 October 2021.

Another noteworthy observation from the case studies is the effectiveness of the ties of loyalty both within the military and towards the commander-in-chief. For example, in The Gambia, when asked about the military's deployment to support Jammeh's efforts to cling on to power after his electoral defeat, the former chief of defence staff stated as follows:

> I'm supporting the commander-in-chief of … the Islamic Republic of the Gambia—whosoever it may be … As we speak now, I'm paid by the government of the day, that is Yahya Jammeh's government. He's my commander-in-chief as we speak now. I have only one commander-in-chief as we speak.[108]

In Maldives, the Progressive Party of Maldives (PPM), a party loyal to former President Gayoom, who was president (and thus, commander-in-chief) for 30 years, was at the forefront of the protests (including members of the military and the police) which led to the ouster of Nasheed.[109] After ousting Nasheed, the post of minister of defence went to Mohamed Nazim, who was a leader of the security forces under Gayoom.[110] It is a matter of conjecture whether Gayoom played a role in engineering the coup against Nasheed, but this could indicate the military's loyalty and relationship to their commander-in-chief of 30 years.

Both issues of fused dominion and loyalty take on a notably distinct character where the civilian head of state/government is a former military official (Ethiopia, Sri Lanka, Thailand) and when former military officials exercise civilian powers. Consider the example of Sri Lanka, where the president, a former military official, appointed members of the same regiment in which he served in the army (the Gajaba Regiment) as the defence secretary and the chief of defence staff cum army commander.[111] Even where checks and balances exist, fused dominion in such situations would appear to be inherently consolidationist in both an effective and perceived sense. Effectively, power can be consolidated through the operation of rank within the military, through ties of loyalty, intra-military loyalty such as regimental ties, and the loyalty between former and present military officials. The presence of military officials could also have a coercive and debilitating effect on civilian authorities, both in terms of weakening checks and balances and creating parallel administrative structures and procedures.[112] Perceptively, the way that a head of state is identified—and self-identifies—would be transformed by their former military

[108] Ruth Maclean, 'Gambian Military Takes Over Offices of Electoral Commission' *The Guardian* (London, 13 December 2016) <www.theguardian.com/world/2016/dec/13/gambian-military-takes-over-offices-of-electoral-commissionyahya-jammeh> accessed 16 October 2021.

[109] Naseem (n 107).

[110] Ibid.

[111] News First, 'Gajaba Regiment Commemorates Its Glorious 38th Anniversary' (*News First*, 14 October 2021) <www.newsfirst.lk/2021/10/14/gajaba-regiment-commemorates-its-glorious-38th-anniversary accessed 17 October 2021.

[112] See Satkunanathan (n 80).

designation. How would armed forces perceive a former member of the military who is a civilian head of state/government? Concomitantly, would a former military official perceive themselves as a civilian head of state/government where they are endowed with the title of commander-in-chief and their military prowess is one of the bases on which they seek election or usurp power? In both these questions, it is more likely than not that perception consolidates power.

One pertinent question that arises from this discussion is where the loyalty of the security sector ought to lie. Here, the experiences of the case-study countries are instructive. Where the security sector is loyal to the government, like public servants, the danger is that this enables *the government* to deploy the military for political purposes as well (Ethiopia, Maldives).[113] Where the security sector is loyal to *the state*, the military may act to safeguard what they determine to be in the national interest, including by intervening to overthrow elected governments (Myanmar, Thailand).[114] The security sector may also be loyal to a person, and this too legitimises the deployment of the military for political purposes and their intervention in the civilian domain. For example, in Thailand, the military is (or perceives itself to be) the 'representative of the king and guardian of the crown'.[115] The king has played a critical role in the balance of civil–military relations, in the context of both military and civilian rule. After the popular uprising against military rule in 1992, the king summoned the leaders of both sides, which led to the resignation of General Suchindra Kra-Prayoon and the non-occurrence of a military coup for another two decades.[116] There have been 12 coups during the tenure of King Bhumibol Adulyadej, and none have succeeded without his endorsement.[117] It is noteworthy that the loyalty of the security sector towards the king is embedded within a consolidationist model of fused dominion, where the king exercises wide-ranging effective power vis-à-vis the armed forces, including the royal prerogative to declare and lift martial law[118] and to appoint and remove officials in the military service.[119]

Such examples can be contrasted with the case of Malaysia, which is an outlier illustrating how the commander-in-chief can advance democratic consolidation. In Malaysia, the security sector appears to be loyal to the institution of the Yang di-Pertuan Agong, who is the supreme commander of the armed forces. The position of Yang di-Pertuan Agong is held only for a period of five years and rotates within the Conference of Rulers, who elect a person to this position.[120] This

113 See also Ronald J May and others, 'Introduction: Democracy and the Military in Comparative Perspective' in May and Selochan (n 2) 21–22.

114 Ibid, 22.

115 See in this collection Tonsakulrungruang (n 37).

116 Ibid.

117 BBC News, 'Thai Coup: Leader Gen Prayuth Receives Royal Endorsement' (26 May 2014) <www.bbc.com/news/world-asia-27572726> accessed 17 October 2021.

118 Constitution of Thailand, s 176.

119 Ibid, s 180.

120 Constitution of Malaysia, arts 32 and 38.

inhibits the creation of ties of loyalty to a person and redirects it to an institution. Executive authority is vested in the Yang di-Pertuan Agong and is exercisable 'by him or by the Cabinet or any Minister authorised by the Cabinet'.[121] In the exercise of their functions under the Constitution and federal law, the Yang di-Pertuan Agong acts in accordance with the advice of the cabinet or a minister, except as provided for in the Constitution, and must accept and act in accordance with advice where the Constitution requires them to do so.[122] Some discretion is retained for the Yang di-Pertuan Agong, both constitutionally[123] and in practice.[124] Finally, the Constitution provides for an 'Armed Forces Council', responsible under the general authority of the Yang di-Pertuan Agong, for the all matters relating to the armed forces including command, discipline, and administration, but excluding matters concerning operations.[125] The loyalty of the security sector towards the Yang di-Pertuan Agong is embedded within this separationist model of fused dominion, demonstrated in the fact that the Yang di-Pertuan Agong constrains the powers of the security sector and other civilian institutions check the power of the Yang di-Pertuan Agong.

In this light, the observation that 'unlike in numerous other states in the region, the [Malaysian] military has neither sought nor exercised any role in the government'[126] is instructive. There have been concerns that broad internal security powers (e.g. as provided for in the NSC Act) would be used to undermine the democratic electoral process, but even after the electoral defeat of former Prime Minister Najib, the security apparatus remained neutral.[127] The Yang di-Pertuan Agong has intervened at crucial moments, in accordance with the constitutional framework, to consolidate Malaysian democracy and balance civil–military relations—for example by rejecting a proclamation of emergency in October 2018 and securing the support of the Conference of Rulers for this decision.[128] This demonstrates the effectiveness of the commander-in-chief in regulating and influencing civil–military relations in ways which promote democratic consolidation but also the crucial role of institutions and checks and balances within which this can be achieved. It also reveals how the personality and ambition of the commander-in-chief could influence civil–military relations.

[121] Ibid, art 39.

[122] Ibid, arts 39, 40(1) and (1A).

[123] Ibid, art 40(2).

[124] See e.g. Joseph Sipalan and Rozanna Latiff, 'Malaysia's King Rejects Emergency Rule in Blow to PM Muhyiddin' (*Reuters*, 25 October 2020) <www.reuters.com/article/uk-malaysia-politics-palace-idUKKBN27A0EA> accessed 18 October 2021.

[125] Constitution of Malaysia, art 137(1).

[126] See in this collection Wilson Tay Tze Vern, Chapter 15 'Making Progress on A Rocky Path: Democratic Consolidation and Constitutional Endurance in Malaysia, 2018–2021'.

[127] Ibid.

[128] Sipalan and Latiff (n 124).

It is fitting to caution that this does not suggest that the separationist model of the commander-in-chief powers is always effective, or as effective, in maintaining balanced civil–military relations. This is analysed further below.[129]

3.1.3 The role of the military

Many of the case-study countries' constitutions contain provisions which directly or indirectly describe the role of the military within the state apparatus.

In Ethiopia, the armed forces are entrusted to protect the sovereignty of the country and to carry out assigned responsibilities during states of emergency subject to the Constitution, and must carry out all their functions in obedience to the Constitution and free of political partisanship.[130] The composition of the armed forces is required to equitably represent the nations, nationalities and peoples of Ethiopia.[131] In this way, the functional role of the armed forces must always be exercised subject to the Constitution and in a politically neutral manner. The armed forces also have a transformative role, by requiring that they equitably represent the diverse Ethiopian communities.

In Maldives, the Constitution requires that the security services—which includes both the military and the police—must be organised as separate services, operate independent of each other, and come under the responsibility of separate ministers.[132] The primary object of the military is to defend and protect Maldives,[133] while the primary objects of the police relate to law and order.[134] In this way, the Maldivian constitutions stresses the functional separation of the military from the police service.

The constitutions of Myanmar and Thailand were both drafted under military rule. For this reason, the provisions they contain relating to the armed forces are revealing as they also indicate the militaries' self-perception as well as the way that they want to be perceived by others. In Myanmar, the defence services are the 'sole patriotic defence force', which are 'strong, competent and modern' and are 'mainly responsible' for safeguarding the non-disintegration of Myanmar, the non-disintegration of national solidarity, and the perpetuation of sovereignty.[135] Where a state of emergency arises that could cause disintegration of Myanmar or of national solidarity, or result in a loss of sovereignty, provisions exist to transfer all legislative, executive, and judicial powers to the commander-in-chief of the defence forces.[136] The defence forces are also responsible for 'safeguarding the constitution'[137] and are foremost in safeguarding Myanmar 'against all internal and

129 See discussion at section 3.2.2.
130 Constitution of Ethiopia, art 87(3), (4), and (5).
131 Ibid, art 87(1).
132 Constitution of Maldives, arts 240 and 242.
133 Ibid, art 243(a).
134 Ibid, art 244.
135 Constitution of Myanmar, art 20(a) and (e).
136 Ibid, art 40(c), 417, and 418.
137 Ibid, art 20(f).

external dangers'.[138] One of the objectives of the union is to enable the defence services to participate in the national political leadership role of the state.[139] In Thailand, the state has a duty to protect and uphold the monarchy, independence, sovereignty, territorial integrity, national honour and interests, state security and public order and, for these purposes, must provide an efficient military and intelligence services.[140] Explicit mention is made of the deployment of armed forces for the purpose of developing the country.[141]

In the examples above, constitutional provisions describing the role of the military regulate and influence civil—military relations in several ways. This could occur by subjecting the functional role of the military to the Constitution and other transformative aspirations; by providing for functional and institutional separation between the military and the police; by entrusting the armed forces with the primary role of safeguarding a state against all internal and external dangers; by making constitutional allowances for a role of the military in the governance and development of a state; and by shaping the perception of, and towards, the military. The effectiveness of such provisions remains ambiguous. For example, in Ethiopia, the ethnic composition of the armed forces is still a contentious issue, and presently, a civil war with ethnic dimensions is being waged between the Ethiopian federal armed forces and the TPLF.[142]

3.1.4 The 'military imprint'

Military involvement in the civilian domain can result in a 'military imprint',[143] which can regulate and influence civil–military relations in both formal and informal ways. First, such an imprint could affect the Constitution and the law, both in terms of substance and procedure. Second, it could also influence the operation of institutions created by the Constitution and the law. Finally, it could operate at the level of ideology, legitimising or delegitimising foundational concepts within a flourishing constitutional democracy, as well as perceptions towards it.

The military imprint is unequivocally evident when armed forces, military officials, and militant groups have directly enacted, been involved in, or provided leadership to the process of enacting constitutions (Ethiopia, The Gambia, Myanmar, Thailand). This could have significant implications for civil–military relations, especially after moments of democratic transition. For example, in Myanmar, the Constitution grants the Tatmadaw a 25 per cent quota in all legislatures (union, state, regional).[144] The Constitution can only be amended with the

[138] Ibid, art 339.
[139] Ibid, art 6(f).
[140] Constitution of Thailand, s 52.
[141] Ibid.
[142] BBC News, 'Ethiopia's Tigray Crisis: TPLF Says 150 Have Died of Starvation' (7 September 2021) <www.bbc.com/news/world-africa-58428711#:~:text=About%20150%20people%20died%20of,from%20federal%20forces%20in%20June> accessed 18 August 2023.
[143] See in this collection Ohn, Janet, and Zulueta-Fülscher (n 8).
[144] Constitution of Myanmar, arts 74, 109, and 141.

approval of more than 75 per cent of the members of the union legislature—thus, giving the military an effective veto over any constitutional amendment.[145] Where the Tatmadaw is able to form a sufficient majority together with other political parties, the Tatmadaw's representation in union, state, and regional legislatures may also block democratically elected leaders from legislating. In The Gambia, the Constitution does not have a term limit for the president, and repressive laws and decrees from the regime prior to democratic transition are still in force.[146]

The military imprint can also operate at the level of institutions and institutional ideology, influencing the role and functioning of such institutions. In The Gambia, commissions mandated to recommend ways of improving police duties have observed that officials in the security sector who were appointed and who functioned during the regime of former President Jammeh should, among other things, be trained and reorientated to operate under a regime with a democratic dispensation.[147] This also reveals how a military imprint may occur through mainstreaming outlooks, approaches more commonplace within the military realm into laws, institutions, and other non-military domains.

Under military rule in Thailand, 'royalist nationalism' was promoted and the king was established as an indispensable part of the nation.[148] Democracy was undermined, and, in its stead, 'Thai-style democracy' was proposed. In Thai-style democracy, rights and liberties are restricted and though periodic elections are held, electoral politics are characterised as being 'dirty'.[149] The king is heralded as being above politics, and the army, proclaimed to be the representative of the king and guardian of the crown, can intervene in such dirty politics where they believe that politicians—whom they portray as corrupt and selfish—are placing the very essence of 'Thainess' in danger.[150] This results in a vicious cycle between coups and elections, which undermines and weakens the political party system and constitutional democracy.[151]

A government's term is often cut short by a coup. An election is therefore an arena for local mafias to violently compete for wealth and connection. Most [political] parties have no discernible ideology, hence no supporting mass. Corruption is rampant, rendering bureaucracy inefficient. Such chaos justifies another coup, which further discourages competent candidates. Upper and emerging middle

145 Ibid, art 436.
146 See in this collection Nabaneh (n 11).
147 See Faraba Banta Commission of Inquiry (1st July–31st August 2018), 'Recommendations on Ways of: (3) Improving Police Duties and Police Crowd Control Capabilities', text accessible at Gambia Times, 'The Faraba Banta Commission of Inquiry Report' *Gambia Times* (17 January 2019) <www.thegambiatimes.com/the-faraba-banta-commission-of-inquiry-report> accessed on 20 October 2021.
148 See in this collection Tonsakulrungruang (n 37).
149 Ibid.
150 Ibid.
151 Ibid.

class, due to electoral violence and bureaucratic incompetence, view democracy with negativity. Thus, the vicious cycle self-perpetuates the next political crisis.[152]

Here, we see evidence of an ideological military imprint. Usually, a shift towards military rule or imbalanced civil–military relations occurs synchronously with techniques and narratives to delegitimise and undermine principles of constitutional democracy, such as a flourishing political party system, fundamental rights and freedoms, periodic elections, and the rule of law. In the example of Thailand, it is also fitting to note how the military imprint interfaces with a form of nationalism, with the armed forces essentialising what it means to be Thai and then anointing themselves as the guardians thereof.

3.2 How Should Constitutions Seek to Regulate and Influence Civil–Military Relations?

3.2.1 Ideal institutions and institutional design

In moments of democratic transition, constitutional reform relating to the security sector would include (i) ensuring democratic, civilian control (and oversight) of the security sector, (ii) separating the functions and roles of security agencies, and (iii) removing the security sector from governance and policymaking.[153] Often, this is achieved through a combination of institutions and institutional design,[154] which may include the following:

1. Ensure clear civilian control and oversight by:
   a. establishing a clear chain of command headed by a civilian;
   b. establishing civilian ministries staffed by professional bureaucrats and led by a cabinet minister, while providing adequate safeguards to protect against partisan abuse by civilian authorities;
   c. granting the legislature powers of oversight vis-à-vis the military, including mandatory reporting, debating security sector legislation, oral hearings, and controlling the budget and expenditure of security sector agencies; and
   d. establishing independent oversight bodies which broadly represent society and consist of, among other persons, civil society representatives.
2. Ensure intra-security sector separation of powers by:
   a. providing distinct constitutional and legal frameworks for each security agency;
   b. appointing separate cabinet ministers for each security agency; and

152 Ibid.
153 Bisarya and Choudhry (n 1) 10–11.
154 Ibid, 17–20.

   c. distinguishing between the functions and roles of each security agency (for example, national security being the responsibility of the military, and law and order being the responsibility of the police) and establishing separate institutional structures for these respective functions or roles.
3. Establish a national security council with a majority of civilians to coordinate security, share intelligence, and respond to threats which require a whole-of-government response (such as terrorism and drug trafficking).
4. Constrain the potential for abuse during states of emergency by:
   a. enacting clear and detailed provisions about states of emergency;
   b. providing for the legislature to exercise oversight during states of emergency; and
   c. limiting executive powers over security sector agencies during the emergencies.[155]

Other aspects of security-sector reform which have constitutional implications include the choice of legal instrument to implement reform (i.e. the Constitution or legislation), questions about sequencing of reform (whether foundational principles and parameters which further democratic reform can be included in the Constitution, with details being left to legislation); providing amnesties and ensuring transitional justice; and constitutional reforms which regulate the economic interests of the security sector.[156]

3.2.2 Contextual factors and the balance of power

It has been rightly acknowledged that contextual factors must foreground democratic consolidation and constitutional reform relating to the security sector.[157] The security situation within a state is one such contextual factor, including whether non-state armed groups exist and whether the armed forces are 'overly bloated and top-heavy'.[158] Other contextual factors include leverage (i.e. the level of power, legitimacy, and influence that the security sector has within society); whether the security sector wishes to abandon political power and the degree of civilian oversight and accountability it is willing to accommodate; whether there are concerns about human rights violations by the security sector and whether amnesties are required to protect the democratic transition; the economic interests of the military; the security sector's normative vision of society and societal values; and whether the security sector should be represented in post-transition reform initiatives.[159] Reflecting on the case-study countries, this list could be expanded to include many other factors such as the self-image of the military (Myanmar, Thailand),

[155] For an excellent discussion, see ibid, from which the list is derived.
[156] Ibid.
[157] Ibid, 15.
[158] Ibid, 15.
[159] Ibid, 15–16.

its socio-economic composition (Ethiopia), society's perception of the role of the military (Thailand), and the military's history with respect to internal and external security operations.

The reason we would suggest as to why contextual factors must foreground democratic consolidation is that such factors determine the effective balance of power between civilian authority and the security sector. Consider the example of Malaysia. As discussed previously, 'the [Malaysian] military has neither sought nor exercised any role in the government'.[160] The security architecture, especially in relation to the separationist model of the commander-in-chief powers[161] and the civilian-majority composition of the National Security Council,[162] conform to the above-described ideals of institutional design. Contextual factors have also lent themselves to the non-intervention of the military. Even though the Malaysian armed forces played a significant role in managing communist insurgencies between 1948 and 1990, these were effectively resolved through a representative peace process that culminated in the Hat Yai Peace Agreement and reintegrated insurgents into the Malaysian population.[163] The Yang di-Pertuan Agong has also played a stabilising role in Malaysian democracy and balancing of civil–military relations.[164] Malaysia can be contrasted with Ethiopia, where the Constitution establishes ideal institutional safeguards—for example requiring that the minister of defence should be a civilian, ensuring that the functional role of the armed forces exclusively relates to national security, and mandating obedience of the armed forces to the Constitution.[165] However, this operates in a context where the armed forces are engaged in civil war with an ethnic group that has historically enjoyed dominance in both governance and control of the armed forces, combined with the fact that the present head of state and commander-in-chief is a former member of the military and not from the said dominant ethnic group. Here, the effective balance of power between the security sector (including actors on both sides of the civil conflict) and civilian authority will certainly be influenced by institutions and institutional safeguards, but it will also be profoundly shaped by contextual exigencies.

Malaysia is an instructive example of balanced civil–military relations in circumstances where institutional arrangements and contextual factors have coalesced. The institutional arrangements, and the pathway by which they were achieved, are

[160] See in this collection Vern (n 126).

[161] See section 3.1.2.

[162] National Security Council Act 2016 (n 12) s 6 (Malaysia).

[163] Ong Weichong, 'Negotiating the End of Cross-Border Insurgency' *Bangkok Post* (2 December 2019) <www.bangkokpost.com/opinion/opinion/1806424/negotiating-the-end-of-cross-border-insurgency> accessed 26 October 2021.

[164] See in this collection Vern (n 126); see also discussion at [p 18 [INTERNAL CHAPTER CROSS-REF]].

[165] See Constitution of Ethiopia, art 87.

not independent of contextual factors. Both the institutional arrangement and the pathway also reveal the balance of power and the effective loci of power. The case of Ethiopia suggests that 'ideal' institutions operate within contextual factors which continue to play a decisive role in shaping the balance of civil—military relations. These examples confront us with the perennial challenge of causation—do institutions shape the balance of power or do institutions reflect the existing balance of power and the ideological universe within which decisions about institutional design were made and the context within which they are enacted?

Answering this question remains beyond the scope of this chapter, but for our present purposes, two comments are fitting. First, the effective balance of power between civilian authority and the security sector (and the relative power of the security sector vis-à-vis other actors) are relevant contextual factors to security sector reform, and this is significant for both democratic consolidation and constitutional endurance. Analysis about militarisation frames this discussion well[166] as it imagines how effective power is influenced by authority, ideology, and legitimacy at both the formal and informal level. Second, this analysis modifies our understanding of an ideal institutional arrangement as any institutional adaptation which shapes the relative balance of power within a specific context. In this sense, states not only design and implement institutional solutions to achieve enduring reform but also calibrate the balance of power. What are some strategies that states can deploy to shape the balance of power, and in what sequence should this be done? We now turn to these issues.

4. Strategies to Balance Civil–Military Relations at Moments of Democratic Transition

4.1 Sequencing of Security-Sector Reform

The importance of sequencing security-sector reform in moments of democratic transition has been well documented.[167] The range of feasible constitutional reforms influencing or regulating the security sector would depend on the extant balance of power between civilian authorities and the military.[168] This has played out in the case-study countries in diverse ways, and in all such instances, it has deeply influenced the endurance of reform and democratic consolidation.

In countries plagued with civil conflict, security-sector reform must be balanced against the interest of strengthening the legitimate role of the armed forces in responding to conflict. In practice, striking this balance at a time where the

[166] See section 1.1.2.
[167] Bisarya and Choudhry (n 1) 22–23.
[168] Ibid.

effective power of (and reliance on) the military is elevated can be a delicate and complex issue. In Myanmar, for example, the constitutional amendments that were proposed by the National League for Democracy (NLD) focused mainly on democratic consolidation, including the sequential removal of unelected military representatives from the legislature. However, the NLD neglected to propose initiatives to advance power-sharing and federalism, which is one of the most important demands of ethnic groups since independence.[169] In fact, the NLD appeared to undermine power-sharing, for example, by appointing NLD chief ministers to the legislatures of Rakhine and Shan States, where they did not have a majority or plurality.[170] Undermining power-sharing causes the unvirtuous cycle of perpetuating (one of) the root causes of the civil conflict—which, in turn, consolidates the power and legitimacy of the security sector. This demonstrates how achieving security-sector reform would sometimes require prioritising other constitutional reforms which address the core issues through which the relative power and legitimacy of the military are elevated and sustained. In the context of civil war and internal disturbances, addressing such core issues become crucial as narratives about 'stability' could be deployed to legitimise incursions into the civilian domain.[171]

Sequencing of security-sector reform is also a salient consideration in accountability and transitional justice initiatives. Pursuing criminal accountability for human rights and other abuses committed by armed forces could be highly contentious, especially after democratic transition in post-conflict and post-authoritarian contexts.[172] Instead of fixating on criminal accountability, it has been suggested that other initiatives which further the right to truth, the right to reparations, the right to justice, and guarantees of non-recurrence can be explored.[173] The case-study countries indicate that although many such countries have experienced military incursions into the civilian domain and the military has allegations of human rights abuses, there have been no serious efforts to pursue accountability for such actions. In Myanmar, Aung Sung Suu Kyi seemed to avoid direct confrontation with the military on such issues, even going so far as praising Tatmadaw actions which resulted in civilian deaths[174] and appearing as the agent for Myanmar and defending the Tatmadaw against accusations of genocide before the International Court of Justice.[175] The Gambia and Maldives are exceptions, having implemented measures to further transitional justice. In The Gambia, a Truth, Reconciliation and Reparations Commission was established following Jammeh's electoral defeat

[169] See in this collection Ohn, Janet, and Zulueta-Fülscher (n 8).
[170] Kyaw Phone Kyaw, 'NLD Goes It Alone, Raising Ethnic Party Ire' (*Frontier Myanmar*, 2 May 2016) <www.frontiermyanmar.net/en/nld-goes-it-alone-raising-ethnic-party-ire> accessed 26 October 2021.
[171] See section 5.2.5.
[172] Bisarya and Choudhry (n 1) 24.
[173] Ibid, 7.
[174] See in this collection Ohn, Janet, and Zulueta-Fülscher (n 8).
[175] Al Jazeera, 'Transcript: Aung San Suu Kyi's Speech at the ICJ in Full' (*Al Jazeera*, 12 December 2019) <www.aljazeera.com/news/2019/12/12/transcript-aung-san-suu-kyis-speech-at-the-icj-in-full> accessed 26 October 2021.

to President Barrow—however, the final report has been delayed,[176] and the fate of such report remains ambiguous following the announcement of a political coalition between President Barrow and former President Jammeh.[177] In Maldives, though a Transitional Justice Act has been enacted, alleged perpetrators of atrocities hold high positions in the government (e.g. the current government coalition consists of politicians who were implicated in the coup against former President Nasheed) and thus, the success of this initiative remains to be seen.[178] The lack of accountability within the case-study countries could reflect the effective balance of power and the unwillingness to confront the armed forces. Not pursuing any forms of accountability and transitional justice may fortify the relative power of the security sectors by elevating them above the reach of the law.

Sequencing is also relevant to coalition-building. This is significant as in all the case-study countries, except for those presently under military rule (Myanmar, Thailand), the moment of democratic transition came about through coalition-building across political parties—and the process of democratic backsliding is often connected to fractures within the coalition. Such intra-coalition fissures may be caused, directly (Ethiopia) or indirectly (Sri Lanka), by attempted security-sector reform and attempts to hold security agencies accountable for alleged atrocities.

Finally, what is relevant is not only the chronology of sequencing but also the means employed to achieve the reform being sequenced. The case studies point to two reasons for this. First, after moments of democratic transition, the constitutionality and legality of acts of the regime are often subject to hyper-scrutiny. Any failure on their part is depicted as a failure of democracy itself. The events that lead to democratic backsliding are often tightly wound up in failures by the ruling regime to hold itself to the standards by which it came to power (Ethiopia, Maldives, Sri Lanka, Thailand). Such self-destruction can sometimes be linked with civil–military relations and security-sector reform. In Thailand, for example, former Prime Minister Yingluck Shinawatra attempted to pass an amnesty law that would pardon all parties of the civil conflict; cease investigation into the atrocities committed by the military; and, at the same time, absolve Thaksin Shinawatra, her brother, from corruption cases.[179] She then attempted to push the bill through the legislature without granting the opposition an opportunity to debate it.[180] Although the bill was later withdrawn, these actions were relied on to mobilise anti-democratic forces and massive protests.[181] Ultimately, General

[176] Ibid.
[177] Ibid.
[178] Mushfiq Mohamed, 'Unpacking the Maldives' Transitional Justice Act' (*Himal Southasian*, 4 June 2021) <www.himalmag.com/unpacking-the-maldives-transitional-justice-act-2021> accessed 26 October 2021.
[179] See in this collection Tonsakulrungruang (n 37).
[180] Ibid.
[181] Ibid.

Prayuth Chan-ocha took over power in a military coup. The second reason that the means employed to achieve the reform may be relevant is that reform in the context of post-military or authoritarian rule may be challenging because of institutional capture and the presence of public officers and officials appointed by the previous regime remaining in power (Maldives, The Gambia, Myanmar). In Maldives, former President Nasheed had to literally padlock the Supreme Court, given the issues caused by the newly independent judiciary and judicial service commission.[182] He then deployed the military to arrest and detain the chief judge of the Criminal Court. Although the exigencies that necessitated such action remain contested,[183] such actions were *prima facie* unconstitutional and were used to justify the coup which ousted him from power. Institutions which emerge after transition are sometimes unable to further democratic consolidation due to (at best) the lack of institutional practice and jurisprudence to guide their decision-making or (at worst) resistance to and undermining of democratic consolidation, while enjoying the operation of democratic principles (such as judicial tenure) which shield them from removal through the operation of multiple checks and balances. Reform is necessary to reverse the effects of military or authoritarian rule, but the pathways to reform may remain captured by the previous regime. However, recourse to extra-constitutional methods can be used as propaganda to delegitimise and undermine democratic governance.

While sequencing is undoubtedly a vital, and perhaps even *the* vital consideration, in transitions and consolidation, there are few clear and universal lessons our case studies, or the literature, have to offer. However, it is clear from our case studies and the literature that the balance between civilian and military centres of power; the institutional and sociological structure of their relationship; and specific features arising from history, geography, political economy, and other 'deep' determinates had profound implications for the relationship between the Constitution and democratic transition, consolidation, and endurance.

4.2 Strategies for Security-Sector Reform

This section is really about the role of agency in shaping these ideas, structures, relationships, and forces. It seeks to distil lessons so those who seek to bend these legacies and structures to further democratic transition, consolidation, and endurance have the benefit of history and comparative experience. Stripped to its core, this section is about strategy: it asks (i) *how* can the civilian sector grow its power vs

[182] See in this collection Mariyam Zulfa, Chapter 11 'Maldives Constitution 2008: Winds of Change at the Fifteenth-Year Crossroads'.
[183] See Naseem (n 107).

the military and (ii) once a satisfactory level of balance (and associated checks) is achieved, *how* can that state entrench this equilibrium?

Unlike Chapters 4 and 5 in this collection, which were concerned with understanding the world, asking *what* and *why* (i.e. analysing, classifying and comparing), this chapter is about praxis. Therefore, it differs somewhat in the way the problem is set up (the immediate challenges facing actors actively shaping events) and method (the elements foregrounded, modes by which inferences are drawn) and be less hesitant in making prescriptions. As Weber reminds us, the politician does not have the choice of inaction. He or she must act, for not acting is itself an action. Choices must be made with the best available information that can be collected and digested in the period within which that choice must be made, whether it be seconds, minutes, hours, or days. As a wazir in ninth-century Baghdad reminds us, 'the basis of government is jugglery. If it works, and lasts, it becomes policy.' In that vein, this section of the chapter concerns how to use the Constitution to juggle one's way into more favourable civil–military relations.

5. Conclusion: The Problem

In order to frame the analytical problem this section seeks to solve, it is best to see the problem from the perspective of the actor who is trying to resolve it. The following is a 'stylised model' (to borrow an economic term) of the situations many such actors in our case studies have confronted.

5.1 The Stylised Model

Either by storming the barricades or by the ballot, a counter-authoritarian movement takes over the state. The movement or party is a broad coalition. It gathers myriad interests, social forces, and personalities, uniting them around the common purpose of regime overthrow. Most of the time, there is broad but vague consensus that democracy must be entrenched, the rule of law upheld, and human rights must reign. Everyone knows that, for this to come to pass, something must be done about the security sector, and more often than not, the military in particular.

An alternative version of this film is the Weimar tragedy, majestically illustrated in the television series *Babylon Berlin*. There are well-intended and often capable leaders in a dysfunctional government who struggle to steer the ship of state that is rotten to, or perhaps from, the core. They endeavour to preserve democracy in the face of threats from within and outside the state. Rumblings from deep within the barracks emerge from time to time. The polity yearns for order and desires nothing more than for the trains to run on time. Gradually, whispers that the military should sort this all out become accepted wisdom. Correspondingly, at embassy cocktail parties, there is an ever-growing semi-circle around the once-ignored general who used to nurse his whiskey quietly in a corner (those in the semi-circle fail to notice the envy in the police chief's eyes when he sees the attention the general gets). The liberal/democratic set, if they are still on talking terms with each other, are either in denial, paralyzed with despair, or worn out by their Sisyphian exertions against the counter-reform elements within the state that seem to know exactly how to block any progress whatsoever. They all agree that something must be done to prevent the security sector from getting out of hand, but the party ends and no decisions have been made.

In other words, everyone sees the writing on the wall, but precisely what is to be done, when, how and by whom is not known. In the case of the movement newly heading but yet to control the state, some leaders have hazy plans, dreamed up during their years in the political wilderness. Those of a more idealistic persuasion may want wholesale, big-bang reform immediately before the counter-revolution can be organised and the mandate for change is fresh. Others, more cautious but not necessarily wiser, may seek to thwart precisely such a counter-revolution emerging by suggesting amnesties, transitional arrangements, and the like to co-opt, or at least placate, these forces. Friendly foreign powers and enterprising UN agencies, depending on the agency and season, may proffer advice supporting versions of these schools of thought. The country's own history offers little guidance: either you have no history of this particular type of political excitement or past attempts have failed, offering few clear lessons. But they know that letting events run their natural course is not an option. So what is to be done?

5.2 Key Features of the Stylised Model

This stylised model highlights a few key features that actors confront when attempting to alter the balance of power in civilian–military relations and shape its structure.

First, the civilian sphere is often more heterogenous than the military. Democratic movements often unite actors with disparate ideological, social, economic, and geographic backgrounds.[184] The military, by contrast, is often drawn from specific demographic groups with shared world views, and the leadership of the military is often carefully socialised through a homogenous process of training and education. As a result, in the civilian sphere, there are not just greater coordination problems with respect to *ends* and *means*; even once these questions are settled, this diversity makes action harder due to lower levels of intra-group trust.

[184] See discussion on sequencing and coalition-building at the end of section 4.1.

When resisting military rule, this heterogeneity can be a source of resilience and strength; the diversity of ideologies and actors complicates the process of repression and makes it easier for democratic movements to appeal to disparate groups and interest in the polity. However, should such a democratic movement succeed in securing control of the state, this becomes a liability when then seeking to establish the military's role post-transition. Different branches of the movement will have different ideological views and interests; the urge will be to focus efforts on areas where agreement is easier to come by, and thus this pivotal element of democratic consolidation is often left aside.

In order to mitigate these liabilities, democratic movements should try as much as possible to incorporate critical elements of civil–military reform in their formal or informal, private or public common minimum platforms. This, at the very least, will require the leaders of groups within the movement to discuss these issues and, by deliberation, identify (and hopefully grow) areas of consensus, thus building trust between actors with respect to this domain. Those 'specialising' in this domain within these groups should also be encouraged to interact on this topic to build relationships and trust that can be harnessed post-transition.

Second, the military benefits from information asymmetry; it has a better understanding of the civilian sphere than the civilian sphere has of the military. All members of the military were once civilians, and they also have friends and family who are civilians. They are surrounded by civilian institution, life, etc. By contrast, understanding of the military—including heterogenous interest groups within the military—is very limited amongst civilians. Therefore, democratic actors often have limited understanding of military actors' interests, priorities, sources of power, and motivations. Those that do not have the benefit of ex-military members or advisors find understanding the military and influencing it particularly challenging; even more so in building trust for the inevitable compromises that are inherent in transition and consolidation processes. Democratic leaders should take great care to develop an understanding of militaries and should secure advisors who possess such knowledge and relationships to act as interlocutors.

Third, there is the question of sequencing and prioritisation. As noted above,[185] there is broad consensus on what the ideal institutional structure for civil–military relations should look like. There should be a clear chain of command with a civilian at the top; a civilian ministry and minister of defence; parliamentary oversight, including over the defence budget; a clear and limited constitutional role, etc. However, the central concern for the actor engaged in transition and consolidation is rather how can the little power they have—that is likely to be at its peak at the moment of authoritarian overthrow—be harnessed to increase the political power of democratic actors and institutions and reduce that of the military? The

[185] See section 3.2.1.

optimal moves will vary from country to country, but some broad principles can be deduced.

5.2.1 *Divide et impera*

Divide et impera is almost always an efficient tool for reducing the power of an overmighty actor. In the case of the security sector, there are five major cleavages which can be harnessed: (i) intra-state (e.g. parliamentary committee versus defence ministry), (ii) intra-executive (e.g. civil servants versus armed forces), (iii) intra-security sector (e.g. armed forces versus police or intelligence, (iv) intra-armed forces (e.g. army versus navy), and (v) intra-service (engineers versus infantry or inter-regimental rivalry).

As a general principle, identifying the strongest and most regressive actor is critical and then harnessing rivalry at the appropriate level. This can be done by allocating honours, attention, and position to those who could be potentially rivalrous to the main actor. Examples of this might include appointing a non-prestige regiment officer as commander of a service, appointing a second-tier service as chief of defence staff.

A further approach is strengthening the position of rivals to the main regressive actor. Examples might include expanding or reducing function (e.g. giving the police greater responsibility) or altering budgets (e.g. giving the navy or foreign ministry a greater share of the security budget or improving the ability of the Treasury to hold the armed forces accountable for their budgets by building their defence economics capabilities).

Establishing this system of decentralised power, combined with checks and balances, not only disempowers actors opposed to the ideal scheme of civil military relations outlined above but also makes the transition easier by already establishing key principles and elements of such a scheme as existing facts on the ground. More importantly, it also allows any formal or informal negotiations with the security sector on constitutional reform to take place bilaterally with the disparate interest groups within the security sector bloc rather than enabling them to create a common front.

5.2.2 Actors within the security sector

There are some actors within the security sector that are especially vital and deserve careful attention. The intelligence services are the prime example. Intelligence services are often a key way in which the military seeks to influence the political realm: they have the ability to shape public perception through a web of influences and slush funds. They also have the ability to intimidate those who are likely to support democratic transition and consolidation. Finally, they have the ability to spread mistrust and discord within the democratic coalition. If possible, the heads of intelligence agencies should be immediately replaced with trusted professionals. Systems of bureaucratic, financial, and parliamentary accountability such as thorough audits and administrative control by the relevant line ministry, security-cleared departments of the national audit office and parliamentary intelligence committee are important measures to ensure that intelligence services perform their constitutional role.

Constitutionally, the role of the intelligence services whose function is the protection of the people (and not a specific government, party, or interest group, or even the state) and thus is accountable to the people through representative institutions e.g. parliamentary committees, civilian minister and civilian controlled ministries and the judicial branch can be established.

5.2.3 Entrenching the balance of power through institutionalisation

Entrench the balance of power at the moment of democratic transition via institutionalisation. The moment of democratic transition is often the point where pro-democratic forces enjoy the greatest popularity, unity, and legitimacy. Conversely, the military is often confused, disunited, and in shock at the change in the status quo. Constitutions often take time and require broad coalition-building; however, ordinary legislation of constitutional significance, including in the realm of civil–military relations, can often be quickly passed to entrench this status quo. Examples of such legislation might include:

- parliamentary oversight committees;
- amendments to the army, navy, air force, police or equivalent acts;
- amendments and publication of the administrative regulations governing the security sector (e.g. police standing orders);
- reversal of secondary legislation calling the armed forces out of the barracks/ states of emergency;
- repeal of key legislation that enables security-sector abuse (e.g. overmighty counterterrorism, surveillance authorisation);
- a legislative bar to military-run enterprises (the actual divestment can take place later);
- a legislative bar preventing the military from holding positions in the civil service;
- budgetary accountability and oversight.

5.2.4 Reducing the size of the military

In many, if not most, transitional democracies, the size of the military and its budgets are disproportionately large relative to security needs.[186] Reducing the size of these budgets is key for placing balanced civil–military relations on a sustainable footing. One important reason for the failure to reduce the defence budget is

[186] Daniel Alphonsus, 'Sri Lanka's Post-War Defence Budget: Overspending and Underprotection' (South Asia Scan No 15, Institute of South Asian Studies 2021).

the lack of expertise among politicians, bureaucrats, and the media as to what an optimal, or at least, efficient military budget would look like. As a result, the executive is not able to effectively perform its constitutional task of integrating disparate domains to make policy on a holistic basis. Nor is the legislature effectively able to perform its constitutional duties with respect to budget-making.

Few civilians or civilian agencies have the expertise to question whether the purchase of fighter jets, tanks, or large infantry recruitments are necessary for achieving the country's security ends. This can be relatively easily mitigated by building the defence economics capacity of defence ministries, finance ministries, and parliamentary committees, including parliamentary committees that have a constitutional role covering budgets and public finance. This can be completed by funding analytic studies on defence economic issues by think-tanks and universities. In addition to acting as a resource for technical advice, multilateral agencies—such as the World Bank, Asian Development Bank, and International Monetary Fund—could also consider asking countries for justification of their spending priorities in this domain as part of lending due-diligence processes.

5.2.5 Diminishing legitimacy for an oversized role

However, before understanding how to limit the military's legitimacy to its security mandate, it is prudent to understand the means by which the security sector influences the balance of power in such a way that it generates, or is endowed with, the legitimacy to command an outsized role.

As discussed, militarisation is a step-by-step process by which not only institutions but also norms and other aspects of society are dominated by the military or militaristic criteria.[187] From this perspective, the effective balance of power is not only determined by institutional dominance but also other techniques which legitimise the forms of authority being exercised. In other words, the arena of the struggle for power is not just institutional but ideological as well. The case-study countries reveal some of the techniques and narratives employed to legitimise (military) rule and military incursions into civilian domains.

Military rulers do not (just) rule extra-constitutionally. They often engage in the process of enacting laws and constitutions to provide legitimacy to their actions—which could perhaps be termed 'legal legitimacy'. The rule of law is dispensed with and replaced with rule *by* law, where law is used instrumentally, among other things, to weaken the opposition, the media, and civil society organisations.[188] Institutions—including the judiciary—are captured and commandeered to fortify the ruling regime, and loyalties are bought through techniques including incentives and the allure of career advancement.[189] All such actions are cloaked with the legitimacy of a legal instrument.

[187] See section 1.1.2.
[188] See in this collection Abebe (n 106).
[189] See in this collection Tonsakulrungruang (n 37).

Military and authoritarian regimes also may subordinate democratic values, fundamental rights, and freedoms to rapid economic development, invoking a form of performative legitimacy.[190] As part of this project, democratic values may also be condemned as antithetical to economic development, and this undermines future democratic consolidation and constitutional endurance.

Another form of legitimacy is invoking stability. For example, the allocation of 25 per cent of seats to the Tatmadaw in the national legislature of Myanmar has been defended as being 'necessary to safeguard Myanmar's stable transition to multiparty democracy' and to 'ensure national stability'.[191] The invocation of stability is especially problematic for several reasons: it dovetails with the legitimate role of the security sector, which poses significant challenges when attempting to demythologise such assertions; and it enables opportunistic officials to create, facilitate, or orchestrate the very conditions which they rely on to seize power.[192]

5.2.6 Claiming legitimacy by employing religious tropes and narratives

In the weeks preceding the coup against former President Nasheed in Maldives, his regime was delegitimised by entities including the 'December 23 Alliance', which constantly portrayed him as anti-Islam.[193] Shortly after the coup, television stations broadcast discussions about the Prophet Mohamed's conquest of Mecca, perhaps drawing an analogy to the way that the god-fearing opposition defended the county from an enemy of Islam.[194] In The Gambia, former President Yahya Jammeh portrayed himself as a 'pious Muslim', dressing in a white Muslim gown with prayer beads and a holy Quran in his hands.[195] He also built a mosque on the State House grounds and declared The Gambia to be an Islamic Republic in 2015.[196] In this way, religious tropes and narratives are deployed to legitimise military incursions into the civilian domain and to delegitimise democratic governance, thus influencing the effective balance of power between civilian authorities and the security sector.

These forms of legal, performative, stability-orientated, and religious legitimacy could continue to exist in varying degrees within public consciousness and ideology even after moments of democratic transition. As a result, various iterations of these can be deployed to undermine democratic governance and foster a yearning to return to military or authoritarian rule. On democratic transition, governments need to re-legitimise legality and the rule of law and delegitimise the

[190] See in this collection Abebe (n 106).
[191] Htet Naing Zaw, 'Military's Parliamentary Quota Necessary as Country Not Yet Stable: Army Chief' (*The Irawaddy*, 18 February 2019) <www.irrawaddy.com/news/burma/militarys-parliamentary-quota-necessary-country-not-yet-stable-army-chief.html> accessed 26 October 2021.
[192] See discussion at the end of section 3.1.1.1; see also in this collection Khemthong Tonsakulrungruang (n 37).
[193] Naseem (n 107).
[194] Ibid.
[195] See in this collection Nabaneh (n 11).
[196] Ibid.

tropes and narratives employed to fortify military rule, or the turn to authoritarian rule, to secure constitutional endurance.

Turning now to the question of diminishing legitimacy for the militaries' oversized role—a professional military's role in a democratic constitutional structure is solely limited to mandated security functions. However, in many transitional states, the absence of capacity and perception of military competence results in widespread legitimacy for military overreach. Improving state capacity *tout court* is beyond the scope of this chapter. However, correcting perceptions is not. Due to their secretive nature, militaries—and especially intelligence agencies—are often far less capable than they appear. This mismatch between appearance and reality allows militaries to receive undue legitimacy for engaging in non-security functions. Therefore, the challenge is to make the security sector more transparent without diminishing its ability to achieve its security function. Here, again, constitutional structures can play a key role, especially by ensuring capable civilian control of public finance, including the defence budget, and reporting and scrutiny mechanisms.

Note that, aside from the legitimacy the security sector might enjoy for non-security functions among actors outside the security sector, there is also the question of the legitimacy of performing non-security functions among actors within the security sector. As we can see from the militaries of our case studies and their influence on constitutional reform, this self-perception can play a vital role in determining the shape and form of constitutional negotiations and outcomes. Here, there are two main ways in which the military's self-perception of its constitutional duty can be shaped. The first is through the curricula of military academies such as staff colleges. These institutions play an important role in forming and socialising identity, preferences, and perceptions among the military. Ensuring that these curricula reflect democratic values can assist in democratic consolidation and endurance. Particular care must also be taken to ensure that members of the military are not too far removed from civilian life. For example, in Myanmar, where children of military families go to military schools, live in military townships, shop in military shops, and then study at military academies, the *other*ing of the civilian population is very profound.

The second is by harnessing the process of isomorphic mimicry to serve democratic consolidation and endurance. This can be shaped by managing the exposure of the military to models or exemplars in civil military relations. For example, militaries that train and have exchanges with countries that have robust democratic traditions of civil–military relations are likely to emulate them more; they are also less likely to learn ways and means of subverting processes of democratic consolidation.

Throughout the constitutional reform, negotiation, and consolidation process, care must be taken to ensure that the security sector believes that it will ultimately benefit from the process too. There are two main types of benefit that can be offered through a process of democratic transition and consolidations.

First, greater military prestige, professionalism, and legitimacy: by ensuring the military performs its constitutional role, the military's professionalism and legitimacy can be burnished. This constitutional process can also enable the military to upgrade partnerships with foreign militaries, enabling greater access to foreign training and exchange opportunities.

Second, representing the country in United Nations (UN) peace-keeping missions, which also provides significant economic benefits: UN peace-keeping missions provide opportunities for the security sector to engage in purposeful activity that boosts its prestige and morale. In lower-income countries, like the countries in our case studies, it also offers members of the security sector an opportunity to obtain significantly higher remuneration than they otherwise would have had.

7

Constitutional Cultures

Cheryl Saunders

1. Introduction

This chapter examines the relevance of culture to the establishment of constitutional democracy and to the extent of its resilience over time. It seeks both to understand the impact of culture on the endurance of constitutional democracy and to identify responses that might be useful to maximise resilience and to minimise decay. In doing so, it contributes to the overall aim of the volume as a whole to better understand the causes of democratic decay and endurance. Consistently with the scheme of the volume, it seeks insights that might have broader relevance from experiences in Asia and Africa, drawing on seven case studies in which opportunities to establish or consolidate constitutional democracy have emerged in recent times with, at best, limited success. The chapter is not prescriptive about where the parameters of constitutional democracy lie but assumes that the overriding goal is to capture its benefits in a form that works in context.[1]

The amorphous quality of culture makes it a challenging subject in any context. Roger Cotterrell once observed, in considering its role in comparative law, that understanding the often-changing and contestable dimensions of culture was like 'trying to nail a jelly to a wall'.[2] In the context of constitutional comparison, culture also can be controversial, on account of the potential of some of its apparent manifestations to cut across what are claimed as universal values.[3] Avoidance is not an option, however, if the goal is to understand causes and solutions with resonance in the real world. To quote Amartya Sen, in relation to the significance of culture to economic development, culture has a 'pervasive influence ... in human life' and 'the real issue ... is how—not whether—culture matters'.[4] This chapter

[1] These issues are explored in Michael W Dowdle and Michael A Wilkinson, *Constitutionalism beyond Liberalism* (Cambridge University Press 2017).

[2] Roger Cotterrell, 'Law and Culture—Inside and Beyond the Nation State' (2008) 31(4) Nordisk Juridisk Tidsssskrift 23.

[3] On the 'false dilemma' created by this apparent dichotomy, see Jean-Francois Bayart, *The Illusion of Cultural Identity* (Hurst & Co 1996) 245, 251.

[4] Amartya Sen, 'How Does Culture Matter?' in Vijayendra Rao and Michael Walton (eds), *Culture and Public Action* (Stanford University Press 2004) 37, 38.

Cheryl Saunders, *Constitutional Cultures* In: *Democratic Consolidation and Constitutional Endurance in Asia and Africa*. Edited by: Tom Gerald Daly and Dinesha Samararatne, Oxford University Press. © Oxford University Press 2024.
DOI: 10.1093/oso/9780192899347.003.0007

proceeds on the premise that culture is a factor to be taken into account in examining constitutional resilience and decay, whether its influence is positive, negative, or neutral.

The chapter is structured as follows. Section 2 explores the concept of culture itself. It begins with a definition of culture, as the term is used in this chapter, exploring those of its properties that might affect analysis of its relevance to the development or decline of constitutional democracy. This section acknowledges the complexity of treating culture as a factor in democratisation but seeks to establish some working assumptions that enable critical inquiry to proceed. This section of the chapter also identifies the variety of communities with which aspects of culture may be associated in the context of constitutional democracy, both general and sectoral. Section 2 concludes with a segment on constitutional culture, which overlaps with those of the relevant communities in some respects but is also, in others, discrete.

Section 3 of the chapter introduces the case studies. It does so by considering the apparent relevance of culture to the emergence of opportunities for democratisation in each of them and to the ways in which such opportunities were handled. A final segment of this section examines the link between democracy and constitutions. As the case studies show, opportunities for democratic consolidation or threats of democratic backsliding are not necessarily in lockstep with constitution-making or constitutional change. In any event, constitutions alone cannot secure democracy, ensure its development, or shield it from decay. On the other hand, constitutions offer critical support to democracy, whatever form it takes. They provide a framework for democratic institutions, they prescribe key democratic ground rules. and they protect both from easy change as a matter of law. Constitutional endurance, understood to include the meaningful operation of constitutions in practice, is a significant part of the puzzle of understanding the dynamics of democratic resilience and decay.

Section 4 of the chapter pursues the theme of constitutional endurance to examine the role that culture plays. To this end, it examines three phases in the timeline for making and maintaining democratic constitutions: the period during which foundations are laid; implementation of a constitution, during transition to the new arrangements; and the period of consolidation, for the rest of a constitution's effective life. Although stylised, this approach is useful to isolate the characteristics of each phase for the purposes of considering the implications of culture. In relation to each phase, the chapter raises two main questions. One is the ways in which culture manifests itself with implications for constitutional resilience. The second is whether—and, if so, how—culture plays a role in strengthening resilience and minimising the chances of decay. A final section 5 of the chapter draws brief conclusions, noting that the chapter still offers only a tentative base on which others may build.

2. Culture

2.1 Meaning, Properties, Use

Culture has been defined, in a way that is useful for present purposes, as encompassing 'values, premises and practices in terms of which members of any given community order their interactions', drawing on 'frames of meaning, moral orders, and tacit understandings'.[5] A helpful disaggregation by Cotterrell identifies four relatively distinct components: beliefs and values; tradition, including historical experience; material culture, including levels of technological and economic development; and 'emotional attachments and rejections'.[6] Understood in this way, it is clear that all communities have 'values, premises and practices' that are cultural in nature.[7] It is also clear that the scope of culture is potentially broad and that it has properties that complicate the task of understanding it and assessing its impact. These are canvassed briefly here and assumed in the rest of the chapter.

First, culture is not homogenous. Aspects of culture may be understood differently within the same community and may be internally contested.[8] This can readily be anticipated where there are perceptible cleavages in society along religious, linguistic, or ethnic lines. Even where a community appears relatively cohesive, however, there may be different attitudes towards aspects of culture that are attributable to differences in circumstances of various kinds, including gender, age, geography, socio-economic opportunities, and exposure to the forces of globalisation. In any community, some versions of culture may be more conducive to constitutional democracy than others, offering opportunities. Some versions may be patently antithetical to democracy, presenting threats which democratisation must meet.

Second, culture is not immutable but changes over time. Sometimes, change occurs gradually, through an evolutionary process, in response to changing attitudes or conditions or exposure to new influences. Sometimes, change occurs more rapidly, in response to stimuli of various kinds, the impact of which cannot always be predicted. There are plenty of gradations in between. Cultures have always blended across communities when they come in contact. Colonisation caused cultural

[5] Roger Ballard and others, 'Cultural Diversity: Challenge and Accommodation' in Ralph Grillo and others (eds), *Legal Practice and Cultural Diversity* (Ashgate Publishing 2009) 9, 15.

[6] Ibid.

[7] See e.g. Alexander Latham-Gambi referring to the 'shared understandings' forming 'a rich fabric of meaning' as a 'constitutional imaginary' across 'modern western societies': Alexander Latham-Gambi, 'The Constitutional Imaginary: Shared Meanings in Constitutional Practice and Implications for Constitutional Theory' (2021) 15 ICL Journal 21.

[8] Thus, Legrand defends the 'legitimacy' of reasonable reference to French culture 'although ... it is obviously multiple, disparate, and labile ... and ever-recommencing': Pierre Legrand, 'The Guile and the Guise: Apropos of Comparative Law as We Know It' (2021) 16 Asian Journal of Comparative Law 155, 168.

change, although, to a degree, that varied with conditions of colonisation and with consequences that are still unresolved.[9] Globalisation is another catalyst for cultural change, mixing cultures in ways that operate unevenly between and within communities. The current phase of globalisation seems particularly significant in this regard, enabling the rapid spread of information and encouraging progressive expansion of broadly shared norms.[10] The extent of cultural convergence nevertheless remains unclear and is one of many contested questions.[11] By its very nature, culture seems likely to be resistant to simple transplantation.[12] Also unsettled is how, and how quickly, culture can alter to meet, for example, the demands of a new constitutional order. This is a core issue for this volume and is taken up in section 4 of the present chapter.

Third, constitutions and culture have a reflexive relationship in which constitutions shape culture and culture shapes constitutions, in both form and operation.[13] The link between the two may be obvious where, for example, a preamble acknowledges culture or cultural norms and institutions are protected in the text.[14] More often than not, however, the relationship is implicit. Culture is assumed in the drafting of a constitution, which it is likely to affect, and cultural change is assumed to follow in the wake of new constitutional arrangements. If culture is relevant to democratic resilience, however, there may be value in a greater consciousness of this relationship and a more realistic appraisal of the opportunities and challenges it presents.

Fourth, the usual lack of a definitive source means that culture may be mischaracterised or even manipulated for instrumental—typically political—ends. In the latter case, claims typically are made to discredit what are characterised as transnational standards for constitutional democracy. Situations of this kind juxtapose local political opportunism, the possibility that some cultural sensitivities are genuinely engaged, and shifts in the understanding of what is core and what is periphery in democracy itself. Ideally, such tensions are resolved by those immersed

[9] Sakul Kundra, 'Cultural Change Transformed Indigenous Tradition: Colonial Encounter' *Australia Today* (3 July 2021) <www.theaustraliatoday.com.au/cultural-change-transformed-indigenous-tradition-colonial-encounter> accessed 13 October 2022. On cultural imperialism more broadly, see e.g. Theresa Weynand Tobin, 'Cultural Imperialism', *Encyclopaedia Britannica* <www.britannica.com/topic/cultural-imperialism> accessed 13 October 2022.

[10] But see the view that this may be more apparent than real and that, in at least some ways, globalisation can heighten consciousness of cultural difference: Uwe Kischel, *Comparative Law* (Oxford University Press 2019) 47–50.

[11] For a useful discussion, with particular reference to legal and constitutional culture, see Wen-Chen Chang and others, *Constitutionalism in Asia; Cases and Materials* (Hart Publishing 2014) 70–76.

[12] David Kenny notes that the generally positive referendum culture in Ireland is 'hard to know fully ... contingent, fragile and may be difficult to replicate': David Kenny, 'The Risks of Referendums' in Maria Cahill and others (eds), *Constitutional Change and Popular Sovereignty* (Routledge 2021).

[13] Günter Frankenberg, 'Comparing Constitutions: Ideas, Ideals and Ideology—Towards a Layered Narrative' (2006) 4 International Journal of Constitutional Law 439.

[14] The examples of the Constitutions and cultures of Timor-Leste, Laos, and Bhutan are cited in Chang and others (n 11) 76–77, but there are many others, including those of Papua New Guinea.

in the relevant cultures, albeit in light of global experience, problematic and slow though such a process may be.[15] It is difficult for others to evaluate the accuracy or weight of cultural claims, whether they have solid foundations or not.

These reflections on the properties of culture suggest that it is relevant in assessing the prospects for constitutional democracy in at least three ways, First, it is important to be conscious of prevailing cultures that may have a bearing on resilience or decay so as to be able to take them into account, whatever that involves. Second, in designing change, there is much to be gained by maximising the opportunities that existing culture offers while minimising unwanted impacts, to the extent that this is possible. Third, it should be assumed that any significant move from the constitutional *status quo* will require cultural change. As a caveat, it might also be noted that cultural difference may sometimes be obscured when local concepts are translated into other languages, presenting them in familiar terms that, in practice, may be deceptive.[16]

2.2 Cultural Communities

Different cultural communities, both general and sectoral, may need consideration in determining the significance of culture to democratic resilience and decay.

A general community comprises the society at large or a distinctive segment of it. The culture associated with a general community is described here as societal culture. Such a community need not be co-extensive with the population as a whole. On the contrary, the population may be divided in ways that reflect quite distinctive cultural attitudes and expectations, as in, for example, Sri Lanka and Myanmar.[17] Even where a community is ostensibly cohesive, there may well be tensions within it over aspects of an otherwise broadly shared culture. An active civil society may further contribute to this complex pattern if there are marked disagreements of a cultural kind between civil society and other segments of the community or within civil society itself. A general community is distinguishable from the sectoral cultural communities considered below on the basis that it has no specific vocational role in a constitutional democratic system. Instead, a general

[15] Chang offers insights into the ways in which these threads might be brought together in the broad context of Asia: ibid, ch 2. For a similar example, in the context of East Asia, see Jiunn-Rong Yeh and Wen-Chen Chang, 'The Emergence of East Asian Constitutionalism: Features in Comparison' (2011) 59 American Journal of Comparative Law 805.

[16] Maartje de Visser, 'Constitutional Comparisons and Language' in Vicki Jackson and Madhav Khosla (eds), *Comparative Constitutional Law: Redefining the Field* (forthcoming).

[17] On the contributions of the Soulbury Constitution to these differences in Sri Lanka, see Roshan de Silva-Wijereratne, 'Dominion Status and Compromised Foundations' in Kevin YL Tan and Ridwanul Hoque (eds), *Constitutional Foundings in South Asia* (Hart Publishing 2021) 121. On Myanmar, see Melissa Crouch, *The Constitution of Myanmar* (Hart Publishing 2019) ch 2. As these pieces show, such divisions often have their origins in colonialism and its immediate aftermath, but they constitute a present reality, nevertheless.

community or communities plays a foundational role as the people, whether *demos* or *demoi*, on whom the continuing legitimacy of governance depends, with all that legitimacy entails.

Not all aspects of societal culture are relevant to the resilience of constitutional democracy. Many are, however; or, at least, may turn out to be. Examples, which are by no means exhaustive, include attitudes of trust or, alternatively, mistrust towards the state or other segments of society; preferences for either confrontational or consensual decision-making; expectations of either personalised or relatively impersonalised politics; historical experience of governance in action; and assumptions about matrilineal or patrilineal societal roles. These and other cultural traits of a general community may have a bearing on the substance of a constitution, including its operation in practice, on the process of constitution-making, on the style of democracy, or on all three.

Many sectoral communities may be relevant to the success or failure of democracy-building. They are grouped here in three categories. One comprises the political classes: those who might be expected to be candidates for elected office and to occupy a position as representatives in governments and legislatures. Hereditary heads of state might be included in this category as well, notwithstanding contemporary expectations of neutrality. This group is the focus of political culture, which may also draw elements from elsewhere, including society as a whole.[18] A second sectoral category comprises those associated with the legal system, including, critically, the judiciary. These generate a legal culture, components of which potentially affect judicial independence and constitutional adjudication, amongst other matters of a constitutional kind.[19] A more amorphous third category comprises other public institutions, including the military, the police, the civil service, and other independent public authorities. While these might be described collectively as having an institutional culture, it is evident that this may often need further disaggregation to isolate, for example, the distinctive role of the military or of an electoral commission. Other sectoral communities may need specific consideration in some contexts, including religious groupings, where these play a role in public life.[20]

The cultures of each of these sectoral communities may present challenges to be noted and either managed or averted in the course of democratic transition. They may also present opportunities to be seized and used to underpin a transition and strengthen its endurance over time. Examples will be drawn out from the case studies, as they are introduced in the next part, but a few may be mentioned now

[18] Lucian W Pye, 'Political Culture' in Joel Krieger (ed), *The Oxford Companion to Politics of the World* (2nd edn, Oxford University Press 2001) <www.oxfordreference.com/view/10.1093/acref/9780195117394.001.0001/acref-9780195117394-e-0596> accessed 13 October 2022.

[19] Chang and others (n 11) 69.

[20] See e.g. the discussion of Sinhala-Buddhist nationalism in de Silva-Wijereratne (n 17).

to illustrate the point. The political culture developed under what effectively was a one-party state in Ethiopia added to the challenges that Abiy Ahmed faced in building on his unexpected elevation as prime minister in 2018.[21] In Sri Lanka, the culture of key independent institutions, including the Electoral Commission, was critical in confirming the election of President Sirisena and thus providing an opportunity for change, even if, in the end, the opportunity proved short-lived.[22] In Thailand, the culture of the military fostered through its long relationship with an interventionist monarchy has played a central role in the cycle of coups and failed constitutions.[23]

2.3 Constitutional Culture

Culture that is labelled 'constitutional' intuitively is relevant to constitutional resilience and decay. The primary purpose of this segment is to consider what it comprises to justify the label. As the parts that follow show, constitutional culture might be used in at least two ways. It has a diagnostic use, to assist understanding of both resilience and backsliding. It also has an instrumental use, to anticipate and maximise opportunities to strengthen a constitutional order and to avoid, or at least manage, pending challenges. In this latter regard, it may contribute to a constitutional imaginary that supports resilience, subject to the caveat that an imaginary may be negative as well.[24]

A generic understanding of constitutional culture links it in some way to constitutions, also understood generically. One way of describing this link is by reference to 'ideas, values, attitudes and opinions ... with respect to ... the constitution'.[25] If the notion of a constitution itself is narrowed, to refer only to those arrangements that potentially satisfy the expectations of liberal constitutionalism, the category of constitutional culture may be refined further still. In these circumstances it is likely to include, for example, cultural traits that have

[21] This observation points to assumptions and practices developed during the long hold on power of the Ethiopian People's Revolutionary Democratic Front (EPRDF), not on any deep-seated authoritarian 'tradition' of the kind criticised in Tobias Hagmann, 'Ethiopian Political Culture Strikes Back: A Reply to J Abbink' (2006) 105 African Affairs 605.

[22] Dinesha Samararatne, 'Resilience through Synergy? The Legal Complex in Sri Lanka's Constitutional Crisis' (12 November 2021) Asian Journal of Law and Society <https://papers.ssrn.com/sol3/papers.cfm?abstract_id=3962700> accessed 13 October 2022.

[23] Nicholas Farrelly, 'Why Democracy Struggles: Thailand's Elite Coup Culture' (2013) 67 Australian Journal of International Affairs 281.

[24] Cheryl Saunders, 'Constitutional Imaginary: A Contribution to a Blog to Honour a Lifetime of Achievements of Professor Roberto Toniatti in Comparative Constitutional Law' (*Roberto Toniatti*, 1 December 2020) <www.robertotoniatti.eu/contributi/constitutional-imaginary> accessed 13 October 2022.

[25] LM Friedman, *The Republic of Choice: Law, Authority and Culture* (Harvard University Press 1990) 4, quoted in Chang and others (n 11) 68.

a bearing on the acceptance of the value of limitations on power, the assumption of individual worth, and compliance with constitutional norms. A nice version of this understanding of constitutional culture refers to 'implicit and explicit ... thoughts, feelings, beliefs, impressions and norms ... about the nature, scope and function of constitutional constraints; the thoughts and feelings about balancing political expediency with constitutional principle; and levels of trust and cooperation, within one's community and also with strangers'.[26] As this quote suggests, these cultural traits may be positive or negative from the standpoint of constitutionalism.

Defined in these ways, constitutional culture is infused by some, but not all, of the cultural attributes of the communities discussed in the earlier part. The attitudes of the political elite towards working within constitutional norms, or of the military towards civilian control, clearly contribute to the prevailing constitutional culture. A preference of the general community for consensual rather than adversarial decision-making may feed into constitutional culture but will not necessarily do so. It is not necessary to draw the borders precisely. It may be accepted that, like law, constitutions operate within a broader cultural context, aspects of which may become relevant in resolving particular problems in particular circumstances. It may also be accepted that, in any polity, the elements of culture combine and interact with each other in ways that constitute a discrete whole, understood as more than a collection of its composite parts. In examining and responding to the causes of resilience and decay, it will sometimes be useful to reflect on constitutional culture in this broad, collective sense. Equally, however, in some cases, there will be additional insights to be gained in isolating and understanding the societal and sectoral cultures that contribute to it.

So far, this segment has focused on the relevance of constitutional culture to resilience or decay in a generic constitutional setting. Often, however, it will be useful, for diagnostic or instrumental purposes, to focus on the character of a particular constitution or particular features of it. Which features of a constitution require particular attention, from the standpoint of culture, depend on context. Likely examples, however, include constitutional settings in which there is a move from autocratic to democratic government, from a unitary to a federal form of the state, from a parliamentary to a presidential system or vice versa, or from a stratified to a more equal society. These and other common constitutional trajectories invariably also require cultural change if they are to succeed, presenting the challenge of whether—and, if so, how—such change can be effected, deliberately and within a transitional time frame.

[26] N Wenzel, 'Towards a Research Agenda on the Emergence of (Informal) Constitutional Culture into (Formal) Constitutional Order' (2012) 5 Studies in Emergent Order 1, 3, quoted in Chang and others (n 11) 68.

3. Democratic Opportunity

3.1 Case Studies

The seven case study countries on which this volume draws for insights into the dynamics of democratic resilience and decay are diverse in many ways: history; geography; experiences during the age of colonisation; legal system; culture; and experience of governance, now and over time.[27] Importantly, however, there are similarities between them as well. In none does constitutional democracy as presently understood have deep historical roots, although all had experience over centuries with other modes of governance before the advent of the age of colonisation. In all of them, written constitutions and elements of democracy were introduced in consequence of Western imperialism, beginning to take their present form within the last century as imperial powers withdrew and independence was achieved.[28] Experience since independence has varied. Even so, however, they share some experiences with democratisation that justify their selection for this volume and help to make comparison productive. These are canvassed below as a means of introducing the salient features of the case studies, as a foundation for the discussions of culture that follow.[29]

First, and most obviously, none of these states presently is a fully developed democracy on any of the common indices of measurement.[30] These indices are imperfect, not least in viewing democracy through a selective lens.[31] In the third decade of the twenty-first century, democracy is at risk in many of even the most apparently established democracies, further blurring the borders between categories.[32] Even so, on any view, in all seven states, the system of government is, or has been, such that new opportunities for democratisation are significant. The nature and extent of the democratic shortfall varies across the cases at the time the events on which the chapter focuses occurred. In all, however, the shortfall involves, in some degree, limited civil and political rights, concentration of power in the executive with corresponding implications for the arbitrary exercise of public power, some

[27] The case studies are Ethiopia, Malaysia, Maldives, Myanmar, Sri Lanka, Thailand, and The Gambia.

[28] Not all were colonised, but colonisation was influential, nevertheless. For an account of the spread of 'modern' constitutions, see Linda Colley, *The Gun the Ship and the Pen* (Profile Books 2021).

[29] In using examples from the case studies for the remainder of this chapter, I draw on the seven country chapters in this volume unless otherwise indicated.

[30] See e.g. the distinction between 'full' and 'flawed' democracies: Economist Intelligence Unit, 'Democracy Index 2020: In Sickness and in Health?' (*Economist Intelligence Unit*, 2020) <www.eiu.com/n/campaigns/democracy-index-2020> accessed 13 October 2022.

[31] Amongst a vast critical literature, see e.g. Carl Henrik Knutsen, 'Measuring Effective Democracy' (2010) 31 International Political Science Review 109.

[32] On the challenges of such measurements, see Todd Landman, 'Developing Democracy: Concepts, Measures and Empirical Relationships' (*International Institute for Democracy and Electoral Assistance (International IDEA)*, 2007) <www.idea.int/sites/default/files/speeches/Developing-Democracy-Concepts-Measures-and-Empirical-Relationships-PDF.pdf> accessed 13 October 2022.

manipulation of the electoral system, and shortfalls in compliance with the rule of law, even in its limited, procedural sense. Another problem, shared by one or more cases, is inequality, including on the basis of ethnic identity, militarisation, and general instability of the constitutional order.

In each case, nevertheless, the democratic glass is, or was, also at least partly full. Even before the opportunity for democracy-building with which each case study deals, there had been some exposure to elected government within a constitutional framework. In two of them, Sri Lanka and Malaysia, elected government had been the norm since independence in 1948 and 1957, respectively. Sri Lanka, although not Malaysia, also had had repeated experiences of peaceful change of government, through election, during that time. In Ethiopia, the Constitution of 1995 ostensibly provided for a federal parliamentary democracy, although in practice the country operated as a centralised one-party state, in which elections became more competitive from 2005. In Thailand, periods of parliamentary government had occurred since the end of the absolute monarchy in 1932, albeit constrained by the monarch and the military and interspersed, astonishingly frequently, with coups. In Maldives, halting progress with constitutional government had been underway since 1932, in a form that served to underpin the legitimacy of strong executive government, whether as a sultanate or a republic, until a more democratic constitution came into force in 2008. In The Gambia, the 22 years of repressive, although formally elected authoritarian government, which came to an end in 2016, had been preceded by decades of multiparty government since independence in 1965, albeit without a change of government. Even Myanmar, with its almost 50 years of effectively military government from 1962, had experienced some, admittedly rocky years of government under a democratic constitution after independence in 1947 and had returned to a form of constitutional government in 2008.

The other shared experience is the presentation of the opportunity for deepening democracy itself. In all states except Thailand and, perhaps, Maldives, this took the form of the emergence of a political leader through political processes framed by an existing constitution, claiming commitment to reforms of a democratic kind. In Sri Lanka, The Gambia, Myanmar, and Maldives the leader emerged through elections: Sirisena in Sri Lanka in 2015, Barrow in The Gambia in 2016, and Suu Kyi in Myanmar in 2015. In a variation on the theme, in Ethiopia and Malaysia, the leadership changed through the internal dynamics of a coalition when Abiy Ahmed became prime minister of Ethiopia and Mahathir in Malaysia, both in 2018. In none of these cases did the elevation to power of a reformist political leader emerge in a vacuum. On the contrary, the development was variously made possible by public protests, the ethical behaviour of independent institutions, the actions of political parties, and international pressure. In Thailand and Maldives, the democratic opportunity was somewhat different to the extent that it took the form of the promulgation of a new, more democratic constitution. The Thai Constitution of 1997, however, was itself made possible by the relative absence of the military from politics following a popular uprising in 1992. In Maldives, the democratic Constitution of 2008 followed the formation of political parties and other liberalising changes in the immediately preceding years. The election of Nasheed, as the first president under the new Constitution, also with a reformist agenda, again highlights the significance of leadership.

In each of these cases, democratisation faltered and the opportunity apparently was lost, prompting the inquiry in this volume into causes. In Myanmar, the slow struggle for both peace and democracy by the National League for Democracy (NLD) government under the 2008 Constitution was brought to an abrupt end by the military coup in early 2021, repudiating the results of the recent elections. In Sri Lanka, the promise of a new constitution dealing with long-running tensions over devolution and the executive presidency came to nothing under Sirisena, power was resumed by anti-reformist groups, and the executive presidency was strengthened. In Maldives, Nasheed was ousted early, setting in train an unproductive pattern of struggles for political power, exposing weak institutions, and failing to further democratic reform. In Malaysia, the Mahathir reforms underdelivered, effectively returning the United Malays National Organisation (UMNO) to the power it had enjoyed since independence. In Ethiopia, the impetus for reform collapsed and ethnic divisions were reignited to the point of civil war, although Ahmed was returned to power and remains in office. In Thailand, the 1997 Constitution was abrogated in yet another coup in 2006, following the controversial premiership of Thaksin, and there has been democratic deterioration since. In The Gambia, a new democratic constitution drafted in a broadly consultative process ultimately failed to pass, when it did not attract the requisite majority in the legislature.

The passage of time already has begun to show that these opportunities were not entirely wasted and that some progress was made, on which the future could build. Most obviously, the Draft Constitution for The Gambia may yet pass, if agreement can be reached on changes to the relatively few, if significant, contested provisions, one of which concerns the backdating of the point for calculation of term limits, to the detriment of the incumbent president. In Malaysia and Ethiopia, the leadership changes broke the hegemony of the respective ruling, ethnically structured coalitions, shifting the goal posts to that extent for the future.[33] In Malaysia, the reduction of the voting age to 18 during the short reform period may also prove to be a significant development. In Maldives, the 2008 Constitution remains in force, and there is active debate about how to improve it in ways that would be likely to deepen democracy, including through decentralisation. In Thailand, too, despite

[33] Following his electoral victory in June 2021, Prime Minister Abiy Ahmed initiated a National Dialogue Commission in Ethiopia to lay the ground for constitutional change, the outcome of which is too early to predict but that is significant for present purposes: Seleshi Tessema, 'Ethiopia Forms 1st-Ever National Dialogue, Reconciliation Commission' (*AA*, 29 December 2021) <www.aa.com.tr/en/africa/ethiopia-forms-1st-ever-national-dialogue-reconciliation-commission/2460635> accessed 13 October 2022.

the discouraging, downward spiral, the still-important precedent of the 1997 Constitution provides some encouragement to democratic forces in what is, at least in part, an intergenerational struggle. In broadly similar vein, in Sri Lanka, the bright spots in the story that began with the election of Sirisena, including the roles of independent agencies together, perhaps, with object lessons from the failures of constitutional reform, provide some fuel for democratic reformers. Arguably, these factors played a role in the fall of President Rajapaksa in July 2022, following widespread public protest, offering some promise, not yet realised, of constitutional reform. Even in Myanmar, where the outlook is particularly bleak, the military takeover has been repudiated by a government with democratic credentials in exile and has consolidated a broad range of opposition forces in ways that provide some encouragement for the future.

3.2 Considerations of Culture

Culture is potentially relevant at several points in the democratisation stories that emerge from the case studies. It may assist to explain the opportunities for democratisation that arose and, by extension, to anticipate the conditions that may facilitate others. Consideration of culture may also assist in understanding the regression that occurred in each case and in developing insights from the understanding that may have future use.

Culture is by no means the only factor in play in either development.[34] Others are reflected in thematic chapters elsewhere in this volume and need only briefly be mentioned here. The practicalities of politics, including intra-coalition relationships, sometimes crosscut by ethnic loyalties, were a major factor both in creating the democratic moment and in causing it to fail in Ethiopia, Sri Lanka, and Maldives. Election outcomes were significant in creating democratic opportunities in The Gambia, Sri Lanka, Myanmar, and Malaysia and contributed to its decline in Sri Lanka, Thailand, and Maldives. The constitutional and legal framework played a role in almost every case, insofar as the actions taken were enabled or, at least, claimed to be consistent with the current Constitution and supporting law. In some cases, including Sri Lanka, Thailand, Malaysia, and Myanmar, other public institutions contributed, for better or worse, to the events that occurred: courts, fourth-branch institutions, the military, and the monarchy. In some, most obviously The Gambia, the people did so as well, through public protests of varying intensity. In all cases, while both the rise and decline of democratic opportunity occurred

[34] An instructive account of the relevance of a broad range of political, economic, and demographic conditions, especially in divided societies, is in Nicholas Haysom, 'Nation-Building and Constitution-Making in Divided Societies' in Asanga Welikala (ed), *The Sri Lankan Republic at 40: Reflections on Constitutional History, Theory and Practice* (Centre for Policy Alternatives 2012) 863.

within states, it did so against a complex regional and international backdrop, exerting pressures towards democracy and occasionally playing an active role, exemplified by the intervention of Senegal in The Gambia.

Even so, culture is part of each story. The roles that it appears to have played differ somewhat between opportunity and regression, which are considered separately in what follows.

Three broad points might be made, with varying degrees of certainty, about the role of culture in the emergence of the democratic opportunities around which the case studies centre. One is that the marked degree of formal constitutional compliance, or claimed compliance, which was sustained even as democratic opportunities eroded, suggests widely held attitudes and beliefs indicative of constitutional culture in this admittedly narrow sense. It manifested itself not only in the way in which key actors worked within the constitutional framework, critically in holding and participating in elections, but also in the pursuit of formal constitutional change when the framework was deemed deficient. In an extreme example, even as the junta stepped in to quash the outcome of the 2021 election in Myanmar, it claimed, however fancifully, to be working within the 2008 Constitution.[35] Thailand, inevitably, is an exception, in which the cycle of coup and post-coup recovery itself has cultural foundations. Even here, however, coups invariably are followed by constitutions, both interim and ostensibly final, with some attention to the suitability of the process by which they are made.[36] This culture of formal, if sometimes contrived, constitutional compliance provided a foundation for all the democratic opportunities in the case studies and, in principle, could do so again.

In a more tentative point about the contribution of culture to democratic opportunity with hindsight, in at least some cases, the democratic moment took its place in a drawn-out, although not necessarily linear, progression towards more limited government by consent. The underlying attitudes and beliefs generated and exemplified by this progression arguably contributed to the will and understanding to take advantage of democratic opportunity, should it occur. The history of Myanmar, Maldives, and The Gambia can be viewed in this way; perhaps also Ethiopia and Thailand. The point is less obvious in Sri Lanka and Malaysia, where democracy has more established roots and the emergence of a reformist leader more obviously occurred in the course of ordinary politics. In either set of cases, however, the broad trajectory of governance suggests a cultural base on which democracy might build.

A third cultural influence on democratic opportunity, which is highlighted by some of the case studies but which may be significant for any democratic transition,

[35] Sebastian Strangio, 'Was Myanmar's Coup Legal? And Does It Matter?' (*The Diplomat*, 17 February 2021) <https://thediplomat.com/2021/02/was-myanmars-coup-legal-and-does-it-matter> accessed 13 October 2022.

[36] Kittipong Thavevong, 'With 20 Constitutions, Thailand Joins a Select League' *The Nation* (10 June 2017) <www.nationthailand.com/perspective/30317723> accessed 13 October 2022.

underpins the actions of key institutions in support of the democratic moment.[37] If, as in so many of these cases, the democratic moment arises from the election of a political leader with a reformist platform, institutions that contribute to success may include courts, electoral bodies, law officers, and, perhaps, the people themselves. In fraught political circumstances, the beliefs and values of each of these groups can influence what they do and how they do it. Examples in the case studies that make the point include the role of courts and fourth-branch institutions in Sri Lanka following the Sirisena election[38] and the mediating role of the monarchy in Malaysia as the Mahathir coalition unravelled. Culture may also underpin inaction. A comparison of the role of the military in civilian life in Malaysia and Thailand makes the point.[39]

Culture also played both a general and more specific role in causing the opportunities for democratisation to be lost. A general factor was the weakness of democratic culture in a form that underpins, for example, acceptance of limitations on power, internalisation of the need for probity, tolerance of decisions of a democratically chosen government, understanding of the need for give and take in achieving change or working within a coalition, and assumptions of the centrality of political equality, irrespective of ethnic or ideological division. Weakness of the culture underpinning general democratic practice, particularly in conditions of stress, contributed to the failure of promised reforms in Sri Lanka, Maldives, Ethiopia, and Malaysia and to the disappointing performance of the governments from which so much had been expected. Ultimately, it also contributed to the collapse of such governments in Maldives, Sri Lanka, Thailand, and Malaysia.

More specific cultural explanations of why these democratic opportunities passed are legion. They include, most obviously, the assumptions of suzerainty by the military in Myanmar, the alliance between the military and the monarchy in Thailand, and indications in, for example, Maldives, that what is involved in judicial independence and impartiality were not adequately grasped.[40] Culture influenced substantive choices as well. So the challenge of agreement on constitutional design was exacerbated in Sri Lanka, Maldives, and Myanmar by hostility to federalism and other forms of effective decentralisation on the part of influential elites and segments of the general community that appear to have cultural dimensions. In a further variation on the theme of the potential relevance of culture, the failures

[37] The 'fourth-branch' or 'guarantor' institutions, which have attracted increasing interest for their potential to support democracy, may have a particular role to play here: see e.g. Tarunabh Khaitan, 'Guarantor Institutions' (2021) 19 Asian Journal of Comparative Law 1.

[38] Samararatne (n 22).

[39] Chin Kin Wah, 'Reflections on the Shaping of Strategic Cultures in Southeast Asia' in Derek de Cunha (ed), *Southeast Asian Perspectives on Security* (ISEAS Publishing 2000) 1, with particularly pertinent observations about Malaysia at 11.

[40] In relation to Maldives, see e.g. 'UN News Service, UN Expert Urges Greater Independence for Courts in the Maldives' (*UN News Service*, 24 February 2013) <www.refworld.org/docid/512dd7bf2.html> accessed 13 October 2022.

of democratic constitutional change in The Gambia, Maldives, Sri Lanka, and Myanmar at critical moments for the deepening of democracy may also be linked with a cultural assumption that parliament or its alter ego[41] has constituent authority, limiting inclusion and transparency and making it significantly more difficult to distinguish negotiations of a constitutional kind from politics as usual.[42]

3.3 Democracy and Constitutions

Democracies are supported by a constitutional framework, underpinned by the rule of law.[43] Typically, a formal, entrenched constitution lies at the core of this framework, albeit embellished by other laws, interpretations, principles, and practices. In reflecting on the causes of democratic resilience and decay, questions arise about how much weight should be placed on the relationship between democracy and constitutions and about the extent to which solutions to problems with democracy are likely to lie in the constitutional protections provided for it.

The cases in this volume offer further insights into the relationship between democracy and constitutions, showing that it is more complex than might at first sight seem, in ways that appear to implicate culture. This section of the chapter concludes with an analysis of the cases from this perspective. It develops three perceptions in particular. One is that at least some of the constitutions under which the democratic moment arose provided for relatively few of the trappings of democracy, apart from elections. The second is that even where the constitutional text seems facially democratic, democracy proved not to be assured. The third is that, while the consolidation of the democratic opportunity required constitutional change in some cases, it did not do so in all of them.

The earlier examination of the cases showed that, in five of them (Ethiopia, The Gambia, Malaysia, Myanmar, and Sri Lanka), the opportunities for strengthening democracy emerged under existing constitutions. These constitutions varied in the extent of their democratic credentials, with Myanmar at the nadir, but all had democratic shortcomings and all provided a framework for a less-than-ideal democracy that the democratic moment had the potential to improve. As noted earlier, the degree of formal constitutional compliance that enabled the democratic moment to emerge seems all the more remarkable in these circumstances, and suggests the influence of a limited form of constitutional culture. The decline that

[41] The reference here is to a legislature that reconstitutes itself as a constitution-making body, a practice that is familiar in Sri Lanka. On the origins of this practice, see Asanga Welikala, 'Specialist in Omniscience?' in Harshan Kumarasingham (ed), *Constitution-Making in Asia* (Routledge 2016) 112.

[42] Cheryl Saunders and Anna Dziedzic, 'Parliamentary Sovereignty and Written Constitutions in Comparative Perspective' in Asanga Welikala (ed), *The Sri Lankan Republic at 40: Reflections on Constitutional History, Theory and Practice* (Centre for Policy Alternatives 2012) 475.

[43] Chris Thornhill, *A Sociology of Constitutions* (Cambridge University Press 2011) 372, describing constitutions as 'functional preconditions for the positive abstraction of political power'.

followed, nevertheless, was consistent with the tenor of each of the constitutions and unsurprising, to that extent. On the other hand, in each of the other two cases, Thailand and Maldives, the democratic opportunity took the form of the promulgation of a new constitution that had a familiar range of democratic features. The decline that followed cannot be attributed to the constitutions alone, suggesting that, in these cases and, almost certainly, in the others as well, additional factors were at work, including—significantly—culture.

Another aspect of the link between constitutions and democracy suggested by the cases is also instructive: the relationship between the democratic opportunity and constitutional change. This relationship takes at least three forms. In two cases, Thailand and Maldives, the democratic opportunity was created by a new constitution and, in that sense, is consistent with orthodox assumptions about the role of constitutions in democratic transition. In another two cases, Sri Lanka and The Gambia, attempts to agree and promulgate a new constitution were a proximate outcome of a democratic opportunity. This also seems broadly consistent with the expected order of things, particularly if the failure of constitutional reform is also equated to the failure of the democratic moment, as was the case in Sri Lanka. In the final three cases, however (Malaysia, Ethiopia, and Myanmar), there was no immediate connection between the democratic opportunity that emerged and a new, or even changed, constitution. Admittedly, the case of Myanmar is ambiguous because the need for constitutional change of some kind in due course seemed evident, and a somewhat half-hearted attempt to change particular provisions of the Constitution failed in the period before the coup. There was no such ambiguity in Malaysia and Ethiopia, where it was assumed at the time that democracy could deepen under the existing Constitution and there were no undertakings about significant constitutional change. The assumptions were not fanciful, even though, in the end, they were not realised.

These seven case studies suggest that constitutional form and substance alone are not determinative in consolidating democratisation. In some cases, impetus for democracy may be productive even under a constitution that has democratic flaws. Conversely, democracy may falter even under a constitution with apparently sound democratic credentials.[44] Culture is an influential factor in each of these scenarios.

At some point in democratisation, nevertheless, in varying degrees, depending on context, constitutions themselves are potentially important. At the very least, they may protect procedures that can act as a catalyst for democracy, provide a framework for the principles and institutions on which democracy depends, and

[44] It may be, of course, that the Constitution does not adequately provide for the requirements of democracy in the particular context, a shortfall that also may have links with culture. On the demands placed on constitutions in deeply pluralist societies, see Welikala, 'Specialist in Omniscience?' (n 41). See also Haysom (n 34).

support the resilience of constitutional democracy over time. Often, they may need to do more, to respond to diversity or to a 'legacy of conflict'.[45] Section 4 considers how that potential can be furthered through understanding and managing the interaction between constitutions and culture.

4. Constitutional Endurance

The relevance of culture to constitutional endurance is explored in this section through three phases in the life cycle of a constitution, described here as the phases during which the foundations are laid, new constitutional arrangements are implemented, and the Constitution is consolidated over time.[46] These phases are treated separately for analytical purposes, even though they are not necessarily either discrete or neatly sequential in lived experience. As the case studies show, some of these phases may not be experienced at all in the course of responding to an opportunity for democratisation. In both Malaysia and Ethiopia, the opportunity arose under relatively established constitutions, during the phase described here as consolidation over time, offering support for taking its potential seriously.

The interaction between constitutions and culture involves consideration of both constitutional substance and process.[47] Process is more obviously significant in the foundational phase, when a constitution is made, but it is potentially relevant in the phases that follow, as the Constitution operates in practice, also if further constitutional change is sought. Intuitively, it seems likely to be useful for a process of constitution-making that has been effective in establishing a foundation for a positive constitutional culture to be reinforced in practice over time.[48] Arguably, for example, in Maldives, the shift in the 2008 Constitution from approval of constitutional change by a Special Majlis to approval by the People's Majlis, as the ordinary legislature, was detrimental in cultural terms, equating constitutional change with ordinary politics and contributing to the deterioration that occurred.[49]

The concept of constitutional imaginary is also a recurring theme, linked to culture, that potentially cuts across all three phases. Jan Komarek's definition of the concept adapts readily enough to constitutional democracy: 'sets of ideas and beliefs that help to motivate and at the same time justify the practice of government

[45] Haysom (n 34) 875.

[46] These three phases are well understood, although the third typically is taken for granted. See e.g. United Nations (UN) Secretary-General, 'Guidance Note on United Nations Assistance to Constitution-Making Processes' (*United Nations and the Rule of Law*, 2009) <www.un.org/ruleoflaw/files/Guidance_Note_United_Nations_Assistance_to_Constitution-making_Processes_FINAL.pdf> accessed 13 October 2022.

[47] Ibid.

[48] The insistence in *David Ndii v Attorney General* [2021] eKLR (13 May 2021) in Kenya that certain types of constitutional change required a process that reflected the original exercise of constituent power is an unusual example of judicial recognition of the significance of continuity.

[49] Constitution of the Republic of Maldives (2008) ch XII.

and collective self-rule'.[50] Many, perhaps most, states have ideas and beliefs, often born of historical experience, on which they might draw to build or strengthen an imaginary that supports a constitutional democratic culture.[51] The proud democratic story of The Gambia in the years immediately following independence is one example. The long, unbroken, history of post-independence parliamentary government in Malaysia is another. The most obvious opportunity to reinforce a positive constitutional imaginary is during the foundation phase when, in addition, it may also be reflected in constitutional text. To enhance resilience, however, it needs continued life over time, with all that 'life' suggests in terms of adaptation and change.

A constitutional imaginary can also have a negative impact on constitutional democracy if, for example, it emphasises the dominance of one community over others for the purposes of 'collective self-rule'.[52] Where such an imaginary is influential, it also needs to be understood and, if possible, countered in strengthening democratic resilience, however gradual a process that may be.

4.1 Foundations

This is the phase during which a new democratic constitution, or constitutional changes with democratising effect, are negotiated, formulated, and brought into operation. During this phase, then, the legal framework for constitutional democracy is settled, at least for the time being. Equally importantly, however, this foundational phase offers opportunities to build commitment to the Constitution, ensure shared understanding of its significance and purpose, and encourage internalisation of what it requires on the part of relevant actors, including the public at large. Both the process by which the Constitution is made and the substance of the Constitution itself are relevant to these ends.

Culture may be significant for both process and substance. Culture, for this purpose, encompasses both societal culture and relevant sectoral cultures. Which aspects of culture are relevant and the roles that they play depend very significantly on context. Any constitutional transition implicates culture in some ways. In some cases, however, the challenges presented by culture are more complex and

[50] Jan Komarek, 'Why Read the Transformation of Europe Today? On the Limits of a Liberal Constitutional Imaginary' (*Imagine: European Constitutional Imaginaries*, 3 September 2020) <www.imagine-const.eu/imagine-working-paper-no-10-why-read-the-transformation-of-europe-today-on-the-limits-of-a-liberal-constitutional-imaginary-by-jan-komarek-icourts-working-paper-series-no-213> accessed 13 October 2022. See also Latham-Gambi (n 7).

[51] There may be overlap here with the idea of a 'critical interpretation of national history' developed by William Partlett and Dinesha Samararatne, 'Redeeming the National in Constitutional Argument' (2021) World Constitutional Law 461.

[52] The 'imaginary' of Sinhala-Buddhist nationalism in Sri Lanka is a case in point: de Silva-Wijereratne (n 17). See also Welikala, 'Specialist in Omniscience?' (n 41) 121.

demanding than others.[53] Most obviously, if new constitutional arrangements involve transition from an undemocratic to a democratic regime, the cultural challenges will be greater than if the changes are made within an existing democratic, or even proto-democratic, order. The precise nature of the challenge will depend on the earlier regime, of which single-party or other forms of authoritarian government, military rule, a history of repeated coups, prolonged internal or external armed conflict, and colonialism are examples. In addition to the cultural opportunities and risks that arise in any constitutional transition, in cases of these kinds, a new democratic culture needs to be built and non-democratic cultures neutralised to the extent that they detract from the operation of the new Constitution.

Four types of measures might be considered during the foundation phase to enhance resilience with an eye to the cultural context.

The first is to understand and be alert to significant aspects of culture that may be engaged in designing and operating new constitutional arrangements. Some of these may concern process: assumptions about modes of decision-making or styles of discussion and negotiation. Some may concern the substance of new constitutional arrangements. Aversion to federalisation in Sri Lanka and insistence on federalism in Myanmar as a *sine qua non* are obvious but superficial examples. They serve also to draw attention to the need to probe more deeply, to consider what 'federalisation' is understood to involve in context and whether there is a shared understanding.[54] Some aspects of culture may be much less obvious or appreciated only with hindsight. The attitudes and habits formed by long periods of rule by a single party or coalition, as in Ethiopia or Malaysia, are possible examples.

Building on this understanding, a second type of measure can maximise the opportunities that culture provides in conducting a meaningful constitution-making process or in determining the principles, institutions, and practices to be included in the Constitution itself. Recourse to a Special Majlis for constitution-making in Maldives is an example of relying on a culturally significant process, but there are other more subtle ways in which culture might have a bearing on process as well. One, perhaps reflected in the process adopted in The Gambia, is to accommodate a cultural assumption that a new constitution requires parliamentary approval, where such an assumption exists, by combining the role of the parliament with an inclusive, consultative, pre-ratification process to distinguish it from ordinary politics and facilitate popular involvement. Where this occurs, however, as the case of The Gambia shows, it is necessary also to anticipate the need to build support

[53] This general idea is sometimes captured by describing the Constitution as 'transformative': for an early and influential formulation, see Pius Lange, 'Transformative Constitutionalism' (*Prestige Lecture*, 9 October 2006) <https://gimmenotes.co.za/wp-content/uploads/2019/01/1238154663PiusLangaSpeech.pdf> accessed 13 October 2022.

[54] In Myanmar, for example, underlying the competing aspirations for a 'democratic federal Union' or a 'federal democratic Union' are different understandings of whether Myanmar should be regarded as a 'coming together' or a 'holding together' federation: Crouch (n 17) 214.

for the draft within the legislature itself, so as to ensure the success of ratification, ideally with significant consensus.

Cultural expectations may offer opportunities in designing the substance of the Constitution as well to the extent that they can be incorporated into new constitutional arrangements. The unusual Malaysian institutions of the Conference of Rulers and the Yang di-Pertuan Agong that it periodically elects are a case in point. There was no comparable arrangement for constituting a head of state elsewhere in the world when these institutions were established in the 1957 Constitution.[55] They drew upon earlier practice in the Malay states, however, and have proved resilient and adaptable enough to remain useful in the slowly evolving Malaysian democracy for more than 60 years, as recent events in Malaysia show.

A third type of measure, also building on the first, involves anticipating any clash between established aspects of culture and new constitutional arrangements and, to the extent possible, guarding against fallout through the constitution-making process, constitutional design, and extra-constitutional measures. Examples that might give rise to such a clash are legion: entrenched assumptions of executive hegemony, inexperience with the self-restraint required when election results change a government or public interests conflict with private interests, and acceptance of regular military involvement in civilian affairs. Overcoming these and other cultural threats to democratisation along whatever lines are desired is easier said than done and may take considerable time. It is unlikely to be a matter for constitutional text alone, although formally prescribed powers and procedures can help in some instances. It may also be necessary to consider, in countering some cultural tendencies, whether the cure might be worse than the disease or, at least, import cultural challenges of its own. In theory, for example, a shift from a presidential to a parliamentary system, as sometimes considered in Maldives, could assist to break down a concentration of executive power, but a parliamentary system requires distinctive cultural attitudes on the part of both legislature and executive which may take some time to develop, if they develop at all.[56]

A final type of measure directly anticipates the need for cultural change to support a new constitution by encouraging broad-based public and elite buy-in to the new arrangements during the foundation phase, ensuring national 'ownership'.[57] Internally, this might be done through the design of an appropriately inclusive constitution-making process, through attempts to build sufficient consensus on key issues and through effective and targeted information and education

[55] Andrew Harding, *The Constitution of Malaysia: A Contextual Analysis* (Bloomsbury 2012) 34.

[56] Elijah Ben-Zion Kaminsky, 'On the Comparison of Presidential and Parliamentary Governments (1997) 27 Presidential Studies Quarterly 221. Semi-presidential systems present different cultural challenges again, depending on the relative power held and exercised by the president. A useful introduction to the genre is Thomas Sedelius and Jenny Aberg, 'Semi-Presidential Systems' (*Oxford Bibliographies*, 3 December 2020) <www.oxfordbibliographies.com/view/document/obo-9780199756223/obo-9780199756223-0271.xml> accessed 13 October 2022.

[57] UN Secretary-General (n 46).

throughout the formative period. There is a message here for external actors as well, defined to mean those involved in the constitution-building process in some way who will not live under the constitution that results from it. National ownership of a kind that supports transition to a new constitutional culture requires external actors to temper the scope and manner of their involvement. It may also mean that they should be wary of overtly, or even covertly, privileging groups already supportive of a more democratic culture over those that are not if, at least, the effect is to achieve constitutional change with significant segments of the community still unsure, unsettled, or undecided. Broad-based national ownership seems more likely to be conducive to constitutional endurance, difficult though it may be to secure.[58]

4.2 Implementation

The implementation phase immediately follows ratification of a new constitution. It lasts until the new constitutional arrangements are bedded down; potentially, a period of years. This is the period during which new institutions are established, new rules promulgated, appointments made, power devolved, and, often, first elections held. In recognition of its significance, some countries establish institutions specifically charged to oversee implementation in the years immediately following introduction of a new constitution.[59] The implementation phase is also a critical period for fostering a culture that is responsive to the new constitutional arrangements, however, of a kind that is conducive to the effective functioning of a democratic state.[60] This is less readily accomplished by a formal implementation process alone, even if its brief reaches beyond technical requirements.[61]

Constitutional culture is not reliant on this phase alone; it is a consideration throughout the lifespan of a constitution. The period immediately following introduction of a new constitution nevertheless offers a valuable opportunity to influence the culture that develops, while some euphoria and memories of what was sought and achieved remain. This is also likely to be a difficult time, however, as the practical realities of operating a new and unfamiliar system of government are encountered. The degree of difficulty is reflected in the case studies: poor

58 Cheryl Saunders, 'International Involvement in Constitution-Making' in David Landau and Hanna Lerner (eds), *Comparative Constitution Making* (Edward Elgar 2019) 69.

59 The Commission for the Implementation of the Constitution in Kenya was an example: Constitution of Kenya (2010) Sch 6 s 6, art 262. For an analysis of its strengths and weaknesses, see Siyu Li, 'An Alternative Constitutional Implementation Mechanism? A Case Study of Kenya's Commission for the Implementation of the Constitution' (2020) 4 Indiana Journal of Constitutional Design, art 2 <www.repository.law.indiana.edu/cgi/viewcontent.cgi?article=1014&context=ijcd> accessed 13 October 2022.

60 Li (n 59).

61 In Kenya, for example, the Commission's functions include working with other commissions 'to ensure that the letter and spirit of the Constitution is respected': Constitution of Kenya (n 59) s 5(6).

relations between the president and the prime minister in the aftermath of the 19th Amendment in Sri Lanka; corruption allegations against governments under the 1997 Constitution in Thailand; and political infighting in Maldives during the implementation period, leading to the ousting of the elected president within three years. More often than not, as the case studies also show, the predictable difficulties of any democratic transition are exacerbated by fraught economic or security conditions that would challenge any democratic system.

The issue of culture therefore arises during this phase primarily in connection with the transfer from the old to the new. At a general level, it involves adapting existing 'values, premises and practices' to those required for the new constitutional order. More specifically, particular impediments to implementation may arise, which also have cultural dimensions.[62] There may be a misunderstanding of what the new Constitution requires, on the part of political actors or courts, or even the public at large. There may be hesitation or reluctance to put aspects of the Constitution fully into effect, a problem frequently encountered in the context of decentralisation or limitations on executive power. There may be deliberate delays in implementation or avoidance of constitutional requirements altogether, eroding the consensus on which the constitution is based, with implications for future resilience. Problems of governance that arise may be used as an excuse for constitutional breach rather than as issues to be managed within the framework of the constitution. The abrogation of the 1997 Constitution of Thailand by military coup in 2006 is an extreme case in point. As these examples suggest, the requirement for cultural adaptation applies across the polity during the implementation phase: most obviously to current and aspiring political actors at all levels of government but also to judges, the administration, fourth-branch institutions, the media, and the public. Depending on context, it may also apply to the military, a monarchy, religious orders, and others who may influence the operations of government.

Some of the measures that might be taken to enhance resilience during this phase, with an eye to the need to strengthen constitutional culture, are relatively straightforward. They apply whether there is a formal implementation process or not. They include both general and sector-specific education and training in the requirements of the new constitutional arrangements, in the light of the purposes they are intended to serve. They also include vigilance in attempting to head off constitutional problems to which culture is a contributing factor that can be anticipated in advance. There is value also in paying particular attention to the importance of early precedents in terms of, for example, peaceful and fair elections in the early years, judicial interpretations that enhance the purposes of the constitution,

[62] Siyu quotes the Kenyan Commission's summary of these, including 'the increasing trend by the Executive and some members of the Legislature to create grey areas regarding the interpretation of the Constitution': Li (n 59) 23.

and responsive patterns of behaviour in the administration. Other measures that are less obvious deserve mention as well. Prioritising effective government is one, including at sub-national levels. A positive constitutional culture is likely to be enhanced if, in its early years, a constitution is seen to provide a framework for a working system of government that actually delivers for its people. Another is that, when things go wrong, as inevitably they will, they should be managed within the confines of the Constitution in a manner that reinforces its legitimacy, rather than detracting from it. In these and other respects, external forces have roles to play as well. In particular, insofar as they can ease economic and security concerns without detracting from the responsibilities of the new political leaders, they should do so, in recognition of the sensitivity of this phase of a constitutional transition.

4.3 Endurance

A final phase encompasses the operation of a constitution for the rest of its effective existence, until it is replaced or, perhaps, significantly amended. During this phase, the constitutional moment, such as it was, has passed and the constitution provides a framework for day-to-day democratic politics, in constantly shifting domestic and global conditions to which it must adapt, formally or informally. No constitution is perfect and, while formal change is appropriate for some imperfections, stable constitutional democracy also involves making do, within constitutional limitations.

Two sets of issues will almost certainly arise during this lengthy phase, with relevance to constitutional endurance. The first involves threats to constitutional democracy, some of which may have been anticipated, although many may not. The variety of possibilities is endless, but the case studies offer a sample. These include emergencies of various kinds that put stress on democratic politics; interruptions and impediments to the democratic transfer of power; corruption; military intervention in civil politics; capture of the institutions of state by one dominant group; internal divisions, sometimes leading to armed conflict and, increasingly, incentivised by cyber campaigns; and destabilisation by other powerful states, including neighbour states. Unless handled effectively, these and other such situations present the risk of democratic backsliding.

A second set of issues with a bearing on endurance presents opportunities for deepening and strengthening democracy. As with threats, some of these may be anticipated, but others may be entirely unexpected. Again, there is a range, although, as the case studies show, one recurring opportunity is the election of a leader with a democratic reform programme. There is some overlap between issues that present threats and those that offer opportunities. Emergencies may be adapted to good purpose to build trust within the polity if the crisis is handled effectively. Usefully also, they may disturb the normal pattern of politics in a way that provides a catalyst for change.[63] An irregular transfer of power may elevate a democratic leader, as in Ethiopia and Malaysia. The intervention of neighbours may be positive, rather than negative, as in The Gambia. In all these cases, the challenge is to maximise the advantage that a democratic opportunity presents rather than to let it slip away.

As noted earlier in other contexts, many factors other than culture are at work in repelling threats and maximising opportunities in the interests of democratisation over the life span of a constitution. Culture has a role to play as well, however. The stronger the constitutional democratic culture developed before such events occur, the greater the likelihood of a positive outcome. Constitutional culture, for this purpose, is not just a general phenomenon reflecting the values, beliefs, and practices of the polity overall. Critically, it also embraces the culture of each of the key sectoral communities. In these conditions, if one community succumbs to a threat, others may assist to counter the problem. If constitutional culture is relatively robust, an opportunity for democratisation that presents itself in connection with the responsibilities of one sectoral community can be supported by others. Both threats and opportunities may be used to build constitutional culture as well, including through development of the constitutional imaginary. A threat that is overcome or mitigated can become a positive element of the national constitutional story. So too, more obviously, can an opportunity for democratisation, even if, in the end, it is not fully taken.

5. Conclusions

This chapter makes a case for the relevance of culture to understanding resilience or backsliding in constitutional democracies. It draws on the experiences of seven African and Asian states, in all of which opportunities to deepen democracy arose in relatively recent times, none of which, ultimately, came to fruition. These cases offered a rich range of experiences through which to explore the implications of culture. While details will differ, there is no reason to think that culture would not be similarly significant for the possibilities of democratisation in other contexts as well.

The chapter raises, but leaves unresolved, some of the more difficult questions about the interaction between culture and the resilience of constitutional democracies. One of the most important is whether—and, if so, how— an adequately supportive constitutional culture can actively be developed over the relatively short period during which new constitutional arrangements are approved and brought

[63] The impact of the earthquake in Nepal on the political deadlock over the new Constitution is an obvious case in point: Michael Hutt, 'Before the Dust Settled: Is Nepal's 2015 Settlement a Seismic Constitution?' (2020) 20 Conflict, Security and Development 379.

into effect. The experiences of established Western democracies offer little assistance in this regard because, in all of them, what now is understood as constitutional democracy evolved gradually, over relatively long periods of time, during which complementary cultures evolved as well. If answers are to be found, they lie in the experiences of states that have sought to democratise more quickly and more recently, typically in the context of decolonisation, adapting existing cultures to quite different constitutional requirements.

This chapter suggests some of the insights, positive as well as negative, that can be drawn from the experience of seven such states. These remain to be tested in other contexts, which are likely to yield insights of their own as well. Ironically, some of the conclusions about culture and constitutional democracy may also prove useful to established democracies as they grapple with their own causes of democratic malaise.

8
The Impact of COVID-19

Joelle Grogan

1. Introduction

The COVID-19 pandemic has placed an extreme degree of stress on states worldwide as it challenged the capacity of their democratic institutions, as well as their health, regulatory, and legal systems, to respond and to adapt to both the uncertainties of viral mutation and its most effective response. Writing in September 2022, the world has counted over 6.5 million deaths and 605 million infections as a result of the SARS-CoV-2 virus,[1] while concerns for further and more infectious variants and mutations of the virus are ever present. Even while vaccination programmes have been actioned and are proving effective at mitigating the worst of the COVID-19 disease in the Global North, efforts to ensure global and equitable access to vaccines have been hampered by 'financial self-interest, fiscal considerations, geopolitics, sovereignty, governance, protectionism, and nationalism'.[2]

The virus did not discriminate between autocratic (or autocratising) and democratic (or democratising) states. However, the global health emergency exposed endemic socio-economic and structural inequalities. Populations in vulnerable circumstances are most at risk due to high rates of exposure, infection, and mortality but also most negatively impacted by the measures adopted in efforts to respond to the pandemic.[3] At state level, the capacity of states not only to respond to pandemic conditions but also to effectively manage an ongoing crisis of the related consequences of measures (e.g. lockdowns resulting in extended periods of a reduction in commercial activity and educational opportunities) is inevitably linked with the resources available to governments to support populations, not only in

[1] 'COVID-19 Map—John Hopkins Coronavirus Resource Centre Statistics' (*John Hopkins University & Medicine*) <https://coronavirus.jhu.edu/map.html> accessed 2 November 2021.

[2] Jerome Singh, 'COVID-19 Vaccines: How Structural Factors Can Vitiate Patient Autonomy and Dictate Vaccine Choice' in Joelle Grogan and Alice Donald (eds), *Routledge Handbook of Law and the COVID-19 Pandemic* (Routledge 2022) 31.

[3] See e.g. Rasha Al Saba, 'Inequality and the Impact of Covid-19: How Discrimination Is Shaping the Experiences of Minorities and Indigenous Peoples during the Pandemic' (Minority Rights Group International 2020); Maria Melchior and others, 'Migrant Status, Ethnicity and COVID-19: More Accurate European Data Are Greatly Needed' (2021) 27(2) Clinical Microbiology and Infection 160; Rasha Al Saba and Samrawit Gougsa, 'Exposing Inequalities: The Experience of Minorities and Indigenous Peoples during COVID-19 Emergencies' in Grogan and Donald (n 2) 399.

Joelle Grogan, *The Impact of COVID-19* In: *Democratic Consolidation and Constitutional Endurance in Asia and Africa.* Edited by: Tom Gerald Daly and Dinesha Samararatne, Oxford University Press. © Oxford University Press 2024.
DOI: 10.1093/oso/9780192899347.003.0008

terms of health-care provision but also in terms of economic support to workers, businesses, schools, and court systems.

Where 'consolidating democracy means reducing the probability of its breakdown to the point where [we] can feel reasonably confident that democracy will persist',[4] the stressors of a global health emergency can reasonably be foreseen to push institutions to their very breaking points. The pandemic tests the capacity of democratic, administrative, and legal systems to adapt to an unpredictable, and highly risk-laden situation, and one which is not often envisioned within constitutional texts determining the division and limitations of power, particularly where constitutions have been drafted before the advent of a globalised, highly interconnected, and digitised world. A reasonable concern at the beginning of a pandemic is that if a democratic state fails to effectively respond, then it will incentivise the population to turn away from democracy.

The practice of democracy is difficult in a pandemic: elections can be delayed or suspended, and where they are not, then they may require individuals to place their personal health in conflict with their right to vote. Campaigning can be restricted where gatherings are not permitted. Opportunistic (and anti-democratic) governments can restrict protests or actions by political opponents with targeted or discriminatory application of rules forbidding gatherings of people. Restrictions on numbers that may gather can also affect democratic institutions and oversight: parliamentary meetings can become limited (particularly where no alternative or support is offered), and courts can be closed. Democratic discourse can also be reduced through conscious deference by democratic actors including parliaments, courts, and civil society to executive decision-making during emergency, or even penalised through laws prohibiting 'fake news' grounded on the justification of stopping the spread of misinformation concerning the virus.

The forms of decision-making, the degree of accountability of those decisions, and the measures adopted as a consequence have, in some cases, revealed systemic weaknesses in governance systems in their capacity to respond to emergency. Such weaknesses do not necessarily reveal a North–South divide but rather a deepening of pre-existing trends towards either democratisation or (more commonly) autocratisation of state governance.[5] However, in states such as Kenya[6] and the Philippines,[7] the pandemic also evidenced the potential for democratic innovation

[4] Andreas Schedler, 'What Is Democratic Consolidation?' (1998) 9(2) Journal of Democracy 91, 95.

[5] See V-Dem Institute, 'Democracy Report 2021: Autocratization Turns Viral' (Democracy Report, 10 March 2021); see e.g. Tom Gerald Daly, 'The Pandemic and the Future of Global Democracy' in Grogan and Donald (n 2) 5; Aurel Croissant and Jeffrey Haynes, 'Democratic Regression in Asia' (2021) 28(1) Democratization 1; Roberto S Foa and Yascha Mounk, 'The Signs of Deconsolidation' (2017) 28(1) Journal of Democracy 5; Lauri Rapeli and Inga Saikkonen, 'How Will the COVID-19 Pandemic Affect Democracy?' (2020) 7(2) Democratic Theory 25.

[6] Tara Imalingat, Nerima Were, and Allan Maleche, 'Political Opportunism and Pandemic Mismanagement in Kenya' in Grogan and Donald (n 2) 181.

[7] Maria Ela L Atienza, 'The Philippines under Lockdown: Executive Dominance and an Unclear Pandemic Response' in Grogan and Donald (n 2) 445.

through civic engagement and localised action even in the face of democratic decline and national level, while Singapore[8] and Taiwan[9] have shown the possibilities of parliamentary innovation and democratic resilience in the event of emergency.[10]

In any consideration of the impact of the COVID-19 pandemic on states and systems, and within the larger picture of democratic consolidation or decline, it is important to reflect on the fact that the pandemic has not 'ended'. Its impact too, on families and the bereaved, on health care, on education, on businesses and organisations, and in the memory of individuals (and voters) will last for many years. Capturing initial assessments is challenging, and any conclusions must be qualified as we cannot be certain. The COVID-19 pandemic happened at a point where, globally, concern for the resilience of democracies was already heightened. Prior to 2020, democracies were already 'struggling to address the diffuse but intensifying challenges of hyper-polarisation, political fragmentation, yawning economic inequality, disengaged and distrustful electorates, a distorted and fractured information landscape hollowing out the shared epistemic basis and trust fundamental to democratic society', and 'the proliferation of neo-authoritarian governments actively dismantling liberal-democratic systems or at least challenging their liberal components; especially counter-majoritarian constraints such as independent courts'.[11]

A reality exposed by the study of governance in a global health emergency is the often narrow range of expertise or voice which exclusively influenced, if not determined, actions taken by governments. States which treated the pandemic as a health crisis relied primarily on the expertise of virologists and epidemiologists often to the exclusion of other experts who would be relevant to understanding and informing pandemic response. In academic discourse too, scholarship was often siloed: interdisciplinary work—particularly as between the sciences and the social sciences—was too often limited. Academic research, too, can often be unsuited to fast-moving changes as publishing schedules are often measured in years, not weeks. This often left a gap where important expertise was unavailable and informed opinion was absent.

The foundation for much of the discourse in this chapter rests on two global symposia (in 2020 and 2021) which cumulatively published over 160 reports from over 120 scholars worldwide on the impact of the COVID-19 pandemic on legal systems and governance, as well as the use of emergency powers in response to the COVID-19 crisis from the perspective of democracy, human rights, and the rule of law. The symposia published reports on over 60 countries, analysing legal

[8] Shirin Chua and Jaclyn L Neo, 'Democracy in the Time of COVID-19: Pandemic Management, Public Trust, and Democratic Consolidation in Singapore' in Grogan and Donald (n 2) 84.

[9] Wen-Chen Chang and Chun-Yuan Lin, 'Taiwan's Effective Pandemic Control with Dialogic Constitutionalism' in Grogan and Donald (n 2) 311.

[10] See Daly (n 5).

[11] Ibid.

measures which impacted nearly 80 per cent of global population. They aimed to provide a kind of 'snapshot' analysis, offering analysis from in-country experts in near-real time of the actions of states in response to the pandemic. In the design of the symposia, a conscious effort was made to ensure that understudied states were represented, to ensure not only that a voice was given to underrepresented scholars and states but also an accurate global picture of response to global pandemic. This was challenging, however, due to limited resources which could be given to support contributors, language barriers, and willingness to participate in an open and public forum, as well as access to authors. It is a testament to the global community of scholars, and to the innovations created as a result of pandemic conditions, that connections could be made. As evidenced, too, by this volume, the study of countries underrepresented in mainstream academic discourse is not justifiable. The insights they offer in terms of democratic consolidation and deconsolidation, as well as constitution-building in the context of emergency conditions, are universal.

With this in mind, this chapter examines the impact of the COVID-19 pandemic on Ethiopia, The Gambia, Malaysia, Myanmar, Maldives, Sri Lanka, and Thailand. As part of this examination, it is important to examine whether the predicted dangers of the abuse of emergency powers took place and whether countries were successful in limiting the potential for abuse as well as preventing or sanctioning it. It examines the wide array of responses to pandemic, contextualising them within the global response and interrogating the extent to which they reflect upon a commitment to democratic principles. This chapter also considers the degree to which constitutional limits on the use of emergency powers in a pandemic in those countries analysed, as well as provisions for legislative oversight and judicial scrutiny, have provided an effective safeguard against the abuse or misuse of power during pandemic. It explores the emerging and common themes of the case studies: (mis) management and public trust, and the interplay of politics and the law in questions of the constitution in a situation of emergency, which heightens both the immediacy and stakes of the exercise of power and its limits.

The chapter concludes with a consideration of whether the countries examined follow the wider global trends towards democratic deconsolidation and rule-of-law backsliding and whether the COVID-19 pandemic has provided a catalyst for (further) decline. It alternatively considers whether the COVID-19 crisis has, instead, served as a motivation for a deeper commitment to constitutional consolidation and proof of the resilience of democratic institutions in Asia and Africa, where such processes reveal a better capacity to respond, reform, and rebuild.

2. Power in an Emergency

During the COVID-19 pandemic, many states quickly adopted measures which would have been considered unfathomable prior to the global health emergency, including national and regional lockdowns and border restrictions, as well as the closure of educational, religious, and commercial premises for extended periods. While, globally, the strategies adopted by states were common across many democracies and autocracies, there was very wide variance in the degree to which there was democratic oversight of the decision-making involved in these strategies, as well as the form of power used to action them. Where constitutions establish boundaries on the division and use of power, provisions can allow for the *exceptional* use of power.

States of emergency (or states of exception, siege, crisis, or other terms within national frameworks) allow for the exceptional use of powers by typically executive authorities and usually within the defined scope of the constitutional regime underpinning it. While there is significant variance in the form, limits, and powers which arise as a consequence of declaring a state of emergency (including, for example, which institution can declare one, which institution must approve one, or the extension of one), there are general and common concerns in the use of exceptional power and safeguards which can be introduced by way of framing the context to any consideration of such a state of emergency.

Where an unexpected emergency situation requires immediate action and the costs of non-intervention or slower action can involve catastrophic harm, parliamentary debate and consultation may prove unsuitable as compared with the speed of decision-making of the executive. In this way, emergencies can incentivise, and even legitimise, the delegation of powers ordinarily exercised by legislatures to the executive. Emergency powers are considered to be exceptional and sit with tension within the ordinary frame of governance as emergency situations can serve to deprioritise the expectations of ordinary governance, including detailed or close legislative scrutiny. Ongoing or extended emergency can further entrench the use of power within the executive, particularly where deference to executive decision-making by the legislative and judicial branches can make effective scrutiny all but moot.[12]

In stable systems of consolidated democracy, an 'emergency' would be considered rare: an often unforeseeable event, which could punctuate longer periods of 'ordinary' governance. However, evidenced by states within this volume, many countries, instead, experience rolling or chronic crisis, sometimes accompanied by ongoing emergency powers. Western liberal constitutional thought has treated the use of emergency powers—especially the potential for extended use and not returning to ordinary governance—with suspicion,[13] emphasising that such powers should be treated as exceptional and require both procedural (e.g. temporal) limits and substantive (e.g. prohibiting the suspension of certain rights) safeguards. Such

[12] David Dyzenhaus, *The Constitution of Law: Legality in a Time of Emergency* (Cambridge University Press 2006) 41–42.

[13] Ibid.

safeguards can exist within constitutional design but also are principles of international human rights law.[14] To prevent abuse, limitations placed on the use of power during emergency are typically in terms of 'necessity, proportionality, exigency in the situation, temporality and a commitment to human rights as a framework for legitimate emergency measures'[15]—contextualising and evaluating the degree of threat as well as the necessity and justification for the (ongoing) use of such powers. As a first stage, the conditions needed for the declaration of a state of emergency, and concomitant limitations on the powers which arise from such a declaration, should act almost as a 'quarantine' on the use of those powers to prevent any abuse or misuse of such power. However, such limitations and conditions are only effective when they are enforced.

Negative historical experiences show us where emergency situations can be abused to consolidate power within the executive. The misuse of emergency power can lead to the excessive restriction of liberties, the unjustified benefit of a majority against minorities, or the failure to readjust following emergency.[16] Continued instability or the political incentive to exercise power with reduced scrutiny and restraint can lead to countries existing in an extended state of emergency. For example, Hungary (since 2016), France (since 2015), and Egypt (near-continuously since 1967) had declared states of emergency *prior* to the pandemic and extended or adapted to 'new' states of emergency through it. In Egypt, we see a failure of the constitutional mechanisms designed to *prevent* such a continued state of emergency. The 2014 Egyptian Constitution introduced the requirement that two-thirds the House of Representatives approved any extension. However, instead of seeking this approval, the President has declared a new state of emergency a few days after the lapse of the last one. The Egyptian government did not declare a state of emergency in response to the pandemic as it was already in one.

Within the states which feature in this book, three declared a state of emergency from the point that the pandemic was identified as an emergency. Maldives declared a public health emergency within days of the identification of the first positive case within the country, which was subsequently extended. In Ethiopia, the federal government declared a state of emergency on 8 April 2020, with minimal involvement of the federal parliament with the initial restrictions imposed in the

[14] See e.g. International Covenant on Civil and Political Rights (opened for signature 16 December 1966, entered into force 23 March 1976) 999 UNTS 171 art 4; European Convention on Human Rights (opened for signature 4 November 1950, entered into force 3 September 1953) ETS 5 art 15; American Convention on Human Rights (opened for signature 22 November 1969, entered into force 18 July 1978) art 27; Arab Charter on Human Rights (adopted on 22 May 2004) art 4; all contain clauses for the temporary suspension of individual rights during a national emergency, but all also identify a subset of rights which are non-derogable in emergencies.

[15] Martin Scheinin, 'COVID-19 Symposium: To Derogate or Not to Derogate?' (*Opinio Juris*, 6 April 2020) <https://opiniojuris.org/2020/04/06/covid-19-symposium-to-derogate-or-not-to-derogate> accessed 4 October 2022.

[16] Eric Posner and Adrian Vermeule, *Terror in Balance: Security, Liberty, and the Courts* (Oxford University Press 2007).

country which had activated its preparations for pandemic, even before the first case in the country was confirmed.[17] In The Gambia, under section 34(1) of the 1997 Constitution, the president of the republic has the exclusive power to make a declaration of a state of public emergency. However, any extension of such a state must be approved by the National Assembly by two-thirds majority vote—ostensibly providing legislative control on the exercise of emergency powers along with the obligation to ensure that all government action complies with the rule of law. Between March 2020 and August 2021, seven such declarations have been made by the President, though it has also been highlighted that negative recent experiences of dictatorship weakened public approval for visibly increased executive powers.[18] Highlighted here is the degree to which the political environment, or even public approval, plays into the use of emergency powers by the executive. It should not be assumed that because an emergency power exists, and there is an emergency, such powers will be exercised without restraint.

Some states did not initially declare a state of emergency in response to the COVID-19 pandemic but instead relied on ordinary legislation in the management of the crisis. For example, and to the arguable surprise of many in Malaysia, the previously unfamiliar Prevention and Control of Infectious Diseases Act 1988 (Act 342) delegated power to the federal government, supported by the armed forces, to effectively impose a nationwide lockdown without a declaration of emergency.[19] Broad powers within this Act to 'direct the isolation, observation, treatment, or surveillance of such persons as may be necessary',[20] and under section 31 to take 'any other measures as the authorized officer considers necessary to control the disease' align with the broad and open-ended terminology relied upon by executives in a significant number of states worldwide to combat the pandemic. Such reliance on open-ended terminology, or sometimes interpretation beyond the boundaries ostensibly intended by the legislature and often accompanied by a *lack* of parliamentary scrutiny, is a point of significant criticism where it raises rule-of-law concerns of both legality and legal certainty.

What this shows is that reliance on ordinary legislation in an emergency does not guarantee the prevention of the risks which emergency power can generate. The initial Malaysian response is not unusual globally, as a number of states (including,

[17] Zemelak Ayele and Yonatan Fessha, 'COVID-19 in Ethiopia: A Year in Review' (*Verfassungsblog*, 20 April 2021) <https://verfassungsblog.de/covid-19-in-ethiopia-a-year-in-review> DOI: 10.17176/20210420-185012-0 accessed 4 October 2022.

[18] Satang Nabaneh, 'The Use of Emergency Powers in Response to COVID-19 in The Gambia' (*Verfassungsblog*, 6 May 2021) <https://verfassungsblog.de/the-use-of-emergency-powers-in-response-to-covid-19-in-the-gambia> accessed 4 October 2022.

[19] R Rueban Balasubramaniam, 'The COVID-19 Emergency: Malaysia's Fragile Constitutional Democracy' in Grogan and Donald (n 2) 423.

[20] Ibid.

for example, Cyprus,[21] Nepal,[22] and Switzerland[23]) witnessed the interpretation of ordinary legislation in ways arguably unexpected by the drafters.

The Malaysian Constitution had created the king, Yang di-Pertuan Agong as a constitutional monarch and head of state who would exercise powers on advice of the prime minister. The constitutional framework also envisions the exercise of political rule as subject to principles of democracy and the rule of law. However, as argued by Wilson Tay,[24] the potential weakness of the design was to grant vast emergency powers to the king, if he is satisfied (under article 150) that there is a serious threat to 'security', 'economic life', or 'public order'. Where the Malaysian parliament is not sitting during the emergency, the king may rule by degree and derogate from the constitutional Bill of Rights. Any such law enacted cannot be invalid 'on the ground of inconsistency with the Constitution' and is immune from judicial review. Following a failed attempt to a request by the Prime Minister for a declaration of emergency in October 2020, the King did so on 14 January 2021. Arguably, however, this declaration was not directly linked with the need to respond to the pandemic emergency and, instead, reflected political instability, particularly where existing laws ostensibly provided sufficient legal basis for requisite COVID-19 measures.

The other case studies of this book provide a contrast in power during an emergency and mutual contrast in how states in the process of democratic consolidation responded to the emergency. In Sri Lanka, no declaration of a state of emergency in response to the pandemic was made. For many states, including geographic neighbours India and Bangladesh, the executive decision not to declare an emergency state was made for political reasons based on negative historical experiences of abuse of powers during an emergency period. Instead, in Sri Lanka, ambiguous and amorphous 'quarantine curfews' have been imposed on large sections of the country, though such orders by the executive do not have clear legal basis[25] and were imposed through press releases of the presidential office and the National Operation Centre for Prevention of COVID-19 Outbreak. These orders with

[21] Constantinos Kombos, 'Constitutional Improvisation and Executive Omnipotence: the Cypriot Handling of the Pandemic' (*Verfassungsblog*, 2 March 2021) <https://verfassungsblog.de/constitutional-improvisation-and-executive-omnipotence-the-cypriot-handling-of-the-pandemic> accessed 4 October 2022.

[22] Iain Payne, 'Emergency Powers in Nepal: An Ordinary Response?' (*Verfassungsblog*, 15 April 2020) <https://verfassungsblog.de/emergency-powers-in-nepal-an-ordinary-response> accessed 4 October 2022.

[23] Felix Uhlmann and Odile Ammann, 'Switzerland and the COVID-19 Pandemic: A Look Back and a Look into the Future (*Verfassungsblog*, 1 March 2021) <https://verfassungsblog.de/switzerland-and-the-covid-19-pandemic-a-look-back-and-a-look-into-the-future> accessed 4 October 2022.

[24] See in this collection Wilson Tay Tze Vern, Chapter 15 'Making Progress on A Rocky Path: Democratic Consolidation and Constitutional Endurance in Malaysia, 2018–2021' [PAGE NUMBER, p.17 manuscript].

[25] Luwie Ganeshathasan, 'Sri Lanka's Legal Response to COVID-19: Past Trends and Future Prospects' (*Verfassungsblog*, 23 March 2021) <https://verfassungsblog.de/sri-lankas-legal-response-to-covid-19-past-trends-and-future-prospects> accessed 4 October 2022.

ambiguous legal foundations (and so questionable democratic oversight by parliaments) were also not unusual, as were the pandemic responses in Turkey and Cameroon. While the executives sought to justify them on the grounds of necessity, they are problematic from a democratic perspective, where they seemingly operate outside of constitutional boundaries and democratic oversight.

How far constitution-building and democratic consolidation could be tested in pandemic conditions cannot be accurately gauged in Myanmar. The government did not initially declare a state of emergency, which would have led to the suspension of parliament and the transfer of legislative, judicial, and executive powers to the commander-in-chief. Reflecting the difficult political environment, and the tensions between burgeoning democratic voice and the military, there were likely incentives to avoid a situation suspending parliamentary democracy. However, in February 2021, in a military coup against the democratically elected government, such a state of emergency was declared. The degree to which this was politically motivated primarily by objection to government policies and democratic consolidation or in response to the pandemic is not questionable. However, the decision to capitalise on the situation of pandemic as a means of anti-democratic ends is certain.

There are certain commonalities in the militarised approach taken by Thailand in response to the pandemic. The initial lackadaisical approach by Payruth's government, opposed to measures which could harm the core tourist industry of the country, was replaced by centralised emergency powers invoked in March 2020. The pre-existing militarisation of Thailand's government was identified as a factor which enabled it to exert a significant degree of control over the initial wave of the virus.[26] Measures including shutdown, travel bans, and border closures were enabled through the use of an emergency decree. The emergency decree authorised an almost unlimited degree of power with little accountability or democratic oversight. This underlined a central concern on the use of such emergency powers without safeguards of limited time for use, which is determined outside of the executive, as there was continued use made of the decree without evident plan or desire by government to return to ordinary governance. However, the capacity to exert control over the population through militarised structures does not necessarily connote control over the disease when paired with other concerning trends including corruption and discriminatory application of the rules.

The continued use of emergency powers, extension of states of emergency, or even reliance on ordinary legislation to provide for *exceptional* restrictions on constitutional liberties with little or no accountability of these decisions, raise significant concerns where such actions (along with the suspension of parliaments) become normalised, leading to what David Dyzenhaus hauntingly warned of as

[26] Khemthong Tonsakulrungruang and Rawin Leelapatana, 'The COVID-19 Emergency: Malaysia's Fragile Constitutional Democracy' in Grogan and Donald (n 2) 168.

the 'permanence of the temporary'.[27] Within the context of the states at focus of this chapter, the concerning signs identified are indicative of the more long-term impact of the pandemic. However, it should be underlined that the form of power—emergency or ordinary—is not innately concerning if it is accompanied by robust democratic oversight and the effective use of safeguards to prevent the abuse of powers.

3. The (In)Effectiveness of Safeguards

Accountability through parliamentary scrutiny is an essential aspect of any parliamentary democracy. The COVID-19 pandemic has had inevitable impact on the practicability and possibility of parliamentary practice globally. Parliaments are fundamentally and functionally envisioned as the assembly of people. Mandates to socially distance, or to restrict the assembly of large groups of people, have inevitably, therefore, had consequences on parliamentary assemblies. The consequences of the pandemic exposed this as problematic where states were unprepared for digital or online sessions or were not constitutionally permitted to assemble remotely as quorum required mandatory attendance.[28] As an accompanying factor in evaluating the health of a democracy, pandemic measures also led to the suspension or delay of elections, for example, within our case studies as seen in Malaysia and Ethiopia. Equally, the use of COVID-19 measures to repress dissent through bans on gatherings (and so public protest) and similarly to delay elections was witnessed in Thailand. Globally, the challenge has been to find a balance between rights—for example, the difficulty of ensuring both public safety and health by encouraging (or mandating) social distancing and restrictions on groups gathering while also enabling democratic protest or campaigning, or even safety at voting booths.

The effect of the suspension of both parliaments and elections is a lessening of democratic oversight. Safeguards on the use of power during the COVID-19 emergency in the form of judicial review or judicial control did not emerge in any of the case studies.[29] The lack of a mandate for the courts to interpret the Constitution in Ethiopia is linked with consequent failure of political compromise or legal resolution.[30] Meanwhile, in Myanmar, the weakness of the judiciary was highlighted

[27] David Dyzenhaus, 'The Permanence of the Temporary: Can Emergency Powers be Normalized?' in Ronald J Daniels and others (eds), *The Security of Freedom* (University of Toronto Press 2001). See also Chua and Lee (n 33) 121.

[28] See Ittai Bar-Siman-Tov, 'COVID-19 Meets Politics: The Novel Coronavirus as a Novel Challenge for Legislatures' (2020) 8 Theory and Practice of Legislation 11, 14–17.

[29] For further analysis, see in this collection Julius Yam, Chapter 5 'Constitutional Courts and the Exceptionality of Regime Change'.

[30] See in this collection Adem Kassie Abebe, Chapter 10 'Ethiopia's Transition: Will the Country Stem Descent to Its Tradition of Authoritarianism?' [PAGE NUMBER [p.14 manuscript].

where its appointment and dismissal was primarily determined by the executive and legislature, hindering effective independence from political interference.[31] While this is not a situation caused by COVID-19, the emergency highlights the weakness in oversight where the separation of powers is weakened or non-existent.

On ensuring the effectiveness of safeguards on the use of power by executives, pro forma, or lip service, adherence to constitutional requirements can serve both to undermine the effectiveness of constitutional safeguards on the use of power and to highlight the essential fact that constitutional democracy (and constitutional consolidation) cannot exist only on the page but must instead be supported by the wider political and social context of the system in which it operates. Malaysia has provided an example in May 2020, while the country was under effectively under nationwide lockdown in response to the pandemic, where the constitutional requirement for there to be no more than six months between sittings of parliament was satisfied by a half-day sitting, which, in turn, prevented any effective opposition from effective action where no substantive motions could be tabled.[32] Such lip service to democratic practices is not unique to Malaysia, as evidenced in Thailand, where intentional disregard and dismantling of democratic institutions and safeguards has the effect of 'emptying the constitution into a mere text instrumental to perpetuate its brutal control'.[33] However, what is also evidenced within the chapters is the extent to which this is not a change so much as a continuation of a pre-existing trend. In this way, we could say that 'the pandemic transformed legal systems, institutions or governments or set in motion a pattern of democratic deconsolidation that was not already visible. Rather, it generally had the effect of accelerating pre-existing trends and exposing the true character of regimes'.[34]

In January 2021, the new Malaysian government moved towards the consolidation of power in the executive branch through a declaration of emergency which suspended parliament indefinitely and postponed elections. While the King had shown the capacity to intervene with both legal and political power, and enjoys large popular support, the emergency decree (ordinance) further empowered the federal government cabinet to rule by decree. On a global level, it has not yet been established in any convincing way that regimes which rule by decree are more effective in tackling the spread of COVID-19. The suspension of parliament removes an essential avenue of accountability of government action.

The reality of the COVID-19 pandemic is that it has made the ordinary functioning of democratic governance—and, within it, accountability—more challenging. Safeguards within constitutional frameworks for the use of emergency

[31] Balasubramaniam (n 19), citing Melissa Crouch, *The Constitution of Myanmar: A Contextual Analysis* (Hart Publishing 2019).

[32] Balasubramaniam (n 19).

[33] Tonsakulrungruang and Leelapatana (n 26).

[34] Joelle Grogan and Alice Donald, 'Lessons for a Post-Pandemic Future' in Grogan and Donald (n 2) 474.

powers, or ordinary checks on power in the context of the ordinary use of power, cannot effectively function where courts or parliaments are suspended, or reduced in function, or unable to operate. Where this is of extended duration, as we are witnessing with the pandemic, this can create a worrying paradigm of removing the expectation of accountability on the use of executive power. It should be noted, however, that in the comparative context of these case studies within the wider world, no single political system has, at this point, stood out as being significantly or consistently more effective at managing the health crisis. They have shown, however, important limitations within the design of constitutions and testing their limits in an emergency situation.

4. Constitutional Questions: Power, Politics, and the Law during an Emergency

The case studies of this book serve to highlight where the pandemic emergency has revealed tensions among state organs, levels of government, and the separation of powers. Such tension between powers can also fuel clearer delineation (or efforts at delineation) of the use of powers or *who* should exercise those powers during an emergency. Such consideration goes to core questions of the separation of powers and which institutions may police the limits of the power of another. While executive powers normally exercise emergency powers, and are the prime decision-makers during an emergency situation, questions may still arise where there is uncertainty as to the extent of powers which may be exercised, their duration, and, in particular, who may call an end (or an extension) to any state of emergency. In Maldives, parliament determined that executive-declared emergencies (outside the *constitutional* state of an emergency) had to be approved by parliament, and extensions to the declared state of a health emergency have been made on that basis.

Further tensions can arise and be exacerbated by questions of interpretation of constitutional requirements, though these, too, likely function as a cypher to larger political tensions. This is evidenced within Ethiopia, and the question of the constitutional obligation to hold an election came into overt conflict with the declaration of a state of emergency and the measures adopted in response to the pandemic. Where the Constitution did not indicate clear direction as to what *should* happen in the event of emergency against the mandate of a maximum five-year parliamentary term, the decision by the House of Representatives (the lower house of the Ethiopian Federal Parliamentary Assembly) to defer the decision to an advisory body, the Council of Constitutional Inquiry (an elected body, charged with investigating constitutional disputes) for final deliberation in the House of Federation (the upper house of the Ethiopian Federal Parliamentary Assembly) seemed ostensibly a politically neutral act—particularly where efforts were made at transparency and wide engagement with relevant experts. Of particular interest, and distinction within the comparative context where certain courts are the sole body constitutionally empowered to interpret the constitution, is the fact that the Ethiopian courts did *not* have the mandate to make such interpretation.

Opposition parties' argument that the resolution *should* have been made through political channels or through a political compromise of a transitional government is especially interesting to note within the wider COVID-19 context of questions of law and politics: where measures and government decisions have been challenged in the courts, very often, the responding argument is that such decisions should be solely understood as a 'political question'. However, within the Ethiopian context, the subsequent and escalating conflict between the federal executive and the Tigray People's Liberation Front (TPLF) party controlling the Tigray state has so far culminated in mutual refusal to recognise the other's power and authority, which could ultimately lead to civil war.

Succinctly, even where there can be awareness, if not consensus, as to the basic constitutional framework, where questions of interpretation arise, many political actors can 'continue to disagree about key aspects of this framework'.[35] The insights exposed by the case studies relate to the continued *uncertainty* as to core constitutional questions. As the case study of Ethiopia evidences, where states are in the process of liberalisation, or of the democratic consolidation, an emergency tests the limits and strengths of the degree to which they have become embedded. While tempting to consider whether this relates to when constitutional documents were adopted, or in light of pushes for reforms, it could, instead, be argued that nearly all questions are contestable: the essential point is a common consensus on the forum whereby such constitutional questions can be considered and resolved.

5. The Wider Context: Public Trust

In any consideration of the global health crisis and its impact on constitutionalism, it is impossible to divorce the negative, and often devastating, impact on public health from the wider social, economic, and political context. As Ramraj and Thiruvengadam argue, legal frameworks do not operate in a vacuum, instead interacting with expertise, public trust in institutions, and the capacity of governments to respond to feedback.[36] This same principle applies within the context of constitutionalism, and the process of democratisation, which rest on legal frameworks but rely on the wider environment of public trust in the institutions and processes of democracy. The economic and social challenges presented by a health crisis can become the most significant challenge to incumbent, as well as new,

[35] See Vern (n 24).

[36] Victor Ramraj and Arun Thiruvengadam, *Emergency Powers in Asia: Exploring the Limits of Legality* (Cambridge University Press 2009) 141.

regimes and challenges frameworks to uphold the democratic values upon which they are assumed to exist.

As highlighted in Myanmar, even where there had been successfully, if not remarkably, low numbers of initial infections, global economic recession, particularly with the economic slowdown of China, has nevertheless had a knock-on effect in further slowing economic growth in the country.[37] The negative impact of the coup on the country's health-care system through the targeting of health-care professionals correlated with surges in infection and death rates and—in line with global trends—has been most noticed among marginalised populations. In Thailand, the restrictive measures adopted under the emergency decree served to reduce infection rates through closures and partial shutdowns, without effective economic stimulus and distribution of relief packages, while having a profoundly negative effect on a population already experiencing one of the worst levels of economic disparity in the world.[38]

Inevitably, and in line globally with the most negative impacts, such economic slowdown will negatively impact economically vulnerable workers and populations. But such immediate economic impact plays out within questions of governance and particularly the accountability of decision-makers in the spending of emergency funds and the rationalisation of resources during an emergency situation. Mismanagement of government funds, and allegations of corruption, as in Maldives, compounded by the challenges posed by COVID-19 restrictions, can presage popular opposition even where the executive government currently enjoys a supermajority in parliament. In The Gambia, the arguably ineffective use of public funds to address direct and basic needs of access to food and basic supplies strained citizens' trust in government and their capacity to respond to the global health emergency.[39] The expectations of a citizen in a democracy or a democratising state, such as an awareness of an upcoming election, may heighten a mutual expectation on the part of the elected representative, as well as the electorate, to deliver on the promise of response to an emergency. Where this is not delivered, a lasting concern is that the blame shifts not to the executive or deficiencies in decision-making but to the institutions which gave them the authority to take action. Political and social instability have always provided opportunity and impetus for populist and anti-democratic forces and the furthering of authoritarian trajectories.

The role of public trust has a wider dimension within the context of the pandemic: it is necessary for public compliance with measures designed to mitigate COVID-19 risk. Where current political leadership is *mismanaging* a situation, it

[37] See in this collection Ohn Mar Zin, Naw Janet, and Kimana Zulueta-Fülscher, Chapter 13 'Myanmar's Transition to Peace and Democracy: The Journey Reversed' [PAGE NUMBER, manuscript pp.22–23].

[38] Tonsakulrungruang and Leelapatana (n 26).

[39] See in this collection Satang Nabaneh, Chapter 9 'Prospects for Democratic Consolidation in The Gambia: A Cup Half Full, Half Empty, or More?'

can—unfairly and unjustifiably—be linked with an incapacity of the *system* to respond to a crisis. One of the earliest concerns, in the first wave of pandemic, for those who advocated democratic consolidation and governance based on the rule of law and fundamental rights was the spreading argument that autocratic regimes were more capable, and more effective, at tackling the spread of the virus. This is not accurate. It has been shown that effective management and response to the health crisis correlates with a boon in public trust and public support for the regime unrelated to the *form* of regime of the state (as in China,[40] New Zealand,[41] and Singapore,[42] and among these case studies, as highlighted by Sri Lanka[43]).

The perceived initial success in response to the health crisis was credited with bolstering President Gotabaya Rajapaksa and his government's popularity, leading to the landslide victory of the party in the August 2020 elections. However, ostensible 'success' in control of the pandemic does not correlate with good legal practices or with constitutional or democratic consolidation, as in Sri Lanka, where the 'executive's proclivity for extra-legal governance [and] bypassing existing legal procedures and the legislature'[44] called into question the credibility of the country as a 'constitutional democracy'. This is particularly so where it becomes a permanent feature of executive style of governance. Some established democracies modelled a response that protected both public health and the 'health' of legal and political institutions, as, for example, witnessed in New Zealand or Taiwan. Others fell disastrously short on both these counts (for example, the United Kingdom or the United States under the Trump administration). In states on the spectrum between authoritarianism and democracy, the pandemic appeared to pull systems in different and sometimes unexpected directions: towards democratic consolidation (e.g. in Singapore) or along the opposite path (as evidenced in this book, in Malaysia). Indecision, and instability, can serve to weaken systemic capacity to respond to crisis, no matter the form of system upon which it is built. The weak response of the Thai government under Prayuth has served to exacerbate existing vulnerabilities in both institutions and further deepen economic disparities and highlight arbitrary and discriminatory application of the law. Where institutions were already weakened, or the trend of governance tended towards autocracy prior to the COVID-19 pandemic, then the weight counted against the process of democratisation.

[40] See e.g. Jaques deLisle and Shen Kui, 'China's Response COVID-19' [2021] Administrative Law Review 19; Xin He, 'The State Advances, the People Retreat: China's Political and Legal Responses to COVID-19' (*Verfassungsblog*, 4 May 2021) <https://verfassungsblog.de/the-state-advances-the-people-retreat> accessed 4 October 2022.

[41] Dean Knight, 'New Zealand: Rendering Account during the COVID-19 Pandemic' in Grogan and Donald (n 2).

[42] Chua and Neo (n 8).

[43] See in this collection Luwie Ganeshathasan, Chapter 12 'Sri Lanka's Chronic Inability to Sustain Democratic Reform'.

[44] Ibid.

Even while COVID-19 measures have served to justify the ban on mass gatherings, protest was widespread and continuing.[45] In Sri Lanka,[46] a crisis can be further exacerbated by mismanagement (and public perception of mismanagement) made evident in the tension and friction arising from the lack of law, rules, and certainty in the face of pandemic. A question was whether it would mean the delay of elections, particularly where the public sentiment of government's handling of the election would directly tie in to result. The possibility of political opportunism for both the consolidation of power in the executive and the voice of the oppositional parties enabled by the circumstances of the pandemic is also arguably evidenced in the case studies examined, particularly where the health crisis 'arrived at a moment of crisis and effectively became the last straw that broke the country's tense political spine',[47] as in the case of Ethiopia, where the indefinite postponement of elections exacerbated existing tensions between federal powers and the Tigray region to the point of violence.

Simply, political and social instability arising as a consequence of an emergency situation have long been able to provide both the opportunity and impetus for anti-democratic or autocratic forces. However, and particularly within the context of the current global health emergency, it is not the cause of democratic deconsolidation and does not mean that it is inevitable.

6. Conclusions

Encapsulated within this is the central question of whether COVID-19 has acted as a catalyst for democratic deconsolidation, the opposite, or—in reflection of the complexity of the pandemic and the responses it has spawned—neither. In such an evaluation, the threats to democratic consolidation have certainly become more evident and the actions of deconsolidating executives more prominent, but the modes of response to the pandemic have also revealed a degree of democratic resilience in some states. At such a magnitude of both global and individual threat, the pandemic has often had the effect of galvanising responses, which (although depending on wider social and political contexts) can have the effect of either enhancing the process of democratic consolidation or hastening deconsolidation.

The exigencies of the pandemic can reveal the true functioning of the executive and the political system. The early state of research on the pandemic has most often sought to test the hypothesis of whether (established) democracies fare better than (pre-existing) autocracies. It has yet to examine in depth the impact of the COVID-19 pandemic on states in transition to democracy or in the context of democratic fragility. The case studies of this chapter have not necessarily presented promising

[45] Tonsakulrungruang and Leelapatana (n 26).
[46] See Ganeshathasan (n 43).
[47] See Abebe (n 30) [PAGE NUMBER, p.15 manuscript].

examples of where the pandemic has provided a catalyst for democratic consolidation, neither have they shown the resilience of democratic institutions in the face of the extreme demands of an emergency situation beyond certain control. Where it has provided an opportunity to consolidate executive power, and limit the potential for accountability, executive powers have capitalised on it (Malaysia, Thailand). The vagaries of the pandemic have also exposed and exacerbated pre-existing political and economic fissures (Ethiopia, Myanmar, and Sri Lanka) and also revealed systemic weaknesses within the legal system to prevent the abuse of power where there is little capacity for opposition in parliament or the courts.

Writing only 20 months following the first emergence of worldwide concerns for the threat of a viral epidemic, it is very early to fully gauge the impact of the pandemic on the longer-term trajectory of both the states examined and where they are fitting within, if not evidencing, larger trends. Public memory of living under an emergency, and particularly the capacity of the executive or government to manage such an emergency and what choices are made during it, is long-lasting and will have both medium-term impacts on political support and success in elections and long-lasting effects in how the public will respond to future emergencies.

The COVID-19 pandemic is on such a scale, scope, and length of impact that it should not be treated or understood as an anomalous event, with quarantined and confined impacts on legal and governance systems, but rather as a constitutional moment which will both define and redefine powers and its limitations. Emergency situations are the litmus test for states and their leaders. They test the resilience of democratic systems, and their capacity to adjustment and readjustment show necessary adaptability to situations of extreme stress. In the focus on the case studies of this volume, we not only see the reflections of decision-making and democratic (de)consolidation echoed throughout the world but also the moments of innovation and capacity for states to change.

A reality of the focus on major states and their actions during emergency, taken as either a model or mode for response, is that the opportunity for learning from the diverse is lost, and the assumption of a common approach is mistaken. However, there is no inevitability in the direction a state may make in the process of democratic consolidation, and there is no certainty in constitutional direction. Within the case studies of this book, we find that the COVID-19 crisis has provided opportunity for both democratic innovation and executive aggrandisement. These are lessons for the future of emergencies. As we face a new age of climate crisis and environmental emergency, it is likely that executives will increasingly seek to rely on emergency powers to adapt to a multitude of interrelated and ongoing crises. It is in this expectation for crisis and emergency that democratic constitutional principles must come to the fore. Effective safeguards against abuse, widely participatory decision-making, and building public trust in the institutions of democratic governments are essential not only to the process of democratic consolidation during emergency but also to ensuring the health of democracy beyond it.

PART II
CASE STUDIES

This Part comprises seven chapters providing case studies of Asian and African states that have experienced an understudied democratising event in the past decade: Ethiopia, The Gambia, Malaysia, Maldives, Myanmar, Sri Lanka, and Thailand. Together, these case studies have informed the thematic chapters, presenting a more granular account of the dynamics of democratic consolidation and constitutional endurance in specific country contexts, and often strongly challenging our existing understandings of political order and constitutionalism (even in the Global South). All case studies have been authored by experts in, or from, each country analysed.

9

Prospects for Democratic Consolidation in The Gambia

A Cup Half Full, Half Empty, or More?

Satang Nabaneh

1. Introduction

On 1 December 2016, The Gambia witnessed the beginning of the demise of the authoritarian regime of Yahya Jammeh, who had ruled the country for 22 years.[1] The rare occurrence in which a dictator loses his own 'window-dressing' election to the opposition is unique. Due to an uneven playing field for political competition and various techniques, elections, held every five years, always led to his re-election.[2] Thus, elections were held not to democratise but to maintain the status quo and legitimise his rule. What happened in The Gambia is the first time in post-colonial Africa's political history that a 'military-turned-civilian' dictator lost an election within a system of a 'politics of permanent fear'.[3] In my view, previous theories about democratic consolidation underestimate the potential for the emergence of a democratic political consensus in such an environment. For this reason, The Gambia, as an understudied context, remains pertinent to problematise assumptions and practices associated with the dominant models related to democratic consolidation and constitutional endurance.

Emerging from two decades of a brutal dictatorship, The Gambia is engaged in an ambitious transition process based on laying the 'foundations for a genuine and durable democracy anchored in a new constitutional framework'.[4] Upon taking over the country's leadership, the new government, under Adama Barrow,

[1] Al Jazeera, 'Yahya Jammeh Loses to Adama Barrow in Gambia Election' (*Al Jazeera*, 2 December 2016) <www.aljazeera.com/news/2016/12/2/yahya-jammeh-loses-to-adama-barrow-in-gambia-election> accessed 15 April 2020. Such elections have taken place in Mexico in 2000, Madagascar in 2001, and Ukraine in 2004.

[2] See Abdoulaye Saine, Ebrima Ceesay, and Ebrima Sall (eds), *State and Society in The Gambia since Independence: 1965–2012* (Africa World Press 2013).

[3] Amos Perlmutter, *Modern Authoritarianism: A Comparative Institutional Analysis* (Yale University Press 1981) 20.

[4] Satang Nabaneh, Adem Abebe, and Gaye Sowe, 'The Gambia in Transition—Towards a New Constitutional Order' in Satang Nabaneh, Adem Abebe, and Gaye Sowe (eds), *The Gambia in Transition: Towards a New Constitutional Order* (Pretoria University Law Press 2022) 1.

Satang Nabaneh, *Prospects for Democratic Consolidation in The Gambia* In: *Democratic Consolidation and Constitutional Endurance in Asia and Africa*. Edited by: Tom Gerald Daly and Dinesha Samararatne, Oxford University Press.
 DOI: 10.1093/oso/9780192899347.003.0009

launched numerous actions geared towards transitioning from authoritarian rule, which had crippled the country, to democratic governance, building a human rights culture and undertaking long-overdue reforms in all sectors.

Given The Gambia's context of the withering of an authoritarian regime and its replacement by a democratic government, this chapter gives an overview of the constitutional change processes, the role of governing and judicial institutions, and the influence of entrenched political culture on democratic constitutional performance after more than two decades of autocratic rule.

I begin by outlining the broader sweep of The Gambia's political and constitutional evolution since its independence in 1965. I then discuss the electoral authoritarian regime under Yahya Jammeh, and the manoeuvres he used to retain power, including the weaponisation of ethnicity and neopatrimonialism. This is followed by the main regime-change event, the 2016 presidential election, and the ensuing reform processes. In conclusion, I review the state of constitutional democracy against backsliding tendencies that may crucially shape any further democratic consolidation.

2. Democracy Manifest: Historical Perspective

Prior to colonialism, the territory considered as The Gambia was under the jurisdiction of different chiefs or kings who represented different empires inhabiting this part of West Africa. Prominent among these were the Mandinka Empire of Kaabu and the Wolof Empire of Jollof.[5] However, there also existed decentralised societies, like the Jola people, who independently ruled themselves without any king or ruler at the head.[6]

The Gambia undoubtedly ranked, for many years, as one of the most valuable yet interesting of the British colonies.[7] The founding of the island of Bathurst (Banjul) in 1816, nine years after the abolition of the slave trade, marked the beginning of British settlement and subsequent control of the entire territory around the River Gambia. Bathurst as a settlement was established 'primarily as [a] fort to prevent the river from being used by other nations for the export of slaves'.[8] The settlement became a Crown Colony in 1821 and formed part of British West African settlements under the jurisdiction of the Governor of Sierra Leone.[9] In 1888, The

[5] Gambia's history is inextricably tied to neighbouring Senegal, given the cultural and historical linkages.

[6] Arnold Hughes and David Perfect, *Political History of The Gambia 1816–1994* (Rochester Studies in African History and the Diaspora 2006) 6.

[7] Satang Nabaneh, 'The Gambia: Commentary' in Rudiger Wolfrum, Rainer Grote, and Charles Fombad (eds), *Constitutions of the Countries of the World* (Oceana 2016) 4.

[8] See Thomas Southorn, 'The Gambia: Background for Progress' (1944) 43(170) Journal of the Royal African Society 10.

[9] Arnold Hughes and David Perfect, *Historical Dictionary of The Gambia* (4th edn, The Scarecrow Press 2008) 13.

Gambia became a colony separate from the administrative control of Sierra Leone. The main features of political dispensation in The Gambia under colonial rule were direct rule of the colony (which was Bathurst and its immediate environs) headed by the governor of the British central government, and indirect rule of the Protectorate (which were the other territories in the hinterland) administered by recognised chiefs. Under this system of 'indirect rule', there was some continuity of the political and social systems before colonial rule.[10]

The Gambia was the last country of the West African States, (Ghana, Nigeria, and Sierra Leone), to gain its independence from the British. Despite the late development of political parties, there was clamour by these parties and mostly Western-educated Gambian elites demanding independence in the early 1960s. There were several proposals to integrate little Gambia into Senegal or form a confederation as it was deemed to be an unviable economic unit, given its size.[11] However, The Gambia eventually became independent on 18 February 1965 through the Independence Constitution Order, 1965. Under this constitution, Queen Elizabeth II remained as head of state, with a governor general serving as her local representative, while the government was headed by an elected prime minister, Sir Dawda Jawara, assisted by a cabinet.

On 24 April 1970, The Gambia became a republic following a majority-approved referendum ushering in the 1970 Constitution.[12] This effectively meant that the Queen was replaced by a president, who was the head of state and government, while the posts of governor general and prime minister were both abolished.

From 1965 to 1994, the country was a multiparty democracy, with the People's Progressive Party (PPP), under the leadership of the late Sir Dawda Kairaba Jawara.[13] Five presidential elections were held under the First Republic, with Jawara winning under the banner of the PPP. During this period, spanning nearly 30 years, The Gambia was able to make distinctive and constructive contributions to the advancement of Africa in relation to democracy, rule of law, and human rights. For example, during the 1978 UN General Assembly, President Jawara, in response to human rights violations happening in the African continent, noted:

> The Gambia ... was under foreign rule for many centuries. Throughout that dark period of our history, colonialism deprived our people of the most basic of human rights, such as the right to choose their own leaders and own their system of government and the right to develop their indigenous culture. Then came the gallant struggle for independence and finally independence itself. With the attainment of self-determination and independence it would indeed be ironic if the freedom

[10] Ibid, 43–44.
[11] See generally Sulayman S. Nyang, 'Ten Years of Gambia's Independence: A Political Analysis' [1977] Présence Africaine 104, 28–45.
[12] The Constitution of the Republic of The Gambia 1970.
[13] See generally Nabaneh, 'The Gambia' (n 7) 3–44.

> gained from the defeat of colonialism should again be denied to our peoples by our own leaders. After centuries of a deliberate policy of dehumanization, subjugation and oppression, the minimum our peoples expect and must have is the full enjoyment of their political, economic, social and cultural rights ... It should be the duty of all of us to strive assiduously to ensure that everywhere in the world today people enjoy to the full their civil and political right ... For us in the Gambia human rights are composite, indivisible and universal, and include also social and economic rights.[14]

Jawara played a leading role in the development of the primary regional human rights treaty, the African Charter on Human and Peoples Rights, also known as the Banjul Charter, named after the capital of The Gambia, where it was adopted in 1981. Consequently, small as the Gambia is in comparison with its great neighbours, it was selected to host the secretariat of the African Commission on Human and Peoples' Rights, the pan-continental human rights entity operating under the aegis of the African Union (then the Organisation of African Unity).

The relative stability of the Jawara era was broken first by a violent and bloody coup attempt in 1981, led by Kukoi Samba Sanyang, who, on two occasions, had unsuccessfully sought election to parliament. After a week of violence, which left several hundred dead, Jawara, who was in London when the attack began, appealed to Senegal for help. Senegalese troops defeated the rebel force and restored the Jawara government to power. After the attempted coup, Senegal and The Gambia signed the 1982 Treaty of Confederation. The result, the Senegambia Confederation, aimed eventually to integrate the two sovereign countries into one political and economic union with cooperation in many areas. However, the confederation came to an end in 1989 due, in large part, to concerns about The Gambia maintaining its sovereignty.[15]

On 22 July 1994, Yahya AJJ Jammeh, a young army lieutenant, led a *coup d'ëtat* which overthrew the Jawara government and suspended the 1970 Constitution, marking the end of the first republic. Following the coup, the military junta, known as the Armed Forces Provisional Ruling Council (AFPRC) dissolved the parliament, banned most political parties, and set up commissions of inquiry to investigate civilian politicians. The AFPRC also selected and controlled the members of the Constitutional Review Commission that drafted the new Constitution, which was followed by a constitutional referendum on 8 August 1996 giving birth to the 1997 Constitution. More than 70 per cent of voters were reported to have endorsed the proposed Draft Constitution at the referendum and the Constitution entered

[14] Alhaji Sir Dawda Jawara, 'Statement at the 33rd Session of the UN General Assembly' (A/33/PV4, 22 September 1978) paras 35–36.

[15] DK Jawara, *Kairaba* (Alhaji Sir Dawda Kairaba Jawar 2009) 355; Arnold Hughes, 'The Collapse of the Senegambian Confederation' (1992) 30(2) Journal of Commonwealth and Comparative Politics 200.

into force on 16 January 1997.[16] As a result of this military-controlled process, even though Jammeh retired from the army to run as a civilian during the 1996 elections, the new Constitution had already birthed the principle of one person reigning supreme over all institutions in government.[17] Being drafted during a period of military rule, the processes which culminated in the 1997 Constitution provide important clues into the Jammeh regime's subsequent governing practices.

The 1997 Constitution of The Gambia proclaims itself to be the supreme law of the land, which espouses the fundamental principles of the rule of law, the separation of powers, democracy, and fundamental rights and freedoms. The Gambia's legal system, like most West African countries, is based on a tripartite system consisting of common law, customary, and *Shari'ah* law, relating to marriage, divorce, and inheritance. In addition to the Constitution, the major sources of law, as provided in section 7, are legislation, judicial precedents, decrees (passed by the Armed Forces Provisional Council between 1994 and 1996), English law, customary law, and *Shari'ah* law.

The constitutional catalogue of rights and freedoms is provided in Chapter IV of the Constitution, which includes rights to life, personal liberty, privacy, and protection from discrimination. Section 25 guarantees freedom of speech, including freedom of the press and other media, conscience, assembly, association, and movement. These freedoms and rights are subject to the law of The Gambia, which imposes on their exercise reasonable restrictions that are 'necessary in a democratic society and are required in the interests of the sovereignty and integrity of The Gambia, national security, public order, decency or morality, or in relation to contempt of court'. This provision was broad enough to allow for the arbitrary application of the law. Jammeh was able to exploit this for his purposes as the Constitution did not define the precise scope of the lawful limitations allowed.

Unlike the 1970 Constitution, which had a hybrid system in which cabinet ministers were elected or nominated members of parliament, the 1997 Constitution established an executive presidential system without the necessary checks and balances. The Constitution did not provide for term limits, even though, when it seized power in 1994, the AFPRC did criticise the 1970 Constitution for lacking such a provision. The military junta claimed that the lack of a provision on term limits resulted in Jawara being in power for 30 years.[18] A simple majority vote ('first-past-the-post') was introduced, which meant that the whole country effectively served as a single constituency.[19]

[16] Nabaneh, 'The Gambia' (n 7) 6.

[17] For example, the presidential term limit was removed before the Draft Constitution 1996 was subject to a referendum.

[18] Saine, Ceesay and Sall (n 2) 28.

[19] The Commonwealth, 'Report of the Commonwealth Expert Team: The Gambia Presidential Election' (*The Commonwealth*, 24 November 2011) 14 <https://production-new-commonwealth-files.s3.eu-west-2.amazonaws.com/migrated/news-items/documents/TheGambiaPresidentialElection2011Final.pdf> accessed 20 April 2018.

The Constitution has guaranteed the right to political participation, including the right to participate in public affairs either directly or through representation and to vote and stand for elections. The Constitution guarantees the right to be registered as a voter and be entitled to vote to take part in elections. In fulfilment of this right, and to conduct all public elections, including the registration of political parties, the Constitution created the Independent Electoral Commission, whose functions are further enunciated in the Elections Act.[20] Section 60 prohibits the formation of a party based on an ethnic, sectional, religious, or regional basis and emphasises the need for the parties to conform to democratic principles. During the 2016 elections, there were at least nine registered political parties,[21] including the former ruling party, the Alliance for Patriotic Reorientation and Construction (APRC), which had won four out of five elections (1997, 2001, 2006, and 2011) amidst claims of unfairness by the opposition.

As of 2006, Schedler categorised The Gambia as an electoral authoritarian regime relative to other countries such as Russia and Singapore and sub-Saharan countries such as Burkina Faso, Cameroon, Chad, Ethiopia, Gabon, Guinea, Mauritania, Tanzania, Togo, and Zambia.[22] Although each has its particularities, electoral authoritarian regimes have a multiparty system and hold regular elections but violate liberal democratic rules so fundamentally that elections become an instrument of authoritarian rather than democratic rule.[23] In Schedler's definition, electoral authoritarianism entail 'elections [that] are broadly inclusive ... as well as minimally pluralistic ..., minimally competitive ..., and minimally open.'[24] The authoritarian regime in The Gambia preserved the facade of democratic institutions and multiparty democracy.

3. The Talking Marbles: Voting Out the 'Billion-Year' Dictator in The Gambia

Although the military rule was short-lived, it was the beginning of authoritarianism in The Gambia. Jammeh usurped power at an early age and without experience, which proved intoxicating.[25] Presidential elections were subsequently held

[20] Elections Decree 1996.

[21] These are the Alliance for Patriotic Reorientation and Construction (APRC), Gambia Democratic Congress (GDC), Gambia Moral Congress (GMC), Gambia Party for Democracy and Progress (GPDP), National Convention Party (NCP), National Reconciliation Party (NRP), People's Progressive Party (PPP), United Democratic Party (UDP) and People's Democratic Organisation for Independence and Socialism (PDOIS).

[22] Andreas Schedler (ed), *Electoral Authoritarianism: The Dynamics of Unfree Competition* (Lynne Rienner Publisher 2006) 3.

[23] Ibid.

[24] Ibid, 382.

[25] See Adam Przeworski, *Democracy and The Market: Political and Economic Reforms in Eastern Europe and Latin America* (Cambridge University Press 1991).

every five years: 2001, 2006, 2011, and 2016. On 1 December 2016, The Gambia became Sub-Saharan Africa's newest democracy, following 22 years of authoritarian rule by former dictator Yahya Jammeh, when the opposition coalition candidate Adama Barrow won the elections.[26] On 2 December 2016, the Independent Electoral Commission (IEC) declared the winner, which was followed by Jammeh accepting the results, only to reverse his position a week later by rejecting the election results as fraudulent and unilaterally cancelling it.[27] Jammeh's action follows the trend in many African countries, where presidential incumbents are not prepared to accept an election defeat, thereby plunging their countries into political crisis and uncertainty.[28] The IEC's announcement prompted this as it had detected some errors in the final tally of votes for each of the three presidential candidates. It re-issued the revised results but still indicated that Barrow had won the elections, albeit with a reduced majority.[29] On 13 December 2016, Jammeh instituted an election petition to contest the validity of the election results.

However, the Gambian Supreme Court, the only court competent to deal with this matter, could not hear the petition due to a lack of a quorum.[30] Five judges are required to constitute a quorum. At the time, there was only one Supreme Court Justice in the country, former Chief Justice Emmanuel Fagbenle, from Nigeria.[31] This situation arose because, in 201,5 President Jammeh sacked two Gambian judges of the Court after the full bench of the Court decided in favour of certain military officers who were convicted of treason and sentenced to death, commuting their sentences to life imprisonment and acquitting and discharging Sarjo Fofana, the then naval commander. Although judges from Nigeria and Sierra Leone were earmarked for appointment to the Court, they never took office.[32]

Having failed to constitute a Court of his liking, the former President argued that he had found a loophole, provided for in section 34 of the Constitution, in

[26] Al Jazeera, 'Yahya Jammeh Loses to Adama Barrow in Gambia Election' (n 1).

[27] Dionne Searcey and Jaime Yaya Barry, 'Yahya Jammeh, Gambian President, Now Refuses to Accept Election Defeat' *New York Times* (9 December 2016) <www.nytimes.com/2016/12/09/world/africa/yahya-jammeh-gambia-rejects-vote-defeat-adama-barrow.html> accessed 4 October 2022. This violated the law which gives only the Supreme Court the power to nullify an election.

[28] Three recent post-election coalitions in Africa stand out. Kenya, Zimbabwe, and Ivory Coast (Côte d'Ivoire) were characterised by violent elections and more violence post the election.

[29] Ruth Maclean, 'Gambian Military Takes Over Offices of Electoral Commission' *The Guardian* (London, 13 December 2016) <www.theguardian.com/world/2016/dec/13/gambian-military-takes-over-offices-of-electoral-commissionyahya-jammeh> accessed 4 October 2022.

[30] The Gambia Constitution (n 12) s 127(1)(c) states: 'The Supreme Court shall have an exclusive original jurisdiction on any question as to whether or not any person was validly elected to the office of President or was validly elected to, or vacated his or her seat in, the National Assembly.'

[31] Lamin Jahateh, 'Gambia Supreme Court Judge Declines to Rule on President's Election Challenge' (*Reuters*, 17 January 2017) <www.yahoo.com/news/gambia-supreme-court-judge-declines-rule-presidents-election-070927457.html> accessed 4 October 2022.

[32] Nicholas Ibekwe, 'Gambia: How Nigeria Blocked Gambian Supreme Court from Sitting for Jammeh' *Premium Times Nigeria* (11 January 2017) <www.premiumtimesng.com/news/headlines/220090-gambia-how-nigeria-blocked-gambian-supreme-court-from-sitting-for-jammeh.html> accessed 4 October 2022.

which the president may 'declare that a state of emergency exists' in the whole or parts of the Gambia. Section 99(2) of the Constitution provides that when the president has declared a state of emergency, the National Assembly may adopt a resolution to prolong its own term for a period of up to three months. Upon the adoption of this resolution, the term of office of the president is then prolonged for the same period. Although the president has the power to declare a state of public emergency, the National Assembly has legislative oversight. The parliament has the obligation to ensure that the actions taken by the executive during an emergency adhere to the dictates of democracy and the rule of law. However, in this particular case, upon Jammeh declaring a state of emergency on 17 January 2017, the APRC-dominated National Assembly approved and extended the term of the parliament and the presidency by 90 days.[33]

Jammeh's refusal to step down led to a political impasse. Troops from neighbouring Senegal, with support from Nigeria, entered The Gambia after Barrow was sworn in as president on 19 January 2017 in the Gambian Embassy in Senegal. This was after he was flown out of the country by the Economic Community of West African States (ECOWAS) for fear for his life.[34] 'I have decided today in good conscience to relinquish the mantle of leadership of this great nation with infinite gratitude to all Gambians':[35] these were the words of former President Jammeh on 20 January 2017 following a last-minute diplomatic persuasion by the international community.[36] Jammeh, after having looted the state's coffers, left The Gambia for Equatorial Guinea.[37] On 26 January 2017, The Gambia's new president, Adama Barrow, returned to the country amidst widespread celebrations.[38]

During his 22 years of rule, Jammeh held five elections, which cemented his regime and gave him a semblance of legitimacy. As noted by Schedler, 'electoral contests are subject to state manipulation so severe, widespread and systematic that they do not qualify as democratic'.[39] Jammeh used all the guises available under 'authoritarian manipulation', state power, and resources to ensure one particular

[33] BBC News, 'The Gambia's President Declares State of Emergency' (17 January 2017) <www.bbc.com/news/world-africa-38652939> accessed 4 October 2022.

[34] Al Jazeera, 'Adama Barrow Sworn in as Gambia's President in Senegal' (*Al Jazeera*, 19 January 2017) <www.aljazeera.com/news/2017/01/gambia-president-adama-barrow-takes-oath-senegal-170119170745954.html> accessed 4 October 2022.

[35] BBC News, 'Yahya Jammeh Says He Will Step Down in The Gambia' (21 January 2017) <www.bbc.com/news/world-africa-38702787> accessed 4 October 2022.

[36] See Joint Declaration by the Economic Community of West African States, the African Union and the United Nations on the Political Situation of the Islamic Republic of The Gambia (African Union, 21 January 2017) <https://au.int/en/pressreleases/20170123/joint-declaration-economic-community-west-african-states-african-union-un-gambia> accessed 4 October 2022.

[37] BBC News, 'Yahya Jammeh: Other Leaders Accused of Looting the Coffers' (23 January 2016) <www.bbc.com/news/world-africa-38717136> accessed 4 October 2022.

[38] Al Jazeera, 'President Adama Barrow Arrives in The Gambia, at Last' (*Al Jazeera*, 26 January 2017) <www.aljazeera.com/news/2017/01/adama-barrow-arrives-capital-banjul-170126133750241.html> accessed 4 October 2022.

[39] Schedler (n 22) 3.

electoral outcome: to win the elections.[40] In this respect, Jammeh's presidency was not only notorious for its disregard of the rule of law but also further distinguished itself by a number of amendments to the Constitution with largely anti-human rights and undemocratic provisions. Through a multiplicity of laws regulating the media, journalists operated in a precarious environment characterised by draconian restrictions (many of which are still in existence) and arbitrary arrests, detentions, and physical assaults against journalists, as well as the closure and burning down of media houses. It is estimated that during Jammeh's rule, three journalists were killed in the line of duty, more than a dozen attempts of murder were made on journalists, at least 89 cases of (mostly arbitrary) arrest and detention of journalists occurred, an estimated 52 cases of violent attacks were recorded, 15 cases of torture,[41] 4 cases of arson attacks on media practitioners and media outlets, and 14 instances of arbitrary closure of media outlets.[42]

He also devised discriminatory electoral rules, such as sweeping reforms to the electoral law, which imposed heavy financial deposits for presidential and National Assembly candidates.[43] He further restricted access to the media and campaign finances for the opposition. The 30 December 2014 attempted coup to overthrow Jammeh by six Gambian dissidents from the United States resulted in him tightening his grip on the country even harder by ordering arbitrary arrests and allowing the national security services to openly brutalise Gambians with impunity.[44]

Furthermore, under Jammeh's rule, the right of people to protest peacefully and open opposition to the government was met with a consistently repressive response over the years.[45] This was the case for Solo Sandeng on 14 April 2016. Sandeng, the then National Organising Secretary of the main opposition, United Democratic Party (UDP), alongside other members, was arrested for leading a peaceful protest for electoral reforms and demanding the resignation of President Jammeh.[46] Two days after the arrest, senior members of the UDP, including the leader Ousainou Darboe, confirmed, in a press conference, the death of Solo Sandeng while in

40 Ibid.

41 See Gambia Press Union (GPU), 'Submission to the Constitutional Review Commission in Response to the Issues Document Presented for the Constitutional Review Consultation' (2018) (on file with author).

42 Some of these include the closure of Citizen FM Radio in 1998, *The Independent* newspaper in 2006, and *The Standard* and *Daily News* in 2012. It has also arbitrarily closed down Teranga FM radio station on at least two occasions without any legal authority. While the *Standard* and Teranga FM were later allowed to resume operations, *The Independent* and the *Daily News* are still closed.

43 Nabaneh, 'The Gambia' (n 7) 23–24.

44 Amnesty International, 'Gambia: Dozens Held Incommunicado, "Disappeared" Reveal Whereabouts of People Arrested after December Coup Attempt' (*Amnesty International*, 27 May 2015) <www.amnesty.org/en/latest/news/2015/05/gambia-dozens-held-incommunicado> accessed 4 October 2022.

45 See *Gambia Student's Association v Inspector General of Police* (26/04/2000); *Peters (Femi) v The State* (HC 195/10/CR/075/BO, Crim Appeal).

46 Human Rights Watch, 'Gambia: Investigate Death in Custody, Free Protesters' (*Human Rights Watch*, 18 April 2016) <www.hrw.org/news/2016/04/18/gambia-investigate-death-custody-free-protesters> accessed 10 May 2018.

detention. Darboe also stated that two detained female protesters were in a coma following their arrest and alleged brutal torture by the security agents. Angered by the harsh treatment of the detainees, Darboe and a group of UPD stalwarts led a protest march but were swiftly rounded up by Gambia's security forces and arrested. Eyewitnesses said the security agents fired tear gas at the crowd to disperse it.[47]

As Jammeh's regime became more repressive in character, it might have been expected that defections and dissent may have been stifled. However, the repressive practices encouraged defections from the regime and citizens to dissent. The irony was that in going too far, Jammeh was viewed as desperate and his regime regarded as vulnerable. This was evident in his expulsion of former APRC National Assembly member for Kantora, Mama Kandeh, which changed the internal dynamics of Jammeh's party.[48] Kandeh later formed his own political party, the Gambia Democratic Congress (GDC) in 2016, a few months before the presidential election. Unlike the traditional opposition parties that maintained a following, Kandeh primarily targeted APRC supporters. His political strategy of appealing to members of the ruling party helped to fragment the APRC as he received 17 per cent of the votes.[49]

Jammeh also took other decisions and actions that might have negatively impacted his broader support. For minority Christian voters especially, this included the unilateral declaration of The Gambia as an 'Islamic Republic' on 11 December 2015.[50] In making the proclamation, Jammeh cited the wishes of the people and the need to distance the country from its 'colonial legacy'.[51] However, there was no indication that the people were consulted. On 4 January 2016, an executive order, leaked to the press, banned all female civil servants from leaving their hair uncovered during working hours. This was later rescinded. The Christian population, estimated at 4.2 per cent of the population, the majority of whom are Roman Catholics,[52] had felt alienated over the years, with a decline in influence in the community from the early 1990s. Thus, after Jammeh's erratic announcement, they

[47] BBC News, 'Gambian Activist "Died in Detention"—Amnesty International' (16 April 2016) <www.bbc.com/news/world-africa-36064276> accessed 10 May 2018.

[48] The Standard, 'APRC Expelled MP Mamma Kandeh Reminds Mayor Colley' *The Standard* (29 June 2016).

[49] Yusef Taylor, '2016 Presidential Elections Results' (*GAINAKO*, 7 December 2016) <http://gainako.com/gambia-elections-results-2016> accessed 10 April 2018.

[50] Alex Vines, 'The Gambia: Africa's New Islamic Republic' (*BBC News*, 26 January 2016) <www.bbc.com/news/world-africa-35359593> accessed 15 July 2018.

[51] The Economist, 'The Gambia Fashions Itself as a Kind of Islamic State' *The Economist* (11 January 2016) <www.economist.com/news/middle-east-and-africa/21685736-how-tiny-west-african-tourist-trap-turning-itself-islamic> accessed 20 July 20 2017.

[52] United States Department of State, '2018 Report on International Religious Freedom: The Gambia' (*United States Department of State*, 2018) <www.state.gov/reports/2018-report-on-international-religious-freedom/the-gambia> accessed 5 April 2019.

were less supportive of him.[53] As noted elsewhere, 'throughout his rule, Jammeh employed various tactics to gain political control and recognition in the Islamic world and among its leaders, using anti-Western rhetoric'.[54] This resonates with the ploy by African leaders to start using Islam as a political tool prior to and after decolonisation.[55] For instance, Jammeh's self-identification as a 'pious Muslim' was exemplified in the way he dresses in a white Muslim gown with long prayer beads and carries a Quran in his hands. He also built a mosque on the State House grounds.

Jammeh, like most political leaders in Africa, has used ethnicity as a weapon to cement power.[56] Ethnic consensus is evident during elections to show allegiance.[57] Gambian political parties are highly tribalised, not necessarily by design but by default. Given the ethnicity of the founder, or the main people behind the formation of the party, it is common for kinsfolks to align themselves with a particular party. For example, APRC draws more passionate support among the Jola community because of Yahya Jammeh, just as UDP enjoys the same support from the Mandinka thanks to Ousainou Darboe. Politicians mobilise along the lines of ethnicity for both personal and political gains.[58] Thus, Jammeh leveraged such a system, in which he mainly channelled government resources to his ethnic supporters to ensure his political survival. During his 2016 'Dialogue with the People Tour', Jammeh delivered one of his most controversial and vitriolic speeches. He threatened to eliminate the Mandinka ethnic group, which forms more than 40 per cent of the population. Jammeh referred to the Mandinka as 'enemies, foreigners' and threatened to kill them one by one and place them 'where even a fly cannot see them'.[59] The United Nations (UN) Special Adviser on the Prevention of Genocide condemned his speech and called it irresponsible and extremely dangerous.[60] Within six months of the elections, Jammeh had alienated Mandinkas, the largest ethnic group in The Gambia, with his derogatory remarks. This angered and roused them to vote for the opposition.

[53] Evangelical Focus, 'Gambia: Religious Freedom at Risk after Islamic State Declaration' (*Evangelical Focus*, 23 February 2016) <http://evangelicalfocus.com/world/1391/Gambia_Religious_freedom_at_risk__after_Islamic_state_declaration> accessed 23 May 23 2017).

[54] Satang Nabaneh, 'The Gambia's Political Transition to Democracy: Is Abortion Reform Possible?' (2019) 21(2) Health and Human Rights Journal 172.

[55] Momodou Darboe, 'Gambia' (2004) 47(2) African Studies Review 73–82.

[56] Robert H Bates, 'Modernization Ethnic Competition and the Rationality of Politics in Contemporary Africa' (1974) 6(4) Comparative Political Studies 457.

[57] See Alex Thomson, *An Introduction to African Politics* (3rd edn, Routledge 2010).

[58] See Westen K Shilano, 'Introduction: Ethnicity and Politics in Kenya' in Westen K Shilano (ed), *Political Power and Tribalism in Kenya* (Palgrave Macmillan 2018) 1.

[59] Niklas Hutlin and others, 'Briefing Autocracy, Migration, and The Gambia's "Unprecedented" 2016 Election' (2017) 116(463) African Affairs 4.

[60] UN News, 'Gambia: UN Adviser Condemns President's Reported Threats against Ethnic Group' (*UN News*, 10 June 2016) <https://news.un.org/en/story/2016/06/531822-gambia-un-adviser-condemns-presidents-reported-threats-against-ethnic-group#.V2HJKPkrLIU> accessed 22 July 2018.

Notwithstanding the unfair playing field, the inability of the opposition to form and remain a viable and effective coalition had meant Jammeh's victory in four consecutive presidential elections. The opposition coalition's decision to unite to contest the 2016 presidential elections was critical in ending Jammeh's rule. The situation was so bad that all parties needed to effect change through cooperation. Against this background, opposition parties had to consider effectively competing against the incumbent dictator.

In contrast to the four previous elections, the opposition united behind a single presidential candidate, leading to Jammeh's loss in the 2016 elections. The opposition's formation of a cohesive coalition party, which they had failed to achieve since 1996, provided a viable alternative to the citizenry.[61] This crucial difference in opposition strategy explains the difference in electoral outcomes in 2016 (when they won) and 1996, 2001, 2006, and 2011 (when they lost).[62] As Diamond argues, 'while an opposition victory is not impossible in a hybrid regime, it requires a level of opposition mobilization, unity, skills, and heroism far beyond what would normally be required for victory in a democracy'.[63] The 'opportunity structures' shifted over time.[64] These included the increased usage of the internet and social media, which gave the diaspora a voice; provided an opportunity for networking, raising funds online, and sending money quickly; and attracted support from external actors due to heightened awareness of government abuse. The actions of the diaspora are in line with the exit-voice theory, which states that even when people leave the country, they can use their voices to shape and nudge politics back home towards a democratic path.[65] Through the Gambia Democracy Fund (GDF), about 4 million Gambian Dalasis (approximately US$ 102,359) was sent to the coalition for the 2016 elections.[66]

From the above, it can be deduced that Jammeh made wrong decisions as to what extent he needed to rely on authoritarian control (strategies for electoral manipulation) and the persuasion of voters (strategies for electoral mobilisation).

[61] 'Strategy' is, here, the overall plan to gain a particular objective, while 'tactics' refer to the means used.

[62] See a similar study, Valerie J Bunce and Sharon L Wolchik, *Defeating Authoritarian Leaders in Post-Communist Countries* (Cambridge University Press 2011).

[63] Larry J. Diamond, 'Thinking about Hybrid Regimes' (2002) 13(2) Journal of Democracy 2, 24. On social organisation and the capacity for collective action, see Stephan Haggard and Robert R. Kaufman, *Dictators and Democrats: Masses, Elites and Regime Change* (Princeton University Press 2016) 79–88.

[64] See Elinor Ostrom, 'Collective Action and the Evolution of Social Norms' (2000) 14(3) Journal of Economic Perspectives 137.

[65] For discussion of this theory, see Steven Pfaff and Hyojoung Kim, 'Exit-Voice Dynamics in Collective Actions: An Analysis of Emigration and Protest in the East German Evolution' (2003) 109(2) American Journal of Sociology 401; Steve Pfaff, *Exit-Voice Dynamics and the Collapse of East Germany: The Crisis of Leninism and the Revolution of 1989* (Duke University Press 2006).

[66] GAINAKO, 'GDF Release Details of Funds Donated to the Coalition from Gambian Diaspora' (*GAINAKO*, 20 December 2016) <https://gainako.com/gdf-release-details-funds-donated-coalition-gambian-diaspora> accessed 4 October 2022.

4. 'New Gambia': The Reform Process

The political watershed in 2016 brought enormous promises for a brighter future for democratic governance in the Gambia. In their 2016 Manifesto, the Coalition was clear in the deliverables listed for attainment once they won the election. In fact, not only did they commit themselves to a three-year transitional agenda, but also the Coalition noted that, within six months of coming to office, they would repeal or reform all laws that infringed on human rights, popular participation, and democracy, including embarking on institutional reforms. Furthermore, a number of provisions in the Constitution, the Elections Act, and the Public Order Act were identified for review to enhance democracy and good governance in the country. After taking office in January 2017, an ambitious transitional justice programme was launched, which saw several reform processes and institutions. To this end, the government is undertaking key constitutional, legal, and institutional reforms to consolidate the democratic gains made by The Gambia.[67]

4.1 Constitutional Amendment: Change of Retirement Age and Removal of Upper Age Limit for Holding Office as President

On 28 February 2017, the National Assembly passed the Constitution (Amendment) Bill 2017. The bill amended section 141(2)(b) of the Constitution to extend the age at which a Supreme Court judge should vacate his or her office from 70 to 75 years. In addition, the amendment also removed the upper age limit of 65 for holding office as president provided under section 62(1)(b).

However, this constitutional amendment was passed in contravention of the procedure. The proposed amendments to sections 62(1)(b) and 141(2), which are not entrenched provisions, fall within the ambit of section 226(2), whose procedures were not followed. Section 226(2) provides:

(a) before the first reading of the Bill in the National Assembly, the Bill is published in at least two issues of the Gazette, the latest publication being not less than three months after the first, and the Bill is introduced into the National Assembly not earlier than ten days after the latest publication;
(b) the Bill is supported on the second and third readings by the votes of not less than three quarters of all the members of the National Assembly.

[67] For a more comprehensive discussion, see Satang Nabaneh and Gaye Sowe, 'The Gambia: The State of Liberal Democracy' in Richard Albert, David Landau, Pietro Faraguna, and Šimon Drugda (eds), *I·CONnect-Clough Center: 2018 Global Review of Constitutional Law* (21 October 2019) 107.

In a televised statement, the then Attorney General and Minister for Justice Tambadou advised President Barrow not to sign the bill with the two amended constitutional provisions because the procedures for amendment were misconceived.[68] This sort of unconstitutional constitutional amendment has a history in The Gambia. In several cases, such as *Independent Electoral Commission v Attorney General*[69] and *Jammeh v Attorney General*,[70] the Supreme Court per Jallow JSC (as he then was) held that:

> [g]iven the supremacy of the Constitution over all other laws and acts or omissions of public authorities, it is important for those involved in the exercise of legislative authority of the state to exercise due care and caution to ensure that such legislation is consistent with the provisions of the Constitution and that it is enacted with regard to the requirements and procedures of the Constitution.[71]

The minister took full responsibility for the error and promised to remedy the situation and avoid such occurrences in the future. He further underscored the urgent need to review the Constitution comprehensively. This public apology and acceptance of responsibility showed the government's responsiveness to citizens' concerns, who lamented the non-adherence to constitutional procedures in passing the amendments.

However, the constitutional debate surrounding this amendment was about the non-compliance with the relevant procedures and the motivation underlying the removal of the upper age limit. People saw the removal of the upper age limit as an amendment for the benefit of one person. The controversies surrounding this came about after the news of the appointment of Fatoumatta Jallow Tambajang as the vice-president on 23 January 2017. The public discussion that ensued focused on whether Tambajang was qualified to be appointed vice-president. It was deemed that she was above the constitutional age of 65 years at the time. Subsequently, a press statement from the spokesperson of the president responded to the outcry stating that the attention of the President had been drawn to the constitutional provisions and that although Mrs Tambajang was well suited for the job, the provisions of the Constitution would be respected.[72]

Interestingly, the Barrow government never appointed a vice-president while that crisis was ongoing because it was widely believed that he still intended to

[68] Kairo News, 'Constitutional Amendment: AG Admits Procedural Error' *Kairo News* (Kairo, 9 March 2017) <www.kaironews.com/constitutional-amendment-ag-admits-procedural-error> accessed 20 May 2019.

[69] Gambia Law Reports [1997–2001] GR 630.

[70] *Jammeh v Attorney General* (2002) AHRLR 72 (2001 GaSC).

[71] Ibid, para. 32.

[72] News24, 'Gambia's New Government Mired in Controversy over Appointed VP's Age' (*News24*, 25 January 2017) <www.news24.com/Africa/News/gambias-new-govt-mired-in-controversy-over-appointed-vps-age-20170125> accessed 13 June 2019.

appoint Mrs Tambajang, and so she was appointed overseer of the office from March 2017. With the eventual passing of the Constitutional (Amendment) Act on 25 July 2017, which was assented to by the President on 27 July 2017, Tambajang was sworn in as vice-president on 9 November 2017.[73]

4.2 Legislative Reform: Electoral Law

As noted above, the Jammeh era witnessed major shrinking of political rights and political space. For example, through a previous Elections (Amendment) Act passed on 7 July 2015, the fee for presidential candidates was raised from D 10,000 (approximately USD 250) to D 500,000 (approximately USD 12,500). The fee for candidates for the National Assembly was increased from D 5,000 (approximately USD 125) to D 50,000 (approximately USD 1,000), and candidates for the local council office were to pay D 10,000 (about USD 200). Opposition political parties regarded the increases as unreasonably high and a ploy by the government to drastically limit the opposition's participation in elections.

The matter was subsequently taken to the ECOWAS Community Court of Justice, in which the plaintiffs alleged that the abovementioned amendments were a violation of article 13 (1)(2) of the African Charter on Human and Peoples' Rights (ACHPR) on the right to participate in one's government freely.[74] The Court declared that it was not competent to deal with the electoral matter as it borders on the internal affairs of The Gambia and is not an issue of human rights violation as envisaged under the Charter. Despite the Court's very progressive jurisprudence, this judgment took a very restricted view on the right to political participation.

In 2017, the National Assembly reversed the exorbitant fees to their initial amounts through the Elections (Amendment) Act of 2017, aimed at encouraging widespread participation of the ordinary citizenry in the new democratisation dispensation.

4.3 'Gambianisation' of the Judiciary

Although the 1997 Constitution provides for the independence of the judiciary, the Gambian judiciary under the former regime was subject to various forms of interference. Consequently, there was little public confidence in the judiciary. Since the new government came into power, there have been considerable efforts to appoint

[73] Since then, Tambajang was removed on 9 July 2018, followed by the appointment of Ousainou Darboe from 9 July 2018 to 15 March 2019; Dr Isatou Touray, who was appointed on 15 March 2019 to 4 May 2022; and now (at the time of writing) the incumbent Badara Joof since 4 May 2022.

[74] *Omar Jallow & Amadou Scattred v Republic of The Gambia* (ECW/CCJ/JUD/06/17).

Gambians at all levels of the judiciary. Departing from the style of the former regime of foreign appointments to the position of Chief Justice, President Barrow appointed a Gambian, Hassan Jallow, former Prosecutor of the International Criminal Tribunal for Rwanda in Arusha, Tanzania. Following this, numerous appointments took place, including at the level of the Supreme Court.

In 2017, 16 superior court judges were appointed, including 14 Gambians.[75] As of September 2020, there are 14 High Court judges (including 2 non-Gambians), 5 Gambian Court of Appeal judges, and 7 Gambians out of the 9 Supreme Court judges, who are all Gambians.[76]

In the backdrop of allegations that, during Jammeh's era, foreign judges were doing the former dictator's bidding, the Gambia Bar Association (GBA), in April 2017, filed a petition with the High Court against a bid to renew the contract of four Nigerian justices.[77] The GBA argued that their appointments were contrary to provisions of the Constitution, such as sections 138, 145, and 229. The argument was that the Judicial Service Commission (JSC) did not follow proper procedures as section 138(2) provides that the president shall appoint all appointments except judges of the Special Criminal Court on the recommendation of the first respondent. The JSC did not have the power to appoint (or renew) judges for the superior courts. The presiding High Court judge declared that the reliefs sought required an interpretation and enforcement of the Constitution and, as a result, referred the matter to the Supreme Court for determination.

The Supreme Court, in its determination, held that since the named judges were no longer in the employment of the judiciary, the issue was moot.[78] Accordingly, the High Court was directed to dismiss the motion, filed and dated on 5 April 2017.[79]

4.4 Dealing with Past Human Rights Violations

Following the enactment of the Truth, Reconciliation and Reparations Commission (TRRC), Act 2017,[80] the Commission was formally launched. The

[75] Nabaneh and Sowe (n 67) 100–01.

[76] Data culled from the judiciary, September 2020. The two foreign judges are from Nigeria (Justice AD Yahaya) and Sierra Leone (Justice NC Browne-Marke), the latter initially appointed by Jammeh on 30 December 2016 to hear the election petition but declined to take up the seat—he was consequently reconfirmed by President Barrow. Their appointments show that judges from common law systems were not barred from serving.

[77] *Rachel Y Mendy, Combeh Gaye & Abdul Aziz Bensouda (as trustees of the Gambia Bar Association) v Judicial Service Commission (1st Respondent) and Attorney General (2nd respondent) in the Matter of Appointment by the Judicial Service Commission of the Edward E Ogar, Mathias O Agboola, Simeon Abi and Martins O Okoi as Justices of the High Court of The Gambia and in the Matter of Sections 138, 145 and 229 of the 1997 Constitution of The Gambia* (Misc App No HC/092/17/MF/0333/A).

[78] *RY Mendy & others v JSC* (SC/SCCS001/2017, 16 July 2020) 10.

[79] Ibid.

[80] Truth, Reconciliation and Reparations Commission (TRRC) Act 2017 <www.lawhubgambia.com/truth-reconciliation-reparations-commission> accessed 5 June 2020.

TRRC Act provided for establishing the historical record of the nature, causes, and extent of violations and abuses of human rights committed during the period July 1994 to January 2017 and considering the granting of reparation to victims. The Commission's mandate included initiating and coordinating investigations into violations and abuses of human rights, the identity of persons or institutions involved in such violations, identifying the victims, and determining what evidence might have been destroyed to conceal such violations.

The hearings, which began on 7 January 2019, served as an initial first step towards securing justice, truth, and reparations in The Gambia.[81] The TRRC provides a foundation, if executed properly, to not only address the structures and causes of violations but also assure victims of past violations of non-repetition. According to an Afrobarometer survey, more than 28 per cent of Gambians say they or a family member suffered at least one form of human rights violation under the regime, including arbitrary arrest or detention without trial (14 per cent); torture, rape, and other brutalities by agents of the state (14 per cent) and intimidation by state agents (13 per cent).[82]

The TRRC worked for more than two years and submitted its Final Report with findings and recommendations to President Barrow on 25 November 2021.[83] A month later, on 24 December 2021, the government, through the Ministry of Justice, made the report public. As per the TRRC Act, the government had six months to issue a White Paper.[84]

4.5 Building a Human Rights Culture

After over two decades of authoritarian rule characterised by gross human rights violations, including torture, enforced disappearance, arbitrary arrests, detention without trial, and murder perpetrated by state agents, the new government has made strides towards building a human rights culture.

[81] The Point, 'TRRC Hearings Begins Today' *The Point* (7 January 2019).

[82] Sait Matty Jaw, 'Gambians Expect the Truth Reconciliation and Reparations Commission to Heal the Nation but Expect Human Rights Violators Prosecuted' (2018) 249 (6) Afrobarometer Dispatch 2 <http://afrobarometer.org/sites/default/files/publications/Dispatches/ab_r7_dispatchno249_gambians_want_national_healing_with_justice.pdf> accessed 5 May 5 2020.

[83] Satang Nabaneh, 'From a "Crusade to Root out Homosexuality Like Malaria" to a "Non-issue": The Absence of Sexual Minority Lawfare in The Gambia' in Adrian Jjuuko and others (eds), *Queer Lawfare in Africa* (Pretoria University Press 2022) 323.

[84] Amnesty International, 'Gambia: Truth and Reconciliation Report Must Lead to Justice and Reparations for Victims' (*Amnesty International*, 25 November 2021) <www.amnesty.org/en/latest/news/2021/11/gambia-truth-and-reconciliation-report-must-lead-to-justice-and-reparations-for-victims> accessed 2 September 2022.

4.5.1 Establishment of the National Human Rights Commission

Following the enactment of the National Human Rights Commission (NHRC) Act 2017,[85] the National Assembly approved the nomination of five candidates with proven records in defending human rights who were sworn into office on 14 February 2019. The Commission's establishment addresses the need for a legal and institutional framework to which a human rights culture will be anchored. The NHRC is authorised to investigate and consider complaints of human rights violations in The Gambia committed by the state, private persons, and entities. During its first year of operation, it focused on formulating standards and guidelines to support rule-of-law actors and strengthen the institutional capacity of law enforcement.[86]

In addition, the Act was amended by the National Assembly on 7 July 2020 and assented to by the President on 23 July 2020.[87] Notable amendments include section 6, which now provides that the Chairperson of the Commission will hold office for five years, while the other commissioners hold office for four years and are eligible for reappointment for one term. Initially, the term in the 2017 Act stated that commissioners could hold office for three years.

4.5.2 State reporting to human rights treaty bodies

It is important to note that in fulfilment of its regional and international human rights obligations, on 23 November 2018, The Gambia became the ninth African country to make the declaration under article 34(6) of the Protocol to the African Charter on Human and Peoples' Rights on the Establishment of an African Court on Human and Peoples' Rights (the African Court) to allow individuals direct access to the Court. The declaration allows the Court to trigger its jurisdictional competency under article 5(3) of the Protocol to allow non-governmental organisations (NGOs) access.

In July 2018, the Human Rights Committee reviewed the implementation of the International Covenant on Civil and Political Rights (ICCPR) in The Gambia. The Gambia submitted a report in response to the list of issues *in lieu* of its second periodic report.[88] The Committee raised concerns that section 18 of the Constitution and sections 15(A) and 72 of the Criminal Code allow for a great deal of discretion in the use of force by law enforcement officials and that sections 2(a) and (b) of the Indemnity Act (as amended in 2001) exonerates all public officials from

85 National Human Rights Commission Act 2017 <www.lawhubgambia.com/national-human-rights-commission> accessed 5 June 2020.

86 See National Human Rights Commission, 'Annual Report 2019' (2020) <www.gm-nhrc.org/annual-reports> accessed 10 September 2020.

87 National Human Rights Commission Act 2020.

88 Human Rights Council, 'Replies of the Gambia to the List of Issues' (CCPR/C/GMB/Q/2/Add1, 12 June 2018). See also Human Rights Committee, 'List of Issues in the Absence of the Second Periodic Report of The Gambia' (CCPR/C/GMB/Q/2, 11 December 2017).

civil or criminal liability for the exercise of their duties with respect to unlawful assemblies, riotous situations, or public emergencies.[89] The Committee made recommendations to The Gambia to revise its laws to bring them in line with international standards.[90]

5. The Constitutional Reform Process

5.1 The Constitutional Review Commission (CRC)

The new government pledged to revitalise the economy, strengthen social cohesion, and transform the economy for the well-being of Gambians.[91] In this regard, the government engaged in a constitution-building process[92] to review the 1997 Constitution and draft a new constitution to address the wishes and aspirations of Gambians. Against this background, the National Assembly enacted the CRC Act in December 2017. In January 2018, President Barrow assented to the CRC Act. In this regard, the CRC was established in June 2018 and its Members were sworn in by the President of The Gambia on 4 June 2018. Its mandate was two-fold: first, to review the 1997 Constitution and draft a new one; and second, to prepare a report in relation to the draft Constitution. Section 21 of the Act empowers the Commission to publish the Draft Constitution and the report in the Gazette and such other manner as the Commission deems fit upon submission to the president. This serves as a safeguard against tampering.

In discharging its responsibilities, according to section 6 of the Act, the Commission was required to seek the opinion of citizens both within the country and abroad. Thus, the Commission used a highly participatory and consultative approach to solicit the views and opinions of Gambians about the constitutional issues they wished to see addressed in the proposed new Constitution of The Gambia. Following these consultations, done both in the country and with Gambians living abroad, the CRC embarked on drafting a new constitution. The proposed first Draft Constitution was published on 15 November 2019 in both print and electronic form and widely distributed in The Gambia and online.[93]

[89] Human Rights Committee, 'Concluding Observations on the Gambia in the Absence of Its Second Periodic Report' (CCPR/C/GMB/CO/2, 30 August 2018) para 29.

[90] Ibid, para 30.

[91] Constitutional Review Commission (CRC) Final Report (30 March 2020).

[92] This 'refers to the processes of negotiating, drafting and implementing constitutions and implies building new structures or re-developing existing ones, enhancing or adding value to governance and the political system': International Institute for Democracy and Electoral Assistance (International IDEA), 'Constitution Building after Conflict: External Support to a Sovereign Process' (*International IDEA*, 2011) <www.constitutionnet.org/sites/default/files/2017-06/cb-after-conflict.pdf> accessed 10 March 2020, 10.

[93] See First Draft Constitution (12 November 2019) <https://crc220.org/wp-content/uploads/2015/12/CRC-DRAFT-CONSTITUTION.pdf> accessed 20 April 2020.

The CRC then embarked on a second and final public consultation around the country from 31 November to 16 December 2019, this time to inform and solicit feedback on the Draft Constitution, in addition to receiving written contributions. In addition, a total of 198 submissions were received from government institutions, civil society organisations, religious bodies, individuals, associations, NGOs, international organisations, and the private sector. The submissions addressed different aspects of the Draft Constitution. The CRC took feedback on the proposed Draft Constitution and prepared the final draft.

On 30 March 2020, the CRC submitted the 'Final Draft Constitution and Report' to the President. In line with requirements in the 1997 Constitution, the proposed Constitution Promulgation Bill, 2020 was twice published in the government Gazette (first on 28 May and then on 28 August 2020),[94] whereafter it was introduced in the National Assembly (section 226). The bill was tabled before the National Assembly on 14 September 2020. Twenty-three lawmakers in the National Assembly voted against the bill, while 31 supported it.[95] However, this was not a big enough majority to meet the threshold requirement of three-quarters of members needed to effect constitutional change. Therefore, the Draft Constitution could not be put to a referendum.

5.2 Overview of the 2020 Draft Constitution

The 2020 Draft Constitution contains provisions in response to the wishes and aspirations of the Gambian people. The preamble provides that Gambians gave themselves and future generations 'this Constitution as a beacon of hope, stability and national unity, progress, peace, and prosperity'.

Chapter I establishes The Gambia as a multiparty democratic state. It notes that sovereign power belongs to the people of The Gambia from whom the organs of government derive their authority and are to be exercised according to the Constitution. The Draft Constitution also recognises the decentralisation of government and the delegation of power to local government areas (LGAs), ensuring the devolution of government.

Unlike the 1997 Constitution, the Draft Constitution introduces a two-term limit for the president. Section 100(1) states 'Subject to subsection (3), the President shall hold office for a term not exceeding five years.' Subsection (2) goes further to state that 'No person shall hold office as President for more than two

[94] Gazette No 88/2020 (28 May 2020) and Gazette No 181/2020 (28 August 2020).

[95] Kebba AF Touray, 'Gambia: Parliament Rejects Draft Constitution Bill 2020' *Foroyaa Newspaper* (22 September 2020).

terms of five years each, whether or not the terms are consecutive.' This is in recognition of Gambia's troubled autocratic past.

In terms of the rule of law and good governance systems, the 2020 Draft Constitution, moreover, includes necessary governance institutions, and checks and balances for the legislature, executive, and judiciary are stipulated. Thus, the Draft Constitution spells out the functional responsibilities, mandates, and jurisdictions of the branches of government. For example, in the Draft Constitution, the president is mandated to nominate and appoint a vice-president (within 30 days) of assuming office and ministers of government (within 60 days) but subject to the confirmation of the National Assembly.[96] Here, we see a shift from the 1997 Constitution, where the president appoints the vice-president and ministers without confirmation from the National Assembly.[97]

The 2020 Draft Constitution also introduced new provisions aimed at ensuring respect for the rule of law and human rights. The protection of fundamental human rights and freedoms is a crucial feature of any democracy. For this reason, Chapter VI provides for these rights and freedoms in two parts in sections 31–73. Part I deals with general human rights and freedoms, and Part II deals with specific ones. Part I provides for the objectives of human rights, the enforcement and implementation of rights guaranteed in the chapter, and the courts' authority in dealing with rights. The chapter further deals with the limitation of specified rights.

In contrast to the 1997 Constitution, the chapter introduces a new provision that imposes a positive obligation on the state to respect and uphold the rights guaranteed under the Constitution. Part II of the chapter provides specific rights and freedoms, including civil and political rights, economic, social, cultural, and group rights. Part II also introduces the right of access to information, and it further defines fundamental rights and freedoms related to the media.

Compared to the 1965, 1970, and 1997 Constitutions, the 2020 Draft Constitution contains novel and progressive provisions as it seeks to reshape the institutions of the modern state, entrench public freedoms and rights, create a real separation of powers, and establish adequate checks and balances. In moving towards democracy, the importance of ensuring periodic democratic elections, which includes establishing term limits for the Office of President, was aptly captured in the Draft Constitution, albeit a contention issue. The absence of term limits in the Gambian Constitution and the requirement for a simple majority greatly hindered the progress and development of democracy in the country.[98] Chapter VIII of the Draft Constitution introduces term limits for the office of president.

96 See Final Draft Constitution (29 March 2020) ss 108, 113 (Law Hub Gambia) <www.lawhubgambia.com/constitutions-2019-2020>.

97 The Gambia Constitution (n 12) s 70.

98 See generally Charles Fombad and Nat Inegbedion, 'Presidential Term Limits and Their Impact on Constitutionalism in Africa' in Charles Fombad and Christina Murray (eds), *Fostering Constitutionalism in Africa* (Pretoria University Law Press 2010) 15.

A review of the parliamentary debates suggests that the primary concern, arguably those of the ruling government, was the retroactive nature of the presidential term limit. This provision would ensure that the first term of President Barrow were counted towards his two-term limit.

Another unexpected outcome of the constitution-building process was the flaring of religious tensions when the minority Christian population raised concerns about the non-inclusion of the word 'secular' in the 2020 Draft Constitution, in contrast to the inclusion of *Shari'ah* courts. Despite Jammeh's previous efforts towards greater state recognition of Islam, generally, The Gambia has been considered a beacon of religious tolerance, where Muslims and Christians live in peace and harmony. However, these notions were challenged as it divided the country into two camps. On the one hand, the pro-secularism camp argued that the exclusion of the term would make The Gambia somewhat of an Islamic state, with the majority of decisions being in favour of Muslims. On the other hand, the anti-secularism camp argued that inclusion of the term would mean acceptance of same-sex relations and inability to practice Islam as it should be practiced.[99] Consequently, while the word 'secular' does not appear in the 2020 Draft Constitution, section 1(1) declares The Gambia as a sovereign republic and also prohibits both the president and National Assembly from establishing any religion as a state religion.[100] In addition, section 49 under the fundamental human rights chapter also guarantees freedom of conscience, religion, thought, belief, and opinion. These provisions attempt to ensure that there are special measures in place to avoid a repeat of past divisive tactics and to guarantee that the fears of pro-secularists are assuaged.

6. Liberal Democracy on the Rise or Backsliding?

Like other electoral authoritarian regimes, Jammeh set up an institutional landscape where the Constitution and its institutional safeguards and weaponisation of ethnicity, coupled with neopatrimonialism, cemented his power. While he manipulated electoral laws and political processes to help him keep a grip on power, elections served as the means of his ouster. Thus, elections are a double-edged sword as they serve both the rise and the decline of authoritarian rule. The case study of The Gambia is a depiction of deviation from 'politics as usual'. It included decisions from the opposition to form a coalition, both online and on-the-ground actions by civil society, including youth movements, and diaspora. Ultimately,

[99] GAINAKO, 'Gambia Supreme Islamic Council (GSIC) Response to the Draft Constitution' (*GAINAKO*, 19 December 2019) <https://gainako.com/gambia-supreme-islamic-council-gsic-response-to-the-draft-constitution> accessed 5 February 2019.

[100] See 2020 Final Draft Constitution (n 96) ss 88(5)(b), 153 (1)(b).

ousting Jammeh and ending his dictatorship of 22 years involved an array of actors, activities, and organisations.

While Jammeh's departure marked a new beginning for The Gambia, the legacy of the authoritarian rule was characterised by gross human rights violations and disregard for laws, and impunity continues to be a challenge in the new government's efforts to consolidate democracy. For instance, a deadly clash between personnel of the Police Intervention Unit (PIU) and the community of Faraba Banta on 18 June 2018 led to the fatal shooting of two men and the injuring of nine others. A Commission of Inquiry was subsequently established with the mandate to investigate the incident.[101] Upon completion of work in 2018, the Commission held that there was no evidence that the police have taken any steps to vet and or screen PIU officers who have been involved or are suspected of being involved in past human rights abuses, nor were they made aware of any programmes in place to train and or reorientate PIU officers in operating under a democratic dispensation.[102] It reiterated the urgent need for security-sector reform.[103] At the time of writing, a *White Paper on the Report of the Faraba Banta Commission of Inquiry* has been published, yet the government still has not taken any appropriate action.[104]

The continuous presence of repressive laws such as the Public Order Act has led to the same repressive response by the Barrow government. Some of these incidents included the denial of a permit for the 'Occupy Westfield' protest against The Gambia's energy company, the National Water and Electricity Company (NAWEC) for security reasons[105] and the regressive decision of the Supreme Court relating to this matter. On 23 November 2017, the Supreme Court unanimously held that the restrictions on the grounds set out in section 25(4) of the Constitution and section 5 of the Public Order Act were reasonably justifiable in any democratic society.[106] The case was brought by Ousainou Darboe, the former opposition party (the UDP) leader against the state, dealing with the right to assembly and expression. They further claimed that the requirement levied on a person to apply for a police permit before holding any public gathering is illegal, unconstitutional, and made in excess of legislative authority. Arguably, the Supreme Court's judgment is a major setback as it is contrary to international and regional human rights standards such

[101] The establishment of the Commission was gazetted on 1 July 2018 and all the commissioners were sworn before the President on 5 July 2018.

[102] 'Report of the Faraba Banta Commission of Inquiry into the Events of Monday 18 June 2018 at Faraba Banta, West Coast Region' (31 August 2018) 59.

[103] Ibid.

[104] Gambia Government, 'White Paper on the Report of the Faraba Banta Commission of Inquiry: Supplement "A" to The Gambia Gazette No 33 of 28 November 2018' (Legal Notice No 47 of 2018) 11–12.

[105] Kebba AF Touray, 'Westfield Protesters Dispersed' *Foroyaa Newspaper* (13 November 2017) <https://foroyaa.net/westfield-protesters-dispersed> accessed 15 May 2018.

[106] *Ousainou Darboe v 19 Others IGP & Inspector General of Police, Director General of National Intelligence Agency & The Attorney General*, CML Suit No: SC 003/2016.

as rule 71 of the Guidelines on Freedom of Association and Assembly in Africa of the African Commission.

The reality is that The Gambia's democracy remains fragile. While the government has undertaken measures to deal with the abuses of the past and to reinstate democratic institutions in the country, there are concerns regarding existing repressive laws that continue to stifle fundamental human rights. The country currently has many laws (including decrees) and practices from the former regime that severely limit and violate human rights and human dignity. Thus, the new democratic government of The Gambia must prioritise the reform of laws and institutions, including the police, judiciary, military, and national intelligence.

Although it is acknowledged that Barrow inherited the monumental task of repairing the damage accumulated from 22 years of dictatorship, the undemocratic actions highlighted above call into question the commitment of the government to democratic system change. Arguably, some of the democratic setbacks are primarily due to the continued existence of repressive laws and the lack of capacity of institutions and actors in The Gambia, as a new democracy, to keep pace with democratic accountability. For the attainment of the vision of 'New Gambia', the Barrow government needs to manifest its acceptance and commitment to democracy and constitutionalism both in theory and everyday practice, including a relinquishing of any attempts that give any semblance to actions undertaken by the previous dictatorship. It is vital to undertake legal and institutional reforms in order to facilitate democratic gains.[107]

[107] See Tom Ginsburg and Aziz Huq, *How to Save a Constitutional Democracy* (University of Chicago Press 2018).

10

Ethiopia's Transition

Will the Country Stem Descent to Its Tradition of Authoritarianism?

Adem Kassie Abebe

1. Introduction

In April 2018, Ethiopia was on the cusp of a transition from authoritarianism to democracy and, according to historical and scholarly insights, at its most vulnerable to conflict. Alas, the sceptics were right as the country descended into widespread civil and ultimately military conflict, and now it faces the twin challenges of transition from conflict to peace *and* to democracy. Enduring contestations over the history and nature of the Ethiopian state, the political form of the state (particularly regarding the place of linguistic identity in organising the federation and broadly underpinning politics), the absence of design of the transition, and a power struggle among old, new, and aspiring powerholders degenerated in November 2020 into what is perhaps the largest civil war in recent African history.

The Ethiopian story reveals and confirms some insights to studies of political transitions and constitutional democracy. First, constitutional arrangements can be critical, even in authoritarian settings. For instance, the federal arrangement provided ambitious individuals within the ruling party with regional apparatus and resources to challenge the dominant forces at the centre. Second, transitions from authoritarianism to peace are moments of vulnerability that require tremendous work to identify and address risks of conflict flare-up. In particular, the absence of a genuine coalition for democracy among key opposition parties (despite their ideological leanings), civil society, and other socio-economic and political leaders not only undermines transitions to democracy but also enhances vulnerability. Third, the most fundamental reforms in transitions need not take constitutional, or even legal, form. The transformation of the ruling party from a coalition of ethno-linguistic parties to an ostensibly individual membership-based party altered the workings of the political system and therefore the calculations of the political actors.

Moreover, while the chapter does not delve into it, political concepts have unique and often skewed meaning and connotation in different contexts. For instance, politics that is not centred on linguistic identity is seen by some actors as

Adem Kassie Abebe, *Ethiopia's Transition* In: *Democratic Consolidation and Constitutional Endurance in Asia and Africa*. Edited by: Tom Gerald Daly and Dinesha Samararatne, Oxford University Press. © Oxford University Press 2024.
DOI: 10.1093/oso/9780192899347.003.0010

'unitary' and 'anti-federal' and even 'liberal'. Engagements with debates about 'unitary vs federal' and 'liberal vs illiberal' should therefore identify and consider these parochialisms. Finally, political and social culture can be extremely sticky. The allures and tradition of authoritarian politics and the permeability of Ethiopian politics to social and religious notions of inevitability and singular/one-right way (among all key actors, and not just the ruling group) have posed profound challenges towards compromise and constitutional democracy, whose hallmarks are uncertainty and constant evolution. The religious fervour of Prime Minister Abiy Ahmed has accentuated these challenges to the success of a peaceful and national dialogue process necessary to extract the country out of conflict and into peace and relative democracy.

Ethiopia is a country unaccustomed to constitutional democracy. The experiment with no-party democracy did not save Emperor Haile Selassie's monarchical regime in 1974. After ruling through brute military force and conflict with a wide range of ethno-linguistic liberation fronts, the successive Dergue communist regime ultimately established a one-party constitutional framework in 1987. But this was too little, too late. With the ethnonationalist forces prevailing in 1991, Ethiopia's future was cast along ethno-linguistic-based federal dispensation under the auspices of the Ethiopian Peoples' Revolutionary Democratic Front (EPRDF), a coalition of four ethno-linguistic parties representing the four main regional states of the country alongside affiliate parties from the five other smaller regions. The coalition was formed under the tutelage of the Tigray People's Liberation Front (TPLF), representing the smallest popular constituency of the four parties by far, but militarily the strongest. The 1995 Constitution established the foundations for a federal, parliamentary, and democratic system of government.[1]

The new constitutional dispensation provided a modicum of linguistic and cultural autonomy to the country's diverse linguistic groups. Beyond this, however, the country was de facto neither federal nor democratic.[2] The EPRDF ruled with an iron fist. Hopes for a more democratic dispensation after relatively competitive elections in 2005 were dashed as a result of extensive and systematic post-election suppression. Nevertheless, the EPRDF continued to face popular resistance. A mere few months after the coalition and its affiliates claimed 100 per cent of seats in all state and federal parliaments in 2015, large-scale protests broke out, first in opposition to a master plan, which would have expanded the capital, Addis Ababa, into the surrounding Oromia region, and quickly morphed into a movement

[1] The Constitution of the Federal Democratic Republic of Ethiopia Proclamation No 1/1995 (FDRE Constitution). For a discussion of key features of the Constitution, see Adem K Abebe, 'The Federal Democratic Republic of Ethiopia: Introductory Note' in Institute for International and Comparative Law in Africa (ed), *Oxford Constitutions of the World* (Oxford University Press 2011).

[2] Ethiopia is consistently classified as 'not free' in Freedom House, 'Freedom in the World' <https://freedomhouse.org/report/freedom-world> accessed 3 October 2022.

against the government, and also expanding into the Amhara and other regions.[3] The popular protests in the biggest two regions, constituting more than two-thirds of the country's population, allowed reformist elements within the ruling coalition to ascend the political mantle. The TPLF leadership eventually gave in, and in April 2008, the EPRDF selected Abiy Ahmed Ali from the Oromo branch of the coalition as prime minister. This reshuffle in power instantly created hopes and opportunities of a new brand of political and democratic culture.

This chapter tells the story of the tumultuous times between Abiy's arrival and September 2021, when Abiy was reappointed in line with elections in June and September 2021, which returned a landslide for the ruling party. Initial euphoria and optimism about a possible transition to democracy and a less identity- and more ideas-based politics have given way to concerns and disillusionment. Abiy took significant symbolic measures, including appointing prominent figures to lead constitutionally independent institutions, such as the National Electoral Board of Ethiopia (NEBE) and the Federal Supreme Court, and promised to deliver free, fair, and competitive elections according to the constitutional timeline (by May 2020). Some controversial laws (such as the law governing political parties, civil society organisations, and the media) were also reviewed, and new ones, such as the administrative procedure law, were adopted. Political prisoners were released and exiled political groups, including armed ones, were invited back.

Nevertheless, major institutional reforms were largely postponed. The disbanding of the EPRDF and its replacement with a new Prosperity Party at the end of 2019 not only effectively cut the cord connecting with the TPLF but also alienated Abiy's key Oromo base, sowing the seeds of intensified ethno-linguistic violence, particularly against regional minorities. The postponement of the May 2020 elections due to the COVID-19 pandemic exacerbated the political fissures, and the brinkmanship between the TPLF and the federal and Amhara regional governments led to a devastating civil war that still rages on.[4]

After providing a brief context to the run up to the April 2018 transition, this chapter outlines the notable symbolic, institutional, and constitutional developments that followed. Sections 2 and 3 explain how the COVID-19 pandemic added fuel to a fiery political arena and tentative outcomes and projections regarding the trajectory of reform prospects. The chapter concludes with some reflections. As at September 2021, the hoped-for transition to a democratic dispensation has stalled at best, and the country is going through active military conflict, which has led to effective stalemate, potentially reviving missed chances for a negotiated political

[3] For a narration of this movement and the eventual outcome, see Jason Mosley, 'Ethiopia's Transition: Implications for the Horn of Africa and Red Sea Region' (Stockholm International Peace Research Institute (SIPRI) Insights on Peace and Security No 2020/5, March 2020) <www.sipri.org/sites/default/files/2020-04/sipriinsight2005.pdf> accessed 5 November 2020.

[4] Tom Gardner, 'Is Ethiopia Headed for Civil War?' (*Foreign Policy*, 5 November 2020) <https://foreignpolicy.com/2020/11/05/is-ethiopia-headed-for-civil-war> accessed 5 November 2020.

settlement. But there is no guarantee that the conflict will end through negotiation, or even at all.

2. Context

While, historically, Ethiopians claim existence as an organised and continuous political entity for over 3,000 years, the country took its modern shape at the end of the nineteenth century. Preceding and following the epic battle of Adwa in 1896 against the invading Italian army, the first time an African nation successfully and decisively defeated a Western colonial force, Emperor Menelik II expanded south, east, and west, bringing under his effective control large swaths of modern-day Ethiopia. Beyond the battle and victory, two factors connected to this formative stage have defined Ethiopian politics and history: the secession of Eritrea in 1993 and the 'question of nationalities' that continues to occupy the heart of the idea and reality of Ethiopia as a polity.

Despite their defeat, the embattled Italians continued to control what is now Eritrea, historically part of the Ethiopian empire, until the defeat of the fascist regime in the Second World War. Following some years of governance as a UN Protectorate, Eritrea was reunited with Ethiopia in 1952 under a federal arrangement.[5] The federation was short-lived and was formally abolished in 1962, with Eritrea made an integral part of Ethiopia. A liberation movement soon emerged from the independence movement that had opposed the initial merger with Ethiopia.

Amidst increasing pressure from the Eritrean independence drive, a growing student movement steeped in socialist ideology, and a tragic famine, a coup d'état removed Emperor Haile Selassie and ended the Ethiopian monarchy and its feudal economic system in 1974.[6] The Dergue military rule that succeeded the monarchy proclaimed scientific socialism as the governing ideology and redistributed the principal means of production, land, through the 'Land to the Tiller' programme.

As it solved one key political demand, 'the land question', the Dergue exacerbated another through pursuing a policy of unifying national ideology through the 'Ethiopia First' and socialist banner, effectively reinforcing perceptions of a single Ethiopian identity that the empire pursued. This was resisted by the Eritrean independence movement but also a litany of armed groups with roots in the

[5] Tekeste Negash, 'Eritrea and Ethiopia: The Federal Experience' (*Nordiska Afrikainstitutet*, 1997) <www.diva-portal.org/smash/get/diva2:272775/FULLTEXT01.pdf> accessed 5 November 2020; Semere Haile, 'The Origins and Demise of the Ethiopia–Eritrea Federation' (1987) 15 Journal of Opinion 9.

[6] Andargachew Tiruneh, *The Ethiopian Revolution 1974–1987* (Cambridge University Press 1993); Stefano Bellucci, 'The 1974 Ethiopian Revolution at 40: Social, Economic and Political Legacies' (2016) 16 Northeast African Studies 1.

'Nationalities Question' famously articulated during the student movement that paved the way for the revolution and coup that removed the monarchy.[7]

While Emperor Menelik hailed from the Amhara region, the (re)conquered lands were inhabited by groups with different language and distinct socio-cultural and political ideals in the south, west, and east. The nation-building efforts that the monarchy and the Dergue pursued were therefore seen by ethno-nationalist leaders as empowering the political, cultural, psychological, and even economic hegemony of Amharas and elites from other groups who were seen to have assimilated. The movement that started with moderate demands for recognition of the Oromo language and identity was quickly suppressed at the end of Haile Selassie's regime. It was never extinguished, though, and later re-emerged with a vengeance with Oromo, Tigray, Eritrean, and other groups launching armed resistance that challenged the Dergue, which could not subdue the rebellions despite building one of Africa's largest armies.[8]

With the collapse of the Soviet Union and drying up of support to the Dergue, while the United States intensified its assistance to the rebels, especially the Eritrean independence movement and the Tigray People's Liberation Front (TPLF) in the north, the Dergue collapsed in 1991 and the ethno-linguistically organised rebels took control. Considering their roots in the 'Nationalities Question', the trajectory of political and constitutional organisation of the country was clear.

The TPLF engineered the birth of the ruling EPRDF coalition after midwifing the formation of pliant ethno-linguistic parties in the three biggest regions, namely, Amhara; Oromia; and the Southern Nations, and the Nationalities and Peoples Region (SNNPR), while systematically outmanoeuvring and suppressing more popular ethno-linguistic parties from Amhara and Oromia, as well as pan-Ethiopian parties.[9]

Following a series of political engagements, the EPRDF led the adoption of a transitional charter as a constitutional framework awaiting the adoption of a final constitution.[10] The charter claimed ethno-linguistic groups as the constituent elements of the Ethiopian state and divided the country into 14 administrative regions, the biggest of which served as a home to the major ethno-linguistic groups, while others contained multiple ethno-linguistic groups. The charter also recognised the right to secession of ethno-linguistic groups.

A new constitution was adopted in 1995, specifically declaring itself as a federal political compact among nations, nationalities, and peoples (linguistic groups)

[7] Wallelign Mekonnen, 'On the Question of Nationalities in Ethiopia' (17 November 1969) <www.marxists.org/history/erol/ethiopia/nationalities.pdf> accessed 5 November 2020.

[8] John Young, 'Ethnicity and Power in Ethiopia' (1996) 23 Review of African Political Economy 531.

[9] Moses Khisa, 'Politics of Exclusion and Institutional Transformation in Ethiopia' (2019) 40 Third World Quarterly 542.

[10] The full text of the Charter is available at ConstitutionNet, 'Interim Constitution—Ethiopia (1991–1995)' (*ConstitutionNet*) <http://constitutionnet.org/vl/item/interim-constitution-ethiopia-1991-1995> accessed 5 November 2020.

and proclaiming their sovereignty.[11] Alongside the emphatic start with 'We, the nations, nationalities and peoples of Ethiopia', the Constitution organises the regional states primarily along linguistic lines and establishes a second chamber, the House of Federation, composed of representatives of linguistic groups—one for each group plus one more for every one million members of the group.[12] The Constitution also guarantees the right of all ethno-linguistic groups to establish their own state and even to secede from the federation, subject only to procedural requirements entirely within the control of the ethno-linguistic group itself.[13] The Constitution combines these corporate or group rights and foundations with the trappings of modern liberal constitutions, notably multiparty elections, fundamental rights, and separation of state and religion.

The Constitution became the fourth basic law in Ethiopia's history. The 1955 Constitution, which replaced the first 1931 Constitution, had introduced a modicum of representative politics through an elected house of deputies under a no-party system. This constitution was swept alongside the monarchy in 1974, and Ethiopia effectively operated without a constitution until 1987, when the embattled Dergue adopted a one-party, socialist, and largely centralised republic in its dying days. The 1987 Constitution provided a modicum of recognition to the rights of ethno-linguistic groups, but this was too little, too late and unable to appease the ethno-linguistic momentum.

The 1995 Constitution elevated the issue of ethno-linguistic identity from the margins of the constitutional framework to the fundamental axis of politics. It establishes a federal system of governance with regions established primarily along linguistic lines, with most of the states named after the dominant group. At the federal level, a parliamentary system of government combines a head of government (prime minister) with a ceremonial president with virtually no executive or legislative powers. The prime minister is appointed by, and accountable to, the House of Peoples' Representatives (HPR), the lower house. While a second House of Federation exists, it is not involved in the regular legislative process, except constitutional amendments. Instead, the House serves as the principal arbiter of constitutional and intergovernmental disputes and issues related to the right to self-determination of ethno-linguistic groups.[14] The House also decides on the formula for the distribution of federal transfers to the regional states, as well as

[11] FDRE Constitution (n 1).

[12] The members of the House are selected by state legislative councils, which could choose to organise elections instead. Because of the ethno-linguistic basis of representation, the capital, Addis Ababa, which is a self-governing entity under federal control, does not select representatives to the House.

[13] FDRE Constitution (n 1) art 39. See Alem Habtu, 'Multiethnic Federalism in Ethiopia: A Study of the Secession Clause in the Constitution' (2005) 35 Journal of Federalism 313.

[14] See Adem K Abebe, 'The Role of Constitutional Review in the Realisation of Human Rights in Ethiopia' (LLD thesis, University of Pretoria 2012) <https://repository.up.ac.za/bitstream/handle/2263/23887/Complete.pdf?sequence=10> accessed 5 November 2020.

determining whether the federal government can enact laws to ensure a single economic community.

While the Constitution sets up a judiciary and guarantees its independence, it effectively excludes it from the process of constitutional adjudication. Instead, the ultimate power of constitutional interpretation belongs to the House of Federation. With a view to ensuring sufficient legal expertise, the Constitution also establishes a Council of Constitutional Inquiry, including the chief justice and deputy, as well as nine other experts, three appointed by the House of Federation from its members and six members appointed by the president of the country upon the proposal of the HPR.

Overall, the constitutional framework combines a decentralised federal structure with a majoritarian political system at the national level. In practice, the EPRDF was founded on the principle of 'democratic centralism', with decisions and political position at the regional state level flowing from the national level, effectively undercutting the federal arrangement. Moreover, the EPRDF was structured in such a way that the four component parties had an equal number of representatives in decision-making institutions of the party. In combination with the principle of democratic centralism, which ensured a rubber-stamp HPR, this effectively established a consociational system among the four, with no formal say for the so-called 'affiliate' parties from smaller regions, eclipsing the largely majoritarian constitutional framework. The system formally empowered the TPLF, by far the smallest of the four parties, which, in practice, exercised an outsized influence in political positions, control of the security sector and policymaking, and the economy. As such, during the EPRDF years, Ethiopia was constitutionally federal and majoritarian, while, in practice, it operated as a centralised and consociational polity.[15]

The dominance of the ruling party and later adoption of a 'Developmental State' rhetoric, while delivering consistently high economic growth rates due to investment in large-scale infrastructure, made the state a tremendous source of rent-seeking and corruption. Despite the establishment of an anti-corruption commission, the rhetoric was used to justify occasional purges from the party and targeted low-level cadres. The rule of law was also largely absent. Since the 2005 elections, the government resorted to rule *by* law to weaken the political opposition, the media, and civil society organisations.[16] In the absence of rule of law, the opposition was decimated, and the fundamental liberties guaranteed in the Constitution remained distant mirages. Critical voices were silenced, jailed, and exiled, and sometimes disappeared. The country was consistently ranked as 'not

[15] Adem K Abebe, 'Introduction' in Adem K Abebe and Amen Taye (eds), *Re-imagining Ethiopian Federalism* (Ethiopian Public and Constitutional Law Series 2019) vol X, 1.

[16] Adem K Abebe, 'Rule by Law in Ethiopia: Rendering Constitutional Limits on Government Power Nonsensical' (Centre for Governance and Human Rights, University of Cambridge 2012) <www.repository.cam.ac.uk/handle/1810/245111> accessed 5 November 2020.

free' in the annual Freedom House democracy rankings and scored extremely low in terms of civil and political liberties.

3. The Regime-Change Event and the Constitutional Reform Process

For two decades, the EPRDF seemed infallible and, through its godfather, former Prime Minister Meles Zenawi, achieved an intellectual, political, and security hegemony. Hopes for democracy in the run-up to the 2005 elections, the most competitive elections in Ethiopian history, were dashed by the post-election crackdown and subsequent sniffing out of any signs of opposition.[17] A slew of new laws regulating political parties, civil society organisations (CSOs) and the media effectively muzzled any legitimate voice outside of the state. The ruling party also turned trade unions, women, and youth organisations, as well as religious entities, into government mouthpieces.

The ruling coalition effectively abandoned democratic credentials as a source of legitimacy. Instead, it started to propagate a form of performance legitimacy founded on a developmental state rhetoric, drawing on, and seeking to imitate, the economic miracles of the East Asian Tigers. Facing criticism that the developmental state rhetoric was incompatible with the democratic aspirations of the Constitution, the late Meles Zenawi argued that Ethiopia could build a *democratic* developmental state.[18]

The massive state investment in public infrastructure projects in line with the developmental state rhetoric delivered successive years of remarkable economic growth in gross domestic product (GDP) but also increased public debt exponentially. At the same time, the state-led and state-controlled growth unduly benefited individuals and companies affiliated with the ruling coalition. Despite the impressive statistics, partly due to the low starting point and partly the skewed growth, a large segment of the population still lived under abject poverty, and inequality visibly expanded. By 2018, the developmental drive had effectively run out of steam.[19]

The developmental state rhetoric was also used to stem the undue emphasis on ethno-linguistic politics and promotion of a more pan-Ethiopian political

[17] See generally John Abbinkm 'Discomfiture of Democracy? The 2005 Election Crisis in Ethiopia and Its Aftermath' (2006) 105 African Affairs 173.

[18] Meles Zenawi, 'State and Markets: Neoliberal Limitations and the Case for a Developmental State' in Akbar Noman, Kwesi Botchwey, Howard Stein, and Joseph Stiglitz (eds), *Good Growth and Governance in Africa: Rethinking Development Strategies* (Oxford University Press 2012). For Meles's critique of the neoliberal paradigm of development, see Meles Zenawi, 'African Development: Dead Ends and New Beginnings' (unpublished master's thesis, 2006) <https://africanidea.org/m_zenawi_aug_9_2006.pdf> accessed 6 November 2020.

[19] Abdulmena Mohammed, 'Ethiopia's Developmental State Model Runs Out of Steam' (*Addis Fortune*, 28 July 2018) <https://addisfortune.net/columns/ethiopias-developmental-state-model-runs-out-of-steam> accessed 6 November 2020.

community. The government launched a 'Flag Day' and started to implement grand projects, notably the Grand Ethiopian Renaissance Dam (GERD) over the Nile River in 2011. Beyond its tremendous expected economic windfalls, the GERD was touted as a crucial nation-building endeavour to stitch back a country fractured along linguistic lines. The fact that Egypt fiercely opposed the construction of the dam and, at times, even threatened the use of force, mobilised the entire country around the dam. Egypt's successful efforts to deny Ethiopia access to international finances to fund the dam further mobilised the country to raise the needed funds (close to five billion USD when completed) from domestic sources.

Nevertheless, the fires of ethno-linguistic politics were hardly extinguished with popular perceptions that ruling elites from Tigray (which dominated political, economic, and security sectors) were unduly benefiting from the economic windfall. When Meles unexpectedly died in August 2012, despite fears of a succession battle, the EPRDF coalition managed to stage an orderly transition, with Deputy Prime Minister Hailemariam Desalegn taking over the premiership.

Like Meles, Hailemariam hailed from the minority Welayta group, and it was public knowledge that the biggest members of the EPRDF coalition, the Oromo and Amhara branches, were unhappy that they did not get their turn. He was likely a compromise candidate—none of the parties rejected him, but none were enthusiastic about him either. The coalition devised two key institutional manoeuvres to ease tensions. Three deputy prime ministers were appointed from each of the three members of the coalition, while Hailemariam represented the fourth. Furthermore, the party amended its internal rules to provide that no person may serve more than two terms as prime minister or minister.[20]

Moreover, lacking a strong constituency and support from the bigwigs of the coalition, Hailemariam sought to pursue a collegial form of governance. While designed to be accommodative, the arrangement worsened perceptions of continued indirect dominance of TPLF elites. It also led to inefficiencies and marked perceptions of lack of leadership. With its ideological father gone and Hailemariam unable to fill Meles's big shoes and the EPRDF effectively running out of ideas, the dominant mantra simply became 'continuing Meles' Legacy'.[21] Over time, factionalism and power struggles within the EPRDF coalition intensified.

A matter of months after the ruling coalition claimed all the seats in the national and all regional parliaments in 2015, a fateful Master Plan for Addis Ababa to expand the capital and developmentally conjoin it with surrounding areas in Oromia region triggered protests as a continuation of historical displacement

[20] Adem K Abebe, 'A True Glimmer of Hope or a Mere Mirage: Term and Age Limits in the "New" Ethiopia' (*Africlaw*, 15 October 2021) <https://africlaw.com/2012/10/15/a-true-glimmer-of-hope-or-a-mere-mirage-term-and-age-limits-in-the-new-ethiopia> accessed 13 August 2020.

[21] Hailemariam vowed, on his inauguration, that Ethiopia would continue Meles's legacy 'without any change': BBC News, 'Ethiopia's Hailemariam Desalegn Sworn in as Prime Minister' (21 September 2012) <www.bbc.com/news/world-africa-19672302> accessed 3 October 2022.

against Oromos, who claim the capital as part of Oromia. The rejection of the plan provided a rallying point for protests and ultimately forced the Oromo People's Democratic Organisation (OPDO), the Oromo branch of the EPRDF coalition, to announce the abandonment of the plan in early 2016. The incident marked a watershed moment as a regional branch of the ruling coalition effectively challenged the central party leadership.

The protests continued and expanded to other regions of the country, including, notably, Amhara areas, calling for the end of oppression, genuine regional self-rule, equality, freedom, democracy, and the release of political prisoners. Together representing more than two-thirds of the population of the country, the Oromo and Amhara joined in grievances of TPLF dominance, a party that represents about 6 per cent of the country's population.

The protests in the two biggest regions emboldened the OPDO and the Amhara National Democratic Movement (ANDM) to challenge the TPLF-dominated central leadership. Despite being hallowed by the dominance of the TPLF and EPRDF's philosophy of democratic centralism, the formal federal structure gave the two parties the platforms and resources to outgrow their beginnings as TPLF creations and challenge its dominance. The parties started to refuse to follow central orders and even supported and protected protesters. While the popular protests unsettled the central government, the two regional parties provided much-needed organisational, institutional, material, and moral support. It would not be an exaggeration to conclude that the change in April 2018 would have been impossible without the federal arrangement, with all its faults.

Unable to quell the protests or effectively lead the coalition, and in a move that blindsided the TPLF, Hailemariam announced his resignation in February 2018.[22] With no clear successor in line and the coalition fracturing, the resignation opened an acrimonious succession battle, with candidates for the premiership emerging from all four member parties of the coalition.

Under the party rules, the chairperson of the EPRDF coalition, who practically became the prime minister due to the coalition's control of the House of Peoples' Representatives, is selected by the executive committee. Despite the tremendous difference in the size of their constituency, each party had an equal number of representatives in the committee, particularly over-empowering the TPLF, the smallest of the parties.

The TPLF supported the candidate from the SNNPR, the third largest region in terms of population and home to over two-thirds of Ethiopia's ethno-linguistic groups. Because of historical suspicion, it was not clear whether the Amhara and Oromo factions of the party would stand together. Ultimately, the Amhara faction

[22] BBC News, 'Ethiopia PM Hailemariam Desalegn in Surprise Resignation' (15 February 2018) <www.bbc.com/news/world-africa-43073285> accessed 6 November 2020.

threw its weight behind the candidate from OPDO, then little known Abiy Ahmed Ali, who won the chairmanship of the EPRDF in March 2018. In April, he was sworn in as prime minister, the first Oromo to become the head of government in Ethiopian modern history.

3.1 Of Symbols

In a speech at his confirmation in parliament, Abiy projected himself as a proud Ethiopian, rather than just an Oromo, and promised to promote a pan-Ethiopian politics that respects but transcends ethno-linguistic politics. In a country that had been gripped by hegemonic ethno-linguistic politics for almost three decades, the symbolic significance of his inaugural and subsequent addresses and expressions dramatically altered the psychic of Ethiopian politics.[23]

Abiy also declared his belief and support for a democratic dispensation and promised to lead the country through a genuine transition. In other symbolic moves, Abiy nominated the first woman president of the country and appointed women to half of his cabinet.[24] He also nominated a former opposition exile as the first woman chair of the National Electoral Board of Ethiopia and the first woman chief justice of the country.

Abiy also apologised for what he admitted was 'state terrorism' against protesters and the criminalisation of dissent[25] and vowed to release political prisoners, encourage the return of exiled political and media groups, engage opposition forces, and reform laws and institutions to pave the way for a democratic dispensation based on free, fair, and competitive elections. He also promised to hold to account those responsible for egregious violations of rights and corruption.

Moreover, Abiy sought to engineer a new political culture of democratic competition and cooperation by rebranding opposition parties as 'competitor' parties, which has a more positive spin. In a country accustomed to labelling anyone with a different political agenda as dissident, 'anti-peace', and, in the past decade, 'terrorist', the value of a change of vocabulary represented a profoundly fresh political breath.

[23] Maria Gerth-Niculescu, 'Can PM Abiy Ahmed Breach Ethiopia's Ethnic Divide?' (*Deutsche Welle*, 3 January 2020) <www.dw.com/en/can-pm-abiy-ahmed-breach-ethiopias-ethnic-divide/a-51877108> accessed 6 November 2020.

[24] Yohannes Gedamu, 'How Ethiopia's Progressive Premier Is Levelling the Gender Playing Field' (*The Conversation*, 6 November 2018) <https://theconversation.com/how-ethiopias-progressive-premier-is-levelling-the-gender-playing-field-106365> accessed 6 November 2020.

[25] Awol K Allo, 'Torture, State Terrorism and Ethiopia's Transformation' (*Al Jazeera*, 23 June 2018) <www.aljazeera.com/opinions/2018/6/23/torture-state-terrorism-and-ethiopias-transformation> accessed 6 November 2020.

3.2 Of Legal and Institutional Reform

Considering that the former government weaponised the law to persecute the principal troika of democratic dispensation (namely, political parties, CSOs, and the media),[26] and the near absence of effective laws to ensure government accountability, Ethiopia's transition from a near-totalitarian state to a democratic country must be founded on the rule of law.

Accordingly, the office of the Attorney General established an Advisory Council for Legal and Justice Affairs, composed of expert volunteers, to identify and propose reforms to laws that required urgent change, and to propose new ones.[27] The council oversaw the revision of many key laws, including the laws regulating the establishment, financing, and operation of non-governmental organisations. Notably, the requirement limiting access to 'foreign' sources of funding to organisations working on human rights, democracy, and security issues only to a maximum of 10 per cent of total budget was scrapped. The process of registration and updating of licenses has also been simplified. The law constituting the Electoral Board was revised and notably sought to require the consultation of opposition parties in the process of appointment of members of the Board. The electoral law was also revised. Notably, the law increased the number of signatures required to establish parties as well as to run as a candidate, effectively seeking to tame the perceived proliferation of parties, triggering criticism from smaller parties. A new media law has sought to make registration and operation of private media more manageable, including potentially easing foreign participation in media business. The anti-terrorism legislation was also revised, and while it remains controversial (notably for maintaining the political process of designating groups as terrorist), it has removed some of the procedural advantages granted to the prosecution in the previous law, including almost unlimited power to use evidence regardless of its source. Nevertheless, the adoption of an anti-hate speech and disinformation law has been criticised for imposing severe restriction on dissemination of information by the media as well as by individuals.[28]

Another notable legislation that has been introduced is the federal administrative procedure law, requiring transparency and consultations in the making, as well as judicial review of, administrative directives and other regulations. Considering the extreme discretion that administrative entities exercise and the reluctance of courts to seriously review their decisions, if implemented properly, the new law may help transform the working of the opaque bureaucracy.

[26] Abebe, 'Rule by Law in Ethiopia' (n 16).

[27] Abadir Ibrahim, 'The Silent Fighters: The Volunteers behind Ethiopia's Democratic Reforms' *Addis Standard* (Addis Ababa, 27 February 2020) <https://addisstandard.com/profile-the-silent-fighters-the-volunteers-behind-ethiopias-democratic-reforms> accessed 6 November 2020.

[28] Tewodros W Workneh, 'Ethiopia's Hate Speech Predicament: Seeking Antidotes beyond a Legislative Response' (2020) 40 African Journalism Studies 123.

Economically, Abiy's government has shifted the focus from a state-led capitalism to a more recognisable role for the private sector, including a privatisation drive to sell parts of shares of large public businesses, such as Ethio-telecom.[29]

3.3 Of Deferred Constitutional Reform

Despite the push from pan-Ethiopian political groups towards a comprehensive constitutional reform, no formal process has been pursued so far. Nevertheless, contestation over the profoundly ethno-linguistic foundations of the constitutional framework continues. While some parties want to see a strengthening of the current system, such as by guaranteeing ethno-linguistic representation at the national government level, others want its dilution (e.g. by ensuring that the biggest ethno-linguistic groups are divided among many states rather than one state) or even its abolition and replacement with a geographic/administrative form of federalism. This contrast has led to acrimonious relations between supposedly 'unitary' and 'federalist' forces, with the latter accusing anyone seeking to tamper with the predominantly ethno-linguistic foundations of the framework as 'unitary'. Abiy and some key opposition parties have also indicated a preference for a presidential system of government, partly with a view to counterbalance the ethno-linguistically organised politics with an office with a decidedly national constituency.[30]

Nevertheless, despite calls for an inclusive transitional arrangement to oversee legal and constitutional reforms as a foundation for free, fair, and competitive elections, Abiy insisted that *his* government was a transitional government and that any reforms should be considered by a government with a popular mandate. Accordingly, the impact of the political transition on the formal constitutional framework is likely to be felt only after the formation of the new government in October 2021 and the end of the civil war. Other than the timing, most parties, even those who defend the ethno-linguistic basis of the federal Constitution, have included in their party manifestos plans for constitutional reform.

While formal constitutional change is yet to materialise, extra-constitutional changes have had a significant impact on the workings of the formal Constitution. First, the transition has created new opportunities for ethno-nationalist forces to assert their influence and pursue long-suppressed demands for self-determination. Notably, the Sidama group was able to successfully exercise its right to form a

[29] Lionel Barber and David Pilling, '"My Model Is Capitalism": Ethiopia's Prime Minister Plans Telecoms Privatisation' *Financial Times* (London, 24 February 2019) <www.ft.com/content/433dfa88-36d0-11e9-bb0c-42459962a812> accessed 6 November 2020.

[30] Adem K Abebe, 'The Threat of Intraethnic Strife in Ethiopia' (*Al Jazeera*, 1 November 2019) <www.aljazeera.com/opinions/2019/11/1/the-threat-of-intraethnic-strife-in-ethiopia> accessed 6 November 2020.

regional state, officially becoming the tenth state.[31] This has unleashed demands for statehood from other groups. Nevertheless, instead of pursuing the rather permissive constitutional procedure to form a new state, the government has sought to find a political solution with a view to limiting the number of new states. This has created instability in parts of the SNNPR of Ethiopia, home to more than two-thirds of the ethno-linguistic groups in the country. A second referendum, held in September 2021, created the eleventh state in Ethiopia out of the southern region. The willingness of the government to allow some groups to form a state, while being reluctant with other groups, shows the combination of continuity and change regarding ethno-linguistic politics. While the symbolic shift towards pan-Ethiopian rhetoric at the federal level works against ethno-linguistic assertiveness, the decades of identity politics also continue to dominate, including in inspiring demands for statehood.

Perhaps the most profound change relates to the nature of the ruling party. The EPRDF was a consociational coalition of four parties representing the four dominant regions, effectively displacing the constitutionally established majoritarian political system at the federal level. The consociational structure of the EPRDF benefited the smallest of the parties, the TPLF, which had as formal an equal say as the other three, each of which represented constituencies more than three times as large.

With Abiy's rhetorical inclination towards a pan-Ethiopian politics, he saw the ethno-linguistic foundations of the EPRDF as parochial and the equal representation of the coalition member parties, regardless of their size, as well as the formal exclusion of the affiliate parties from the five other regions, as inequitable. He also saw it as a critical reform drive to weaken the formal powers of the TPLF and enhance the corresponding powers of the Oromia branch, the largest. Abiy therefore led the transformation of the EPRDF into an individual membership-based party—the Prosperity Party—in late 2019.[32] This transformation triggered the formal and acrimonious departure of the TPLF from the ruling party. The transformation also led to divisions within Abiy's Oromo Democratic Party. In particular, the former president of Oromia Regional State and Abiy's former boss, Lemma Megersa, who was serving as defence minister at the time of the transformation, opposed the move. The Oromo opposition groups also derided the dismantling of the EPRDF coalition as undermining the ethno-linguistic foundations of the Ethiopian federation and serving Abiy's centralising proclivity.[33]

[31] Adem K Abebe, 'What Ethiopians Can Learn from Sidama's Thorny Statehood Journey' (*Al Jazeera*, 18 September 2019) <www.aljazeera.com/opinions/2019/9/18/what-ethiopians-can-learn-from-sidamas-thorny-statehood-journey> accessed 6 November 2020.

[32] Yohannes Gedamu, 'Why Abiy's Prosperity Party is Good News for Ethiopia' (*Al Jazeera*, 18 December 2019) <www.aljazeera.com/opinions/2019/12/18/why-abiy-ahmeds-prosperity-party-is-good-news-for-ethiopia> accessed 6 November 2020.

[33] Rebecca Zerihun, 'A New Dominant Party Delays Democratisation' (*Ethiopian Insight*, 18 March 2020) <www.ethiopia-insight.com/2020/03/18/a-new-dominant-party-delays-democratization> accessed 6 November 2020.

The contestation around the transformation of the party, notably the departure of the TPLF from national politics and the hardening of intra-Oromo divisions, has soured the political and security discourse in the country. There was, nevertheless, hope among the TPLF and the Oromo opposition that the expected 2020 elections would provide them with the opportunity to challenge the ruling party. However, the announcement that the elections would be held in August 2020, amid the rainy season in large parts of the country, created opposition complaints. All past elections had been held in May, just before the start of the rainy season. The decision to hold the elections in August was necessitated by the need to give the Electoral Board, as well as newly founded parties, time to prepare. Nevertheless, it also meant that the electoral logistics, as well as the last months of campaigning, would be during the rainy season.

Some parties therefore called for the postponement of the elections and establishment of a transitional government. As the contestation was heating up, the COVID-19 pandemic was announced and reached Ethiopia's shores in March 2020, just a few weeks after the announcement of the election timeline. In response to initial measures by both the federal and regional governments and disruption of international and national supply chains affecting the recruitment of poll workers and procurement of election amenities, NEBE was forced to suspend preparations and cancel the timeline.

4. Of COVID-19: The Last Straw

The cancellation of the election timeline added fuel to an already tense political environment. Under the Constitution, the term of the federal parliament, and the government formed under it, is a maximum of five years. This meant that if elections could not be held before September 2020 and a new parliament not constituted before 5 October, there would be a violation of the Constitution. While controversy over the five-year term limit was ongoing, the government declared, in April 2020, a five-month state of emergency, which imposed severe restrictions, including on public meetings, transport, and other activities necessary to deliver on the elections.

There was some suspicion that the government would use the formal declaration of emergency to extend the term of parliament and the government. While the TPLF rejected the effective postponement of the elections, many opposition groups called for the formation of a transitional government as the Constitution does not appear to establish any specific exception to the five-year term of parliament. Instead, the government presented four possible options: a constitutional amendment, using the state of emergency to justify extension, constitutional interpretation, or dissolving parliament. The House of Peoples' Representatives chose to refer the issue for constitutional interpretation to the Council of Constitutional

Inquiry, an advisory body providing initial interpretation of the Constitution for final deliberation and approval by the House of Federation—the second chamber, which has the exclusive and ultimate power to interpret the Constitution. While the Council includes the chief and deputy chief justice, alongside six legal experts appointed by president and three members of the House of Federation, the courts do not have the mandate to interpret the Constitution.

Despite opposition to the mandate of the Council to issue what many considered was a request for advisory opinion, the Council quickly announced that it had the mandate, requested submissions from legal experts, and proceeded to hearings with selected experts, individuals who were part of the constitution-making process, the Electoral Board, and health authorities. Interestingly, the Council refused to invite or hear political parties, which was severely criticised. Despite the efforts to create a sense of impartiality and transparency (the proceedings were broadcast and streamed live for the first time ever), opposition parties dismissed the process as a sham and called for a political solution.[34] This is partly because of the realisation that the Council includes individuals who are, or were, members of the ruling party. Crucially, the final authority lay with the House of Federation, which is a purely political body dominated by the ruling party. This was thought to likely serve as a downstream constraint on any hopes for an independent assessment from the Council.

The Council ruled that the term of parliament can be extended; that federal and state governments, as well as parliament, will continue with their full power; and that elections should be held within 9–12 months of a time when COVID-19 was thought not to pose any serious danger to life and health. This decision was endorsed by the House of Federation and effectively extended the term of government indefinitely and without any formal or informal role for opposition parties.

Many opposition parties rejected the decision and threatened not to recognise the government at the end of its original term. In particular, the TPLF, which controls the Tigray region, announced that it would proceed with regional elections regardless of the decision. Amid this intense political confrontation, a political assassination of a prominent Oromo musician in June 2020 unleashed attacks on ethno-linguistic minorities in the region, with hundreds killed. The government responded by arresting prominent Oromo and other opposition leaders for hate incitement of violence and deploying highly armed security forces across Oromia.

The TPLF went ahead and organised elections in defiance of the federal authorities. The regional government argued that they had the right to self-determination that precedes any authority's mandate. The federal government, in contrast, argued that the mandate to adopt electoral laws and administer elections, including

[34] Jawar Mohammed, 'Ethiopia's Impending Constitutional Crisis and Why We Need a Political Solution' *Addis Standard* (3 May 2020) <https://addisstandard.com/opinion-ethiopias-impending-constitutional-crisis-and-why-we-need-a-political-solution> accessed 6 November 2020.

regional elections, belongs to the federal authorities. Accordingly, when the Tigray government formally requested the Electoral Board to organise regional elections, the Board declined, noting the decision of the House of Federation to postpone the elections. Despite repeated warnings and the threat of invoking federal intervention for undermining the constitutional order from the federal authorities, the region went ahead and established its own election commission, adopted electoral laws and organised elections in September 2020.

Following the end of the original term of the national parliament and government, the Tigray region announced that it did not recognise federal political institutions. Subsequently, the federal government similarly denied recognition to the regional government and announced that federal subsidies would not be transferred to the region and that it would explore ways of transferring subsidies directly to local authorities in Tigray. The brinkmanship, alongside a military build-up in Tigray region, exacerbated political and security tensions, and in early November, a full-blown civil war erupted.[35]

In Oromia and other regions, tension among ethno-linguistic forces continues to escalate, with an armed Oromo Liberation Army continuing to create insecurity in large swaths of the region, even with the massive deployment of the security forces.

The COVID-19 pandemic arrived at a moment of crisis and effectively became the last straw that broke the country's tense political spine.

5. Transition Outcomes

The political reforms and rise of Abiy Ahmed as prime minister of Ethiopia heralded a tremendous opportunity to transform the country's authoritarian and centralised governance into a democratic and genuinely federal framework. It promised to build the institutions necessary to enable a political and economic system founded on the rule of law, political equality, and popular accountability. It also created hopes for transformation of the politics of the ethno-linguistic division, genuine cooperation, and free political competition. More than three years down the line, reality has hit hard, and it is now clear that the expectations were unrealistic. There is nothing as revealing of this shift than the change of tone in Abiy's public utterances from one of togetherness, hope, and reconciliation to a sense of dismissiveness, aloofness, and finger-pointing, particularly in the contestation with the TPLF.

[35] International Crisis Group, 'Ethiopia's Clash with Tigray: Getting to a Ceasefire and National Dialogue' (*International Crisis Group*, 5 November 2020) <www.crisisgroup.org/africa/horn-africa/ethiopia/ethiopias-clash-tigray-getting-ceasefire-and-national-dialogue> accessed 6 November 2020.

The initial euphoria that greeted the political change has given way, again, to doubt and even despair, with the country witnessing repeated bouts of conflict, skirmishes and confrontation, and ultimately civil war.[36] While Abiy still enjoys pockets of support, as partly evidenced in the outcomes of the June and September 2021 elections, where the Prosperity Party won decisively, even in places where elections were relatively free and fair, such as the capital Addis Ababa, the promised institutional reforms have largely stalled. In particular, other than the symbolic changes, the politicisation of the security forces, the prosecution, the bureaucracy, and the rubber-stamping parliament, as well as a partisanship of the public media, have not changed. So far, the reform has delivered neither peace nor democracy, and the country seems to be where it started—perhaps even more fragmented, along with heavily armed regional ethno-linguistic forces occupying a central stage in the security architecture and potentially capable of challenging the national army.

Moreover, the political discourse has also returned to the toxicity of yesteryear, of the desire for total victory and annihilation of the perceived opponent, and of the loyal and disloyal to the Ethiopian cause. With Abiy facing strong resistance from an organised Tigray, suspicion from his principal Oromo constituency, and mistrust even from the moderate opposition, the government has increasingly reverted to old habits of ruling by fiat, through rampant deployment of the security forces, as well as instrumentalisation of the law to undermine even the moderate opposition groups.

Under pressure, and distrustful of institutions and even political allies, Abiy has sought to take a more direct role, especially in governance and decisions regarding developmental projects and the politics of Addis Ababa, with the city's administration largely puppets. He has consistently gone around institutions and pursued unilateral courses of action. Most notoriously, he told parliament, in October 2020, that the members could not ask him about projects he was implementing on public land and resources with money raised through public donations because parliament 'did not give him one penny'.

The postponed elections were held in June 2021 amid a tense political environment, insecurity across the country, and, notably, electoral boycotts from the main opposition parties in Oromia. The elections produced an astonishing result in favour of the ruling party, which won more than 94 per cent of the seats at the federal level.[37] Unexpectedly, it also won all the seats in the capital, Addis Ababa. The second phase of elections was held on 30 September 2021 in areas where they were

[36] Abel Abate Demissie and Ahmed Soliman, 'Unrest Threatens Ethiopia's Transition under Abiy Ahmed' (Chatham House, 24 July 2020) <www.chathamhouse.org/2020/07/unrest-threatens-ethiopias-transition-under-abiy-ahmed> accessed 6 November 2020.

[37] Al Jazeera, 'Ethiopia's Ruling Party Wins Landslide Election Victory' (*Al Jazeera*, 10 June 2021) <www.aljazeera.com/news/2021/7/10/ethiopias-ruling-party-wins-national-election-in-landslide> accessed 30 July 2021.

not held in June for different reasons. In the Somali region, the main opposition party boycotted the elections. The outcomes of these elections are unlikely to dent the dominance of the ruling party. While the ruling party has promised to include opposition figures in the national and federal governments, hopes for a competitive political dispensation have effectively disappeared.

It is important to note that the country's challenges do not emanate only from Abiy's style of governance. If anything, he has slowly slid into a governance habit only too familiar in Ethiopia's political history. The challenge is one of political culture that is profoundly undemocratic and founded on total victory, mistrust of political adversaries, and extreme political paternalism towards the people.

The result is that hopes for heralding a new politics founded on constitutional democracy have been dashed and popular disillusion has returned. Some have even started to reminisce about the 'old good days' under EPRDF authoritarianism, and some analysists have even suggested that Abiy should openly resort to overt 'benevolent' authoritarianism to tackle what they consider to be a more existential threat—violent ethno-linguistic nationalism.

As the new government is constituted in October 2021, the spirit of freedom, hope, and competitive politics that characterised the second half of 2018 and the first half of 2019 has effectively faded. The party–state separation remains as blurred as ever, and the state and party structure continue to churn out propaganda depicting Abiy's messianic persona as only hope for the country, with his images adorning public spaces. Without a radical turn of events, Ethiopia seems to be retreating to its old authoritarian roots. As of September 2021, the hopes and rhetoric of the rule of law and constitutionalism has decidedly reversed gear to Ethiopia's historic default practice of rule by law and virtually unlimited and—even worse—personalised governance system.

6. Reflection: Back to the Beginning

Looking back, the internal party reshuffle that was consummated in April 2018 with the selection of Abiy Ahmed as prime minister was a combination of popular pressure and intra-party dynamics within the ruling party. While the country's ethno-linguistic-based political system did not prevent the centralisation of power, the federal arrangement provided the structural and resource springboard for junior partners in the ruling coalition to orchestrate a successful ouster of the TPLF-minority-dominated government under the EPRDF. It is practically impossible to imagine the changes without the formal federal arrangement, regardless of how battered it was in its implementation. The key lesson, therefore, is that constitutional frameworks are critical even in authoritarian regimes. A pretentious federal system where power remains centralised is still important as it can enable new ambitious arrivals to challenge the centre.

While the symbolic shift from an ethno-linguistic to pan-Ethiopian rhetoric and legal and institutional reforms were notable, the most significant change has been in the transformation of the ruling party from a consociational coalition of ethno-linguistic-based parties to a single unified party. This change has aligned the political system with the constitutional framework, which is principally majoritarian at the federal level, although the absence of any single majority in the country—Ethiopia is a country of minorities—always necessitates ethno-linguistic coalitions at the federal level. The second key lesson, therefore, is that the absence of formal constitutional change should not detract observers from fundamental shifts in the workings of the political system.

Third, the failure of the opposition to align on the issue of transition to democracy has allowed Abiy Ahmed and his Prosperity Party to effectively renege on promises of democratisation. The contestation on substantive policy issues and the differences between perceived ethno-nationalists and pan-Ethiopian opposition groups saw them vying for influence and prominence, in the process weakening both forces and strengthening the ruling clique. The absence of a unified coalition for democracy meant that the opposition camp was divided and competing fiercely, at times trying to use the state apparatus to weaken ideological competitors in the opposition.

Fourth, and related to the above, the hopes for a democratic transition have waned significantly. While Abiy continues to invoke the vocabulary of democracy, little has been institutionalised. Even institutions where prominent figures were appointed, such as the Electoral Board and the Supreme Court, have struggled to mark their influence, and their ability to deliver justice, limited government, or free, fair, and competitive elections are increasingly seen as far-fetched due to reasons beyond their control—effective manipulations of the state apparatus, especially law enforcement agencies and media. Indeed, the results of the June 2021 elections are seen as the demonstrating the difficulty of midwifing genuinely competitive politics, even with relatively autonomous institutions.

For many in the opposition, the transition has effectively been derailed, and Ethiopia is once again reversing to its authoritarian ways.[38] With hopes for a democratic dispensation fading, Abiy appears to be seeking to legitimise his power based on a pan-Ethiopian rhetoric and historical pride, leading the country into a controversial renaissance and portraying a persona capable of delivering growth. This harks back to the performative legitimacy that the EPRDF regime he replaced consistently invoked (perhaps with an enhanced role for the private sector).

While it is too early to tell, the new regime has been unable to effectively stem conflict among ethno-linguistic groups, and political violence and insecurity has

[38] Jawar Mohammed, 'How Ethiopia's Transition to Democracy Derailed' *Addis Standard* (28 October 2020) <https://addisstandard.com/in-depth-how-ethiopias-transition-to-democracy-derailed-reflections-by-jawar-mohammed> accessed 5 November.

heighted. In particular, the confrontation between the federal government and the heavily armed Tigray region has spiralled the country into a dangerous and intractable civil war, which has already produced a humanitarian apocalypse. Moreover, the military build-up in the states—with each state strengthening its special forces—also poses serious risks of destabilisation in the long term. Accordingly, it may well be that the transition is towards an ineffective and potentially unstable authoritarianism.

Overall, despite the hopes, Ethiopia's transition to democracy was always opaque without some form of basic understanding over its past and a transitional arrangement in which all major political groups are represented, rather than a single group insisting on midwifing it. Any hopes to salvage the derailed transition and prevent a tragic repeat of squandered opportunities may therefore lie in a national dialogue.

The ruling party has indicated that such dialogue will be organised once the new government is constituted in October 2021. With a civil war raging and prominent opposition leaders in jail, the inclusivity and usefulness of any dialogue remains unclear. Unless the war sees a negotiated settlement, and opposition leaders are brought into the fold of dialogue, the country's problems are unlikely to go away. Abiy's promise of peace, democracy, and prosperity remains a distant dream, and an inclusive dialogue could hold the key. This would require nothing less than a return to the politics and language of compromise and reconciliation that characterised his first few months. Without a grand bargain towards a political settlement on key issues, such as the structure of the state, while also developing consensus on democracy as the only game in town, the country may simply have reset the countdown to another transition, if it survives the conflict and a new phase of authoritarianism.

11

Maldives Constitution 2008

Winds of Change at the Fifteenth-Year Crossroads

Mariyam Zulfa

1. Introduction

Maldives had a new constitution promulgated on 7 August 2008. The tenets of a multiparty democracy bar one fundamental right—freedom to choose one's religion—have been conferred unto the people of Maldives in this sixth and latest Constitution.[1] In 2008, newly formed political parties vigorously competed in presidential elections and returned Maldives' so-called first democratically elected president,[2] Mohamed Nasheed, leader of the Maldivian Democratic Party (MDP), as the winner.

Barely three years into his presidency, on 7 February 2012, Nasheed was ousted in a coup d'état-style uprising, orchestrated by political opponents joined together with some elements in the military and police forces.[3] The balance of the five-year term was completed by Dr Mohamed Waheed, his vice-president, who was accused by Nasheed of disregarding the Constitution and alleged to have played a major role in his removal.

Nasheed himself was accused of unconstitutionally dismissing an allegedly recalcitrant criminal court judge and forcibly disappearing him.[4] The 28-day-long protest leading to the ousting of Nasheed was purportedly kick-started as a result of this incident, with the opposition parties protesting the blatant disregard to the Constitution by the executive. Calls for early elections by the MDP went unheeded and elections were held as scheduled in 2013. Nasheed faced defeat, with the Progressive Party of Maldives (PPM)—the party of Maumoon Abdul Gayoom, the president who ruled Maldives for 30 years—coming back into power.

[1] Constitution of the Republic of Maldives (2008).

[2] As described on the Maldives Parliament website, '19th Parliament Speaker' (*People's Majlis*, 2018) <https://majlis.gov.mv/en/19-parliament/speaker> accessed 25 September 2021.

[3] BBC News, 'Maldives President Mohamed Nasheed Resigns Amid Unrest' (7 February 2012) <www.bbc.com/news/world-asia-16922570> accessed 25 September 2021.

[4] BBC News, 'Maldivian Army Arrests Senior Judge Abdulla Mohamed' (17 January 2012) <www.bbc.com/news/world-asia-16589429> accessed 25 September 2021.

Mariyam Zulfa, *Maldives Constitution 2008* In: *Democratic Consolidation and Constitutional Endurance in Asia and Africa*. Edited by: Tom Gerald Daly and Dinesha Samararatne, Oxford University Press. © Oxford University Press 2024. DOI: 10.1093/oso/9780192899347.003.0011

The presidential candidate of that party was Gayoom's brother, Abdulla Yameen. As matters unfolded, Gayoom and Yameen soon parted ways in a bitter dispute. Yameen procured a court ruling to install himself as the PPM's leader, forcing Gayoom out of the party,[5] and incarcerated leaders of political parties opposing him, including Gayoom and Nasheed.[6] Under Yameen, Maldives left the Commonwealth,[7] citing interference in internal affairs. Decentralisation, commenced according to the provisions of the Constitution in 2008, was circumscribed.[8]

Despite the tumultuous path facing Maldives as a country grappling with the changeover from authoritarian rule, party politics have gained ground. Multiparty democracy, which was introduced just prior to the new Constitution coming into effect, is now generally accepted as the norm, with the previous president, Gayoom, forming his own party. Prior to multiparty democracy, parliament members proposed a name for the president by secret ballot and, once endorsed, a public referendum to approve was taken.[9] Today, presidential candidates are nominated from political parties, and they reach out directly to the public to win votes.

Historically, from the inception of the first Constitution in 1932 until 2005, only one political party briefly existed (from 1950 to 1953), the Muthagadhim Party, which was formed in 1950 by Mohamed Amin Didi, Maldives' first president. As the then prime minister, he initiated a new constitution in 1953 that brought an end to monarchical rule in 1953. Amin Didi's presidency was short-lived, and Maldives reverted to a sultanate in the same year. After Amin Didi's fall from power, the Muthagadhim Party was wound down.[10] No other political party ever existed until 2005, demonstrating the public's hesitation to engage publicly in political commentary.[11]

Since 2005, however, political party formation has been robust. In a span of 15 years, 10 political parties have come into existence, fostering greater

[5] Mohamed Afrah, 'Civil Court Orders Handover of PPM Reins to President Yameen' (*Public Service Media News*, 16 October 2016) <www.psmnews.mv/en/18288> accessed 30 August 2022.

[6] Mohamed Junayd, Shihar Aneez, and Peter Graff, 'Maldives Police Arrest Former President Gayoom: Spokesman' (*Reuters*, 6 February 2018) <www.reuters.com/article/us-maldives-politics-gayoom-idUSKBN1FP2IZ> accessed 25 September 2021.

[7] See Eva Namusoke, 'The Maldives Leaves the Commonwealth' (Institute of Commonwealth Studies 21 October 2016) <https://commonwealthoralhistories.org/2016/the-maldives-leaves-the-commonwealth> accessed 25 September 2021.

[8] Law on Decentralised Administration of Maldives Law No 7/2010 was amended by Law No 15/2015, third amendment to Law No 7/2010 gazetted on 25 June 2015, which stipulated that functions of local councils shall henceforth be determined by the president in consultation with the cabinet.

[9] Choosing a president via referendum has been prescribed in every constitution since the abolition of the sultanate in 1968 and until the 2008 Constitution.

[10] In 1968, another prime minister, Ibrahim Nasir (appointed to serve Sultan Mohamed Farid Didi), introduced a new constitution and abolished the monarchy. Nasir was the second president and remained in power for two terms.

[11] There is no constitutional bar to forming an association for public participation. The first party, the Maldivian Democratic Party (MDP), was registered on this basis at the Ministry of Home Affairs under a special decree of the President as there was no legislation, at the time, regulating political parties.

engagement by Maldivians overall in party politics, reflecting the flourishing nature of democratic consolidation. To a large extent, Maldivians are now enjoying their constitutionally guaranteed rights to freedom of association and freedom of speech, and privately owned media (whereas, previously, media was state-owned or state-sponsored) engaging arduously in critical commentary. This shift signifies the Maldivian public's desire for more openness and newfound keenness to participate in decisions affecting them.

This chapter traces the political developments in Maldives since the inception of multiparty democracy and multi-candidate elections, illustrating that constitution-making processes are sites for power play by political elites. While political parties create a space for greater public participation, something more is required for the true benefits of individual rights guaranteed by the Constitution to flow to the people and for institutional resilience to set in.

2. Historical Context of Constitution-Making in Maldives

The Republic of Maldives is an Indian Ocean archipelago of approximately 1,200 small islands[12] (out of which about 200 are inhabited by citizens and some 170 are island resorts, devoted entirely to international tourism) arranged, uniquely, in 26 ring-like natural geographical atolls. A constitution-making process was initiated in 1931 for the first time in Maldives by Sultan Mohamed Shamsudeen III. Maldives had been a protected state of the British government since 1887, therefore British assistance was also sought.[13]

According to many historians, a written constitution was required because of uneasiness felt by political elites of the day due to the growing role of the prime minister, Abdul Majeed Didi (who resided in Egypt but travelled back and forth) and questions around the suitability of Crown Prince Hassan Izudeen to succeed to the throne.[14] Maldives' first ever Constitution was given royal assent in 1932,[15] codifying the hereditary but 'elected monarchy' of Maldives.[16]

[12] John Stanley Gardiner, 'The Formation of the Maldives' (1902) 19(3) Geographical Journal 277, 296.

[13] As a protected state, oversight of Maldives was conducted through the governor and commander in chief of the Island of Ceylon, Maldives' closest neighbour and a colony of Great Britain: see Colonial Office, 'Maldives Islands: Correspondence regarding the Agreement of 1887' (CO 882/19, 1887).

[14] Husnu Al Suood, *Political System of the Ancient Kingdom of Maldives* (Maldives Law Institute 2018); see also Shamsul Falaah, 'Towards a Maldivian Nation-State: The Constitutions of 1932 and 1968' in Kevin YL Tan and Ridwanul Hoque (eds), *Constitutional Foundings in South Asia* (Hart Publishing 2021).

[15] Constitution of Maldives (1932).

[16] Historically, names for a monarch were chosen from amongst senior members of the ruling family and voted by what was called a Supreme Council of the Realm, which consisted of senior royals: email from HRH Chris Abdul-Wahhab to the author, on file with the author (17 December 2017).

As defined in this first Constitution, the sultan was to be elected by a two-thirds majority of an august gathering convened in the palace for such a purpose, comprising members of the cabinet, legislative assembly, nobles in Male' at the time, learned persons, and noteworthy persons in the community (*kamuvoshi vegenvaa meehun*).[17] Notably, the first Constitution established a bicameral legislature—a legislative *majlis* or assembly and an elected people's *majlis*. This constitution is regarded as 'foundational' in that it transformed the political status of Maldivians from subjects to citizens, enshrined a bill of rights, established an independent judiciary, and marked the beginning of constitutional rule in Maldives.[18]

Sovereignty previously vested in the sultan came now to be expressed as 'originating from the people': the Constitution provided that all the powers of the state shall henceforth originate from the people, with the sultan listed at the apex of the power structure administering affairs of the state.[19] This meant that the people's wishes must now not be disregarded in matters of state. Another significant feature of the 1932 Constitution was that it included an entrenchment clause that prevented amendments or alterations unilaterally. Any alteration to the Constitution can only be made by a two-thirds majority of the special *majlis* convened expressly for such purpose and was composed of members of parliament (people's *majlis*), legislative *majlis*, learned persons who were present on Male' at the time, and decorated individuals.[20]

Not long after promulgation, though, disagreements arose between the political elites and the Sultan about whether the sultan should occupy the head of the executive branch in a symbolic position or remain de facto king.[21] Growing discontent was also felt regarding some of the legislation (mainly trade laws) that was rapidly passed.[22] The Constitution was rejected and ceremoniously torn up in a public uprising backed by the Sultan and his son. The uprising escalated and culminated in an impasse amongst the political elites. An angered mob demanded that some ministers, who were accused of failing to be true to the people's wishes, be dismissed and arrested. However, these ministers were taken, in the dead of the night, to a government-owned ship and later taken to Ceylon to remain there until the

[17] Constitution of the Republic of Maldives (1932) art 26. (Interestingly, members of parliament or the people's *majlis* were not included in this list). Customary bestowing of titles by the sultan on individuals who made noteworthy contributions to the community is a tradition handed down over centuries. Such persons commanded respect in the community and were invited to the palace for gatherings held at the pleasure of the sultan. Learned persons, who were very few in number, were those who had had the benefit of a foreign education and their disciples.

[18] Falaah (n 14). Jury trials were introduced by this constitution, a first for Maldives.

[19] Constitution of Maldives (1932) art 23.

[20] Ibid, art 92.

[21] Falaah (n 14) 218.

[22] At the time, the economy was supported by Indian Borah merchants who had trading entities in Maldives. Presumably their financial affiliations with the business and political elites were deeply entrenched and the laws affecting trading vehemently opposed.

heat died down.[23] Subsequently, the Sultan was forced to abdicate and was exiled with his son to Fuamulak Island, in the south of Maldives. The ministers sent off to Ceylon were then returned.

After the uprising was quashed, Prime Minister Abdul Majeed Didi, who was at odds with the Sultan, resigned and left for Egypt to be with his family there.[24] In the meantime, the 1932 Constitution was re-enacted with some amendments and a new king, Sultan Hassan Noordeen II, was appointed in 1935. The ex-prime minister's influence was felt as his eldest son, Mohamed Farid Didi, became prime minister and his second son, Hassan Farid Didi, appointed the minister for the portfolios of finance and foreign affairs.[25]

In the reign of Sultan Hassan Noordeen II, a new constitution-making process was again initiated. Abdul Majeed Didi came back to Maldives to assist with the drafting process. The new Constitution, when ratified in 1942, vested the powers of the state in the sultan, the foreign minister, and the people's *majlis*; thus, a dilution of monarchical powers was made. The Sultan abdicated in 1943.[26] The country was then governed by a three-member Council of Regency chaired by Hassan Fareed Didi. As events precipitated, Hassan Farid Didi was presumed lost in 1944 while on a British navy ship that was torpedoed and sunk during the Second World War.[27] In 1944, Abdul Majeed Didi was voted as sultan-elect. This time, he preferred to reside in Ceylon (living in Colombo with his family until he died in 1952) but continued in his role as monarch, travelling to Maldives intermittently. The people's *majlis* appointed Mohamed Amin Didi as prime minister. Amin Didi was a charismatic figure with modern ideas of statecraft, who initiated work on a new constitution with the aim of introducing a republican form of governance to Maldives.

When the 1953 Constitution was ratified, some prerogatives of the sultan were renounced, and, in their place, a people's assembly of 47 members was established (the lower house, called *rayyithunge ge*) as well as an upper house (called the senate), which consisted of 18 members, of whom 9 were nominated by the

[23] As Maldives was a British protected state at the time, affairs relating to Maldives were overseen by the British governor based in Ceylon (Sri Lanka as it was then known, which was a British colony). It was likely that the Maldives government would have sought the assistance of the Ceylonese government in this context, with the ambassador from Maldives to Ceylon, Hussain Hilmy Didi, overseeing the contingent.

[24] Historian Mohamed Farook writes that Abdul Majeed Didi 'resigned as prime minister and left the country, ostensibly to educate his young son in Egypt but, in reality, to escape from questioning from the new legislative *majlis* regarding his misuse of Government finances when he was prime minister'. See Mohamed Ismail Didi, *The Motorboat Revolt, the Demise of the First Constitution of Maldives* (Mohamed Farook tr, first published 1966, KDP Print US 2021) 9.

[25] Ibid.

[26] The abdication itself is a vivid indication of the negotiations at play, first in diluting the powers of the Sultan and second in the installing of an influential foreign minister (Majeed Didi's son) to deal with the British government on behalf of the Sultan.

[27] On 27 March 1944, Hasan Farid Didi was onboard HMS Maaloy en route from Maldives to Sri Lanka when the ship came under attack from the German U-boat U-510: <https://threadreaderapp.com/scrolly/1592130525506207744> accessed 8 October 2023.

president. It was seen as a compromise amongst the elitist rivals.[28] Amin Didi, formerly prime minister, was ushered in as the country's first president, under the new Constitution. The title bestowed upon the president was 'Waly-ul-Amr'—a reference to the president as the authority or head of state as well as the executive.[29]

The 1953 Constitution conferred vast powers upon the *Waly-ul-Amr*, including the right to appoint half of the membership of the legislative assembly and the power to dissolve parliament.[30] A prime minister would be appointed by the *Waly-ul-Amr* who was designated to head the cabinet of ministers.[31] The role of the prime minister may be assumed by the *Waly-ul-Amr* himself if a resolution of the people's *majlis* enabled it.[32] Provision was also made for a vice-president to assist the *Waly-ul-Amr*.[33] Hence, it was an ambitious superstructure that enabled power-sharing between the head of state and a prime minister, with a vice-president in attendance.

The first republic established under the 1953 Constitution, however, was short-lived. The state reverted to a sultanate on 1 March 1954 with the creation of a unicameral parliament.[34] Amin Didi was ousted in a mob-style civic uprising, one of the darkest episodes of Maldives' political history. Amin Didi was banished to an uninhabited island and died on 18 January 1954 (at the age of 43) because of illness exacerbated by injuries sustained during the heated public revolt. Monarchy once again prevailed, however, with the prime minister taking on a more pronounced role in governing. The amended Constitution of 1954 gave powers to the prime minister to appoint ministers, and the prerogative of appointing the prime minister remained with the sultan.[35] In effect, executive powers vested largely in the prime minister and the role of law-making was held by parliament. Included in the 54 members of parliament were 6 appointees of the sultan and 2 elected from the business sector.[36] A new, amended Constitution in 1964 gave wider powers to the prime minister.[37]

In summary, Maldives has a history of monarchical political systems built on undemocratic constitutional rules evolved over eight centuries.[38] The *Dhivehi Tarikh* records that 89 sultans and three sultanas reigned over the islands from 1153 to

[28] Urmila Phadnis and Ela Dutt Luithui, *Maldives, Winds of Change in an Atoll State* (South Asian Publishers 1985) 22.

[29] Constitution of Maldives (1953) art 5 (refers to the Waly-ul-Amr's jurisdictional powers as 'hurihaa gothakun', literal meaning 'in every way').

[30] Ibid, arts 20 and 22.

[31] Ibid, arts 11 and 15.

[32] Ibid, art 16.

[33] Ibid, art 5.

[34] On 7 March 1954, in a constitutional amendment.

[35] Constitution of Maldives (1954), art 58; previously one elected member from the business community and no appointees by the president except for the senate.

[36] Ibid, art 51.

[37] Ibid, art 43.

[38] Athaulla Rasheed, 'An Institutionalist Approach to Understand the Recent Political Changes in the Maldives' (2012) Law Asia Journal 159.

1968,[39] and a hereditary oligarchy formed as the resultant legacy.[40] Bicameralism was introduced in the first Constitution of 1932 but institutional resilience never set in; it was again reintroduced in 1953, with a senate as the upper house and a people's assembly as the lower house. The first republic was dissolved, and the 1953 Constitution suspended by those opposed to Amin Didi's rule. The monarchy was restored but with many prerogatives of the sultan diluted and with more powers granted to the prime minister, again by constitutional amendment, to assist him with executing the affairs of state.[41]

A new constitution in 1968 abolished the monarchy and resumed the unicameral system of parliament. Ibrahim Nasir, the prime minister who initiated the constitution-making process in the 1960s, was in power for almost 20 years (with 10 years as prime minister and two terms of five years each as president under the 1968 constitution). Nasir changed the presidential term from four to five years during his tenure.[42] Nasir is credited in Maldives' history with having quashed a rebellion in the south of Maldives to secede[43] and for ending the protected status from the British government and securing independence, thereafter causing Maldives to take up membership of the United Nations in 1965. Nasir, when needing to travel abroad for medical treatment, has amended the Constitution three times, allowing vice-presidents to govern in his absence. Such provision, not to be construed as power-sharing or a variation in governance structure, was designed solely to ensure continuity of the powers of the executive president.

The 1968 Constitution was first amended in 1970, creating a bar on the freedom of press.[44] In 1972, a further amendment to the Constitution was made and the new post of prime minister created. Some executive powers were delegated to the prime minister. Ahmed Zaki, who was Nasir's minister for foreign affairs, was appointed to the position. This new office lasted only three years. Nasir's prime minister and some senior executives were dismissed and banished for attempting to overthrow the presidency. In April 1975, special *majlis* was reconvened to amend the Constitution once more. The prime minister's role was terminated and provision

[39] *Dhivehi Tarikh* is the official record of Maldives history (in Dhivehi) beginning from 1153, when Maldives converted to Islam: Naibu Tuttu and others (eds), *Dhivehi Tarikh* (Government of the Maldive Islands 1902).

[40] Phadnis and Luithui (n 28) 94: An abridged version of *Dhivehi Tarikh* in English is available in Harry Charles Purvis Bell, *The Maldive Islands: An Account of the Physical features, Climate, History, Inhabitants, Production & Trade* (Government Press, Colombo 1883).

[41] Constitutional amendment of 1954.

[42] Constitution of the Republic of Maldives (1968) art 47 states that the presidential term is four years. This was changed to a five-year term in a 1972 amendment.

[43] The people of the three southernmost atolls, Thinadhoo, Addu, and Fuamulak Atolls, who formed a breakaway government, United Suvadives Republic, allegedly with assistance from the British, for a brief period of time. For a full account of this separatist history, see Seena Zahir *Addu Radhun* (self-published 2018).

[44] Article 15, which was repealed, refers to the freedom as permitted for the procuring, printing, and dissemination of books and newspapers in a manner that does not contravene legislation.

for four vice-presidents was made instead. This experiment also did not last long—the four vice-presidents were redesignated as ministers.[45]

Nasir resigned in 1978 for reasons of ill health and a new president-elect, Nasir's then Minister for Transport, Maumoon Abdul Gayoom, was endorsed by *majlis* and approved by public referendum. He took the oath of office in November 1978. Work on a brand new constitution was begun by Gayoom in 1980. Drafted again by the constitutionally required special *majlis*,[46] this constitution was promulgated in 1998.[47] The 1998 Constitution, though more progressive in outlook than previous ones, still called for eight members of parliament to be appointed by the president, illustrating very vividly Max Weber's notion of 'sultanism without sultans'.[48] The executive was still the central apparatus of state, led again by a powerful head of state, in whom was also vested the authority to control the judiciary, with no independent institutions in place to check and balance that power. The Constitution has therefore served as a tool to confer legitimacy unto powerful heads of state.

In 2008, when the MDP first came to power, it faced many challenges in successfully instituting the steps outlined for completion in the interim period of the Constitution (a two-year time limit). First, with a year left to fully activate the provisions of the interim chapter, it faced defeat in the parliamentary elections of 2009 (always held a year after the presidential elections in Maldives), compounding its inability to govern smoothly. As the MDP did not have a majority in parliament, blockage of legislation, disapproval of cabinet members, and delays in matters such as passing the budget happened frequently, coercing Nasheed (the president at the time) to take drastic measures to simply govern. Heavy recourse was made to the powers granted to the president in the Constitution.[49]

3. Regime Change and the Constitutional Reform Process

As has been the legacy of the foundational 1932 Constitution, the 1968 Constitution also mandated that any change to the Constitution can only be made by a constituent assembly called the *khaassa majlis* (special *majlis*). Such *majlis* comprised all ministers of the cabinet, members of parliament, plus two additional elected members from each atoll, and eight members appointed by the president.[50] The purpose of the *khassa majlis* was to conduct the sole business of amending the Constitution or to form a new one. Thus, a wide degree of representation was

[45] Anand Kumar, *Multi-Party Democracy in the Maldives and the Emerging Security Environment in the Indian Ocean Region* (Pentagon Press and Institute for Defence Studies and Analysis 2016) 12.
[46] As required by art 87 of the 1968 constitution.
[47] Constitution of the Republic of Maldives (1998).
[48] Max Weber, *The Theory of Social and Economic Organisation* (The Free Press 1964).
[49] Constitution of the Republic of Maldives (2008) art 115.
[50] Constitution of the Republic of Maldives (1968) art 87.

required to bring about change[51] or as much representation as could be achieved in the absence of political parties or any apparent opposition to the president.

The 1998 Constitution was 18 years in the making, and by the time it was promulgated, Gayoom had served his fourth five-year term (through the method of referenda). This method of choosing the president was the same as under previous constitutions—by ballot in parliament followed by referendum. Gayoom's name has been endorsed by parliament for a fifth as well as a sixth term, with public referenda returning over 90 per cent approval rating every time, when politics took a very different turn in 2005. Political parties came into existence, precisely with the determination of changing an authoritarian head of state. A call for a new constitution based on the rule of law was then heeded and a new special *majlis* reconstituted. The constitution-making process in 2005 attempted to give more power to the people. The 2008 Constitution was drafted by a special *majlis* that included members who belonged to the newly formed political parties—the MDP registered on 26 June 2005 and Gayoom's Dhivehi Rayyithunge Party (DRP) came into being on 21 July 2005. Pressurized by newly formed political parties, Gayoom initiated what was known as a 'Roadmap for Reform Agenda'.[52]

A significant reform that took place consequently was the separation of police and military forces; police forces were assigned under the Ministry of Home Affairs and military under the auspices of the Ministry of Defence & National Security. Previously, they had operated as one force, headed by the president—the ex-officio commander-in-chief of the armed forces and minister of defence (Gayoom retained the portfolio by powers granted by the Constitution). Under the reform agenda, a judicial services commission was formed with the ambition of creating an independent judiciary (which was later formalised in the 2008 Constitution). Further, in August 2007, a decision was made to hold a public referendum for Maldivians to decide on a governance system. The vote had returned the preference for a presidential system.[53] Hence, it is only logical that executive powers of the president remain extensive in the Constitution.

The making of the 2008 Constitution began in 2004 and sought to establish a presidential form of governance. This time, however, the special *majlis* included members who openly identified themselves as those opposed to the president (Gayoom). When ratified, it was no surprise that the provision for presidential appointments of members to parliament was eliminated. Despite this change, the 2008 Constitution contained immense powers granted to the executive position of the president, reflecting the constitutional culture ingrained from centuries

[51] Ibid, arts 82 and 83.

[52] Strategic Communications Unit, President's Office, 'Roadmap for Reform Agenda, Ushering in a Modern Democracy' (27 March 2006).

[53] Held on 18 August 1987; Stephen Abbott, 'Voters Choose Presidential System in Maldives Referendum' *The Guardian* (London, 23 August 2007) <www.theguardian.com/world/2007/aug/22/uk.stephenabbott> accessed 24 December 2021.

of authoritarian rule. Notably, the new Constitution no longer required a special *majlis*—amendments to the Constitution can simply be effected by a majority vote in parliament, leaving the door wide open for a president whose party had a majority in parliament to lean towards hyper-presidentialism.[54]

Looking back, it would seem that the democratic dispensation launched in 2008 has been derailed somewhat with the ousting of Nasheed in 2012. The remainder of the term, headed by Nasheed's Vice-President Waheed, who, at this time, was head of his own party (Itihaad Party) was marked with immense chaos. An 'All-Party Talks' initiated by the government to address issues of discontent arising as a result of the fall of Nasheed's government failed, and when the cabinet was reformulated in 2012 by Waheed, no MDP ministers were retained. The MDP, although the largest party in Maldives, was sidelined from any political appointments for the remainder of the 2008–2013 term. There was no legal framework to give guidance as to what happens to the composition of ministers and political appointees in the event that the president resigns. When Nasheed resigned, all MDP executives were dismissed or requested to tender resignation. Filing for unfair dismissal was not an option as appointees served at the pleasure of the president.

When elections were held in September 2013, Nasheed attained 46 per cent, short of the 50 per cent + 1 required by the new Constitution.[55] Chaos ensued, with the candidate who achieved third highest, Qasim Ibrahim, leader of the Jumhooree Party (JP) disputing the results in the Supreme Court. The attorney general of Waheed's government took the bold and unprecedented step of supporting a leader of a political party, in the highest court of the land, invoking public interest.[56] As a result of the court case, the first round of elections was annulled by the Supreme Court.[57] Waheed also ran as a presidential candidate but did not win much support. A coalitional arrangement was inevitable as contenders for the presidency jostled for power.

A number of complaints from political parties were lodged at the Elections Commission, causing a major conundrum and multiple delays for fresh elections. The elections commissioner at the time, Fuwad Thowfeek, attempted to hold subsequent rounds of presidential elections within constitutionally prescribed timelines. However, the Maldives Police Service, on the orders of the Supreme Court, intervened and curtailed the Commissioner's actions, literally confiscating ballot boxes

[54] This involves presidents testing the limits of their power by subverting constitutional and legal structures designed to check and balance them: see Susan Rose-Ackerman, Diane A. Desierto, and Natalia Volosin, 'Hyper-Presidentialism: Separation of Powers without Checks and Balances in Argentina and Philippines' (2011) 29 Berkeley Journal of International Law 246, 247.

[55] Constitution of the Republic of Maldives (2008) art 111.

[56] The Prosecutor-General Office and Elections Commission are the appropriate institutions to initiate lodgement; however, in this instance, JP applied directly to court. The attorney general joined the proceeding under art 133(d) of the 2008 Constitution.

[57] BBC News, 'Maldives Court Annuls Presidential Election Result' (7 October 2013) <www.bbc.com/news/world-asia-24436773> accessed 9 October 2023.

packed for shipment to constituencies and declared the Elections Commission suspended.[58] The Supreme Court ruled *suo moto* that the Commissioner was in breach of his mandate and dismissed the Commissioner and the vice-president of the Elections Commission, thereafter sentencing the Commissioner to incarceration. Assuming a law-making role, the Supreme Court issued regulations, to which, in its opinion, the Elections Commission must adhere. The Supreme Court's exertion of authority over the state's independent institutions has thus begun very starkly.

The deadlines provided in the 2008 Constitution for holding elections passed and, presumably exercising caution, Waheed, with the assistance of a Supreme Court order, deemed it proper to remain in office despite parliament deliberating that the speaker of the people's *majlis* must take over as caretaker to fill the constitutional void created and must do so until election results were cleared. Parliament's decision was not heeded as the speaker did not follow up on its own ruling. Matters were complicated by further delays caused in investigating hundreds of complaints filed at the Elections Commission by the PPM and JP.

After the constitutionally prescribed deadlines had passed, presidential elections were finally held on 9 November 2013. Nasheed won 46 per cent (again, short of the 50 per cent + 1 requirement), with Yameen and Qasim attaining 25 per cent and 24 per cent, respectively, leading, once again, to the inevitable dilemma of coalition amongst political parties. After vigorous negotiations with Qasim, Nasheed was unsuccessful in reaching agreement. Yameen, the candidate with the second highest number of votes, was able to announce a coalitional arrangement with JP for the purpose of winning round two, enabling him to secure just over 51 per cent and form a government, which he did.[59]

The resultant coalition, just like the coalition that brought Nasheed into the presidency in 2008, fell apart very shortly. Disagreements arose very quickly after elections, amongst Yameen, Gayoom (both then of the PPM) and Qasim (of JP). The brothers Gayoom and Yameen disagreed on two constitutional amendments that Yameen proposed and speedily passed: capping of the age limit of presidential candidates at 65 years and permitting the sale of state land to foreign investors.[60] The age cap was ostensibly to prevent both Gayoom and Qasim, who were over 65 years old, from running for the office of president. This amendment, widely

[58] See J.J. Robinson, 'Maldives Police Halt Presidential Election; Britain, United States Denounce delay' (*Reuters*, 19 October 2013) <www.reuters.com/article/maldives-election-idINDEE99100O20131019> accessed 30 August 2022.

[59] Cited in Kumar (n 45) 16. For results notifications, see Elections Commission <www.elections.gov.mv> accessed 9 October 2023.

[60] A constitutional amendment was made to allow the sale of land providing that an investment of US $1 billion dollars on land approved for projects by parliament guaranteed the right to own land in free hold. The 2008 Constitution's original provision prohibiting foreign ownership of land (art 251) was changed to 'except' what was termed 'project land'. All approved projects under this amendment attached 'project rights', which included the right to own land in freehold. This amendment is now repealed by the new government of Ibrahim Mohamed Solih (Law No 3/2019 of 23 April 2019).

believed to violate the fundamental rights chapter of the Constitution, has now been repealed. Nonetheless, it marked the beginning of the severing of allegiances between Yameen and Gayoom and between Qasim and Yameen.

Yameen began his campaign to stay in power for a second term early on, having achieved a majority in parliament. He appointed a loyal supporter from his own party, the PPM, as the new Elections Commissioner. The leaders of all four opposition political parties were incarcerated on charges of various kinds. With pressure from the international community, two of these leaders, Qasim and Nasheed, were allowed out of the country, Qasim to Germany and Nasheed to the United Kingdom.

Dr Willy Mutunga, a former Chief Justice of Kenya, announced (during his own retirement speech) that he had accepted an appointment by the Commonwealth as a special envoy to Maldives in 2016, to try and bring together the political leadership of Maldives and to assist with the process of reorientating the country to constitutional democracy and democratic transition.[61] His mandate was to 'support a sustainable political dialogue process leading to a stronger climate of pluralism and inclusive elections in 2018, and to encourage the strengthening of democratic institutions and culture in Maldives'.[62] Mutunga's appointment was rendered null as Yameen caused Maldives to leave the Commonwealth in October 2016.[63]

Meanwhile, the Supreme Court ruled that Yameen was the rightful leader of the PPM, forcing Gayoom out of the very party he had formed, making it the second time in history for the same predicament to befall Gayoom as he had to part ways with his first party, the DRP, in a similar case of factionalisation. The DRP's major players later joined the MDP, and the party now remains in the hands of some former disgruntled MDP members. The DRP at times leans towards the ruling coalition but wields no real power as it had not been successful in gaining seats in parliament. After Gayoom left the PPM, Yameen took over the leadership and dismissed all those loyal to Gayoom. Gayoom formed a new party again, the Maldives Reform Movement (MRM), and worked with other parties to defeat Yameen at the ballot box through forming a coalition agreement prior to (rather than after) the election.

The PPM, as the ruling party, had its own challenges. Party elites competed for lucrative state contracts and sought business opportunities bypassing established legislative processes. In October 2014, the auditor-general uncovered corruption within the state-owned tourism promotion company, Maldives Marketing &

[61] National Assembly of Zambia, 'Kenyan Chief Justice Mutunga Appointed as Commonwealth Secretary-General's Special Envoy to Maldives' (Parliament of Zambia 20 June 2016) <www.parliament.gov.zm/node/5179> accessed 30 August 2022.

[62] Willy Mutunga, 'Farewell Statement to the Judiciary and Kenyans' (The Judiciary, Republic of Kenya, 16 June 2016).

[63] Shihar Aneez, 'Maldives Quits Commonwealth, Weeks after Democracy Warning' (*Reuters*, 14 October 2016) <www.reuters.com/articles/us-maldives-commonwealth-idUSKCN12D1QS> accessed 30 August 2022.

Public Relations Corporation.[64] The auditor-general faced dire consequences as a result, with the president swiftly dismissing him from his role. The tourism minister (who was later appointed to the post of vice-president) was implicated in the misappropriation of funds and was subsequently prosecuted and incarcerated.

Supreme Court judges, bolstered by the precedent of supremacy created during the former regime, took an activist role again, this time turning against Yameen, ordering the release of incarcerated opposition leaders, and ruling that the 2015 conviction of Nasheed was unconstitutional. The executive did not allow the Supreme Court's ruling to be enforced and Yameen declared a state of emergency, giving the security forces a wide range of powers to make arbitrary arrests and ban public assembly.[65] The chief justice and the justices associated with the judgment were subsequently remanded, prosecuted, and eventually incarcerated.

4. A Tumultuous Political Context

Against this tumultuous background, the major parties formed a pre-agreed coalition to defeat Yameen in the elections of 2018. A coalition partnership between the MRM, MDP, JP, and a minority party, the Adalat Party (AP), endorsed a candidate fielded by the MDP, Ibrahim Mohamed Solih, and a vice-presidential candidate, Faisal Naseem of the JP. Nasheed's name as a presidential nominee was not possible at the time because of the constitutional bar on persons convicted.[66] Solih and Faisal Naseem both campaigned fiercely, promising decentralisation as a key election pledge, amongst other things, and won with a clear majority—avoiding a second run-off, as was the case in the previous two elections held under the new Constitution. A coalition cabinet was thus formed in accordance with the coalition agreement.

Although both Solih and Nasheed claimed there were no rifts within the MDP, Nasheed has openly denied the existence of a formal coalition agreement to form government, making Solih's position with the rest of the coalition leaders seem shifty. For the parliamentary elections, coalition partners demanded a proportionate retention of seats in parliament and to restrict competition by agreement. However, the MDP, with pressure from Nasheed, disregarded the demand and put forward candidates for all constituencies. Nasheed's stance gained traction and was cause for celebration within the MDP as the parliamentary elections returned a

[64] Maldives Independent, 'Court Hears Challenge to Former Auditor-General's Removal' *Maldives Independent* (29 February 2016) <www.maldivesindependent.com/politics/court-hears-challenge-to-former-auditor-generals-removal-122490> accessed 30 August 2022.

[65] Yameen concluded that the release of leaders of major political parties was tantamount to a threat to his government, and thereby a 'threat to national security', in justifying the imposition of a state of emergency under art 253 of the 2008 Constitution.

[66] Constitution of the Republic of Maldives (2008) art 109(f).

supermajority (65 per cent of seats) to it, giving the party vast scope to change the Constitution, pass laws, and remove cabinet appointees if it considered it was necessary to do so.

Nasheed himself, after having his conviction overturned by the incoming Solih government, contested in parliamentary elections as an MDP candidate and won a seat for the constituency of Malé. He was selected by the party as the speaker of parliament, with the deputy speaker also appointed from among MDP members of parliament. Nasheed, as the current speaker and the MDP's leader, is advocating for a parliamentary system of governance, a view not yet formally endorsed by Solih given that his coalition partners are opposed to the proposition. Although the MDP has retained a supermajority of members in parliament, that position is therefore threatened with factional divisions looming within the MDP and putting pressure on members. Solih, as the president whose allegiance is to the coalition agreement, has remained silent on this issue so far, understandably so as none of the coalition leaders support a parliamentary system of governance, despite Nasheed's best efforts to lobby them.

While dissatisfaction amongst members of the MDP has continued since the elections, Nasheed met with an accident in May 2021 and nearly lost his life due to an improvised explosive device (IED) planted near his car, blasting just minutes before he approached the scene. Ongoing investigations have not revealed the perpetrators; nor have they uncovered evidence of the identity of any potential financial backers, despite the demands of Nasheed's supporters. A parliamentary inquiry stated that negligent conduct on the part of some members of the administration was apparent.[67] Solih has remained cautious on taking heed of the recommendations of the parliamentary inquiry report, with supporters of Nasheed criticising his inaction, once again causing friction within the MDP as members align their loyalties and question who the real leader of the MDP is.

Today, criticism of Solih's government emanates from all quarters, with accusations of inaction, corruption, nepotism, misuse of courts and government funds, and the abuse of constitutional powers to delay local council elections, further complicated by COVID-19 restrictions and budget cuts to decentralisation projects. Events that arose because of the COVID-19 outbreak have compelled parliament to declare successfully that any emergencies announced by the government outside of the constitutionally permitted state-of-emergency imperatives must first be approved by parliament. Thus, the question of parliamentary sovereignty in the face of a constitution articulating a presidential system has been bluntly posed.

[67] Police inquiry into the incident does not implicate government officials. See Ahmed Naish, 'Maldives Police Say Bomb Blast Targeting Nasheed 'Act of Terror' (*Al Jazeera*, 7 May 2021) <www.Aljazeera.com/news/2021/5/7/Maldives-police-say-bomb-blast-targeting-nasheed-act-of-terror> accessed 9 October 2023.

Despite the precepts of the rule of law and separation of powers enshrined in the 2008 Constitution, democratic backsliding has not been entirely stemmed. The tendency for manoeuvrability by presidents who seek to subvert democratic institutions and use legislative means and courts as tools to justify authority is rife. Maldives' experience since the separation of powers in the 2008 Constitution shows that executive powers concentrated in the position of the president have been heavily relied upon by every government to control and exercise authority over other branches of the state when it sees fit. Parliament, the judiciary, and independent institutions also have their own vestiges of power, and at times they are utilised in varying degrees by political leaders. Political leaders in Maldives, as elsewhere, have found creative ways to garner power through manoeuvring these institutions. Once garnered, due regard to the Constitution and its provisions is not often given.

One debate that keeps surfacing and resurfacing in the political arena is whether Maldives should embrace a parliamentary system of governance. To view the introduction of such a change in governance structure as the panacea to cure the dilemma that every president has faced since the inception of the Constitution—the inevitability of coalition-forming—is akin to ignoring the fundamental shortcomings of the Constitution and looking for solutions elsewhere. The framers of the Constitution may not have foreseen how onerous it would be for one single leader or party to achieve success with the 50 per cent + 1 formula, given the relative novelty of political parties in Maldives. Nasheed, who has been a consistent proponent of parliamentary sovereignty, is finding it difficult to mount support, with his motives questioned, given the current apparent frictions with Solih. But the situation may change.

The MDP's own party manifesto for governance, circulated for purposes of campaigning for the presidential elections of 2018, specified the promise of a parliamentary system. However, such a call is inoperable under the coalition arrangement as it is now a combination of parties that bear the responsibility of governing; the respective weight to be given to each party's manifesto is thus in legal limbo and administratively a headache for the president.[68] The legal weight of the coalition agreement that brought Solih to power is contestable considering the silence in the Constitution for coalitional governance (although it does not bar it). Solih is, on the one hand, duty-bound to his own party's manifesto, yet, on the other, obliged to honour the coalition agreement to maintain the cohesion of his government. Opinions are divided amongst MDP members over the governance structure issue, with those loyal to Solih and Nasheed falling into two separate camps. Any resultant fracture within the MDP may cause divisions, forcing members of

[68] Government of Maldives, 'Strategic Action Plan 2019–2023' <www.presidency.gov.mv/SAP> accessed 9 October 2023.

parliament to regroup, with history repeating itself, as has happened with the PPM under Yameen.

On 17 November 2018, Solih was sworn in as the third elected president of Maldives under the 2008 Constitution. The people of Maldives voted for Solih on a promise to unseat Yameen and to end the perceived invincibility of Yameen's power, demonstrating that political parties can, indeed, work together to deliver the benefits of democracy to the people. The device of coalition agreements, however, continues to stand on weak legs as there is no mention of power-sharing nor a prescribed structure of governance in the Constitution. Power-sharing amongst political parties remains, at best, a matter for private law and is open to limitless directions as both the executive and parliament can initiate legislation to bear upon it. Contract law doctrine suggests that parties are not on an equal footing when agreeing to the arrangement, given the immense powers granted by the Constitution to the president. A creative approach to maintaining contractual coalitional arrangements and preventing them from fraying was seen in the introduction of the anti-defection law introduced by Yameen (now repealed by Solih).[69] This law was purportedly intended to prevent floor-crossing by members of parliament and their potential buyout.

Coalition-making has been experimented with both 'after' and 'before' forming government, with the difference in timing creating very different dynamics within leading political parties. The three cycles of presidential elections since the new Constitution have resulted in no one candidate receiving a clear 50 per cent + 1 majority and gaining legitimacy. The result is that the ongoing political instability in Maldives continues to mar democracy.

5. Decentralisation: First as Development, Now a Vehicle for Democracy?

Solih's campaign platform was primarily premised on the delivery of democracy through decentralisation. Although the 2008 Constitution had its detailed chapter on decentralisation, it took two further years for enabling legislation—the Decentralisation Act—to be enacted,[70] a clear indication that prior agreement was not reached between the executive and legislature on the key features to be implemented with the roll-out of the decentralisation architecture, contrary to what may have been envisaged by the framers of the Constitution.

Decentralisation undoubtedly works well in both parliamentary as well as presidential systems if cooperation and agreement amongst stakeholders is facilitated.

[69] Anti-Defection Law (Law No 2/2018), gazetted on 14 March 2018, was repealed on 13 November 2018.

[70] Act on Decentralization of the Administrative Divisions of Maldives 2010.

It may well be the case that those who vouched for a presidential system in 2007 required the chapter on decentralisation in the Constitution to be interpreted narrowly and applied only via an executive delegation of authority. They did not intend to grant complete autonomy to the island councils, created by the decentralisation chapter of the Constitution. This argument is substantiated as, contrary to the provisions of the Constitution, the president arbitrarily created a provincial layer—in effect, a fourth layer—to sit atop island councils and atoll councils, and appointed state ministers accountable to the government to head each province.[71] The Local Government Authority (LGA), members of which were appointed by the president, and its head, an ex-officio government minister, sit at arm's length to the executive, with appointed state ministers heading the provinces. The prerogatives of the president in the 2008 Constitution were used substantively in this instance, with the governance system tilting towards hyper-presidentialism.

Historically, it was the 1998 Constitution that enabled the precursor to decentralisation—the concept of national development planning in Maldives. Regional development was set out in the Maldives' Sixth National Development Plan, the drafting of which was begun in 2000. Two regions covering thirteen atolls each, the Northern Development Region and the Southern Development Region, were formed. The criteria for selecting islands that were to be included for benefiting from a planned agglomeration of services were (i) existing populations of significant sizes and (ii) availability of land or reclaimable lagoon area for expansion.[72] Given the smallness of disbursed populations over the 200 inhabited islands, and taking into account that the capital, Malé, is geographically located in the centre of the archipelago, the government at the time designated Malé to operate as the centre for planning and then extended development axiomatically to the northern- and southern-most points.[73]

The 1998 Constitution, however, made no mention of the institutional architecture for either regional development or local governance. The mandates of the regional development offices were assigned to the then Ministry of Atolls Administration, a government department created at the pleasure of the president.[74] The decentralisation system did not achieve much success at the grassroots

[71] No mention of provinces is made in Chapter VIII or any part of the 2008 Constitution; 7 provinces were created out of the 20 atolls, and this was done using presidential prerogatives granted in art 115 of the 2008 Constitution.

[72] Maldives Ministry of Planning and National Development, 'Key Priorities and Sectors in the Seventh National Development Plan 2006–2010', in *A Background Paper for the Maldives Partnership Forum to Be Held in the Maldives* (26 June 2006).

[73] During the Sixth National Development Plan period, the government established 2 development regions consisting of 13 atolls: the Northern Development Region (NDR), covering Haa Alifu, Haa Dhaal, and Shaviyani atolls; and the Southern Development Region (SDR), which includes Gaafu Alifu, Gaafu Dhaal, Gnaviyani, and Seenu atolls. The regional capital for the NDR is Kulhuduffushi in Haa Dhaalu Atoll and for the SDR is Hithadhoo of Seenu Atoll: ibid.

[74] The last minister of Atolls Administration prior to the Ministry's dissolution was MW Deen, a noteworthy protagonist for local government in Maldives. Deen served as vice-president to President Waheed after Nasheed's ouster.

level precisely due to this top-down approach in introducing it. Partnerships were not enabled by constitutional powers at the local level, thereby resulting in the system being 'less decentralised'.[75]

The need to expand the tourism industry (the country's major income earner) and establish an atolls-wide network to support it was felt by many as the key driving factor necessitating decentralisation. The tourism industry itself had considerable barriers to entry as, traditionally, the government controlled the industry and expansion was strictly limited. As can be expected, the business elite who were allowed to participate in the industry had vested interests in keeping such barriers checked. With political parties coming into existence in 2005, the call for expanding tourism to all atolls and allowing a greater number of participants in the industry became prominent. As a result, lobbying for expansion of tourism was caused through political parties. Decentralisation came to be promoted as the vehicle for democracy, at the heart of this drive the desire for greater access to economic wealth by more citizens.

Decentralised administration is yet to take off successfully. Interference in the running of the LGA has been widespread across all three presidencies since the 2008 Constitution. Recourse to winding down funds for councils and reverting many of their legislatively authorised functions to the government ministry has been common, thereby crippling the structure intended to perform the delivery of services to local island communities.[76] It seemed that decentralisation was only allowable with 'centralising controls'.[77] Solih's government too, despite his election promise, was forced to cut funding previously earmarked for decentralisation as a result of budgetary restraints caused by loss of income from tourism due to border closures during the COVID-19 crisis.

6. Outcomes

Since the inception of the 2008 Constitution, political parties in Maldives have grown from strength to strength. New political party formation has been robust to date, and the aspiration is that a single leader who will achieve success with the 50 per cent + 1 requirement may emerge momentarily. Funding for political parties has come to be provided by the state after taking into consideration party membership numbers. Moreover, parties adopt their own methods of raising additional

[75] See Cheryl Saunders, Constitutional Design, Options for Decentralising Power (Constitution Transformation Network, Policy Paper No 2, March 2018) <https://law.unimelb.edu.au/data/assets/pdf_file/0006/2698854/CTN-Policy-Paper-2-Decentralisation-Approaches-Feb-18.pdf> accessed 30 August 2022.

[76] United Nations Children's Fund, *Study on the Decentralisation Process in the Maldives with Reference to the Impact on Services to Children* (UNICEF 2013).

[77] Merilee S Grindle, *Going Local, Decentralisation, Democratisation, and the Promise of Good Governance* (Princeton University Press 2007) 34.

funding; with no legal bars to disclose sources, many parties were supported or owned by the business elite. The MDP calls itself a centre-left outfit, although party formation and coalition-making have shown no bearing whatsoever on ideological leanings.

The merging of political and business elites has seen party politics in Maldives become somewhat of a lobby for the protection of business interests. The most glaring example is that of the JP; its leader, Qasim, Solih's coalition partner (who owns several tourist resorts, an airport, and an airline) securing a cabinet position for his wife, Aishath Nahula, a member of JP, as the Minister of Transport & Civil Aviation, and appointing another senior party member and former employee of Qasim's business to the position of Minister of Tourism. Two other political parties are owned by business operators in the tourism industry. Any effort to follow the decentralisation chapter of the Constitution with the objective of expanding tourism to all atolls may be open to capture by business elites unless checks and balances are introduced.[78]

The 2008 Constitution was predicated on a presidential system of governance, with no reference to power-sharing in the event of a presidential candidate not achieving the required majority of votes in the first round. All presidents since 2008 have had to resort to coalition-making and experience has shown that whether agreements were reached before or after the elections, political instability and mistrust by the grassroots members of parties of presidents eventuated. Legitimacy and trust to govern must be bestowed on winning leaders. This has been challenging for all incoming presidents after the 2008 Constitution as no one party on its own has so far achieved success with the 50 per cent + 1 formula.

Under the current presidential system, independent institutions such as the Human Rights Commission, the prosecutor general, the auditor-general, and the Anti-Corruption Commission have thrived less. A precedent is now set concerning the Supreme Court's assertions of its superiority over the functioning of independent institutions, most notably the Elections Commission. The public's trust in the integrity of judges and independence of the judiciary has not materialised, despite the separation of powers granted by the 2008 Constitution. The procedures for appointing judges as per the steps to be followed in the Constitution's interim period from inception (the first two years) were not properly followed.[79]

[78] See Ibrahim Athif Shakoor, 'The Tourism Industry of Maldives—Have We Gone Beyond "Regulatory Capture"?' (2020) 8(1) Maldives National Journal of Research 213.

[79] Article 149(a) prescribes the qualifications of judges: 'A person appointed as a judge . . . must possess the educational qualifications, experience and recognized competence necessary to discharge the duties and responsibilities of a judge and must be of a high moral character.' Several judges lacked formal qualifications and, further, disagreements arose as to whether 'high moral character' should be narrowly or broadly interpreted as the Judicial Service Commission (JSC) in May 2010 publicly adopted narrow criteria. See International Commission of Jurists, 'Maldives: Securing an Independent Judiciary in a Time of Transition' (22 February 2011) 14 <www.icj.org/maldives-securing-an-independent-judiciary-in-a-time-of-transition>.

While an official review of the experiences since the Constitution's inception has not been made, it has been identified that a re-evaluation of the functions and composition of the judicial services commission is now needed.[80]

The ease with which the 2008 Constitution can be amended (i.e. with a two-thirds majority vote) serves as an added advantage for any incoming president whose party had a majority in parliament, leaving the door wide open to possible misuse. Yameen was the first to introduce constitutional amendments, most notably enabling the sale of state land, which was seen to violate the spirit of the Constitution. The MDP, with a supermajority in parliament, has not yet proposed any major amendments, although Nasheed has proposed a debate on parliamentarism versus presidentialism within the party with a view to implementing a change to parliamentary democracy via a constitutional amendment. The MDP's 2022 Congress decided to postpone the debate until after the elections of 2023.

Constitution-making has historically been utilised as a means of conferring legitimacy unto a powerful head of state. The first president of the first republic, Amin Didi, who had considerable powers as prime minister previously, introduced the 1953 Constitution, abolished the sultanate, and amassed more powers unto the position of president, not dissimilar to those of the sultan. Nasir, prime minister under the last sultan, Mohamed Farid Didi, promulgated the 1968 Constitution and became the president of the second republic. The constitution's framers did not see it necessary to separate the three branches of state and held onto the legacy of a fused system. The chief justice remained as a cabinet minister and part of the executive, and the auditor-general served at the pleasure of the president. Parliament, to a large extent, served as a rubber stamp for the executive. Once he resigned after ten years as president, the incoming president, Gayoom, initiated a constitution-making process which took 18 years for the 1998 Constitution to see the light of day.

With the 1998 Constitution, the fusion of the executive and judiciary had remained, and furthermore, the president was conferred the role of the final arbiter of justice; once the office of the chief justice has made its ruling, final appeals were allowed to be made to the president. The president also retained the role of commander of the armed forces. The procedure for choosing a president continued as before, via parliamentary ballot and confirmed by referenda, and Gayoom completed five terms under these arrangements when the device of political parties was used to stir citizens into a new frame of thinking about affairs of the state. The first party to be formed was the MDP and, very shortly thereafter, Gayoom organised his supporters and registered the DRP. These two parties were the two major contenders in 2008 with the JP as the third.

[80] Ibid.

Maldives' experience since the introduction of multiparty democracy has shown that it did not matter whether coalition agreements were formed before or after the elections—they were problematic for presidents either way. The first president under the 2008 Constitution, Nasheed, disbanded his coalition arrangement early on in his term and caused his entire cabinet to resign en masse.[81] He faced many challenges in governing as parliamentary elections did not return a majority for his party. His fate was sealed when all major parties colluded successfully to unseat him midway through his term. Yameen, who parted ways with founders in his own party and did not honour his first coalition agreement, faced a similar predicament. Unlike Nasheed, Yameen, had a majority in parliament, hence he completed his first term successfully with a second coalitional arrangement but was defeated in the contest for a second. Solih, who has come in on a prearranged coalition, is now facing challenges from within his own party, but despite that, he has publicly announced the desire to seek a second term in 2023.[82]

7. The Impact of COVID-19

Maldives reported its first two cases of COVID-19 on 7 March 2020.[83] On 12 March 2020, a state of public health emergency was declared by the Minister of Health.[84] On 26 April 2020, parliament approved a motion to suspend, by one year, Article 32, sections (a), (d), and (e) of the Fiscal Responsibility Act to allow the government to take long-term loans from the country's Reserve Bank, Maldives Monetary Authority, in order to manage the cash flow of the state and to fund events required to control the COVID-19 pandemic.[85]

The approval to suspend certain clauses of the Fiscal Responsibility Act allowed the government to take a long-term loan of 272 million US dollars in 2020 from the Reserve Bank.[86] The motion was passed by the parliament, with votes from

[81] This incident was reported as an exercise in protest against parliament, blocking the government's policies. See BBC News, 'Maldives Cabinet Stages Mass Resignation' (29 June 2010) <www.bbc.co.uk/news/10452297> accessed 30 August 2022.

[82] The 2008 Constitution allows two terms, art 107(a): 'The president shall hold office for a term of five years and no person elected as president pursuant to this constitution shall serve for more than two terms in office, whether consecutive or otherwise.'

[83] Reuters, 'Maldives Confirms First Two Corona Virus Cases; Two Resort Islands Locked Down' *Economic Times* (*Reuters*, 8 March 2020) <https://web.archive.org/web/20200319211647/https://economictimes.indiatimes.com/news/international/world-news/maldives-confirms-first-two-coronavirus-cases-two-resort-islands-locked-down/articleshow/74535526.cms> accessed 25 September 2022..

[84] Section 33 of the Public Health Act 7/2012 grants the Minister of Health the power to declare a public health emergency. This emergency was lifted on 13 March 2022.

[85] Article 32, Law No 7/2013 (Fiscal Responsibility Act of Maldives) refers to limitations on borrowing. Section (a) limits borrowings to 1 per cent of gross domestic product (GDP) at rates not lower than market rate. Section (d) limits borrowing to purposes of improving productivity and national development only and section (e) limits repayment periods.

[86] Finance Committee, Parliament of Maldives, 'Report on the Review and Decision on Parliament's Extension of Deadline for Suspending the Stipulations and Principles Provided for in Sections (a),

60 members out of the 69 members present at the sitting demonstrating that, in a national emergency, warring factions in political parties set aside their differences for political expediency. The suspension was extended to 31 December 2023. The President has, quite conveniently, utilised the time period to pass supplementary funds required to manage the economy in subsequent years. This was conspicuous in the way in which the budget for 2023, an election year, was passed in parliament in November 2022.[87]

Due to the unprecedented spread of COVID-19 globally, tourism, just as in travel destinations all over the world, came to a standstill. The country had to close its borders, with stringent public-health measures taken to curb the outbreak. Border closure for international tourists was made subjectively initially. Arrivals from China were banned on 4 February 2020, and by the third week of March, arrivals from affected regions of South Korea, Italy, Iran, Bangladesh, affected areas of Germany, France, Spain, Malaysia, and the United Kingdom were banned.[88] From 27 March 2020, Maldives suspended on-arrival visas to visitors. A partial lockdown was in place in Male' and Greater Male' and in tourist resorts. Controls were more relaxed, with make-shift isolation facilities created on some tourist islands. Given the geographical separation of islands, isolation measures taken were hailed by the government as successful and effective in containing the epidemic as well as causing the recovery of tourism. After 110 days of closing the borders, on 15 July 2020, Maldives reopened its borders.

8. Reflections

The experiences since the inception of the Constitution that brought multiparty democracy to Maldives in 2008, as reflected upon in the current context, have provided elements of a rich case study of how a long-established society adapts to change and one from which many lessons can be learnt. The lack of an embedded constitutional culture due to centuries of monarchical and later authoritarian rule, a lack of inclusiveness of members of the public in the process of changing constitutions, the relative youthfulness of political parties manifested in their lack of liberal ideological bearings, and the continued factionalisation and disagreements amongst party elites, are all signposts for review as the democratisation process embraces more citizen participation.

(d) and (e) of the Fiscal Responsibility Act', Parliament Report No M19/ML/2021/09 of 17 November 2021 (in Dhivehi).

[87] Ibid.

[88] Health Protection Agency, 'Public Health Interventions to Prevent COVID-19 Transmission in the Tourism Sector, Version 4' (Ministry of Health, 28 September 2020) <www.file:///C:/Users/mariy/OneDrive/Desktop/Covid%20booklet%20Healthy%20Ministry.pdf> accessed 25 September 2022.

Constitutionalism was introduced to Maldives over 90 years ago with an impressive first governance structure instituted under its first Constitution of 1932. Since then, political elites, traditionally formed from within circles close to the sultan, have exerted various levels of influence in changing the architecture of state and, indeed, as to who wielded power over which institutions. In its constitutional history, Maldives' politics has witnessed its fair share of violent overthrows that saw sultans dethroned as well as presidents abruptly ousted. Three viciously orchestrated dismissals were those of Sultan Shamsudeen in 1933, and Presidents Amin Didi and Nasheed (in 1953 and 2012, respectively). On all these occasions, the constitutions in place were fittingly sound. The events were demonstrations of how vehement public reactions to newly introduced changes can escalate to alarming proportions, urged on by political elites. Constitutionalism itself was not at fault, but the context in which political actors engaged with the Constitution needed examination.

In that context, political parties play a major role in advancing democracy[89] or, to put it differently, the roles which political parties are assigned in reality—to animate the rights granted by the Constitution and the governance structures enabled by it in the furtherance of democracy—are critical. The first political party in Maldives was formed in the 1950s by Amin Didi, who was instrumental in bringing the monarchy to an end. After the demise of Amin Didi, the Muthagadhdhim Party wound down. The reason why the party did not prosper to make a significant enough mark on the body politic is compelling. Party politics in the context of entrenching democracy was relatively unexplored in Maldives until after 2005. The MDP was formed in 2005 with the broad aim of introducing greater engagement by a larger number of citizens in governance. However, its ethos in the beginning was fuelled by the energies of personalities enthused to bring down a president who had been in power for 30 years (6 terms). It was only much later that the MDP styled itself as a centre-right party. Political party resurgence has therefore come about with a defensive mindset and was not necessarily ideology-based—a factor that can be seen to hinder maturation.

The first constitution-making process of 1932 saw a small but significant widening of the political elite structure. From then on, the pressure for inclusion of members of the wider public in affairs of governance has become more and more pronounced, with the latest Constitution in 2008 culminating in the call for decentralisation. The debate today has come to rest on the question of whether a parliamentary or a presidential system can best deliver the benefits of decentralisation. At the heart of it lies the issue of how the Constitution can articulate a form of democracy that best represents the people it serves. Three cycles of presidential elections

[89] Tom Gerald Daly and Brian Christopher Jones, 'Parties Versus Democracy: Addressing Today's Political Party Threats to Democratic Rule' (2020) 18(2) International Journal of Constitutional Law 509.

since the 2008 Constitution saw presidential candidates who received around 25 per cent of the people's vote in the first round vie successfully for a second round to the exclusion of the candidate who was supported by a much more significant number of votes (over 45 per cent) in the first round. Hence, a true representation of the people's decision is denied in governance, calling into question the strength of the legitimacy of presidents so elected. The Constitution does not lend itself to providing solutions to the dilemma.

Frequent leadership contestation and infighting within political parties are common in Maldives as elsewhere. It is weakening the general public's trust in the elected president's ability to govern. Party infighting and leadership contestation popularly occurs in parliamentary systems of governance and is often viewed as a healthy feature of a robust democracy insofar as the executive is not hindered in effectively managing the affairs of state.[90] Given the absence of any reference to governance structures in the current Constitution, nothing short of a major overhaul could address the current dilemma of coalition-making (a feature of parliamentary and not presidential systems).

Constitutional democracy can mature only if the resilience of democratic institutions is allowed to set in, without one institution unjustifiably encroaching on the legitimate operations of the other. The spirit of the Constitution has been diluted as extensive uses of presidential powers granted in the Constitution has led to autocratic legalism on many occasions. Experience from three presidencies since the 2008 Constitution indicates that the predilection to resort to these powers emanated from presidents whose allegiance to the coalition arrangement was somehow called into question, for whatever reason—be it pressures from the president's own party or others. Any review of the Constitution will need to address the receding of legitimacy as well as the increased trust issues caused by the inevitable coalition-making that follows from the 50 per cent + 1 stipulation.

Endurance of the Constitution and resilience of institutions enabled by it are facilitated once the Constitution itself truly delivers what it purports to. The separation of the three branches of state is one fundamental feature that it promised to the people. Currently, the role assigned to parliament by virtue of several of the Constitution's provisions has belied true separation. The composition of the judicial services commission is one example in which the speaker and three other members endorsed by parliament are included, tilting the balance towards parliament's favour.[91] Parliament's role for endorsing nominees for judges, cabinet, and other executive positions to head state institutions contradicts the presidential format of governance upon which the Constitution is predicated.

[90] Tarunabh Khaitan, 'Political Parties in Constitutional Theory' (2020) 73(1) Current Legal Problems 89.

[91] Constitution of the Republic of Maldives (2008) art 158 includes the speaker and a member of parliament, as well as a member of the public, appointed by parliament.

Prior to multiparty democracy, in the 1970s, power-sharing through the introduction of a prime minister's office within the presidential system was experimented with. This structure proved that the context encouraged political actors to vie for the presidential powers granted in the Constitution and did not necessarily advance or provide benefits of democracy to the people. The prime minister and the president clashed, with the result that constitutional amendments were swiftly introduced, dissolving the prime minister's office altogether. Today, political parties have come into existence providing a wider opportunities for citizen engagement, as can be viewed in their representation in parliament under the current Constitution. A possible power-sharing role between a prime minister and a president in today's context may prove fruitful if a parliamentary system of governance is, indeed, made possible by a 'yes' vote in a referendum.

From the very first experience with constitutionalism in 1932, every constitution-making process has had the benefit of a constituent assembly or a special *majlis* structure put in place for purposes of review, debate, and amendment of the Constitution. The 2008 Constitution discarded this requirement. This may be due to a wish held by the framers to leave the door open to facilitate frequent change as processes settled. If special *majlis* existed, then it could have reviewed the constitution's wherewithal as it matured, preventing the deadlock during the two-year interim period. If it existed now it could act as a vehicle for further review and make recommendations, even for a new constitution if need be. There was little prospect of smooth sailing in the early part of Maldive's constitutional journey. The voyage was delayed but not denied. With the winds of change blowing in countless positive directions today, a safe harbour may soon be found if the captaincy were to be resolute.

12

Sri Lanka's Chronic Inability to Sustain Democratic Reform

Luwie Ganeshathasan

1. Introduction

This chapter will discuss Sri Lanka's 2015–2018 constitutional reform process. The catalyst for this reform process was the election of President Maithripala Sirisena in January 2015. Sri Lanka has seen several unsuccessful attempts at reforming its present Constitution. These reform efforts have centred around efforts to ensure greater devolution of power and on reducing the power of the executive presidency. This chapter will explain the modalities of the 2015–2018 constitutional reform process and analyse the reasons for its failure, which ultimately resulted in the electoral success of the main political configuration that opposed the said process. The chapter will also trace how mismanaging a reform effort predicated on institutional reform for good governance significantly undermined public confidence in democratic institutions.

Section 2 of this chapter explains the country context in Sri Lanka, beginning with a brief comment on its demographic characteristics. This section briefly discusses Sri Lanka's constitutional evolution since its Independence Constitution, grounding this discussion in Sri Lanka's fraught ethnic relations, majoritarian politics, and secessionist claims.

Section 3 discusses the change in the political regime that occurred after the election of President Maithripala Sirisena in January 2015. Thereafter, this section discusses the reform process that was undertaken both in terms of the constitutional amendment that was passed between the two elections in 2015 and the longer-term project of drafting a new constitution. Finally, this section considers the manner in which the political opposition to these reforms manifested itself both within and outside the government.

Section 4 discusses the Nineteenth Amendment to the Constitution, which was the main outcome of the 2015–2018 reform process, and the different positions taken by parties in the interim report of the Steering Committee of the Constitutional Assembly. The chapter will then provide a brief comment on Sri Lanka's response to the COVID-19 pandemic and its impact on constitutional governance in Sri Lanka.

Luwie Ganeshathasan, *Sri Lanka's Chronic Inability to Sustain Democratic Reform* In: *Democratic Consolidation and Constitutional Endurance in Asia and Africa*. Edited by: Tom Gerald Daly and Dinesha Samararatne, Oxford University Press. © Oxford University Press 2024. DOI: 10.1093/oso/9780192899347.003.0012

Finally, section 5 reflects on the reasons for the failure of the 2015–2018 reform effort. It discusses the failures, in terms of both process and substance, that allowed the momentum and public support for curtailing the powers of the executive president to be completely squandered and provided ammunition for a counter-narrative as to why a stronger executive president was, in fact, needed.

2. Country Context

The Democratic Socialist Republic of Sri Lanka (Sri Lanka) is an island nation in South Asia, located in close proximity to India. It was under colonial rule from the sixteenth century, first under the Portuguese, then the Dutch, and finally the English, from whom it gained independence in 1948. The Sinhalese are the majority ethnic community in Sri Lanka whilst the Sri Lankan Tamils are the largest minority community.[1] A significant portion of the Muslim community live in the Eastern Province but are, in general, more evenly distributed across all nine provinces of Sri Lanka. The Upcountry Tamil community predominantly live in the central highlands of Sri Lanka. Sinhala, Tamil, and English are the main languages used in Sri Lanka. Both Sinhala and Tamil presently enjoy constitutional recognition as National and Official languages, whereas English is recognised as a 'link language'.[2] Sinhala is the predominant language among the population, with significant parts of the population also using Tamil and English.[3]

Sri Lanka's post-independence history is marred by turbulent political contestations on the nature of the state, several racial pogroms, two youth-led Marxist insurrections, and a three-decade-long civil war that ended in May 2009.

Contestation about the nature and structure of the Sri Lankan state pre-dates its independence from colonial rule in 1948. The first serious political articulation of the idea for a federal state was by SWRD Bandaranaike[4] in 1926.[5] Bandaranaike would later go on to become the leader of the Sri Lanka Freedom Party (SLFP), prime minister, and architect of the controversial 'Sinhala Only' language policy,

[1] According to the latest census (2012), the total population of Sri Lanka is 20,359,439, of which Sinhalese are 74.9 per cent, the Sri Lankan Tamils 11.15 per cent, Sri Lankan Moors (Muslims) 9.3 per cent, and the Up Country or Indian Tamils 4.12 per cent: Department of Census and Statistics, *Census of Population and Housing of Sri Lanka, 2012*, Table A3 <http://www.statistics.gov.lk/Resource/en/Population/CPH_2011/CPH_2012_5Per_Rpt.pdf> accessed 5 May 2020.

[2] The Constitution of the Democratic Socialist Republic of Sri Lanka adopted and enacted on 7 September 1978 (Second Republican Constitution), arts 18 and 19 (as amended).

[3] See Department of Census and Statistics (n 1), Table A33 and A34 for language distribution (age ten and above).

[4] Solomon West Ridgeway Dias Bandaranaike, was prime minister of Sri Lanka from 1956 until his assassination in 1959. He graduated with Honours in Modern Greats from the University of Oxford where he was also elected as part of the Oxford Union.

[5] Rohan Edrisinha and others, *Power-Sharing in Sri Lanka: Constitutional and Political Documents, 1926–2008* (Centre for Policy Alternatives 2008) 26–59.

which established Sinhalese as the only official language of Sri Lanka in 1956. This policy is widely considered as one of the early trigger points for the ethnic conflict between the Sinhalese and Tamil communities.[6]

The Independence Constitution of Sri Lanka (or Ceylon, as it was known then)[7] set up a Westminster style of parliamentary democracy with a cabinet form of government.[8] In 1949, the Federal Party of Sri Lanka[9] was founded by a group of Tamil politicians and based as its founding ideal the goal of establishing a federal Sri Lanka.[10] This was based on the widely held opinion among Tamil nationalists that despite the Independence Constitution not containing an explicit provision on the issue, it had established a unitary form of government modelled on that of the United Kingdom. Sinhala nationalists, however, agitated for explicit constitutional recognition of the 'unitary status of Sri Lanka'.

The first mainstream political demands for secession were articulated during the late 1960s. These demands were primarily a response to the 'Sinhala Only Act' and the failure of subsequent measures promised by Sinhala leaders to address the inequality created by the operation of the Act.[11] These initial demands for secession were explicitly rejected by the Federal Party (ITAK) manifesto in the 1970 election, which called for a new constitutional arrangement based on a federal structure of government and requested the people to vote against all candidates who campaigned for secession.[12] The Federal Party won 13 of the 16 seats contested in the Northern and Eastern Provinces.[13]

Contestations between Sinhala and Tamil nationalists on the question of the nature of the Sri Lankan state played out during the drafting of Sri Lanka's first Republican Constitution between 1970 and 1972. The Federal Party submitted a proposal to the Constituent Assembly in the form of a 'Memorandum and a Model Federal Constitution'. The proposal was defeated by an overwhelming majority of

[6] Ketheshwaran Loganathan, *Sri Lanka; Lost Opportunities, Past Attempts at Resolving Ethnic Conflict* (Centre for Policy Research and Analysis 1996) 12–18.

[7] Ceylon (Constitution) Order in Council 1946 www.lawnet.gov.lk/1947/12/31/ceylon-constitution-order-in-council-3 accessed 9 October 2023.

[8] Leonard James Mark Cooray, *Constitutional Government in Sri Lanka 1796–1977* (Lake House Investments 1984) 10.

[9] The Tamil name of this party is 'Illankai Tamil Arasu Kachchi' (ITAK), which translates into 'Tamil State Party of Sri Lanka'.

[10] Edrisinha and others, *Power-Sharing in Sri Lanka* (n 5) 208–15.

[11] For a history of the operation of the Sinhala Only Act, see Nesiah Devanesan, 'Tamil Language Rights in Sri Lanka: Part I' (*Sri Lanka Guardian* 7 March 2012) <http://www.srilankaguardian.org/2012/03/tamil-language-rights-in-sri-lanka.html> accessed 20 November 2023. For a history of secessionist claims based on language discrimination, see Asanga Welikala and Rajavarothiam Sampanthan, 'The Ilankai Thamil Arasu Katchi (Federal Party) and the Post-Independence Politics of Ethnic Pluralism: Tamil Nationalism before and after the Republic: An Interview with R. Sampanthan' in Asanga Welikala (ed), *The Sri Lankan Republic at 40: Reflections on Constitutional History, Theory and Practice* (Centre for Policy Alternatives 2012) <http://republicat40.org/wp-content/uploads/2013/01/The-Ilankai-Thamil-Arasu-Katchi1.pdf> accessed 9 October 2023.

[12] Ibid, 949.

[13] Loganathan (n 6) 46.

the assembly and the Federal Party discontinued its engagement with the process shortly thereafter.[14]

The government of the day, which was led by the SLFP, had more than a two-thirds majority in parliament, enacted the first Republican Constitution, which established a heavily centralised form of government, and explicitly recognised Sri Lanka as a unitary state.[15] Like the Independence Constitution, the First Republican Constitution was also based on a parliamentary form of government, with the National State Assembly (parliament) being the 'Supreme instrument of State power', exercising the legislative, executive, and judicial power of the people.[16]

The First Republican Constitution also entrenched the 'Sinhala Only' policy into the Constitution, with some cosmetic measures recognising the 'reasonable use of the Tamil Language in the Northern and Eastern Provinces'.[17] The First Republican Constitution also gave Buddhism 'the foremost place' in the new republic and placed a duty on the state to 'protect and foster' it, while assuring the right of thought, conscience, and religion to all citizens.[18] Consequently, both the Federal Party and its subsequent political incarnations continued to deny the legitimacy of the First Republican Constitution.[19]

The Vaddukoddai Resolution adopted in 1976 marked a turning point in Sri Lankan political history. The resolution called for the creation of a 'Free, Sovereign, Secular and Socialist state of Tamil Eelam' within the territory of Sri Lanka.[20] The resolution called on the Tamil United Liberation Front (TULF)[21] to establish a political plan to achieve secession and called on Tamil youth to 'fully throw themselves to the struggle of establishing the separate state of Tamil Eelam'.[22]

Peaceful protests by the TULF were repressed by the government, including through emergency regulations which made it an offence to advocate for a separate state.[23] The late 1970s and the early 1980s saw the rise of several Tamil youth-led militant organisations, which, in addition to fighting the Sri Lankan state, also fought each other to claim the title of 'sole representative of the Tamil people'.[24]

14 Edrisinha and others, *Power-Sharing in Sri Lanka* (n 5) 232–53; Asanga Welikala, 'The Sri Lankan Conception of the Unitary State: Theory, Practice, and History' (2016) 1 CPA Working Papers on Constitutional Reform 8–9 <www.cpalanka.org/wp-content/uploads/2016/06/CPA-Working-Paper-1.pdf> accessed 9 October 2023.

15 Constitution of the Republic of Sri Lanka (Ceylon, adopted and enacted by the Constituent Assembly on the 22nd of May 1972, arts 42, 44, and 45 <https://bit.ly/3jE1ldh> (First Republican Constitution).

16 Ibid, art 5.

17 Ibid, art 7.

18 Ibid, art 6 read with art 18(1)(d).

19 Welikala and Sampanthan (n 11); Loganathan (n 6) 54–60.

20 Edrisinha and others, *Power-Sharing in Sri Lanka* (n 5) 254–59.

21 The TULF was a political coalition comprising the Federal Party (ITAK), the All Ceylon Tamil Congress, and the Ceylon Workers Congress.

22 Ibid.

23 Ibid, 261.

24 Loganathan (n 6) 77–87.

A deadly racial pogrom against the Tamil minority in July 1983 saw increased support for these militant organisations from among the Tamil community, particularly towards the Liberation Tigers of Tamil Eelam (LTTE). During this period, the LTTE operated quickly to brutally crush other militant organisations and absorb their cadres.

The United National Party (UNP), which seized a five-sixths supermajority in parliament in 1977, enacted the Second Republican Constitution, which continues up to this date, having been amended 20 times. This constitution shifted the balance of power from parliament to the 'executive president' with substantial powers over parliament and the cabinet of ministers, the judiciary, and the public service. The executive president also enjoyed immunity for all official and private acts done whist in office. The Second Republican Constitution, unlike its predecessor, also contained a justiciable bill of fundamental rights, an electoral system based on proportional representation, and a limited form of pre-enactment judicial review of legislation.

One of the most significant amendments to the Second Republican Constitution was through the Thirteenth Amendment to the Constitution, which devolved some executive and legislative power to subnational units named provincial councils.[25] There are nine such provincial councils. The Thirteenth Amendment was the result of the Indo-Sri Lanka accord of 1987 which dealt with a broad range of issues relating to security and bilateral cooperation. The Thirteenth Amendment was strongly resisted by Sinhala nationalists and disappointed Tamil nationalists as it did not go far enough in terms of establishing a federal form of government. Despite this, the amendment continues to remain as part of the Constitution, although successive governments have used legislative and administrative mechanisms to undermine the Thirteenth Amendment, and parts of it remain 'unimplemented'[26] since its inception.

The next significant change to the structure of governance set up by the Second Republican Constitution was through the Seventeenth Amendment, which was enacted in September 2001. The Seventeenth Amendment sought to limit the powers of the president in relation to appointments made to several key institutions and positions in government. The amendment, which was enacted when the government of the day, did not have a working majority in parliament and was passed with all but one member of parliament voting in favour. The amendment was, however, undermined and ignored for the most part of the subsequent nine years.[27]

[25] The Thirteenth Amendment to the Constitution was enacted on 4 November 1987. The provisions introduced by this amendment are textually similar to the provisions of devolution of power in the Indian Constitution at the time.

[26] See Appendix I [Law and Order] and Appendix II [Land and Land settlement] of the Nineth Schedule to the Constitution (the Provincial Council list).

[27] Rohan Edrisinha and others, 'The Continuing Violation of the Seventeenth Amendment: Yet More Unconvincing Excuses' (*Groundviews*, 2 March 2008) <https://groundviews.org/2008/03/03/the-continuing-violation-of-the-seventeenth-amendment-yet-more-unconvincing-excuses> accessed 30 August 2020; 'Centre for Policy Alternatives, 'President Violates 17th Amendment to the

In 2010, the SLFP-led United People's Freedom Alliance (UPFA) government, which almost won a two-thirds majority in parliament, enacted the Eighteenth Amendment, which repealed the Seventeenth Amendment.[28] The UPFA was able to make up the requisite two-thirds majority by engineering crossovers from the UNP and other minor parties.

The Seventeenth Amendment prohibited the president from making appointments to several identified independent institutions,[29] except on a recommendation[30] of the 'Constitutional Council', and allowed the president to make certain other appointments only after the Constitutional Council approves the president's nomination.[31] Three members of the Constitutional Council were appointed *ex officio*,[32] whilst the remaining seven members were intended to be 'persons of eminence and integrity who have distinguished themselves in public life and who are not members of any political party'.

In terms of the Eighteenth Amendment, the president was only mandated to seek 'observations' of the 'Parliamentary Council' when making appointments to the institutions and officers. As the observations of the Parliamentary Council are non-binding, the president can disregard these 'observations'. Furthermore, whilst the 'Constitutional Council' required seven members to be appointed who were not 'members of any political party', the Parliamentary Council established by the Eighteenth Amendment consisted of five members who were all members of parliament.[33]

There have been several failed attempts to repeal and replace the Second Republican Constitution, the most recent of which was the now failed constitutional reform process undertaken between 2015 and 2018.[34]

Constitution—12th April 2006' (Centre for Policy Alternatives, 25 May 2009) <www.cpalanka.org/president-violates-17th-amendment-to-the-constitution12th-april-2006> accessed 30 August 2020.

[28] For more detailed analysis on the impact of the Eighteenth Amendment, see Rohan Edrisinha and Aruni Jayakody (eds), *Eighteenth Amendment to the Constitution: Substance and Process* (Centre for Policy Alternatives 2011) <http://constitutionalreforms.org/the-eighteenth-amendment-to-the-constitution-substance-and-process>; Rohan Edrisinha and Asanga Welikala, 'The 18th Amendment to the Constitution: Process and Substance' (*Groundviews*, 2 September 2010) <https://groundviews.org/2010/09/02/the-18th-amendment-to-the-constitution-process-and-substance> accessed 10 May 2019.

[29] See e.g. Election Commission, National Police Commission, Human Rights Commission, Permanent Commission to Investigate Bribery and Corruption.

[30] See s 2 of the Seventeenth Amendment to the Constitution, art 41B: '*No person shall be appointed by the President* as the Chairman or a member of any of the Commissions specified in the schedule: to this Article, *except on a recommendation of the Council*' (emphasis added).

[31] See e.g. all judges of the Supreme Court (the apex court) and Court of Appeal, members of the Judicial Service Commission, the attorney general, and the auditor general.

[32] The speaker of parliament, the prime minister, and the opposition leader.

[33] The speaker of parliament, the prime minister, and the opposition leader were members *ex officio* and the two other members of parliament, one each nominated by the prime minister and the opposition leader.

[34] 'News18, 'Sri Lanka's New Constitution a Non Starter, Says Opposition Leader Rajapaksa' (*News18*, 27 January 2019) <www.news18.com/news/world/sri-lankas-new-constitution-a-non-starter-says-opposition-leader-rajapaksa-2015849.html> accessed 6 May 2020.

3. The Regime-Change Event and the Constitutional Reform Process

3.1 The Change in the Political Regime

Having removed the two-term limit through the Eighteenth Amendment, President Mahinda Rajapaksa called for an early presidential election in January 2015 in the hope of being elected for a third term. However, Maithripala Sirisena, the general secretary of President Rajapaksa's own political party, who was also a senior minister in his government, defected to the opposition and successfully contested the presidential election. The election of President Maithripala Sirisena in January 2015 was on the back of promises for ambitious reforms.[35]

The coalition that supported the election victory of President Maithripala Sirisena was formed within a short period of time.[36] It comprised a broad alliance of political parties and civil society organisations with significantly varying views on a variety of issues, including the ethnic conflict and the economy. An important figure in the process was the Buddhist monk Maduluwawe Sobitha Thero, who initially launched and sustained a campaign to abolish the executive presidential system several months before the presidential election in January 2015.[37] Maduluwawe Sobitha Thero was the catalyst to an otherwise fragmented opposition, which shared a common pursuit of opposition to the increasingly authoritarian regime of President Rajapaksa, coalescing around the idea of 'good governance' and the need to abolish the executive presidency.

The slogan of 'good governance' was useful both as a unifying political imperative and as the main vector of attack against President Rajapaksa's regime, which, by that time, was widely perceived to be corrupt. This rhetoric, while necessary for—and ultimately successful in—the immediate goal of regime change, proved to be an insufficient catalyst for the reform project. In fact, the term 'good governance'

[35] Colombo Telegraph, 'Maithripala Sirisena's 100 Day Work Programme; Detailed Diary Description' *Colombo Telegraph* (Colombo, 20 December 2015) <www.colombotelegraph.com/index.php/maithripala-sirisenas-100-day-work-programme-detailed-diary-description> accessed 30 January 2017; New Democratic Front, 'Manifesto: A Compassionate Maithri: Governance Stable Country' (*Groundviews*) <http://groundviews.org/wp-content/uploads/2014/12/MS-2015.pdf> accessed 30 January 2017.

[36] The cabinet spokesperson indicated about early elections in October 2014: BBC News, 'Sri Lanka Calls Early Presidential Election' (20 October 2014) <www.bbc.com/news/world-asia-29693336> accessed 9 October 2023; the election was officially announced in November 2014: Al Jazeera, 'Sri Lanka President Calls Early Election' (*Al Jazeera*, 20 November 2014) <www.aljazeera.com/news/asia/2014/11/sri-lanka-president-calls-early-election-201411201320399688850.html> accessed 9 October 2023.

[37] Nalaka Gunawardene, 'Maduluwawe Sobitha Thero (1942–2015): The Monk Who Ended Sri Lanka's Decade of Darkness' (*Groundviews*, 8 November 2015) <https://groundviews.org/2015/11/08/maduluwawe-sobitha-thero-1942-2015-the-monk-who-ended-sri-lankas-decade-of-darkness> accessed 1 September 2020; H.L. Seneviratne, 'Maduluwawe Sobitha, From Nationalist To Democratic Activist' *Colombo Telegraph* (Colombo, 10 November 2015) <www.colombotelegraph.com/index.php/maduluwawe-sobitha-from-nationalist-to-democratic-activist> accessed 1 September 2020.

and its Sinhala equivalent, 'Yaha Palanaya', proved to be a potent weapon in the hands of the Rajapaksa-led opposition parties between 2015 and 2020 to criticise the corruption of the government led by President Maithripala Sirisena and Prime Minister Ranil Wickremesinghe.

Soon after his victory in the January 2015 presidential elections, President Sirisena became the leader of the SLFP and the UPFA. These two entities had worked against him during a bitterly contested election.[38] Despite losing the presidential election, former President Mahinda Rajapaksa continued to enjoy the support of a large part of the party machinery and voter base. Rajapaksa's support within the party and country at large contributed to President Sirisena's decision to allow his predecessor to contest the parliamentary elections of August 2015 under the UPFA. The main contenders in the parliamentary election were the UNP-led United National Front (UNF) coalition and the SLFP-led UPFA coalition. The election did not yield a clear winner; however, the UNP-led coalition won the largest number of seats (106) and the UPFA secured 95 seats in the 225-member parliament.[39]

The result, whilst not overwhelming, still affirmed the mandate given at the January elections. It also ensured that the two main parties were reliant on each other to govern the country and confirmed the continued popularity of former President Mahinda Rajapaksa, despite the loss at the presidential election.

With neither of the two main coalitions being able to form a government on their own,[40] the UNP (the main constituent party of the UNF) and the SLFP (the main constituent party of the UPFA) signed a memorandum of understanding (MoU) to form a National Unity government for the period of two years.[41] This historic move was the first time the SLFP and the UNP had entered into a coalition to form a government but was also met with opposition by a section of the UPFA, which continued to sit in opposition (described as the joint opposition). This group, with the leadership of former President Mahinda Rajapaksa, would later go on to form their own political party, the Sri Lanka Podujana Peramuna (SLPP).

[38] INFORM, 'Repression of Dissent in Sri Lanka: 22 Nov 2014–31 January 2015 Presidential Election Coverage' (*INFORM*, February 2015) <https://ihrdc.files.wordpress.com/2015/05/repression-of-dissent-in-sri-lanka-22nov2014-31jan2015-election-special-edition-english-08march2015.pdf>; Asian Mirror, 'Dummy Sirisena Swallows Rs. 2 Million Public Money' *Asian Mirror* (1 February 2015) <https://asianmirror.lk/index.php?option=com_k2&view=item&id=6778:dummy-sirisena-swallows-rs-2-million-public-money&Itemid=162> accessed 30 January 2017; Lahiru Fernando, 'Abducted Child Used to Defame Presidential Candidate Alleges Mother' *Sri Lanka News—Newsfirst* (2 January 2015) <http://newsfirst.lk/english/2015/01/abducted-child-used-defame-presidential-candidate-alleges-mother-watch-report/70489> accessed 30 January 2017.

[39] The Election Commission, 'Final Results of 2015 Parliamentary Election' <https://results.elections.gov.lk/#App> accessed 31 August 2020.

[40] UNP-106 seats, UPFA-95 seats, ITAK-16 seats, JVP-6 seats, SLMC-1 seat, EPDP-1 seat: see ibid.

[41] Tharushan Fernando, 'UNP and SLFP Reach a Two-Year Agreement' *Sri Lanka News—Newsfirst* (21 August 2015) <www.newsfirst.lk/2015/08/21/unp-and-slfp-reach-a-two-year-agreement> accessed 31 August 2020.

3.2 The Nineteenth Amendment to the Constitution

Immediately after the presidential election, both President Sirisena and the new government, led by the UNP, faced significant challenges in the process of fulfilling the promise of constitutional reform. The government had to accommodate differing views within a politically diverse coalition and also an opposition that continued to have a significant majority in parliament.[42] Although many expected the members of parliament of the UPFA to move towards its new leader, a variety of factors led to a significant part of the UPFA parliamentary group continuing to support former President Rajapaksa or remaining noncommittal in their support.[43] Inevitably, this impacted the content of the proposed reforms.[44]

Despite the commitment to 'good government', the process of drafting and passing the Nineteenth Amendment was shrouded in secrecy.[45] This lack of official and authoritative information was problematic as it prevented the government from galvanising support for the proposals and countering the opposition against it. This also allowed the bill's opponents to spread misinformation about its content and implications.[46] Whilst the amendment was eventually passed in parliament, with overwhelming support, the secretive process allowed the opponents of the amendment to continue to attack its legitimacy.

3.3 The Scope of Reform Introduced by the Nineteenth Amendment

The final text of the amendment was the result of a political compromise,[47] which, despite the chaotic

[42] After the presidential election of 2015, some members of the SLFP-led UPFA joined the government and took up cabinet positions, whilst other sections of the UPFA opted to sit in the opposition. See Economic Times, 'Mahinda Rajapaksa Loyalists Seek Ouster of Sri Lankan Opposition Leader Nimal Siripala de Silva Read' *Economic Times* (7 April 2015) <http://economictimes.indiatimes.com/articles how/46838378.cms?utm_source=contentofinterest&utm_medium=text&utm_campaign=cppst> accessed 9 October 2023.

[43] President Maithripala Sirisena was elected primarily on the support of the UNP. This was seen as a betrayal by the SLFP/UPFA members, who supported former President Rajapaksa during the elections.

[44] The main change pushed by the UPFA was with regard to the composition of the Constitutional Council, specifically the reduction in the number of non-political appointees on the Council.

[45] Aruni Jayakodi, 'The Process of Constitutional Reform: January to May 2015' in Asanga Welikala (ed), *The Nineteenth Amendment to the Constitution: Content and Context* (Centre for Policy Alternatives 2016) <http://constitutionalreforms.org/2016/05/10/chapter-1-the-process-of-constitutional-reform-january-to-may-2015> accessed 30 January 2017; Kelum Bandara, '19A Riddled with Confusions, Complications and Contradictions' *Daily Mirror* (London, 3 April 2015) <www.dailymirror.lk/68407/19a-riddled-with-confusions-complications-and-contradictions>.

[46] Camelia Nathanial, '19-A: Threat To National Security—Sarath Weerasekera' *Sunday Leader* (3 May 2015) <www.thesundayleader.lk/2015/05/03/19-a-threat-to-national-security-sarath-weerasekara>.

[47] A total of 174 amendments had been submitted for consideration during the committee stage of the Bill (63 amendments by the government and 111 by the opposition).

process,[48] received near-unanimous support within parliament. Some important areas provided in the Nineteenth Amendment include the removal of the president's immunity for official acts,[49] reducing the president's power in relation to parliament,[50] reintroducing term limits for the office of the president,[51] taking away the sole power of the president to make appointments to key independent institutions,[52] improving transparency in the law-making process,[53] and granting constitutional recognition to the right to information. Furthermore, whilst the president retained power over other aspects of cabinet appointments,[54] the president was required to act on the advice of the prime minister in identifying specific MPs for appointment as cabinet and other ministers.

The Nineteenth Amendment resulted in imposing the most significant limitations on the powers of the office of the executive president under the Second Republican Constitution. Despite all holders of the office between 1994 and 2019 promising to abolish the executive presidency, the Nineteenth Amendment constitutes the most significant curtailment of the powers of the presidency that was undertaken within this period.

3.4 Towards a New Constitution

Within six months of the parliamentary election in August 2015, the government appointed the Public Representations Committee on Constitutional Reform (PRC). The PRC comprised professionals and academics and was tasked with gathering representations from citizens from across the country on proposals for a new constitution.[55] The government also presented a resolution to parliament, which was adopted unanimously, to establish a Constitutional Assembly to formulate a

[48] Through the chaotic process of the Committee stage, the changes being made to the bill were unclear for almost three weeks. See Jayakodi (n 45).

[49] The president's official acts were specifically made subject to the Fundamental Rights jurisdiction: s 7 of the 19th Amendment to the Constitution of Sri Lanka.

[50] Section 17 of the 19th Amendment, which amended art 70(1) of the Constitution.

[51] Section 4 of the 19th Amendment, which amended art 31(2) of the Constitution.

[52] Section 7 of the 19th Amendment, which amended art 35 of the Constitution.

[53] Constitution of Sri Lanka, art 41.B(1).

[54] The president—the head of the cabinet—appoints the prime minister. The president determines the number of cabinet ministries and the assignment of subjects to ministers, and retains the power to change the assignment of subjects and functions for such ministries. However, the president can appoint a member of parliament as a minister only on the advice of the prime minister and can only dismiss such a minister on the advice of the prime minister. Furthermore, the president does not have the power to dismiss the prime minister.

[55] 'According to our records, over 2,500 persons/organizations have appeared before us and made oral and written representations. Further, over 800 presentations were received via e-mail, 150 by way of fax messages, 60 by telephone messages, and 700 representations by post or handed over at the office': Public Representations Committee on Constitutional Reform, 'Public Representations Committee on Constitutional Reform' (May 2016) <http://constitutionnet.org/sites/default/files/sri_lanka_prc_report-english-final.pdf> accessed 9 October 2023.

new constitution.[56] The Constitutional Assembly, in turn, appointed the Steering Committee of the Constitutional Assembly (the Steering Committee) comprising 21 members.[57] The role of the Steering Committee was to consider the different reports developed by the relevant subcommittees and its own deliberation and to submit a report to the Constitutional Assembly, including possibly providing the Assembly with 'a draft constitutional proposal'.[58]

In the most optimistic sense, the Steering Committee represents an attempt to gain broader cross-party political consensus for constitutional proposals. Perhaps this was envisaged as the only viable model for constitutional reform in Sri Lanka, particularly considering the failures of the past when attempting constitutional reform which impacts the nature of the state. Perhaps it was also an attempt to build on the experience of passing the Nineteenth Amendment to the Constitution, which included political compromise between the different groups in parliament.

The membership of the Steering Committee comprised eight members from the UNP, three from minority parties allied to the UNP,[59] five from the UPFA, which included three members who were part of the UPFA in the National Unity government and two members who were part of the 'joint opposition'; one member from the Eelam Peoples Democratic Party, which was alighted with the 'joint opposition'; and two each from the Tamil National Alliance (TNA) and the Janatha Vimukthi Peramuna (JVP). Whilst, on first blush, it might seem like those supporting a new constitution were the overwhelming majority, with only the two members of the joint opposition seemingly opposed to the reform process, the reality of the process was much more complex.

First, the two joint opposition members were not openly adversarial to the reform process, including in their public comments. In fact, the members were part of key subcommittees proposing reform on devolution, which were more progressive than the existing devolution framework. Second, whilst the three members of the UPFA who were also in the National Unity government seemingly supported the reform effort, they continuously delayed the process. In the end, all three of these members switched allegiances to the SLPP and became vociferous critics of the reform process. Third, a member who was part of the UNP also defected to the SLPP and became a critic of the process. Despite official change of party affiliation happening some time after the reform effort had collapsed, it was increasingly

[56] K Venkataramanan, 'In the Throes of Political Reform' (*The Hindu*, 6 January 2016) <www.thehindu.com/opinion/op-ed/In-the-throes-of-political-reform/article13984280.ece> accessed 30 January 2017; The Hindu, 'Sri Lanka Kick-Starts Process to Adopt a New Statute' (*The Hindu*, 9 January 2016) <www.thehindu.com/news/international/Sri-Lanka-kick-starts-process-to-adopt-new-statute/article13990310.ece> accessed 9 October 2023.

[57] 'Parliament of Sri Lanka—Constitutional Assembly' <www.parliament.lk/constitutional-assembly> accessed 31 August 2020.

[58] The Resolution of Parliament appointing a Constitutional Assembly, cl 16.

[59] This included one each from the Sri Lanka Muslim Congress, All Ceylon Makkal Congress, and the Tamil Progressive Alliance.

clear, during the process, that his loyalties did not rest with formulating a new constitution.

The negotiations were particularly fraught on the dual issues relating to abolishing the executive presidency and devolution of power. The issue of devolution of power has historically been a contentious issue,[60] but some progress was seemingly being made on that front (at least between the UNP and the SLFP). However, the SLFP and the section of the UPFA within the national government wanted to trade concessions on devolution to retain the executive presidency in its post-Nineteenth Amendment form.[61] There was also clear disagreement between the TNA, on one hand, and the UNP and SLFP, on the other, as regards the extent of devolution of power and in relation to whether the Constitution would continue to have the label of a unitary state. Additionally, the joint opposition as a group, went into the Steering Committee process with several non-negotiable preconditions, which left little room for negotiation and change on the issues of devolution of power and the executive presidency.[62]

Another point of contention was regarding the new electoral system. Whilst the Steering Committee was divided on the proposed new electoral system, amendments were made to the Local Authority Elections Acts and the Provincial Councils Elections Act to introduce a system based on mixed-member proportional representation.[63] Whilst the claim was made that this was to 'try out this system' at local elections, considering the context in which they were passed, this claim sounded dubious at best.[64]

3.5 Opposition to the Constitutional Reform Process

Opposition to the constitutional reform process started immediately after the PRC was announced and was sustained throughout the constitutional reform process. The opponents of the constitutional reform process started on a stronger footing than those who supported a new constitution. In October 2016, only 33.9 per cent of Sri Lankans agreed that Sri Lanka needed a new constitution, whilst 33.6 per cent stated the current Constitution should continue with 'needed changes' and 13.7

[60] Edrisinha and others, *Power-Sharing in Sri Lanka* (n 5).

[61] Chamikara Weerasinghe, 'SLFP Backs Executive Presidency, Broader Power to PCs' *Daily News* (30 May 2016) <www.dailynews.lk/?q=2016/05/30/political/83151>.

[62] Shamindra Ferdinando, 'Constitution Making Process: JO Spells Out Non-negotiable Conditions, Urges Govt. to Reveal UNP–SLFP Proposals' (*The Island*, 21 December 2016) <www.island.lk/index.php?page_cat=article-details&page=article-details&code_title=157575> accessed 9 October 2023.

[63] One positive and important change in both these laws was to introduce a quote for female representatives in local authorities and provincial councils.

[64] Centre for Policy Alternatives, 'CPA Statement on Passage of Provincial Councils Elections Amendment Act' (Centre for Policy Alternatives, 25 September 2017) <www.cpalanka.org/cpa-statement-on-passage-of-provincial-councils-elections-amendment-act> accessed 2 September 2020.

per cent stated that the Constitution did not need any changes.[65] However, a few months later, in March 2017, only 23.5 per cent of Sri Lankans agreed on the need for a new constitution, whilst 38.9 per cent stated that the current Constitution should continue with 'needed changes' and 8.7 per cent stated that the Constitution did not need any changes.[66] In this backdrop, the sustained attacks by members of 'the Joint opposition',[67] civil society organisations supportive of Sinhala nationalist causes, and members of the Buddhist clergy[68] hastened the building of public opinion that there was no need for a new constitution.

The political negotiations in the Steering Committee did not proceed at the expected pace and the government missed its own timelines.[69] The Steering Committee met 73 times between April 2016 and September 2017.[70] In September 2017, an Interim Report[71] of the Steering Committee was tabled in the Constitutional Assembly outlining proposals for a future constitution and positions expressed by the different political parties represented in the Sri Lankan Parliament on them. A reading of the Interim Report lay bare the political disagreements that plagued the reform effort.[72] However, more crucially, the political landscape in the country had begun to change drastically, with the UNP-led government becoming increasingly unpopular, increasing tensions between the president and the prime minister in relation to issues of governance and increasing public support to former President Mahinda Rajapaksa and the SLPP.

The opposition to the interim report was swiftly mobilised, with the joint opposition members attacking[73] the proposals together with sustained opposition from

[65] Centre for Policy Alternatives, 'Opinion Poll on Constitutional Reform: Top Line Report' (*Social Indicator*, Centre for Policy Alternatives 2016) 18 <www.cpalanka.org/wp-content/uploads/2016/10/Opinion-poll-on-Constitutional-Reform_Final_Oct-16.pdf>.

[66] Ibid.

[67] Sinhalanet.Net, 'Constitutional Reform a Sinister Smokescreen' (*Sinhalanet.Net*, 27 January 2016) <www.sinhalanet.net/constitutional-reform-a-sinister-smokescreen> accessed 20 October 2020; Meera Srinivasan, 'Rajapaksa Slams Draft Proposals for Constitution' (*The Hindu*, 5 December 2016) <www.thehindu.com/news/international/Rajapaksa-slams-draft-proposals-for-Constitution/article16765014.ece> accessed 1 September 2020.

[68] 'Sunil, 'MS, RW Urged to Give Buddhism, the Foremost Place' *Daily Mirror* (London, 10 January 2016) <www.dailymirror.lk/breaking_news/ms-rw-urged-to-give-buddhism-foremost-place/108-102445> accessed 20 October 2020.

[69] Srinivasan, 'Rajapaksa Slams Draft Proposals for Constitution' (n 67). This involved a delay of almost two months to pass the framework resolution and set up a constitutional assembly.

[70] See the Steering Committee of the Constitutional Assembly of Sri Lanka 2017, 'The Interim Report of the Steering Committee of the Constitutional Assembly of Sri Lanka' (Introduction) <https://english.constitutionalassembly.lk/interim-report-of-the-steering-committee> accessed 9 October 2023</IT>.

[71] Ibid.

[72] The position of the Joint Opposition on devolution and electoral reform remained irreconcilable with those of the Steering Committee interim report. The SLFP, which was part of government, diverged on the issue of devolution with the interim report. This meant that the required votes for a draft constitution to pass in parliament (two-thirds majority) were not available, at least in terms of the issues of devolution and electoral reform.

[73] News18 (n 34); Yusuf Ariff, 'Proposed Constitutional Reforms Could Lead to Catalonia-Style Split: MR' (*Ada Derana*, 16 October 2017) <www.adaderana.lk/news/43611/proposed-constitutional-reforms-could-lead-to-catalonia-style-split-mr> accessed 1 September 2020.

outside, including from leading Buddhist monks[74] and from professionals associated with links to the joint opposition.[75]

3.6 Constitutional Reform Derailed

The most significant blow to the constitutional reform process occurred with the results of the local authority elections in February 2018. The UNP only obtained 32.6 per cent of the vote, whilst the newly formed SLPP[76] obtained almost 45 per cent of the vote.[77] The election was conducted to elect members to 340 local authorities;[78] of this, the SLPP gained control of 231, and the UNP only got control of 34 local authorities.[79] Whilst the SLPP could not obtain an absolute majority, in terms of the votes cast on its own, together with the SLFP/UPFA its share of the total vote jumped to 58 per cent of the vote.

The results of the local authority elections also hastened the consolidation of the SLPP over the membership of the SLFP/UPFA. It further aggravated the discord between President Sirisena and Prime Minister Wickremesinghe, with speculation about the former wanting to remove the latter immediately after the local authority elections.[80] Prime Minister Wickremesinghe himself survived a vote of no confidence in parliament, moved by the SLPP, only to have the president unconstitutionally remove him from office in October 2018.[81]

[74] Daily FT, 'No Need for a New Constitution, Buddhist Prelates Decide' *Daily FT* (London, 19 October 2017) <www.ft.lk/front-page/No-need-for-a-new-Constitution---Buddhist-prelates-decide/44-641820> accessed 1 September 2020.

[75] Panchamee Hewavissenti, 'Constitution Law Expert Manohara R. De Silva, PC Says One Govt in "Unitary" Several Govts in "United"' (*Sinhalanet.Net*, 1 November 2017) <www.sinhalanet.net/constitution-law-expert-manohara-r-de-silva-pc-says-one-govt-in-unitary-several-govts-in-united> accessed 1 September 2020; LankaWeb, 'LankaWeb—BASL Expresses Grave Concern over Proposed Constitutional Changes' (*LankaWeb*, 23 October 2017) <www.lankaweb.com/news/items/2017/10/23/basl-expresses-grave-concern-over-proposed-constitutional-changes/comment-page-1/#comments> accessed 1 September 2020.

[76] The group, styling itself as the 'joint opposition' under the leadership of former President Mahinda Rajapaksa, formed the SLPP in late 2016. The party was de facto controlled by Basil Rajapaksa (brother of Mahinda Rajapaksa). See also Daily FT, 'Podujana Peramuna Channels Mahinda, Seeks to Become the 'True' SLFP' *Daily FT* (London, 18 November 2016) <www.ft.lk/front-page/podujana-peramuna-channels-mahinda-seeks-to-become-the-true-slfp/44-580879> accessed 23 September 2022.

[77] Ada Derana, 'Local Authorities Election 2018 Results—Sri Lanka' (*Ada Derana*, 2018) <www.adaderana.lk/local-authorities-election-2018> accessed 1 September 2020.

[78] The Election Commission of Sri Lanka 2019, 'Performance Report of the Election Commission for the Year 2018' <https://elections.gov.lk/web/wp-content/uploads/pdf/admin_reports/AR2018_E.pdf> accessed 9 October 2023.

[79] *Ada Derana* (n 77).

[80] Dharisha Bastians, 'Removal of PM: Experts Warn President's Options Limited by 19A', *Daily FT* (14 February 2018) <www.ft.lk/front-page/Removal-of-PM--Experts-warn-President-s-options-limited-by-19A/44-649409> accessed 1 September 2020.

[81] BBC News, 'Fears of 'Bloodbath' in Sri Lanka Crisis' (30 October 2018) <www.bbc.com/news/world-asia-46019280> accessed 1 September 2020.

3.7 An Illegal Transfer of Power and Unconstitutional Dissolution of Parliament

After months of deepening divide between them, on the 26 October 2018 President Sirisena removed Prime Minister Wickremesinghe from office and appointed former President Rajapaksa as prime minister.[82] The president did not have the power to remove the prime minister due to the checks introduced by the Nineteenth Amendment to the Constitution.[83] This created a constitutional crisis, with two individuals claiming to be prime minister. The President then proceeded to prorogue parliament, thereby preventing the members of parliament from expressing their confidence in one of the two individuals claiming to be prime minister. This move was ostensibly done to give former President Rajapaksa enough time to 'win over support'. Thereafter, on 9 November 2018, President Sirisena yet again violated the Constitution and dissolved parliament, prematurely calling for elections outside the process provided for in the Constitution.[84]

Several petitions were filed in the Supreme Court and Court of Appeal challenging the several unconstitutional acts by the President. The Supreme Court ruled in a unanimous judgment by seven judges of the Court that the dissolution of parliament was unconstitutional.[85] Before the final judgement, the Supreme Court had already stayed the operation of the presidential decree dissolving parliament and allowed parliament to reconvene. When parliament reconvened, chaos ensued, with members engaging in fisticuffs; however, through the chaos, a majority of members were able to pass a resolution removing former President Rajapaksa as the prime minister.[86] After the decision of the Supreme Court on the dissolution of parliament, former President Rajapaksa resigned as prime minister (weeks after he was removed by a vote of no confidence) and President Sirisena reappointed[87] Mr Wickremesinghe as prime minister, bringing to an end the political crisis, albeit with significant economic costs.[88]

[82] Asanga Welikala (ed), *Constitutional Reform and Crisis in Sri Lanka* (Centre for Policy Alternatives 2019).

[83] 'Groundviews, 'The Constitutional Crisis: A Round Up' (Groundviews, 2 November 2018) <https://groundviews.org/2018/11/02/the-constitutional-crisis-a-round-up> accessed 1 September 2020.

[84] Jayadeva Uyangoda, 'The Gravest Crisis' (*Groundviews*, 10 November 2018) <https://groundviews.org/2018/11/10/on-dissolution-of-parliament-2> accessed 1 September 2020.

[85] Meera Srinivasan, 'President Sirisena's Dissolution of Parliament Illegal, Rules Sri Lanka Supreme Court' *The Hindu* (Colombo, 13 December 2018) <www.thehindu.com/news/international/president-sirisenas-move-to-dissolve-parliament-illegal-rules-sri-lanka-supreme-court/article25733773.ece> accessed 1 September 2020; *Rajavarothiam Sampanthan and Others Vs The Hon Attorney General and Others* (2018) Supreme Court Minutes SC FR 351-356/2018, SC FR 358- 361/2018 (Supreme Court of Sri Lanka).

[86] Michael Safi and Amantha Perera, 'Sri Lanka MPs Pass No-Confidence Vote against Disputed PM Rajapaksa', *The Guardian* (London, 14 November 2018) <www.theguardian.com/world/2018/nov/14/sri-lanka-parliament-no-confidence-pm-mahinda-rajapaksa> accessed 1 September 2020.

[87] Ibid.

[88] Mangala Samaraweera, 'Sri Lankan Economy after the October Coup', *Colombo Telegraph* (Colombo, 21 February 2019) <www.colombotelegraph.com/index.php/sri-lankan-economy-after-the-october-coup> accessed 8 May 2019.

4. Outcomes of the Reform Process

The main outcomes of the reform process were the changes introduced by the Nineteenth Amendment to the Constitution. However, several provisions of the Nineteenth Amendment were the result of a political compromise and were interim measures pending the new Constitution. Thus, the main failure of reform effort was its inability to deliver on the promise of a new constitution.

During the time period it was in operation, the results of the Nineteenth Amendment were mixed. Several concerns have been raised about the Constitutional Council, particularly in relation to its composition.[89] Although no serious concerns about the character and independence of the specific appointments made through the Constitutional Council process have been raised,[90] significant delays were evident with the appointment process, and questions were posed about the lack of transparency in its decision-making process.[91] The injudicious[92] conduct of some appointees raised concerns about their apparent bias, which was also used as ammunition by the opponents of the Nineteenth Amendment to undermine it. The functioning of independent institutions has also seen mixed results, with some commissions being assertive and robustly fulfilling their mandate,[93] whilst others were largely ineffective.[94] Furthermore, several independent commissions were hampered by the delay in enacting enabling legislation.[95]

The constitutional scheme established by the amendment did create ambiguity in relation to the division of executive power between the office of the president and of the prime minister.[96] The power balance was such that it required a good

[89] Both the domination of political actors (seven political actors vs the three non-political appointees) and the inclusion of members of the cabinet of ministers in the Constitutional Council. Conversely, there is also the criticism, by those opposed to the Nineteenth Amendment, that it should consist entirely of members of parliament.

[90] Except in the case of the appointment of the Inspector General of Police Pujith Jayasundara. See Dharisha Bastians, 'Police Chief under Fire over "Phone Gate" Scandal', *Daily FT* (3 December 2016) <www.ft.lk/article/583814/Police-Chief-under-fire-over--phone-gate—scandal> accessed 9 October 2023.

[91] Nihal Jayawickrama, 'The Constitutional Council Fiasco' (*The Island*, 6 February 2016) <www.island.lk/index.php?page_cat=article-details&page=article-details&code_title=139922> accessed 9 October 2023.

[92] The conduct of the then inspector general of police, Pujith Jayasundara, was particularly problematic. See Colombo Telegraph, 'Social Media Outcry Over IGP's Phonegate Scandal' *Colombo Telegraph* (Colombo, 1 December 2016) <www.colombotelegraph.com/index.php/social-media-outcry-over-igps-phonegate-scandal> accessed 23 September 2022.

[93] The Human Rights Commission of Sri Lanka has been particularly assertive in carrying out its functions. See Hunter S. Thompson, 'Restriction of Access to Legal Assistance', *Ceylon Today* (1 October 2016) <www.ceylontoday.lk/print20160701CT20161030.php?id=6476> accessed 30 January 2017.

[94] The Public Service Commission and Procurement Commission. Also there has been considerable criticism of the National Police Commission.

[95] No legislation has been brought to establish the National Audit Commission. See Ashanthi Warunasuriya and Amavasya Sirisena, 'New National Audit Bill: Boon or Bane?', *The Sunday Leader* (17 July 2016) <www.thesundayleader.lk/2016/07/17/new-national-audit-bill-boon-or-bane> accessed 9 October 2023

[96] See Public Representations Committee on Constitutional Reform (n 55).

working relationship between the two individuals who hold these offices. Whilst the reform enacted through the Nineteenth Amendment helped prevent[97] the unconstitutional acts of President Sirisena and ensured constitutional governance,[98] its effectiveness in doing so made it the target of sustained attacks. This resulted in a sustained campaign against the Nineteenth Amendment, including during the presidential election of 2019 and parliamentary election of August 2020,[99] and ultimately led to its repeal[100] in October 2020.

As mentioned previously, the constitutional reform effort fizzled out after the local authority elections of 2018, and it was clear, in early 2019, that there was no viable path towards a new constitution.[101] The falling per capita gross domestic product (GDP) growth rate and deepening economic crisis,[102] and the government disastrous failure to prevent the Easter Sunday terrorist attacks, ensured that the constitutional reform effort never made a comeback during the rest of the government's tenure.

Gotabaya Rajapaksa, who was the SLPP candidate and the brother of former President Mahinda Rajapaksa, won the presidential election held in November 2019.[103] President Gotabaya Rajapaksa was particularly critical of the Nineteenth Amendment and campaigned to abolish the changes made by the amendment.[104] However, his official election manifesto, which was the basis of the SLPP's election platform at the August 2020 Parliamentary election,[105] touted a new constitution

[97] Particularly through removing the immunity of the president's act from judicial review and through widening participation in a more broad-based process for judicial appointments to the superior courts.

[98] Ashraf Hegazy and Gary Milante, 'Resilience in Sri Lanka' (*Groundviews*, 14 December 2018) <https://groundviews.org/2018/12/14/resilience-in-sri-lanka> accessed 2 September 2020.

[99] Indian Express, 'Sri Lankan President Gotabaya Rajapaksa Vows to Abolish 19th Amendment' *Indian Express* (Colombo, 20 August 2020) <https://indianexpress.com/article/world/sri-lankan-president-gotabaya-rajapaksa-vows-to-abolish-19th-amendment-6563179> accessed 2 September 2020.

[100] Within two months of its landslide win in the 2020 August general election, the SLPP had enacted the Twentieth Amendment to the Constitution. This enactment was in line with the rhetoric deployed by the SLPP during the presidential election of 2019 and the general election in 2020. See Centre for Policy Alternatives, 'A Brief Guide to the 20th Amendment to the Constitution' (Centre for Policy Alternatives 2021) <www.cpalanka.org/a-brief-guide-to-the-20th-amendment-to-the-constitution> accessed 9 October 2023.

[101] Ashwin Hemmathagama, 'Legislative Lane for New Constitution Faces Snags', *Daily FT* (12 January 2019) <www.ft.lk/top-story/Legislative-lane-for-new-Constitution-faces-snags/26-670711> accessed 2 September 2020.

[102] WA Wijewardena, 'Sri Lanka's Deep Economic Crisis: Wasted Four Years and a Wasting Election Year', *Daily FT* (7 January 2019) <www.ft.lk/columns/Sri-Lanka-s-deep-economic-crisis-Wasted-four-years-and-a-wasting-election-year/4-670265> accessed 2 September 2020; World Bank, 'GDP per Capita Growth Annual (2011–2019) Sri Lanka' (*World Bank*) <https://data.worldbank.org/indicator/NY.GDP.PCAP.KD.ZG?end=2019&locations=LK&start=2011&view=chart> accessed 2 September 2020.

[103] Asad Hashim, 'Gotabaya Rajapaksa Wins Sri Lanka Election' (*Aljazeera*, 17 November 2019) <www.aljazeera.com/news/2019/11/17/gotabaya-rajapaksa-wins-sri-lanka-election> accessed 20 October 2020.

[104] Indian Express (n 99).

[105] SM Wijayaratne, 'SLPP to Use Presidential Polls Manifesto' (*Daily News*, 22 July 2020) <www.dailynews.lk/2020/07/22/political/223919/slpp-use-presidential-polls-manifesto > accessed 20 October 2020.

to restore 'smooth functioning of the government'.[106] Almost immediately after winning a two-thirds majority in the August 2020 parliamentary election, the SLPP government enacted the Twentieth Amendment to the Constitution, which effectively repealed the reform enacted by the Nineteenth Amendment.

5. The Impact of COVID-19

Sri Lanka's response to the spread of COVID-19 has deteriorated with each progressing wave. The government responded relatively well to the first wave (March 2020–September 2020), curtailing and preventing the spread of the disease within the country, including by conducting an effective tracing mechanism. However, repeated failures to increase capacity within the health sector, especially in relation to testing, and questionable policy decisions relating to boarder control saw repeated outbreaks in October 2020 and then again in April 2021. The government's initial response, at least prior to September 2020, helped buttress the popularity of President Gotabaya Rajapaksa's government, eventually resulting in a landslide election victory for the SLPP at the August 2020 parliamentary elections.

Despite this relative success, there have been several concerning trends which directly impact governance and the rule of law. In light of the exceptional challenges posed by COVID-19, the SLPP's governance style was not met with any significant and visible backlash from the public. However, this situation changed during June–August 2021, wherein the visible policy incoherence and economic anxiety damaged the government's image considerably and resulted in a series of protests against government policy.

A key concern during this period was the lack of a functioning parliament for more than five months. President Gotabaya Rajapaksa issued a proclamation dissolving parliament on 2 March 2020[107] and calling for elections at the earliest opportunity available to him to do so. The election commission soon concluded that elections could not be held within the three-month period mandated by the Constitution and requested the President to seek appropriate directions from the Supreme Court. The President did not accede to this request.[108] The elections were eventually conducted on 5 August 2020, after several postponements,[109] and were widely considered to be free and fair.

[106] Gotabaya Rajapaksa, 'Vistas of Prosperity and Splendour, Election Manifesto of Gotabaya Rajapaksa' (2019) <www.presidentsoffice.gov.lk/wp-content/uploads/2019/16/Gotabaya_Manifesto_English.pdf> accessed 9 October 2023.

[107] Gazette (Extra Ordinary) No 2165/8 (2 March 2020) <https://www.parliament.lk/en/election-2020/dissolution-of-the-8th-parliament> accessed 9 October 2023.

[108] See <www.documents.gov.lk/files/egz/2020/4/2172-03_E.pdf> accessed 9 October 2023.

[109] See <https://elections.gov.lk/web/wp-content/uploads/publication/ext-gz/PE_2020_E.pdf> accessed 9 October 2023.

The absence of a functioning parliament raised several concerns. First, there were several options available to the president to resummon parliament; however, the President actively refused to do so.[110] Several petitions filed in the Supreme Court for inter alia an order to have parliament summoned immediately were also dismissed at the threshold stage after almost 11 days of hearings, without any reasons being provided.[111]

Second, it raised serious concerns regarding public finance, particularly as to the basis on which the executive was continuing to spend public money in the absence of appropriations being made by parliament.[112] Third, the government essentially governed by press release, with little or no opposition or inquiry as to the legal basis of its decisions, ranging from the imposition of 'quarantine curfew' across the country[113] to providing debt relief.[114] In most instances, the decisions in question were necessary; however, the striking feature was that they were made in an extra-legal manner when there was a clear and simple legal procedure to be followed.

In addition to the disregard for the rule of law, the other overarching feature of Sri Lanka's response to COVID-19 was the increased militarisation of the pandemic response. The national security state, which established itself as a political power centre soon after the end of the civil war in 2009, saw a setback in light of the change in government in 2015.[115] There was, however, no concerted effort to reform the security apparatus, which, in turn, staunchly resisted even the minimal reform initiatives.[116] After the Easter Sunday attacks, the national security establishment had reasserted itself in the public discourse and publicly stated its displeasure over the limited attempts at reform.[117]

[110] Asanga Welikala and Suren Fernando, 'Balancing Efficiency with Law and Liberty: Dealing with the Pandemic without Democratic Backsliding', *Daily FT* (8 April 2020) <www.ft.lk/opinion/Balancing-efficiency-with-law-and-liberty--Dealing-with-the-pandemic-without-democratic-backsliding/14-698609> accessed 12 September 2020; Centre for Policy Alternatives, 'Evolving Legal Issues in the Context of COVID-19' (Centre for Policy Alternatives 2020) <www.cpalanka.org/wp-content/uploads/2020/03/Brief-Guide-I-_Evolving-Legal-Issues-in-the-Context-of-COVID-19.pdf.

[111] Meera Srinivasan, 'Sri Lanka's Top Court Dismisses Petitions Challenging Poll Date', *The Hindu* (Colombo, 2 June 2020) <www.thehindu.com/news/international/sri-lankas-top-court-dismisses-petitions-challenging-poll-date/article31733871.ece> accessed 18 October 2020.

[112] Asanga Welikala and Suren Fernando, 'Public Finance in Times of Crisis: The Constitutional Functions of President and Parliament', *Daily FT* (31 March 2020) <www.ft.lk/opinion/Public-finance-in-times-of-crisis-The-constitutional-functions-of-President-and-Parliament/14-698254> accessed 12 September 2020; Centre for Policy Alternatives, 'Evolving Legal Issues' (n 110).

[113] 'Centre for Policy Alternatives, 'Brief Guide III Curfew in Response to COVID-19: Legal Framework and Relevant Questions in Sri Lanka' (Centre for Policy Alternatives 2020) <www.cpalanka.org/wp-content/uploads/2020/04/Brief-Guide-III-CURFEW.pdf> accessed 9 October 2023.

[114] NewsWire, 'Former Air Force Officer Files Case against CBSL & Private Bank over Violation of COVID-19 Concession Scheme' (*Newswire*, 14 September 2020) <www.newswire.lk/2020/09/14/21450-cbsl> accessed 18 October 2020.

[115] Jayadeva Uyangoda, 'Reform Resistance in Sri Lankan Politics' (*Groundviews*, 26 March 2018) <https://groundviews.org/2018/03/27/reform-resistance-in-sri-lankan-politics> accessed 10 May 2019.

[116] Ibid.

[117] In an interview soon after the Easter Sunday attacks, when questioned as to why Sri Lanka was targeted by ISIS, the Army Commander responded: 'Too much of freedom, too much of peace for the last 10 years. People forget what happened for 30 years. People are enjoying peace and they neglected

The presidential election in 2019 and subsequent change in government saw the national security establishment returning to the centre of civilian life across the country. With the threat of COVID-19, security forces personnel were mobilised for a wide array of functions, including the use of intelligence agencies for testing and tracing functions.[118]

6. Reflections

The main lesson from the failed 2015–2018 constitutional reform effort is that mismanaging a reform effort predicated on institutional reform for good governance has the potential to significantly undermine public confidence in democracy and democratic institutions.

In this case, the scale of mismanagement was such that it completely squandered the momentum and public support for curtailing the powers of the executive president and provided ammunition for a counter-narrative as to why a stronger executive president was needed. The indecision and corruption of the government, and its failure to prevent the Easter Sunday terrorist attacks, was used by its political opponents to discredit not only the individuals who wielded governmental power but also the foundational idea on which that government was built, namely, 'good governance'. In this way, the failures of the government came to be portrayed as the undesirability, and or even unsuitability, of the types of reform proposed by that government for Sri Lanka.

Opinion polls indicate an increased discontent among the public in Sri Lanka towards democratic institutions and a growing support for governance by a 'strong ruler' which pre-dates the Sirisena–Wickremesinghe government.[119] This trend is particularly acute among the Sinhalese community.[120] One possible explanation for this propensity could be the effective branding by Sinhala nationalists, who

security'. See The Hindu, 'Suicide Bombers Visited Kashmir, Kerala, Bengaluru: Sri Lankan Army Chief', *The Hindu* (Colombo, 5 May 2019) <www.thehindu.com/news/international/suicide-bombers-visited-kashmir-kerala-bengaluru-sri-lankan-army-chief/article27036863.ece> accessed 10 May 2019.

[118] The Army commander was appointed head of National Operations Centre for Prevention of COVID-19 Outbreak: Daily FT, 'Govt. Launches National Ops. Centre to Counter COVID-19', *Daily FT* (18 March 2020) <www.ft.lk/news/Govt-launches-National-Ops-Centre-to-counter-COVID-19/56-697707> accessed 20 October 2020. For military personnel being appointed to key positions within government, including the Ministry of Health Chathuranga Hapuarachchi, see 'Sri Lanka News—Newsfirst, 'Major General Sanjeewa Munasinghe Assumes Duties as the New Health Secretary', *Sri Lanka News—Newsfirst* (11 May 2020) <www.newsfirst.lk/2020/05/11/new-director-general-of-army-health-services-appointed> accessed 20 October 2020.

[119] Pradeep Peiris, Sakina Moinudeen, and M Krishnamoorthy, 'Authoritarianism Is No Remedy to the Country's Wounded Democracy' (*Groundviews*, 14 June 2020) <https://groundviews.org/2020/06/14/authoritarianism-is-no-remedy-to-the-countrys-wounded-democracy> accessed 2 September 2020.

[120] Ibid.

have sought to create a strong association between a powerful executive president and the pre-colonial Sinhala Buddhist monarch.[121] Beyond opinion polls, the result of the presidential election of 2019 and the parliamentary election of August 2020 also lent credence to this idea. The SLPP's winning campaign, in both instances, was that the party represented strong, stable, and secure leadership and that it was seeking a mandate to repeal the Nineteenth Amendment, which was a barrier to effective government. However, Sri Lanka has seen such swings in the past, particularly in 2010, immediately after the end of the war. As such, it is too early to assume that these perceptions are indicative of long-term trends.

Another important lesson is the fact that a regime such as the Sirisena–Wickremesinghe government, which lacked credibility, especially among the Sinhala Buddhist voters when it came to constitutional reform relating to the nature of the state, should have been more proactive and transparent in explaining its position on those issues.

As discussed previously, the Sri Lankan polity outside the Northern and Eastern Provinces have a fraught and contentious history concerning the devolution of power and fears about secession. In this context, the secretive Steering Committee process provided the perfect opportunity for the SLPP to discredit the constitutional reform process, which it did. Additionally, a new constitution abolishing the executive presidency and providing for meaningful devolution of power would have anyway required approval by the people at a referendum.[122] As such, it is truly baffling as to why the Sirisena–Wickremesinghe government did so little to broaden the discourse on these issues by explaining its vision to the electorate and attempting to proactively deal with misinformation circulated by the opponents of the reform effort.

Completely relying on the secretive Steering Committee process to evolve a consensus and the government's inability to communicate its policy direction allowed the opposition to set the narrative. It further undermined public confidence in the government's reform efforts and gave credence to the opposition's claims about the constitutional reform process. The result of this was a lack of understanding of the reform effort, even among members of parliament within the government.

[121] Asanga Welikala, 'Nation, State, Sovereignty, and Kingship: The Pre-Modern Antecedents of the Presidential State' in Asanga Welikala (ed), *Reforming Sri Lankan Presidentialism; Provenance, Problems and Prospects*, Vol 1 (Centre for Policy Alternatives 2015); Asanga Welikala and Roshan de Silva-Wijeyeratne, 'The Past and the Present in the (Re)Constitution of the State' (*Groundviews*, 25 August 2020) <https://groundviews.org/2020/08/25/the-past-and-the-present-in-the-reconstitution-of-the-state> accessed 2 September 2020.

[122] This is because moving beyond the devolution framework already in the Constitution and the Provincial Councils Act will require a referendum based on the interpretation of art 2 of the Constitution in the majority decision of *In Re the Thirteenth Amendment to the Constitution and the Provincial Councils Bill (1987)* 2 Sri LR 312 (a full Bench decision of the Supreme Court), and converting the presidency into a titular presidency would also require a referendum in terms of the decisions of the Supreme Court in *In Re the Nineteenth Amendment to the Constitution* (2002) 3 SLR 85 and *In Re the Nineteenth Amendment to the Constitution* (SC SD 04/2015, 19 April 2015).

A third lesson from this reform process was that a government which is elected on the basis of democratic reform should do everything possible to be seen as adhering to democratic ideals. The Sirisena–Wickremesinghe government seriously harmed its image and democratic credentials by failing to hold local government elections on time and permanently postponing provincial council elections.[123] Worse still was the fact that the government abused the law-making process in order to be able to enact legislation that postponed provincial council elections.[124] Despite the government citing various reasons for the delays in elections, it was plainly evident that the UNP and the SLFP were concerned about their own electoral prospects in light of the growing popularity of the SLPP. These delays entrenched the narrative that the government was undermining representative democracy and that the government itself had lost its legitimacy.

Ultimately, the forgoing analysis of the Sirisena–Wickremesinghe government's staggering failure raises the question as to whether there was actually political will to carry through the far-reaching reforms promised by the government or whether it was merely an electoral platform designed to attract broad support and win an election. This is even more problematic when considering the fact that the government showed much more urgency and willingness to expend political capital whilst pushing through several economic reform efforts.[125] As a result of these failures, Sri Lanka is presently stuck on the brink of possible constitutional reform that not only undoes the democratic gains achieved between 2015 and 2018, but also could potentially entrench strong-form presidentialism with increasingly authoritarian powers, significantly undermine the existing limited framework of devolved government, and further entrench Sinhala–Buddhist nationalistic ideology within the institutional architecture of the state.[126]

As was detailed earlier, the oscillation between curtailing the powers of the president (through the Seventeenth and Nineteenth Amendments) to further expanding the powers of the president (through the Eighteenth and Twentieth Amendments) was primarily driven by Mr Mahinda Rajapaksa's and Mr Gotabaya Rajapaksa's ability to consolidate the Sinhala–Buddhist voters in Sri Lanka. When they have succeeded, they have been able to procure significant majorities in

[123] Centre for Policy Alternatives, 'CPA Statement on Passage of Provincial Councils Elections Amendment Act' (n 64).

[124] Ibid.

[125] 'EconomyNext, 'Sri Lanka Domestic Tax Collections Grow 20.6-pct in 2019' (*EconomyNext*, 20 January 2020) <https://economynext.com/sri-lanka-domestic-tax-collections-grow-20-6-pct-in-2019-40925> accessed 20 October 2020; The Hindu, 'Sri Lanka, China Sign $1.1 Billion Hambantota Port Deal', *The Hindu* (Colombo, 29 July 2017) <www.thehindu.com/news/international/sri-lanka-china-sign-11-bn-hambantota-port-deal/article19385932.ece> accessed 20 October 2020; BBC News, 'Sri Lanka Signs Deal on Hambantota Port with China' (29 July 2017) <www.bbc.com/news/world-asia-40761732> accessed 20 October 2020.

[126] Asanga Welikala, 'The Coming Constitution of the Civilization-State' (*Groundviews*, 8 July 2020) <https://groundviews.org/2020/07/08/the-coming-constitution-of-the-civilization-state> accessed 2 September 2020.

parliament which allowed them to expand the powers of the presidency. The SLPP government has used its majority in parliament to undo most of the changes enacted by the Nineteenth Amendment and has undertaken its own process to draft a new constitution.

It is unclear as to whether the proposed constitutional reform proposals will lead to intractable change or whether it is part of the oscillation Sri Lankan democracy has been through across several decades of its post-independence history. It is also unclear as to how this further entrenchment of Sinhala Buddhist nationalism will impact existing divisions within Sri Lankan society, particularly between the different ethnic groups. Will it reignite the cycles of violence that have plagued Sri Lanka's post-independence history, will the reform have finally reached a sufficient intractability to compel acquiesce from a sufficient mass of dissidents, or will it crumble under the weight of its own expectation as it grates against the 'deeply rooted tradition of electoral democracy in a plural polity'.[127]

[127] Ibid.

13

Myanmar's Transition to Peace and Democracy

The Journey Reversed

Ohn Mar Zin, Naw Janet, and Kimana Zulueta-Fülscher

1. Introduction

On 1 February 2021, the Myanmar armed forces took over power in a coup d'état, arresting President U Win Myint, State Counsellor Daw Aung San Suu Kyi, and other high-level government officials. The date of the coup was not a coincidence. 1 February was the day that the newly elected members of parliament were to convene in their first session.[1] Security forces guarded them in their residences and effectively impeded their commute to the parliamentary complex.

In the meantime, the first vice-president, U Myint Shwe, a former lieutenant general, was appointed acting president and declared a nationwide (and unconstitutional) state of emergency. Under the 2008 Constitution, in a state of emergency, executive, legislative, and judicial powers are transferred to the commander-in-chief, in this case Min Aung Hlaing.[2] Initially, the Commander-in-Chief declared that the state of emergency would last for one year, and elections would be held after a number of tasks have been achieved, including the restoration of 'eternal peace'.[3] On 1 August 2021, however, Min Aung Hlaing declared himself interim prime minister, a position not provided for in the 2008 Constitution; extended the state of emergency for two more years, until August 2023; and announced that elections would be held afterwards.[4]

Min Aung Hlaing allegedly declared a state of emergency, following the coup d'état, because of the failure on the part of relevant officials, from the Speaker of

[1] ABC News, 'Myanmar's Military Takes Power in Coup, Detains Suu Kyi' (2 February 2021) <https://www.columbian.com/news/2021/feb/02/myanmars-military-takes-power-in-coup-detains-suu-kyi> accessed 17 November 2023.

[2] Constitution of Myanmar (2008) art 418(a).

[3] Republic of the Union of Myanmar, Office of the Commander-in-Chief of Defence Services, Notification No 1/2021 (1 February 2021).

[4] AP News, 'Myanmar Military Extends Emergency, Promises Vote in 2 Years' (1 August 2021) <https://apnews.com/article/business-health-elections-coronavirus-pandemic-myanmar-8504af88bd5b2c2c2b30c7da5baa8ad5> accessed 16 September 2021.

Ohn Mar Zin, Naw Janet, and Kimana Zulueta-Fülscher, *Myanmar's Transition to Peace and Democracy* In: *Democratic Consolidation and Constitutional Endurance in Asia and Africa*. Edited by: Tom Gerald Daly and Dinesha Samararatne, Oxford University Press. © Oxford University Press 2024. DOI: 10.1093/oso/9780192899347.003.0013

the Union Parliament to the Chair of the Union Election Commission (UEC), to deal with alleged (and never proven) election fraud. In his view, the fact that the newly elected members of parliament were still convened for the third session of the Union parliament, and for the formation of a new government, represented a type of action meant 'to take over the sovereignty of the Union by wrongful forcible means', which therefore justified the takeover.

National and international observers, including the Carter Center,[5] however, recognised the general elections held on 8 November 2020 as relatively free. This was the case despite a number of challenges incurred because of the constraints imposed by the COVID-19 pandemic, the conflict situation in some of the countries' states and regions,[6] and, particularly, multiple errors in the voter lists that were mostly corrected throughout the campaign period.[7] For the second time since the 2008 Constitution entered into force, the National League for Democracy (NLD) won by a landslide with 79.5 per cent of the elected seats in the Union parliament.[8]

The 1 February coup, in essence, halted Myanmar's incipient and only one-decade-long transition to peace and democracy.[9] But it was not accepted either by elected officials or by the wider population. Since the coup, a parallel interim government of National Unity has been established, and a preliminary Federal Democracy Charter agreed upon, which describes both the interim governance framework as well as the road map for the drafting of a new (transitional) constitutional framework for Myanmar.

In this chapter, in Section 2, the authors explain Myanmar's historical context from the time it was a British colony to the adoption of the 2008 Constitution and the start of a military-controlled transition process to peace and democracy. Section 3 continues by exploring the first elected civilian-led government since 1962, and its impact on the ongoing peace process, and the intention to amend the 2008 Constitution. When exploring the outcomes of these difficult transitions in Section 4, we cannot but refer to the 1 February 2021 coup d'état as not only a setback but also the point of emergence of a new and better organised democracy movement. In Section 5, we briefly deal with the way the civilian government

[5] 'Carter Center, 'Preliminary Statement on the 2020 Myanmar General Elections' (*Carter Center*, 8 November 2020) <www.cartercenter.org/news/pr/2020/myanmar-111020.html> accessed 13 September 2021.

[6] BBC News, 'Myanmar Election: No Evidence Fraud in 2020 Vote, Observers Say' (17 May 2021) <www.bbc.com/news/world-asia-57144397> accessed 16 September 2021.

[7] San Yamin Aung, 'Myanmar Election Officials Scramble to Correct Error-Riddled Voter Lists', *The Irrawaddy* (6 August 2020) <www.irrawaddy.com/elections/myanmar-election-officials-scramble-correct-error-riddled-voter-lists.html> accessed 17 September 2021.

[8] Zsombor Peter, 'Aung San Suu Kyi, NLD Win Second Landslide Election in Myanmar' *VOA* (15 November 2020) <www.voanews.com/east-asia-pacific/aung-san-suu-kyi-nld-win-second-landslide-election-myanmar> accessed 16 September 2021.

[9] Kimana Zulueta-Fülscher, 'The Struggle for Legitimacy in Post-Coup Myanmar' (*Carnegie Europe*, 14 April 2021) <https://carnegieeurope.eu/2021/04/14/struggle-for-legitimacy-in-post-coup-myanmar-pub-84302> accessed 16 September 2021.

dealt with the COVID-19 pandemic, the planned November 2020 elections, and the manner in which the military completely lost control of the situation after the coup. With constantly changing circumstances on the ground, we conclude with some reflections, conscious that the latter may already be outdated once the book goes to press.

2. Context

Myanmar is a highly diverse country of 54 million people. The exact number of ethnic groups is a matter of controversy, but in a 1983 census, 135 ethnic groups were officially recognised, including 8 major ethnic groups: Kachin, Kayah, Kayin, Chin, Mon, Bamar, Rakhine, and Shan.[10] These ethnic groups speak different languages and practice different religions, though Burmese is the *lingua franca* and Buddhism is the religion of the majority. The Bamar hold a majority of two-thirds.

Coexistence between the different groups has not always been easy. After the British annexation of Burma in 1885, the country was divided between the Frontier Areas, with hills and mountains to the west, north and east of the country, inhabited mainly by minority ethnic groups; and Burma Proper, mostly in the centre and south of the country, inhabited mostly by the majority Bamar.[11] While Burma Proper was governed through a highly centralised colonial state administration, local political systems functioned in the remote and rural Frontier Areas, with high levels of autonomy under a system of British indirect rule.[12] Before granting independence, the British required Bamar nationalists that had emerged out of a new independence movement (led by General Aung San, the founder of the Myanmar armed forces) to engage in consultations with minority ethnic groups from the Frontier Areas on the structure of the state as the latter favoured a continuation of a decentralised system of government.[13]

A conference of nationalities held in February 1947 resulted in the Panglong Agreement, where leaders of some, but not all, ethnic nationalities (specifically the Chin, Kachin, and Shan) agreed to join the Union of Burma, which would, in turn, guarantee a certain level of autonomy to these groups.[14] The Constitution, which entered into force in January 1948, provided some states with a degree of

[10] Sai Wansai, 'Clarifying Myanmar's Complex Ethnic Makeup' *Asia Times* (7 December 2017) <https://asiatimes.com/2017/12/myanmars-controversial-135-ethnicity-count-needs-clarity> accessed 19 April 2020.

[11] Sarah Clarke, Seng Aung Sein Myint, and Zabra Yu Siwa, 'Re-Examining Ethnic Identity In Myanmar' (Centre for Peace and Conflict Studies 2019) <https://reliefweb.int/sites/reliefweb.int/files/resources/Ethnic-Identity-in-Myanmar.pdf> accessed 10 April 2020. See also Thant Myint-U, *The Hidden History of Burma* (Atlantic Books 2020) 12–31.

[12] Clarke, Sein Myint, and Yu Siwa (n 11) 16.

[13] Ibid, 18–20.

[14] Ibid, 20.

self-governance and a right of secession after ten years from the Constitution coming into operation.[15]

However, since independence, and even before, a number of insurgencies emerged, partly due to their discontent regarding the actual level of autonomy provided to ethnic nationalities. The resulting instability eventually led the *military* (in turn, led by General Ne Win) to briefly take power in 1958 by instituting a military caretaker government. They restored power to a democratically elected government in 1960 but permanently assumed power in 1962 after a coup. Post-1960, discussions among ethnic groups meant to decide on a road map towards federalism motivated the military to take over as, at the time, they saw federalism as the ultimate source of chaos and instability.[16]

Following 1962, Myanmar was governed under a military regime with a centralised command structure for more than six decades.[17] The 1947 Constitution was suspended, and the bicameral parliament was dissolved. In January 1974, the military adopted a new constitution, based on the 1962 'Burmese Way to Socialism',[18] which introduced a one-party system led by the military-led Burma Socialist Programme Party (BSPP) and established a unicameral legislature, the Pyithu Hluttaw. The 1974 Constitution was suspended in 1988, after a student-led uprising called for democracy and an end of the one-party rule. The demonstrations were violently suppressed, with thousands of casualties,[19] and resulted in mass imprisonments, including the house arrest of Aung San Suu Kyi (daughter of General Aung San), who, by that time, had emerged as the leader of the newly established National League for Democracy (NLD).[20] Ne Win resigned and the military regime dissolved the Pyithu Hluttaw. The BSPP was replaced by the also military-led State Law and Order Restoration Council (SLORC), which called for elections, held in May 1990.[21]

Despite numerous constraints, the NLD won the 1990 elections by a landslide (60 per cent of the vote), with ethnic parties winning around 35 per cent of the vote.[22] The SLORC, though, did not recognise the results, arguing post hoc that a new constitution had to be adopted in advance and inaugurating a National Convention in 1993 that mostly included military appointees and less than 100

[15] The Constitution of the Union of Burma (1947) Chapter X.

[16] Clarke, Sein Myint, and Yu Siwa (n 11) 22. See also Melissa Crouch, *The Constitution of Myanmar: A Contextual Analysis* (Hart Publishing 2019) 22.

[17] Su Mon Thazin Aung and Matthew Arnold, *Managing Change: Executive Policy Making in Myanmar* (The Asia Foundation 2018) 5–12. See also Ye Htut, *Myanmar Political Transition and Lost Opportunities* (Institute for Southeast Asian Studies 2019) 8–9.

[18] See Fred R von der Mehden, *Religion and Nationalism in Southeast Asia. Burma, Indonesia, The Philippines* (University of Wisconsin Press 1963); Josef Silverstein, 'First Steps on the Burmese Way to Socialism' (1964) 4(2) Asian Survey 716.

[19] Clarke, Sein Myint and Yu Siwa (n 11) 25.

[20] Aung San Suu Kyi, 'In Quest of Democracy' 3(1) (January 1992) Journal of Democracy, 5–14.

[21] Clarke, Sein Myint, and Yu Siwa (n 11) 25.

[22] Ibid, 26.

of the 1990-elected representatives. The National Convention ran until July 2007 but was suspended between 1996 and 2004.[23] After the National Convention came to a close, with little participation of ethnic minorities, new mass demonstrations erupted in response to an increase in fuel prices.[24] Led by Buddhist monks, the so-called 'Saffron Revolution' was again met by high levels of violence. The Constitution was subsequently adopted in May 2008, after a contested national referendum held just days after Cyclone Nargis had rampaged through the south of the country.

The 2008 Constitution was a step towards multiparty democracy at the time, but it also guaranteed key institutional powers to the military. The Constitution was based on the 2003 military-drafted 'Seven Step Roadmap to Disciplined Democracy',[25] which mandated a new constitution to be drafted according to the basic principles agreed by the National Convention, to be followed by a nationwide referendum, and free and fair elections, held in 2010.

2.1 Structure of Government under the 2008 Constitution

The 2008 Constitution formally divided power between the executive, the legislature, and the judiciary. Voters used to elect their representatives in both the Union and state/region parliaments using a first-past-the-post electoral system. The Union Hluttaw was divided into three caucuses, namely, elected members of each house and the military-appointed members of both houses, which then elected the president and two vice-presidents. The president could only be removed from office via impeachment under limited though ill-defined grounds. At all times, three key ministries were appointed and controlled by the commander-in-chief—defence, home affairs, and border affairs. The commander-in-chief also had the power to appoint at least 25 per cent of all seats in legislatures at both national and regional levels, which, at the national level, gave military representatives, who remained under command by the military chief, a veto on constitutional amendments. The executive at the state/regional level was headed by a chief minister, appointed by the president with the approval of the state/regional parliament. The latter, however, could only refuse approval under very limited grounds, and hence the chief minister was responsible to the president rather than to the directly elected region/state parliament.

The independence of the judiciary, and also fourth-branch institutions like the UEC, was curtailed by both the executive and legislature being responsible for

[23] Ye Htut (n 17) 9–22.

[24] Clarke, Sein Myint, and Yu Siwa (n 11) 28.

[25] David Arnott, 'Burma/Myanmar: How to Read the Generals' "Roadmap"' (*Scribd*, 10 March 2008) <www.scribd.com/document/2250232/7-Step-Road-Map-of-Burmese-Regime> accessed 15 August 2020.

appointing and dismissing judges and other officials and for their control upon legal and administrative procedures.[26] The Constitutional Tribunal, specifically, constituted by nine members, three appointed respectively by the president, the speaker of the lower house, and the speaker of the upper house, had a term of five years that coincided with the parliamentary term. When there was a clear majority in parliament, as had been the case since the Constitution entered into force, appointments to the Constitutional Tribunal were primarily based on political interests. The members of the UEC were also directly appointed by the president. Beyond this, the fact that members of these institutions could be impeached by the president, give again limited but ill-defined grounds, tied their rulings to presidential policies and further curtailed their independence.[27]

2.2 The First Quasi-Civilian Government (2010–2015)

The 2010 general elections were the first elections held after the adoption of the 2008 Constitution. Despite criticisms by both Myanmar and international observers regarding the nature of the elections,[28] they marked the start of a transition from military to civilian rule. Thirty-seven parties participated in the elections;[29] all except for the main opposition party, Aung San Suu Kyi's NLD, which boycotted these elections.[30] Thein Sein of the United Solidarity and Development Party (USDP), former prime minister of the military government (2007–2010), became the first elected president since 1960 and initiated a course of economic and political reforms.[31]

It was only in early 2012, when the NLD decided to run in the by-elections, that the new constitutional order gained some legitimacy in the eyes of the public and the international community. The NLD saw its participation as an opportunity to enter the legislature and push for constitutional amendments. The NLD won 43 out of 45 contested seats, and Aung San Suu Kyi—who was released from house arrest

[26] Crouch (n 16).

[27] Gabriela Marti, 'The Role of the Constitutional Tribunal in Myanmar's Reform Process' (2015) 10(1) Asian Journal of Comparative Law 153.

[28] Myanmar and international observers criticised the elections for several reasons, including the fact that the election laws restricted the registration of political parties and candidates, the Union Election Commission was appointed by the military government, the campaign period had not been officially declared, there was a lack of transparency, and there was a low voter turnout. See Monique Skidmore, Nick Cheesman, and Trevor Wilson (eds), *Ruling Myanmar: From Cyclone Nargis to National Elections* (Institute of Southeast Asian Studies 2010) chs 1 and 15.

[29] Kudo Toshihiro, 'Myanmar Results of the 2010 Elections in Myanmar: An Analysis' (*IDE-JETRO*, January 2011) <www.ide.go.jp/library/English/Research/Region/Asia/pdf/20110104.pdf> accessed 15 April 2020.

[30] Ibid, 1.

[31] Marco Bunte and Jorn Dosch, 'Myanmar: Political Reforms and the Recalibration of External Relations' (2015) 34(2) Journal of Current Southeast Asian Affairs 3, 4–13.

in 2010—became a member of parliament.[32] In July 2013, the USDP-controlled parliament decided to initiate a constitutional amendment process,[33] which, while fairly inclusive, was not overly successful. Out of 34 amendment proposals to the main text of the Constitution (and more than 50 amendment proposals to schedules 2 and 5, all of which were approved)[34], only one minor change to the main text passed the 75 per cent majority required for constitutional amendments, and this did not enter into force as the required referendum was never held.[35]

In parallel, President Thein Sein also engaged ethnic armed organisations (EAOs) in negotiations aimed at ending the world's longest civil war and at achieving sustainable peace in Myanmar.[36] Fourteen bilateral ceasefire agreements were signed from 2011 to 2013 with some EAOs.[37] In 2013, Thein Sein's government initiated talks with 18 EAOs that were to result in the signing of a Nationwide Ceasefire Agreement (NCA).[38] The drafting of the NCA took two years,[39] and only eight EAOs signed it on 15 October 2015.[40]

3. The Transition Trumped

3.1 Democratic Transition after 2015

The 2015 general elections were held shortly after the NCA was signed. The results marked a critical change in Myanmar's recent political history. For the first time since the 1960 elections, Myanmar voters were able to elect a civilian

[32] BBC News, 'Aung San Suu Kyi: Myanmar Democracy Icon Who Fell from Grace' (23 January 2020) <www.bbc.com/news/world-asia-pacific-11685977> accessed 15 April 2020.

[33] Andrew Harding and Khin Khin Oo (eds), *Constitutionalism and Legal Change in Myanmar* (Hart Publishing 2019) 71–82.

[34] Global New Light of Myanmar, 'Parliament Approves Amendment to Schedules 2 and 5 of Section 436(b)' (9 July 2015) <www.burmalibrary.org/sites/burmalibrary.org/files/obl/docs21/GNLM2015-07-09-red.pdf> accessed 8 April 2020.

[35] San Yamin Aung, 'How Does the NLD's Push to Amendment Myanmar's Constitution Differ from the USDP's?', *The Irrawaddy* (14 February 2020) <www.irrawaddy.com/opinion/analysis/how-does-the-nlds-push-to-amend-myanmars-constitution-differ-from-the-usdps.html> accessed 8 May 2020.

[36] Ei Ei Toe Lwin and Andrew Kaspar, 'From Panglong I to Panglong II: A Timeline' *Myanmar Times* (30 August 2016) <www.mmtimes.com/national-news/22202-from-panglong-i-to-panglong-ii-a-timeline.html> accessed 7 April 2020.

[37] John Buchanan, 'Militias in Myanmar' (Asia Foundation 2016) <https://asiafoundation.org/wp-content/uploads/2016/07/Militias-in-Myanmar.pdf> accessed 12 April 2020.

[38] Institute for Security & Development Policy, 'Myanmar's Nationwide Ceasefire Agreement' (Institute for Security & Development Policy, October 2015) <https://isdp.eu/content/uploads/publications/2015-isdp-backgrounder-myanmar-nca.pdf> accessed 12 April 2020.

[39] Toe Lwin and Kaspar (n 36). See also Ardeth Maung Thawnghmung, 'Signs of Life in Myanmar's Nationwide Ceasefire Agreement? Finding a Way Forward' (2017) 49(3) Critical Asian Studies 379, 379–95.

[40] The Karen National Union (KNU), the KNU/Karen National Liberation Army Peace Council (KNU/NNLA PC), the All Burma Students' Democratic Front (ABSDF), the Arakan Liberation Party (ALP), The Chin National Front (CNF), the Democratic Karen Benevolent Army (DKBA), the Pa-O National Liberation Organisation (PNLO), and the Restoration Council of Shan State (RCSS).

government—Aung San Suu Kyi's NLD won by a landslide.[41] Elections were also followed by a peaceful handover of (at least some) government functions in March 2016.[42] The outgoing USDP saw its representation in parliament significantly reduced (from 79 to 8 per cent), but also the ethnic political parties (with few exceptions) fared poorly in both union and state parliament elections.[43] Indeed, the NLD—and Aung San Suu Kyi specifically—was perceived by many as the only political force able to end the military era and bring about much-needed reforms.[44]

Aung San Suu Kyi herself, however, was not eligible to become president,[45] and hence a new position was created for her (state counsellor), which allowed her to act as the *de facto* president (in parallel with a proxy president).[46] At the same time, the ministries of defence, home affairs, and border affairs remained under the control of the military.[47] To a certain extent, starting in 2015, Myanmar had a double executive, one led by the NLD and one led by the military. The NLD, though, was critically dependent on the military because not only did the latter control the entire security apparatus but also the NLD's majority in parliament was still insufficient to amend the Constitution without the agreement of the military. Moreover, many senior positions in Union and state/regional administrative structures, the parliament, and independent institutions had been filled by retired military personnel, and many of them clearly retained their loyalty to the military, as became obvious after the 2021 coup.

Despite these constraints, which were, of course, known long before the 2015 elections, the NLD's 2015 Election Manifesto articulated a series of fairly ambitious priorities that included national reconciliation, internal peace, constitutional amendment, and socio-economic development.[48] These priorities were seen as interrelated: the final peace agreement was meant to result in constitutional amendments that would, in turn, impact the socio-economic development of the country.[49]

41 Transnational Institute, 'The 2015 General Election in Myanmar: What Now for Ethnic Politics?' (*Transnational Institute*, 17 December 2015) 6.

42 Kyaw Sein and Nicholas Farrelly, 'Myanmar's Evolving Relations: The NLD Government' (Institute for Security & Development Policy 2016) <https://isdp.eu/publication/myanmars-evolving-relations-nld-government> accessed 13 October 2022.

43 International Crisis Group, 'The Myanmar Elections: Results and Implications' (*International Crisis Group*, 9 December 2015) <www.crisisgroup.org/asia/south-east-asia/myanmar/myanmar-elections-results-and-implications> accessed 13 October 2022.

44 Transnational Institute (n 41) 12–14.

45 Article 59(f) of the 2008 Constitutions sets out that the president's parents, spouse, and legitimate children or their spouses shall not owe allegiance to a foreign power and not be subject of a foreign power or citizen of a foreign country.

46 Sein and Farrelly (n 40) 9.

47 Ibid, 26–27.

48 Ibid, 9–10.

49 Min Min, 'Aung San Suu Kyi "Path to Democracy" Speech Highlights' (*Mizzima*, 12 August 2017) <www.mizzima.com/news-domestic/aung-san-suu-kyi-%25E2%2580%2598path-democracy%25E2%2580%2599-speech-highlights> accessed 10 May 2020.

3.2 The Peace Process

As soon as the NLD took power in March 2016, it set out to build on the peace process and the implementation of the 2015 NCA inherited from Thein Sein's government.[50] This initially included drafting a framework for political dialogue, organising national-level political dialogues, holding Union peace conferences (UPCs), and signing a Union Peace Accord and ratifying it in the Union parliament, as well as implementing the Union Accord and integrating the ethnic armed forces into the security sector.[51]

The twenty-first-century Panglong conferences (or UPCs) were initially announced to be held twice a year (in accordance with the requirements in the Framework for Political Dialogue), but only four conferences took place from August 2016 to August 2020. In these conferences, the parties managed to agree to a total of 71 basic principles on political, social, economic, and environmental issues.[52] These principles, however, were vague, partly reaffirming provisions already included in the NCA, and therefore failed to significantly support a transition to federalism as envisioned by many of Myanmar's ethnic minorities.[53]

The NLD was also unable to avoid two key signatory EAOs—the Karen National Union (KNU) and the Restoration Council of Shan State (RCSS)—from suspending their (formal) participation in the peace negotiations in October 2018. The peace process was, in turn, deadlocked for over a year over issues ranging from general disagreements with the implementation of the NCA, the exclusion of some EAOs from the formal peace process, the inability to conduct national political dialogues, and more substantive issues related to the right to secession of ethnic states from the union, the right to self-determination, and the sequencing of security-sector reform (SSR) and disarmament, demobilisation, and reintegration (DDR).[54]

Both the RCSS and the KNU only resumed their participation in the formal peace negotiations at the end of 2019,[55] which enabled the negotiating parties to reach eight agreements in January 2020, including the commitment to convene

[50] International Crisis Group, 'Myanmar's Peace Process: Getting to a Political Dialogue' (*International Crisis Group*, 19 October 2016) <www.crisisgroup.org/asia/south-east-asia/myanmar/myanmar-s-peace-process-getting-political-dialogue> accessed 13 October 2022.

[51] Nationwide Ceasefire Agreement (2015) ch 5 art 20.

[52] National Reconciliation and Peace Centre (NRPC), '7 Points Signed as Part of Pyidaungsu Accord' (*NRPC*, 2017) <www.nrpc.gov.mm/en/node/226> accessed 15 May 2020; NRPC, '14 Points Signed as Part II of Union Accord' (*NRPC*, 2018) <www.nrpc.gov.mm/en/nca-part-ii> accessed 15 May 2020.

[53] BNI Multimedial Group, 'CA-Signatory EAOs Agree to Resume Official Peace Talks with Govt, Military' (*BNI Multimedia Group*, 15 October 2019) <www.bnionline.net/en/news/nca-signatory-eaos-agree-resume-official-peace-talks-govt-military-0> accessed 23 May 2020.

[54] Gumn San Awng, Mi Aye Khine, and Nyan Tun Aung, 'The Deadlocking Factors in Myanmar's Peace Process' (Friedrich Ebert Stiftung, Peace Leadership & Research Institute 2019) 6–8 <http://library.fes.de/pdf-files/bueros/myanmar/15639.pdf> accessed 25 May 2020.

[55] Nyein, 'Rebel Groups Told to Unite to Save Myanmar's Peace Process' (*The Irrawaddy*, 17 January 2020) <www.irrawaddy.com/news/burma/rebel-groups-told-unite-save-myanmars-peace-process.html> accessed 15 June 2020.

the fourth Peace Conference, clarify some of the terms and definitions in the NCA, commit to implementing the NCA in 2020 and beyond, and include non-signatories in the peace process.[56] Due to the COVID-19 pandemic, the Peace Conference only took place in August 2020, shortly before the November general elections.[57]

3.3 The Constitution-Building Process

While initially, constitutional amendments were to follow the Union Peace Accord, lack of progress in the peace process likely motivated the NLD to pursue constitutional amendments directly through the Union parliament. On 29 January 2019, NLD member of parliament U Aung Kyi Nyunt submitted an emergency motion to the Union parliament to establish a Joint Parliamentary Committee for Constitutional Amendment (JPCCA).[58] The aim of this committee was to review the Constitution, report any findings, and draft an amendment bill based on the findings.[59] The committee was formed on 19 February 2019 and comprised 45 members representing all parties in the Union parliament. While both the military and the USDP opposed the process,[60] they sent representatives to attend—but not actively participate in—the committee's meetings.[61] Both parties presented amendment bills directly to the Union parliament.[62]

[56] The eight-point agreement includes the following: (i) creation of a framework for Nationwide Ceasefire Agreement (NCA) implementation; (ii) continuation of the process beyond 2020; (iii) step-by-step implementation of the NCA; (iv) agreement on part three of the Union Accord, which includes a framework for political dialogues and ceasefire monitoring; (v) convening the fourth session of the Union Peace Conference during the first four months of 2020; (vi) formation of a working group for interpretation of terms used in the NCA; (vii) work for all-inclusion of non-signatory ethnic armed organisations (EAOs); and (viii) holding Union Peace Dialogue Joint Committee (UPDJC) and Joint Monitoring Committee meetings within two months.

[57] Myat Thura, 'Govt Plans Fourth Panglong Session for July', *Myanmar Times* (1 June 2020) <www.mmtimes.com/news/govt-plans-fourth-panglong-session-july.html> accessed 26 May 2020.

[58] Ye Mon, 'Parliament Approves Committee to Amend Constitution' (*Frontier Myanmar*, 19 February 2019) <https://frontiermyanmar.net/en/parliament-approves-committee-to-amend-constitution> accessed 26 May 2020.

[59] San Yamin Aung, 'Parliament's Constitution Amendment Panel Completes Review of Charter' (*The Irrawaddy*, 14 June 2019) <www.irrawaddy.com/news/burma/parliaments-constitution-amendment-panel-completes-review-charter.html> accessed 26 May 2020.

[60] Shoon Naing and Poppy McPherson, 'Myanmar Suu Kyi's Party Clashes with Military over Proposal to Change Army-Drafted Charter' (*Reuters*, 29 January 2019) <www.reuters.com/article/us-myanmar-constitution/myanmar-suu-kyis-party-clashes-with-military-over-proposal-to-change-army-drafted-charter-idUSKCN1PN0C2> accessed 27 May 2020.

[61] Nay Lwin, 'Military Lawmakers to Outnumber Others in Charter Amendment Debate', *The Irrawaddy* (25 July 2019) <www.irrawaddy.com/news/military-lawmakers-outnumber-others-charter-amendment-debate.html> accessed 28 May 2020.

[62] San Yamin Aung, 'USDP and Military Propose 4 New Charter Amendments', *The Irrawaddy* (29 May 2019) <www.irrawaddy.com/news/usdp-military-propose-4-new-charter-amendments.html> accessed 26 May 2020.

The initial JPCCA report, submitted to the Union parliament on 15 July 2019, contained 3,765 amendment proposals. These proposals were to be debated and voted upon within the committee, and those proposals approved by an absolute majority of the committee members were to be made part of an amendment bill.

The committee's decision-making rules, perceived by some as non-inclusive, resulted in five members of the JPCCA withdrawing from the committee between September and December 2019.[63] The majority threshold within the committee allowed the NLD, with the support of a small number of other parties, to approve any given proposal. Indeed, only those amendments proposed by the NLD in July 2019 made it into the final amendment bills. Hence, only 114 out of 3,765 amendment proposals were endorsed by the committee.[64]

The content of these amendment proposals merits attention. The NLD mainly focused on constitutional amendments that would advance Myanmar's democratic consolidation, for instance, by sequentially eliminating unelected military representatives from state institutions. At the same time, the NLD did not propose changes that would advance Myanmar's federalisation, one of the most important demands from ethnic minority groups since independence and a central issue in the peace negotiations.[65] The USDP and the military took advantage of this gap and proposed constitutional amendments that addressed some of these ethnic demands, particularly regarding the election of the chief minister in states and regions, currently appointed by (and accountable to) the president.

Only four very minor amendments were finally adopted in the Union parliament.[66] The military again exercised its structural veto on constitutional amendments. The NLD did not support the five amendment bills submitted by the USDP and neither did the military.

[63] These included one member from the National Unity Party, two from the Arakan National Party, and one from the USDP, respectively: San Yamin Aung, 'Myanmar's Main Opposition Party Quits Amendment Committee' (*The Irrawaddy*, 17 December 2019) <https://www.irrawaddy.com/news/burma/myanmars-main-opposition-party-quits-charter-amendment-committee.html> accessed 26 May 2020.

[64] Kimana Zulueta-Fülscher, 'Looking Back at the Myanmar Constitution Amendment Process' (*International Institute for Democracy and Electoral Assistance* (*International IDEA*), 2020) <www.idea.int/news-media/news/looking-back-myanmar-constitution-amendment-process> accessed 29 May 2020.

[65] International IDEA, 'Constitutional Amendment Bills in Myanmar, 27 January 2020: Interim Report' (*International IDEA*, 2020) <http://constitutionnet.org/sites/default/files/2020-04/constitutional-amendment-bill-in-myanmar-v2.pdf> accessed 29 May 2020.

[66] Please check the voting results of the amendment proposals here: International IDEA, 'Myanmar 2008 Constitution Amendment Proposals and Voting Results of Union Parliament (For 436(a))' (*International IDEA*, 2008) <http://constitutionnet.org/vl/item/myanmar-2008-constitution-amendment-proposals-and-voting-results-union-parliament-436a> accessed 13 October 2022 and here: International IDEA, 'Myanmar 2008 Constitution Amendment Proposals and Voting Results of Union Parliament (For 436(b))' (*International IDEA*, 2008) <http://constitutionnet.org/vl/item/myanmar-2008-constitution-amendment-proposals-and-voting-results-union-parliament-436b> accessed 13 October 2022.

3.4 The NLD and the Opposition in the Union Parliament

Since the 2008 Constitution came into force, the issue of civilian control over the military has been intensely and increasingly debated. As explained above, the Constitution guaranteed a certain type of power-sharing between the elected civilian government and the armed forces in the legislature at both Union and state/regional levels and in the executive.[67] The Constitution furthermore provided for the defence services 'to be able to participate in the National political leadership role of the State' (article 6(f)) and to 'independently administer and adjudicate all affairs of the armed forces' (article 20(b)), as well as to take over state power in case of a state of emergency that could endanger the Union, national solidarity, or general loss of sovereign power (article 40(c)). This constitutionally guaranteed power-sharing arrangement—or rather, division of powers—has since constituted a critical constraint on any civilian government decision-making process.

At the same time, the ample majority won by the NLD in the 2015 elections allowed it to pass ordinary legislation on its own, despite disagreements with the military and other parties. The latter were unable to stop the NLD from creating the position of state counsellor,[68] for instance, or effectively block the establishment of the JPCCA.[69] While the military held the baton on constitutional amendments, the NLD was still able to pass laws and somewhat change the practice of constitutional implementation. They did this, for instance, when transferring the critically important General Administration Department (GAD) from operating under the military-led Ministry of Home Affairs to be coordinated under the civilian Ministry of the Union Government, praised as one of the most significant policy decisions of the NLD government.[70] These and other NLD legislative initiatives were a constant source of tension between the NLD and the Myanmar military and proxy parties.

The relationship between the military and the NLD was indeed complex. The NLD's ultimate aim to return the military to the barracks was often combined with declarations, from both sides, on their willingness for reconciliation and coordination regarding both peace-building and democratic consolidation. Aung San Suu Kyi tried to avoid direct confrontation with the military, especially regarding matters related to security and conflict management, by, for instance, remaining silent on—or sometimes approving—the military's actions against the Arakan Army in Rakhine and Chin State,[71] which led to a high number of civilian deaths.[72]

[67] Crouch (n 16) 37.

[68] Min Than, 'The Tatmadaw in the Hluttaw' (2018) 73 Institute of Southeast Asian Studies 5.

[69] Naing and McPherson (n 60).

[70] Frontier Myanmar, 'Govt Reveals Plan to Bring GAD under Civilian Control' (*Frontier Myanmar*, 22 December 2018) <https://frontiermyanmar.net/en/govt-reveals-plan-to-bring-gad-under-civilian-control> accessed 26 May 2020.

[71] Nyein Nyein, 'In Western Myanmar, State Counselor's Praise for Tatmadaw Causes Unease' (*The Irrawady*, 23 April 2020) <https://www.irrawaddy.com/opinion/analysis/western-myanmar-state-counselors-praise-tatmadaw-causes-unease.html> accessed 27 August 2020.

[72] Human Rights Watch, 'Myanmar: Civilians Caught in Surge of Fighting' (*Human Rights Watch*, 4 March 2020) <www.hrw.org/news/2020/03/04/myanmar-civilians-caught-surge-fighting> accessed 5 June 2020.

All other political parties were only able to attain minority representation in the Union parliament in the 2015 elections. The USDP sometimes attempted to maintain an oversight role in parliament, also objecting to a number of legislative proposals presented by the NLD, such as the establishment of the JPCCA, the establishment of the Kofi Annan-led Rakhine Advisory Commission and Independence Commission to investigate human rights violations in Rakhine State,[73] or the proposal for joining the International Covenant on Civil and Political Rights (ICCPR).[74]

Since 2010, however, ethnic parties, on the other hand, have had generally weak representation in parliament.[75] In the 2015 elections, a total of 13 ethnic-based parties, out of more than 90, gained representation in parliament at both union and region/state level, winning only 11 per cent of all elected seats. In preparation for the 2020 elections, many parties from major ethnic areas merged into party coalitions to try to improve their chances of being elected—the first-past-the-post (FPTP) electoral system favours those candidates that win the highest number of votes.[76] At the same time, some ethnic parties, such as the Shan Nationalities League for Democracy (SNLD), attempted to redefine themselves from an ethnic-based party to a 'state-based party' aiming to represent all ethnic groups residing in Shan State.[77]

The electoral results were highly disappointing, not only for the newly created ethnic coalitions but also for other parties, such as the USDP. Counting all seats won in the Union parliament in 2015 and in 2020, both the USDP and ethnic parties/coalitions lost about 20 per cent of their 2015 Union parliament seats to the NLD,[78] with many ethnic (minority) voters supporting the NLD rather than the political party that purported to represent the respective ethnic group.

[73] Advisory Commission on Rakhine State, 'Towards a Peaceful, Fair and Prosperous Future for the People of Rakhine: Final Report of the Advisory Commission on Rakhine State' (*ReliefWeb*, August 2017) <https://reliefweb.int/report/myanmar/towards-peaceful-fair-and-prosperous-future-people-rakhine-final-report-advisory> accessed 6 June 2020, 16.

[74] Htet Naing Zaw, 'USDP, Military Lawmakers Slam NLD Call for Myanmar to Join Int'l Rights Pact' (*The Irrawaddy*, 11 September 2019) <www.irrawaddy.com/news/burma/usdp-military-lawmakers-slam-nld-call-myanmar-join-intl-rights-pact.html> accessed 27 May 2020.

[75] Kristian Stokke, 'Political Representation by Ethnic Parties? Electoral Performance and Party-Building Processes among Ethnic Parties in Myanmar' (2020) 38(3) German Institute for Global and Area Studies 307.

[76] Nan Lwin, 'Ethnic Political Parties Merge to Seek Stronger Representation in 2020 Election' (*The Irrawaddy*, 11 September 2018) <www.irrawaddy.com/news/politics/ethnic-political-parties-merge-to-seek-stronger-representation-in-2020-election.html> accessed 28 May 2020.

[77] Sithu Aung Myint, 'Ethnic Parties Face Stacked Odds' (*Frontier Myanmar*, 29 June 2019) <https://frontiermyanmar.net/en/ethnic-parties-face-stacked-odds> accessed 30 May 2020.

[78] Union Election Commission Myanmar, 'Announcement No 266/2020' (*Union Election Commission Myanmar*, 17 November 2020) <www.uec.gov.mm/news_preview_detail.php?action=news_detail1&news_id=J%2Fny6jIgSNZKRGL8rz3C81rZ7hopEVYUpBA9Pd2uf1Y%3D> accessed 16 September 2021. See also Transitional Institute, 'The 2020 General Election in Myanmar: A Time for Ethnic Reflection' (Transitional Institute, 24 December 2020) 12–14 <www.tni.org/files/publication-downloads/myanmar_policy_briefing_24_the_2020_general_election_in_myanmar.pdf> accessed 16 September 2021,.

3.5 The Difficult Road to Federalism

The appointment of chief ministers by the president, with little regard for parliamentary support, significantly limited chief ministers' responsiveness and accountability to voters. In other words, chief ministers were accountable to the president rather than to the constituencies that elected state/regional parliaments.[79] Ethnic minority political parties may have expected their representation to increase to the extent that would enable them to become legislative kingmakers at both union and state level and, if they were to win a plurality/majority in state parliaments and the Constitution was finally amended, to choose their own chief minister.[80] But, as mentioned above, these parties fared poorly in the 2020 elections.

In 2016, the NLD could theoretically have appointed chief ministers that had the support of (a majority in) the given state/region parliament. No constitutional amendment would have been needed. Instead, in the two states the NLD did not win a majority or plurality of the seats (Rakhine and Shan State), they appointed an NLD representative as chief minister. This was highly contentious and discouraging not only for those ethnic parties that had won a plurality of seats in their respective state parliament—the Arakan National Party in Rakhine State and the USDP and SNLD in Shan State—but also for all other ethnic political parties, who saw their chances to select their state's chief minister dwindle.[81] The NLD demonstrated its winner-takes-all approach and interest to control state/regional governments, just as the USDP had done in the previous administration.

Beyond the latter, ethnic parties/coalitions hoped that a higher representation in state parliaments would give them more clout when negotiating the actual division of powers between the centre and state/regional governments and parliaments. While the Constitution included schedules with exclusive lists of power for the Union and the state/regional parliaments, the Union parliament was often involved in local affairs.[82] The oversight role of state/regional parliaments vis-à-vis state/region governments was also often uncertain, partly stemming from the fact that the Union and state/regional governments were often at odds regarding who is responsible for what.[83] This was an additional reason for ethnic political parties to

[79] Interestingly, under both USDP and NLD-led governments, the major opposition party—the NLD during the USDP-led government and the USDP during the NLD-led government—proposed amendments to art 261, which, in both cases, failed to be approved.

[80] Myint, 'Ethnic Parties Face Stacked Odds' (n 77).

[81] Ei Ei Toe Lwin and Wa Lone, 'NLD Control over Chief Ministers Riles Ethnic Parties' *Myanmar Times* (29 March 2016) <www.mmtimes.com/national-news/19694-nld-control-over-chief-ministers-riles-ethnic-parties.html> accessed 29 May 2020.

[82] Pyae Thet Phyo, 'Mon Bridge Name a State Matter: Union Minister' *Myanmar Times* (17 March 2017) <www.mmtimes.com/national-news/25361-mon-bridge-name-a-state-matter-union-minister.html> accessed 29 May 2020.

[83] Tinzar Htun and Mael Raynaud, 'Schedule Two of the 2008 Constitution Avenues for Reform and Decentralization and Steps Towards a Federal System' (*Konrad Adenauer Stiftung*, 2018) 37.

continue to demand more autonomy and greater (and clearer) responsibilities for the states and regions under the 2008 Constitution.

3.6 Formal or Informal Oversight Institutions

While the Constitutional Tribunal was formally responsible for resolving disputes between the Union and state/regional governments and parliaments, it was an institution subordinate to the Union executive and legislature.[84] Provisions related to the appointment and removal of judges of the Constitutional Tribunal, as well as the fact that their term coincided with the term of the Union legislature, further contributed to this perception. Access to the tribunal was also centralised and dependent, for the most part, on the approval of either the president or the speaker of the lower or upper house of the Union parliament. Hence, if representatives of a state/regional parliament wanted to bring a case to the Constitutional Tribunal, they would need the consent not only of the speaker of the state/regional parliament but also of the speaker of the Union parliament.[85]

The relative lack of independence, though, was not only an issue with the Constitutional Tribunal but also with the entire court system, including, critically, the Supreme Court, High Courts in states and regions, and courts in districts and townships. Timid attempts to reform the judiciary were also hampered by the fact that many judges appointed by Thein Sein's administration were still in office.[86] The NLD also aimed to increase public trust in the judiciary, for instance, by developing an ethics code for judges in 2018, which was meant to help tackle widespread corruption within the legal profession.[87] However, none of these initiatives had sufficient time to be implemented and evaluated against set targets.

At the same time, before the coup, and after decades of military rule, the exercise of oversight of and among state institutions was only embraced half-heartedly. Initiatives, such as the establishment of the Myanmar National Human Rights Commission (MNHRC) in 2014, which were aimed at protecting and promoting citizens' fundamental rights, were positive signs but were subsequently questioned by civil society organisations for lack of independence, lack of transparency in the membership selection process (mostly civil servants), and slow implementation.[88]

[84] Crouch (n 16) 163.

[85] Ibid, 169.

[86] Tin Htet Paing, 'Legal Experts Reject Govt Claims of Judiciary Reform' (*The Irrawaddy*, 23 March 2017) <www.irrawaddy.com/news/legal-experts-reject-govt-claims-of-judiciary-reform.html> accessed 24 May 2020.

[87] Ben Dunant, 'How the Rule of Law Was Lost' (*Frontier Myanmar*, 31 May 2019) <https://frontiermyanmar.net/en/how-the-rule-of-law-was-lost> accessed 29 May 2020.

[88] Nyein Nyein, 'Reform of Myanmar Human Rights Commission Lacks Transparency, Critics Say' (*The Irrawaddy*, 15 January 2020) <www.irrawaddy.com/news/burma/reform-myanmar-human-rights-commission-lacks-transparency-critics-say.html> accessed 26 May 2020.

This commission, for instance, failed to investigate alleged human rights violations in conflict-affected areas, including Rakhine, Kachin, Shan, or Karen states.[89] In Rakhine, its inaction was particularly noticed, also internationally, as the military's response to the August 2017 Arakan Rohingya Salvation Army (ARSA)[90] attacks ended up with almost a million Rohingya refugees forcibly displaced across the border in Bangladesh and thousands of civilians killed.[91] This crisis was followed by Aung San Suu Kyi personally leading a defence of the Myanmar government (including the military) in front of the International Court of Justice in The Hague in December 2019.[92]

An initiative where the NLD administration showed greater ambition related to the 2014-established Anti-Corruption Commission (ACC), which the NLD reformed in 2017 by giving it broader authority to undertake investigations.[93] While its 12-person membership was fully appointed by the president, it still received a total of 9,394 complaints in 2019 alone[94] and succeeded in investigating a number of high-ranking officials, also from the NLD.[95] Moreover, the ACC established corruption prevention units within 14 ministries to monitor and report bribery.[96] In 2019, the country ranked 130 out of 180 countries in the Transparency International Corruption Perception Index, an improvement of 14 points since

[89] United Nations, Human Rights Council, 'Situation of Human Rights in Myanmar (A/HRC/40/L.19)' (*ReliefWeb*, 9 March 2019) <https://reliefweb.int/report/myanmar/situation-human-rights-myanmar-ahrc40l19> accessed 15 May 2020; Zaw Zaw Htwe, 'Myanmar Human Rights Commission Ineffective, Needs Reform: Civil Society Groups' (*The Irrawaddy*, 9 December 2019) <www.irrawaddy.com/news/burma/myanmar-human-rights-commission-ineffective-needs-reform-civil-society-groups.html> accessed 29 May 2020.

[90] Formed in 2013, ARSA was declared a terrorist organisation on 25 August 2017 and has never been part of any peace negotiations with either the Myanmar government or the military: Anti-Terrorism Central Committee Order 2017.

[91] BBC News, 'Myanmar Rohingya: What You Need to Know about the Crisis' (23 January 2020) <www.bbc.com/news/world-asia-41566561> accessed 29 May 2020.

[92] UN News, 'Aung San Suu Kyi Defends Myanmar from Accusations of Genocide, at Top UN Court' (11 December 2019) <https://news.un.org/en/story/2019/12/1053221> accessed 29 May 2020.

[93] May Thu Htet and Myo Min Htun, 'Big Moments of Anti-Corruption under the USDP and the NLD Administrations' (*Inya Economics*) <www.inyaeconomics.com/blogs/big-moments-of-anti-corruption-under-the-usdp-and-the-nld-administrations> accessed 5 May 2020.

[94] Anti-Corruption Commission, 'Report of Anti-Corruption Commission for 2020 from January to July' (Anti-Corruption Commission 2020) <www.accm.gov.mm/acc/index.php?route=cms/article&path=43&article_id=637> accessed 2 August 2020.

[95] Frontier Myanmar, 'Tanintharyi Chief Minister Arrested on Corruption Charges' (*Frontier Myanmar*, 11 March 2019) <https://frontiermyanmar.net/en/tanintharyi-chief-minister-arrested-on-corruption-charges> accessed 29 May 2020. Further reading: Myanmar Times, 'FDA Director General Charged with Bribery' *Myanmar Times* (20 May 2020) <www.mmtimes.com/news/fda-director-general-charged-bribery.html accessed 29 May 2020>; Ye Mon, 'Yangon Attorney General, Five Others Arrested for Corruption over Dropped Murder Case' (*Frontier Myanmar*, 14 September 2018) <https://frontiermyanmar.net/en/yangon-attorney-general-fiveothers-arrested-for-corruption-over-dropped-murder-case> accessed 29 May 2020; San Yamin Aung, '5 Water Resources Officials Face Corruption Charges' (*The Irrawaddy*, 11 April 2019) <www.irrawaddy.com/news/5-water-resources-officials-face-corruption-charges.html> accessed 29 May 2020.

[96] Htet and Htun (n 93).

2012.[97] After the coup, a military-established ACC was instrumentalised to make unfound corruption charges against high-level NLD officials, including Daw Aung San Suu Kyi.[98]

With reference to the ability of non-governmental institutions and private individuals to make state institutions and officials accountable, there has been some modest change over time, but there have also been setbacks. Media freedom, for example, appears to have declined during part of the NLD administration.[99] Two Reuters journalists received a seven-year prison sentence under the Burma Official Secrets Act in September 2018 for trying to investigate a massacre of Rohingya civilians—they were pardoned in April 2019. Their case led other journalists to conduct self-censorship.[100] Journalists were also often prosecuted under article 66(d) of the Telecommunications Act.[101] Beyond that, a large number of individuals have been prosecuted for criticising government institutions or high-level officials under a range of restrictive laws, including the Anti-Defamation Law, the Unlawful Association Act, the Counter-Terrorism Law, or the Penal Code. These laws are still currently used to prosecute and detain anyone that dares to publicise any criticism against the junta.[102]

4. Outcomes

A preliminary, if somewhat brisk, conclusion is that a very narrow transition took place in 2015, when Myanmar moved from a government dominated by former military officers to a government led by long-time democracy advocates, limited by the very rigid 2008 Constitution. Even though this transition was a welcome transformation in Myanmar's political history, much work was still to be done for Myanmar to become a genuine democracy. At the same time, when looking at the general state of Myanmar's democracy, according to Polity IV, Myanmar improved its democratic status substantially (12 points in a 20-point scale) in the period from

97 Transparency International, 'Corruption Perceptions Index 2019: Myanmar' (*Transparency International*) <www.transparency.org/en/countries/myanmar> accessed 15 June 2020.

98 The Irrawaddy, 'Myanmar Regime Delays Trial of Daw Aung San Suu Kyi until September' (*The Irrawaddy*, 23 August 2021) <www.irrawaddy.com/news/burma/myanmar-regime-delays-trial-of-daw-aung-san-suu-kyi-until-september.html> accessed 16 September 2021.

99 Reporters without Borders, 'World Press Freedom Index: Myanmar' (*Reporters without Borders*) <https://rsf.org/en/myanmar> accessed 16 September 2021.

100 E Tammy Kim, 'Myanmar's Other Reporters' (*Columbia Journalism Review*, 13 August 2019) <www.cjr.org/special_report/myanmars-other-reporters.php> accessed 5 June 2020.

101 Article 66(d) of the Telecommunication Law states that 'any person shall be punished a maximum of three years in prison, a fine or both if that person is found guilty for extorting, coercing, restraining, wrongfully defaming, disturbing, causing undue influence or threatening any person by using any telecommunications network': Telecommunication Law 2013 (amended in 2017) ch 18 art 66(d).

102 The Guardian, 'The Darkest Days are Coming: Myanmar's Journalists Suffer at Hands of Junta' *The Guardian* (London, 7 June 2021) <www.theguardian.com/global-development/2021/jun/07/the-darkest-days-are-coming-myanmars-journalists-suffer-at-hands-of-junta> accessed 16 September 2021.

2010 to 2017.[103] International IDEA's Global State of Democracy 2020 indicated that Myanmar had been rated a weak/low-performing democracy since 2015, in contrast to some of its neighbours in southeast Asia, such as Cambodia, Laos, Thailand, and Vietnam, all of which were categorised as authoritarian regimes.[104] In 2021, Myanmar was rated an authoritarian state, but until then, Myanmar scored mid-range on democratic aspects related to the representativeness of its government and general checks and balances, which resulted from having held relatively clean elections.[105] Areas related to fundamental rights scored lower but were slowly improving, specifically on social rights and equality, freedom of movement, personal integrity and security, and the general protection of human rights.[106] Particularly in 2020, scores for electoral participation, civil society participation, and local democracy remained low but in an upward trend. Only the scores on direct democracy continued to decrease.

Before the 2020 elections, it appeared that democratic consolidation in Myanmar would mostly depend on how the peace process would evolve (i.e. on whether the gaps between the government, the military, and more than 20 EAOs could be bridged) and whether a significant agreement on both process and content could be signed. At the same time, an important question was whether or not the NLD would manage to successfully position itself as the party of all Myanmar people and not just the Bamar majority. Would the reforms the NLD tried to achieve be generally perceived as benefiting all Myanmar people?

After the elections, it appeared that a majority of Myanmar voters, including a significant percentage of ethnic minority voters, had responded affirmatively to the last question. The NLD was perhaps seen by the electorate as the only viable (if not ideal) option to continue Myanmar's reform processes, including a much-expected transition to a federal state. It won approximately 60 per cent of the votes and almost 80 per cent of all eligible seats.[107] The fact that the peace process was still struggling to significantly build trust among key stakeholders and the process of constitutional amendment had all but failed appeared to matter little for most voters. The military was, of course, central to both of these processes. The military and the USDP, on the other hand, rejected the election results, alleging 'fraud and irregularities that undermined the credibility and fairness of the electoral

[103] Center for Systemic Peace, 'Polity IV Country Report 2010: Myanmar (Burma)' (Center for Systemic Peace) <www.systemicpeace.org/polity/Myanmar2010.pdf> accessed 26 July 2020; Monty G Marshall and Gabrielle Elzinga-Marshall, 'Global Report 2017: Conflict, Governance, and State Fragility' (*Center for Systemic Peace*, 27 August 2017) 32 <www.systemicpeace.org/vlibrary/GlobalReport2017.pdf> accessed 26 July 2020.

[104] International IDEA, 'The Global State of Democracy Indices: World Map' (*International IDEA*, 2020) <www.idea.int/gsod-indices/#/indices/compare-attributes> accessed 13 October 2022.

[105] International IDEA, 'The Global State of Democracy Indices: Myanmar' (*International IDEA*, 2019) <www.idea.int/gsod-indices//#/indices/countries-regions-profile?rsc=%5B775%5D&covid19=1> accessed 13 October 2022.

[106] Ibid.

[107] Peter (n 8).

process and its outcomes'.[108] On 1 February, as mentioned in the introduction, the Commander-in-Chief unconstitutionally assumed all powers.

But by 1 February 2021, Myanmar was not the same country the military had ruled with an iron fist for five decades until 2010. Myanmar had opened up to the world for a decade, and a new generation of young people were unenthused about the fact that uniformed men would suddenly take charge of *their* country. As a result, a broad-based Civil Disobedience Movement (CDM) emerged, and massive demonstrations were held across the country.[109] The military responded violently, killing more than 2,000 and arresting more than 15,000 peaceful demonstrators to date.[110] On 5 February 2021, elected NLD members of parliament announced the establishment of the Committee Representing the Pyidaungsu Hluttaw (Union parliament) or CRPH as the sole legitimate body representing the people of Myanmar.[111] Although the CRPH initially only included NLD members, it soon expanded its membership by including elected representatives from three ethnic political parties.[112] It engaged with other (unelected) ethnic political parties, EAOs, General Strike Committees,[113] and other democratic forces and formed a broad collation of collaboration amongst these parties in order to build an inclusive federal democracy union.[114]

On 31 March, the CRPH declared the nullity of the 2008 Constitution and released the first version of the Federal Democracy Charter (FDC), setting out interim government arrangements and a road map for a future constitution-building process.[115] On 16 April, the CRPH, in consultation with the newly created National Unity Consultative Council (NUCC)—composed of representatives of the CRPH,

[108] Zulueta-Fülscher, 'The Struggle for Legitimacy in Post-Coup Myanmar' (n 9).

[109] Tommy Walker, 'How Myanmar's Civil Disobedience Movement Is Pushing Back against the Coup' (*VOA*, 27 February 2021) <http://How Myanmar's Civil Disobedience Movement Is Pushing Back Against the Coup | Voice of America - English (voanews.com)> accessed 16 September 2021.

[110] Assistance Association for Political Prisoners, 'Daily Briefing in Relation to the Military Coup' (*Assistance Association for Political Prisoners*, 10 September 2021) <https://aappb.org/?p=17578> accessed 10 September 2021.

[111] Committee Representing Pyidaungsu Hluttaw, 'Statement Number 2/2021' (*Committee Representing Pyidaungsu Hluttaw*, 5 February 2021) <https://crphmyanmar.org/statement-number-2-2021-5-feb-2021> accessed 17 September 2021.

[112] Committee Representing Pyidaungsu Hluttaw, 'Who We Are' (*Committee Representing Pyidaungsu Hluttaw*) <https://crphmyanmar.org/who-we-are> accessed 18 September 2021.

[113] Eleven Media Group, 'A General Strike Committee Formed, Made Up of Student Leaders and Political Parties' (*Eleven Media Group*, 21 February 2021) <https://elevenmyanmar.com/news/a-general-strike committee-formed-made-up-of-student-leaders-and-political-parties> accessed 23 September 2021.

[114] Tea Circle, 'Hopes for a New Democracy in Myanmar: Multiethnic Unity against Military Power' (*Tea Circle*, 19 March 2021) <https://teacircleoxford.com/2021/03/19/hopes-for-a-new-democracy-in-myanmar-multiethnic-unity-against-military-power> accessed 17 September 2021.

[115] Committee Representing Pyidaungsu Hluttaw, 'Announcement No. 19/2021, Federal Democracy Charter' (*Committee Representing Pyidaungsu Hluttaw*, 31 March 2021) <https://crphmyanmar.org/wp-content/uploads/2021/04/Federal-Democracy-Charter-English.pdf> accessed 17 September 2021; Myanmar Now, 'CRPH Expected to Announce Interim Cabinet Lineup on Friday' (*Myanmar Now*, 16 April 2021) <https://www.myanmar-now.org/en/news/crph-expected-to-announce-interim-cabinet-lineup-on-friday> accessed 17 September 2021.

CDM, EAOs, state/regional governments, general strike committees, and civil society representatives—and in accordance with the FDC, established the interim National Unity government, which operates partly in liberated territories and partly in exile and is in charge of implementing the political objectives and road map prescribed in the FDC, working with local ethnic group administrations wherever they exist.[116]

In conclusion, one could say that the reform processes that were initiated in 2010, and consolidated in 2015 with the election of the first civilian-led government in Myanmar since 1962, were a tremendous success as the return to military rule is being resisted not only by EAOs, ethnic political parties, and the democracy movement (including the NLD) but also by a much wider segment of society. At the same time, since the entry into force of the military-drafted 2008 Constitution, the military has continuously been in control of the transition to both peace and democracy as well as the social and economic development of the country, which led it to believe that it could take back power at will. The military now still has control over much of the security apparatus but, according to the Special Advisory Council for Myanmar, has decreasing territorial (and administrative) control in much of the country as a result of the resistance.[117] The resistance forces, including the National Unity government and the NUCC, are doing their utmost to turn the tide, having established the People's Defence Forces in May 2021[118] and having called for an uprising against the military in September 2021.[119]

5. The Impact of the COVID-19 Pandemic

The COVID-19 pandemic had a relatively light footprint in Myanmar until approximately August 2020. Numbers of infections and deaths remained low. The impact of the pandemic was, however, immediately noticed in a number of different areas, from delays in the peace process, to a critical slowdown of the economy, with

[116] Myanmar Now, 'CRPH Announces Lineup of Interim National Unity Government' (*Myanmar Now*, 16 April 2021) <https://www.myanmar-now.org/en/news/crph-announces-lineup-of-interim-national-unity-government> accessed 17 September 2021; National Unity Government, 'About NUG' (*National Unity Government*) <https://gov.nugmyanmar.org/about-nug> accessed 17 September 2021.

[117] Special Advisory Council for Myanmar, 'Briefing Paper: Effective Control in Myanmar' (Special Advisory Council for Myanmar, 5 September 2022) <https://specialadvisorycouncil.org/wp-content/uploads/2022/09/SAC-M-Briefing-Paper-Effective-Control-in-Myanmar-ENGLISH-1.pdf?fbclid=IwAR0oyDxGAd9nk-2CG6DmOjv4WHFKbWclRM4FAuM8yF5xJksyrER6KKklVZU> accessed 14 September 2022.

[118] Sebastian Strangio, 'Can Myanmar's New "People's Defense Force" Succeed?' (*The Diplomat*, 6 May 2021) <https://thediplomat.com/2021/05/can-myanmars-new-peoples-defense-force-succeed> accessed 17 September 2021.

[119] Al Jazeera, 'Myanmar Shadow Government Calls for Uprising against Military' (*Al Jazeera*, 7 September 2021) <www.aljazeera.com/news/2021/9/7/myanmar-shadow-government-launches-peoples-defensive-war> accessed 17 September 2021.

the gross domestic product (GDP) growing by only 3.3 per cent in 2020,[120] partly due to the economic slowdown in China and around the world, with international trade and investment plummeting as a result.[121]

Myanmar was also one of the last countries to announce its first positive cases, on 23 March 2020. Around the same time, the state counsellor's office established a high-level committee, headed by Aung San Suu Kyi herself, which implemented some mitigation measures, including the closing of airports, cancelling the annual festivities of Thingyan, and night-time curfews. The government did not declare a nationwide lockdown, neither did it declare a constitutional state of emergency.

At the end of March 2020, the government established the first civil–military emergency task force, which was supposed to boost the response to the pandemic. On 27 April 2020, the President's Office established a committee meant to coordinate with EAOs on a number of different issues, including the sharing of information on migrant workers returning to Myanmar, suspected COVID-19 cases, and treatment protocols and contact-tracing.[122] Beyond the establishment of this committee, there were instances of informal collaboration between the government and the EAOs.

The military, on the other hand, declared a nationwide ceasefire in early May, after much pressure from Myanmar but also international stakeholders, allegedly to support the response to the pandemic, though excluding those areas in Rakhine and Chin State where conflict had flared up. This ceasefire was meant to last until 31 August 2020 but was repeatedly extended even beyond the November elections.[123] As mentioned above, the pandemic had quite a crucial impact on the peace process, which was just about to formally resume at the start of 2020 after more than one year of standing still. The UPC finally took place on 19–21 August, though participation in the UPC was limited to one-third of the usual participants, and all national political dialogues were suspended. None of the non-signatory EAOs attended the UPC, partly because of health concerns related to the COVID-19 pandemic but partly also because the Arakan Army had not been invited to take part in the negotiations. The attending parties, though, managed to agree to the third part

[120] Asian Development Bank, 'Economic Indicators for Myanmar' (*Asian Development Bank*) <www.adb.org/countries/myanmar/economy> accessed 17 September 2021.

[121] World Bank Group, 'East Asia and Pacific in the Time of COVID-19' (*World Bank Group*, 2020) <https://openknowledge.worldbank.org/handle/10986/33477> accessed 13 October 2022, 185.

[122] Myanmar Peace Monitor, 'Government's Overture: COVID-19 Prevention Coordination Committee to Cooperate with EAOs' (*Myanmar Peace Monitor*, 6 May 2020) <www.bnionline.net/en/news/governments-overture-covid-19-prevention-coordination-committee-cooperate-eaos> accessed 17 September 2021.

[123] International Crisis Group, 'Conflict, Health Cooperation and COVID-19 in Myanmar' (*International Crisis Group*, 19 May 2020) <www.crisisgroup.org/asia/south-east-asia/myanmar/b161-conflict-health-cooperation-and-covid-19-myanmar> accessed 15 June 2020; Myanmar Peace Monitor, 'Another Tatmadaw Ceasefire Declaration Leaves Arakan in Apparent Exclusion' (*Myanmar Peace Monitor*, 2 December 2020) <www.bnionline.net/en/news/another-tatmadaw-ceasefire-declaration-leaves-arakan-apparent-exclusion> accessed 17 September 2021.

of the Union Peace Accord, setting the stage for more direct negotiations planned for after the elections.

With infections rising in September 2020, some called for a delay of the November elections.[124] The UEC, though, rejected these calls, and announced that elections would be held as planned on 8 November 2020.[125] Some of the reasons for holding these elections were related to the importance of holding regular elections and concerns about additional expenses to be incurred with an extended electoral period but also, quite critically, fears of an institutional vacuum as the Constitution does not provide for an extension of the parliamentary mandate.[126] But, at the same time, a new suspension of national travel starting in August 2020, stay-at-home orders that affected a large number of townships and hampered face-to-face campaign events, and other government guidelines and regulations aimed at curbing the effect of the pandemic on the holding of elections clearly affected the electoral environment and process.[127]

The newly elected legislature, however, never made it to the parliamentary complex. The COVID-19 pandemic had nothing to do with this. The military, which had previously appealed for a postponement of the elections, was not happy with the result and decided to take over power. The effects of the coup were soon to be noticed in the country's health-care system, shattered after the coup, as doctors and nurses were first in joining the Civil Disobedience Movement and have been one of the military's main targets since.[128] Starting in mid-June 2021, infection and death rates in Myanmar surged, reaching a peak in mid-July with more than 7,000 new recorded cases in one day, and close to 400 daily recorded deaths recorded by the end of July.[129] The impact of this surge was particularly noticed with Myanmar's most marginalised populations, including among a rapidly increasing number of political opponents imprisoned by the regime.[130] Beyond this, there were reports of the military intentionally blocking the acquisition of medical supplies and access of patients to hospitals, further raising the death toll.[131]

[124] Asean Post, 'Calls Grow for Myanmar Election Delay' *Asean Post* (16 September 2020) <https://theaseanpost.com/article/calls-grow-myanmar-election-delay> accessed 17 September 2021.

[125] San Yamin Aung, 'Myanmar's Election Commission Rules out Postponing Election due to COVID-19' (*The Irrawaddy*, 21 September 2021) <www.irrawaddy.com/elections/myanmars-election-commission-rules-postponing-election-due-covid-19.html> accessed 17 September 2021.

[126] Michael Lidauer and Gilles Saphy, 'Running Elections under Stringent COVID-19 Measures in Myanmar' (*International IDEA*, 8 July 2021) 8 <www.idea.int/sites/default/files/elections-under-stringent-covid19-measures-in-myanmar_0.pdf> accessed 23 September 2021.

[127] Ibid.

[128] Reuters, 'Myanmar COVID-19 Outbreak Hits Health System Shattered after Coup' (*Reuters*, 30 May 2021) <www.reuters.com/world/asia-pacific/myanmar-covid-19-outbreak-hits-health-system-shattered-after-coup-2021-05-30> accessed 30 May 2021.

[129] Worldometer, 'COVID-19 Data' (*Worldometer*) <www.worldometers.info/coronavirus/country/myanmar> accessed 17 September 2021.

[130] Manny Maung, 'COVID-19 Surge in Myanmar's Prisons' (*Human Rights Watch*, 16 August 2021) <www.hrw.org/news/2021/08/16/covid-19-surge-myanmars-prisons> accessed 17 September 2021.

[131] Time, 'Myanmar's Military Has Weaponized COVID-19' (*Time*, 5 August 2021) <https://time.com/6087689/myanmar-military-weaponizing-covid-19> accessed 18 September 2021.

6. Reflection

Myanmar was, until recently, presumed to be a country in transition: a transition from war to peace, a transition from military rule to fully fledged democracy, and a transition from a poor to a higher-income country. To be sure, none of these transitions were unequivocal, and parties engaged to varying degrees of commitment, depending on a number of different factors, from personal to group interests. The coup on 1 February 2021 halted and reversed all of these transitions.

The erstwhile peace process structures and mechanisms have been suspended. The ten NCA signatory EAOs announced on 23 February 2021 that they would not be part of any peace negotiations as long as all stakeholders were not invited back to the negotiation table.[132] The Peace Process Steering Team, the coordinating body of the NCA signatories, officially declared the temporary cessation of the NCA implementation and the peace negotiations with the junta on 7 July 2021.[133] It is to be noted that not all of the more than 20 currently existing EAOs—and not all of the NCA signatory EAOs—support the CRPH, the interim National Unity government (NUG), and the process these groups embarked on of creating a federal democratic union, following the recently released FDC.[134] Disagreements amongst EAOs have, though, been part of their history, as they have, in the past, struggled to find consensus on a vision for the country, each with a different history of joining alliances, reaching agreements, and attaining concessions from both the Myanmar government and the military. EAOs have also had disagreements on key substantive issues related to the way in which they envision federalism to respond to their particular needs and demands.

In relation to the democratisation process, while relatively free and fair elections were held over the past decade, with a change in government in 2016, the fact that the military retained significant powers in state institutions hampered a full transition to civilian rule and the consolidation of Myanmar's fledgling democracy. Not only was a majority in parliament unable to amend the Constitution without the consent of military representatives, but also the whole security apparatus had always been controlled by the military rather than civilian authorities. Even the all-important GAD, which changed hands at the end of 2018, when it became the responsibility of the civilian-controlled Ministry of the Union government, still

[132] Myanmar Peace Monitor, 'EAOs Suspend Negotiations with Tatmadaw' (*Myanmar Peace Monitor*, 23 February 2021) <www.bnionline.net/en/news/eaos-suspend-negotiations-tatmadaw> accessed 17 September 2021.

[133] Myanmar Peace Monitor, 'PPST Formally Ends Peace Talks with Burma Army' (*Myanmar Peace Monitor*, 12 July 2021) <www.bnionline.net/en/news/ppst-formally-ends-peace-talks-burma-army?fbclid=IwAR34ZRLn_LGn3xDq-PYym4NP0Zj8bM-TIEAPMCiRWYU05vGdGrmKo7lhNgU> accessed 17 September 2021.

[134] Ye Myo Hein, 'Visions of a Federal Future for Myanmar Are Fading Fast' (*The Irrawaddy*, 1 September 2021) <www.irrawaddy.com/opinion/guest-column/visions-of-a-federal-future-for-myanmar-are-fading-fast.html> accessed 17 September 2021.

included large numbers of retired military officers or staff with military connections and would have needed years, if not decades, to be modernised and made more responsive as well as transparent and accountable to the citizens.[135]

Moreover, the 2008 Constitution failed to establish strong checks and balances, oversight, and accountability mechanisms for state institutions and their staff. Given the sustained popularity of the NLD and Daw Aung San Suu Kyi, as the 2020 elections demonstrated, the military and military-supported political parties and high-level officials were unable to constitutionally curb or diminish the NLD's overwhelming and increasing majority in parliament and thereby their increasing power to appoint high-level officials in the executive, the judiciary, and fourth-branch institutions. The commander-in-chief, Min Aung Hlaing, took it upon himself to put an end to these developments. With the detention of many key NLD decision-makers on 1 February 2021, the Commander-in-Chief established the State Administration Council (SAC) as the military-led governing body in Myanmar and appointed judges and other high-level officials himself. On 1 August, the SAC was transformed into a caretaker government, and Min Aung Hlaing became the new prime minister of Myanmar.[136]

Even before the COVID-19 pandemic struck, and despite some progress in terms of economic development partly stemming from the opening of the country a decade ago, after many years of economic shut down and international sanctions, Myanmar was struggling in its transitions to peace, democracy, and economic development. The somewhat unexpected NLD landslide in the 2020 elections was then trumped by the military's coup, but the success of the coup has been overtaken by the unwillingness of a wide majority of Myanmar citizens to be governed once again by a military junta—resistance mounting as we write. But how successful will the resistance be in taking power back from the military? And how will the various forces establish a federal democratic union?

The military has been financially autonomous, extracting rents from oil and gas exploration, jade and other precious gems, and timber and hydropower sales to countries in the neighbourhood.[137] International sanctions and trade bans have the potential to curtail the military's revenue flow but will not have the expected impact unless every key member of the international community consents.[138] The

[135] Lachlan McDonald, 'Making the Most of GAD Reforms' (*Frontier Myanmar*, 11 June 2020) <www.frontiermyanmar.net/en/making-the-most-of-gad-reforms> accessed 20 July 2020.

[136] Eleven Myanmar, 'SAC Announces Establishment of Caretaker Government' (*Eleven Myanmar*, 1 August 2021) <https://elevenmyanmar.com/news/breaking-sac-announces-establishment-of-caretaker-government> accessed 17 September 2021.

[137] Zachary Abuza, 'Authoritarianism and Resistance in Myanmar' (*War on the Rocks*, 20 August 2021) <https://warontherocks.com/2021/08/totalitarianism-and-resistance-in-myanmar> accessed 17 September 2021.

[138] Stephanie Nebehay, 'UN Rights Expert Urges Sanctions on Myanmar's Oil, Gas Sectors' (*Reuters*, 7 July 2021) <www.reuters.com/business/media-telecom/un-rights-chief-urges-asean-move-myanmar-dialogue-2021-07-07> accessed 17 September 2021.

hope is that once the military's financial autonomy is significantly reduced, the leadership may be keener to engage in negotiations and to ultimately concede their defeat.

Over the past decades, the military has appeared to be a fairly cohesive force, 'supported by a system of rewards and punishments and a rigorous indoctrination process'.[139] It is currently unclear whether the coup is supported by a majority of officers and soldiers, despite being a decision made by the top leadership, or to what extent current defections are significant enough to question its cohesiveness.[140] With a force of about half a million men and (few) women, understanding what percentage may be willing to join the resistance is crucial to understanding the likelihood that the military may fracture from within.

But at the moment, most eyes are on the interim NUG and the NUCC and their capacity to (i) convince groups that have not yet openly joined the resistance—mainly NCA signatory and non-signatory EAOs—to do so; (ii) coordinate actions to both politically and militarily impair the military junta's grasp on power; (iii) attain international recognition as the only legitimate government of Myanmar; and (iv) come to an agreement on both the content of the future constitutional framework and, critically, on the constitution-building process itself, including the level of elite inclusion and public consultation.

Before the coup, there was broad agreement that the future National Peace Accord would be followed by a constitutional amendment process in the Union parliament. This process would have transformed Myanmar into a democratic federation, the details of which still needed to be negotiated. The situation has changed quite radically after the coup. If federalism is still the ultimate goal of the democratic resistance, the latter, in all its diversity, will need to make further progress in forging the agreement on both the process and key constitutional design issues that will set the stage for a future federal union of Myanmar. Even though long-standing demands of ethnic minority groups have been included as principles in the new Federal Democratic Charter, the parties still need to continue building a coherent and common vision for the new country as well as a concrete plan to make that future process as inclusive as circumstances may allow.

139 Natasha Lindstaedt, 'Could Defecting Security Forces Bring Down the Military in Myanmar?' (*IPI Global Observatory*, 23 April 2021) <https://theglobalobservatory.org/2021/04/could-defecting-security-forces-bring-down-military-myanmar> accessed 17 September 2021.

140 Hannach Beech, 'Inside Myanmar's Army: "They See Protesters as Criminals"' *New York Times* (New York, 28 March 2021) <www.nytimes.com/2021/03/28/world/asia/myanmar-army-protests.html> accessed 17 September 2021.

14
Coup and Decay
How Thai-Style Democracy Abuses Constitutionalism

Khemthong Tonsakulrungruang

1. Introduction

Once a democratic beacon of Southeast Asia, Thailand's liberal democracy has rapidly declined. This chapter documents that decay through the drafting of the 2017 Constitution reforms and the subsequent 2019 election, the latest development of Thailand's protracted political crisis. This chapter argues that Thailand's democratic decay is carefully crafted by the military, the judiciary, the senate, and anarchical demonstrators. Thailand is torn between two ideologies: first, Thai-style democracy as held by the royalist conservative camp, who favoured placing the king above electoral politics; second, as advocated by diverse groups of progressive minds, liberal democracy that believes in equality and civil rights. Since 2005, the aforementioned network renewed an effort to permanently install Thai-style democracy through a campaign of constitutional reform.

This chapter begins with an introduction to key actors of Thai-style democracy and its origins. Then, it discusses the coup, the constitutional reforms, and the outcome. Finally, it demonstrates the ill caused by the undemocratic arrangements and the reaction to such abuses.

2. Thai-Style Abusive Constitutionalism

Thailand is obsessed with writing a constitution (20 in total), hoping that a new charter would introduce liberal democracy: a free and fair periodic election, independent judiciary, and robust protection of rights and liberties, as well as supremacy of the Constitution itself. In reality, hyper-constitutionalism[1] seemingly fails to safeguard democracy. The 2014 coup d'état vowed to restore true democracy, but the 2017 Constitution marks the latest milestone in Thailand's democratic decay.

[1] See e.g. Duncan McCargo, *Fighting for Virtue: Justice and Politics in Thailand* (Cornell University Press 2020).

Khemthong Tonsakulrungruang, *Coup and Decay* In: *Democratic Consolidation and Constitutional Endurance in Asia and Africa*. Edited by: Tom Gerald Daly and Dinesha Samararatne, Oxford University Press.
DOI: 10.1093/oso/9780192899347.003.0014

Thailand is experiencing abusive constitutionalism—the use of constitutional mechanism to undermine democracy. Illiberal constitutional change—either an amendment or a replacement—has become a potent tool for authoritarian leaders to rule since a traditional military coup is increasingly unpopular. Abusive constitutionalism entrenches autocratic leadership and undermines institutions.[2]

In Thailand's case, the process of constitutional change is not entirely legal. A constitution is abolished by a coup, but the junta displays great faith in drafting a democratic charter. The problem is that their version of democracy, so called Thai-style democracy, looks very different from the liberal version.

3. Network of Thai-Style Democracy

Amidst the Great Depression and the wave of independence in Asia, the People's Party—a group of progressive revolutionaries—ended absolute monarchy of the Chakri dynasty through a bloodless revolution on 24 June 1932.[3] However, the People's Party made a compromise with King Prajadhipok by allowing the constitutional monarch to reign 'above' politics.[4] Soon, the royalists were able to make a pact with the army to stage a counter-coup, in 1946, that effectively ended the People's Party's effort and plunged the country into decades of military dictatorship.[5] Not only did the royalists regain political power, but they also produced an ideology rivalling liberal constitutional democracy—Thai-style democracy. At the centre of Thai-style democracy sits the monarchy, specifically King Bhumibol, who ascended to the throne when the royalist conservatives were rebuilding the royal hegemony.[6] His Majesty gained reverence and love from continuous charitable works and virtuous behaviours.

In principle, the Kingdom of Thailand has always been a bicameral parliamentary system. The House of Representatives is elected, while the senate is appointed by the prime minister. The judiciary and other constitutional watchdogs impose checks upon political branches. Recently, the judiciary was accused of expanding its jurisdiction and asserting its personal preference into the political sphere, a

[2] David Landau, 'Abusive Constitutionalism' (2013) 47 University of California Davis Law Review 189, 191.

[3] Benjamin Batson, *The End of Absolute Monarchy in Siam* (Oxford University Press 1984).

[4] Eugénie Mérieau, 'The 1932 Compromise Constitution: Matrix of Thailand's Permanent Constitutional Instability' in Kevin Tan and Bui Ngoc Son (eds), *Constitutional Foundings in Southeast Asia* (Hart 2019).

[5] Kevin Hewison and Kengkij Kitirianglarp, 'Thai-Style Democracy: The Royalist Struggle or Thailand's Politics' in Søren Ivarsson and Lotte Isager (eds), *Saying the Unsayable: Monarchy and Democracy in Thailand* (Nordic Institute of Asian Studies 2010) 184–86.

[6] Thak Chaloemtiarana, *Thailand: The Politics of Despotic Paternalism* (Silkworm Books 2007) 204–18.

phenomenon known as judicial activism.[7] In reality, Thailand's democracy was often interrupted by military coups.[8]

The period between 1992 and 2006 was marked by a long absence of the military in politics, the result of the 1992 popular uprising against General Suchinda Kraprayoon.[9] This allowed Thailand to experiment with democratisation. The 1997 Constitution designed strong checks and balances to eradicate corruption.[10] It had a robust and progressive bill of rights.[11] The 1997 Constitution proved hugely popular, but it failed to contain Thaksin Shinawatra, whose economic development policies were loved by the rural majority but whose corruption and human rights abuses were hated by the upper middle class. He was the first populist autocrat.[12] Moreover, Thaksin's popularity was said to compete with that of the ageing King. The military, accusing Thaksin of disloyalty and corruption, ousted him in 2006, the watershed year of Thailand's democratic decay.

One ideology that binds the anti-Thaksin camp together is Thai-style democracy, which is inspired by royalist nationalism. Royalist nationalism regards Thailand as unique among its Southeast Asian neighbours because it survived the colonial era while remaining independent. This is because of the monarchy's benevolence and intelligence, which led the nation through various crises. The monarchy, therefore, is an indispensable part of Thainess, and Thais owe their prosperity to the able kings. Royalist nationalism was an essential part in building Thailand's modern nation state, while maintaining its traditional socio-political hierarchy.[13]

Thai-style democracy aims to preserve that socio-political hierarchy. Based on the premise that commoners are unreliable, democracy cannot be wholly embraced. Because the King is the most virtuous, he may intervene in politics for the greater good of the nation. As result, Thai-style democracy delivers a hybrid arrangement. An election is held periodically, but a coup is justified. Rights and liberties are guaranteed unless the junta limits them. The judiciary is independent from political influence but serves under the King. Most importantly, the supremacy of the Constitution is compromised by the King's traditional authority.[14]

[7] Bjoern Dressel, 'Judicialization of Politics or Politicization of the Judiciary? Considerations from Recent Events in Thailand' (2010) 23 Pacific Review 671.

[8] Dan Slater, 'Democratic Careening' (2013) 65 World Politics 729.

[9] See the second part of Eugénie Mérieau, *Constitutional Bricolage: Thailand's Sacred Monarchy vs. The Rule of Law* (Bloomsbury 2021).

[10] Borwornsak Uwanno, คำอธิบายวิชากฎหมายรัฐธรรมนูญ [*Lecture on Thai Constitutional Law*] (Thai Bar Association 2010) 40–41.

[11] Andrew Harding and Peter Leyland, *The Constitutional System of Thailand: A Contextual Anaylsis* (Hart 2011) 222–23.

[12] See Kim Lane Scheppele, 'Autocratic Legalism' (2018) 85 University of Chicago Law Review 545, 545–46.

[13] Thongchai Winichakul, 'Siam's Colonial Conditions and the Birth of Thai History' in Volker Grabowsky (ed), *Unravelling Myths in Southeast Asian Historiography* (Rivers Books 2011); Benedict Anderson, 'Studies of the Thai State: The State of Thai Studies' (Conference on the State of Thai Studies, Chicago, 30 March 1978) 197–99 <www.zenjournalist.org/wp-content/uploads/2012/10/Anderson-Studies-of-the-Thai-State.pdf> accessed 10 October 2023.

[14] Winichakul (n 13); Dressel (n 7); Mérieau, '1932 Compromise Constitution' (n 4).

The royalist elites formed a vast network with King Bhumibol as the epicentre to dominate Thai politics.[15] Two major pillars are the army and the judiciary. The army understands itself as the guardian of Thainess, especially the throne.[16] Such belief allows the army, in peaceful times, to carry out a coup to correct political ills and, in critical moments, to commit atrocious crimes. Once a coup happens, King Bhumibol always accepted a junta leader as a legitimate leader. The 2006 and 2014 coups are described as the royalist coups to get rid of an opponent of the crown.[17] Throughout modern Thai history, the army has led several major massacres, notably in 1973, 1976, 1992, 2009, and 2010, as well as many more minor forced disappearances, tortures, unlawful detentions, and murders.[18] The excuse to safeguard the monarchy gives it absolute impunity.[19] In addition to political power, the army is driven by avarice—to amass a huge amount of wealth from both legal and extra-legal activities within and across the border.[20]

Thailand's military regime threatens democratisation in the region. It supports Myanmar's junta and Cambodia's strongman prime minister in cracking down on anti-government activists, to which both countries reciprocated.[21]

An equally important partner is the judiciary, which has always faithfully confirmed the legality of a coup.[22] King Bhumibol inculcated a good relationship with the judiciary by granting judges regular audiences and visits.[23] As a result, the judiciary, which prides itself for its service to His Majesty, has become the bastion of royalist conservatives who are willing to accept a junta order as law.[24] The judiciary's deference to a military dictator contrasts sharply with its aggressive review of civilian politicians under the claim to uphold the rule of law.[25]

[15] Duncan McCargo, 'Network Monarchy and Legitimacy Crises in Thailand' (2005) 18 Pacific Review 499.

[16] Paul Chambers and Napisa Waitoonkiat, 'The Resilience of Monarchised Military in Thailand' (2016) 46 Journal of Contemporary Asia 425.

[17] Ukrist Pathmanand, 'A Different Coup d'État?' (2008) 38 Journal of Contemporary Asia 124.

[18] See Tyrell Haberkorn, *In Plain Sight: Impunity and Human Rights in Thailand* (University of Wisconsin Press 2018).

[19] Ibid.

[20] Napisa Waitoolkiat and Paul Chambers, 'Arch-Royalist Rent: The Political Economy of the Military in Thailand' in Paul Chambers and Napisa Waitoolkiat (eds), *Khaki Capital: The Political Economy of the Military in Southeast Asia* (Nordic Institute of Asian Studies 2017).

[21] Pavin Chachavalpongpun, 'How Generals Plot Together, in Myanmar and Thailand' *New York Times* (New York, 23 April 2021) <www.nytimes.com/2021/04/23/opinion/myanmar-thailand-asean.html> accessed 10 October 2023; Surasak Glaharn, 'Hun Sen Learns How to Fake Democracy' *Bangkok Post* (Bangkok, 14 November 2019) <www.bangkokpost.com/opinion/opinion/1793859/hun-sen-learns-how-to-fake-democracy> accessed 10 October 2023.

[22] McCargo, *Fighting for Virtue* (n 1) 91–94.

[23] Ibid, 56–79.

[24] Piyabutr Saengkanokkul, ศาลรัฐประหาร: ตุลาการระบอบเผด็จการ และนิติรัฐประหาร [*Court of Coup: Judiciary, Dictatorship, and the Judicial Coup*] (Same Sky Book 2017).

[25] See Khemthong Tonsakulrungruang, 'Entrenching Minority' (2017) 26 Washington Journal of International Law (2017) 247.

Political monopoly leads to economic oligopoly. Sino-Thai conglomerates with connection to the network access privileges and capital.[26] Oligopoly leaves Thailand with one of the worst levels of economic and social disparity in the world.[27] Major public policies, such as industry hubs and concessions, are catered to big businesses at the sacrifice of the poor, who enjoy few spoils from their hard labour. The upper class thus strongly supports an authoritarianism that preserves its business empires.[28]

Once a coup is institutionalised, it significantly weakens the political party system and discredits constitutional democracy. An election is simply an arena for local mafias to violently compete for access to wealth and connection.[29] Most parties have no discernible political ideology, hence no supporting mass. Such chaos justifies another coup, which further discourages competent candidates. Upper and emerging middle classes, due to electoral violence and bureaucratic incompetence, view democracy with negativity.[30] Thus, the vicious cycle self-perpetuates the next political crisis.

Antagonists of Thai-style democracy share common beliefs in the supremacy of a constitution and electoral governance, as well as rights and liberties. But they are by no means a united front.[31] They all reject extra-constitutional changes. Some of them are Thaksin's supporters, who benefited from his economic policies, hence their appreciation of electoral democracy.[32] Others are pro-democratic progressives, for example academics, activists, and the middle class, whose Western education and cosmopolitan world view convince them to disagree with Thai-style democracy. Some of the latter might even have been critics of Thaksin, but the highly-polarised politics left no middle ground for those who disagreed with the royalist conservatives. Younger generations increasingly lean towards the progressive camp. They go as far as supporting the reform of the army and monarchy.

[26] Kevin Hewison, 'Crazy Rich Thais: Thailand's Capitalist Class, 1980–2019' (2019) 51(2) Journal of Contemporary Asia 262; Phongpaichit Pasuk, 'Inequality, Wealth, and Thailand's Politics' (2016) 46 Journal of Contemporary Asia 405.

[27] Phongpaichit (n 26) 407–13.

[28] Ibid, 411.

[29] See Prajak Kongkirati, 'Murder and Regress: Violence and Political Change in Thailand' in Michael Montesano, Terence Ang, and Mark Heng Shu Xun (eds), *After the Coup: The National Council of Peace and Order Era and the Future of Thailand* (Institute of Southeast Asian Studies 2019) 202–09; Duncan McCargo, 'Alternative Meanings of Political Reform in Contemporary Thailand' (1998) 13 Copenhagen Journal of Asian Studies 5, 10–11.

[30] Thorn Pitidol and Chanon Techasunthornwat, 'The Rise of the Thai Upper Middle Class and Its Turn against Democracy' in Montesano, Ang, and Heng Shu Xun (n 29) 49–53.

[31] See Claudio Sopranzetti, 'Mass Politics and the Red Shirts' in Pavin Chachavalpongpun (ed), *Routledge Handbook of Contemporary Thailand* (Routledge 2020) 158.

[32] Apichart Satitniramai, 'Yellow vs. Red and the Rise of a New Middle Class in Thailand' in Ward Berenschot and others (eds), *Citizenship and Democratization in Southeast Asia* (Brill 2016) 291–99.

4. The Regime Change and Constitutional Reform (2014–2019)

This section showcases how the royalist network abused the idea of constitutionalism through both democratic and undemocratic means. Three interconnected events mark Thailand's regime change and constitutional reform: the 2014 coup, the royal succession, and the drafting of the 2017 Constitution.

4.1 The 2014 Coup

The 22 May 2014 coup was premediated.[33] It was a continuation of the 2006 coup, which ousted Thaksin but failed to prevent his proxies from returning to power, notably, his youngest sister and Thailand's first female prime minister, Yingluck Shinawatra (2011–2013). In late 2013, Yingluck pushed for the controversial amnesty bill that would pardon her brother, thus allowing him to return from an exile.[34] She abused her majority status by hastily ushering the bill through the House without giving the opposition a chance to debate. Yingluck's miscalculation triggered a massive protest by radical royalist-nationalist groups, collectively known as the People's Democratic Reform Council (PDRC).

PDRC supporters held a deep distrust of electoral politics and longed for a Buddhist-style virtuous leader above written rules. They made several demands, from Yingluck's resignation, to her exile, then to indefinite suspension of the Constitution and, ultimately, for a coup.[35] Meanwhile, the judiciary undercut Yingluck by barring her from exercising an emergency power, blocking another election, and ultimately removing her from the office.[36] After a protracted negotiation, Prayuth Chan-ocha declared a coup.

The National Council for Peace and Order (NCPO) subdued the angry crowd through a combined use of brutal force and law. It invoked the martial law to summon or detain hundreds of potential dissidents.[37] Detainees were released only after signing a statement that they would no longer get involved in politics.

[33] Chris Baker, 'The 2014 Thai Coup and Some Roots of Authoritarianism' (2016) 46 Journal of Contemporary Asia 388, 390–93.

[34] Ibid, 391.

[35] Veerayooth Kanchoochat and Kevin Hewison, 'Introduction: Understanding Thailand's Politics' (2016) 46 Journal of Contemporary Asia 371, 374–75; Prajak Kongkirati, 'Thailand's Failed 2014 Election: The Anti-Election Movement, Violence, and Democratic Breakdown' (2016) 46 Journal of Contemporary Asia 467, 474–76.

[36] Const Ct Decision 9/2557 (2014); Const Ct Order 36/2557, 37/2557, 45/2557, 50/2557 (2014).

[37] Amnesty International, 'Thailand: Attitude Adjustment: 100 Days Under Martial Law' (2014) <www.amnesty.org/download/Documents/8000/asa390112014en.pdf> accessed 10 October 2023. In total, at least 902 were visited by the NCPO: see <http://freedom.ilaw.or.th/blog/902abusedbyncpo> accessed 10 October 2023.

A few individuals disappeared and were probably summarily executed,[38] while others were charged with various offences, a protracted trial of which effectively impeded political activities.[39] Many fled abroad. This brutality can be explained by a determination to permanently subjugate liberal democracy.[40] The NCPO learned from its 2006 predecessor's mistake of returning to democracy too soon, thereby allowing Thaksin's proxy to regain power.[41] As the reign of King Bhumibol was coming to an end, there was a sense of urgency to facilitate a smooth succession to Prince Vajiralongkorn and maintain the status quo.[42] The NCPO would draft a new rule that guaranteed its success in a coming election.

Unlike many strong men, who successfully mixed their authoritarianism with personal charm to lure the populace, Prayuth seriously lacked leadership skills. He was crass, almost comical, and yet so violent. Prayuth was incompetent, yet his regime survived because the monarchical network endorsed him. The PDRC believed that he was Bhumibol's choice.[43] Prayuth never stopped expressing his loyalty, which convinced them to overlook many policy blunders and corruption scandals. Right-wing radicals were willing to accept whatever choice as long as it was not Thaksin. Moreover, the NCPO's policies favoured a few large conglomerates which reported significant growth during the period, even though the overall economy nosedived.[44]

4.2 Constitutional Reform

The NCPO promised a thorough political reform that would restore Thailand to democracy. However, it was cautious not to commit to a concrete timeline or to the content of the next constitution.[45]

The core of the junta regime was the NCPO, the supreme body of Prayuth and other commanders of the army, navy, and air force. It enjoyed ultimate power and absolute impunity.[46] The NCPO promulgated the 2014 Interim Constitution, which

[38] See Front Line Defenders, 'Case History: Den Kamlae' (*Front Line Defenders*) <www.frontlinedefenders.org/en/case/case-history-den-khamlae> accessed 10 October 2023.

[39] Bangkok Post, 'Bring an End to Lawfare' *Bangkok Post* (Bangkok, 31 January 2020) at <www.bangkokpost.com/opinion/opinion/1847319/bring-an-end-to-lawfare> accessed 10 October 2023.

[40] Federico Ferrara, 'The Logic of Thailand's Royalist Coups d'État' in Chachavalpongpun, *Routledge Handbook of Contemporary Thailand* (n 31) 81–82.

[41] Kanchoochat and Hewison (n 35); Baker (n 33) 389.

[42] Kevin Hewison, 'Managing Vajiralongkorn's Long Succession' in Pavin Chachavalpongpun (ed), *Coup, King, Crisis* (Yale Southeast Asia Studies 2020) 118.

[43] A rumour circulated among royalists that the King's dog licks his face. See <www.bangkokbiznews.com/news/detail/722881> accessed 10 October 2023.

[44] Prajak Kongkirati and Veerayooth Kanchoochat, 'The Prayuth Regime: Embedded Military and Hierarchical Capitalism in Thailand' (2018) 1 TRaNS 14–22.

[45] Asian Network for Free Election (ANFREL), 'The 2019 Thai General Election: A Missed Opportunity for Democracy' (ANFREL Election Observation Mission Report, 2019) 20.

[46] Interim Charter of Thailand BE 2557 (2014) ss 42, 43, and 44 (2014 Interim Charter).

laid out the mega-structures. The NCPO appointed 200 members of the National Legislative Assembly (NLA). Despite the Interim Charter's mandate that the NLA must represent diversity, in reality, appointees came from three main sources.[47] More than half were from the armed forces, siblings and colleagues of Prayuth, and friends; the other two groups were former bureaucrats and sympathisers of the coup. Many were present on the PDRC's rallying stage.[48] They represented the uppermost echelon of Thai political and economic class.[49] The NLA then voted Prayuth to be prime minister. The cabinet's membership overlapped with much of the NCPO itself, with a few additional economic and legal technocrats.

The reform was supervised by the National Reform Council (NRC), which would outline the new Constitution and approved the final draft. Again, more than half of the NRC were retired generals, bureaucrats, and PDRC sympathisers.[50] The final body was the Constitution Drafting Commission (CDC). The NRC nominated a chairman and 20 other members.[51] Five each were nominated from the National Legislative Assembly (NLA), the NCPO, and the cabinet. Many were veteran legal and political science experts, but others were army generals.

It was obvious that loyalty was the most important quality for the junta. Appointments were based on personal relationship and a shared ideology. These bodies presented more or less similar faces. None represented pluralism. Regardless of elaborate procedures, the NCPO had *de facto* total control over the reform process. Except for a few staged forums, the public held back opinions due to fear of harassment.

There was no consensus on what the new constitutional order should be like. Thais were divided over questions of a coup, Thaksin, and—most critically—the role of the monarchical network in democracy. Nonetheless, the Interim Charter instructed the CDC that the draft must be compatible with Thai context.[52] This mandate reflected the ideological basis of the NCPO's constitutionalism. It possibly gave leeway to circumvent or ignore a thicker version of democracy and to justify undemocratic features under Thai-style democracy. The drafters' main objective was to prevent another parliamentary dictatorship, so they introduced an electoral system that favoured small parties and, therefore, weakened the political branches.[53] Those who were to assume public office were to undergo rigorous

[47] Ibid, s 7.
[48] Khemthong Tonsakulrungruang, 'Thailand's National Legislative Assembly' (*New Mandala*, 25 August 2014) <www.newmandala.org/thailands-national-legislative-assembly>.
[49] Pasuk (n 26) 415–19.
[50] Kongkirati and Kanchoochat (n 44) 8; Khemthong Tonsakulrungruang, 'Constitutional and Political Reforms in Thailand: Deconstructing the Junta's Vision' (*ConstitutionNet*, 29 October 2014) <http://constitutionnet.org/news/constitutional-and-political-reforms-thailand-deconstructing-juntas-vision> accessed 10 October 2023.
[51] 2014 Interim Charter (n 46) s 32.
[52] Ibid, s 35(2).
[53] Duncan McCargo, 'Peopling Thailand's 2015 Draft Constitution' (2015) 37 Contemporary Southeast Asia 329; Puangthong Pawakapan, 'Will Thailand's New Constitution Be a Return to Authoritarianism?' (ISEAS Perspective 2015).

moral vetting through a national virtues board. The hyper-moralistic draft stressed the moral duty of Thais.

The original timeline could have returned Thailand to an election by early 2016. But when the NCPO felt that the 2015 draft was so unpopular that it might not pass the referendum, nor was it likely to ensure an electoral victory, the NCPO signalled to the NRC to reject the draft, hence, its first default of a constitutional deadline.[54] This rejection defied a usual pattern of a quick alternation between a coup and an election. Prayuth decided to delay a plan and withstand growing domestic and international pressure. Unfortunately, the West was facing its own democratic challenges in the United States and Europe, so the pressure was light. The junta quickly found a new partnership in China.[55] The NCPO then appointed the second CDC.

The second draft echoed the conservatives' mantra that wisdom of the majority cannot be trusted; an election does not equate to real democracy, so the CDC should focus on how to prevent the *vox populi* from self-harm and should emphasise its anti-corruption efforts. The more cynical motive was for this Constitution to mitigate the majority and inflate the minority's voice so that the elite could maintain its rule legitimately.[56] Yet, the new Constitution had to be democratic enough to make the NCPO presentable. The result was one of the most complex constitutions Thailand has ever had. The 2016 draft adopted a proportional representation electoral system that favoured small-to-mid-sized parties, allegedly benefiting the NCPO's proxy party competing against existing major parties.[57] Parties and candidates were subject to a long list of restrictions. All 250 senators were appointed, a significant setback after the 1997 Constitution introduced a senate election. The draft placed more limits on rights and liberties, especially on freedom of expression and religion, under the pretext of civic duties and Thainess.[58] The CDC expanded the role of the judiciary and watchdog agencies into moral policing. The Constitutional Court and the National Anti-Corruption Commission could remove politicians should they act immorally.[59]

A new constitution would not immediately end the NCPO's regime. It set an unusually lengthy transitional period of 15 months before the first election.[60] The

[54] McCargo, 'Peopling Thailand' (n 53) 347.

[55] Kasian Tejpira, 'A Tick on the Dragon's Back: How Siam Bonded Itself to China's Political and Economic Supply Chains' (2020) 13 Situations 5, 17–24.

[56] Duncan McCargo, 'Ordering Peace: Thailand's 2016 Constitutional Referendum' (2017) 39 Contemporary Southeast Asia 65, 68–71; Eugénie Mérieau, 'Thailand in 2018: Military Dictatorship under Royal Command' (2019) Southeast Asian Affair 326, 329–31.

[57] Siripan Nogsuan Sawasdee, 'Electoral Integrity and the Repercussions of Institutional Manipulations: The 2019 General Election in Thailand' (2019) 20 Asian Journal of Comparative Politics 1, 3–5.

[58] Khemthong Tonsakulrungruang, 'Life under Thailand's 2016 Constitution' (*New Mandala*, 5 February 2016) <www.newmandala.org/liberties-and-rights-lost-under-thailands-2016-constitution> accessed 10 October 2023.

[59] Constitution of Thailand BE 2560 (2017) ss 234(1) and 235(1).

[60] Ibid, ss 267 and 268.

period was purported to allow the NLA and CDC to prepare organic laws concerning political parties, an election, and watchdog agencies, during which the NCPO retained absolute power. Technically, the NCPO could even override the Constitution. Worse, for the first five years, the first senate would be appointed by Prayuth, with six seats reserved specifically for army commanders, and the NCPO suggested that the first senate should be authorised to vote for the prime minister.[61] For the first five years, the prime minister did not have to be elected, providing more leeway for Prayuth to not compete in an election. The point was so contentious that the CDC decided to put it up for the referendum. Any incoming government would find its room for policymaking very limited. The draft created the National Reform Committee that prepared the 20-year plan, covering all subjects from corruption to the economy, from education to health care.[62] The 2016 draft was basically a manual for constitutional authoritarianism with only a flimsy democratic gloss.

4.3 The 2016 Referendum

Two years into the coup, the NCPO grew more confident. It had firm support from the monarchical network. Watchdog agencies refused to investigate high-profile corruption scandals.[63] The judiciary raised no objection to its intimidation and suppression of human rights. The right-wing masses were willing to overlook any flaw as long as the NCPO persecuted Thaksin's men. Thaksin made a strategic mistake, too, telling his supporters to lie low and wait for the next election. He was confident that his team could beat the NCPO with brilliant populist economic policies, as it had always done.

The 2016 referendum was only the second in Thai political history. The first one was in 2007 by the 2006 junta. In both instances, the referendums took place under the watch of military juntas, who severely restricted freedom of speech. Therefore, critics considered a referendum as simply a rubber stamp for an undemocratic charter.

The 2016 referendum asked two questions. The first, main, question was straightforward: do you approve the whole draft of the constitution? But the NRC framed the second question as follows:

> Do you approve or not that, for the benefit of continuity in reforming the country according to the national strategic plan, within the first 5 years since the first

[61] Ibid, s 272.
[62] Ibid, ch 16.
[63] See Bangkok Post, 'NACC Explanation of Watches Case Draws Flak' *Bangkok Post* (Bangkok, 30 May 2020) <www.bangkokpost.com/thailand/general/1926796/nacc-explanation-of-watches-case-draws-flak> accessed 10 October 2023.

Parliament under this constitution, the joint meeting between the two Houses should be the one that decides the prime minister candidacy?

The wording was confusing and that confusion might be deliberate. In other words, can the senate be permitted to join the House of Representatives in selecting a prime minister? But the NRC was careful not to mention the senate. Nor did it explain that the first senate was an exception because it would be appointed by Prayuth Chan-ocha.

The NCPO mobilised every state organ to get the draft approved.[64] The government involved existing governmental networks, including public school teachers, local headmen, and even high-school students, to distribute its propaganda.[65] Up to 1.93 million personnel were trained and ordered to relay the message throughout the country.[66] There were songs and parades as well as radio and TV programmes.[67] These communications were criticised for misinformation, exaggerating the good while ignoring any down side.[68] There was no independent forum or channel where dissenters could speak openly.[69] The NLA promulgated the 2016 Referendum Act, which criminalised distribution of false information.[70] Having a differing opinion about the draft could be deemed a distorted fact and, thus, punishable.[71] A group of NGOs and activists challenged the constitutionality of the Act in the Constitutional Court but the Constitutional Court held that such an overbroad offence was constitutional.[72] With an endorsement from the Constitutional Court, more than 212 people, non-governmental organisations (NGOs), activists, and local politicians were arrested.[73] News of arrest had a chilling effect, discouraging open discussion about the draft. Information was, as a result, scarce and often skewed in favour of the government.

Yet, the success of the referendum was partly due to voter passivity. Uncertainty and fear were the NCPO's two main tactics.[74] The NCPO withheld information about its post-referendum plan should the draft be rejected. It might, or might not, appoint another CDC, and the duration of any appointment was unclear. No

[64] See Hataikarn Treesuwan, 'Cultural Politics of Thailand's Constitutional Referendum in 2016' (MA thesis, Thammsat University 2017) ch 3.

[65] Ibid, 116–56.

[66] Ibid, 196.

[67] Ibid, 119–24.

[68] McCargo, 'Ordering Peace' (n 56) 71; ANFREL, 'Thailand Constitutional Referendum: A Brief Assessment Report' (2016) 11 (ANFREL Referendum Report).

[69] See Treesuwan (n 64) 156–93; McCargo 'Ordering Peace' (n 56) 74–75.

[70] Referendum Act, s 61.

[71] ANFREL Referendum Report (n 68) 7.

[72] Const Ct Decision 4/2559 (2016); Khemthong Tonsakulrungruang, 'Thailand's Referendum Roadblock' (*New Mandala*, 4 August 2016) 3 <www.newmandala.org/false-serious-business-thailands-referendum> accessed 10 October 2023.

[73] iLaw, 'Tables of Arrest Related to 2016 Referendum' (*iLAW*, 2 August 2016) <https://freedom.ilaw.or.th/blog/referendum_charge> accessed 10 October 2023.

[74] Treesuwan (n 64) 222–29.

one was certain what the next constitution would look like in terms of its democratic quality. It may never allow another referendum. The junta was unpopular, so no one wished it to stay in power any longer. Many concluded that accepting the draft was the best option to vote the military out of politics. Some of them, perhaps the majority, never read the Draft Constitution, either in a leaflet or in full—a fact later revealed when they expressed shock in the 2019 election. The silent majority may have voted to avoid disorder, as the junta threatened. They did not want to see mass street protests return. Thaksin's supporters strategically voted for the draft in a hope that they could beat the junta in a general election regardless of an unfair electoral rule.[75] This was a toxic combination of cynicism on the junta's part and dangerous naivety on the part of the general public. This costly mistake allowed the NCPO to entrench itself.

The polling day went smoothly despite some minor errors. Voter turnout was lower than expected at 59.40 per cent.[76] The majority voted in favour of both questions. For the first question, 61.35 per cent voted for the Draft Constitution; while for the second question, concerning the selection of the prime minister, 58.07 per cent voted in favour.[77] The outcome was a big relief to the government as well as a bitter defeat for anti-junta activists.

4.4 Royal Succession

Democracy did not return as quickly as the NCPO promised. First, the NCPO failed to present the draft to the ailing King Bhumibol in time. Bhumibol's death on 13 October 2016 further complicated the road map. The NCPO put all political process on hold until Vajiralongkorn ascended the throne in late November. Royal succession had long been a contentious issue among the royalist network, who feared that the heir apparent, Vajiralongkorn, would not be able to command the same love and reverence as his father did.

Upon his ascension, Vajiralongkorn suggested that the draft be amended in matters concerning his power; first, in a time of crisis, the king may retain the privilege to intervene in politics; and second, the king may be absent from the country without appointing a regent.[78] While the government explained to the public that the changes were minor and irrelevant to the public, the amendment after the referendum showed that the people's will could be overridden by the monarch's wish, suggesting that sovereignty might not belong to the people as the Draft

[75] McCargo, 'Ordering Peace' (n 56) 81.
[76] ANFREL Referendum Report (n 68) 14.
[77] Ibid, 14.
[78] Eugénie Mérieau, 'Thailand's New King Is Making a Power Grab' (*The Diplomat*, 4 February 2017) <https://thediplomat.com/2017/02/thailands-new-king-is-making-a-power-grab> accessed 10 October 2023.

Constitution itself said.[79] After a long pause, Vajiralongkorn signed the draft into the 2017 Constitution on 6 April 2017, significantly later than the original plan.

Unsurprisingly, the NCPO did not honour the 15-month transition commanded by the Constitution. According to the timeline, when the Constitution was promulgated in April 2017, all the organic laws had to be passed by January 2018, and an election was to be held by the end of 2018. But in January 2018, the NLA announced a 90-day extension for political parties and concerning agencies to enable better preparation.[80] Thailand had not had an election since February 2014, and political parties had been suspended after the coup. But the real reason was perhaps less benevolent. The NCPO was founding a new party as its proxy for the upcoming election, so it needed more time for preparation. Finally, in November 2018, the NCPO set the election date for 24 February 2019.

The NCPO would postpone the election date again in January 2019, citing a scheduled conflict with Vajiralongkorn's coronation in May 2019.[81] Again, it seemed that the real reason was that its newly created party, the Palang Pracharath Party (PPRP), needed more time to usher more money through its canvassers to ensure a victory.

5. Elections and Consolidation of Thai-Style Democracy

The first half of 2019 was about the transition of Prayuth from a military dictator to a civilian prime minister. Then, Thailand witnessed the long consolidation of Prayuth's power, as the opposition was crushed, watchdog agencies and the judiciary were tampered with, and constitutional norms were undermined, in effect fuelling further decay.

5.1 The 2019 Election

Historically, the military's proxy parties have never performed well in an ensuing election.[82] But the NCPO was callous. It made no rushed exit, painstakingly

[79] Reuters, 'Thailand to Begin Amending Draft Constitution on King's Request' (*Reuters*, 17 January 2017) <www.reuters.com/article/us-thailand-king-constitution-idUSKBN15115D> accessed 10 October 2023.

[80] Aekarach Sattaburuth, 'NLA Votes on Bill That Will Delay Election to February' *Bangkok Post* (25 January 2018) <www.bangkokpost.com/thailand/politics/1401922/nla-votes-on-bill-that-will-delay-election-to-february> accessed 10 October 2023.

[81] Pravit Rojanaphruk, 'NLA Expects to Pass "Election Delay" Despite Objection' (*Khaosod English*, 25 January 2018) <www.khaosodenglish.com/politics/2018/01/25/nla-expects-pass-election-delay-despite-objections> accessed 10 October 2023.

[82] Prajak Kongkirati, 'Why Thailand's Generals Fail to Co-opt Elections' (*New Mandala*, 15 January 2019) <www.newmandala.org/why-thailands-generals-fail-to-co-opt-elections> accessed 10 October 2023.

designing the most favourable rules and obedient rule enforcers. The NCPO's seven years in power granted it an unprecedented advantage to tilt the playing field in its favour. The unusually long transition period of 15 months plus subsequent delays allowed it to appoint sympathisers to various offices, importantly including the Election Commission (EC) and the Constitutional Court.[83] The NCPO then ordered the EC to gerrymander.[84] As predicted, the 2016 referendum and the 2017 Constitution did not return Thailand to democracy.

The NCPO hatched a new party to compete with Thaksin's popular Pheu Thai (PT). Although Prayuth was not officially the party leader, the link between the PPRP and the NCPO was clear. Four members of his cabinet formed the core of PPRP, named after Prayuth's populist economic policy (People—State Power).[85] The PPRP announced its support for Prayuth as the next prime minister in advance. It enjoyed privileges of exception and impunity. PPRP was the only party able to campaign while other parties were still under a ban.[86] Corporations and government agencies made large donations, in clear violation of campaign finance laws, but the EC refused to convict the PPRP.[87]

Ironically, the PPRP copied much of Thaksin's party model. It promised heavily populist handouts, most of which would not be delivered at all. Moreover, it bought many of Thaksin's former men into its camp.[88] Those who joined would be cleared of impending criminal cases. Thus, through a *quid pro quo*, the PPRP was able to acquire large numbers of vote canvassers in a short period.

But PPRP did not sail into victory. There emerged a new contender, the radically progressive Future Forward Party (FFP), led by Thanathorn Jungrungraungkit and Piyabutr Saengkanokkul, a pro-democratic tycoon and a law scholar, respectively. Its progressive anti-coup stance, as well as its clean record from previous conflicts, attracted a huge following, principally youths but also many anti-coup individuals who had lost trust in Thaksin as well as former anti-Thaksin voters, who looked for a new alternative to the corrupt Prayuth.[89] By now, the polarisation seemed to fall along the generational divide as well. The younger generation became very critical of the current state of affairs, questioning the political role of the monarchy

[83] iLaw, 'The 2019 Elections, of the NCPO, by the NCPO, and for the NCPO' (*iLaw*, 7 November 2018) <https://ilaw.or.th/node/5004> accessed 10 October 2023.

[84] Siripan (n 91) 10.

[85] Duncan McCargo and Saowanee T Alexander, 'Thailand's 2019 Election: A State of Democratic Dictatorship?' (2019) 26 Asia Policy 89, 95.

[86] Ibid, 94–96; Jacob I Ricks, 'Thailand's 2019 Vote: The General's Election' (2019) 92 Pacific Affairs 443, 450–51.

[87] Bangkok Post, 'EC: No Foreign Donors, No Grounds to Dissolve PPRP' *Bangkok Post* (Bangkok, 12 March 2019) <www.bangkokpost.com/thailand/politics/1643252/ec-no-foreign-donors-no-grounds-to-dissolve-pprp> accessed 10 October 2023.

[88] Duncan McCargo, 'Southeast Asia's Troubling Elections: Democratic Demolition' (2019) 30 Journal of Democracy 119, 127.

[89] Prajak Kongkirati, 'Overview: Political Earthquake' (2019) 41 Contemporary Southeast Asia 163, 166; Anyarat Chattharakul, 'Social Media: Hashtag #Futurista' (2019) 41 Contemporary Southeast Asia 170, 171–72.

and the army. The older generation was seen as clinging on to power regardless of the damage inflicted upon the country. This is what FFP exploited.[90] Naturally, it became the main target of the anti-democratic campaign, with hateful propaganda and lawsuits. The FFP directly and openly challenged the conventional *status quo* of the monarchy, the army, and the judiciary, calling for them to be more transparent and to modernise.[91] But the FFP challenged Thaksin's PT, too, with its more radical reformist agenda as a selling point.

The Palace was implicated in the election shenanigans too. The army commander, the *de facto* Palace's representative, publicly condemned the democratic front.[92] The Constitutional Court dissolved Thai Raksa Chat, PT's sister party, after the King admonished the party for nominating his elder princess as a prime ministerial candidate.[93] On the eve of the voting day, King Vajiralongkorn recommended that Thais should choose good people to run the country. While he never mentioned the name, the public understood the speech as anti-FFP, creating a backlash that the king should not interfere.[94]

The EC proved itself incapable of handling a free and fair election. There were reports of errors, some probably genuine mistakes while others were possibly deliberate. The tallying process was so rife with mistakes that the count was halted midway.[95] The EC never released the official figures.

The PT, PPRP, and FFP were the big winners. But none received enough seats to form a government without the senate's approval according to the 2017 Constitution. Formation of a government was further complicated by the EC's arbitrary calculation of party list members of parliament. Overly complex electoral rules allowed the EC to give at least one seat to every party.[96] The EC deducted these seats from larger parties, effectively reducing the seats of PT and the FFP. The Constitutional Court refused to review the EC's calculation.[97] Almost all 20 single-seated parties pledged their support to Prayuth. In May 2019, the NCPO released a list of 250 senators. More than half were military friends of the NCPO and the rest its cronies.[98] All 250 of them, together with small parties, voted for Prayuth Chan-ocha to be the next prime minister.[99]

[90] Anyarat (n 89) 172.
[91] Ricks (n 86) 452.
[92] Ibid, 452–53; McCargo and Alexander (n 85) 96–97.
[93] McCargo, 'Southeast Asia's Troubling Elections' (n 88) 128–29; Const Ct Decision 3/2562 (2019).
[94] Kongkirati, 'Political Earthquake' (n 89) 167.
[95] Siripan (n 91) 11.
[96] Ibid, 7; McCargo and Alexander (n 85) 98–99.
[97] Const Ct Decision 6/2562 (2019).
[98] Prachatai, 'All Goes Wrong with Unelected Thai Senate' (*Prachatai*, 16 May 2019) <https://prachatai.com/english/node/8049> accessed 10 October 2023.
[99] Prachatai, 'Even without a House Majority, Junta Can Still Function Minimally' (*Prachatai*, 18 June 2019) <https://prachatai.com/english/node/8103> accessed 10 October 2023.

5.2 Consolidation

Little has changed under the Prayuth II government, which continued to suppress political expression. Attacks, and even forced disappearances, occurred regularly and openly.[100] The reinvigorated monarchical network displayed its power more regularly, too. The legislature approved bills that transferred wealth and security forces to the King's personal keep. The King's men were appointed to key positions in the administration. Prayuth showed no respect to constitutional norms. During the audience with the King, the cabinet did not swear to uphold the Constitution and refused to correct the mistake, which was vindicated when the Constitutional Court suggested that oath-taking was a matter between the king and the prime minister.[101] This expansion of the king's territory into electoral politics is described as indicative of a virtual absolute monarchy regime.[102]

Prayuth ignored other democratic norms as well. One of his deputy ministers had been convicted of heroin smuggling into Australia, where he was imprisoned for four years.[103] He was later implicated in a murder but was mysteriously reinstated.[104] But Thammanat, the controversial minister, made it known that he oversaw the coffers, paying small coalition parties for their obedience.[105] Several PPRP members of parliament deliberately obstructed the work of the House committees, especially on the subject of corruption and scandals related to Prayuth.[106] When the PPRP lost the vote on a budget bill, with the Constitutional Court's blessing, it simply requested a new vote until it won.[107]

Meanwhile, the network concentrated its efforts to dismantle the FFP. Charges were filed on two counts: that Thanathorn still held shares in a now defunct magazine company and that Thanathorn illegally lent his money to the FFP. These charges relied on minor, rather frivolous, offences set by the 2017 Constitution to

[100] International Crisis Group, 'COVID-19 and a Possible Political Reckoning in Thailand' (Asia Report No 309, 2020) 13–14.

[101] Const Ct Order 36/2562 (2019).

[102] Prachatai, 'เกษียรเตชะพีระ: สาธารณรัฐจำแลงกับเสมือนสัมบูรณาญาสิทธิ์' ['Kasian Tejapira: Pseudo-republic and Virtual Absolute Monarchy'] (*Prachatai*, 24 June 2021) <https://prachatai.com/journal/2021/06/93654> accessed 10 October 2023.

[103] Michael Ruffles and Michael Evans, 'From Sinister to Minister: Politician's Drug Trafficking Jail Time Revealed' *Sydney Morning Herald* (Sydney, 9 September 2019) <www.smh.com.au/national/from-sinister-to-minister-politician-s-drug-trafficking-jail-time-revealed-20190906-p52opz.html> accessed 29 January 2020.

[104] Ibid.

[105] Michael Ruffles and Michael Evans, 'Drug crime a small issue as Thai PM stands by minister once jailed in Sydney' *Sydney Morning Herald* (Sydney, 10 September 2019) <www.smh.com.au/national/drug-crime-a-small-issue-as-thai-pm-stands-by-minister-once-jailed-in-sydney-20190910-p52pwu.html> accessed 10 October 2023.

[106] See e.g. Thai PBS World, 'Flare-Up at Meeting of House Anti-Corruption and Misconduct Committee' (*Thai PBS World*, 16 January 2020) <www.thaipbsworld.com/flare-up-at-meeting-of-house-anti-corruption-and-misconduct-committee> accessed 10 October 2023.

[107] Const Ct Decision 2-3/2563 (2020).

'cleanse' Thai politics.[108] The Constitutional Court found Thanathorn and the FFP guilty on both counts, disqualifying him from being a member of parliament and dissolving the FFP, respectively.[109] Notwithstanding the official charge, it appears that the real crime of the FFP was disloyalty, failing to conform to the theatrical act of paying respect to the nation, the army, and the king. The government benefited from the FFP's dissolution by buying some of its members of parliament. While the junta supporters cheered the death of the FFP, the pro-democratic masses began to lose trust in the judiciary and the present Constitution.

With its power firmly consolidated, Prayuth should have ruled with ease. However, the rise of Thai-style democracy brought a backlash from the progressive wing of the polity, which found the decay of democratic norms installed in 1997 unacceptable. Notable among the dissidents were thousands of the younger generation, who saw the monarchy's involvement in politics as unacceptable, that coup and corruption stole from them their future. They were fed up with diminishing rights and liberties, that they could be abducted or silenced if being too honest about their criticism of power.[110] Thailand's largest protest ever erupted. From February 2020 to the first half of 2021, thousands of protests sprung across the country, involving several tens of thousands of protesters, mostly from the younger generation.[111] The government responded, as usual, with violence and lawsuits. There seems to be no peaceful exit in sight.

6. COVID-19: Policy Blunder and Economic Gap

The COVID-19 pandemic saw Prayuth's biggest blunder, which cost many lives and widened the already terrible economic gap. Yet, the polarised polity meant that his supporters remained loyal to the terrible regime, allowing Prayuth to worsen the catastrophe.

Thailand's militarised nature enabled the government to control the first wave of the pandemic.[112] Prayuth invoked the emergency decree, which granted him

[108] Khemthong Tonsakulrungruang, 'Thailand's Obsession with Clean Politics Dismantles Its Democracy' (*Verfassungsblog*, 3 March 2020) <https://verfassungsblog.de/thailands-obsession-with-clean-politics-dismantles-its-democracy> accessed 10 October 2023.

[109] Const Ct Decision 14/2562 (2019) and Const Ct Decision 5/2563 (2020). See Khemthong Tonsakulrungruang, 'Anakot Mai: 'Lawfare' and Future Forward Party's Legacy' (*New Mandala*, 28 February 2020) <www.newmandala.org/anakot-mai-lawfare-and-future-forward-partys-legacy> accessed 10 October 2023.

[110] Kanokrat Lertchoosakul, 'The White Ribbon Movement: High School Students in the 2020 Thai Youth Protests' (2021) 53 Critical Asian Studies 206.

[111] Duncan McCargo, 'Disrupters' Dilemma? Thailand's 2020 Gen Z Protests' (2021) 53 Critical Asian Studies 175.

[112] Khemthong Tonsakulrungruang and Rawin Leelapatana, 'Health before Rights and Liberties: Thailand's Response to COVID-19' (*VerfassungsBlog*, 8 May 2020) <https://verfassungsblog.de/health-before-rights-and-liberties-thailands-response-to-covid-19> accessed 10 October 2023.

unlimited power with little liability. He imposed several immediate measures to halt the spread of the disease, including a partial shutdown, total border shutdown, curfew, and travel ban.[113] Thailand was suddenly plunged back into the authoritarian regime under which it had been previously. These drastic measures resulted in a sharp drop of new cases. However, they brought grave side-effects as most businesses were suspended and millions of Thais and immigrant workers found themselves jobless.[114]

In 2020, Thailand had one of the worst levels of economic disparity in the world.[115] Five years under the NCPO significantly widened that gap as most policies were favourable to Prayuth's allies in large conglomerates.[116] Most Thais had too little savings to last more than three months.[117] Reports of suicides poured in.[118] But the government was unmoved. Its economic stimulus package was too little, too late. It took a long time to formulate and the package was paltry.[119]

Despite its early success, Prayuth was in no hurry to terminate the emergency decree. Neither did he try to prepare the country for the next wave of the pandemic. No extra medical supplies were procured. There was no plan to replace the emergency decree with ordinary law. Worse, the government refused to procure adequate amounts of good-quality vaccines. Thailand's vaccine programmes are linked to those with business or political connections to the government, raising questions as to potential conflict of interests.[120]

All the major waves of the pandemic can be traced to either corruption or Prayuth's cronies. The first major wave, in April 2020, was from the army's boxing event, despite the government's plea to ban a public gathering event.[121] The second wave, in December 2020, was from human trafficking and gambling dens.[122] The

[113] Regulation No 1 issued under s 9 of the Emergency Decree on Public Administration in Emergency Situations BE 2548 (2005) 29 March 2020.

[114] International Crisis Group, 'COVID-19' (n 100) 17–19.

[115] World Bank, 'Taking the Pulse of Poverty and Inequality in Thailand' (5 March 2020) <www.worldbank.org/en/country/thailand/publication/taking-the-pulse-of-poverty-and-inequality-in-thailand> accessed 10 October 2023.

[116] Shawn Crispin, 'Thailand's Five Families Poised to Profit on the Plague' *Asia Times* (8 May 2020) <https://asiatimes.com/2020/05/thailands-five-families-poised-to-profit-on-the-plague> accessed 10 October 2023.

[117] Siam Commercial Bank, *Outlook Quarterly 1/2020* (SCB Economic Intelligence Center 2020) 90–103.

[118] Anna Salva, 'Thailand: The Corona Virus Suicides' (*The Diplomat*, 11 May 2020) <https://thediplomat.com/2020/05/thailand-the-coronavirus-suicides> accessed 10 October 2023.

[119] International Crisis Group, 'COVID-19' (n 100) 19–20.

[120] Thitinan Pongsudhirak, 'No Duopoly in Thai Jab Procurement' *Bangkok Post* (Bangkok, 27 May 2021) <www.bangkokpost.com/opinion/opinion/2122703/no-duopoly-in-thai-jab-procurement> accessed 10 October 2023.

[121] Marwaan Macan-Karkar, 'Coronavirus exposes Thai Military's Off-the-Books Enterprises' (*Asia Nikkei*, 31 March 2020) <https://asia.nikkei.com/Spotlight/Coronavirus/Coronavirus-exposes-Thai-military-s-off-the-books-enterprises> accessed 10 October 2023.

[122] Punchada Sirivunnabood, 'Thailand's Second Covid-19 Outbreak: Corruption and Its Consequences' (*Fulcrum*, 20 January 2021) <https://fulcrum.sg/thailands-second-covid-19-outbreak-corruption-and-its-consequences> accessed 10 October 2023.

most serious wave, in April 2021, was first detected among one of Prayuth's cabinet members, who went to a party which clearly defied a lockdown order.[123] None of those involved were held accountable.

By April 2021, Thailand's early reputation was in tatters. The death toll steadily rose, peaking in August. Hospitals were filled up. Many perished while waiting at home or even by the roadside. Meanwhile, the government was in denial. It failed to adjust its vaccination plan in response to the crisis.

COVID-19 represented a godsent gift to the Prayuth government. By February 2020, the country was on the verge of potential mass-scale protest after the FFP's dissolution. COVID-19 provided Prayuth with a pretext to discourage political assembly. The emergency decree is an effective tool to suppress a dissenting crowd.[124]

7. Reflection: Towards a Crisis

Thailand's democratic decay serves as a reminder of how potent ideology can be. The 1992 Revolution, for the monarchical network, is a festering wound that, in 2021, they attempted to permanently settle. Thai-style democracy is a counter-revolution, and later, a counter-democratisation discourse that successfully radicalised a significant portion of Thais to shun liberal democracy. They irrationally forego civil rights, to their own detriment. Unfortunately, Thailand's most successful civilian politician is Thaksin Shinawatra, whose terrible record of corruption and human rights abuses matches him perfectly to the image of a bad politician. Anti-Thaksin sentiment conveniently grows into the anti-democratic movement.

After seven long years, and the engineering of law, lobbying, and a blatant disregard of norms, the government of Prayuth Chan-ocha appears more secure than ever. Laws, watchdog agencies, and politicians are all on his side, leaving the opposition no chance to challenge his further sabotaging of remaining democratic norms. But this becomes a pyrrhic victory. The more he asserts pressure to institutionalise Thai-style democracy, the stronger the resistance grows.

Though sporadic, Thailand has experienced short stints of democracy, most critically, that of the 1997 Constitution. Albeit weak and brief, these moments convince the younger progressive minds and the grassroots majority alike that a better alternative to authoritarianism is possible—that ideas of rights and liberties, equality, the rule of law, stability, and transparency can be implemented.

[123] Channel News Asia, 'Bangkok Nightlife Clusters Expose Thailand's COVID-19 Stumbles' (*Channel News Asia*, 15 April 2021) <www.channelnewsasia.com/asia/bangkok-nightlife-clusters-expose-thailand-covid-19-stumbles-220416> accessed 10 October 2023.

[124] International Crisis Group, 'COVID-19' (n 100) 21–22.

Now, the monarchical network is ruling over a divided nation. It depletes the credibility of public institutions (i.e., the judiciary and the watchdog agencies), whose professionalism and impartiality are crucial to a functioning society. This is a dangerous strategy as Prayuth may need a more credible state apparatus than ever. Thai-style democracy relies heavily on the personal charisma of a single man, who was succeeded by a new figure with a different personality and charisma. The network has obviously lost its hegemonic authority. The narrative of the righteous king versus corrupt politicians no longer works to the desired effect. The country is rapidly declining under Prayuth's many policy blunders. But the network seems unaware of the changing circumstances.

When the political ideology of the ruling network no longer works but they still wish to cling on to power, the ruling network resorts to brute force and the abusive application of law. But cruelty and injustice upset the public further. This model is pushing the network to collide with the people. This collision might end the pattern of democratic careening but with a result no one can predict.

15

Making Progress on a Rocky Path

Democratic Consolidation and Endurance in Malaysia, 2018–2021

Wilson Tay Tze Vern

1. Introduction

The peaceful, democratic change of government that took place in Malaysia in May 2018 was heralded as a watershed moment in the country's history, marking the first time that the ruling political coalition had lost power at federal level since independence in 1957. The defeat of the long-entrenched incumbents, who had become mired in maladministration and a staggering corruption scandal that drew worldwide attention, was meant to usher in a new era of reform, constitutional governance, democracy, and transparency under the stewardship of the victorious opposition, who made these values the centrepiece of their electoral platform.

In less than two years, these prospects had all but collapsed. The reforms touted at the hustings in 2018 proved, for various reasons, to be long on promises and short on delivery. Instead, ethno-nationalist sentiments, which notoriously permeate the Malaysian body politic, were adroitly exploited by opponents of the new administration to destabilise it and to stymie efforts to achieve real reform. The new administration, meanwhile, did itself no favours with its tardy pace of reform and internal bickering amongst coalition partners, which left the electorate increasingly restless and disillusioned.

The culmination of this was the collapse of the new administration in February 2020 as a renegade faction within that coalition abruptly changed sides, forcing the resignation of the prime minister, Dr Mahathir Mohamad, and his cabinet. What followed was an extraordinary—and unprecedented—fortnight in which the Yang di-Pertuan Agong, the constitutional monarch of Malaysia ('hereinafter the Agong') personally intervened in order to establish who actually commanded the requisite parliamentary support to take over as prime minister under the provisions of the Federal Constitution. Ultimately, a new government was formed under the premiership of Muhyiddin Yassin, comprising the renegade faction (led by Muhyiddin himself), the former ruling coalition that previously lost power in the general election of 2018, and the Pan-Malaysian Islamic Party (PAS). Thus, most

Wilson Tay Tze Vern, *Making Progress on a Rocky Path* In: *Democratic Consolidation and Constitutional Endurance in Asia and Africa*. Edited by: Tom Gerald Daly and Dinesha Samararatne, Oxford University Press. © Oxford University Press 2024. DOI: 10.1093/oso/9780192899347.003.0015

of the 'reformist' coalition that had won in 2018 were cast into the political wilderness, bringing a premature end to what had once been a promise of reform. By January 2021, this new government had consolidated its power through a proclamation of emergency (ostensibly due to the COVID-19 pandemic), which had the effect of suspending parliament, postponing elections, and giving the federal government the power to rule by decree.

Then, in July 2021, an internal putsch within this newly formed and somewhat uneasy coalition toppled Muhyiddin from the prime minister's position. Once again, the Agong was compelled to ascertain who had the majority support to be the next prime minister, but not before His Majesty had become embroiled in an astonishing public spat with Muhyiddin's government, which led directly to the latter's downfall. Into the prime ministership stepped Ismail Sabri Yaakob, a vice-president of the United Malays National Organisation (UMNO), thereby completing a remarkable turnaround in which UMNO regained control of the position it had held for 61 years before losing it in 2018. Thus, as from August 2021, the political parties that had been ousted in the 'watershed' election of 2018 were essentially back in the driver's seat.

From a constitutional and democracy-building perspective, Malaysia's journey in 2018–2021 is a truly remarkable one. On the one hand, the failure of the promise of reform in 2018 clearly holds lessons in how *not* to go about the process of reforming a troubled democracy. Yet, on the other hand, the persistence of constitutional government—and the continued reference to constitutional due process by all parties involved—throughout the tumultuous years (and the onset of a pandemic) also underlines the resilience of the basic constitutional framework, even as Malaysians and other stakeholders continue to disagree about key aspects of this framework.

This chapter continues this collection's study of the complex relationship between constitutional democracy and the forces arranged against its social entrenchment—particularly populism, ethno-nationalism, and authoritarianism, in the context of Malaysia. The chapter is organised as follows: with the landmark events of 2018–2021 sketched out above as a background, section 2 identifies the salient features of the Malaysian constitutional and political context which facilitate our understanding of the significance of what transpired in this period. Section 3 focuses on the 'regime-change event'—the watershed general election of 2018 and its aftermath. Section 4 assesses the outcomes of these events to draw out the various reasons why the promise of democratic renewal in Malaysia did not get off the ground and what can be learnt from this experience in terms of constitution-building. Section 5 examines the Malaysian experience of dealing with the COVID-19 pandemic and the constitutional and legal mechanisms employed for this purpose. Section 6, the conclusion, reflects on what the Malaysian experience may signify for our understanding of constitutional endurance and the entrenchment of democracy.

2. Context

Malaysia is a federal constitutional monarchy of 13 states, with a population of approximately 32.7 million as of July 2020.[1] Malaysia is ethnically and religiously heterogenous; about 69.6 per cent of the population is classified as *Bumiputera* (literally 'princes of the soil'), a term used by the Malaysian government to refer to the country's majority Malay community, plus other indigenous Austronesian ethnic groups inhabiting the country. Ethnic Chinese (22.6 per cent) and Indians (6.8 per cent) form sizeable minorities in Malaysia. Approximately 61.3 per cent of the population adheres to the Islamic faith, with Buddhism (19.8 per cent), Christianity (9.2 per cent), and Hinduism (6.3 per cent) also practised by significant sections of the population. Malaysia is classified as an upper-middle-income country and has a 'very high' score of 0.81 on the United Nations Development Programme's Human Development Index (HDI).[2]

Understanding the ethnic and religious composition of Malaysia is essential because of how these influence constitutionalism and politics in the country. The ethnocentric nature of politics and governance in Malaysia is underlined by the traditional dominance of political parties based explicitly on ethnicity, such as the UMNO, the Malaysian Chinese Association (MCA), the Malaysian Indian Congress (MIC) and, of late, the Malaysian United Indigenous Party ('Bersatu'). The Alliance Party, a coalition comprising UMNO, MCA, and MIC, held power with broad-based support at the independence of the erstwhile Federation of Malaya in 1957 and later became the core of an expanded National Front (Barisan Nasional or BN) coalition, which retained power at every general election until 2018. BN's model of governance was an overtly ethnocentric one in which cabinet positions and patronage were allocated on the basis of power-sharing between the various ethnicities in Malaysia, represented by the leaders of the ethnic-based political parties.[3]

Likewise, several of the major political parties in opposition to the BN are also closely associated with particular ethnicities, such as the PAS, which, by virtue of its Islamist platform, almost exclusively comprises ethnic Malay Muslims.[4] The Democratic Action Party (DAP), although multiracial, has constantly struggled to

[1] Department of Statistics Malaysia, 'Current Population Estimates, Malaysia, 2020' <www.dosm.gov.my/v1/index.php?r=column/cthemeByCat&cat=155&bul_id=OVByWjg5YkQ3MWFZRTN5bDJiaEVhZz09&menu_id=L0pheU43NWJwRWVSZklWdzQ4TlhUUT09> accessed 15 February 2021.

[2] CIA.gov, 'The World Factbook—Malaysia' <www.cia.gov/the-world-factbook/countries/malaysia> accessed 15 February 2021; United Nations Development Programme (UNDP), *Human Development Report 2020* (UNDP 2020) 385 <http://hdr.undp.org/sites/default/files/hdr2020.pdf> accessed 15 February 2021.

[3] Andrew Harding, *The Constitution of Malaysia: A Contextual Analysis* (Hart Publishing 2012) 59–60.

[4] Malay ethnicity in Malaysia is legally intertwined with the religion of Islam, since the Federal Constitution of Malaysia, art 160(2) defines 'Malay' as 'a person who professes the religion of Islam' (among other criteria).

shed its image as a 'Chinese' political party due to its historically close association with that community—a problem that dogged its brief stint in federal power, as will be further discussed below. With the probable exception of Mr Anwar Ibrahim's People's Justice Party (Parti Keadilan Rakyat—PKR), genuinely multiracial political parties have struggled to gain traction at federal level in Malaysia in recent decades. This has created a situation whereby an ethnic community's perceived political influence is inextricably intertwined with the electoral performance of that community's proxies in the form of the communally based political parties and the role that these parties play in government.

Political contestation in Malaysia takes place in the context of a constitutional system that explicitly establishes 'the special position of the Malays and natives of any of the States of Sabah and Sarawak (Malaysia's two states on the island of Borneo)', enabling the government to reserve positions in the public service, places in higher education institutions, scholarships, permits, and licences in favour of these ethnic groups.[5] Decades of affirmative action policies assisting the Malay and native communities (collectively termed the *Bumiputera*) have also created a perception, if not an expectation, that these ethnicities occupy a special position as compared to ethnic minorities. This is, in turn, linked to a metaphorical 'social contract' dating back to the eve of independence in 1957, whereby acceptance of the special position of the Malays (and later the natives of Sabah and Sarawak as well) was seen as a trade-off, among other elements, in exchange for the liberal grant of citizenship of the new nation to the non-Malay communities.[6]

At the same time, there have also been efforts by previous administrations to centralize the position of Islam, which is constitutionally enshrined as 'the religion of the Federation', albeit that 'other religions may be practised in peace and harmony in any part of the Federation'.[7] Somewhat unusually, the Malaysian Constitution also ties together two potent forces—ethnicity and religion—by expressly defining a 'Malay' as, among others, 'a person who professes the religion of Islam'.[8] Alongside the close association of Islam with the state, this creates a situation whereby issues of public importance involving ethnic Malays can rapidly acquire a religious dimension and vice-versa.

Since independence, Malaysia has more or less successfully maintained a multiparty parliamentary democracy organised broadly along the Westminster model instituted by the British, the former colonial power.[9] The only exception was an

[5] Federal Constitution of Malaysia, arts 153(1), 153(2), and 153(8A).

[6] See e.g. Harding, *Constitution of Malaysia*) (n 3) 70; Karl von Vorys, *Democracy without Consensus: Communalism and Political Stability in Malaysia* (Princeton University Press 1975).

[7] Federal Constitution of Malaysia, art 3(1).

[8] Ibid, art 160(2). See also n 4 above. Consequently, the term 'Malay' in the context of Malaysia is not a purely ethnic identifier, but carries religious implications as well. See e.g. *Lina Joy v Majlis Agama Islam Wilayah Persekutuan* [2007] 4 MLJ 585 (Federal Court). Besides ethnic Malays, there are also Muslims of other ethnic backgrounds in Malaysia.

[9] The Federation of Malaya evolved into the present Federation of Malaysia through the merger of Malaya, North Borneo (now Sabah), Sarawak, and Singapore on 16 September 1963, although

interregnum between 1969 and 1971, when parliamentary democracy was suspended following serious inter-ethnic bloodshed in the capital, Kuala Lumpur. The Constitution adopted at independence (with adjustments for the evolution from Malaya to Malaysia in 1963) continues to be the supreme law, and unlike elsewhere in the region, the military has neither sought nor exercised any role in government.

In this context, the BN, continuing from its predecessor the Alliance Party, governed uninterrupted until 2018, with UMNO undoubtedly playing the leading role by virtue of its consistently commanding significantly more parliamentary seats than any of its coalition partners. There were transitions of power from one prime minister (invariably the current UMNO president) to another, and some state governments within the federation were, from time to time, held by opposition parties.[10] However, until the twelfth general election in 2008, the BN not only retained power but also maintained a two-thirds majority in the federal parliament, enabling it to amend the Federal Constitution with ease.[11] The BN's supermajority was lost in the election of 2008, a precursor to its outright loss of power ten years later.

A defining feature of Malaysia's political system is the tremendous power that has accrued, over the decades, to the post of prime minister. In the Westminster model of constitutionalism, the prime minister is *primus inter pares* among his cabinet colleagues, but in the context of Malaysia, the prime minister's tremendous powers of patronage (such as the ability to select cabinet ministers, senators, ambassadors with ministerial rank, the attorney general, etc) and the outsized importance of the prime minister's department (which also controls economic planning, parliamentary affairs, the public service department, and federal-level religious affairs, among others), as well as the prime minister's role as leader of the house (capable of determining when, and for how long, the lower house of parliament sits), make the position a commanding one indeed.[12] When combined with a strong majority in the lower house, the post has, indeed, been likened to 'a sun around which the planets revolve'.[13] Understanding this is important in appreciating the

Singapore was later detached from the Federation in 1965. For a comprehensive account, see JC Fong, *Constitutional Federalism in Malaysia* (Thomson Sweet & Maxwell 2008) ch 1.

[10] Each of the 13 states in Malaysia has its own elected legislative assembly and its own state-level cabinet, which can become controlled by political parties in opposition to the federal government. At present, the state of Penang is governed by the DA, and Selangor by the PKR (both in opposition at federal level).

[11] A total of 42 amending Acts were passed, and more than 600 textual amendments made to the Federal Constitution between 1957 and 2008: Harding, *Constitution of Malaysia* (n 3) 103. In contrast, the United States Constitution has been amended only 27 times since 1789.

[12] See e.g. Harding, *Constitution of Malaysia* (n 3) 57–59. From 1998 to 2018, there was also the practice of the prime minister concurrently holding the portfolio of finance minister, which led directly to the 1 Malaysia Development Berhad (1MDB) episode (discussed below).

[13] Shad Saleem Faruqi, 'Keystone of the Govt Arch' *The Star* (25 March 2001) <http://lib.perdana.org.my/PLF/Digital_Content/Prominent_Leaders/Mahathir/News_1968-2004/2001-2005/2001/00001713.pdf> accessed 10 December 2021.

significance of the events involving the appointment (and fall) of prime ministers in 2018–2021.

The BN's grip on power weakened with the 'retirement' of strongman Dr Mahathir Mohamad, Malaysia's fourth prime minister from 1981 to 2003, who presided over the most rapid period of the country's economic development to date. His successor, Abdullah Badawi, was blamed for losing the parliamentary supermajority as well as an unprecedented number of regional state governments to an increasingly cohesive political opposition in 2008. Najib Razak then became the sixth prime minister in 2009, replacing Abdullah. An economist by training, Najib implemented several ambitious 'Transformation Programmes', attempting to improve government service delivery and move the country away from its traditional dependence on petroleum revenue and palm oil exports.

However, Najib soon became embroiled in the 1MDB fiasco. This corruption scandal of worldwide proportions involved a supposed sovereign wealth fund (1MDB), from which more than US$ 4.5 billion was allegedly embezzled with the connivance of top Malaysian government officials.[14] The investigation into 1MDB drew in law enforcement agencies in the United States, Switzerland, and Singapore, among others, and was described by the then US Attorney General Jeff Sessions as 'kleptocracy at its worst'.[15] As the prime minister, finance minister, and also chairman of the 1MDB board of advisers at the time of the alleged wrongdoing, Najib was heavily implicated in the scandal, and subsequent revelations by the *Wall Street Journal* that up to RM 2.6 billion (US$700 million) had allegedly been deposited into his personal bank account at the height of the scandal outraged Malaysians.

Najib's response, however, was to dismiss any members of his cabinet who dared to question his involvement in the 1MDB scandal. He also dismissed the then attorney general, whose handpicked replacement promptly declared Mr Najib's innocence and halted all domestic investigations into the prime minister.[16] Against a backdrop of mounting public discontent, the Election Commission (EC) then commenced a re-delineation of the country's electoral boundaries, producing some severely imbalanced constituencies which immediately raised allegations of

[14] For an outline of the now-notorious scandal, see e.g. Hannah Ellis-Petersen, '1MDB Scandal Explained: A Tale of Malaysia's Missing Billions' *The Guardian* (London, 28 July 2020) <www.theguardian.com/world/2018/oct/25/1mdb-scandal-explained-a-tale-of-malaysias-missing-billions> accessed 10 December 2021.

[15] Reuters, 'Jeff Sessions Calls Malaysia's 1MDB Scandal "Kleptocracy at Its Worst"' (*Reuters*, 5 December 2017) <www.reuters.com/article/us-malaysia-scandal-doj-idUKKBN1DZ0MX> accessed 15 February 2021.

[16] See e.g. Al Jazeera, 'Malaysian PM Cleared of Wrongdoing over $681m Donation' (*Al Jazeera*, 26 January 2016) <www.aljazeera.com/news/2016/1/26/malaysian-pm-cleared-of-wrongdoing-over-681m-donation> accessed 20 December 2021. The attorney general has the prosecutorial discretion to institute or discontinue any proceedings for an alleged offence: Federal Constitution of Malaysia, art 145(3).

deliberate gerrymandering.[17] Existing internal security laws were also beefed up, including new legislation which gave the prime minister the power to proclaim emergency-like measures 'in the interest of national security'.[18] This sparked concern that preparations were being made for a refusal to hand over power in the event of the BN losing the next general election, scheduled for 2018.

3. The Regime-Change Event and the Constitutional Reform Process

3.1 The Pact of Hope

Against this backdrop, an unlikely 'saviour' stepped up to challenge Najib and the BN's hegemony: former Prime Minister Dr Mahathir Mohamed, aged 92 at the time of the general election in 2018, came out of retirement to organise a new political party, Bersatu, and to unite the main political opposition to Mr Najib under a single coalition, Pakatan Harapan (Pact of Hope—PH). At the time of the general election (Malaysia's fourteenth, hence its moniker of 'GE14'), PH comprised Bersatu, the DAP, PKR, and Parti Amanah Negara (National Trust Party—'Amanah'). It was also in alliance with a regional party, Parti Warisan Sabah (Sabah Heritage Party—'Warisan'). Through adroit use of social media, so-called 'alternative media', and mass-messaging technology, PH successfully portrayed itself as the champion of reform, good governance, and accountability. Its election manifesto, *Buku Harapan* (*Book of Hope*) contained more than 60 reform-orientated pledges, envisioning a 'new Malaysia' in which corruption would be tamed and the welfare of the people prioritised.[19]

This set-up, however, contained the seeds of its own destruction because it brought together parties with deeply inconsistent ideologies, united only by a common enmity with the BN and the Najib administration, and a desire to capture federal power. The DAP, the oldest party in the coalition, is an ethnic Chinese-led

[17] Malaysia practices a purely first-past-the-post electoral system for elections to the federal parliament and to each of the state legislative assemblies. The re-delineation exercise of 2016–2018 produced a situation in which the largest constituencies (which also happened to be opposition strongholds) had up to 6.5 times the number of electors in the smallest constituencies (which conveniently happened to be strongholds of the incumbent). For further discussion, see e.g. Kai Ostwald, 'Electoral Boundaries in Malaysia's 2018 General Election' (University of British Columbia, 20 February 2020) <https://sppga.ubc.ca/news/electoral-boundaries-in-malaysias-2018-election-malapportionment-gerrymandering-and-umnos-fall> accessed 10 December 2021; Harry Jacques, 'Malaysia Election Falls Prey to "Gerrymandering"' *Financial Times* (London, 8 May 2018) <www.ft.com/content/ecb87f18-51d7-11e8-b3ee-41e0209208ec> accessed 10 December 2021.

[18] National Security Council Act 2016 (Act 776) s 18(1). Strengthening amendments were also made to the Prevention of Crime Act 1959 (Act 297) and the Prevention of Terrorism Act 2015 (Act 769).

[19] Pakatan Harapan, 'Buku Harapan: Rebuilding our Nation, Fulfilling Our Hopes' (*Pakatan Harapan*, 2018) <https://dl.dapmalaysia.org/repository/Manifesto_PH_EN.pdf> accessed 15 February 2021.

(albeit officially multiracial) social democratic party dedicated to the idea of a secular 'Malaysian Malaysia' in which every citizen would have 'equal and equitable rights'.[20] The PKR is a multi-ethnic outfit dedicated to the causes of institutional reform and social justice,[21] although it is almost inextricably associated with the personal political struggle of its founder, Anwar Ibrahim, who was jailed during the Najib administration on charges of sodomy, which many consider to have been highly questionable.[22] The significantly smaller Amanah is a splinter of the PAS, officially positioning itself as a moderate Islamist party.

But the latest component party, Dr Mahathir's Bersatu, is an exclusively ethnic Malay and indigenous party dedicated explicitly to the promotion of the interests of these communities; in other words, an ethnic-based political party in exactly the same mould as the UMNO, its chief rival. In addition, Bersatu was (and still is) led by ex-UMNO leaders who either fell out with Mr Najib or decided to hitch their wagons to the new party's star, ditching the perceptibly waning influence of the UMNO at the time. This mix of personalities also meant that decades of bitter political rivalry and mudslinging that had taken place between Bersatu leaders, especially Dr Mahathir himself, and those of the DAP, PKR, and Amanah, were seemingly swept under the carpet in the quest to unseat Mr Najib.

The choice of Dr Mahathir as PH's prime ministerial candidate, if it won GE14, was also an interesting one because during his earlier premiership (as president of the UMNO), Dr Mahathir himself was responsible for establishing many of the practices and mechanisms that were now being criticised. For example, it was Dr Mahathir who initiated the practice of the prime minister concurrently holding the portfolio of finance minister—the system by which Mr Najib came to wield almost unchecked power in the 1MDB episode. Dr Mahathir also presided over dark episodes in Malaysian constitutional history such as the 1988 'judicial crisis', in which the then Lord President and two other Supreme Court justices were controversially dismissed from office, and 'Operation Lalang' of 1987, wherein scores of opposition politicians, journalists, and academicians—including, ironically, some of his new-found allies in PH—were detained without trial under draconian internal security legislation.[23]

[20] DAP, 'The Party' <https://dapmalaysia.org/en/about-us/the-party> accessed 15 February 2021; DAP, 'Our Objectives' <https://dapmalaysia.org/en/about-us/vision-mission/our-objectives> accessed 15 February 2021.

[21] Constitution of Parti Keadilan Rakyat, Part II, 3–5 (in Malay) <https://keadilanrakyat.org/wp-content/uploads/2016/10/Perlembagaan-Parti-Keadilan-Rakyat.pdf> accessed 15 February 2021.

[22] See e.g. BBC News, 'Anwar Ibrahim: A Long-Held Dream to Lead Malaysia' (25 September 2020) <www.bbc.com/news/world-asia-16440290> accessed 10 December 2021; Jonathan Edward, 'Malaysia Welcomes Anwar Ibrahim: "Free at Last"' (*Al Jazeera*, 16 May 2018) <www.aljazeera.com/news/2018/5/16/malaysia-welcomes-anwar-ibrahim-free-at-last> accessed 10 December 2021.

[23] For a discussion of the 1988 judicial crisis, see e.g. FA Trindade, 'The Removal of the Malaysian Judges' (1990)106 Law Quarterly Review 51; Andrew Harding, 'The 1988 Constitutional Crisis in Malaysia' (1990) 39 International & Comparative Law Quarterly 57. On 'Ops Lalang', see Harding, *Constitution of Malaysia* (n 3) 173–74; Kua Kia Soong, *The Malaysian Civil Rights Movement* (Strategic Information Research Development 2005) ch 7.

Notwithstanding this, PH secured significant electoral success in GE14, capturing (together with its ally Warisan) an outright parliamentary majority and unseating the BN from federal power for the first time in Malaysia's history. PH secured 45.68 per cent of the popular vote, with its Warisan allies contributing a further 2.32 per cent. The BN took 33.8 per cent of the vote, and the PAS drew 16.9 per cent. This gave the PH–Warisan bloc a 9-seat parliamentary majority, enabling Dr Mahathir to be sworn in once again as prime minister; at 92 years of age, he became the oldest person to be appointed prime minister in the world.[24] Ministerial positions were distributed among the PH component parties and Warisan, but with a clear disproportionality in favour of Bersatu, the prime minister's party.[25] For the DAP, PKR, and Amanah, it was the first time their leaders had tasted power at federal level, having warmed the opposition benches for decades.

In the early days, the new administration did, indeed, set about implementing its reform agenda. An Institutional Reform Committee (IRC) and an Electoral Reform Committee (ERC) were established to examine the ways in which the reforms pledged by PH could best be brought to fruition. Up to 11 new parliamentary select committees were established, including committees dedicated to 'Fundamental Liberties and Constitutional Rights' and 'Finance and the Economy', among others, and the British practice of having an opposition member of parliament chair the Public Accounts Committee (PAC) was instituted.[26] Controversial appointees of the former regime, such as the then Chief Justice of Malaysia and the President of the Court of Appeal (the top two posts in the judicial hierarchy, respectively), the former attorney general, as well as the entire Election Commission, were quickly replaced. In the name of protecting the public purse, several high-profile projects of the previous regime, such as the high-speed rail (HSR) link between Kuala Lumpur and Singapore, the Eastern Corridor Rail Link (ECRL), and the Klang Valley Mass Rapid Transit (KVMRT), were either renegotiated, rerouted to deliver cost savings, or (in the case of HSR) scrapped altogether. The PH government also promptly abolished the deeply unpopular goods and services tax (GST), which had been introduced by the Najib administration in 2015, and even granted a three-month 'tax holiday' on consumption before the pre-GST sales and services tax (SST) was reinstated. Most notably, investigations into former Prime Minister

24 David Stubbings, 'Oldest Prime Minister Records as Mahathir bin Mohamad Becomes Malaysia's Leader Aged 92' (*Guinness World Records*, 11 May 2018) <www.guinnessworldrecords.com/news/2018/5/oldest-prime-minister-records-as-mahathir-bin-mohamad-becomes-malaysias-leader-a-525206> accessed 10 December 2021.

25 In the cabinet formed in stages until July 2018, Bersatu held 4 ministries (in addition to the prime minister's post), including the important portfolios of home affairs and education, despite that party contributing only 13 out of PH's 113 seats. In comparison, the DAP contributed 42 seats but received 5 ministerial portfolios. PKR, which contributed 47 seats, received 6 portfolios (in addition to the deputy prime minister's post).

26 See e.g. The Sun Daily, 'Malaysian Parliament to Witness More Transformations' *The Sun Daily* (9 November 2021) <www.thesundaily.my/home/malaysian-parliament-to-witness-more-transformations-CJ8319859> accessed 20 December 2021.

Najib's alleged wrongdoing with regard to 1MDB were resumed, ultimately resulting in his indictment and conviction by the High Court on various charges of criminal breach of trust and money-laundering.[27]

As might have been expected, resistance soon began materialising against the reform initiatives. An effort to repeal the 'Anti-Fake News Act 2018'[28]—another deeply unpopular legacy of the Najib era—was voted down in the senate, the upper house of parliament, which was still dominated by appointees of the previous administration. This delayed the repeal for over a year before the lower house was able to exercise its constitutional override of the senate's rejection.[29] An effort by the new government to ratify the International Convention on the Eradication of Racial Discrimination (ICERD) and the Rome Statute of the International Criminal Court (ICC) provoked considerable public backlash, adroitly exploited by PH's political rivals, over fears that it could erode the 'special position' of Malaysia's majority *Bumiputera* community and threaten the position of the Malay Rulers.[30] Further, a proposal to amend the Federal Constitution to restore the position of Sabah and Sarawak—Malaysia's two resource-rich states on the island of Borneo—as distinct entities from the other eleven states of the federation failed to garner bipartisan support and thus fell well short of the necessary two-thirds majority.[31]

However, one successful reform initiative which may yet prove a lasting contribution of the PH era was a constitutional amendment to lower the age of eligibility to vote and stand for elections to the federal and state legislatures from 21 to 18 years of age. This had been a key pledge in PH's electoral manifesto, and it appeared well positioned to tap into PH's perceived support amongst younger voters at the time. Bipartisan support was marshalled for the amendment by acceding to the BN and PAS's demand for a simultaneous implementation of automatic voter registration.[32] This enfranchisement of a very significant segment of

[27] *Public Prosecutor v Dato' Sri Mohd Najib bin Hj Abd Razak* [2020] 11 MLJ 808 (HC). This decision was affirmed by the Court of Appeal on 8 December 2021 and, at the time of writing, is currently pending appeal to Malaysia's apex court, the Federal Court. Note also that there are other charges against Najib, also relating to 1MDB, which are currently pending before the courts.

[28] Act 803.

[29] Similar to the position in the United Kingdom, the unelected upper house of parliament (the senate) can delay non-money bills for at least one year, but it cannot ultimately block the bill if the elected lower house (the House of Representatives) passes the same bill again after the stipulated interregnum: Federal Constitution of Malaysia, art 68(2).

[30] See e.g. Channel News Asia, 'Malaysia U-turns on Decision to Join War Crimes Court after Political Pressure' (*Channel News Asia*, 5 April 2019) <https://www.channelstv.com/2019/04/06/malaysia-makes-u-turn-on-war-crimes-court/> accessed 20 December 2021.

[31] See e.g. Channel News Asia, 'Bill to Make Sabah, Sarawak Equal Partners Rejected in Malaysia Parliament' (*Channel News Asia*, 10 April 2019) <www.channelnewsasia.com/asia/sabah-sarawak-equal-partners-bill-fails-to-get-two-thirds-885216> accessed 20 December 2021.

[32] See e.g. Wilson Tay Tze Vern, 'Bipartisan Support for Constitutional Amendment to Lower Voting Age in Malaysia: Consensus Is the Way Forward in a Developing Democracy' (*ConstitutionNet*, 1 August 2019) <https://constitutionnet.org/news/bipartisan-support-constitutional-amendment-lower-voting-age-malaysia-consensus-way-forward> accessed 20 December 2021.

the population brings Malaysia in line with mature democracies such as the United Kingdom, Australia, India, the United States, and most of the European Union[33] and augurs well for efforts to raise constitutional awareness amongst the younger generation.

Then, everything fell apart. On 24 February 2020, PH was rocked by the departure of Bersatu, the Prime Minister's own party, from the coalition, accompanied by a significant number of defectors from the PKR. This was the so-called 'Sheraton Move', named after the hotel in the suburb of Petaling Jaya where the manoeuvre was strategised by its key movers. Thus deprived of his slim parliamentary majority, and having by then already lost control over most of Bersatu, Dr Mahathir tendered the resignation of the PH cabinet on 24 February.[34] This necessitated the appointment of a new prime minister; under the Federal Constitution, this must be a member of parliament who, in the judgement of the Agong, 'is likely to command the confidence of the majority of [the House of Representatives]'.[35] It was, however, unclear as to who commanded majority support—Dr Mahathir and PH's Anwar Ibrahim were early frontrunners, but there were other contenders as well, and none could conclusively establish majority support.

At this juncture, the Agong intervened by summoning the country's MPs to an audience at the palace, personally interviewing each of them in an effort to establish which candidate had majority support. This was an extraordinary intervention, made possible by a combination of Malaysia's constitutional framework on the formation of cabinets; an apex court decision, stemming from a state-level constitutional crisis eleven years earlier, to the effect that the head of state can determine the issue of confidence otherwise than through a vote in the legislature;[36] plus Malaysia's arcane rules on the summoning of a special session of parliament to deliberate this issue.[37] The Agong also called a meeting of Malaysia's nine hereditary

33 Sharon Omondi, 'Legal Voting Age By Country' (*WorldAtlas*, 7 September 2017) <www.worldatlas.com/articles/legal-voting-age-by-country.html> accessed 21 December 2021.

34 Under Malaysia's Federal Constitution, if the prime minister ceases to command the confidence of the majority of the House of Representatives then unless at the prime minister's request the *Agong* dissolves parliament, the prime minister shall tender the resignation of the cabinet: art 43(4). Here, it was perhaps questionable whether Dr Mahathir himself had already ceased to command the confidence of the majority, given that parliament not in session at the time. It was possible that, despite the actions of the renegade faction in Bersatu, there was still adequate support for Dr Mahathir from other then opposition parties, such as PAS, to maintain his majority. Nonetheless, in his statement accompanying his resignation, Dr Mahathir insisted that he had lost majority support.

35 Federal Constitution of Malaysia, art 43(2)(a).

36 *Dato' Seri Ir Hj Nizar bin Jamaluddin v Dato' Seri Dr Zambry bin Abdul Kadir (Attorney General, Intervener)* [2010] 2 MLJ 285 (Federal Court).

37 Dr Mahathir had actually called for an urgent sitting of parliament to determine the question of confidence in the next prime minister, but the Speaker blocked this on grounds of procedural noncompliance: Damodaran Kanyakumari, 'Malaysia's Speaker of Parliament Says There Will Be No Special Sitting Next Monday on PM Position' (*Channel News Asia*, 28 February 2020) <www.channelnewsasia.com/asia/malaysia-speaker-parliament-special-session-mahathir-781356> accessed 20 December 2021.

Rulers (each the sovereign of their respective states in the federation)[38] to seek their input.

Following these consultations, it was announced, on 29 February, that the Agong was satisfied that Muhyiddin Yassin, the president of Bersatu, had majority support to be appointed as prime minister, and the swearing-in ceremony was completed the next day. This capped a week in which the Malaysian political landscape was dramatically altered with the departure of Bersatu and its supporters from the PH coalition, the formation of a new Perikatan Nasional (National Alliance—PN) coalition headed by Bersatu, and a new network of political alliances which allowed Muhyiddin to claim a majority. The net effect of this was to restore the same parties who had 'lost' the election of 2018—the BN in particular—to federal power (see Table 15.1 below).

3.2 Causes of the Pact of Hope's Collapse

The root causes of PH's collapse, and the stunning reversal of the results of 2018, are multifarious, and it would be beyond the scope of this chapter to analyse each of them in detail. Three primary factors, however, can be outlined.

3.2.1 Ethno-nationalist agitation

This was epitomised by the mobilisation of public opinion among Malaysia's majority Malay community to oppose the PH administration's proposed ratification of ICERD and the Rome Statute of the ICC, culminating in a large demonstration ('The Anti-ICERD Rally') in Kuala Lumpur on 8 December.[39] Although the PH administration supposedly heralded an era of non-ethnicity-based governance, in contrast to the policies of the overtly monoethnic BN component parties, there was a marked increase in racial rhetoric in public discourse during PH's administration, culminating in a 'Malay Dignity Congress' on 6 October 2019, which was framed as a 'response to challenges against Malays'.[40] Notably, Dr Mahathir himself

[38] Four of Malaysia's 13 states—Penang, Malacca, Sabah, and Sarawak—are former British Crown Colonies and do not have hereditary rulers.

[39] See e.g. Kate Mayberry, "Malaysia: Malays Rally Amid Worries over Government 'Weakness'" (*Al Jazeera*, 8 December 2018) <www.aljazeera.com/news/2018/12/8/malaysia-malays-rally-amid-worries-over-government-weakness> accessed 20 December 2021.

[40] Mohsin Abdullah, 'Bersatu and the Malay Dignity Congress' (*The Edge Markets*, 4 October 2019) <www.theedgemarkets.com/article/bersatu-and-malay-dignity-congress> accessed 20 December 2021. Other instances, such as the death of an ethnic Malay firefighter in a riot that erupted over the attempted demolition of a Hindu shrine in Selangor, and the supposed uncovering of a cell of Liberation Tigers of Tamil Eelam (LTTE) sympathisers (despite the LTTE having long been defeated in the Sri Lankan civil war), also quickly became racialised: see e.g. Tashny Sukumaran, 'In Malaysia, a Firefighter's Death Threatens to Set Off Long-Standing Racial Tensions' *South China Morning Post* (18 December 2018) <www.scmp.com/news/asia/southeast-asia/article/2178566/malaysia-firefighters-death-threatens-set-long-standing> accessed 20 December 2021; Hew Wai Weng, 'The Politics of Muslim Majoritarianism' (*AsiaLink*, University of Melbourne, 6 April 2020) <https://asialink.unimelb.edu.au/insights/the-politics-of-muslim-majoritarianism2> accessed 20 December 2021.

Table 15.1 In Summary—The Shifting Sands of Power in Malaysia, 2018–2021

Alliance	Characteristics	Notes
BN *Barisan Nasional* (National Front) Status: in government	Ethno-nationalist Grew out of the independence-era Alliance Party Reduced to 4 component parties after defeat in the 2018 general election (down from 13 previously) UMNO is the largest and most influential component party	• Lost power after the watershed 2018 election. • Regained power after February 2020 • Regained PM position in August 2021
PH *Pakatan Harapan* (Pact of Hope) Status: in opposition	Reformist pledges Originally comprised the DAP (social democratic), PKR (multiracial), *Amanah* (moderate Islamist) and *Bersatu* (Malay nationalist) In electoral cooperation with Sabah regional party *Warisan*	• Won power in the 2018 election • Lost power after *Bersatu* ditched the coalition in February 2020 and allied itself with BN and PAS
PN *Perikatan Nasional* (National Alliance) Status: in government	A new coalition spearheaded by *Bersatu* after the events of February 2020 Comprises the ethno-nationalist *Bersatu*, PAS (the Pan-Malaysian Islamic Party), and smaller, less influential parties	• In alliance with BN to maintain federal power to the exclusion of PH • Held prime minister's position (February 2020–August 2021) because *Bersatu*'s leader, Mr Muhyiddin, was appointed by the *Agong* • Was opposed by BN in state-level elections in Sabah and Malacca but maintains cooperation with it at federal level
GPS *Gabungan Parti Sarawak* (Coalition of Sarawak Parties) Status: in government	The former wing of BN in Sarawak state, comprising four component parties Remains relatively influential because of its strength in Sarawak state-level politics (and the size and resources of Sarawak state)	• Immediately broke away from BN after the coalition's defeat in the 2018 election • After the events of February 2020, GPS allied with BN and PN to form the new federal government (but is not part of either coalition)

Source: Table compiled by the author based on first-hand observation of the events as a Malaysian academic based in the country. For further reading on these developments, see e.g. Tricia Yeoh, 'Malaysian Politics: What Just Happened and the Political Outlook' (Heinrich Böll Stiftung Southeast Asia, 20 October 2021) <https://th.boell.org/en/2021/10/20/malaysian-politics-what-just-happened-and-political-outlook> accessed 20 December 2021; Bridget Welsh, 'Malaysia's Political Polarization: Race, Religion, and Reform' (Carnegie Endowment for International Peace, 18 August 2020) <https://carnegieendowment.org/2020/08/18/malaysia-s-political-polarization-race-religion-and-reform-pub-82436 accessed 20 December 2021.

was invited to, and did, officiate at the launch of the congress. The PH administration failed to effectively restrain the 'racialization' of major public controversies during its time in office.

3.2.2 Internal dissent within PH

A long-standing issue that plagued the PH administration was the supposed agreement that in the event of the coalition's victory, Dr Mahathir would become prime minister for the time being, secure a royal pardon for the jailed PKR leader Anwar Ibrahim, and then hand over the prime minister's position to Anwar at some point. The first two parts of the deal were duly delivered; Anwar was released and made a comeback to parliament via a by-election. However, Dr Mahathir refused to even indicate a time frame for the handover of power to Anwar. This was not at all surprising considering the long history of animosity between the two leaders stemming from Anwar's dismissal, arrest, and imprisonment by Dr Mahathir in 1998. By the second year of PH's term, agitation within the PKR for the promised handover led to countermoves within Bersatu to defend Dr Mahathir's position, and thus open in-fighting between PH component parties. Also fraying ties within the coalition was Bersatu's practice of accepting members of parliament (MPs) 'defecting' from other parties, especially the UMNO, which steadily increased Bersatu's parliamentary numbers—and hence its negotiating position—vis-à-vis its coalition partners.

3.2.3 Slow pace of reform

Despite a promising early start, many of the electoral pledges made by PH on the campaign stump remained unfulfilled well into its second year in power.[41] Dr Mahathir himself stated that the coalition made too many promises without expecting that it would actually win power and that its manifesto was 'not a bible' but only a guide.[42] Despite the establishment of the high-profile IRC, the ERC, and a 'Council of Eminent Persons' (CEP) to look into reforms, these committees' reports were never made public. PH also made no move towards abolishing draconian legislation such as the Sedition Act 1948 and the Official Secrets Act 1972 once in power, despite its leaders having advocated this while in opposition.

[41] In addition to institutional reforms, PH also made populist promises such as reduction of highway toll charges and abolishment of higher education loans, which proved difficult to implement in the prevailing economic circumstances.

[42] See e.g. The Straits Times, 'Malaysian PM Mahathir Admits Pakatan Harapan Made Promises without Expecting to Win Election' *The Straits Times* (16 August 2018) <www.straitstimes.com/asia/se-asia/malaysian-pm-mahathir-admits-pakatan-harapan-made-promises-without-expecting-to-win> accessed 20 December 2021; The Sun Daily, 'Mahathir: Manifesto Not a bible, Only a Guide' *The Sun Daily* (17 July 2018) <www.thesundaily.my/archive/mahathir-manifesto-not-bible-only-guide-NUARCH564580> accessed 20 December 2021.

A string of by-elections in 2019, in which BN candidates won convincingly, had indicated growing discontentment among Malaysians at the new state of affairs.[43]

3.3 Postscript

Despite drastically reshaping the political landscape, the 'Sheraton Move' ultimately also failed to produce political stability. Doubts persisted over whether Muhyiddin Yassin actually had a parliamentary majority to justify his appointment; these concerns were only exacerbated by repeated delays in reconvening parliament through 2020, ostensibly due to the threat of COVID-19. Eighteen months after the 'Sheraton Move', Muhyiddin's government fell when the UMNO publicly withdrew its support, after the administration had earned itself a rare royal rebuke from the Agong for having pre-empted His Majesty on the issue of revoking emergency decrees that had been promulgated to deal with the COVID-19 crisis.

After another exhaustive round of interviewing MPs, in August 2021, the Agong called upon Ismail Sabri Yaakob, a vice-president of the UMNO, to form a government. This completed a remarkable turnaround in which the UMNO (and the BN) now regained the prime minister's position, which had been lost in the election of 2018. At present, the BN maintains federal power through an uneasy alliance with Bersatu and its PN coalition, which includes the Islamist PAS; this is so despite the BN and PN contesting against each other in state-level elections in Sabah (September 2020) and Melaka (November 2021).

4. Outcomes

The outcome of the 'regime-change event' in Malaysia in May 2018 cannot fairly be characterised as a complete success or an utter failure. It is true that, at the time of writing, the 'reformist' coalition which spearheaded the supposed 'regime change' has itself been driven from power, to be replaced by an ad hoc ethno-nationalist alliance comprising many who were on the losing side in the 2018 election. On that account, the outlook for reforms and democratic consolidation appears bleak.

Nevertheless, the changes of government in May 2018, February 2020, and August 2021 also underlined, in many ways, the extent of constitutional endurance and the stabilising role of key constitutional institutions, particularly the monarchy, in Malaysia. First, it demonstrated to a once jittery electorate that peaceful

[43] In Cameron Highlands, Rantau, Semenyih, and Kimanis, BN candidates defended these constituencies with comfortable majorities. Significantly, on 16 November 2019, BN also recaptured the ethnically mixed constituency of Tanjung Piai, indicating that sentiment was shifting even among the Chinese community, which had fulsomely supported PH in the general election of 2018.

and orderly regime change at federal level is possible via the existing constitutional process. This is particularly important in the context of Malaysia because before 2018, the only occasion on which the incumbents had come close to losing federal power (in May 1969) had resulted in deadly ethnic riots immediately afterwards. The 'spectre of May 13' (referring to the ethnic clashes), as a propaganda threat against a change of government at the ballot box appears to have been finally laid to rest. This has significant implications for the electoral accountability of future governments holding federal power. From 2018 onwards, no political party or coalition can claim a birth right to govern Malaysia.

Second, the regime-change events demonstrate that the mechanisms for transition of power provided for in the Federal Constitution actually work and therefore that political contestation via constitutional avenues does matter. This is important because of the real concerns, particularly around GE14, that the broad internal security powers currently available to an incumbent government could be used to block the results of the democratic process. As it happened, however, all parties abided by the outcome of the election, the internal security apparatus stayed strictly neutral, and the new government was duly sworn in. This reiterates that political contestation can be effectively channelled within the avenues provided for in Malaysia's Westminster-model constitutional system, strengthening the legitimacy of these avenues of political participation.

Third, the actions of the Agong in the events of February 2020 (when the PH government fell), October 2020 (when the PN's first attempt to secure a proclamation of emergency failed), and July 2021 (when the Agong and his brother Rulers resolved to put an end to the then ongoing state of emergency) highlight the crucial stabilising role that Malaysia's constitutional monarchy can play at times of political crisis in the country, whilst staying broadly within the framework of the Malaysian Constitution. The Agong's personal and much-publicised interventions in ascertaining who commanded the majority in the wake of the PH government's collapse bought precious time for the constitutional process to unfold and also dissuaded any extra-constitutional measures that might have been contemplated at these moments of grave political uncertainty. Furthermore, the Agong's adroit marshalling of Malaysia's hereditary Rulers behind key decisions concerning the formation of governments sent a clear message that the monarchy can, both legally and practically, intervene when necessary to facilitate the constitutional process in Malaysia. Separately, this also marks a further step in the remarkable revival of the monarchy's fortunes after earlier constitutional crises in which their powers and influence were progressively curbed by the first Mahathir administration.[44]

[44] See e.g. Hoong Lee, *Constitutional Conflicts in Contemporary Malaysia* (Oxford University Press 2017) chs 2–4; Andrew Harding, '"Nazrinian" Monarchy in Malaysia: The Resilience and Revival of a Traditional Institution' in Andrew Harding and Dian AH Shah (eds), *Law and Society in Malaysia: Pluralism, Religion, and Ethnicity* (Routledge 2017).

A further significance of the 'regime-change events' of 2018 and 2020 was the drastic reshaping of the Malaysian political landscape. The fragmentation of what had once been a dominant party scenario has produced a proliferation of new political parties catering to a broad range of interests, including regional states' rights[45] and youth-led reform,[46] which now compete with existing parties and ideologies in the marketplace of ideas. Even the realignment of existing political forces has heralded a new era in which there are at least three real alternatives—the BN, PH, and PN—as exemplified by state-level elections in Melaka in November 2021, when all constituencies witnessed at least three-way contests between these power blocs.

Above all, Malaysian voters proved that they could decisively break free of the BN power-sharing model, which is based on overtly ethnic-based political parties acting as proxies for their respective communities. Thus, the ethnocentric 'power-sharing' model first propagated by the Alliance Party and continued by the BN is no longer the only game in town. Instead, the political space has opened up for a wider contestation of ideas relating to good governance. With that said, from the point of view of Malaysia's ethnic minorities, this may represent a leap into the unknown. The current PN government—which emerged holding the reins of power in 2020—lacks component parties with any meaningful claim to represent Malaysia's sizeable ethnic Chinese and Indian minorities since these communities overwhelmingly voted for the 'reformist' PH coalition in 2018. Although ethnic Chinese and Indian ministers have been co-opted into Prime Minister Muhyiddin's cabinet to give a semblance of multi-ethnicity, the question of how—and, indeed, whether—Malaysia's ethnic minorities will continue to be represented in future governments remains to be seen. Also significant in this regard is how the post-2018 developments highlighted that, under Malaysia's current demographics and electoral delineation, ethnic Malay and indigenous political parties (the UMNO, Bersatu, PAS, and GPS) can secure a parliamentary majority without having to rely on the support of their ethnic Chinese and Indian-based counterparts.

The outcome of 'regime change' in Malaysia in 2018 can thus be described as a mixed one, which underscored the endurance of the country's Westminster-model constitutional system but also illustrated how this very system could be manipulated by reactionary, ethno-nationalist forces to produce outcomes antithetical to democratic consolidation. Nonetheless, in demonstrating that peaceful change is possible via the ballot box, and by disposing of an old regime that had grown deeply decayed and complacent in power, 'regime change' has permanently altered the way in which democratic discourse is conducted in Malaysia. Insofar as it inspires

[45] In addition to Warisan and GPS, which have already been discussed, there are also numerous new political parties dedicated explicitly to regional interests, such as the Sarawak United Party (PSB), the 'Love Sabah Party' (PCS), the Bumi Kenyalang (Sarawak) Party (PBK), and the Sarawak People's Aspiration Party.

[46] The Malaysian United Democratic Alliance (MUDA) is a newly registered youth-based reformist party. 'Muda' means 'young' in the Malay language.

greater political awareness (especially among the younger generation); emphasises the democratic accountability of incumbent governments; and contributes to a freer, more vibrant atmosphere of political discourse, it is suggested that the events of 2018 and 2020 have, on the whole, taken the country in a positive direction.

5. The Impact of the COVID-19 Pandemic

The novel coronavirus ('COVID-19') pandemic reached Malaysia in January 2020, and subsequently, a large religious gathering in Kuala Lumpur in late February (contemporaneous with the political crisis of that month) triggered a massive spike in transmissions.[47] By March 2020, there were over 2,000 cases across the country.

Malaysia's battle against COVID-19 took place against the backdrop of the ongoing political uncertainty discussed in section 3 above. The pandemic, and its economic and social fallout, became the main operational (as opposed to political) challenge facing Mr Muhyiddin's administration, which took office in February 2020.

Two main mechanisms—legislative and executive—have been used in Malaysia's ongoing response to the pandemic. The legislative mechanism is the Prevention and Control of Infectious Diseases Act 1988[48] ('the Act'), which the federal government invoked to proclaim a series of movement control orders (MCOs) throughout the country. Under the Act, the minister for health can proclaim any area within Malaysia as an 'infected local area' and prescribe measures to control or prevent the spread of disease.[49] The Act also gives broad powers to direct the isolation, observation, treatment, or surveillance of such persons, as may be necessary, and to take 'any other measures as the authorised officer considers necessary to control the disease'.[50]

On 16 March 2020, the government gazetted the entirety of Malaysia as an 'infected local area' and imposed progressively stringent measures such as suspending all international travel in and out of Malaysia, drastically reducing business hours (except limited 'essential services'), closing public parks and amenities, restricting public transportation, banning inter-state travel, and eventually limiting daily activities to a 10km radius of one's home. The Malaysian army was deployed to support the police in enforcing these movement controls.

[47] See e.g. Hisham Atan Edinur and Sabreena Safuan, 'Sri Petaling COVID-19 Cluster in Malaysia: Challenges and the Mitigation Strategies' (2020) 91(4) Acta Biomedica <www.ncbi.nlm.nih.gov/pmc/articles/PMC7927555> accessed 10 December 2021.

[48] Act 342.

[49] Ibid, s 6(1).

[50] Ibid, s 31(2).

The executive mechanism is the National Security Council (NSC), which became the day-to-day coordinating body for the government's response to COVID-19. The Senior Minister (Defence and Security) served as the *de facto* spokesperson of the NSC, communicating the federal government's agenda, strategy, and directives on a regular basis via the media. Today, the NSC's role has been replaced with that of the National Recovery Council (NRC) as Malaysia transitions into the 'recovery phase' of the pandemic.

Many Malaysians would have been surprised to discover that a hitherto little-known statute could confer on the federal government the power to impose what was effectively a nationwide lockdown, backed by the armed forces, without the need to proclaim a state of emergency or even to invoke internal security legislation. As it turned out, the Act clearly empowered the government to take all the action necessary to control the outbreak, despite imposing considerable limitations on economic activity and the freedom of movement. The so-called 'first lockdown' apparently succeeded as daily infections reached low double digits by May.

That changed drastically, however, with a political crisis in the state of Sabah in July 2020, wherein the BN successfully undermined the Warisan state government through the defection of several state legislators. In response, the Warisan chief minister managed to secure the dissolution of the state legislature, triggering state-level elections that duly took place in September. The intense election-related activities that took place were the precursor to a fresh wave of infections nationwide, which soon dwarfed the earlier outbreak; by 7 January 2021, Malaysia recorded more than 3,000 new infected cases daily. On 11 January, a nationwide state of emergency was proclaimed, which lasted until 1 August. The MCOs and restrictions, which had earlier been progressively relaxed, were reimposed in earnest. The state of emergency came to an end on 1 August as scheduled, after Malaysia's Rulers made it clear that their Royal Highnesses would not countenance an extension.[51]

It could be argued that the COVID-19 pandemic has given the PN government, whose parliamentary majority has always been somewhat doubtful, a convenient pretext for avoiding accountability to the legislature. This is because the prime minister—who is leader of the House in Malaysian parliamentary practice—can decide when the House is convened and for how long it sits on each occasion. The only limitation on this discretion is that no more than six months shall elapse between meetings of parliament,[52] but that restriction can be easily outflanked by simply calling a pro forma sitting of the House.

[51] The Star, 'No Need to Extend Emergency beyond Aug 1, Say Malay Rulers' *The Star* (16 June 2021) <www.thestar.com.my/news/nation/2021/06/16/no-need-to-extend-emergency-beyond-aug-1-say-malay-rulers> accessed 20 December 2021.

[52] Federal Constitution of Malaysia, art 55(1).

To illustrate, during the first MCO period in March 2020, the parliamentary session scheduled to begin on 18 May—during which Dr Mahathir and other opposition law-makers had proposed motions of no confidence in Muhyiddin's government—was converted (by order of the government) to a mere half-day sitting in which no substantive motions were allowed. This satisfied, on paper, the constitutional requirement that no more than six months shall lapse between sittings of parliament whilst buying time for the PN government to shore up its support through the use of patronage and government spending power. It was not until 13 July—more than four months after the new government was formed—that its majority could be tested in a regular sitting of parliament. By this time, the PN government had consolidated enough support not only to see off challenges to its legislative agenda but also even to remove the then Speaker, who had been nominated by the previous PH government.

The government's ability to evade parliamentary scrutiny becomes even more manifest when a state of emergency is invoked. This is because, under the Federal Constitution, when a state of emergency is proclaimed, the Agong (in reality the cabinet since the monarch acts on advice)[53] can effectively rule by decree through the use of emergency ordinances, which carry the same force and effect as an Act of Parliament and can therefore dispense with the need for parliament to be summoned.[54] Moreover, the Constitution is silent on the need to summon parliament in a state of emergency.[55] With the proclamation of emergency in January 2021, an ordinance was swiftly promulgated on 14 January, indefinitely suspending parliament and all the state legislative assemblies, besides postponing all elections due to be held (the term of the state legislature of Sarawak was to have expired in June).[56] The suspension of parliament attracted some criticism because, first, it is not clear how this would help control the spread of COVID-19; sittings of the legislature have not been suspended in other comparable democracies and the suspension removes a key avenue for securing the accountability and testing the legitimacy of the government. Second, it has been pointed out that the 1988 Act and the MCOs issued under it, as well as other laws such as the National Security Council Act 2016, already give the government the wide powers its needs to combat the pandemic without having to proclaim a state of emergency.[57]

[53] Ibid, art 40(1). See also e.g. *Teh Cheng Poh v Public Prosecutor* [1980] AC 458 (Privy Council) per Lord Diplock.

[54] Federal Constitution of Malaysia, art 150(2B), (2C).

[55] At independence, art 150 contained provisions requiring parliament to be summoned as soon as reasonably practicable, but these were subsequently deleted via constitutional amendments.

[56] Emergency (Essential Powers) Ordinance (2021) ss 12–15.

[57] See e.g. Andrew Khoo, 'Is the Emergency Proclamation Truly Justified?' (*Malaysiakini*, 11 February 2021), reproduced with permission at <www.malaysianbar.org.my/article/news/legal-and-general-news/members-opinions/is-the-emergency-proclamation-truly-justified-> accessed 15 February 2021.

6. Concluding Reflections

The overall outcome of the 'regime-change event' in Malaysia following the landmark general election of 2018 can be described as mixed. Although the 'reformist' camp did not ultimately maintain its grip on power long enough to implement its promises of change, the turbulence of 2018–2021 also demonstrated that constitutionalism and democracy remain alive and well in Malaysia. The pre-2018 political alliances in the country have been radically reshaped, giving rise to what could be an exciting new era of genuine multiparty democracy. In essence, the 'regime-change event' of May 2018 underlined that a two-party system is here to stay. The 'Sheraton Move' of February 2020 and its aftermath presage what may yet blossom into a *three*-party system in which the PN, BN, PH, and a host of smaller parties compete to give voice to Malaysians' aspirations. Such broadening of the democratic space in Malaysia, together with the successful reduction of the voting age, which has now enfranchised a large proportion of Malaysia's relatively young population, augurs well for the democratic process in the country.

Parliamentary democracy in Malaysia has proved resilient enough to withstand three transitions of power in as many years and finally looks to be on firm ground as the curtain falls on 2021. On each occasion, the rise and fall of each administration was debated, explained, and justified by all the constitutional actors involved—including the Agong—strictly in terms of the constitutional provisions applicable. Calls for what would have been a one-man dictatorship, in the guise of a 'non-partisan unity government', were rightly ignored.[58]

Still, not all is rosy on the horizon. The post-2018 political realignment has given new vigour to ethno-nationalist forces, now united with Islamist and ultraconservative elements in their common determination to prevent the 'reformist' faction from ever pulling off a repeat of 2018. Should they decide to energise their base by resorting to more ethnocentric and/or fundamentalist policies, this will not bode well for Malaysia's multicultural identity and may increasingly impinge on the interests of ethnic minorities.

The extraordinary intervention of Malaysia's hereditary Rulers in the political crises of 2018–2021 has reinvigorated discussion around the practice of constitutional monarchy in the country. The Rulers (and the Agong in particular) proved to be a constant pillar of constitutionalism amidst the political hullaballoo and, in so doing, have regained a considerable amount of prestige and political influence

[58] See e.g. Today Online, 'Risk of Power Abuse, Dictatorship Tendencies: Pundits Caution against Mahathir's Unity Govt Idea' (*Today Online*, 27 February 2020) <www.todayonline.com/world/risk-power-abuse-dictatorship-tendencies-pundits-caution-against-mahathirs-unity-govt-idea> accessed 20 December 2021; Soo Wern Jun, 'PKR Veep: Dr M Planned Unity Govt All Along, with an Eye to Axe Pakatan Leaders' *Malay Mail* (28 February 2020) <www.malaymail.com/news/malaysia/2020/02/28/pkr-veep-dr-m-planned-unity-govt-all-along-with-an-eye-to-axe-pakatan-leade/1841736> accessed 20 December 2021.

that appeared to have been lost to them in earlier constitutional crises.[59] The uses to which this influence will be put remain to be seen.

Malaysia's 'regime-change event' of 2018 thus illustrates how a democratic transition of power under a Westminster-model constitution can trigger a series of consequences highly specific to the constitutional context involved. It illustrates how a 'reformist' initiative must constantly evolve to deal with context-specific challenges and reactionary measures thrown at it by its opponents. The obvious point that, in order to succeed, the reformist leadership must be genuinely united with a common reform agenda appears to have been overlooked, thereby setting in motion a train of events that made collapse an inevitability. Nevertheless, the watershed events of 2018 and 2020 proved the resilience of constitutionalism and democracy in a country situated within a regional context where the endurance of these values can by no means be taken for granted.

[59] For context on these events, see e.g. Hoong Lee, *Constitutional Conflicts in Contemporary Malaysia* (2nd edn, Oxford University Press 2017) chs 2 and 3; Abdul Aziz Bari, 'The 1993 Constitutional Crisis: A Redefinition of the Monarchy's Role and Position?' in Hoong Lee and Andrew Harding (eds), *Constitutional Landmarks in Contemporary Malaysia: The First 50 Years* (LexisNexis 2007) ch 15.

Index

For the benefit of digital users, indexed terms that span two pages (e.g., 52–53) may, on occasion, appear on only one of those pages.

Tables and figures are indicated by *t* and *f* following the page number